CADOGAN

KU-515-421

Scotland: Highlands & Islands

Introduction	1
Travel	3
Practical A–Z	9
History	25
Topics	35
Perthshire: Gateway to the Highlands	45
Southwestern Highlands	79
Central West Highlands	105
Central Highlands	127
Wester Ross and the North West Highlands	143
Inverness and Around	159
Sutherland and Caithness	189
Islands	211
Skye	249
Outer Isles	267
Northern Isles	297
Clans and Families	321
Scottish Monarchs and Chronology	329
Glossary and Further Reading	332
Index	337

Cadogan Guides
West End House, 11 Hills Place, London W1R 1AG
becky.kendall@morrispub.co.uk

The Globe Pequot Press
246 Goose Lane, PO Box 480, Guilford,
Connecticut 06437–0480

Copyright © Richenda Miers 1998, 2000

Design by Animage

Maps © Cadogan Guides, drawn by Map Creation Ltd

Cover Photographs: Travel Ink/David Martyn Hughes (*front*)
Travel Ink/Leslie Garland (*back*)

Chapter title pages designed by Kicca Tommasi
Maps © Cadogan Guides, drawn by Map Creation Ltd

Editorial Director: Vicki Ingle
Series Editor: Linda McQueen
Editor: Catherine Charles

Proofreading: Mary Spicer Lambert
Indexing: Angie Hipkin
Production: Book Production Services

ISBN 1-86011-951-4

A catalogue record for this book is available from the British Library

The author and publishers have made every effort to ensure the accuracy of the information in this book at the time of going to press. However, they cannot accept any responsibility for any loss, injury or inconvenience resulting from the use of information contained in the guide.

Printed at Cambridge University Press

All rights reserved. No part of this publication may be reproduced, stored in a retrieval system, or transmitted, in any form or by any means, electronic or mechanical, including photocopying and recording, or by any information storage and retrieval system except as may be expressly permitted by the UK 1988 Copyright Design & Patents Act and the USA 1976 Copyright Act or in writing from the publisher. Requests for permission should be addressed to Cadogan Guides, West End House, 11 Hills Place, London W1R 1AG in the UK, or The Globe Pequot Press, 246 Goosel Lane, PO Box 480, Guilford, Connecticut 06437–0480 in the USA.

Acknowledgements

For their valuable help, I would like to thank Fiona and Alick Barratt, Angus Fairrie, Ann and Christopher Thompson, Sir Ilay Campbell, Rachel Clough, and the Rev W.F.Harris. I am also grateful to members of the Scottish Tourist Board, particularly: Debbie Forbes, Fiona Meikle, Sarah Seaton, Lisa-Rose Moller, Michael Hart, Mary Ann MacIver, Brian Kemp, Alison Leith, Mrs Aitcheson, and Jennifer Macrae. I am indebted to my patient editor, Catherine Charles, who has managed to unscramble my illegible handwriting without complaint and who ought to be a diplomat. Most of all, my thanks go to my daughter Mary, without whose hard work, tactful (usually) advice and knowledge of Scotland this book could never have been written.

About the Author

Richenda Miers is a novelist, freelance journalist and travel writer. Part English and part Scottish, she divides her time between the two countries, and has spent many years living 'north of the border'. She has many ties to the country she loves: her husband served in a Highland regiment; her son was born in Inverness; two of her daughters went to school in Aberdeen; and two of her children studied at Scottish universities. The Miers family share a home in the Outer Hebrides.

In memory of Father John Tranmar SJ and Mary Jane Duncan. Two dear friends.

Contents

Introduction 1–2

Travel 3–8

Getting There 4
Getting Around 5
Specialist Tour Operators and Special-interest Holidays 8

Practical A–Z 9–24

Climate 10
Food and Drink 10
Historic Scotland 13
Maps 13
National Trust for Scotland 13
Packing 13
Public Holidays 14
Shopping 14
Sports and Activities 14
Tourist Offices 22
Tracing your Ancestors 22
Where to Stay 23

History 25–34

From the Ice Age to Christianity 26
The Birth of Scotland 27
The Stewarts 28
Union and Enlightenment 31

Topics 35–44

Céilidh 36
Clans and Tartans 36
Crofting 37
Gaelic 37
The Highland Clearances 38
Highland Wildlife 39
Johnson and Boswell 39
The Napier Commission 41
Piping 42
Religious Differences 42
Seers 43
Sorcerers and Superstition 44

Perthshire: Gateway to the Highlands 45–78

Perth 48
Perth to Balmoral 55
Perth to Pitlochry 58
Dunkeld 59
Pitlochry 60
Pitlochry to Rannoch 61
Pitlochry to Killin 62
Pitlochry to Blair Atholl 67
Perth to Crieff 70
The Trossachs and Breadalbane 73
The Trossachs 74

Southwestern Highlands, Argyll and Loch Lomond 79–104

Loch Lomond 80
Loch Lomond to Loch Fyne 83
Dunoon 85
West Loch Fyne 88
Inverary 88
Oban 92

Southwestern Highlands, Argyll and Loch Lomond (*cont'd*) 79–104

Around Oban 93
Oban to Kintyre via Lochgilphead 94
Knapdale 97
Kintyre 99
Oban to Appin 102

Central West Highlands 105–126

Fort William 106
Fort William to Ballachulish 110
Balllachulish to Glencoe 113
The Rough Bounds 116
Fort William to Mallaig 116
Morar and Knoydart 119
Fort William to Moidart, Sunart and Ardnamurchan 121

Central Highlands 127–142

The Great Glen—Fort William to Inverness 128
Lochaber 128
Invergarry to Kyle of Lochalsh 135
Invergarry to Inverness 137
Fort Augustus 137
Loch Ness 139

Wester Ross and the North West Highlands 143–158

Kyle of Lochalsh 144
North of Kyle of Lochalsh 146
Ullapool 152
North of Ullapool 153

Inverness and Around 159–188

Inverness 160
Around Inverness 166
Nairn 170
Inverness to Newtonmore 171
Kingussie 171
West from Inverness 174
Beauly to Kyle of Lochalsh 177
North from Inverness 179
Easter Ross 183
Tain 185

Sutherland and Caithness 189–210

Dornoch 190
Dornoch to John O' Groats 192
Helmsdale 194
Dunbeath 197
Wick 199
John o'Groats to Cape Wrath 202
Thurso 203

Islands 211–248

Islands of the Clyde 215
Great Cumbrae 215
Arran and Holy Island 216
Bute 220
Inner Hebrides 223
Gigha 223
Islay 225
Jura 229
Colonsay and Oronsay 230
Mull 232

Islands (*cont'd*) 211–248

Iona 238
Coll and Tiree 242
Rum 245
Eigg 246
Canna 247
Muck 248

Skye 249–266

Kyleakin and Sleat Peninula 253
The Cuillins 256
Portree 256
Trotternish 257
Waternish 259
Durinish 261
Raasay 262

The Outer Isles 267–296

Lewis and Harris 270
Lewis 272
Harris 277
Berneray 282
North Uist 282
Benbecula 285
South Uist 287
Eriskay 292
Barra 293
St Kilda 295

The Northern Isles 297–320

Orkney 299
Mainland Orkney 300
Kirkwall 300
Islands South of the Mainland 305
Islands North of the Mainland 307
Shetland 311
Mainland 314
Fair Isle 320

Clans and Families 321–28

Scottish Monarchs and Chronology 329–31

Glossary and Further Reading 332–34

Maps

Perthshire 46–7
Perth 51
Argyll and The Western Highlands 81
Central West Highlands 109
Central Highlands 129
Wester Ross 145
Inverness 161
Inverness and Around 167
Sutherland and Caithness 191
Inner Hebrides and the Islands of the Clyde 213
Skye 251
Outer Hebrides 269
Orkney 301
Shetland 313

To the southern inhabitants of Scotland, the state of the mountains and the islands is equally known with that of Borneo and Sumatra: of both they have only heard a little, and guess the rest.

Dr Samuel Johnson, 1773

The further you go from the main hubs of activity, the more you discover the Highlands proper: golden eagles gliding over bleak moorland inhabited mostly by sheep; stark mountains streaked with snow-filled corries, dramatic against incandescent skies; turbulent rivers and waterfalls swirling through steep-sided glens to feed peat-dark, trout-filled lochs; an island-fringed west coast, bordered by shell-sand beaches and sheer cliffs eroded into stacks and arches,

Introduction

undermined by caves, where the raucous cries of sea-birds drown the boom of thunderous waves.

The enigma of the 'Highland Line' is explained by a geological fault running diagonally, and curvaceously across Scotland from around Helensburgh on the Clyde estuary to the Moray Firth, near Nairn. In this book, the Highlands lie west and north of this line, a capricious division that excludes mountainous Grampian but includes flat Caithness and all the islands.

Tourism is one of the main industries in the Highlands today and is expanding fast. Around the chief tourist centres there are myriad attractions catering for almost every taste: historic buildings, museums, leisure and craft centres, gardens, nature reserves, theme parks and much else.

A superficial grasp of the history of the Highlands and Islands, often darkened by violence, tragedy and treachery, and illuminated by heroism and romance, greatly enhances appreciation of this mystical land. The gaunt ruin of a once-mighty fortress, blown up by government soldiers, peopled by the ghosts of persecuted Jacobites, holds far more fascination than mere remains on a lonely hillside; a scattering of tumbled stones in a remote glen makes little impact unless one knows that a thriving community lived here until it was evicted to make way for thousands of lucrative sheep. This book tries to bridge some of these gaps.

Until relatively recently, the Highlands and Islands were so isolated that few outsiders ventured into them. Hostile mountain ranges, numerous lochs, rivers and bogs made intercommunication arduous and it was not until after the first Jacobite rising in 1715 that travel became easier.

General Wade, Commander in Chief, North Britain in 1724, built 240 miles of military roads and 40 bridges in the Highlands, to try to control rebellious Highlanders, allowing travellers such as Johnson and Boswell to explore this untapped source of purple prose. These formed the nucleus from which today's network of roads evolved.

Main roads are excellent now, though not always dual carriageway, and it is sometimes necessary to drive many extra miles to circumnavigate lochs and mountains when the linear distance is a mere stone's throw. The loveliest areas are often unapproachable except along single-track roads, on foot or by boat. This inaccessibility has helped to preserve rare species of land-birds, flora and fauna in some of the last wildernesses in Europe and to harbour vast colonies of sea-birds, unknown on more populous coasts. Of the 790 islands that fringe the northern and western shores, only about 130 are inhabited—not all served by public transport.

Agriculture, fishing and tourism are the main occupations of today's Highlanders. In the remoter parts, not much has altered in the last century. Television brought some changes, particularly to community life, but a strong sense of national pride remains, and Highland hospitality is unrivalled. There are modern hotels with *en suite* bathrooms and thick pile carpets, but round the back you may find a dozen discarded vehicles peacefully rusting away; and the detritus of crumpled beer cans, tattered polythene and empty bottles is more likely to be left by locals than by ecologically-aware tourists.

In the western Highlands, and particularly in the islands, there are still bards and story-tellers who sing and recite the songs and folklore that have been passed down by word of mouth over generations. The best fiddlers and pipers have their roots in areas that were untouched by the Reformation and by the Calvinists' stern suppression of gaiety. Highland games are popular in the summer, those in remoter parts being less showy and more spontaneous than smarter gatherings around Royal Deeside. They originated in early times when competitions for strength, speed and dexterity gave clan chiefs an opportunity to talent-spot men fit for their armies. Such dangerous encouragement of martial arts was quashed with the Act of Proscription and revived in its present form when Sir Walter Scott masterminded a romantic, tartan renaissance, keenly perpetuated by Queen Victoria and her descendants.

Except for guaranteed sunshine, holidaymakers can find every type of attraction in the Highlands and Islands. International climbers train in the Cuillins; the skiing can be excellent, although you have to be tough; hill walkers are spoilt for choice; windsurfers flock to Tiree; fishermen cross the world for Scottish salmon and trout; sailors and divers find endless scope off the west coast; naturalists and ornithologists find many species of rare bird, insect and plant in the blanket bog of the Flow Country and in other remote parts of the country.

Local ingredients enhance gourmet food, and distilleries look after the inner man. An enthusiastic revival of Gaelic culture is manifest in public *céilidhs* but even better, if you are lucky, you can sit in a croft-house kitchen, pungent with acrid peat-smoke, and listen to Gaelic songs and stories from the past. In the north, in the right conditions, you can witness that elusive stunt, the *Aurora Borealis* (Northern Lights), when shafts of coloured lights, mostly green and red, flash across the sky like an unearthly pageant of searchlights.

Let yourself be guided by the philosophy of the Highlander: *ùine gu lèoir* is Gaelic for 'time enough', and *uisge beatha*, 'water of life' has given us 'whisky'. With all that the Highlands and Islands have to offer, what more could anyone want?

Getting There 4

Getting Around 5

Specialist Tour Operators
and Special-interest Holidays 8

Travel

Getting There

By Air

Scotland has a reasonable choice of direct air links with cities in the UK, Europe and North America; tourists from other countries must fly via one of the English international airports. Scotland's main airports are Aberdeen, Edinburgh, Glasgow and Inverness, with good connections from each airport to the city, either by train, bus or airport taxi. Cars can be hired from the airports, either in advance through your travel agent or through the airport information desks on arrival. Aberdeen, Edinburgh and Glasgow airports have bureau de change facilities.

From the UK

You can fly direct to Edinburgh and Glasgow from London daily (Heathrow, Gatwick, London City, Luton and Stansted), and from Belfast, Birmingham, Bristol, Cardiff, East Midlands, Leeds, Manchester, Southampton and Channel Islands; and to Aberdeen from most of them. There are daily flights to Inverness from Gatwick and Luton; to Dundee from London City, to Wick from Birmingham, Edinburgh and London; and to the Northern Isles from London and Birmingham, via Aberdeen/Glasgow. Flights to the Western Isles are via Glasgow.

Most airlines offer economy fares with conditions (no change, no cancellation). For example, **British Airways**, ✆ 0345 222 111, offers 'Apex' return fares from London to Edinburgh or Glasgow, booked at least two weeks in advance, for £117 (full fare £240, standby £160, special restrictions £68). **EasyJet**, ✆ 01582 700 053, flies to Edinburgh and Glasgow from Luton on a first-come-first-served basis for £29 single. **Ryanair**, ✆ 0541 569 569, offers return fares at £59 to Glasgow with a return fare to any station in Scotland for an extra £5 (very good value). There are also many special package offers, some of which include return fare, self-drive car and a tank of petrol, accommodation and insurance. **Scotsell Ltd**, ✆ (0141) 772 5928, offers flight, car hire and accommodation packages.

British Airways European Air Pass allows up to 12 flights within Britain and the Channel Islands for overseas visitors, valid for a period from 7 days to 3 months, eg. London–Edinburgh–Aberdeen–Shetland–Orkney–Inverness–Stornoway–Glasgow–London for £416. Tickets must be bought at least a week before arrival in Britain, and only for scheduled flights.

From North America and Canada

There are some direct flights to **Glasgow Airport**, ✆ (0141) 887 1111/information ✆ (0141) 848 4552/travel ✆ (0141) 848 4330. Flights from New York take about 6hrs, or 7 from Chicago, and 10 from LA; other cities directly linked to Glasgow include Boston, Denver, Las Vegas, New Orleans, San Francisco, Seattle, Toronto, Vancouver and Washington.

transport from the airport

Aberdeen (7 miles): taxi, £10; frequent coaches;

Edinburgh (7 miles): taxi, £15; shuttle bus every 15mins;

Glasgow (8 miles): taxi, £12; coach every 15mins;

Inverness (8 miles): taxi, £8; coaches meet scheduled flights except Sun;

Prestwick (30 miles to Glasgow): taxi, £40; hourly coach.

By Train

National rail enquiries: ✆ 0345 484 950

There are regular train services from Kings Cross, London, to Edinburgh taking just over 4hrs, and from Euston, London, to Glasgow taking about 5hrs. There are also high-speed trains from London to Aberdeen and Inverness. Trains also run from other major cities such as Birmingham, Carlisle, Crewe, Manchester, Newcastle, Penzance, Peterborough, Preston, Plymouth, York. The inter-city trains are modern and comfortable and serve food and drinks. It's a good idea to book seats in advance. Special-offer tickets are frequently available, eg. London–Edinburgh/Glasgow return: Apex, booking at least a week ahead, for certain trains only, £49; Supersaver, valid for a month with restrictions, £71; Saver, valid for same day or within one month with no restrictions, £79.

Overnight **sleeper services** from London operate to Edinburgh, Glasgow, Aberdeen, Fort William and Inverness. A second-class sleeper costs £109 return (first-class £159 return). Sleepers should be booked well in advance.

Aberdeen, ✆ (01224) 594 222; credit card bookings, ✆ (01224) 582 005;

Edinburgh, ✆ (0131) 556 2451;

Glasgow, ✆ (0141) 204 2844; credit card bookings, ✆ 0800 450 450;

Inverness, ✆ 0345 212 282; credit card bookings, ✆ (01463) 242 124.

By Bus or Coach

Eurolines is the main company offering scheduled coach services from most European cities to London, affiliated to **National Express**, Victoria Coach Station, London, ✆ (020) 7730 0202, and ✆ 08705 808 080, which runs coaches from London to Scotland. Several coach companies operate between London and Scotland, usually running at least one day coach and one overnight. The journey from London to Edinburgh takes about 8hrs, and to Glasgow about 7½hrs, including 'comfort stops'. The coaches are reasonably comfortable, with toilets. Some have a snack service and show a film. Prices vary and there are often special offers. An average return ticket London–Edinburgh/Glasgow costs from £30, London–Aberdeen £44. The 'Explorer' Pass gives unlimited travel on all services operated by **Scottish Citylink**, ✆ 0990 505 050, costing from £30 (3 days), to £120 (15 days), and less for holders of discount cards which are available to students and OAPs.

By Car

An excellent network of motorways means that you can drive comfortably from London to Edinburgh in 7hrs, sticking to the 70mph speed limit. The M1, A1(M) and A68 is the quickest route to Edinburgh, and the M1, M6 and A74 to Glasgow.

Getting Around

In remote areas it is always wise to consult the tourist office for the best way of getting around.

By Air

There is an internal air network connecting the islands and regional airports to the main airports at Edinburgh, Glasgow, Aberdeen and Inverness. Most are operated by British

Airways or Loganair, ✆ 0345 222 111. **British Airways Express Highland Rover** allows travel on any five single flights within Scotland for £189 (with restrictions); you must book this ticket before arriving in Scotland.

British Airways: Aberdeen Airport, ✆ (01224) 722 331; Edinburgh Airport, ✆ (0131) 333 1000; Glasgow Airport, Abbotsinch, ✆ (0141) 887 1111; Inverness Airport, ✆ (01463) 232 471; Wick Airport, ✆ (01955) 2215.

Loganair: Aberdeen Airport, ✆ (01224) 723 306; Glasgow Airport, Abbotsinch, ✆ (0141) 889 3181; Kirkwall Airport, Orkney, ✆ (01856) 872 494; Stornoway Airport, Lewis, ✆ (01851) 703 673.

By Ferry

Caledonian MacBrayne: The Ferry Terminal, Gourock, PA19 1QP, ✆ (01475) 650 100; car reservations, ✆ 0990 650 000

P&O Scottish Ferries: PO Box 5, Jamieson's Quay, Aberdeen AB9 8DL, ✆ (01224) 572 615

Orkney Ferries Ltd: Head Office, Shore St, Kirkwall KW15 1LG, ✆ (01856) 872 044

Shetland Islands Council: Shetland Isles Tourism, Market Cross, Lerwick ZE1 0LU, ✆ (01595) 693 434

Scotland has 130 inhabited islands, most of them around its west coast. Of these, 23 are served by Caledonian MacBrayne ferries, with rail and coach links from many of the mainland terminals. They also operate mainland ferry services. The summer timetable runs from 5 April to 12 October inclusive; a reduced service operates in the winter. All crossings except the very shortest must be booked in advance. Return fares usually work out cheaper than singles. Car fares are calculated according to the length of the vehicle. MacBrayne's, or CalMac as it is known, also offers economy Island Hopscotch tickets, and Island Rover tickets for unlimited travel over a set period, both of which offer considerable savings. It publishes a comprehensive brochure with details of schedules, prices and special offers, some of which change seasonally as well as annually.

P&O Scottish Ferries sail out of Aberdeen or Scrabster to Orkney and Shetland. They have a comprehensive brochure and also offer cruises and inclusive holidays to the islands.

Links between the islands are operated in Orkney by Orkney Ferries Ltd, and in Shetland by Shetland Islands Council.

Detailed information on how to reach a particular island is given with its entry in the guide.

For sailors there is probably nowhere in the world more beautiful (or challenging) than around Scotland's islands, and there are many sheltered anchorages from which to explore.

By Train

Scotrail: ✆ 0345 484 950

As well as the main inter-city routes, branch lines run through the very best of highland scenery. Trains run as far as Thurso and Wick via Inverness and Lairg, in the far northeast, and to Oban, Fort William, Mallaig and Kyle of Lochalsh in the west. Aberdeen–Inverness, Glasgow–Stranraer, Glasgow–Oban and Perth–Inverness are all beautiful journeys. The Kyle Line runs from Inverness across a lovely stretch of country to Kyle of Lochalsh. The famous

West Highland Line from Glasgow to Fort William and on to Mallaig is worth doing just for the beauty of the journey, and the trains themselves—beautifully preserved locomotives and coaches. British Rail offer all sorts of excellent bargain tickets; check at any station.

There are other travel passes worth enquiring about. North Americans can buy a Brit Rail Pass through their travel agents. There is also a motor-rail service to the main cities.

The **Highland Rover** (from £39) and **Festival Cities Rover** (from £29) allow unlimited travel on a regional basis. The **Freedom of Scotland Travelpass** (from £69) gives full inclusive travel on all scheduled rail services, Caledonian MacBrayne ferry services and some Scottish Citylink coach routes.

By Bus

Scottish Citylink: ✆ 0990 505 050

Stagecoach: ✆ (01463) 239 292 (Inverness), and ✆ (01862) 892 683 (Tain)

Buses serve most of Scotland. In very rural areas there is usually a **postbus** service which carries fare-paying passengers as well as mail—an experience which can be fun in itself and is a good way of meeting locals. Call ✆ (0131) 228 7407, or ✆ (01463) 256 273, for timetables, or enquire locally and at tourist offices.

Scottish Citylink runs coaches between most towns, and there are local bus services which vary enormously. Ask about discount and flexible tickets.

Stagecoach has very good bargains and special unlimited travel offers, which can be bought direct from the bus driver.

Tourist offices have details of special **summer bus services**—The Trundler, The Heather Hopper, The Speyside Rambler and The Border Harrier—which operate in 'scenic' areas.

By Car

Car hire firms operate from the airports and stations, and it is worth considering local firms: usually, the more rural, the better the bargain. A car is essential for anyone wishing to explore the Highlands and larger islands. You drive on the left in Scotland, as in the rest of the British Isles, and by law drivers and all passengers must wear seat belts. Road signs are similar to those in Europe. There is a mandatory speed limit of 70mph on all motorways and 60mph on other roads. Parking in towns is usually restricted to parking meters and car parks. A single yellow line by the kerb means you can't park by day; a double yellow line (and zigzag lines by pedestrian crossings), means no parking at any time. The police in Scotland are very hot on drink-driving and speeding.

Main roads are generally good, although many are not dual carriageways. In rural areas there are many single-track roads with passing bays. These should not be used for parking, but are also for slow cars to pull into, to allow faster ones to overtake. When touring in the far north, remember there are not many petrol stations and that some remain closed on Sundays.

hitch-hiking

It is neither more nor less chancy to thumb a lift in Scotland than anywhere else. In populated areas, be extremely wary. In the islands, however, locals will invariably stop and offer a lift without being thumbed; it is part of their instinctive hospitality.

Specialist Tour Operators and Special-interest Holidays

Tour operators offer many travel-inclusive packages: golfing and fishing holidays, historic and castle trails, scenic tours, etc; many firms will arrange individual tours tailored to suit personal requirements. Consult your travel agent or the Scottish Tourist Board for details.

specialist tour operators in the USA

Abercrombie and Kent, ✆ 800 323 3602, runs tours through lovely Highland scenery in *The Royal Scotsman*, a restored steam train.

Caravan Tours, ✆ 800 621 8338, offers a 15-day holiday which includes the air fare from New York, escorted motorcoach tours of Scotland and Ireland, free entrance fees, evening entertainment and first-class hotels.

specialist tour operators in the UK

There are package tours arranged from all over Britain, ranging from luxury coach tours with scheduled itineraries and first-class accommodation, to cheaper less ritzy tours with accommodation to match. The following minibus companies run tours from Edinburgh for 'independent travellers': **The Haggis Backpackers**, ✆ (0131) 557 9393; **Rabbies Trail Burner Tours**, ✆ (0131) 554 2612; **MacBackpackers**, ✆ (0131) 558 9900; and **Going Forth**, ✆ (0131) 226 4848.

Alfa Travel, 6 Golden Hill Lane, Leyland, Lancs PR5 2NP, ✆ (01772) 621 622, runs luxury coach tours and arranges accommodation.

Clansman Monarch Holidays, Central Reservations, St Andrews Square Bus Station, Edinburgh EH1 3DU, will arrange coach tours and accommodation.

Hi-Line, ✆ (01253) 290 431, runs a holiday advisory service and can tell you everything you want to know about a holiday in the Highlands and Islands. Staff will also make all bookings for you.

National Holidays, ✆ (01924) 383 838 (West Yorks), or (01942) 44246 (Lancs), operates an extensive choice of tours from all over the country.

Special-interest Holidays

If you like to build your holiday round a theme or particular activity, the Scottish Tourist Board, PO Box 15, Edinburgh EH1 1UY, publishes an excellent free brochure, *Adventure and Special-interest Holidays in Scotland*, with details of dozens of ideas for different holidays, and addresses to contact.

Hebridean Island Cruises, ✆ (01756) 701 338, offers cruises on the western seaboard in the *Hebridean Princess*, a floating luxury hotel with a crew of 30 serving 40 passengers. If you are lucky with the weather and can afford luxury prices, this is an ideal holiday for idle hedonists. There are plenty of opportunities for a run ashore.

Climate 10
Food and Drink 10
Historic Scotland 13
Maps 13
National Trust for Scotland 13
Packing 13

Practical A–Z

Public Holidays 14
Shopping 14
Sports and Activities 14
Tourist Offices 22
Tracing your Ancestors 22
Where to Stay 23

Climate

A popular postcard shows someone sitting in a deck chair under an umbrella in pouring rain, with the caption 'Having plenty of weather here in Scotland'. In fact, with a bit of luck, you can return from a holiday in Scotland with a tan not entirely inflicted by wind, and memories of blue sky and brilliant sunshine. Unpredictability is the main drawback, often with wide contrasts in one place in a day. When the weather is good, no other country compares. When the weather is bad and people struggle against piercing wind and relentless rain, and a damp chill pervades to the marrow, Siberia would be preferable. It is worth remembering that places in the north of the country have an average of 18 to 20 hours of daylight in the summer, and resorts on the east coast are noted for their hours of sunshine. In the far north, in the middle of the summer, it is never completely dark. In spite of the Gulf Stream, whose warm waters are alleged to lick the western shores of Scotland, the sea is gelid.

In general, the west is wettish, and mild enough in some coastal regions to support palm trees and tropical vegetation. The east is drier with a more bracing climate and colder winds. Winter in the Highlands, when the precipitation is mainly snow, can be very beautiful, with clear skies and sun, though temperatures may seldom rise above freezing.

An unfortunate side-product of the moist, mild weather in the west is the 'midge', a particularly virulent breed of gnat unequalled in persistence anywhere else in the British Isles. Grown men have been reduced to gibbering wrecks under their vicious attacks. They are at their worst in warm, humid conditions; they hide when it is windy and sometimes, though not always, in very bright sunshine. Anyone contemplating camping or picnicking during the midge season should have lots of the strongest possible repellent. In truth, midges can completely ruin an outdoor holiday; even the natives retreat indoors when they are marauding. The surest means of escape is to take to the sea—they won't follow a boat offshore.

Food and Drink

Fair fa' your honest, sonsie face,
Great chieftain o' the puddin' race!
Aboon them a' ye tak your place,
Painch, tripe, or thairm:
Weel are ye wordy o' a grace,
As lang's my arm.

from 'Address to a Haggis', by Robert Burns

National Dishes

Scotland has an unmatched reputation for salmon, both fresh and smoked. The development of fish farming has increased the availability but it has to be said that 'wild' salmon is usually nicer than that which has been reared in a farm. Apart from the salmon, national dishes include trout, sea fish, shellfish, game, beef, lamb and venison. Almost without exception you should go for these served simply in the traditional ways. Poached salmon with mayonnaise, new potatoes and cucumber; a freshly caught mackerel, fried so that its skin is crisp and curling, with wedges of lemon and watercress; an Aberdeen Angus fillet steak, medium-rare, an inch thick, with a green salad of lettuce, chives and a hint of garlic; well-hung roast grouse with game chips, fresh petits pois, fried breadcrumbs, bread sauce, and gravy. These will linger on the taste buds as well as in the memory long after any dish wrapped up in an exotic sauce and given a pretentious name.

Everyone should try **haggis**—if only once. It is made of the heart, liver and lungs of a sheep, mixed with suet, oatmeal and onion, highly seasoned and sewn into the sheep's stomach. Traditionally, it is eaten with 'bashed neeps' (mashed turnip; turnip, in Scotland, is what the English call swede) and washed down with neat whisky. Try black pudding, too: its unusual flavour is strangely addictive.

Arbroath smokies are fresh haddock, dry salted and smoked in pairs; a delicate, mild flavour makes them particularly delicious and the best way to eat them is cold, with brown wholemeal bread and butter, a generous squeeze of lemon juice and plenty of freshly ground black pepper.

Porridge is no longer a national habit but you can usually get it in hotels. The popular myth that Scotsmen eat their porridge with salt, standing up or walking about, is quickly disproved when you discover how many of them sit down and tuck into it heaped with sugar and cream and sometimes even syrup.

Scottish **cheeses** are worth pursuing. Crowdie is unique to Scotland, a creamed cottage cheese, made from skimmed milk. Dunlop cheese, originally made in an Ayrshire village of the same name, is now also made in Orkney, Arran and Islay. Caboc is a rich double-cream cheese rolled in pinhead oatmeal. Galic and Hramsa are both soft cream cheeses flavoured with wild garlic and herbs.

Oatcakes are unsweetened biscuits made with oatmeal, best eaten with cheese, honey or marmalade. Brand-named oatcakes can be dull compared with delicious local and home-made varieties that crumble and melt in the mouth. **Shortbread** originated in Scotland and is known all over the world. You will find many local variations.

Soups include cock-a-leekie, made with chicken and leeks; Scotch broth, made with mutton stock and barley; cullen skink—delicious—made with smoked haddock; and partan bree, made with crab.

Scotch pies are to be found all over the country—small round pies made of hot-water pastry filled with minced meat, eaten hot. Bridies are pies made with a round of pastry folded over, filled with meat, sometimes padded with potatoes and vegetables.

Cranachan, if properly made, is memorable; double cream, and sometimes crowdie, is mixed with toasted oatmeal, sweetened and eaten with fresh soft fruit, preferably raspberries—another of Scotland's specialities.

The Scottish Tourist Board brings out a '**Taste of Scotland**' booklet every year offering details of over 200 hotels and restaurants specializing in good Scottish cooking.

Eating Out

You can choose between *haute cuisine* that will satisfy any gourmet, good plain cooking at a reasonable price, bar meals, and fast-food. In the cities, meals are served at fairly flexible hours, but in smaller places you should aim to have lunch between 12.30 and 2pm, and dinner between about 7 and 9pm. If you know you will be late it is wise to make arrangements in advance. Some of the country's best restaurants are to be found tucked away in out-of-the-way places. These are mentioned in the relevant sections of the guide.

Drink

Inspiring, bold John Barleycorn!
What dangers thou canst make us scorn!
Wi' tippenny [ale], we fear nae evil;
Wi' usquabae [whisky], we'll face the devil!

from 'Tam o' Shanter', by Robert Burns

Among the myths that need to be taken with a pinch of salt is the **whisky** myth. The average canny Scot will go for the two bottles of cut-price blended whisky that he can get from the supermarket, for the price of one bottle of vintage malt. On the whole, except among the rich, malt whisky is kept for very special occasions, bought as presents for other people—or exported. There are over a hundred malts and every connoisseur will swear to the unquestionable superiority of his particular fancy. However, experiments involving the transfer of a 'favourite' malt into a bottle with a rival label will often prove that it is the eye rather than the taste-buds that dictate preference.

Most of the distilleries are on Speyside, northeast of Aviemore in the north, or on the islands of Islay and Jura, and a large number of them run guided tours lasting about an hour, complete with a free dram, showing the process of whisky making. The Malt Whisky Trail, on Speyside, is a 70-mile voyage of discovery, taking in eight distilleries. Tourist information centres will provide details.

Traditionally, malt whisky should be drunk neat or with a little water. Purists will tell you that any other additions spoil the flavour. No other country in the world has the essential ingredients for that unique taste that makes Scotland's whisky so special: a blend of snow melt, peaty water and carefully malted barley. A Scotsman will never ask for 'Scotch'—unless he is abroad and in danger of being served with a foreign impostor.

Drambuie is a whisky liqueur, very drinkable for those who enjoy 'stickies'. Gingermac or whisky-mac is a mixture of whisky and ginger wine which is very warming on cold days.

Scotsmen prefer to drink seriously, in bars, though wine bars and English-type pubs are mushrooming. You may hear someone ordering 'a pint of heavy and a chaser'. This will be a pint of bitter and a dram of whisky—the accepted way to spin out the precious *uisge-beatha*—the 'water of life'. Often the dram is not sipped and savoured, but tossed down in a single reviving gulp. In the old days, when the licensing laws were restrictive, there was no time for leisurely drinking. Now licensing laws in Scotland permit public houses to stay open for 12 hours a day, or longer with special extensions, but not all of them choose to do so.

Generally, a bar will be open from 11am to 2.30pm, and from 5pm to about 11pm, with reduced hours on Sunday. Most city centre bars will stay open till at least midnight, and residents in licensed hotels can buy drinks at any time. Children under 18 may not be served drink in a public house or restaurant, nor may they be sold alcohol in a shop. Some establishments provide special family rooms where children can join their parents, but they must not drink alcohol here. Landlords risk losing their licences if they break the law in this respect.

Sláinte (pronounced slahn-tchuh) is Gaelic for 'health' and is often heard as a toast.

Historic Scotland

Historic Scotland is a division of the Scottish Office Environment Department, responsible for the care and upkeep of many of the country's historic ruins, buildings and sites. Some castles and historic houses open to the public are privately owned and each has its own opening times and admission charges. Wherever possible, this book gives an idea of opening dates but these change from year to year and should be checked in advance, as should opening times. There is an 'open to view' ticket which entitles you to free entrance to 563 places of historic interest: castles, abbeys, stately homes, famous gardens, etc., in Scotland, England, Wales and Northern Ireland. These can be bought from major tourist information centres. Many castles, historic houses and smaller museums close for the winter.

Doors Open Day is Scotland's contribution to 'Heritage Days', two weekends every September when Europe's finest buildings are open free to the public. You can explore historic churches, towers, country houses, breweries, power stations and many more. Find out dates and details from local tourist information centres.

Maps

Good maps are essential if you are to enjoy your holiday to the full. Bartholomew's half-inch maps are good but you need many of them and they are expensive. There is a very adequate Ordnance Survey Motoring Atlas, 3 miles: 1 inch (Scottish Highlands and Islands, 7 miles: 1 inch), available from most garages and bookshops. A 'tourist map' of the whole of Scotland, marking special attractions, is useful. Maps of each region are obtainable from the relevant tourist information centre. If you plan to walk or climb then you should get the appropriate Ordnance Survey sheets, scale 1:50,000.

National Trust for Scotland

Many of Scotland's historic buildings and much of its conserved land is under the care of the National Trust for Scotland (NTS), a charity formed in 1931 to promote the preservation of the country's heritage. Over a hundred properties, including castles, small houses, islands, mountains, coastline and gardens, come under the protection of the NTS. Most are open from April to October, and admission charges vary. Annual membership admits one person free to all NTS properties, and to all National Trust properties in England, Wales and Northern Ireland. Write to the National Trust for Scotland Head Office, 5 Charlotte Square, Edinburgh EH2 4DU, ✆ (0131) 226 5922.

Packing

Because of the unpredictability of the weather, sweaters and waterproof clothing are essential all year round if you are to enjoy the country to the full, as are comfortable, sturdy shoes. Remember Scotland is famous for its woollen industry so if you intend to buy Fair Isle, Shetland, Cashmere and tweed, pack the minimum. Rubber boots are useful but uncomfortable for walking long distances—they are cheap to buy locally if wet weather looks relentless. Go prepared for rain and cold; the chances are you will have hot sunshine and drought. Scottish waters are cold, but if the sun shines you might regret not bringing bathing things.

Public Holidays

New Year's Day is the only statutory public holiday in Scotland. Bank Holidays are mainly for banks only and include: 2 January, the Friday before Easter, the first Monday and last Monday in May, the first Monday in August, 30 November (St Andrew's Day), and 25 and 26 December. Most towns and districts have local public trades' and other holidays which vary from place to place and from year to year. Tourist offices can supply the annual leaflet, *Public Holidays in Scotland.*

Shopping

As well as the tourist-traps, there are still a few sheds and cottage parlours where weaving is done on hand looms, mostly in the islands and parts of the Highlands. They are invariably signposted from the road. Hardwearing **Harris tweed** is acclaimed all over the world: to be authentic it should be woven in the home of the crofter on a hand loom with Scottish wool (but not necessarily wool from Harris).

Some Scottish **glass** is beautiful. At Caithness Glass in Perth, Oban and Wick, factory tours show all the processes of glass-blowing, moulding and engraving, and there are shops selling the finished products. **Potter**'s workshops can be found all over Scotland.

Traditional accessories to Highland dress, set with cairngorms and amethysts, in wrought silver and gold, can be bought from most jewellers. **Jewellery** made from local stones can be found in workshops and craft shops throughout the country. With such a large deer population, both decorative and functional objects carved from horn are made all over Scotland. Take home a shepherd's crook, a crommach, with a handle carved from ramshorn or, if you're travelling light, go for a horn salt spoon or drinking bowl.

Try to squeeze a side of **smoked salmon** into your suitcase but make sure it is well wrapped. Good quality isn't cheap. Buy shortbread, oatcakes and Dundee cake, in tins. They are a good reminder of a Scottish holiday. In the duty-free shop at the airport your choice lies between the **malt whisky** you have adopted as your 'special' (if in doubt, Glenmorangie won't let you down) and Drambuie, Scotland's whisky liqueur.

Sports and Activities

The **Scottish Sports Council**, 1–3 St Colme Street, Edinburgh, ✆ (0131) 225 8411, can provide information on sports and activities throughout Scotland. For full details of water sports on offer, get the **Scotland Holiday Afloat** booklet from the Scottish Tourist Board.

canoeing

This is possible all round the coast and on many of the rivers, where the fast flow is often ideal for 'white-water' canoeing. There are many water-sport centres. The Scottish Sports Council (*see* above) runs outdoor training centres where courses include canoeing.

climbing and walking

From the gentlest stroll to the toughest climb, Scotland, small as it is, has as much to offer as any country, and a lot more than most. The scenery is unbeatable, the terrain everything from easy to dangerously challenging. The choice is endless. The one drawback may be the capricious weather. A day that begins in brilliant sunshine can end in freezing rain.

Unfortunately there are still a number of people who don't take the dangers of climbing and hill walking in the Highlands and Islands seriously. They set out ill-equipped and with insufficient skills and knowledge of the terrain and often get into difficulties. Frequently it falls to the brave men and women of the mountain rescue services to extricate these foolhardy people, often at the risk of their own lives.

There are a few simple **rules** that, if observed, could save lives, money and tempers:

1. Get a weather forecast for the area in which you intend to walk or climb. Watch the weather the whole time you are out and be prepared to turn back if conditions become dangerous, for example if visibility decreases, the wind gets up, or the temperature falls dramatically.

2. Plan your route carefully, remembering that rivers and burns can fill quickly after a rainstorm and cut you off, and peat bogs and rocks can be exhausting to walk over.

3. Tell someone where you are going, when you expect to return, and how many there are in your party. Leave a clearly visible note in your car with this information. And don't forget to tell your informant that you've come back! It's not unknown for such forgetfulness to send rescue services out on a wild goose chase looking for someone who is happily propping up a bar.

4. Take appropriate clothing and equipment: even in summer a sweater and waterproofs are essential. On any serious hillwalk or climb take gloves, hat, waterproof and windproof jacket and trousers. Wear proper walking boots with good ankle support and a sole with a good grip. Take enough food and drink to see you through a crisis: high-energy rations such as chocolate and dried fruit are useful. Take a torch, a first-aid kit, whistle and survival bag. These precautions could save your life.

5. Always carry a map—Ordnance Survey maps are ideal—and a good compass, ideally with a protractor, and be sure you know how to use them properly. It is easy enough to find your way when you can see where you have been and where you are going, but if the mist or a blizzard closes in, as they frequently do, you could spend the rest of a short life wandering around in small circles feeling extremely unhappy. For serious mountain-climbing, take an ice axe and crampons and don't set out unless you really know how to use them.

It would be impossible to list the literally thousands of walks and climbs in the Highlands and Islands. There are 279 peaks over 3,000ft (914m)—seven of them over 4,000 ft/1,230m—in Scotland. These are called **Munros** after the mountaineer Sir Hugh Munro who first listed them. Munro bagging, as it is called, is a popular pastime and most of them are reasonably accessible, often within easy reach of public roads.

The Cuillins, in Skye, have provided a testing training ground for some of the world's top mountaineers. The Arrochar Alps, the peaks northwest of Loch Lomond, particularly the Cobbler, 2,891ft (867m), and the Trossachs are both popular and accessible, as is Ben Vorlich, 3,231ft (969m), near Lochearnhead. North of Loch Tay, Ben Lawers, with its exceptional alpine flowers, is another Munro at 3,984ft (1195m), looked after by the National Trust for Scotland. Perthshire has a number of hills, including Schiehallion, 3,554ft (1,066m), near

Loch Rannoch. The hills around Glen Lyon are also good and Glencoe has a variety of challenging peaks. Further north, Ben Nevis, 4,406ft (1,322m), is Scotland's highest mountain, with several routes up including a well-marked tourist route. There are a number of other high hills in Lochaber. To the northwest, the highest peaks of the Grampians are truly arctic in the winter, but splendid for experienced climbers. The eastern edge of the Grampians, around Glen Clova, and the Lochnagar area, accessible from Deeside, are also popular. North of the Great Glen, Torridon, in the west, offers spectacular rock scenery, equalled only by the peaks of the Inverpolly Nature Reserve north of Ullapool, including the distinctive Stac Polly, 2,009ft (603m), Canisp, 2,779ft (834m) and Guilven, 2,399ft (720m). Ben Hope, southwest of Tongue, is Scotland's most northerly Munro, at 3,042ft (913m).

There are coastal footpaths, nature trails, woodland trails and long-distance footpaths, including the **West Highland Way**, which runs for 95 miles from Milngavie on the outskirts of Glasgow to Fort William at the south end of the Great Glen. It includes a marvellous range of lowland and highland scenery, on old drove roads, forestry tracks, an old military road and a railway track bed. The nanny state has published a leaflet trying to spoil the fun of this walk: no dogs on a few stretches (even on the lead), how to pee without upsetting the environment, etc. so be prepared! There are places to stay along the way. The **Speyside Way** runs for 30 miles, from Tugnet to Ballindalloch, then a further 15 miles to Tomintoul, with splendid and very varied scenery along the route.

Ski lifts for walkers are available at Cairngorm, Glencoe and Glenshee. These chair-lifts are open for hill walkers out of season only and give easy access to the higher terrain.

The Scottish Tourist Board issues a booklet, *Walking*, with details of walks, places to visit, etc. There are a large number of firms specializing in guided walking holidays, details of which are included in the booklet. The **Mountaineering Council of Scotland**, 4a St Catherine's Road, Perth, PH1 5SE, ✆ (01738) 638 227, is another useful organization. For an up to the minute **Winter Road Check**, call ✆ (01898) 654 610 (Highland); ✆ (01898) 654 620 (Grampian).

curling

Scotland's traditional winter game has been played in Scotland for over 450 years and is described as 'a sort of bowls on ice'. These days it's usually played on indoor rinks. For information on where to go to watch or participate contact the Scottish Sports Council, *see* above.

diving

The wonderful clarity of the sea around the coast, full of highly coloured sea animals and plants, makes Scottish waters among the best in the world for diving. There is a wide choice of good places where you can dive. The places listed here are outstanding. In the north there is **Scapa**, in Orkney. Four ships of the sunken German fleet, scuttled at the end of the First World War, lie untouched below the clear waters of this huge anchorage and offer marvellous scope for wreck diving. You can charter boats and get air from several places around the coast. On the west coast the waters around **Oban** are excellent, with a good air supply and boats to charter in Oban. The **Sound of Mull** is littered with wrecks, and there is sub-aqua cliff scenery. **Ailsa Craig** and the **Firth of Clyde** are also good diving sites. The **Summer Isles**, in the northwest, are also ideal for diving. For more information contact the **Scottish Sub-aqua Club**, 16 Royal Crescent, Glasgow, ✆ (0141) 332 9291.

Lord, suffer me to catch a fish,
So large that even I,
When talking of it afterwards,
May have no need to lie.

'A Fisherman's Prayer', Anon

In the first half of the 19th century southern fishermen began making the stagecoach trek to Scotland to ply for salmon with rod and line. The industrial revolution had begun to pollute England's great salmon rivers, and was to wipe the salmon out in many of them by the turn of the 20th century. The Scottish lairds had been accustomed to sending forth their 'sealgairs' (hunters) to procure fish and game for them, frequently disdaining such activities themselves. They were amazed and delighted to be paid by these newcomers for the right to dangle their baits in the water.

Much has changed since Scotland made its name as the world's best fishing venue. The night-time revellers who hunted spawning salmon in their breeding places with lamps and pronged spears have been replaced by fishermen and women throwing out high-tech fishing lines with rods made of supremely light, flexible and strong new materials. Whereas once the huge bulk of Scottish salmon was caught by estuary nets, now salmon nets (challenged by the low price of farmed salmon) are becoming uneconomic; many have fallen into disuse, or been bought up and laid to rest by the rod angling fraternity. The silver king of the river is chiefly valuable as a game fish, and the value of fishing rentals to Scotland, apart from the benefits fishing brings to many sideline economies, is enormous. The capital value of salmon fishing in Scotland has been calculated at close to £1 billion.

It is no exaggeration to say that in the valleys of some of the great rivers like the Spey and Tay, the way of life is chiefly determined by the fishery. Fishing hotels and lodges occupy strategic positions above the precious waters, and ghillies' and water bailiffs' houses are never far from the fish that sustain their livelihood. In many villages on rivers the focal point is the tackle shop, trading not only in fishing paraphernalia, but also in gossip about pools in which fish have been caught and the flies that have caught them. The news of big hauls is particularly influential with trout fishermen, and round any little loch in which someone has struck lucky, large concentrations of anglers are to be observed days later, trying in vain to repeat an individual's one-off glory.

The joy of a river is that its course connects contrasting parts of the country. The sources of many of Scotland's great rivers are swampy spring-fed patches in hanging valleys high in the mountains, or even springs in the floors of lochs. Many Scottish rivers can be fished from the mountain burns near the headwaters right through to the wide, sleepy stretches flowing through farmland nearer the coast. In some places fishermen use rod and line to spin for migratory fish in the sea off the river mouths, usually for seatrout. Seatrout are the members of the native brown trout family which choose to migrate to sea, but—unlike the Atlantic salmon which forage as far as the Greenland shelf to feed—seatrout winter offshore, generally returning in spring and early summer. In seeking enjoyment from duping fish, many methods have been devised to balance the challenge of a catch with applications of physical dexterity and manual skill. Fishing is an outwitting art, and man delights in playing the deceiver.

Salmon fishing in Scotland is classically associated with the wet fly, a contraption of feathers and other titbits which need bear no resemblance to any known insect or creature, but for certain well-tested reasons rouses fishes' aggressive urge. On the bigger rivers spinning is practised in slow, wide pools; but fly fishing is in the ascendancy, and spinning increasingly frowned on. The ancient practice of worming, which is suited to deepening pools where the worms twirl enticingly in the current, is discouraged even more.

Dapping is a technique developed for catching seatrout and brown trout in windy conditions on lochs. By deploying a loose silky cord from a pole-like rod, the fly can be made to dance over the surface like an insect blown from land and trying unsuccessfully to rise. Nymph fishing employs a wingless body in imitation of the fly at larval stage. When a trout takes a nymph it is capitalizing on the momentary opportunity offered by a fly as it rises from the riverbed prior to hatching on the surface. Dry fly, like nymph, is imitative, and although in most Scottish salmon rivers the water is too cold for dry fly to be successful, trout fishermen use it productively on warm evenings on the lochs, when the puffed-up wings of the dry fly keep it popped up on the surface.

The water surface to all fishermen is a hypnotic thing, always moving, always changing with the shifting light in the sky. Cunliffe Pearce has written evocatively of 'the top of the water, that magic looking-glass through which trout and man mysteriously make acquaintance with each other'. In Scotland there is the extra factor of supreme scenery. The Highland lochs—Loch Lomond, Loch Awe—are famed for beauty, yet also loved in a different way by connoisseurs for the fishing they offer. Some of the far north rivers—Helmsdale, Brora, Naver, Dionard—open out through heather moorland, and become faster as they drop through rocky passages before entering the sea. The outer isles have magnificent salmon and seatrout fishing, and it is on the magical Grimersta, where running fish can stream by in a seemingly endless flow, that the British record catch by one man in a day was recorded—52 salmon. Some of the most exciting trout lochs are those gem-like bodies of water in the far north, famous for being dour and uncooperative in one mood, then exploding into action the next. A hundred fish in a day to two rods is not unimaginable.

Scottish salmon fishing is not, as is sometimes said, the preserve of rich tenants on famous water. There are thousands of miles of fishing in Scotland, and many opportunities for those who seek them out. The game fishing magazines, *Trout and Salmon* and *Salmon Trout and Seatrout*, advertise plenty of rentable fishing and, once embarked on the salmon fishing circuit, chances spring up for keen fishermen through contacts made along the way. Some local councils own water, and many rivers are open to day-ticket fishermen either through angling associations, fishing hotels, local river boards, or private riparian owners. Salmon fishing permits start at around £10 per day. Trout fishing is available in greater supply than is ever utilized, particularly in the far north and west of Scotland, and some of the famous fishing hotels have access to numerous remote lochs which never see a fisherman year-round. A boat on a loch costs around £10 a day, bank fishing around £8. Tourist information centres circulate fishing information, as well as details of self-catering accommodation which is accompanied by trout fishing. The more expensive salmon fishing possibilities are marketed through the main sporting agencies, and often sold in exclusive packages based in neighbouring fishing lodges.

The salmon fishing season varies from river to river, starting in January in some places and as late as March in others. Trout fishing is from 15 March to 6 October. Sea fishing is extensive, with such a length of coastline. Porbeagle shark, halibut, cod, bass, hake, ling, skate and turbot are but a few of the many species of fish you can expect to find. There is never a shortage of charter boats or, in most places, of experienced locals to take you out. There is no closed season: weather and availability are the only limitations. Again, ask at your hotel, or in the tourist information centre.

Useful Addresses

Central Scotland Anglers Association, 53 Fernieside Cres, Edinburgh, ✆ (0131) 664 4685.

Scottish Anglers National Association, 307 West George St, Glasgow, ✆ (0141) 221 7206.

Scottish Federation for Coarse Angling, TighnaFleurs, Hill o' Gryfe Road, Bridge of Weir, Renfrewshire, ✆ (01505) 612 580.

The Scottish Federation of Sea Anglers, 18 Ainslie Place, Edinburgh, ✆ (0131) 225 7611.

golf

The monarch in these parts is **Gleneagles**, in the lee of the Ochils. The Kings and the Queens are as fine a pair of courses as you will come across in a day's march, and the combination of great golf and good living is hard to beat, if you can afford it.

At **Nairn** there is a highly regarded links course, which on more than one occasion has played host to the Scottish Championships. **Boat of Garten**, in the Spey Valley, is a relatively short course, but a joy to play. James Braid designed it, and there are superb views.

North of Inverness, **Fortrose** and **Rosemarkie**, **Muir of Ord** and **Strathpeffer Spa** all offer a pleasant 18 holes, but **Tain** is the choice if time is short. A new bridge at Tain has cut an hour from the journey north to **Royal Dornoch** and made this magnificent links more accessible. But for its location, Dornoch would be the choice for the most important championships, and indeed the Amateur Championships were played there for the first time in 1985.

Golf on the islands should not be ignored. Arran has seven courses, of which **Blackwaterfoot**, **Lamlash** and **Brodick** are the pick. Then there is **Machrihanish** on the Mull of Kintyre and the **Machrie** on Islay. Islay has just the one course and eight distilleries, so care is needed with your priorities if the golf is to be enjoyed.

sailing

Sailing off the west coast of Scotland and among the western and northern islands is so beautiful that it makes cruising among the admittedly warmer and more glamorous locations further south, such as the Greek Islands, something of an anticlimax. The weather can be tricky, of course, but this should not deter experienced sailors and there will be many fine days to enjoy. Experience is also necessary to navigate the rocks, currents and whirlpools that make these waters such a challenge. Proper maritime charts are essential. Those less certain of their abilities should stick to the lochs and inshore waters.

Once you are afloat with a good skipper and navigator there could be no better way of exploring this incomparable coastline. Seen from the sea the scenery is somehow even more magnificent than it appears from the land, and you will be able to explore sealochs that are virtually inaccessible by overland routes. As well as dozens of harbours and official moorings there are innumerable sheltered anchorages far from any human habitation. Here you can drop anchor and swim in the cold waters with only seabirds and sheep to see you, before going ashore to enjoy a supper of freshly caught mackerel cooked on an open fire as you listen to the eerie sound of seals calling to each other.

There are marinas and sailing centres around the coast from the Clyde to Ullapool, and on many of the larger lochs. If you haven't got your own boat you can charter from a variety of places, either a fully manned boat or one to crew yourself. *On the water in Scotland* is a directory of watersports facilities in Scotland. It lists names and addresses of firms that hire boats of all categories, for all uses, together with information about slipways, chandlers, moorings, canals, and so on. It is available from the Scottish Tourist Board, *see* below.

Useful Addresses

Royal Yachting Association (Scotland), Caledonia House, South Gyle, Edinburgh EH12 9DQ, ✆ (0131) 317 7388.

North of Scotland Yachting Association, 18 Crown Avenue, Inverness IV2 3NF.

shinty or shinny

Scotland's version of Irish hurling is said to derive from cries used in the game: shin ye, shin t'ye. It's like hockey, with a leather ball and curved sticks.

shooting and stalking

The terrain is ideal, with farmland, mixed woodland and moorland, and Scotland has a long tradition of good game-management. The estuaries and marshes provide excellent scope for wildfowlers, and there are plenty of deer. Stalking, for the uninitiated, involves spending all day wriggling through wet undergrowth until your prey is within range and then, at a signal from the keeper, missing it, or wounding it and spending the night following it to administer the *coup de grâce*. Stalking with a camera instead of a rifle can be infinitely more rewarding. Game-shooting species include pheasants, snipe, grey partridge, woodcock, grouse, capercaillie and ptarmigan. Permitted wildfowl species include many varieties of duck and geese. Rough shooting is for wood pigeon, rabbit and hare. Deer species include red deer, roe, fallow and sika. All other species of wildlife, both bird and mammal, are strictly protected in Scotland by the Wildlife and Countryside Act. No game shooting is allowed on Sundays and a certificate is required by anyone owning or using either a rifle or a shotgun. Before you shoot game you must get a game licence, which is available in all main and branch post offices throughout the country. Some hotels will arrange shooting and stalking, and local tourist boards will advise on contacting estates and on shooting seasons.

skiing

There are five ski centres in the Highlands: Glencoe, the Nevis Range (Aonach Mor), Cairngorm, Glenshee and the Lecht. All have excellent runs and lift networks, as well as equipment hire and ski schools. First-timers should note that the picture-postcard conditions often found in the Alps are not so common in Scotland. At times only the most enthusiastic of skiers will enjoy their sport here, when the slopes are icy, balding and pitted with rocks and tree stumps and a piercing wind cuts through even the best thermal clothing. But on the many good days, skiing in Scotland is good fun, amongst some of the most beautiful scenery in the world.

Ski Hotline Scotland gives information on road and snow conditions and weather forecasts in the five ski centres. For all areas, ✆ 09001 654 654.

Glencoe is situated on the A82 about 95 miles north of Glasgow and 25 miles from Fort William. The centre is open five days a week from Thursday to Monday inclusive during the season, and every day over the Easter period. There are 15 runs (including a particularly easy one called Mugs' Alley), and six lifts. There is a log cabin restaurant and a Museum of Scottish Skiing and Mountaineering. **Ski Hotline**: ✆ 09001 654 658; general information, ✆ (01855) 851 226

The Nevis Range is 125 miles from Glasgow and 5 miles north of Fort William off the A82. The access road, signposted Aonach Mor, is seldom affected by snow. The centre is open throughout the season, which can last from as early as October to as late as May. There are 18 runs of all standards and nine lifts. There is also a 250ft (75m) dry ski slope. A crèche for three- to seven-year-olds is open from 9 to 12am and from 1 to 4pm. The Snowgoose Restaurant and Bar seats over 200 and there is also a snack hut. **Ski Hotline**: ✆ 09001 654 660; general information, ✆ (01397) 705 825

Cairngorm is situated off the A9, 135 miles from Edinburgh, 28 miles from Inverness and 9 miles from Aviemore. There are plans for a £15 million redevelopment, but there are already plenty of good runs of all categories. There is a day-lodge with licensed restaurant, shop and ski hire, and snack bars on the slopes. **Ski Hotline**: ✆ 09001 654 655, general information, ✆ (01479) 861 261

Glenshee is 80 miles from Edinburgh, 105 miles from Glasgow, 40 miles from Perth and 12 miles from Braemar on the A93. Spread over three valleys, it has the widest selection of runs in Britain, 38 in all, ranging over all categories. There are 26 lifts. There is a licensed restaurant and cafès, ski schools, a shop and a crèche in high season. **Ski Hotline**: ✆ 09001 654 656, general information, ✆ (01339) 741 320

The **Lecht** is 100 miles from Glasgow, 50 miles west of Aberdeen and 7 miles from Tomintoul on the A939. It has 12 lifts and 17 runs of varying degrees of difficulty. There is a summer ski slope and night skiing on three of the runs. Facilities include a licensed day lodge, shop and ski hire, and a crèche. **Glen Mulliach**, 4 miles north of the Lecht, is the centre for Nordic cross country skiing. **Ski Hotline**: ✆ 09001 654 657; general information, ✆ (01975) 651 440; for cross country, ✆ 09001 654 659

surfing

Surfing in Scotland hardly conjures up images of Hawaiian shores and hot weather, but the north of Scotland can lay claim to some of the best surfing waves in Europe. In fact, the European Amateur Surfing Championships were held in Thurso in 1981. Any exposed part of Scotland's long coastline has the potential for excellent waves, but the northernmost section—from Bettyhill almost to John O'Groats—has a reputation for the most consistent swells and variety of breaks. There are waves to suit everyone, from gentle beachbreaks to massive reefs, point breaks and river mouths. This is wild-frontier surfing against stunning back-drops of mountains and castles. The water is a slightly off-putting brown, but don't be alarmed because it's only coloured by peat washed down from the hills. There are very few local surfers, but they are very friendly.

Tourist Offices

For tourism purposes, Scotland is divided into regions covered by Area Tourist Boards; each has its own Tourist Information Centre and publishes its own free brochure with local information and a fully comprehensive accommodation guide. Readers are strongly advised to use these brochures to supplement the recommendkations made in this book. Information centres will also advise on routes, sporting permits and local events, and will book accommodation.

The Scottish Tourist Board's Scottish Travel Centre, 19 Cockspur Street, London SW1 5BL (*open Mon–Sat throughout the year*) provides a full range of information, advice and literature. It also helps with route planning, and has a travel agency where you can make reservations for accommodation and transport. for phone queries call, ✆ (0131) 472 2035.

Also in London is the **Britain Visitor Centre**, 1 Regent Street, W1 (*open daily*). Here the British Tourist Authority provides a comprehensive booking service covering rail, air and sea travel, sightseeing tours, theatre tickets and accommodation. They also change currency.

For drivers using the M6 route north, **Southwaite Tourist Information Centre**, in the Southwaite Service Station, a few minutes south of the border near Carlisle, offers full information on all areas in Scotland, as well as accommodation services.

The main **Tourist Information Centre** for the whole of Scotland is Edinburgh Marketing in Waverley Market, 3 Princes Street (*open Oct–May daily except Sun, personal callers only*). Run in partnership with American Express and Europcar, it offers advice to tourists in all areas, accommodation and travel booking, route planning, a Scottish bookshop, currency exchange and car hire. The head administrative office of the **Scottish Tourist Board** is at 23 Ravelston Terrace, Edinburgh, EH4 3EU, ✆ (0131) 332 2433.

These are the area tourist boards for the regions covered in this book. Details of local tourist information centres can be found in the relevant sections throughout the guide:

Perthshire Tourist Board, Lower City Mills, West Mill St, Perth PH1 5QP, ✆ (01738) 450 600, 🖷 444 863.

Argyll, the Isles, Loch Lomond, Stirling, Trossachs Tourist Board, Old Town Jail, St John St, Stirling FK8 1EA, ✆ (01786) 445 222, 🖷 471 301/446 325.

The Highlands of Scotland Tourist Board, Peffery House, Strathpeffer IV14 9HA, ✆ (01997) 421 160, 🖷 421 168.

Western Isles Tourist Board, 26 Cromwell St, Stornoway, Isle of Lewis HS1 2DD, ✆ (01851) 703 088, 🖷 705 244.

Orkney Tourist Board, 6 Broad St, Kirkwall, Orkney KW15 1NX, ✆ (01856) 872 856, 🖷 875 056.

Shetland Islands Tourism, Market Cross, Lerwick, Shetland ZE1 0LU, ✆ (01595) 693 434, 🖷 695 807.

Tracing Your Ancestors

For many reasons, not least the Highland Clearances in the 17th and 18th centuries, a large number of exiled Scots, and descendants of exiled Scots, return to the land of their origins hoping to trace their family history. Write to the **Keeper of the Records of Scotland**,

Scottish Record Office, Her Majesty's General Register House, Princes Street, Edinburgh EH1 3YY, ✆ (0131) 557 1022. Send all the information you have on your ancestors. Many clans have their own clan historian/library and will give advice.

The Highland Folk Museum in Kingussie is running a Root-finding project. Ring Paul Basu, ✆ (01540) 662 435, for details.

Where to Stay

The choice of accommodation in Scotland is enormous, ranging from a few superb, luxury hotels to simple bed and breakfasts, or self-catering. The price is not always a reliable guide. The accommodation guides in the local brochures give full details of price and facilities. This guide gives only a very small selection.

As little as £15 a night can buy bed and breakfast in a clean house, with a warm welcome and a thumping good breakfast. £120 can buy a night in a four-poster bed, or over £200 a suite with a jacuzzi. You can rent a whole house or cottage from as little as £60 a week to well over £1,000. Prices often vary seasonally: single rooms are usually more expensive, per head, than double. You can even get good value in a hotel for as little as £15 a night in some areas.

A static caravan costs from £50 a week upwards, and campsites charge from about £5 a night for visiting caravans. Campsite facilities vary enormously. Some are good, others not, but often the scenery makes up for primitive plumbing.

Many bed and breakfast places serve an evening meal, and all hotels provide full service. In the more rural areas, and indeed in the towns, don't be put off by the lack of en suite bathrooms in the smaller hotels. What they lack in modern facilities is invariably made up for in the friendly hospitality of the staff. Very often 'public bathroom' means sole use of a bathroom across the passage.

Prices

Prices change frequently. In this guide accommodation is loosely graded into three categories, based on the price of bed and breakfast for one person in a single room—double rooms are almost always cheaper per person. Many hotels do special bargain breaks, so it is well worth enquiring about these.

expensive	You won't see much change from £70 at the bottom end of this range, and at the other end, the sky's the limit.
moderate	About £30 to £70 should buy you a comfortable night.
cheap	As little as £15 a night if you are lucky, otherwise up to about £30. Some of the cheapest are often surprisingly good.

Scottish tourist board accommodation gradings

An impartial team of inspectors visits hotels, guest houses, bed and breakfast and self-catering establishments, to assess their quality. They award classifications ranging from one to five stars, and gradings from 'Approved' to 'Highly Commended', depending on the standard and facilities. Full details can be obtained from the Scottish Tourist Board, 23 Ravelston Terrace,

Edinburgh EH4 3EU, ✆ (0131) 332 2433. Visitors should be aware that these awards are based on a set range of standards and facilities such as: TV, shoe-cleaning kit, full-length mirror, trouser press, luggage stand, hospitality tray, etc., as well as the more obvious requirements such as heating and towels. They do not apply to character and soul. It is therefore possible to opt for a Highly Commended, five-star hotel only to find yourself in a sweltering, double-glazed bedroom crammed with gadgets and electric goodies, totally lacking in atmosphere. Equally, an old-fashioned, slightly shabby ex-shooting lodge, as full of Highland character and hospitality as you could ever wish for, with blazing log fires instead of central heating, pure cotton sheets, early-morning tea brought to you, and delicious home cooking, may be excluded from the Scottish Tourist Board's list because of its lack of tangible 'facilities'.

Wolsey Lodges

Wolsey Lodges are private homes where guests are made welcome as friends, entertained as family and often dine with their hosts and other guests. The atmosphere is generally like an informal country house party. Wolsey Lodges vary from grand country houses to more modest homes and often include antiques, fine paintings, silver and glass. The standard of cooking is high, usually done by the hostess—or host—using as many local ingredients as possible. There is often a trust bar. Some houses are licensed, but if not guests may bring their own drink. Prices vary but are always reasonable for what is offered.

youth hostels

There are dozens of Scottish Youth Hostel Association hostels, marked on most maps by a triangle. They fall into three grades, A, B and C, some having central heating, hot showers, carpets, etc., and all offering dormitory accommodation and self-catering facilities. Anyone over the age of five may use a youth hostel. The one on Loch Lomond is very high class and so is Carbisdale Castle, near Bonar Bridge. For full details, you can write to the **Scottish Youth Hostel Association**, 7 Glebe Crescent, Stirling FK8 2JA, ✆ (01786) 891 400. To find out about the availability of rooms at a variety of hostels at the same time, you can phone central reservations on ✆ (0541) 553 255.

There are also a large number of independent hostels/bunkhouses/bothys, and it is well worth getting brochures from Scottish Tourist Board Information Centres. Prices range from £5 up to about £12 and there is often a choice of dormitory bunk room, family room or twin room. Some include breakfast and bed linen, some charge extra. Almost all provide self-catering facilities. They offer an excellent way of seeing Scotland on the cheap.

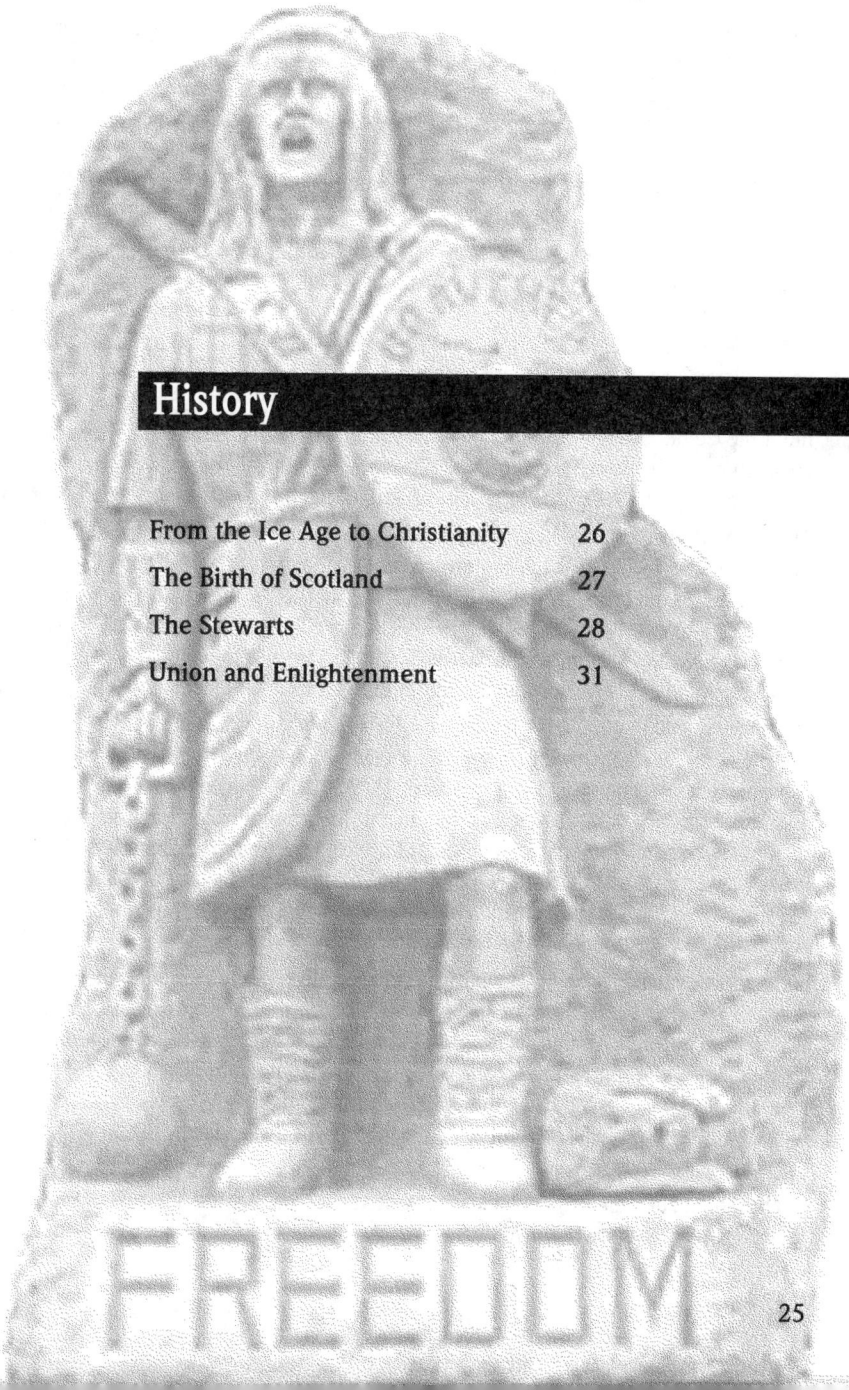

History

From the Ice Age to Christianity 26

The Birth of Scotland 27

The Stewarts 28

Union and Enlightenment 31

From the Ice Age to Christianity

The Ice Age eradicated evidence of any previous habitation in Scotland. **Stone Age** settlers, at least 7,000 years ago, were the first to leave clues to their existence. Burial sites and middens (rubbish heaps) from those times have thrown up enough to tantalize archaeologists, but not enough to leave more than a shadow of their identity. They came from Asia and Europe, through England and Ireland, wave after wave of them, creeping up the coast in dug-out canoes, settling for long enough to leave traces of their culture and way of life, before vanishing into obscurity. They lived off deer and wild boar, fish and crustaceans. Some only stayed a short time, living in caves. An excavated house in Grampian dates from 7000 BC, a round stone building about 25ft (8m) across. Later, farmers came from the Continent and introduced agriculture. People settled for longer periods, burning forests and enriching the land with potash.

After the hunters and gatherers came the **Beaker People**, who laid beakers in the tombs of their dead. They were skilful engineers, and historians puzzle over their mysterious stone circles and monoliths, and over the true purpose of their brochs (massive stone towers built near the sea in the far north, about 2,000 years ago). Metal was introduced about 1,000 years before Christ, and with it the sword and shield. Scotland, on the trade route between Ireland and Scandinavia, was able to barter food and hides for bronze and copper. During this millennium the Celtic-speaking Britons arrived, a sturdy, fair-haired race, combative and quick to attack in order to acquire precious land. The local people built defensive forts, with ditches and ramparts, such as the ones on Barry Hill and Finavon, and skirmishing became part of life.

The **Romans** arrived in AD 82 and with them came the first record of Scottish history, written by the historian Tacitus. Tacitus describes how his father-in-law, Agricola, defeated an army of tall, red-haired men on an unidentified hillside in the northeast, in the Battle of Mons Graupius. The exact location of this battle is debatable, but it was somewhere in today's Grampian, so called from a misprint of 'Graupius' by a 16th-century chronicler. Roman remains were found as far north as the Moray Firth and Tacitus recorded that they 'discovered and subdued' Orkney.

The Romans called their victims *picti*, the painted ones, from which the name 'Picts' is thought to derive, and failed to subdue them. Highly trained legionnaires could not compete with hostile tribes who faded into the mountains, forests and marshes, refusing to fight army-to-army, preferring to lay cunning ambushes for their aggressors. The Romans fell back having, it has long been believed, lost the entire Ninth Legion in a savage massacre. In fact, evidence of their having been merely posted elsewhere was unearthed recently when traces of their later existence were found around the Danube.

Four races dominated Scotland, then called Alba, or Alban in the years after the Romans withdrew. The **Celtic Picts** were the most powerful, occupying the land from Caithness to the Forth; the **Teutonic Angles**, or **Anglo-Saxons**, occupied Bernicia, south of the Forth; the **Britons**, another Celtic race, occupied the western lands south of the Clyde. Finally there were the **Scots**: Celts who had come over from Ireland during the 3rd and 4th centuries and settled north of the Clyde, establishing the **Kingdom of Dalriada** and eventually giving their name to all Scotland.

St Ninian founded the first Christian centre at Whithorn, near the Solway Firth, in 397, and started the daunting task of converting the pagans. Then came **Columba**, a clever man of royal birth, who was exiled from Ireland and arrived in Scotland in 563. He established himself on the island of Iona, continuing St Ninian's work, and sent missionaries to the mainland and to the other islands. They penetrated further and further into Pictland. Columba's influence was political as well as religious and he did much to consolidate the strength of the Scots.

By the end of the 7th century the four kingdoms of Alban were nominally converted to Christianity—a Celtic Christianity, not yet in line with that dictated by Rome.

The Birth of Scotland

At the end of the 8th century Norsemen began to attack from the north, conquering Orkney and Shetland, the Western Isles, Caithness and Sutherland, while the four kingdoms continued to fight amongst themselves, weakening their resistance to outside attack.

In 843 **Kenneth Macalpine**, King of the Scots, achieved some sort of union between Scots and Picts, making himself king over all the territory north of the Forth and Clyde, which then became Scotia. The Picts, who had been dominant for more than 1,000 years, vanished for ever. They remain an enigmatic people whose history is unrecorded and unknown; an elusive ghost-race who will perhaps never be fully understood. It was not until 1018, however, that **Malcolm II** defeated the Angles and brought Bernicia, or Lothian, into the kingdom. He was succeeded in 1034 by his grandson **Duncan I** who already ruled the Britons, and so the four kingdoms were finally united into one Scotland, except for those parts occupied by the Norsemen. The country was divided into seven main kingdoms, of which Fife was the strongest, plus a few smaller ones, each ruled by a *mormaer*. The *Ard Righ* or High King was their overlord—King of the Scots, but not of Scotland, for each *mormaer* owned his land. In those days, under a remarkable clan system in which no one was subservient and each played an important part, Scotland was truly democratic. Duncan I was killed in 1040 by **Macbeth**, whose portrayal by Shakespeare should not be taken too literally. He was the last Celtic king and his 17-year reign was chronicled as a time of plenty. He was killed by Duncan's son, **Malcolm Canmore**, with the help of the English, in 1057. *Ceann Mor* is Gaelic for big head, referring to Malcolm III's status rather than any anatomical defect, or conceit.

Malcolm Canmore's second wife, **Margaret**, was a refugee from the Norman conquest of England. She imported English clergy and established an English court, transforming Scotland into a kingdom similar to Norman England. The Lowland clans gave up their democracy: *mormaers* became earls and established a feudal system, while the Highlands and Islands retained the old, patriarchal clans. **David I**, ninth son of Malcolm Canmore, inherited the throne in 1124. He had been brought up in England and gave away large Scottish estates to his Anglo-Norman friends. The Highlanders took little notice of these southern interlopers.

Malcolm IV was 13 when he inherited the throne from his grandfather, David I. Known as Malcolm the Maiden, he was nevertheless a brave young man, whose courage inspired many of his followers. Gentle and religious, he ruled for only 12 years before he died, to be succeeded by his brother, **William the Lion**, who launched an ill-conceived expedition into Northumberland in 1174. It failed, William was captured, and he was forced to sign the humiliating Treaty of Falaise, placing Scotland under feudal subjection to England.

Alexander II succeeded to the throne in 1214 and directed his attention to the Western Isles, whose lords gave their allegiance to Norway. It was his son, **Alexander III**, however, who managed to expel the Norsemen from the Hebrides by defeating old King Haakon IV of Norway in the **Battle of Largs** in 1263. The Hebrides became part of the Kingdom of Scotland again, though the Lords of the Isles continued to pay little heed to any authority but their own.

When **Edward I** of England declared himself to be overlord of Scotland there were several claimants to the throne, the strongest being **John Balliol**, son of the regent, and **Robert the Bruce**. Edward insisted that Scotland should contribute to English defence costs and join with them in an invasion of France. Rather than do this the Scots instead formed an alliance with France in October 1295. The **Auld Alliance**, as it became known, was between two independent kingdoms, rather than being forced by a stronger state on a weaker one, as England had sought to do to Scotland. Edward saw it as practically a declaration of war.

In 1296 Edward's army progressed through Scotland, compelling nobles and lairds to sign the **Ragman Roll** acknowledging him to be their king. He then returned to England, taking with him what he thought to be the Stone of Destiny, brought from Ireland seven centuries earlier and believed to embody special powers of sovereignty. It had always been used in the coronation of Scottish kings. Edward was convinced he had finally conquered Scotland.

Robert the Bruce, grandson of John Balliol's rival, became Guardian of Scotland, alongside Balliol's nephew, Red John Comyn. Bruce resigned the guardianship in 1302 and went over to Edward's side. In 1306 Bruce and Red Comyn met at Greyfriars Kirk, in Dumfries, but they quarrelled and Bruce killed Comyn, possibly because of his refusal to help Bruce in a campaign for the Scottish throne. Seizing the initiative, Bruce went to Scone and had himself crowned King of Scotland in March 1306, but Edward hurried north and defeated Bruce a month later at Methven. Outlawed, his friends and allies dead, Bruce went into hiding but, following the example of a persistent spider, he returned to reclaim his crown in 1307. He overcame all other claimants to the throne and defeated Edward I's successor, Edward II, at **Bannockburn** in 1314.

Bruce was succeeded by his young son, **David II**, with **Thomas Randolph, Earl of Moray**, as regent. The 42 years of David's reign were troubled times for Scotland. He was captured by the English at the **Battle of Neville's Cross** in 1346 and spent the next 11 years in England as a captive. Following his ransom and release in 1357, David was offered easier terms for the ransom's repayment if he would name Edward III or one of his sons as his successor. Not surprisingly, the Scottish parliament rejected this notion. David reigned until his death in 1371, to be succeeded by his nephew and steward, Robert.

The Stewarts

The Stewarts were a family of incoming Normans named FitzAlan who became hereditary High Stewards to the kings of Scotland, and changed their name accordingly. **Robert**, the first Stewart king, was a better regent than monarch. Anarchy, rebellion and internal squabbles disturbed the peace he strove for. **Robert II** died in 1390 and was succeeded by his son, **Robert III**. Crippled by a kick from a horse, Robert was in poor health and much of the responsibility of government passed to his brother, the Duke of Albany. The ailing Robert III sent his son and heir, **James I**, to France in 1406, fearing Albany had plans to remove him from the succession, but the young prince was captured by pirates and handed over to the English. Robert died a month later, leaving Albany in full power for 18 years while James was held hostage. Powerful nobles seized the opportunity to consolidate their strength. They expanded their estates and built up private armies, many of them becoming as powerful as kings. Most notable among them was the **Douglas** family, whose lands and subjects rivalled those of the king. Meanwhile, in the northwest, the Lords of the Isles allied themselves with the English and continued to live their own lives with little regard for central government.

James I returned to his throne in 1424, aged 29, to find his country in turmoil. His first step was the execution of the Albany family in 1425 and the seizure of their considerable estates. In 1427 he summoned the Highland chiefs and arrested 40: Alexander of the Isles retaliated by burning Inverness. Further rebellion from the west was subdued and James redressed the balance of power in the Lowlands by annexing many of the earldoms that threatened his supremacy. His policies earned him many enemies, and in 1437 three of them stabbed him to death, leaving his six-year-old son **James II** as his heir. James II came to the throne in 1449 at the age of 19. He continued the reforms so dear to his father, but was threatened by an alliance between the Douglases, Crawfords and John of the Isles. James was killed in 1460 when a cannon exploded during the siege of Roxburghe.

James III was nine when his father died and, until his accession at the age of 19, Scotland was once more ruled by regents. He married the King of Norway's daughter, whose dowry included Orkney and Shetland. James was an intellectual, better fitted for academic life than a crown. He survived one attempt to dethrone him but six years later his son led a successful coup against him, becoming James IV in his place. James III was killed in mysterious circumstances at the decisive battle of Sauchieburn, a parliamentary inquiry recording simply that the King 'happinit to be slane'.

James IV, most popular of the Stewart kings, was 15 when he came to the throne. He was clever and charming, a good leader, pious and energetic, generous, flamboyant and sensual. The arts and education blossomed and James led the way. He authorized the building of palaces and churches. His court was elegant and cultured and the country was peaceful and prosperous. But the peace was not absolute: on the doorstep the Lords of the Isles continued to live as they always had: fiercely patriarchal, their loyalties rooted in their clans and chieftains. James, who had learnt Gaelic, decided to visit the Western Highlands and Islands, hoping to win the friendship of the clans. His attempts were viewed with suspicion, so he desisted and appointed overlords to rule them. This resulted in an uprising of the Macdonalds and Macleans who stormed and burned Inverness in 1503.

In that same year James married 12-year-old Margaret Tudor and signed a Treaty of Perpetual Peace with England, but in 1511 his brother-in-law, Henry VIII of England, joined the Pope, the King of Spain and the Doge of Venice in a Holy League against France. James passionately desired a united Europe and, determined to maintain a balance of power, renewed the Auld Alliance with France and tried, in vain, to mediate. In 1513, threatened from all directions, France appealed to Scotland for help. James in turn appealed to Henry, who replied with insults.

Against advice, in August 1513, James led a Scottish army across the Tweed, to **Flodden Field**, where they were massacred by the superior forces of the English. The king, his nobles and most of Scotland's best men were killed in a battle as pointless as it was valiant: it was perhaps Scotland's greatest tragedy. The country was left leaderless, its army slain, its new king, **James V**, a toddler and its regent, Margaret Tudor, with divided loyalties.

There followed a period of more turmoil until the king was old enough to take office and try to restore order. His second wife, **Marie de Guise-Lorraine**, bore him two sons, both of whom died, and a daughter, **Mary, Queen of Scots**, only a few days old when her father died after his army was defeated by Henry VIII at Solway Moss in 1542.

Henry VIII, determined to absorb Scotland, proposed a marriage between Mary and his delicate son, Edward, but the Scottish parliament rejected such a proposal and renewed instead the Auld Alliance with France. Mary, aged five, was sent to France for safety, where she stayed for 15 years, marrying the French Dauphin. While she was away, Protestantism was gaining power in Scotland. In 1554 Marie de Guise-Lorraine, the dowager Queen Mother, replaced Arran as Regent. The presence of many French officials in the Regent's government greatly upset the Scottish nobility. Several of them, calling themselves 'The Lords of the Congregation', declared their support for the Protestant religion. In 1559 **John Knox**, a powerful Reformer, delivered a fiery sermon in Perth, denouncing the Church of Rome.

Mary's French husband died at the end of 1560 and she returned to her country as queen in 1561—no longer Mary Stewart, but Mary Stuart, the French form of her name which was adopted in England. A devout Catholic, she had no desire to tangle with the Protestants and merely wished to be allowed to practise her own religion in peace. This horrified John Knox and his followers, who found her light-hearted ways obnoxious. In 1567 an ill-advised marriage to the Earl of Bothwell sparked off an inferno of protest from both Catholics and Protestants. Mary was imprisoned and Bothwell forced into exile. Humiliated, Mary was forced to abdicate in favour of her baby son, **James VI**. Her half-brother, James Stewart, Earl of Moray, bastard son of James V, was proclaimed Regent. Mary fled to England and threw herself on the mercy of her cousin, Elizabeth I. Elizabeth, without an heir, could not forget Mary's claims to the English throne, and had her imprisoned for 20 years before ordering her execution.

James VI proclaimed himself king in 1585 and found himself head of a country divided between Catholics and Protestants. He aspired to impartiality, incurring the animosity of both factions. A Protestant in name, if not belief, James had no wish to antagonize his Protestant cousin Elizabeth of England and spoil his chances of inheriting her throne. He concluded an alliance with England and made no more than a formal protest when Elizabeth agreed to the execution of his mother in 1587.

The Protestant religion in Scotland now presented problems. It was divided between the extreme Presbyterians, who wanted a religion of the purest simplicity with equality of ministers and no bishops or elaborate ritual, and James' English form of Protestantism, with bishops appointed by the Crown and a formal liturgy. He tried to impose his will on the Kirk, but failed. In 1603 Elizabeth I died, appointing James her heir. Thus he became James VI of Scotland and I of England. He hurried to London and only returned to Scotland once, preferring the magnificence of the English court, and the ritual of the Church of England. But he still tried to foist Episcopacy on his northern subjects and re-instate formal worship. He died in 1625 and his son, **Charles I**, succeeded him.

Charles had no love for the Kirk. When he went north for his Scottish coronation, his subjects were scandalized by the 'popish' practices he brought with him. Thousands flocked to Greyfriars Kirk in Edinburgh in February 1638 to sign the National Covenant, condemning all Catholic doctrines and upholding the 'True Religion'. The Covenant, however, was somewhat ambivalent: its signatories swore, not only to uphold the True Religion, but also to be loyal to a king who demanded the Episcopacy they shunned. Loyal subjects of the Crown thus found themselves torn between obedience to the king and obedience to their new religion.

When civil war broke out in England, the Covenanting Scots agreed to help the English Parliamentarians. In 1649 Charles I was defeated by Cromwell and executed. The Scots grasped this opportunity to advance their quest for stability and invited his exiled son, **Charles II**, to Scotland as king, on condition that he supported the Covenant. Furious, Cromwell invaded Scotland. Charles went back into exile and Cromwell ruled both countries until he died in 1658. The Restoration in 1660 brought Charles II to the throne. He ignored the promises he had made, and sought to reintroduce Episcopacy, rekindling the fervour of the Covenanters, who fled to the hills and worshipped in secret 'Conventicles'. In 1670 these conventicles were declared treasonable, and there followed the **Killing Times**, when thousands of Covenanters were slaughtered.

Charles II died of apoplexy in 1685 and was succeeded by his brother, **James VII/II**, Scotland's first Catholic sovereign for 120 years, who tried unsuccessfully to introduce tolerance for all religions. He was deposed in 1688 by his Protestant daughter, Mary, and her Dutch husband, William of Orange, and fled to France. Some Scots, mostly Highlanders, remained true to James. The **Jacobites**, as they were called, rose, under Graham of Claverhouse and almost annihilated William's army in a savage battle at Killiecrankie in 1689. But Claverhouse was killed, leaving them leaderless, and they lost heart and returned to their Highlands.

The government, uneasy about the rebellious Highlanders, issued a proclamation ordering all clans to take an oath of allegiance to the Crown by the first day of 1692. Circumstances prevented **Alisdair MacIain of Clan Donald** from taking the oath until after the deadline. This provided the government with a chance to intimidate the Highland clans. A company of Campbell soldiers, commanded by a relation of MacIain's, Captain Robert Campbell of Glenlyon, billeted themselves on the MacDonalds in Glencoe. They rose at dawn and slaughtered their hosts. The barbarity of the Massacre of Glencoe produced public outcry, not so much because of the number killed—38 out of about 150—but because of the abuse of hospitality. The king denied all foreknowledge: as a gesture, he sacked his Secretary of State, the Master of Stair, who had instigated the deed.

Union and Enlightenment

Between 1698 and 1700 Scotland's economy was shattered by an unsuccessful attempt to colonize the Darien coast on the isthmus of Panama. Scotland, bankrupt and plunged into political crisis, was forced to accept the Treaty of Union in 1707, uniting the parliaments of England and Scotland. This carefully worded document brought advantage to both countries, giving Scotland a badly needed boost to her economy and the right to Presbyterianism, and removed the threat of further war between the two countries.

The signing of the Treaty of Union forced the Scots to accept a Hanoverian succession, but Jacobite loyalties still prevailed in the Highlands. **James Edward Stuart**, son of the deposed James VII/II, was regarded by many as Scotland's true king. The Old Pretender, as he was called by the Hanoverians, made three unsuccessful attempts to regain his throne. (Pretender is from the French *prétendre*—to claim, not from the English word for make-believe.) His expedition from France in 1708 only got as far as the Firth of Forth. In 1715 the Earl of Mar, upset by his treatment at the hands of the Hanoverian George I, raised the Pretender's banner and proclaimed James king. The rising looked promising but, after an inconclusive battle at **Sheriffmuir**, support for it dwindled. The Old Pretender put in a brief appearance in Scotland but soon returned to France. In 1719 a final attempt was made, backed by the Spanish; but the supporting fleet was lost in a storm and the Highlanders dispersed.

Stringent measures were taken to quell the clans. Between 1726 and 1737 General Wade built military roads, bridges and forts, linking strategic strong points at Fort William, Fort Augustus and Fort George and opening up the Highlands. He raised a regiment of clansmen loyal to the Whig government, the Black Watch, whose duty was to keep order among the resentful clans.

George I was an unattractive German who disliked the British as much as they disliked him. When he died, his son **George II**, equally Germanic and unsuitable to rule over Highlanders, gave them excuse enough to cling to their Jacobite dreams. Exiled in Rome, the Old Pretender's son, **Prince Charles Edward Stuart**, was a brave young man with charisma and magnetism. He pawned his mother's rubies, set sail for Scotland and landed in Eriskay on 23 July 1745, determined to win the crown for his father.

At first his reception was daunting: Macdonald of Boisdale told him to go home. 'I am come home', he retorted. MacLeod and Macdonald of Sleat refused to help, but Macdonald of Clanranald stood by him. Cameron of Lochiel was reluctant to encourage what he believed to be romantic folly, but he was won over and on 19 August the standard was raised in **Glenfinnan**, the Old Pretender proclaimed King James VIII/III, and Prince Charles his regent. Subsequent events are well known. The prince attracted support as he advanced on Edinburgh, but his army probably never exceeded 8,000 men. Capturing Perth on the way, he held glorious court at Holyrood, defeated General Cope's soldiers at **Prestonpans** and inflamed Jacobite hearts with optimism.

On 1 November Prince Charles led his motley army south with the intention of taking London, hoping to woo more Jacobites on the way. Meeting little resistance, but picking up disappointingly few recruits, they reached Derby on 4 December, only 127 miles from their target. At this point Charles' prudent advisers insisted that to go further was madness. On 6 December he agreed reluctantly and the Highlanders turned round to march in an orderly retreat back to Scotland. On 17 January 1746 the Jacobites won their last battle, defeating Cope's successor, General Hawley, at Falkirk. Hearing news of the advance of the Duke of Cumberland's army from England, the Prince took his army back into the Highlands, capturing Inverness on 21 February. On 16 April Cumberland marched towards Inverness, his forces meeting the Jacobite army on Drummossie Moor, south of **Culloden**. Outnumbered and out-gunned, the Jacobites were soon defeated. Defeat turned into a rout in which Cumberland's men showed no mercy to their opponents. The Prince escaped, with a price of £30,000 on his head, and spent the next five months in hiding in the Western Highlands and Islands. Aided by brave **Flora Macdonald**, he escaped eventually to Europe where he lived in squalid exile for the rest of his life, dying in Rome in 1788.

The English and the Lowland Scots were determined to squash the rebellious Highlanders for ever. They enforced the **Act of Proscription** in 1747, banning the wearing of tartan and Highland dress and the bearing of arms, with later measures to abolish the hereditary jurisdiction of the chiefs. Jacobites who had not died at Culloden were either executed or transported. The old way of life was dead. The act was repealed in 1782, largely thanks to the intervention of the Highland Society of London, but by this time it was no longer relevant: the **Highland Clearances** had begun.

Between 1780 and 1860 thousands of crofters were evicted from their homes in the Highlands and Islands to make way for sheep. Many others emigrated voluntarily, to escape persecution, to Canada, America, New Zealand and Australia. In the mid 19th century Ireland's potato famine reached the Highlands, resulting in appalling hardship and causing further emigration. By the end of the 19th century the rural Highlands and Islands were almost deserted.

A flourishing cotton industry collapsed in the 1860s when the American Civil War cut off supplies of raw cotton, and heavy industry developed instead. Glasgow, once the biggest tobacco importer in Britain, led the world in shipbuilding. Expanding industries meant expanding labour forces; there were concentrations of population in industrial areas, fed by refugee Highlanders and Irish. Shipbuilding and engineering developed rapidly from the mid 19th century until, by the beginning of the 20th century, some 100,000 jobs were related to Clydeside shipbuilding alone. The Steel Company of Scotland, founded in 1871, replaced iron, and the entire economy of west and mid Scotland depended on Glasgow's heavy industry. The First World War took its toll of Scottish manhood, but it needed a constant supply of arms and ships and machinery and there was more than enough work for those left behind.

It was the Great Depression in the 1920s and 1930s that dealt Scotland a mortal blow. After the Wall Street Crash in 1929 the global wave of economic disaster washed over Clydeside, and by 1936 the output from the shipyards had fallen from three-quarters of a million tons to less than 60,000, with at least two-thirds of the workforce unemployed. In order to try to increase efficiency and generate more trade, firms merged and pruned their labour forces still further, resulting in more job losses. Not surprisingly, socialism flourished, passionately fuelled by leaders like **James Maxton** and **Emmanuel Shinwell**. Public opinion favoured the plight of the workers, and by the end of the 1930s things were beginning to look up. The Second World War brought with it a fresh demand for armaments and ships: Clydeside boomed and Scotland grew prosperous again. But after the war competition from abroad began to steal trade. Shipyards, steelworks and factories closed; less coal was needed so coalmines closed. The oil boom in the 1970s brought new prosperity for a while but this was short-lived.

A new generation of enterprising minds, particularly from Glasgow, turned the tide of apathy. Diversification spread a rash of light industry throughout the country, and workers are now more inclined to negotiate for rights than to cripple their livelihood with strikes. Politically, Scotland leans to the left and juggles with nationalism. Those in favour of autonomy hold that they are the poor relations of politicians at Westminster, whose survival-of-the-fittest policies make no allowance for Scotland's circumstances. But when, in 1979, they were first invited to vote for devolution, over 36 per cent didn't bother to vote and the Nationalists lost through the nation's apathy.

There were further stirrings of nationalist feeling prior to the general election of 1992, when it seemed likely that the Conservative Party's 13-year grip on government would be loosened. The opposition parties were united in offering greater or lesser degrees of autonomy to the Scottish people, but these promises came to nothing when the Conservatives, although winning a mere 11 of Scotland's 72 seats in Parliament, were once again returned to power in the south.

In the 1997 general election, New Labour led by **Tony Blair** won a landslide victory in Britain, wiping out all Tory constituencies north of the border. Most of Scotland's most able MPs won seats in England, leaving no obvious national leader. A referendum was held in the September of Election year and the Scots voted by 74 per cent for a Scottish Parliament and by 63.5 per cent for that parliament to have tax-raising powers. The outcome was greeted with widespread jubilation and celebration, but there remained a number of questions to be answered before 1999 when the first Edinburgh Parliament assembled, among them the 'West Lothian Question': why should Scottish MPs continue to vote on English matters at Westminster, while English MPs are denied reciprocal rights in Edinburgh? As yet there are no answers.

Scottish Nationalists continue to hail devolution as the first, irrevocable step on the road to independence. They believe that an alliance with Europe would be better than union with England, whose rulers seem sometimes aloof. The governing Labour/Liberal coalition is already at loggerheads over university tuition fees, which will set Scottish students apart from their contemporaries in the rest of the UK. And there is dispute about the new Scottish parliament buildings at Holyrood. The winning design was submitted by a Spaniard, over the heads of many excellent Scottish designers. The spiralling cost of this extraordinary edifice, due to open in 2002, has resulted in some drastic pruning: no bars for the MSPs to relax and refuel in; no ceremonial entrance (£3 million). Meanwhile, in a secret cavern somewhere in the Scottish hills, the true Stone of Destiny gathers dust...waiting.

The Stone of Destiny

Traditionally, the **Stone of Destiny** was the pillow on which Jacob laid his head when he dreamt about the ladder of angels reaching from earth to heaven. Its subsequent history is shadowy. It floated round the world carrying mystical powers of sovereignty until it arrived in Ireland, whence it was brought to Dunadd by early missionaries and used as a throne in the coronation of Scottish kings.

In those days *mormaers* owned their kingdoms and the High King was their overlord, King of the Scots but not of Scotland. At the coronation each *mormaer* filled a shoe with earth from his kingdom and poured a little into a footprint carved into a rock. The king sat on the Stone of Destiny and put his foot over this cocktail of Scottish soil.

From here the Stone was moved to Dunstaffnage. In the 9th century Kenneth Macalpine took it to Scone where it continued to be a coronation throne for the united Scots and Picts. Edward I, believing firmly in its mystical powers, pinched what he thought to be the Stone of Destiny during one of his ravages of the north and whisked it off to become part of the Coronation Chair in Westminster Abbey. It has been there ever since, except for a brief hiatus in 1950 when Scottish Nationalists kidnapped it and hid it for about three months in Arbroath. The canny Scots had almost certainly hidden the original stone: the one in London, a rather dull lump of plain sandstone, is not even a replica, because the true stone was intricately carved. It is safe, in a secret cavern, and will be brought out by its hereditary guardians when the time is right.

O Flower of Scotland when will we see your like again
That fought and died for your wee bit hill and glen
And stood against him proud Edward's army
And sent him homeward tae think again.

The hills are bare now and autumn leaves lie thick and still
O'er land that is lost now which those so dearly held
Those days are passed now and in the past they must remain
But we can still rise now and be the nation again.

'Flower of Scotland' by The Corries

Topics

Céilidh	36
Clans and Tartans	36
Crofting	37
Gaelic	37
The Highland Clearances	38
Highland Wildlife	39
Johnson and Boswell	39
The Napier Commission	41
Piping	42
Religious Differences	42
Seers	43
Sorcerers and Superstition	44

Céilidh

Céilidh (pronounced kayly) is a Gaelic word meaning visit. In winter, when nights were long, crofters gathered in one of the houses when darkness fell, packed in round the central fire. One of the older members, often a bard or musician, acted as the master of ceremonies, and everyone was expected to contribute to the entertainment. The women knitted or spun, men repaired fishing nets or whittled wood; everyone listened. Stories, songs, poems, proverbs and legends were recited, passing history, folklore and tradition from one generation to the next. Their music stirred the soul: mouth-music, straight from the heart; Gaelic songs; pipe, harp and fiddle music. Children grew up steeped in the past and could tell you who their great-great-great-grand-uncle was and whose sweetheart he had run off with. The practice is dying now, thanks to television, and *céilidhs* tend to be commercial shows, staged in halls and hotels.

Clans and Tartans

The Scottish clan system was once an integral part of the Highlands and Islands. Every member of the clan bore the name of the chief, whether related by blood or by allegiance, and each was an equal member of the clan family (Mac means 'son of'). The chief was the father, ruler and judge, and the strength of the clan lay in his justice, kindness and wisdom, and in the loyalty of the members of the clan, to him and to one another. Rents were mostly paid in kind or man-rent and, in return for his patronage and protection, the chief could call on his people at any time to form an army and fight for him.

It is known that Highlanders wore some sort of brightly coloured, striped and checked material as far back as the 13th century, though whether the designs, or 'setts', were related to clans or to territories is not known for certain. The Suppression of the Highlands after Culloden in 1746 broke up clans, forbade tartan and highland dress to all civilians, and led to the death of the clan system. During the 36 years Highland dress was banned, many of the old setts were lost or forgotten.

However, the Highland regiments were exempt from the ban, and it is through them that the kilt survived. The early regiments all wore the Government, or Black Watch, tartan, sometimes introducing coloured overstripes to differentiate one regiment from another. It was not until Hanoverian George IV appeared at Holyrood in 1822 in an astonishing Highland outfit that the fashion for tartan was revived: in a wave of enthusiasm a large number of tartans were hastily designed, and adopted by Highlanders, and even by Lowlanders whose ancestors would have died rather than be seen in Highland dress. It is these relatively modern patterns that make up most of today's enormous range of tartans, which can be seen all over the world, in cloth and adorning luggage, footwear and a staggering range of souvenirs. The average Scotsman doesn't stride over his native hills swathed in tartan; on the whole kilts are kept for ceremonial or formal occasions, or for 'Sunday best', and many Scotsmen don't even own one.

Clan feelings still run strong, but the clan name is now no more than an umbrella for clan societies, museums, annual gatherings and ceremonial, with the chief as a figurehead, in his tartan costume. The mystique that has grown up round clan tartans is put into perspective by the apocryphal story of the irate chieftain, towering over one of a coach party visiting his ancestral castle: *'By what right are you wearing my tartan, my man?' 'By the ri' o' purrchis, at fifteen pounds a yard, my lord.' See* also 'Clans and Families' pp.321–8.

Crofting

Since the Highland Clearances, croftland tenure has been strictly controlled to protect the rights of the tenant. A croft is a smallholding in the Highlands, with a few acres, as many sheep as the land will support, and sometimes cows and poultry. If there is arable land it will be tilled. In the old days, *feannagan* (inappropriately named 'lazy-beds'), were dug for potatoes, involving much hard work, deep digging and the carting of heavy creels of seaweed for fertilizer. Some of the work on the croft is still done communally—sheep-dipping and shearing for instance, and cutting the peat and haymaking. Peat is still used as fuel in some areas. Composed of partially rotted vegetation, compressed in waterlogged conditions in temperate or cold climates, it takes a year to form 5mm, so peat-bogs are running out. In the spring it is cut into oblong slabs, using a special spade, and stacked *in situ* on end like miniature wigwams until dry. Sometimes machines are used for cutting, but this device has not yet been perfected and the resulting sausages of peat are too small, don't store well and there is a lot of wastage. In a wet summer the peat can still be lying late into the year. Once dry, it is built into neat beehives. As recently as the 1970s hay was cut with scythes, and is still sometimes turned with pitchforks until dry.

The family dwelling is the croft-house—often mistakenly called the croft. Less than 50 years ago, many Highlanders still lived in a *tigh dubh* or black house, now almost extinct except as a folk museum or byre. It had thick, double walls, about 6ft (1.8m) high, made of local stone and packed with earth and rubble. Unlined on the inside, it had rounded corners, no gables, and a reed- or heather-thatched roof anchored by boulders tied to ropes of plaited heather. Inside, the furniture was functional and, in the outer isles where there were no trees, often made of driftwood: a dresser, box-beds, a bench, stools, rat-proof meal chests, coffers and a spinning wheel. A peat fire was laid on a stone slab on the earthen floor in the middle of the room, the smoke escaping out of a hole in the thatch or left to seep out through cracks. The accumulation of this smoke gave the black houses their name. In earlier times, light came from a *crùisgean*—a lamp fuelled with fish-liver oil burning on a wick of plaited rushes. Even during the 20th century, in some island communities the beasts shared the family house, penned at one end with the floor sloping down towards them and the effluent running out through holes in the wall.

The crofter is the owner or tenant of the croft. These days most crofters have a subsidiary job as well: fishing, building or public works. Since the Clearances, the Crofting Commission has kept very careful control of crofters' rights.

Gaelic

Gaelic is still the first language in the Outer Hebrides, but even there, with an influx of non-Gaelic speakers and television, the children are growing up speaking English among themselves. Elsewhere it is no longer a living language, though many people are trying to revive it and there are many great Gaelic scholars. Sabhal Mor Ostaig, in Skye, is a popular and very successful Gaelic college; television and radio have a lot of Gaelic slots. It is taught in schools and in adult classes and there are a large number of Gaelic publications. It is an almost impossible language to 'pick up' by ear and eye because the spoken word bears little resemblance to the written. Recently a crop of new notices appeared in some of the islands, proclaiming place names in Gaelic. They must have cost a fortune; local people don't need them, and visitors can neither understand, nor pronounce them.

Gaelic, which is much older than English, stems from the Goidelic branch of Celtic languages, which were an offshoot from the earlier Indo-European language. Scottish Gaelic became a distinct dialect separate from Irish around the 13th century, but there are still many similarities. With the revival of Gaelic has come a revival of Gaelic culture. Groups like Runrig and Capercaillie, who perform modern-style Gaelic music, are enormously popular and an important part of the Scottish music scene.

The Highland Clearances

'The Clearances' are an emotive subject, and it has to be remembered that the first emigration ship sailed out of Fort William as early as 1773. There were several reasons for the depopulation of the Highlands after Culloden. Some Jacobites who had escaped execution found it expedient to go abroad for a few years; others were transported. Many Catholics, unable to practise their religion publicly at home, sought the liberty to do so across the ocean. The Proscription Act of 1747 suppressed the Highlands and broke up the clan system, depriving chiefs of their hereditary status as patriarchs. Many drifted south to become London Scots.

Away from the womb of the clan and the benefits of feudality, however, they felt the pinch financially. Vast, infertile estates in the north, overpopulated by impoverished peasants, brought in little or no revenue. Rents paid in kind were no use to those trying to keep up with society in fashionable assembly rooms or pay off gambling debts in gentlemen's clubs. Sheep farmers from the south offered good rent for sheep-runs in the north, but they wanted land free of people. Highland landowners, desperate for money, began to evict their tenants. Some built resettlement towns and villages for them and established new livelihoods such as fishing; some merely served eviction notices and employed agents to enforce them; some offered to assist with fares to new countries. Hundreds of crofting communities—those which relied entirely on their smallholdings for a living—broke up and scattered. Those who didn't emigrate flocked to the cities in the hope of finding work, or to settlements, mainly on the coast, where the land was unsuitable for sheep.

Meanwhile, in the islands landlords basked in a false prosperity from the kelp industry. Seaweed, of which there was an apparently inexhaustible supply, was collected after each tide, burned in kilns, processed into valuable fertilizer and exported. All that was needed was a huge labour force to cut, carry and burn it. Island proprietors with an eye to the main chance offered tiny plots of land to dispossessed crofters from the mainland. They charged high rent and deliberately ensured each tenant had not enough land for self-sufficiency, forcing them to work at the kelp. By 1812 the islands were crammed with people entirely dependent on kelp for their living.

After the Napoleonic Wars import duty was abolished and cheap foreign kelp flooded the market: prices plummeted; people starved. Proprietors and politicians, faced with the problem of destitute multitudes, offered inducements to encourage emigration, and many people went. The final blow came in 1846. The potato famine had already decimated Ireland; now wind-born spores drifted across the sea and descended on Scotland, half of whose population lived on potatoes. For the already starving Highlanders and Islanders, the effect was catastrophic. Many of those who had managed to stay on, often surviving several evictions, were forced to join their compatriots in Canada, America, Australia and New Zealand. By the end of the 19th century, the rural Highlands and Islands were almost completely deserted.

Highland Wildlife

The relative remoteness of the Highlands and Islands has guaranteed that they have remained largely unspoiled, with a range of wildlife unparalleled elsewhere in Britain. Keen eyes can spot rare birds almost anywhere in the Highlands; a pair of good binoculars and a willingness to walk away from the crowds are your only requirements.

Go to Shetland, Orkney, St Kilda or the Western Isles for seabirds such as skuas, puffins and gannets. Aviemore is a popular centre for inland birds, including crested tits, crossbills, golden eagles and capercaillie. The extraordinary sawing sound of the corncrake, now almost extinct in the rest of Britain, can still be heard in the Western Isles. The mudflats of Findhorn Bay at the mouth of the River Lossie, and the shingle and lagoons around the Spey estuary attract geese, waders, terns and many more, including the osprey, once extinct in Scotland. Loch Garten has a closed-circuit television trained on an osprey eyrie. Lochs in the peatlands of Sutherland and Caithness are good for red- and black-throated divers. Perhaps the most rewarding place for birdwatchers is Fair Isle, staging post for a vast number of migratory birds.

Mammals of the Highlands and Islands include species rarely seen in more populated parts of Great Britain. Deer are, if anything, too numerous here, and can often be seen near roads and habitations in winter. Polecats are becoming a menace, devastating domestic poultry; pine martens, red squirrels, wildcats and otters can be seen more and more frequently and there are still some feral goats. Mink farms flourished in Scotland in the 1950s and many escaped or were let loose into the wild. Seals, dolphins, porpoises and whales are not uncommon around the coasts and can often be seen from boats and sometimes from the land, especially around the Western Isles, the Grampian coast, the Moray Firth and the Cromarty Firth.

Adders and the harmless slow worm, actually a legless lizard, not a snake, may be spotted sunning themselves on rocks or in heather. Other species of lizard may also be seen. Among the rarer butterflies to be seen in woodlands and elsewhere are several varieties of argus, fritillary and skipper. The emperor moth, magpie moth and northern eggar are conspicuous on moorland. Scotland is famous for its salmon, trout and sea trout. Other river and loch fish include brook lamprey, pike, eel, three-spined stickleback, minnow and the rare Arctic char, a relic of the ice ages.

Botanists come a long way to see the rich variety of plants that grow in profusion throughout the Highlands and Islands, in spite of pressures from grazing sheep, cattle and deer. The machair of the Outer Hebrides, especially South Uist, produces carpets of rare wild flowers, including orchids. The blanket bog peatlands of Caithness and Sutherland are particularly noted for their sphagnum mosses, which keep the surface moist and acid, slowing the decay of plant remains. Here, sundews, butterworts and bladderworts trap and digest insects. The native woodland that once covered Scotland has almost all been destroyed. The birch survives, together with pines, oak, alder, ash, hazel, rowan, aspen, wych elm and willow.

Johnson and Boswell

When Dr Samuel Johnson, English critic, poet and lexicographer, aged 63, and his companion 32-year-old James Boswell, Scottish lawyer, writer and Johnson's biographer, set off on their journey to the Hebrides in 1773, the first emigrant ships had already sailed and the Highlands were rapidly losing the character Dr Johnson wished to observe. The Act of Proscription imposed after the 1745 Jacobite Rising had virtually wiped out the clan system and everything that went with it. What they found was a wild land, totally foreign to Johnson's experience. He was a fierce supporter of the underdog, whether slave or victim of the Clearances, and his account of their journey, read in parallel with Boswell's, gives a graphic picture of the Highlands in the latter part of the 18th century.

Boswell was a well-born snob who had 'collected' Johnson some ten years before they set out on their journey. Whether he actually liked Johnson or not is disputable. After their first meeting in 1763, he described him thus: 'Mr Johnson is a man of most dreadful appearance. He is a very big man, is troubled with sore eyes, the palsy and the King's evil (scrofula). He is very slovenly in his dress and speaks with a most uncouth voice. Yet his great knowledge and strength of expression command vast respect and render him very excellent company.'

The unlikely pair set off on their journey—the frighteningly literate Johnson, dogmatic and irascible, susceptible to female charms and careful of his health; and Boswell, intelligent but largely self-taught, sensitive to the opinions of others, punctilious, over-fond of alcohol, randy as a goat and syphilitic. They left Edinburgh on 18 August 1773 and travelled via St Andrews and Montrose up the east coast to Aberdeen. From here they visited Slains Castle. Johnson was intrigued by the architecture and by the local features. Boswell was more concerned with the discomfort of his room and the smell of his pillow. As they continued through Forres they both record a mention of Macbeth. Johnson noted that they were approaching 'a prelude to the Highlands, leaving fertility and culture behind with nothing ahead but a great length of road, nothing but heath.' At Nairn they saw their first peat fires and first heard the Gaelic language.

In Inverness Boswell was embarrassed by Johnson's espousal of the benefits gained by Scotland following the Act of Union in 1707. From Inverness they rode on horseback down Loch Ness. Passing a druid's temple Johnson commented, 'To go and see one druidical temple is only to see that it is nothing, for there is neither art nor power in it; and seeing one is quite enough.' They visited an old woman in a bothy, where Johnson first discovered the primitive conditions in which the peasants lived. He was interested to know where the old crone slept but she suspected his motives and he withdrew. Boswell was less tactful and inspected her humble sleeping area by the light of a taper.

From Fort Augustus they travelled west. On this part of their journey Johnson noted that the country was 'totally denuded of its wood, but the stumps both of oak and firs, which are still found, shew that it has been once a forest of large timber'. They passed an evening with a party of soldiers in a pub in Glenmorison, where their host bemoaned the fact that the rent for his farm had gone up to 20 pounds from 5 pounds in 20 years.

As they progressed into the 'bosom of the Highlands' Johnson recorded that they now had 'full leisure to contemplate the appearance and properties of mountainous regions, such as have been, in many countries, the last shelters of national distress, and are everywhere the scenes of adventures, stratagems, surprises and escapes.' He was amazed to see snow on the peaks and to learn that it might stay there until added to by the following winter's snows.

They then crossed to Armadale in Skye where they were welcomed by Sir Alexander Macdonald and entertained by bagpipes. They encountered the beginnings of the island winter of wind and rain, in contrast to the Highland winter of snow and ice. On the island of Raasay they were lavishly entertained by the laird, Mr McLeod, and his family of three sons and ten daughters. They dined and danced and listened to Gaelic songs. While exploring the island, Boswell discovered the ruins of Castle Brochel, complete with inside lavatory, a facility rarely found in the houses of Scotland at the time. 'Sir,' he said to his host, 'you take very good care of one end of a man, but not the other.' From Raasay they made their way anti-clockwise around Skye and called on Macdonald of Kingsborough and his wife, Flora. She, renowned for her part in the escape of Bonnie Prince Charlie after the failure of the '45, so impressed Johnson that he wrote of her: 'Flora Macdonald, a name that will be mentioned in history and if courage and fidelity be virtues, mentioned with honour.'

On they went to Dunvegan where they found 'Lady MacLeod, who had lived many years in England and who knew all the arts of southern elegance and all the modes of English economy.' Johnson found Dunvegan so comfortable that Boswell had to prod him into continuing their journey. As they travelled on Johnson noted details of the agriculture and the Highlands generally, while Boswell noted the hangovers that resulted from over-indulgence in bowls of punch. A storm during their crossing to Coll frightened Boswell more than Johnson, who retired to his berth and ignored it. Bad weather kept them on Coll longer than either of them found amusing.

They sailed for Mull on 14 October. Travelling across the island put Johnson in a bad humour, partly because his horse was too small for him and could hardly bear his weight and partly because he lost the oak stick he had brought from London. They crossed to Iona by moonlight. Johnson said, 'if this be not roving among the Hebrides, nothing is'. Both men were deeply moved by 'treading that illustrious island which was once the luminary of the Caledonian regions whence savage clans and roving barbarians derived the benefits of knowledge and the blessings of religion.' They spent the night in a barn and the next day explored the monastery, abbey and other buildings. Boswell was disappointed to find it all so broken down and was unimpressed by the uninscribed gravestones of the kings. He had expected marble monuments such as those found in Westminster Abbey. They returned to Mull where they were entertained by the Laird of Lochbuy, described by Boswell as a 'bluff, comely, noisy old gentleman, proud of his hereditary consequence and a very hearty and hospitable landlord'. Johnson was not pleased to be offered cold sheep's head for breakfast. They inspected the castle and Johnson recorded a general description of castles in the Highlands and Islands.

From Mull they crossed to Oban on the mainland, somewhat relieved to be not so much at the mercy of the elements. They were amused to read in a newspaper that they were thought to be still weather-bound on Skye. At Inverary they were entertained by the Duke of Argyle, whom Boswell knew, and were well pleased with his hospitality. Continuing on horses supplied by the Duke they crossed the Rest and Be Thankful and descended to Loch Lomond. The remainder of their journey took them out of the Highlands, south to Ayrshire and so back to Edinburgh. Boswell recorded that Johnson had told him that the time he had spent on his journey was the most pleasant part of his life.

The Napier Commission

Open rebellion by some communities (*see* Battle of Braes, pp.252) against draconian landlords at the climax of the Clearances, attracted the attention of the contemporary 'media'. Unwelcome publicity, coupled with unrest over the demand for Irish Home Rule, forced Gladstone's government to set up a Royal Commission of Inquiry in 1883, with Lord Napier in the chair. The Commission comprised two landowners who were sympathetic to the crofters' problems, two Gaelic scholars and an MP who was also a member of the Highland Land Law Reform Association. These men toured the Highlands and Islands during 1883 and 1884 (once being shipwrecked off Stornoway), collecting overwhelming evidence in favour of reform. With the extension of the parliamentary franchise in 1885, entitling crofters to vote, the crofter question became a dominant issue in the general elections of 1885 and 1886, with a new political party emerging. As always, Scottish affairs seldom received priority at Westminster, but public opinion was by now so strong that the Crofters' Holdings (Scotland) Act was passed, in which crofters were granted security of tenure and a Crofters Commission was appointed to fix fair rents. There were inevitable teething problems, but by the end of the century crofters' rights were secure and peace prevailed.

Piping

Two kinds of bagpipes are played in Scotland these days, the 'warm wind' and the 'cold wind'. The Highland bagpipe, being mouth blown, is 'warm wind'; the Lowland or Border bagpipe is blown by a bellows operated by the piper's right elbow, hence 'the cold wind pipes'. The Highland bagpipe is designed to be played out of doors; the Lowland is essentially an indoor instrument. Recent improvements in the manufacture of the Highland bagpipe, along with the higher standards now being demanded by audiences, have altered the tone of the instrument until it can be listened to with pleasure indoors, where the most prestigious piping events are held. The Highland bagpipe no longer 'skirls'. The 'Small Music' of the Highland bagpipe includes marches and dance tunes in differing tempi; the *ceòl mor*, the 'Great Music' (usually anglicized as 'pibroch' from *pïobaireachd*, meaning piping) comprises tunes constructed on a theme followed by up to ten variations.

Pibroch pieces date from the late 15th century and their names commemorate great events in Highland history. Pibroch is listened to in silence. It is unwise for the visitor to interrupt, even by a whisper. The Lowland pipes are intended to accompany social events indoors and fit in well with the folk music groups now popular in Scotland and beyond. Their tone is sweet and mellow and the repertoire includes the ancient Border ballads from the days of the cross-border raids and feuds, as well as a wide range of dance music and song airs. Both instruments are taken seriously in Scotland, for their own sake as well as for their traditional connotations. Derogatory comment is not appreciated, especially if voiced in the accents of south Britain. The pipes were never specifically proscribed by the Disarming Act of 1747, but it would have been a brave piper who played within earshot of a Government post. The oldest thesis on pipe music was written during the proscription, and several pibroch pieces were composed while the Act was still in force.

Religious Differences

In the Highlands and Islands, where communities tend to be slow to change, there are predominantly Catholic areas, where they rejected the Reformation and reconverted, and other areas which, following the laird, became Protestant. On the whole, Catholics and Protestants live together happily with few of the sectarian problems experienced in Ireland. Sometimes, however, there is a conflict between the strict Sabbatarian beliefs and practices of a few Presbyterians and the more liberal Catholics, and invariably the media manage to stir up an 'incident'.

In the Outer Hebrides, South Uist, Eriskay and Barra are almost entirely Catholic. In their belief God belongs to every day and Sunday is for celebration, both in church and out. North Uist, Harris and Lewis are Presbyterian and the most rigid Protestants in Britain. Their interpretation of the Fourth Commandment is stringently enforced by the Lord's Day Observance Society, who exert moral, social and political pressure. Sunday is for long sermons in church, full of the threat of damnation; for reading the Bible and holy tracts; for dark clothes and solemn faces. No work must be done, not even cooking; washing must come in off the line; fishing boats must lie at anchor and swings are padlocked.

Until fairly recently, no ferries ran to the islands on Sundays. When Caledonian MacBrayne announced a changed schedule including some Sunday sailings, the uproar was clamorous with huffings and puffings and threats of barricades. Running in tandem with this dispute, was friction over a new £12 million school, built at tax-payers' expense, on the island of Benbecula, mid-way between the Catholic south and Protestant north and serving both. The predominantly Protestant Western Isles Council would not employ supervisory staff on Sundays, so no one could use the school's leisure facilities, swimming pool, cafeteria, games hall, library, etc. Catholics protested that their beliefs allowed them to have fun on Sundays and they saw no reason why Sabbatarian rules should prevent them from doing so. The situation was satisfactorily resolved in the end, but not without damage to the hitherto dignified, *laissez-faire* attitudes that enabled such extreme creeds to live side by side in harmony.

The majority of Scots belong to the Established Church of Scotland, or Presbyterian Church, and its many breakaway sects. The Episcopal Church, with its bishops, is the equivalent of the Church of England. The Free Presbyterian Church of Scotland (Wee Frees) is a tiny, fundamentalist sect whose members believe that the Pope is 'Antichrist' and the Mass 'the most blasphemous form of religious worship that Satan ever invented; an offence unto God and destructive of the souls of men.' In 1989 Britain's Lord Chancellor, Lord Mackay of Clashfern, a member of this strict sect, was castigated by fellow members of his congregation because he attended Requiem Masses for two of his Catholic friends. The Free Church Synod suspended him from his position as a senior Elder of the Kirk, and from Communion. Lord Mackay, who once said his Church gave 'the most tender love that has ever been described', was forced to resign from it.

Seers

The second sight, *taibhsearachd* in Gaelic, goes hand in hand with sorcery. Among the many seers who emerged from the Celtic mists were **Thomas the Rhymer** and the Brahan Seer. Thomas, born in 1220, lived for nearly 80 years, and earned himself the title 'True Thomas'. He predicted the death of Alexander III and the Battle of Bannockburn. Traditionally, he had a passionate affair with the Fairy Queen and went off to live with her for three years in Elfland, deep in the Eildon Hills.

The **Brahan Seer**, Còinneach Odhar, is an enigmatic figure from the 17th century, known for the uncanny accuracy of many of his prophecies about the Highlands, some of which are still to be fulfilled. He fell asleep, so it is said, on an enchanted hillside; when he awoke he was clutching a stone with a hole in it, through which he could see the truth and the future. Among the events he foretold that have already happened are the depopulation of the Highlands, the demise of crofting, the arrival of rich landowners, and the making of the

Caledonian Canal. He said that when it was possible to cross the River Ness in Inverness dryshod in five places, a terrible disaster would strike the world. There were four bridges over the Ness until a fifth was erected to replace one about to be demolished. This was opened at the end of August 1939: on 1 September Hitler marched into Poland.

The Brahan Seer met his death by antagonizing his patroness, the Countess of Seaforth. The Earl visited France soon after the Restoration of Charles II in 1660, and had not returned. The Countess sent for the Brahan Seer and asked what her husband was doing. When he was reluctant to say, she pressed him until he revealed that the Earl was in a sumptuous gilded room, grandly decked out in velvet, silk and cloth of gold, with a voluptuous lady on his lap. The Countess was furious, accused him of malice and ordered him to be burnt in a barrel of tar at Fortrose. Before he died he predicted the downfall of the Seaforth Mackenzies, whose line came to an end after a dramatic chain of events, precisely following the prophecy, in 1815.

Sorcerers and Superstition

Communities lived in terror of Devil-worshippers and sorcerers, whom they believed could control the elements and cause plague, famine, drought, miscarriages and crop failure. In the Middle Ages fertile Celtic minds were fed by inherited paganism, folklore, ignorance and religion. This was particularly so in Galloway and the Highlands, where remote communities were separated by vast tracts of moor, hill and loch, far from urban influence, schools and the steely eye of the Church. Every act from pre-birth to death was vulnerable, and the power of evil had to be propitiated. Offerings of food, herbal potions, benisons, gestures, talismans and rites were employed in the hope of warding off supernatural ills. Curiously shaped stones had magic properties. Certain lakes and wells were thought to be especially efficacious. Pilgrims brought their sick and their petitions and tied votive offerings to trees and bushes. People still go to some of the *Clootie Wells* as they are called. At Culloden coachloads of people arrive on or around May Day, the Celtic Beltane, and throw money into the well. Superstition or not, when the Highland Division was being pounded on the beaches of St Valéry-en-Caux, in the summer of 1940, the Culloden Clootie Well attracted throngs of petitioners. Another, on a back road in Rossshire, is so festooned with squalid old rags it looks like a tinkers' tip, yet even today no one removes them for fear of reprisals from the god of the well.

It was by no means just ignorant peasants who believed in sorcery. Macbeth's encounter with the three witches was not a figment of Shakespeare's rich imagination. His source for the story was Holinshed, the 16th-century chronicler, who describes 'three women in strange and wild apparel, resembling creatures of eldritch world', who 'vanished immediatlie' having delivered their prophecies. The last execution for witchcraft in Scotland was believed to be in Dornoch in 1727, when a mother was found guilty of riding upon her daughter, who had been transformed into a pony and shod by the Devil. She was burned in a barrel of pitch having first warmed her cold feet at the fire that was to consume her.

Perth 48
Perth to Balmoral 55
Perth to Pitlochry 58
Dunkeld 59
Pitlochry 60
Pitlochry to Rannoch 61
Pitlochry to Killin 62
Pitlochry to Blair Atholl 67
Perth to Crieff 70

Perthshire: Gateway to the Highlands

The Trossachs and Breadalbane 73
The Trossachs 74

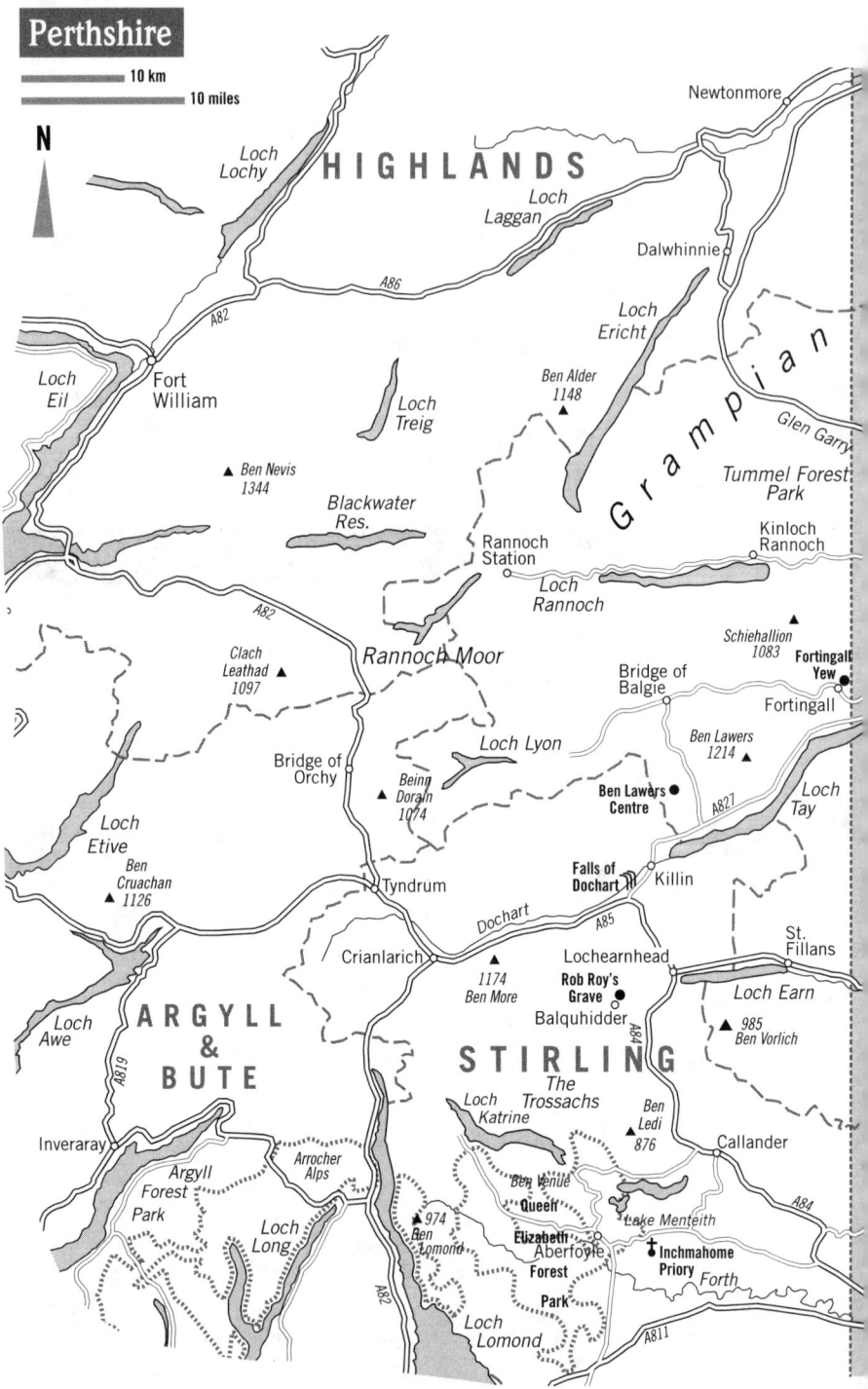
Perthshire
10 km
10 miles
N
HIGHLANDS
Newtonmore
Loch Lochy
Loch Laggan
Dalwhinnie
A86
A82
Loch Ericht
Loch Eil
Fort William
Loch Treig
Ben Alder 1148
Grampian
Glen Garry
Tummel Forest Park
Ben Nevis 1344
Blackwater Res.
Rannoch Station
Kinloch Rannoch
Loch Rannoch
Schiehallion 1083
Fortingall Yew
Clach Leathad 1097
Rannoch Moor
Bridge of Balgie
Fortingall
Ben Lawers 1214
Loch Lyon
Bridge of Orchy
Beinn Dorain 1074
Ben Lawers Centre
A827
Loch Tay
Loch Etive
Ben Cruachan 1126
Tyndrum
Falls of Dochart
Killin
Dochart
A85
St. Fillans
Crianlarich
Lochearnhead
1174 Ben More
Rob Roy's Grave
Loch Earn
Loch Awe
ARGYLL & BUTE
Balquhidder
A84
985 Ben Vorlich
STIRLING
A819
The Trossachs
Loch Katrine
Ben Ledi 876
Inveraray
Arrocher Alps
Callander
Argyll Forest Park
Ben Venue
Queen Elizabeth Forest Park
Lake Menteith
A84
Loch Long
974 Ben Lomond
Aberfoyle
Inchmahome Priory
Forth
A82
Loch Lomond
A811

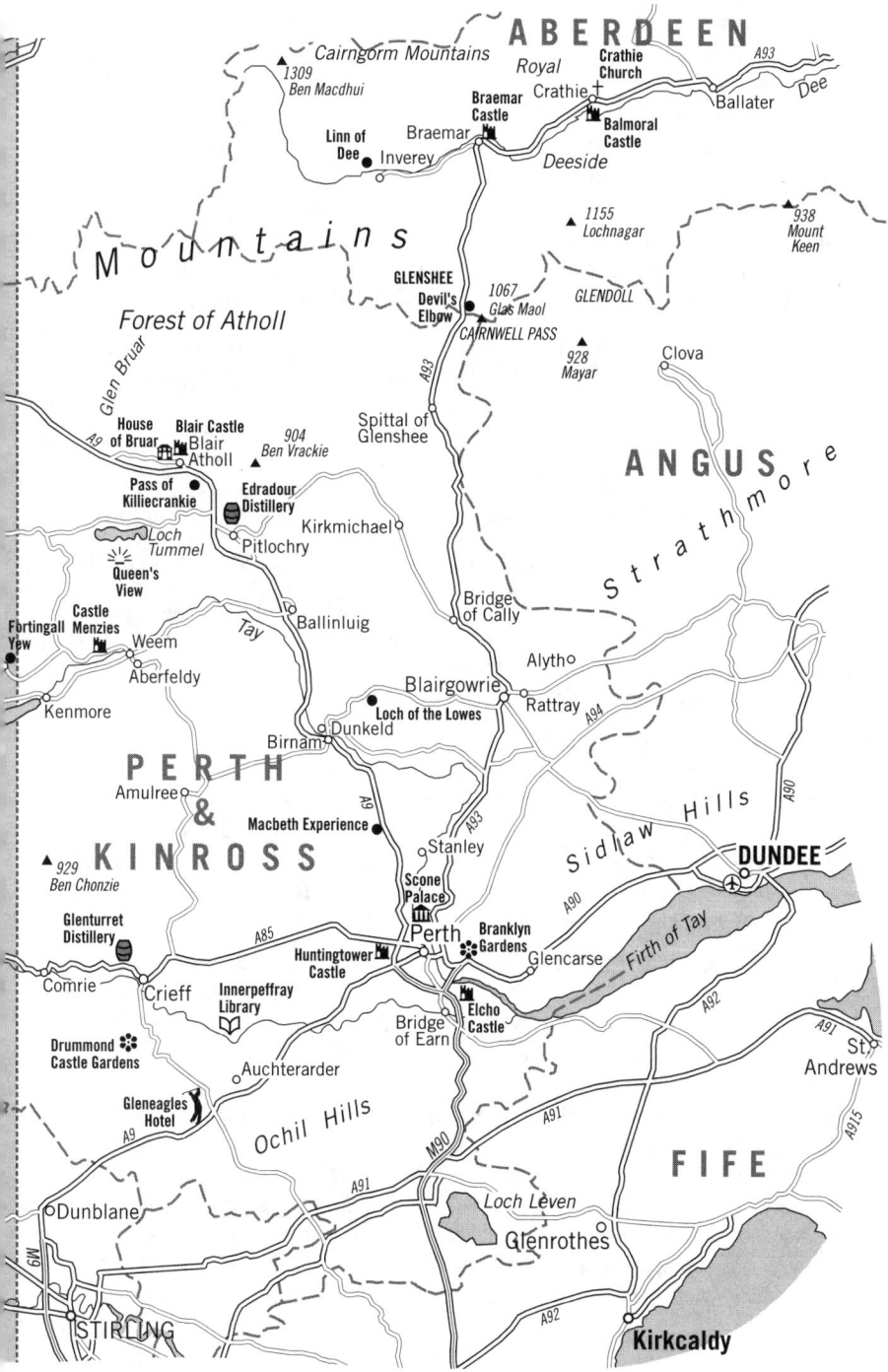
ABERDEEN
Cairngorm Mountains
1309
Ben Macdhui
Royal
Crathie
Crathie Church
A93
Ballater
Dee
Braemar Castle
Balmoral Castle
Linn of Dee
Braemar
Inverey
Deeside
1155
Lochnagar
938
Mount Keen
Mountains
GLENSHEE
Devil's Elbow
1067
Glas Maol
GLENDOLL
CAIRNWELL PASS
Forest of Atholl
928
Mayar
Clova
Glen Bruar
A93
House of Bruar
Blair Castle
Blair Atholl
A9
904
Ben Vrackie
Spittal of Glenshee
ANGUS
Strathmore
Pass of Killiecrankie
Edradour Distillery
Kirkmichael
Loch Tummel
Pitlochry
Queen's View
Bridge of Cally
Castle Menzies
Fortingall Yew
Weem
Tay
Ballinluig
Aberfeldy
Alyth
Blairgowrie
Rattray
A94
Kenmore
Loch of the Lowes
Dunkeld
Birnam
PERTH & KINROSS
Amulree
A9
Macbeth Experience
A93
Stanley
Sidlaw Hills
A90
DUNDEE
929
Ben Chonzie
Scone Palace
Glenturret Distillery
A85
Perth
Branklyn Gardens
Huntingtower Castle
Glencarse
Firth of Tay
Comrie
Crieff
Innerpeffray Library
Elcho Castle
Bridge of Earn
A92
Drummond Castle Gardens
Auchterarder
A91
St Andrews
Gleneagles Hotel
Ochil Hills
A9
M90
A91
A915
FIFE
Dunblane
Loch Leven
Glenrothes
M9
STIRLING
A92
Kirkcaldy

Perthshire and its borders represent the overture to the Highlands. Some of the scenery is grand enough, but the traveller is beckoned onwards, aware that this is a mere foretaste of what lies beyond. The city of Perth is the rather stern dowager who, late in a long life, is making a valiant effort to adjust to the 20th century—just as the 21st century begins. With Royal Deeside to the northeast, the area attracts well-born settlers and its estates offer a variety of expensive sport to smart sportsmen. To the southwest, the Trossachs lure and cater for too many people—best avoided by seekers of peace and solitude who should head north and northwest. Here, with the massive Grampians, torrential rivers, dark mysterious lochs and the moonscape to the west of Rannoch, you can get away from it all and begin to discover the Highlands proper.

Perth

We very soon came upon Perth, the situation of which is quite lovely; it is on the Tay, with wooded hills skirting it entirely on one side, and hills are seen again in the distance, the river winding beautifully. Albert was charmed, and said it put him in mind of the situation of Basle.

Queen Victoria, on first seeing Perth, September 1842

Perth is the self-styled gateway to the Highlands. Reached in a flash from Edinburgh and Glasgow, it is an ideal centre from which to explore the more popular areas of the Southern Highlands. Parts of this area are not, strictly speaking, truly Highland, but they masquerade as such well enough to serve as a fitting prelude to the northern hills.

Coming down into Perth from the M90 you get a fine view of the town, spread out around the Tay. This view, afforded by the building of the motorway, is in fact the same as that extolled not only by Queen Victoria (bestowing her greatest accolade on the place with the final observation quoted above), but also by Sir Walter Scott in the first few pages of his introduction to *The Fair Maid of Perth.* Two wide green parks, North and South Inch, unfold on either side, with a collage of spires reaching for the sky. 'Inch' derives from the Gaelic for island: in times of flood the Inches were cut off from the town.

Perth was the first place where the river could be bridged easily. It was a thriving port in the old days and is now an important livestock market at the centre of a productive agricultural area. First linen and then cotton were once the chief manufacturing industries. Perth used to be renowned for fulling and dyeing the cloths: Pullars of Perth is still here, though much less important now than it used to be. Bells Whisky have their administrative headquarters in the town and are about to open a Bells Whisky Heritage Centre at Cherrybank. Its fine setting earned Perth the title 'The Fair City' (although it's also known as St John's Toun—the football team is St Johnstone) and recent refurbishment has done much to restore it to that status. In the days before conservation became fashionable, many of its old buildings were replaced by utilitarian monstrosities—developments that were little short of architectural vandalism. When a new Marks and Spencer store was being built in the High Street some time ago, the remains of a medieval market were unearthed, resulting in a valuable stay of execution for several fine buildings.

Now, with a new bypass considerably easing traffic congestion in the town centre, traffic-free shopping streets, and award-winning floral displays, Perth is once again an attractive town, particularly when the sun is shining. If you poke around, you can still find traces of the past: there are some splendid late-Georgian terraces, especially around the Inches, with charming vistas of the river.

History

Traces of an old city wall in Albert Close, off George Street, indicate that there was a Roman camp here, although Perth doesn't appear in the records until the 12th century. The name derives from Aber-tha—the mouth of the Tay, which became 'Bertha' in Roman times, and then Perth. A devastating flood destroyed Old Perth in 1210, remembered in the song:

Says the Shochie to the Ordie,
'Where shall we meet?
'At the cross o' Perth,
When a' men are fast asleep.'

William the Lion granted a Royal Charter to the town that was built in its place the same year. It was the capital of Scotland and a town of ecclesiastical importance until the middle of the 15th century: Greyfriars, Blackfriars, Whitefriars and Carthusians all had establishments within the walled city. James I, unpopular for his draconian attempts to subdue his fractious subjects, was assassinated at Blackfriars in 1437. (A 16th-century legend tells the story of Catherine Douglas, Catherine 'Bar-Lass', who supposedly tried to bar the door to the murderers by using her arm as a bolt in the hasps.) John Knox initiated the Reformation in Perth in 1559 (*see* St John's Church) and can be held responsible for the destruction of many sacred treasures, including the Abbey of Scone.

Brave Bargain at the Battle of the Clans

One of the more colourful events in the city's history was the Battle of the Clans in 1396, woven by Scott into the convoluted story of *The Fair Maid*. This was a contest between the Clans Chattan and Quhele (pronounced Kay), to establish who should take precedence in battle—a hotly disputed honour in those swashbuckling days. Thirty men from each side were to fight in a tournament on the North Inch, watched by King Robert III, his wife and the court. At the last moment, one of the Clan Chattan lost his nerve and fled. The rule was that the two sides must be matched man-for-man, so a wee bandylegged blacksmith, Hal o' the Wynd, offered to stand in, for the small fee of half a French crown. All but one of the Quhele Clan were slaughtered. Among the survivors of the Chattans was the blacksmith who, for such a meagre price, had done more than anyone else to secure the victory.

The mysterious drama of the Gowrie Conspiracy took place in 1600 in Gowrie House, now demolished. James VI was lured to an upstairs room by the Earl of Gowrie and his brother Alexander Ruthven (to rhyme with 'driven'), and his life was in some way threatened. From an upstairs window he shouted for his lords, who rescued him, killing Gowrie and Ruthven in the scrimmage. The whole affair provoked much speculation, with hints of homosexual motivation mingling with suggestions that the king staged the event to rid himself of the brothers, whose ruthless political ambition was notorious. Andrew Lang, the Victorian journalist, reported an old Scottish lady as declaring:

> *It is a great comfort to think that at the Day of Judgement we shall know the whole truth about the Gowrie Conspiracy at last.*

Legend has it, albeit hotly refuted by music historians, that Gaetano Donizetti (1797–1848), the prolific composer of *bel canto*, was descended from a Perthshire adventurer named Izatt, or Izett, who served with the Spanish army in Italy and was known as Don Izetti. There are still Izatts or Izetts around in Perth today.

Tourist Information

Lower City Mills, West Mill Street, PH1 5QP, ✆ (01738) 450 600. You can get good city maps and planned walks about Perth here.

Visiting the Town

St John's Kirk (*open April–Oct 10–12 and 2–4*) was founded in 1126 by David I. The present building dates from the 15th century. The War Memorial Chapel was designed by Robert Lorimer when the church was restored in 1923. Edward III is said to have killed his brother the Earl of Cornwall here in 1335. It was in this now plain church that John Knox preached his iconoclastic sermon in 1559, urging his followers to purge the churches of idolatry; this sermon led to the destruction of many of the churches and monasteries in the area and helped fuel the Reformation. St John's had at least 40 richly decorated altars dedicated to saints and it is heart-breaking to think of the treasures that were lost. Of the few that were rescued are the 16th-century German Cellini Cup, given to Mary of Guise-Lorraine by the Pope, 17th-century chalices and a 16th-century baptismal basin. The church is used for Festival concerts and makes an excellent theatre for productions of plays like *Murder in the Cathedral.* Up-to-date leaflets are always available, either in the Tourist Information Centre or in the church.

The Fair Maid's House (*closed at present*) can be seen from outside. It is behind Charlotte Street in North Port and was the home of virtuous Catharine Glover, the Fair Maid herself. Standing on the site of a 13th-century monastery it is a mere cottage and of little interest beyond its literary association, but there are still traces of its medieval origins. **Balhousie Castle**, a heavily restored 15th-century Scottish Baronial castle beyond Rose Terrace on the west side of North Inch was the home of the Earls of Kinnoull. Now the regimental headquarters of the Black Watch, it houses its **Regimental Museum** (*open May–Sept Mon–Fri 10–4.30; Oct–April Mon–Fri 10–3.30*). The Black Watch—so called because of their dark tartan—was raised in 1739 to help the government pacify the restless Highlanders who were gathering momentum for their final bid for independence in 1745. The museum has a comprehensive display of the history of this famous regiment, with uniforms, weapons, pictures, documents, photographs and trophies, recording its many honours and triumphs.

The Art Gallery and Museum, in George Street (*open all year Mon–Sat*), has a changing selection of paintings of local interest, some very fine, as well as good examples of Perth silverware, the natural and social history of the town and its surroundings, and furniture. **Fergusson Gallery** in the Round House in Marshall Place (*open all year Mon–Sat; closed Sun*) is devoted to the work of the Scottish painter and leader of the Scottish 'Colourist' movement, J.D. Fergusson (1874–1961) and his contemporaries. Fergusson's statuesque

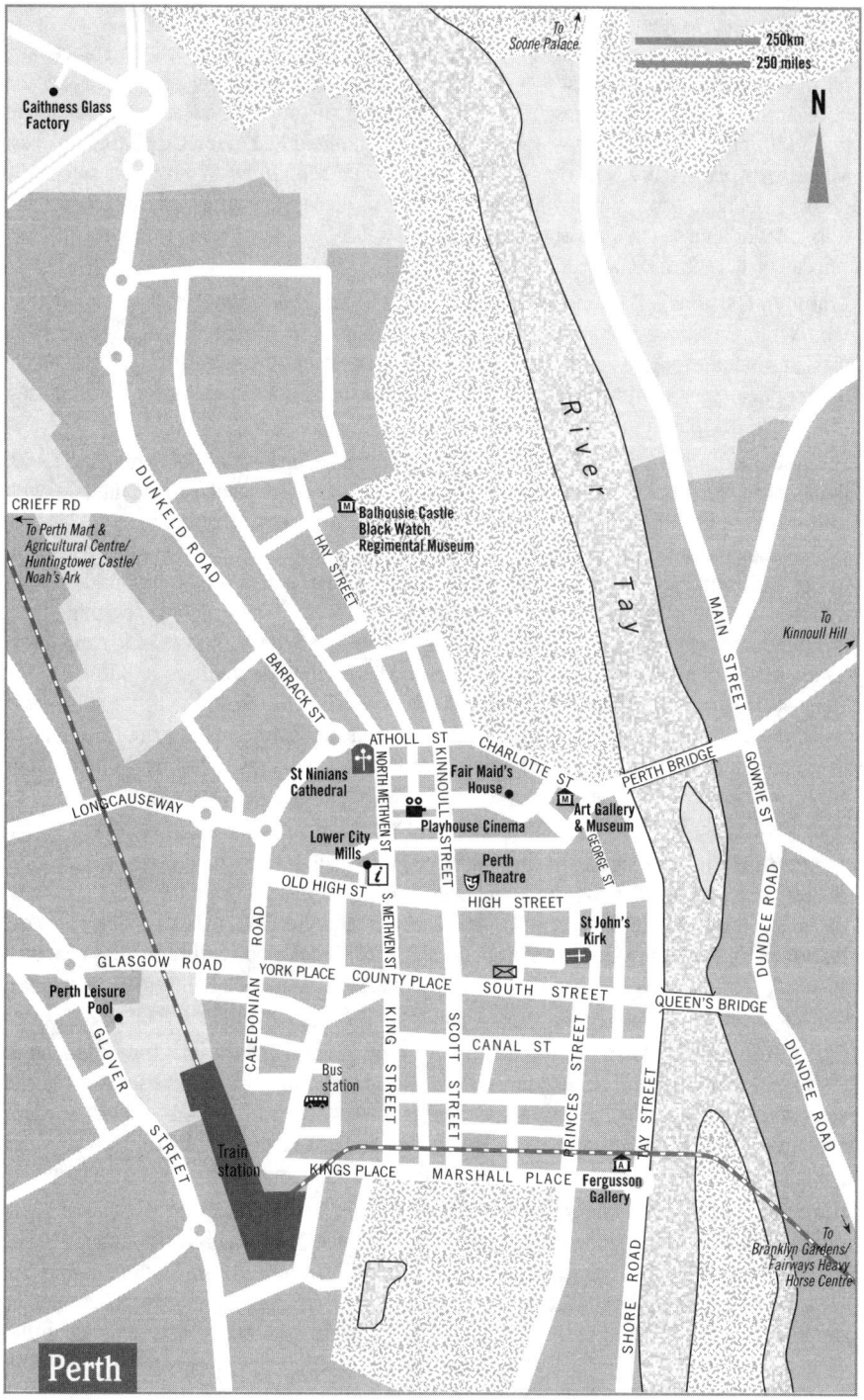
To Scone Palace
250km
250 miles
N
Caithness Glass Factory
River Tay
CRIEFF RD
To Perth Mart & Agricultural Centre/ Huntingtower Castle/ Noah's Ark
DUNKELD ROAD
Balhousie Castle Black Watch Regimental Museum
HAY STREET
MAIN STREET
To Kinnoull Hill
BARRACK ST
ATHOLL ST
CHARLOTTE ST
PERTH BRIDGE
GOWRIE ST
St Ninians Cathedral
NORTH METHVEN ST
KINNOULL STREET
Fair Maid's House
Art Gallery & Museum
LONGCAUSEWAY
Playhouse Cinema
Lower City Mills
GEORGE ST
Perth Theatre
OLD HIGH ST
S. METHVEN ST
HIGH STREET
St John's Kirk
ROAD
GLASGOW ROAD
YORK PLACE
COUNTY PLACE
SOUTH STREET
DUNDEE ROAD
QUEEN'S BRIDGE
Perth Leisure Pool
CALEDONIAN
KING STREET
SCOTT STREET
CANAL ST
PRINCES STREET
GLOVER STREET
Bus station
HAY STREET
DUNDEE ROAD
Train station
KINGS PLACE
MARSHALL PLACE
Fergusson Gallery
To Branklyn Gardens/ Fairways Heavy Horse Centre
SHORE ROAD
Perth

round-bosomed women are not to everyone's taste, but his landscapes are lovely and some of his sculpture very fine. He was a Perthshire man, though he worked mostly in France, in a bright Fauvist/postimpressionist style. **The Round House** used to be the city waterworks and from a distance resembles a mosque with its minaret. It still has a spherical water monument in front inscribed *Haurio et haereo*—I draw water and hold it. **Lower City Mills**, in West Mill Street (*open April–Nov Mon–Sat 10–5; adm; mill shop open all year*), is a splendidly restored Georgian oatmeal mill which once produced the porridge for prisons all over Britain. It is still working, with its massive waterwheel driven by the Town's Lade (millstream), and you can watch the miller at work.

Branklyn Gardens, off Dundee Road (*open Mar–Oct daily ; adm*) were designed in 1910 by John Renton, a local estate agent, and his wife. Although only covering about 2 acres, skilful planning and unexpected vistas make them seem much larger. At **Bridgend**, at the east end of Perth Bridge, there is an old toll house which still has the notice of charges for sheep, horses, etc., which put inflated modern prices to shame.

Scone Palace (*open Easter–Oct daily 9.30–4.45; adm*) is 2 miles north of Perth on the A93. Pronounced 'Scoon', it is a 19th-century restoration of 16th-century and earlier buildings, with battlements, a toy-fort façade and the original gateway. A popular tourist attraction, this neo-Gothic pile is of historical rather than aesthetic interest, though it has some fine porcelain, ivories and memorabilia (including Marie Antoinette's writing desk) on display inside. Prince Albert is said to have used the ancient bog-oak floor of the long gallery as a curling rink. Probably once a Pictish capital, Scone became an important centre of the Celtic church and Kenneth Macalpine brought the Stone of Destiny here from Dunstaffnage in 850 (*see* 'The Stone of Destiny' p.34). Edward I, greedy for loot, stole what he thought to be the stone, now called the Stone of Scone, and installed it in Westminster Abbey, but coronations continued here until that of Charles II in 1651. Alexander I established a priory of Augustinian canons here in 1120, which became an abbey in 1160. This and its adjacent palace were destroyed by John Knox's followers after his sermon in St John's in 1559.

The **Perth Hunt Racecourse**, the most northerly in Britain, is in the grounds of Scone Palace. Steeplechase only, the Perth Races attract many runners (*April/May and Aug/Sept*), drawn by the quality of its old-established turf. Other places to visit within the environs of Perth include: **Fairways Heavy Horse Centre**, Glencarse (*open daily; adm*); and **Caithness Glass Factory** (*open all year daily; ✆ (01738) 637 373*), off the bypass at the turn-off to Inverness, where you can watch glassware being made, buy it from the shop or try it out in the restaurant.

Climb **Kinnoull Hill** for an excellent bird's-eye view of Perth and the countryside around it. It's an easy stroll from the car park in Corsie Hill Road and from the extensive summit you can define the geological 'Highland Line' that divides the Highlands from the Lowlands. The two follies, very visible from the A90, were built by the Earl of Kinnoull and by Lord Gray, owner of Kinfauns Castle, to make work for the local poor and in memory of a visit to the Rhine.

Huntingtower Castle (*open April–Sept daily; Oct–Mar Mon–Sat and Sun pm; closed Thurs pm and Fri; adm*) is 3 miles northwest of Perth on the Crieff Road. Built by the Ruthven family in the 15th century and formerly called House of Ruthven or Ruthven Castle, this was the scene of the Ruthven Raid in 1582 when the Earl of Gowrie and several Protestant nobles captured and held 15-year-old James VI for 10 months as a hostage against a demand that some of the royal favourites be dismissed. The earl was executed two years later for his part in the kidnap but as if to make sure the family were tamed, the succeeding earl and his brother were subsequently killed as a result of the Gowrie Conspiracy in 1600 (*see* above). James then proscribed the name Ruthven and the castle became Huntingtower. In 1670 it passed to the Earl of Atholl, whose grandson, Lord George Murray, Prince Charles' commander, was born here in 1694. The castle fell into ruin but was rescued by the state in 1900 and still has very fine painted walls and ceilings. Nearby, the **Perth Mart and Agricultural Centre** has a visitor centre, restaurant and shops (*open all year*).

Elcho Castle (*open April–Sept daily 9.30–6.30*), a ruin 4 miles southeast of Perth, on the south bank of the Tay, is one of the more interesting of the later Scottish castles, incorporating both a defensive structure and palace-like comforts. James III granted the lands of Elcho to John de Wemyss in 1468. The square tower with a crow-stepped gable dates from that time. A subsequent Sir John became the first Earl of Wemyss under Charles I but sided with the Parliamentarians in the Civil War. The huge kitchen has a fireplace as big as a small room. The bedrooms had en-suite garderobes.

Perth ✆ (01738–) ***Sports and Activities***

Perthshire Activity Days, ✆ (01577) 861 186, will arrange anything from flying, hang-gliding, parachuting and seaplane trips, to camps, archery, abseiling, clay-pigeon shooting, falconry, riding, biking, climbing and off-road driving. All ages catered for.

Perth Leisure Pool, in Glover Street (*open daily; adm*), is very sophisticated, with flumes, a wild water channel, whirlpools, an outdoor pool open in winter, a picnic area, a crêche (✆ 492 410), and a **Health Oasis** for every sort of self indulgence (✆ 635 454). **Splash**, ✆ (01887) 829 706, at Stanley about 5 miles to the north, is an excellent place for white-water rafting over a fairly easy 5-mile stretch of the river Tay.

The **Perth Mart Visitor Centre** (*open daily*) in East Huntingtower (near the castle) is a celebration of Scotland's farming heritage. The **Perth Bull Sales**, held here in February and October, attract farmers from all over Britain—and beyond—where they pay astronomical prices for the best bulls in the land. The sales are great fun: the atmosphere and the concentration of characters would befit a painting by David Wilkie. There are also other livestock, farm machinery and motor car auctions. In the summer they stage the Highland Farm Life Show which children enjoy.

The **Perth Repertory Theatre**, ✆ 621 031, maintains a high standard of performance and varied programme. It also has a bar, coffee house and restaurant.

The **Perth Sculpture Trail** runs for about a mile along the river, with permanent artworks dotted along the way, enhanced by gardens and greenery. There is a Trail Guide with details of the artists, available at Lower City Mills tourist office.

The **Perth Playhouse Cinema**, ✆ 623 126, has recently been refurbished and is now a 7-screen multiplex cinema.

Noah's Ark, at Glendevon Farm, Western Edge, Perth, ✆ 445 568, is an excellent indoor adventure play area (*open daily 10–6.30*). There are three separate areas, for up to 3 years, under 5s and 5–12 year olds. Each session is 1½ hours (adults free), and there's a restaurant. Next door is **Noah's Ark Indoor Karting**, with a 320 metre track and a fast food café.

The nicest accommodation is in fact on the city's perimeter.

expensive

Ballathie House Hotel is at Kinclaven, Stanley, not far north of Perth, ✆ (01250) 883 268, 🖷 883 396, *www.ballathiehousehotel.co.uk.* An overgrown Victorian shooting lodge in 1,500 acres overlooking the Tay, it is elegantly furnished with proper antiques and four-poster beds. It won a Macallan 'Taste of Scotland' award for its haute cuisine, and offers lots of outdoor activities, including salmon fishing. **Kinfauns Castle**, on the outskirts of Perth, ✆ 620 777, 🖷 620 778, *www.kinfaunscastle.co.uk*, is very up-market and worth the £200–£300 you might pay for a double room, if you can afford it.

moderate

Murrayshall House Hotel, at Scone, ✆ 551 171, 🖷 552 595, has two 18-hole golf courses within its 300-acre grounds. Very comfortable, with good wholesome food, it offers everything a golfer could want including a club house with a bar and snacks. **Campsie Hill**, at Guildtown, ✆ (01821) 640 325, is a Wolsey Lodge owned and run by Garry and Jenny Barnett. Garry was brought up here and it is still very much a family home with the emphasis on hospitality and relaxation. The attractive, recently modernized house has gardens overlooking the Tay and views stretching 30 miles to the west. **Dupplin Castle**, near Perth, ✆ 623 224, was rebuilt in 1969 on the site of the original castle, in lovely grounds and parkland only 10 minutes from Perth. Another Wolsey Lodge, it is run by Derek and Angela Straker who make you feel very much at home. The food is excellent, and the ambience gracious.

cheap

Isle of Skye Toby Hotel, 18 Dundee Road, Perth, ✆ 624 471, 🖷 493 902, is large, impersonal and comfortable and you can see the Tay from some of the rooms. It's rather busy but is close to the town centre. **Sunbank House Hotel**, 50 Dundee Road, Perth, ✆/🖷 442 515, is a bit cheaper, only a short walk from the town centre, with a proper garden and views of the Tay. The house is early Victorian and the food is excellent. **Salutation Hotel**, 34 South Street, Perth, ✆ 630 066, 🖷 633 598, has a strong historic association with the Jacobites. It was established in 1699, is one of several hotels which claim to be the oldest in Scotland, and was Prince Charles' headquarters for a while (he stayed in room 20 and his operations room is now a meeting room).

Perth ✆ (01738–) ***Eating Out***

Let's Eat, 77 Kinnoull Street, ✆ 643 377, is *the* place to eat, and has won national awards in recent years to prove it. It is an informal bistro-type restaurant and the food is first class. **Let's Eat Again**, in George Street, ✆ 633 771, sister to Let's Eat, is another excellent choice, and reasonably priced, especially for bar meals. Fish and seafood are their speciality.

Marcello's, in South Street, does excellent take-away pizzas. **Betty's**, opposite the art gallery in George Street, is a tea-room serving memorable home-made cakes as well as more savoury snacks. **Greyfriars** in South Street is intimate and convivial—one of the best pubs in Perth. **Mucky Mulligan's**, 97 Canal Street, ✆ 636 705, is a lively Irish pub serving food.

Tourist Information

Blairgowrie: at Well Meadow, ✆ (01250) 872 960 (*open all year*); **Braemar**: The Mews, Mar Road, ✆ (013397) 41600 (*open all year*); **Crathie**: Balmoral Castle Car Park, ✆ (013397) 42414 (*open end Mar–mid Nov*).

Blairgowrie to Braemar

Blairgowrie is a popular tourist centre (especially with golfers) about 16 miles north of Perth on the A93, beside the fast-flowing Ericht Water. Old mills stand along the river, some derelict, some converted into dwellings (*at least one is open to the public*). The Highlands beckon—there is skiing to the north, at Glenshee. This is also the centre of the Scottish soft fruit industry thanks to the fertile soil. With rivers cascading through steep mountain glens and sudden glimpses of snow-capped peaks massing on the horizon, it's magical walking country.

While you are in the area, you should climb one of the many surrounding hills: make a detour east from Blairgowrie on the A962 to Kirriemuir and take the B955 north up Glen Clova. Go right to the end of the road where there is a car park near the youth hostel and have a go at Driesh and Mayar, part of the great rolling tableland of the White Mounth, south of Deeside. A track called Jock's Road goes on past Acharn through Glen Doll. Ignore all side tracks, including the fork where Jock's Road branches right to Deeside. Cross the White Water and walk along Fee Burn up towards Corrie Fee. The rest is obvious and you can choose where you go towards the top. Allow about 6 hours if you want to enjoy the summits.

From spring through autumn the A93 to Braemar—Britain's highest main road—is a spectacular route. It once included the Devil's Elbow, a hair-raising zigzag that trapped large vehicles and was often cut off by snow. This has now been ironed out, but you can still see bits of it as you flash past on the new road. As you look across to the remains of the old road, spare a thought for Queen Victoria, who used to travel up here with her entourage in their carriages, before they braved the new railway. They changed horses at Blairgowrie, stopped for lunch at the inn at Spittal of Glenshee, and trundled on north through the magnificent scenery. Escorted by locals on foot in case they got into difficulties, they negotiated the Devil's Elbow to reach Cairn Wall (Cairnwell), which marked the watershed. From here it was easier going for the horses, as they carried the royal party on to Braemar and Balmoral.

Glenshee is one of Scotland's main skiing resorts. Its challenging pistes are often icy and demanding—especially the Tiger run, which is best left to experienced skiers—but in the right conditions there is scope for every ability. There are three valleys and four mountains with the largest network of lifts in Scotland—26 in all. Weather conditions can be extreme, roads sometimes becoming impassable in snow. For skiing information, ring the Blairgowrie Tourist Information Office or the Ski Hot Line, ✆ 09001 654 656. In summer take the chairlift at **Cairnwell** for panoramic views and invigorating walks. **Strathardle** forks off northwest of Glenshee from **Bridge of Cally**, on the A924, where the River Ardle and Black Water converge: another good launching pad for climbs and walks in lovely surroundings.

Braemar, some 17 miles north of Glenshee on the A93, is not really in the purist's Highlands, but it certainly was for Queen Victoria, together with her beloved Balmoral. It was fortunate that the queen was hardy: Braemar has the record for Britain's lowest recorded temperature at –27°C. Royal Deeside is certainly scenic, although it is both too popular and too smart for some tastes, falling into the category of Designer Highlands.

Braemar Castle (*open May–mid Oct daily except Fri; adm*) is a massive, turreted fortress built by the Earl of Mar in 1628. It was burnt by the Farquharsons in 1689 and garrisoned by the English after the Jacobite risings in 1715 and 1745 to protect the military road from Perth. The castle has barrel-vaulted ceilings, a sinister pit prison, spiral stairways and gun loops. Look for the carved graffiti on the internal woodwork, left by off-duty soldiers in the 18th century. Keen Jacobites should visit the **Invercauld Arms**, on the spot where the Earl of Mar raised the Jacobite standard in 1715: a plaque commemorates the occasion.

Braemar Royal Highland Gathering is held every year on the first Saturday in September, drawing upwards of 20,000 people. It includes all the traditional events, both athletic and musical, together with plenty of stalls and sideshows. The Royal Family attend the games, which might be why it is one of the biggest events of its kind in Scotland, though perhaps one of the least reminiscent of those original games in the 11th century, when Malcolm Canmore held contests to find the best soldiers for his struggles against the Normans. For less showy, more authentic games, you must head north and west, away from the more popular areas.

Lochnagar is a good hill to climb if you have a spare day. The north peak of the White Mount has a fascination that seems to draw artists and poets as well as climbers. It even inspired the Prince of Wales to write a children's story. The climb takes about 7 or 8 hours, and you need a good map. Start at Invercauld Bridge where the A93 crosses the Dee, 3 miles east of Braemar. Take one of the two forest roads by the bridge—they join up south of the old bridge—into Ballochbuie Forest, bought by Queen Victoria in 1878 to preserve it from being felled. Take the right fork after about half a mile, and cross over the next intersection. Keep left at the hairpin bend, passing the Falls of Garbh Allt, and rejoin the forestry road higher up. You must use your map and follow your nose, but it isn't difficult, and the top is lovely.

A circular tour of about 12 miles west from Braemar, through the wooded Dee Valley, includes the **Linn of Dee**. A 'linn' is a waterfall, a gorge, or a pool below a waterfall—this is all three, and consequently very popular. The narrow, rocky gorge is about 150 yards long. The river boils through this bottleneck in a tumultuous frenzy, filling the air with noise and a haze of spray. You won't find solitude here, though, unless it's early or late in the day. Follow the track west along the Dee to White Bridge, where it crosses the river and turns away to the south. You can walk for miles along here, with tracks leading off up into the hills to the east.

Another good walk from the Linn of Dee is the track south from Inverey, up Ey Water to The Colonel's Bed (less than 2 miles). The Colonel was John Farquharson of Inverey, known as the Black Colonel, who rode his horse up sheer rock slopes and used to summon his servants by firing at a wall-mounted shield which rang like a bell when hit by the bullet. The Colonel's Bed is a ledge of rock in a gorge through which the Ey runs. He hid here after his castle had been burnt down by government troops following the Battle of Killiecrankie in 1689.

Balmoral

Balmoral Castle (*grounds and paintings in ballroom open mid April–July daily 10–5; adm*), about 9 miles northeast of Braemar, is so familiar from photographs and chocolate boxes that its reality is almost an anti-climax. Queen Victoria lost her heart to Balmoral in 1848 when it was 'a pretty little castle in the old Scottish style', leased by Victoria and Albert on the advice of their doctor as the perfect place for those with rheumatism. In the early days of their marriage, the family holiday at Balmoral was the highlight of the year, but as the royal children multiplied it became clear that the castle was inadequate. In 1852 they bought the Balmoral estate of some 17,400 acres for 30,000 guineas, demolished the old castle and built the present one, designed by William Smith of Aberdeen, with the Prince Consort breathing over his shoulder. The result, vast and imposing in pale grey ashlar, capable of housing well over 100 people, is not beautiful but has a certain endearing solidity. Albert oversaw the landscaping of the grounds, working from a model made from sand, and they are now well endowed with every sort of statue and memorial to various members of the royal household, including dogs. There were to be only seven autumn holidays in the new castle before Albert died of typhoid in 1861, and during these Victoria collected enough happy memories to last her through her long, lonely widowhood. Her visits to Balmoral became an almost sacred memorial to her beloved Albert, and, imposing as it now seems, one should picture how it must have been before it was more accessible to the public and seething with security precautions. In those halcyon days the Queen was able to roam freely and she drew strength from 'this dear paradise', attended by the faithful servant John Brown. Balmoral is still the Royal Family's holiday home.

Crathie Church, just north of the castle, was built in 1895 to replace a series of previous churches whose origins date from the 9th century. The Royal Family attend the Church of Scotland Sunday service here, ensuring a good turn-out of fellow worshippers during their annual holiday. This is where the royals made their first appearance following the death of Diana, Princess of Wales. Princess Anne, the Princess Royal, married her present husband Commander Tim Laurence here, prevented by her previous divorce from a second marriage in the Anglican church. In the graveyard beside the Dee by the ruins of an older kirk John Brown is buried, Queen Victoria's devoted servant and companion after Albert's death. Theirs was a unique relationship (beautifully portrayed in *Mrs Brown*), unsullied by the malicious whisperings of contemporary gossips. Despite his abrasive tongue and his weakness for a dram, Brown was the Queen's most loyal subject, helping to soften the grief of her widowhood.

Blairgowrie ✆ (01250–) ***Where to Stay***

expensive

Kinloch House Hotel, by Blairgowrie, ✆ 884 237, 🖷 884 333, *www.kinlochhouse.com* is an early Victorian country house well appointed for gracious living with baronial oak panelling. The focus is on fishing and the cuisine is high class. **Ballathie House**, Kinclaven, near Blairgowrie, ✆ 883 268, 🖷 883 396, *www.ballathiehouse-hotel.co.uk*, is a rich man's mecca—all you could ask for including excellent food and a lovely atmosphere. Fishing available.

moderate

Ashintully Castle, Kirkmichael, Blairgowrie, ✆ 881 237, dating from 1583, was modernized in 1969 without spoiling its character. It's a Wolsey Lodge, well secluded, in 3,000 acres run as a sheep farm and sporting estate. Cordon Bleu food and lots of outdoor activities, including a tennis court, make this a fine resting place. **Angus Hotel**, Blairgowrie, ✆ 872 455, 🖷 875 615, *www.theangus.freeserve.co.uk*, is large and rambling, with an indoor swimming pool, sauna, solarium and spa bath. It is convenient and extremely comfortable, and there's golf and fishing on the doorstep.

Moorfield House Hotel, Myreriggs Road, Coupar Angus, by Blairgowrie, ✆ (01828) 627 303, 627 339, is family run, friendly and comfortable. **Dalmunzie House Hotel**, Spittal o'Glenshee, ✆ 885 224, 885 225, is a sprawling country house with a 9-hole golf course and a relaxed atmosphere, well situated for skiers.

Perth to Pitlochry

Tourist Information

Dunkeld: The Cross ✆ (01350) 727 688; **Pitlochry**: 22 Atholl Road, ✆ (01796) 472 215/472 751.

Perth to Dunkeld

The A9 is the main road north from Perth with good stretches of dual carriageway interspersed with frustrating single-lane sections, which can slow you down considerably in the tourist season. Like many Scottish roads, however, it is well landscaped. On your way north you could look in at Bankfoot, signed off the A9, where you will find **The Macbeth Experience** (*open Easter–Sept 9–8; Oct–Mar 9–7; adm*), which includes a multi-media production about 'the real Macbeth'. Not for the true historian but nevertheless fun for the kids on a dull day.

Birnam

Be lion-mettled, proud, and take no care,
Who chafes, who frets, or where conspirers are:
Macbeth shall never vanquish'd be until
Great Birnam wood to high Dunsinane Hill
Shall come against him.

William Shakespeare, *Macbeth*, Act IV, Scene 1

Birnam, about 14 miles north of Perth, bypassed by the main road, is familiar to all lovers of Shakespeare. From Birnam Hill, Dunsinnan, or Dunsinane Hill—opinions vary on the spelling—is about 12 miles to the southeast. Macbeth, in his castle on Dunsinane Hill, confidently believed the witches' prophecy that he was immortal until 'Birnam Forest come to Dunsinane'. Meanwhile, Malcolm was busy instructing his soldiers to camouflage themselves with branches from the trees in Birnam Wood and march on Dunsinane—which they did. A messenger brought the news to Macbeth: 'As I did stand my watch upon the hill, I look'd toward Birnam, and anon methought the wood began to move.' There are remains of a fort on Dunsinane Hill which was probably Macbeth's, and some of the trees in Birnam Wood are thought to date from the original forest. Queen Victoria, whose yardstick for approval was the opinion of Prince Albert, recorded of Birnam: 'Albert said, as we came along between the mountains, that to the right, where they were wooded, it was very like Thüringen, and on the left more like Switzerland.'

A newly refurbished **Beatrix Potter** exhibition is due to open at Birnam in 2001. The writer and her family used to spend long summer holidays in the area and it was here that she developed her passion for wildlife. It was also from here that she wrote a picture letter to a friend and called it *The Tale of Peter Rabbit.*

Dunkeld

A mile or so on from Birnam, Dunkeld (the fort of the Celts) is an old cathedral town with an ecclesiastical history that goes back to the Celtic Church, possibly as far back as the time of St Columba. Sheltered by wooded hills and straddling the River Tay, Dunkeld is a popular centre for fishermen.

When Norsemen drove the monks from Iona in 729, they fled here and founded an abbey in which they enshrined holy relics of their founder, St Columba. Columba himself may have come to Dunkeld, possibly a few years before his death when he met up with St Mungo to discuss parish boundaries, and it is believed that the two men may have founded some sort of religious establishment then. There is a St Colm's Well nearby, though Scotland has many St Colm's Wells not necessarily related to a visit from the saint himself. Dunkeld suffered badly during the Covenanting Wars. It was here that the Cameronians, extreme Covenanters, held the town against a troop of Highlanders in 1689. Triumphant after Killiecrankie, the Highlanders stormed the town, whereupon the Cameronians set fire to most of its buildings, driving the Highlanders out and eventually securing supremacy for William and Mary.

Dunkeld Cathedral (*open daily*), dating from the early 12th century, is a substantial ruin on shady lawns beside the river. It took about 200 years to build and was reduced to a ruin during the Reformation. The choir has been restored and is now the parish church. The nave and great northwest tower date from the 15th century. The recumbent effigy in the choir is thought to be that of Alexander Stewart, the notorious 14th-century 'Wolf of Badenoch'. Ironically, Stewart earned his sobriquet for being a keen destroyer of towns and churches, including Elgin Cathedral, in retaliation for being excommunicated for abandoning his wife.

The Little Houses lining Cathedral Street were built after the destruction of the town in 1698 and were saved from demolition by the National Trust for Scotland in 1950. Well restored and privately occupied, these harled cottages with outside stairs form a delightful approach to the cathedral and give an old-world charm to this part of the town.

Niel Gow, the well-known 18th-century fiddler immortalized in portrait by Raeburn, was born at Inver, south of the Tay below Dunkeld. A ferry crossed the river here until Thomas Telford built the bridge downstream in 1809. Unless you are addicted to sentimental restoration, don't bother with The Hermitage, also called Ossian's Hall, signed as a tourist attraction off the A9 just after Dunkeld. This folly built by the Duke of Atholl in 1758 lies along a well-trodden trail, less than a mile from where you leave your car. It was probably once very charming in a whimsical way when it used to have mirrors reflecting the water. These were vandalized long ago and now the whole place, together with Ossian's Cave beyond, is no longer worth the stroll when there are so many other glorious places to walk.

A couple of miles northeast of Dunkeld, the **Loch of the Lowes**, formed by receding glaciers, is a nature reserve where ospreys can be watched from a hide. These large brown and white sea-eagles, cousins to the falcon, are common in America where they nest on every available navigation mark in the estuaries and wreak havoc on the fish. Here they are a rare, protected species, though their numbers are increasing slightly now that their nesting sites are fiercely protected by law. Eventually they will probably become as much of a threat to fishing as cormorants and herons. There is a **Wildlife Centre**, ✆ (01350) 727 337 (*open April–Sept daily; adm*).

Pitlochry

Thirteen miles north of Dunkeld on the A9, Pitlochry lies in the heart of Scotland, cradled by hills, with Ben Vrackie (2,759ft/849m) looming to the north. With hours of sunshine above the average and below-average rainfall, this has been a popular holiday town since Queen Victoria, staying at Blair Atholl nearby, declared it to be one of the finest resorts in Europe. The royal stamp of approval resulted in many fine houses and mansions being built in the area, with spas that are now hotels. Today it is hard to believe it was once a remote hamlet: there were no roads north of Dunkeld until General Wade built his network of military roads after the Jacobite uprisings. Despite its popularity—it gets very crowded in the summer—it manages to retain a leisurely, strolling atmosphere and is a good centre from which to explore the Highlands if you want your base to be at the hub of things. The rivers Tummel and Garry converge from their valleys into Loch Faskally, 2 miles to the north, and hurry through the town to join the Tay at Ballinluig to the south. The main street is cheerful with its bright façades, hotels and shops, distilleries and, not far off the road, hydroelectric development.

The Hydroelectric Dam and Fish Ladder (*open year round*) has an observation chamber from which you can see the ingenious method of ensuring the salmon cycle is not broken. Thousands of salmon are 'lifted' annually and you can watch them through glass walls. Sometimes you can see sealice clinging to the fish, proving that they have come fresh from the sea. There is a Visitor Centre and Exhibition (*open Easter–Oct daily*), with a description of activities throughout the country, particularly around the Loch Tummel area.

There are distilleries in the area, open to visitors with conducted tours and usually with the offer of a free dram. The **Edradour Distillery** (*open Easter–Oct daily; Nov and Dec Mon–Sat*) is the smallest in Scotland, hidden in the hills less than 3 miles east of Pitlochry. A small complex of white-washed buildings under neat grey slate roofs, tucked into a hollow beside the Edradour Burn, it was founded in 1825 by local farmers. After a conducted tour of the distillery, virtually unchanged since Victorian times, you get your free dram in front of a peat and log fire in a cosy barn. There is also the **Blair Athol Distillery** close by, ✆ (01796) 482 003 (*open daily; adm*).

Walking in this area is endlessly rewarding: every path you choose reveals fresh beauty and unexpected views. There are waterfalls and gorges, festooned with lush ferns, woods and hills and rivers running fast and shallow over rocky beds.

Pitlochry ✆ (01796–) ***Where to Stay***

expensive

Hilton Dunkeld House, Dunkeld, ✆ (01350) 727 771, 🖷 728 924, once the home of the Duke of Atholl, is on the banks of the Tay in 280 acres with every sort of comfort and leisure facility—indoor pool, sauna, spa bath, steam room and gym, and masses of outdoor activities including fishing. It's very luxurious and grand. **Kinnaird**, Dunkeld, ✆ 482 440, 🖷 482 289, *www.kinnairdestate.com*, is a former shooting lodge run as a private country house with all the trimmings—if you can afford it, go for it. **Pitlochry Hydro Hotel**, Knockard Road, Pitlochry, ✆ 472 666, 🖷 472 788, is a large, imposing and very comfortable building above the town, with indoor pool, jacuzzi, sauna, solarium and gym. Now owned by Shearings.

Auchnahyle, Pitlochry, ✆ 472 318, is a Wolsey Lodge in an 18th-century farmhouse with a garden surrounded by fields and lovely views. Penny and Alastair Howman are hospitable hosts and make you feel completely at home as you enjoy their delicious food. **Atholl Palace Hotel**, Atholl Road, Pitlochry, ✆ 472 400, 🖷 473 036, *www.corushotel.com*, is a large pile in 48 acres surrounded by a wooded park. Rather over-enthusiastic décor and not very cosy, but every sort of indoor and outdoor activity is on offer in nice surroundings.

Pine Trees Hotel and Garden Restaurant, Strathview Terrace, Pitlochry, ✆ 472 121, 🖷 472 460, *www.pinetrees-hotel.demon.co.uk*, is a Victorian country house in 19 acres of well-kept garden; it has garnered some praiseworthy awards for its cooking and welcome. **Queen's View Hotel**, Strathtummel, by Pitlochry, ✆ 473 291, 🖷 473 515, is very well run and welcoming, in a marvellous position above Loch Tummel.

Pitlochry to Rannoch

If you take the B8019 west from Pitlochry you should start humming Harry Lauder's famous song 'The Road to the Isles': 'by Tummel and Loch Rannoch and Lochaber I will go...' The drive out to Rannoch Station, on the northern side of lochs Tummel and Rannoch, to where the road ends and back along the south side, is a round trip of about 65 miles. The scenery is beautiful, so you won't be alone during the tourist season. The great cone of **Schiehallion** dominates the landscape to the south, there is a kaleidoscope of vistas through the trees and the moonscape wasteland of Rannoch Moor stretching away to the west. Loch Tummel is less dramatic than Loch Rannoch, its gentler scenery reshaped by hydroelectric development. **Queen's View**, 2 miles up from the dam, was so called before Queen Victoria visited it in 1866: perhaps Mary, Queen of Scots also stood on the promontory and looked down on the water glinting in the sunlight far below during one of her royal tours.

The **Loch Tummel Forest Centre** (*open April–Sept daily; donation box*) is at the southeast corner of the loch. Here you can learn about the geography and ecology of the area and how to find the Black Wood, south of Loch Rannoch, with part of the remains of the old Caledonian Forest. Harry Lauder's Road to the Isles was the old, much-used route to the west across the moors; the modern road ends at Rannoch Station. One hopes he had stout, waterproof boots and a good map: it is about 13 or 14 miles across to the A82, east of Glencoe, and if you don't stick to the path you'll finish up in a bog.

If you want exercise, Schiehallion is fun, easy and takes less than 5 hours. The best way goes from Schiehallion Road, the minor road that crosses its northern slope to link with the B846 to Kinloch Rannoch. Start from the Braes of Foss car park, just east of the farm of that name, and follow the path. There's a path or marker cairns all the way. It is interesting to note that while the Astronomer Royal was doing a few experiments on the estimation of the mass of the earth in 1774, one of his helpers, Charles Hutton, looked at Schiehallion with its regular cone shape and, with a flash of inspiration, invented contour lines for maps.

Go to the **Rannoch Smokery**, in Kinloch Rannoch, run by Leo and Sarah Barclay, who sell all sorts of delicious smoked game and meat, and excellent pâté.

Kinloch Rannoch ✆ (01882–) ***Where to Stay***

moderate

Loch Rannoch Hotel, Kinloch Rannoch, ✆ 632 201, 🖷 632 203, was a Victorian shooting lodge. It is a convivial hotel and the food is good. **Bunrannoch House**, Kinloch Rannoch, ✆/🖷 632 407, is the place to stay if you can get in (not to be confused with Bunrannoch Hotel), for hospitality at its best. It's a tall, thin, Victorian ex-shooting lodge, run by Mrs Jenny Skeaping, who is an excellent hostess and cook.

Pitlochry to Killin

Tourist Information

Aberfeldy: The Square, ✆ (01887) 820 276; **Killin**: Breadalbane Folklore Centre, ✆ (01567) 820 254 (*open Mar–Nov daily; Feb Sat and Sun*).

Pitlochry to Aberfeldy

Five miles south of Pitlochry, the A827 takes you 10 miles west to Aberfeldy and then out through Strath Tay to Loch Tay and a choice of two roads to Killin, one north and one south of the loch. Both are attractive drives, especially in late summer, winding through small villages with the river shaded by overhanging trees, backed by the hills beyond. For a more dramatic route, however, take the B846 from Aberfeldy north of the Tay and branch off at Keltneyburn to Fortingall, where you follow the sign to Glen Lyon. At Bridge of Balgie, take the left fork south and drive through the hills, round the flank of Ben Lawers and down to Loch Tay at Milton Morenish. Much of this area is part of **Breadalbane**, a large, beautiful tract of the central Highlands once dominated by the Campbells of Glenorchy, created Earls of Breadalbane in 1681. At one time their lands extended from the east coast to the west coast but the estates were broken up and sold in the late 19th and early 20th centuries.

Aberfeldy

Let Fortune's gifts at random flee,
They ne're shall draw a wish frae me,
Supremely blest wi' love and thee
In the birks of Aberfeldy.

Robert Burns, 'The Birks of Aberfeldie'.

Aberfeldy is a pleasant little town on the Urlar Burn at its confluence with the River Tay. Burns' poem might refer to the silver birches beside the burn above the town, which is claimed as the local beauty spot, but some say Burns may have been writing about the birks (beeches) of Abergeldie. Dorothy Wordsworth averred that while there were lots of beeches on the Dee at that time, there were none at all on the Tay. General Wade's bridge over the Tay was designed for him by William Adam. It is said to be Wade's finest bridge. On the south bank stands the **Black Watch Monument**, with a kilted highlander standing on a cairn. It was erected in 1887 to commemorate their founding in 1739 to keep the peace in a country where the Highlanders were ripe for rebellion. There is the ubiquitous restored watermill in the town. The **Glengoulandie Deer Park**, Aberfeldy, on the B846 (✆ *(01887) 830 261;*

open Easter–Sept; adm) is a good trip for children and adults. As well as deer there are Highland Cattle and rare breeds of domestic animals.

Castle Menzies, pronounced 'Mingies' (*open April–mid Oct daily; adm*), is a mile west of the town on the north side of the Tay past Weem. It gets its name from a cave, now blocked up, which is said to have an underground passage through to Loch Glassie. Castle Menzies is a 16th-century, Z-plan fortified tower house with carved gables over its dormers. The central block has flanking towers at diagonally opposite corners, and the west wing was added in 1840 together with the present entrance porch, designed by William Burn. The Menzies family lived here for 400 years but it became almost derelict until it was rescued in 1972. They started the long, arduous and expensive task of restoration and the results are praiseworthy, particularly because it has not been over-restored or filled with the irrelevant and bogus clutter so prevalent in some clan centres. Here and there are showcases of memorabilia, but on the whole the rooms are empty. There is Prince Charlie's Room, complete with four-poster bed, where the prince stayed for two nights on his way to Culloden in Febuary 1746. The chief, Sir Robert Menzies, took no part in the Jacobite cause but was sympathetic to it and entertained his guest with a day's hunting. All the Menzies in the district were 'out' for the prince and the chieftan, Archibald Menzies of Shian, took 700 men to join the Atholl Brigade. He died while sheltering in a bothy after the battle, torched by the government troops. Cumberland garrisoned some of his men here after the battle in August. Among the memorabilia in the castle are a claymore believed to have been used by a Menzies at Bannockburn, a cast of Mary, Queen of Scots' hand, and two ancient shoes found in the walls during restoration. One of the turret rooms has an en suite garderobe with no less than three holes.

Continue west a few miles along the Tay, and turn left just before Keltneyburn; after about 3 miles you will come to **Kenmore** at the head of Loch Tay, built for the estate workers of Taymouth Castle in 1760 by the fourth Earl of Breadalbane, and now a conservation village.

Taymouth Castle

Taymouth Castle, one of the most magnificent of Scotland's neo-Gothic palaces, has had a long and complex architectural history as the centrepiece to a bowl-shaped landscape in which many lodges and other ancillary buildings play an important part in the overall design. The 20th century saw it used as a Polish hospital during the war and a civil defence school. Since then the castle has sat largely disused for many years surrounded by a golf course, its deteriorating condition causing considerable angst to conservationists. Thieves have robbed it of some of its fittings. It is welcome news then that it has recently been put on the market. You can see the castle from the outside by driving through the gate to the golf course and along the drive.

Head of the Campbells of Glenorchy, the first Earl of Breadalbane was described as: 'grave as a Spaniard, cunning as a fox, wise as a serpent and slippery as an eel'. In 1733 he employed William Adam to smarten up what was then Balloch Castle, a 16th-century keep. Adam added two classical wings to the medieval tower. In 1799 the 3rd Earl demolished most of the old castle, leaving only Adam's two wings. The architect John Paterson started work on a new central block, but this was dismantled when he got the sack and James and Archibald Elliot took over in 1806. From then on a succession of architects altered and added to the castle. James Gillespie Graham, with help from Augustus Pugin, remodelled the interior with an extensive and richly carved library and a great Gothic chapel with splendid woodwork screens. Much of the plasterwork executed by Bernasconi in 1809 still remains. Queen Victoria came here on her first Highland tour in September 1842. She was delighted by the castle and its lovely surroundings and by the hospitality of Lord Breadalbane who laid on a fantastic welcome with kilted Highlanders, pipers and guns, bonfires and fireworks. A whole new wing had been built in her honour with painted and gilded ceilings, and she was the first to dine in the new dining room and sleep in the new apartments. The grounds were embellished with pavilions and parterres by Adam, and some of the follies still survive, including a quartz-covered rustic dairy, now a private house, which delighted Victoria— 'a kind of Swiss cottage... very clean and nice'.

Before leaving Kenmore turn left out of the gate to the castle and follow the loch round on the minor road a few hundred yards to the **Crannog** (*open April–Oct 10–5.30, last entry 4.30; adm*). It would be easy to miss: it looks like a make-shift boat house or shelter, but is in fact a brilliant reconstruction of a crannog based on careful underwater research. Wooden piles driven into the bed of the loch hold the framework of a surprisingly large timber-frame hut connected to the land by a timber walkway slung between poles. The hut is conical, its thatched roof rising to quite a height above thatched walls, its interior divided by semi-partitions. There is a central fire on a stone base, a scatter of hay on the timber floor and room for several families. The stone lumps we see in lochs today and call crannogs are now thought to be the detritus that built up after the huts were erected. Excavations have proved this theory correct. The reason for these dwellings' situation seems to have been defensive, one narrow causeway surrounded by water affording considerably more protection than a land-based building.

Fortingall

Fortingall is little more than a hamlet, but it contains Glen Lyon House, seat of the perpetrator of the massacre of Glencoe, unusual English Arts and Crafts-style thatched cottages, and the much publicized 'oldest living thing in Europe'. The latter is a pathetic vestige of a 3,000-year-old yew tree (some say 9,000) in the churchyard, enclosed by railings and propped on stones. It isn't much to look at, but it is awe-inspiring to think that it was here in the time of King Solomon and that its circumference once measured over 60ft. The inner core is gone, burnt out long ago by Beltane fires apparently, and all that is left is a fragmented shell, reminiscent of 'coppicing'. Of much greater interest, though seldom mentioned, is the rough stone font outside the church porch on the right, attributed to Adamnan, St Columba's biographer and champion, who did as much for the Celtic Church in the 7th century as his better-known predecessor. Whether or not Adamnan (the little Adam) administered the sacrament of baptism from this crude font, one reaches out to touch it with reverence. Some say that Pontius Pilate was born in Fortingall, son of a Roman officer who had been sent on a peace mission to the Picts in Dun Geal, a fort on the rocky hill behind the village, and who married a local lass.

If the spirit of Adamnan intrigues you, continue west on the twisty road from Fortingall, about 10 miles along beautiful Glen Lyon to 19th-century **Glen Lyon Church** at Innerwick. They say Adamnan ended his days here. He came to these parts from Iona some time before 704 and established a church at Milton Eonan just west of here; its bell now hangs behind a grid in the porch of the church. That first church was then moved, with this bell, to Kerrowmore, down the road. After lying abandoned for centuries, the bell was finally rescued and preserved here. It's rather a drab little thing but, as with the font at Fortingall, one is moved to touch it and consider the extraordinary faith and determination of those early Christian missionaries. If you feel energetic, and want to bag a Munro, leave your car opposite the church and take off along the marked track north into the hills, 8 miles due north to Loch Rannoch, through the steep-sided Lairig Chalbhath. You'll need someone to pick you up at Carie, the other end.

From Innerwick, drive on west for a mile and turn left—due south—at **Bridge of Balgie**. The lush prettiness of Glen Lyon is rapidly replaced by a desolate moonscape with more Munros to conquer. **Ben Lawers** towers to the east, 3,984ft (1,226m; at its foot is the National Trust for Scotland's Visitor Centre, from which the climb takes about 3 hours. On a clear day you can see from the Atlantic to the North Sea. There are masses of mountain flowers and birds, including kestrel, buzzard, red grouse, golden plover and curlew. Don't be intimidated by the somewhat dog-in-the-manger attitude you may detect in the dismal visitor centre. Conservationists are obsessed by keeping the public from eroding their natural heritage, and are not over anxious for you to explore the area for fear of the damage you might do. Pictures illustrate how to walk on paths, not verges; notices command you to keep dogs on leads; advice is given on what to wear and take if you climb the hill. (This last is understandable: the Mountain Rescue people are frequently called out to risk their lives rescuing idiots who ought to confine their outdoor activities to their gardens.) Some of the displays of local geology, flora and fauna are interesting, as is their audio-visual programme, accompanied by the inevitable booklets and information sheets. There is great conservation work in progress, replanting native woodlands.

This mountain detour takes you down to **Loch Tay**, a long, dark snake of water where there are all types of water sports, as well as excellent fishing. Go west on the A827, through Morenish, about 5 miles to Killin.

Killin

Killin is attractively grouped around an old bridge astride the Falls of Dochart, which carry the River Dochart in a tumble of falls and rapids, swirling down through the village into Loch Tay. This is not, in fact, in Perthshire, but is only a whisker into Breadalbane. White-harled cottages with pretty gardens, jolly hotels and tartan-hung tourist traps complete the picture-postcard scene. On a fine day when there is snow on the hills around, there is an almost alpine feel here, no doubt remarked upon by Prince Albert when he and Queen Victoria trundled through on their first visit in 1842. On **Inchbuie**, the lower of the two islets below the old bridge, is the burial ground of the MacNabs, an aggressive clan who lived at nearby Kinnell and were powerful in the district until they emigrated to Canada in the 19th century, oppressed by the even more powerful Breadalbane Campbells of Glenorchy. These Campbells, including one called Black Duncan of the Cowl, lived at 16th-century **Finlarig Castle**, hidden among trees on a primrose-carpeted mound, half a mile north of Killin past the cemetery, and now a dangerous and rather sinister ruin. All that remains is a stark keep and a building with a coat of arms on it, possibly a chapel. Close to the tower you can still see a gruesome 'beheading pit'. It was the privilege of the gentry to be beheaded, while the common people were hanged from a tree. Beyond the ruin are two 20th-century graves with simple Celtic crosses inscribed for Sir Gavin Campbell, Marquess of Breadalbane and his wife of 50 years, Lady Alma. St Fillan, who died around 777, is thought to have lived nearby and there are eight 'healing stones' near the Bridge of Dochart that bear his name. Each stone represents the part of the body it will heal.

The Breadalbane Folklore Centre (*open Mar–Oct daily; Nov–Feb Mon–Fri; closed Jan; adm*) gives a good insight into the life and legends of Breadalbane, covering the history of the clans of the area, stories of the saints, and details of nature and wildlife. **Moirlanich Longhouse**, on the Glen Lochay road, off the A827 northwest of Killin (*open Easter Sun and May–Sep Wed and Sun 2–5; adm*) dates from the mid 19th century and is a good example of the old buildings in which the family and their livestock lived together under one roof. Most of the original features are preserved, and there is an exhibition of working clothes in the shed next door.

From Killin you can go on west to Crianlarich and the coast, south to Callander and the Lowlands, or back eastwards to Pitlochry along the south side of Loch Tay.

Sports and Activities

Croft-na-Caber, ✆ (01887) 830 588, about a mile along the south side of Loch Tay, is a very good watersports centre, with white-water rafting down the Tay, water-skiing, windsurfing and lots more. They also provide chalet accommodation and a restaurant. **Boreland Farm Park**, at Fearnan, ✆ (01887) 830 212 (*open mid Mar–Oct*) is a good way of occupying the kids when they are bored—and also offers pony trekking and hacking. The Farm Park is predictable (pets corner, etc.) but they do rides and lessons for children, which you must book.

Killin ✆ (01567–)

Where to Stay

expensive

Farleyer House, nr Aberfeldy, ✆ (01887) 820 332, 🖷 829 430, *www.farleyer.com*, is a gracious 15th-century country house in 30 acres of garden with some good salmon fishing on the Tay.

moderate

Ailean Chreggan Hotel, Weem, by Aberfeldy, ✆ (01887) 820 346, is small and friendly, family-run by the Gillespies, with comfortable rooms facing south. The food is excellent, especially if you choose a day when they've been across to the west coast for fresh fish. They can arrange fishing nearby. **Kenmore Hotel**, ✆ (01887) 830 205, 🖷 830 262, is an old inn, said by some to be Scotland's oldest, which people come back to for its old-fashioned values and comfort. In pride of place hangs an original poem by Robert Burns. Now recently refurbished and under new ownership.

Fortingall Hotel, ✆/🖷 (01887) 830 367, just next door to the famous yew tree, is splendidly informal, cosy, unspoilt and not too grand, comfortable and friendly. Also under new ownership. **Morenish Lodge Highland House Hotel**, near Killin, ✆/🖷 820 258, was built in 1750 as a shooting lodge for the Earl of Breadalbane and looks south over Loch Tay, with Ben Lawers to the north. Lorna and Carew Thomas have made this a really comfortable, attractive haven with pretty bedrooms and very good food. **Ardeonaig**, Loch Tay, ✆ 820 400, 🖷 820 282, is a splendid hotel on the south of the loch, with great hospitality, good food and beautiful scenery.

moderate–cheap

The **Killin Hotel**, ✆ 820 296, 🖷 820 647, on the riverbank, is homely and good value, with a bistro overlooking the water. **Dall Lodge Country House Hotel**, Killin, ✆ 820 217, 🖷 820 726, is a country mansion with great views. **Easter Cloanlawers**, Lawers,

✆ 820 522, is a traditional stone farmhouse and converted barn, overlooking Loch Tay. Run by Ken and Beth Miles as a Wolsey Lodge, it is cosy and relaxed. Ken speaks French and German, and Beth is an imaginative cook. No smoking.

cheap

Clachaig Hotel, ✆ 820 270, 🖷 820 439, overlooking the Falls of Dochart in Killin, is an 18th-century coach house with good food and friendly owners. **Morenish House**, Killin, ✆ 820 220, on the north side of Loch Tay, is the nicest self-catering place in the area. It's an old farmhouse beautifully converted and well equipped, with Clanranald himself, the landlord, next door.

Pitlochry to Blair Atholl

Pass of Killiecrankie

Six thousand Veterans practised in War's game,
Tried Men, at Killicranky were arrayed,
Against an equal Host that wore the Plaid,
Shepherds and Herdsmen— Like a whirlwind came
The Highlanders, the slaughter spread like flame.

from a sonnet by William Wordsworth.

Continuing north from Pitlochry, the A9 climbs along the upper slope of the Pass of Killiecrankie, a section of road that cost a great deal of money and took considerable engineering skill to construct. It clings precariously to the densely wooded gorge where, far below, the River Garry cuts its way through to join up with the Tummel. At the far end of the pass, about 3 miles from Pitlochry, there is a National Trust for Scotland Visitor Centre (*open May–Oct daily*) with a pictorial description of the history of the Battle of Killiecrankie. John 'Bonnie Dundee' Graham of Claverhouse and his brave Jacobite Highlanders charged the British Army under General Mackay in 1689, in an attempt to depose William of Orange and restore James VII/II to the throne. Outnumbered by more than two to one, Claverhouse's strategic cunning won the day. Waiting until the setting sun was in the eyes of their enemies, the Highlanders charged them with shot and broadsword until the dead and dying choked the pass. The British were almost annihilated by the Highlanders, but casualties were great on both sides and Claverhouse was mortally wounded. His death, leaving his army leaderless, ensured the subsequent victory three weeks later at Dunkeld of the government troops, who had fled to Aberdeen and recruited a new army. Bonnie Dundee had his darker side: descended from Robert III and a staunch Royalist, he commanded a Troop of Horse raised to suppress the Covenanters' conventicles during the notorious Killing Times. He was also known as 'The Bluidy Clavers' for the atrocities he committed, although it is said that he urged moderation in order not to alienate the people of Scotland. His wife came from a Covenanting family but the final four months of his life, spent rallying the Jacobite cause, established him as a brave, charismatic Highlander. Walk down to the river from the visitor centre, past the terrifying **Soldier's Leap**, an 18-foot jump across the gorge, said to have been made by one of Mackay's soldiers, escaping from the Highlanders. Queen Victoria walked along this path and noted its beauty in her journal: 'Albert was in perfect ecstasies.'

Blair Castle

Three miles north of Killiecrankie, the new road bypasses the village of Blair Atholl giving a good view of Blair Castle from across the river. This white, turreted baronial castle (✆ *(01796) 481 207; open April–Oct daily; adm*), home of the Dukes of Atholl, dates from the 13th century, though it has been much Victorianized. In 1267 John Comyn of Badenoch built a tower on Atholl land while the then Earl of Atholl was away on duty. The earl was justifiably annoyed and complained bitterly to King Alexander III, but the tower remained, now incorporated as Cumming's Tower into the present castle which grew round it. It underwent a series of alterations, including the decapitation of its top storeys in the mid 18th century. Queen Victoria described it as 'a large plain white building' and David Bryce, one of Scotland's leading Victorian architects, was commissioned to baronialize it. This he did, with the help of his brother John, adding the imposing entrance, the castellations and other embellishments so admired by his contemporaries. The effect, though hardly beautiful, is certainly splendid.

The castle has seen many royal visitors: Edward III; Mary, Queen of Scots, who was entertained by a deer and wolf hunt in which 360 deer and five wolves were killed; Claverhouse before the Battle of Killiecrankie (it was here that his body lay before burial in the churchyard of old St Bride's Church in Blair Atholl); Prince Charlie, on his march south in 1745; Cumberland, who garrisoned his troops here the following year, during which time the Duke of Atholl's brother, Lord George Murray, inflicted severe damage on the castle in his attempts to win it back for the Jacobite cause. When Queen Victoria visited the castle in 1844 she and Prince Albert explored the area enthusiastically, escorted by Lord Glenlyon, heir to the Duke of Atholl. Later she presented his bodyguard of highlanders with a pair of colours, bestowing on him the privilege of being the only British subject allowed to retain a private army, the Atholl Highlanders. This honour was revived in 1966 by the late Duke of Atholl and the army numbers some 50 men who appear on parades and have their own pipe band. Membership is highly prized and consists of former servicemen, local lairds and kinsmen of the late Duke.

This is one of Scotland's top historic attractions: the rooms are numbered and there is an excellent new coffee table-style guide book. Look for the Tapestry Room, hung with tapestries and furnished with a sumptuous four-poster bed topped by two vases of ostrich feathers. The Old Scots Room is reconstructed in the style of a simple cottage living room, complete with box bed, cradle and spinning wheel. The castle is stuffed with the usual historic memorabilia: arms and armour, Jacobite relics, china, toys, furniture, lace and paintings, including portraits by Lely, Ramsay and Raeburn. There is even a natural history museum. One of the highlights is a very early example of taxidermy—an 18th-century stuffed polar bear at the bottom of a stairwell. It is rather motheaten and tired-looking now, in need of more stuffing, but endearing nonetheless. The self-service restaurant is licensed and, if you really want to impress your friends, there is a separate dining room for private parties of up to 50 people. If you want to splash out, you can also use the ballroom for up to 200 people, a noble setting for a knees-up, its panelled walls bristling with a forest of antlers and acres of ancestral portraits under a timber-ribbed roof.

If this feast of history gives you dyspepsia, there is a good stroll to the **Bruar Falls** about 3 miles to the west, although even here you will be walking in famous footsteps. Park by the road and it is not far up to the falls, where the River Bruar cascades down through rocky chasms and over gleaming slabs of granite. Robert Burns came up here when he was a guest of the Duke of

Atholl. He was so disgusted by the bare moorland that then surrounded the falls that he dashed off a poem, 'The Humble Petition of Bruar Water', and dispatched it to the Duke:

Would then my noble master please,
To grant my highest wishes,
He'll shade the bank wi' towering trees,
And bonnie spreading bushes.

This plea, as you will see, found its mark and inspired the fourth Duke to plant the trees now growing there. Walk on beyond the falls up the path for another mile or so, through birches and rhododendrons. A bridge takes you over the stream and down the other side, making a round trip of just over 2 miles. You can get a good pub lunch down by the car park.

You can't miss **The House of Bruar** which stands prominently beside the A9 at Blair Atholl. This is a serious shopper's paradise and people drive miles to visit it. In a spectacular building, designed for conversion into an hotel should the present venture ever fail, there are dozens of different shops: country clothes of every possible sort, cashmere, tweed, woollens, china and glass, gifts, a gourmet food hall, a restaurant, a wild flower nursery and a library. You won't find many bargains here, and don't expect to pick up anything so humble as bread and butter for your picnic in the food hall. It has been dubbed 'The Harrods of the North'.

The drive from here to Newtonmore takes you through a diversity of true Highland scenery. The road is so good and fast now that one is through in a flash without realizing what lonely grandeur and solitude lie around as far as the eye can see. (General Wade was responsible for this route.) After the Drumochter Pass you come to Dalwhinnie Moor, a place of the utmost desolation especially in the old days when the previous road wound tortuously across it and a breakdown was a nightmare. The intrepid German writer, Theodor Fontane, described crossing Dalwhinnie in a coach in 1858, packed so tightly on to the roof that those on the outside had only one cheek on the seat. He called it 'the Grampian waste' and said it was the most lonely country he had ever seen.

Pass of Killiecrankie ✆ (01796–) ***Where to Stay***

moderate

The Killiecrankie Hotel, Pass of Killiecrankie, ✆ 473 220, 🖷 472 451, *www.killiecrankiehotel.co.uk*, is a Victorian manse in lovely surroundings, with awards for its food and recommendations in most of the good food and hotel guides. Prices range upwards from moderate. **Atholl Arms Hotel**, Blair Atholl, ✆ 481 205, 🖷 481 550, *www.athollarmshotel.co.uk*, in the main street opposite the castle, has been recently renovated and has a splendid dining room in what once served as the castle ballroom. It's become quieter since the through road was diverted some years ago. The hotel is about to change hands. **Bridge of Tilt Hotel**, Bridge of Tilt, ✆ 481 333, 🖷 481 335, is smaller, slightly cheaper, but just as pleasant and convivial, owned by coach company Grand UK Holidays.

cheap

Dalgreine, off St Andrew's Crescent, Bridge of Tilt, ✆ 481 276, is a very comfortable, very good value villa with a pretty garden. No dogs and no smoking.

Tourist Information

Crieff: Town Hall, High St, ✆ (01764) 652 578; **Dunblane**: Stirling Rd, ✆ (01786) 824 428 (*open May–Sept*); **Auchterarder**: 90 High St, ✆ (01764) 663 450.

Crieff

Crieff (from Crubha Cnoc—Hill of Trees) is about 16 miles west of Perth on the A85 and used to hold the biggest cattle tryst in Scotland in the days when sturdy black cattle were the principal currency of the Highland economy. For most of the summer months drovers from all over the Highlands and Islands would drive their herds over inhospitable, almost impassable tracks to the market to sell to men from the south. The fair earned such a reputation for violent behaviour that it was moved to Falkirk in the 1770s. Crieff is an attractive, lively town on the south-facing foothills of the Grampians, looking down over the valley of the River Earn. The Knock of Crieff, 911ft (280m), dominates the north, a wooded hill with footpaths and good views from the top. The town was sacked and destroyed by Highlanders during the Jacobite rebellion and little remains from before the 19th century. Later a bleaching and tanning industry brought prosperity to its people and it became a popular spa town in the 19th century, attracting a number of good schools into the area, including Morrison's Academy. Echoes of its Victorian heyday linger on in the Crieff Hydro Hotel, perched above the town and embellished with glass domes and pavilions, which opened in 1868 as the Strathearn Hydropathic, 12 years after the arrival of the railway.

The **Crieff Visitor Centre** in Muthill Road is a popular attraction, ✆ (01764) 654 014. It incorporates Perthshire Paperweights, Scotland's oldest working pottery, a show room, an audio-visual presentation and a garden centre. There is a factory shop and a licensed restaurant. Further along Muthill Road is the **Stuart Crystal Factory Shop** (*open daily*) which incorporates a **Falconry Centre** (*open April–Oct; adm*). The **Strathearn Gallery and Pottery**, 32 West High Street (*open daily*) is a gallery of contemporary art and a working pottery. The **Glenturret Distillery** (*open Feb–Dec daily; Jan–Feb Mon–Fri; adm*) is also worth a visit—it's the oldest distillery in Scotland, established in 1775.

Around Crieff

Innerpeffray Library (*open daily except Thurs; adm*), 4 miles southeast of the town off the B8068, is a gem and easy to miss. An unlikely track through farm buildings takes you down to the oldest lending library in Scotland, entirely isolated in its little complex of house, chapel and schoolhouse, with the ruins of Innerpeffray Castle a few hundred yards away (*not open to the public*). It is hard to believe that in Roman times this was on the main route from England to the north. The first Lord Madderty (or Madertie) built the castle in 1610 as his family home. About 50 years later his grandson, the 3rd Lord Madderty, established a library in St Mary's chapel in the burial ground nearby, along with a school. In his will in 1691 he bequeathed 5,000 Scots merks (about £277) in trust for the upkeep of the library and school, for the education of the people, especially young students in the area. His nephew and heir, William Drummond, 2nd Viscount Strathallan, honoured his uncle's wishes in spite of legal difficulties, and added to the endowment to preserve the library and maintain the school. For some 70 years the library was housed in the chapel and in the small house at the east end of the churchyard. In 1762 the present building was completed, adjacent to the chapel, by Robert Hay Drummond, Bishop of Sarum and later Archbishop of York. All the books were moved into the new house and the library flourished until after the First World War, when the public's reading habits changed and were better served by municipal lending libraries. The last books were borrowed in 1968, and now the library is only available for reference and as a museum for bibliophiles. Ted Powell, the present curator who lives in the school house, knows every volume and shows them off with loving pride and great scholarship. Some 3,000 of the 4,400 books are pre-1800 and include many rare and priceless works. Some belonged to Montrose, including the bible he carried throughout his campaigns, which bears his signature. There are 'Treacle Bibles'—those printed in early times before treacle was translated as balm, as in Jeremiah 8, v. 22... 'is there no treacle in Gilead; is there no physician there?' (Ted Powell will show you an old agricultural encyclopaedia in which there is a recipe for treacle, which involves pounding up vipers, used as a salve, particularly against venomous bites and malignant diseases.) There are the collected works of King James VI (James I of England) which include his declamation against smoking, so recently brought to England by Sir Walter Raleigh: 'A custome loathsome to the eye, hatefull to the nose, harmefull to the braine, dangerous to the lungs, and in the blacke stinking fume thereof, neerest resembling the horrible Stigian smoake of the pit that is bottomlesse.' How the Nanny State would have loved him. There is a borrower's record book in which, among others, were numerous loans, mostly historical and religious, to James Michell, student, who went on to be tutor to Sir Walter Scott. From 1747 to 1800, almost 300 people—of which 11 were women—borrowed books. **St Mary's Chapel**, rebuilt in 1508 on an earlier site, is charmingly unspoilt and bare, with a medieval altar and traces of painted frescoes. The original library was in the 17th-century laird's loft.

Drummond Castle Gardens (*open Easter–Oct 2–6; adm*) is about 3 miles south of Crieff on the A822, approached up a mile-long tree-lined avenue. The castle (*not open to the public*), dates from about 1490 with a mixture of later additions. James IV came here often, courting Margaret Drummond. Some say they were secretly married; she almost certainly had his child. She and her two sisters Euphemia and Sibilla were poisoned in the castle, probably by those who saw her as a threat to the king's marriage to Margaret Tudor. All three are buried in Dunblane Cathedral, commemorated by brass plaques. The castle is set in a designed landscape and is renowned for its terraced gardens created by John Drummond, 2nd Earl of Perth in 1630, influenced by French and Italian designs and recreated in 1832. A grand flight of steps leads down three terraces to the formal garden adorned with topiary yews and hollies, many statues, sculpture and architectural features. The gardens were used as the setting at the end of the film *Rob Roy*. They are best appreciated from above.

The Sma' Glen

There is a pretty excursion from Crieff along the A822 up the Sma' Glen towards Amulree. The River Almond thunders down from the hills on its way to meet the Tay above Perth, with rapids and waterfalls and a good salmon leap at Buchanty Spout in Glenalmond, on the B8063. On the right of the road, about a mile south of Newton Bridge, you can see **Ossian's Stone**, by the river. It doesn't look much but is said to have once marked the grave of Ossian, the legendary Gaelic hero and bard who spent many years in fairyland until he was baptized by St Patrick. It was moved here by General Wade's road-builders when it blocked the path of one of their constructions. Traces of a prehistoric burial, found when they lifted the stone, were given a reburial in a secret place by local Highlanders who were convinced they were indeed the remains of the poet. Wordsworth thought so too:

In this still place, remote from men
Sleeps Ossian, in the narrow Glen.

Comrie

Comrie, 6 miles west of Crieff along the River Earn, is an attractive conservation village. At Hogmanay they have the unique Flambeaux Procession, when villagers parade around by torchlight with much revelry. This custom has its roots in the ancient pagan fire-festivals, held to drive off evil spirits for the coming year. Because it lies on the Highland Line—the geological fault that divides Highland and Lowland Scotland—more seismological tremors have been recorded here than anywhere else in Britain. Shocks were especially common during the 19th century; in recent years tremors have never done more than rattle the village teacups. **Earthquake House** was built in 1874 to house one of the earliest seismometers in the world. They have a model of the original instrument as well as a modern one, in use, and a chart recorder. You can't go in but there are exhibits on view from outside.

Drummond Trout Farm and Fishery, a mile west of Comrie just off the A85 (*open summer daily 10–10; winter daily 10–5*) is a good day out for children and adults. It offers free tuition throughout the season, with prizes. There are fly ponds, bait ponds, beginners' ponds, rod hire, a salmon ladder, and an underwater camera. There is a farm shop (*open daily*) with not only fish, but also game and venison. **Auchingarrich Wildlife Centre**, in Comrie (*✆ (01764) 679 4669; open mid Mar–mid Nov; adm*) is 100 acres containing an amazing collection of animals you don't expect to see in Scotland: arctic foxes, wallabies, llamas, racoons, porcupines, chipmunks and many more. Between Easter and October you can even watch eggs hatching.

Just north of Comrie up Glen Lednock is the **Devil's Cauldron**, an impressive waterfall that carries the River Lednock down towards the River Earn. This road takes you on up the glen to Loch Lednock which is a reservoir and quite pretty. **St Fillans** is about 5 miles west of Comrie, a cluster of houses and hotels around the eastern end of **Loch Earn**, very popular for water sports in summer and best avoided if you prefer solitude. The A85 takes you along the north of the loch to **Lochearnhead**. There are quite a few places to stay around here, as well as people keen to hire boats and craft of all sorts. Half way along the southern shore road is the start of a good climb up Ben Vorlich, a popular Munro in the area. From Lochearnhead you can take the A85 westwards to Crianlarich, or the A84 14 miles south to Callander.

Crieff ✆ (01764–) ***Where to Stay***

expensive

If you can afford it, **The Gleneagles Hotel**, ✆ 662 231, ℻ 662 134, *www.gleneagles.com*, is an experience in itself. Once inside its maw it would be possible to live there happily ever after and not be bored. Its golf courses are world renowned, along with its reputation as one of Scotland's best hotels. There is, quite literally, everything here that a hedonist could possibly want, and the staff are remarkably un-stuffy. **Auchterarder House**, Auchterarder, ✆ 663 646, ℻ 662 939, *www.wrensgroup.com*, is another luxurious hotel which is very cosy.

moderate

Crieff Hydro Hotel, ✆ 655 555, 🖷 653 087, *www.crieffhydro.com*, still run by descendants of its founders, is set in 800 acres high above the town, with its own golf course and a mass of indoor and outdoor leisure facilities, including a riding school and sports hall. The Brasserie has an AA Rosette. It's geared towards families. **Murraypark Hotel**, Connaught Terrace, ✆ 653 731, 🖷 655 311, is a pink-stoned Victorian house in attractive grounds. Now owned by the Crieff Hydro, it's very friendly and also does good food.

The **Royal Hotel**, Comrie, ✆ 679 200, is a good place to go for stylish good food with a splendid pub-bar. **The Four Seasons Hotel**, St Fillans, ✆ 685 333, 🖷 685 444, faces south across Loch Earn and is well run by its new owners. It has 2 Rosettes from the AA and is a member of the Scotch Beef Club, which means that it is popular, so book well ahead. They also have A-frame chalets behind the hotel which give a bit of privacy and are cosily decorated. **Kippenross**, Dunblane, ✆ (01786) 824 048, is a lovely Georgian house in a family estate, not in the Highlands but near enough to make it worth the detour. It is a Wolsey Lodge run by Mr and Mrs Stirling-Aird, who make you feel very much at home. No smoking.

cheap

Meadow Inn Hotel, Burrell St, Crieff, ✆ 653 261, is a traditional town-centre hotel on a corner site. It's convivial and very convenient, if not that peaceful. **Merlindale** (formerly Lediffton House), Perth Road, Crieff, ✆ 655 205, is a Georgian house close to the town centre, proud of its cordon bleu cooking. **Leven House Hotel**, Comrie Road, Crieff, ✆ 652 529, is a pleasant, old-fashioned little house with a garden.

The Trossachs and Breadalbane

The rest of this chapter is not, strictly speaking, Perthshire, but it seems most sensible to include it at this point.

Tourist Information

Callander: Rob Roy and Trossachs Visitor Centre, Ancaster Square, ✆ (01877) 330 342 (*open Mar–Dec daily; Jan and Feb Sat and Sun*).

Callander

Callander, 34 miles from Crieff and some 40 miles from Perth, is a popular tourist centre for the Trossachs. It is a sturdy town overshadowed by Ben Ledi to the northwest, which owes its design to the commissioners for forfeited Jacobite estates, who authorized its development on forfeited Drummond land in the 18th century. They favoured a spacious layout rather than that of former times with huddled houses on narrow streets, which were much easier for rebels to defend. Television addicts might recognize the *Tannochbrae* of 'Dr Finlay's Casebook', and scenes from *The Country Diary of an Edwardian Lady.*

There are lots of good walks around here. For a quick stroll, go up to the Bracklinn Falls about a mile to the northeast, on Keltie Water. They say Sir Walter Scott once rode his horse across here for a bet. (To give someone *keltie* is to force a large alcoholic drink on a teetotaller or to give a double dose of punishment.) The Falls of Leny, a couple of miles on up the A84, are too near the road and too well-signed—and therefore rather over-run, but you can climb Ben Ledi (2,875ft/884m) from here, on a reasonable path. During the tourist season, Callander offers a variety of entertainment such as *ceilidhs*, open-air pipe band concerts and Highland dancing, as well as wildlife slide shows. The Callander International Highland Games are in August.

Callander ✆ (01877–) ***Where to Stay***

expensive–moderate

Roman Camp, ✆ 330 003, 🖷 331 533, *www.roman-camp-hotel.co.uk*, is a mixture of 17th century, Victorian and modern, behind the Main Street. It's not noisy, and has a nice relaxed atmosphere, enhanced by cosy log fires. James Barrie once stayed in the Barrie Suite in the Victorian part. The food is excellent.

moderate

Invertrossachs Country House, on Loch Venachar near Callander, ✆ 331 126, 🖷 331 229, is a large Edwardian house with lots of character in 33 acres of woods and garden. It also has self-catering apartments. **Dundarroch Country House**, at Brig O'Turk near Callander, ✆ 376 200, is a cosy Victorian stone house in a rural setting. with a river frontage, free trout fishing, mountain views and a pretty garden. The **Leny Estate** (contact Mrs F. Roebuck, Leny Estate Lodges, Leny House, Callander, ✆ 331 078) has a range of first-class self-catering establishments (from houses to log cabins). **Leny House** (same ✆), a very comfortable country mansion in parkland with good views, offers B&B.

Myrtle Inn, south of Callander on the A84, is probably the best place to eat. Alternatively, **Ben Ledi Café**, on the main street near the square, serves good plain food, and **The Café** in Brig O'Turk, ✆ 376 267, is very popular: book in advance.

The Trossachs

Tourist Information

Tyndrum: Main Street, ✆ (01838) 400 246 (*open April–Oct*).

A Literary Introduction

It has to be said that if it hadn't been for Sir Walter Scott, and to a lesser extent Wordsworth and his sister Dorothy, the Trossachs would never have appeared so indelibly on the tourist map, although travellers had become obsessed by the idea of the Highlands since the publication of James Macpherson's 'translation' of Ossian's epic in 1762. When *The Lady of the Lake* was first read by an avid public, the Trossachs became the 'in' place for travellers north and its unsurpassed beauty became legend. They flocked here from the south and eulogized the places where fair Ellen Douglas was courted by James V, disguised as James Fitzjames. The 'beauty spot' image stuck, heartily endorsed by local innkeepers and hoteliers, assisted by the fact that the area was so conveniently situated for the increasingly densely populated towns to the south. Pretty though the Trossachs is—particularly at first and last light, when there are fewer people to share it with—there are countless other more dramatic spots more worthy of admiration. (H. V. Morton, writing in 1921, disagreed, calling The Trossachs 'a synopsis of Scotland'.)

Although the tourist brochures tend to refer to the whole area between Callander and Loch Lomond as the Trossachs, in fact the Trossachs proper is only the gorge that runs from Loch Achray to Loch Katrine, a rugged pass barely a mile long. Locals will give two meanings for this strange name: 'bristly country' or 'the crossing place'; no one is sure. It is narrow, rocky, rather bosky and unremarkable, but now and then you get a hint of the magic that so enchanted Scott. The road twists and climbs through gorse, bracken and emerald green moor, past rhododendrons, with a number of inviting footpaths leading off.

Loch Katrine

Nine miles west of Callander, this loch was the main setting for *The Lady of the Lake*, with Ellen's Isle named after its heroine. From April to September, the Victorian steamer *Sir Walter Scott* runs 45-minute trips daily along the length of the loch from Trossachs Pier to Stronachlachar (*Sun–Fri 11, 1.45 and 3.15, Sat 1.45 and 3.15; ✆ (01877) 376 316*). As you pass Ellen's Isle remember how, when James Fitzjames blew his horn to summon help:

From underneath an aged oak,
That slanted from the islet rock
A Damsel guider of its way,
A little skiff shot to the bay
That round the promontory steep
Led its deep line in graceful sweep...

A prosaic guide will tell you that this loch is also Glasgow's water supply. Because of this there is a large notice at the pier forbidding you to swim, paddle, picnic, fish, camp, light fires, or throw coins into the loch. There is a café at the pier as well as the obligatory souvenir shops. To get the best view of the loch, forget the boat trip and put on your boots. There is a splendid, very easy climb up **Ben Venue** (2,393ft/736m) from Achray, on the western shore of Loch Achray about 8 miles west of Callander on the A827: it's just over 5 miles and takes under 5 hours. Take the track from behind the Loch Achray Hotel and head west through the Pass of Achray. There are a variety of ways up and it can become quite boggy in places, but the views from the two peaks are well worth the climb.

Aberfoyle

Aberfoyle, 5 miles south of the Trossachs, is another tourist centre for the area with all the lively trappings that implies. Walter Scott made his first notes for *Rob Roy* in the village manse. There is a **Scottish Wool Centre** (*open daily; adm*) telling you all you may want to know about sheep over the past 2,000 years, with films, sheepdog demonstrations, spinning and weaving, a children's farm, shop and restaurant.

Queen Elizabeth Forest Park Visitor Centre is a modern stone building just before Aberfoyle, with an ornamental lake, walks and all the usual displays illustrating flora and fauna. The park lies to the west, all 75,000 acres of it. Although very much Designer Highlands, with numerous waymarked trails, cycling routes, a forest drive, picnic areas and conservation rules, it still has bits off the beaten trail and some good hills to climb with staggering views: Ben Lomond (3,192ft/974m) and Ben Vrackie (1,922ft/591m) are two of the best. **Ben Lomond** is the most southerly Munro, ascended by two well-trodden paths, one from Rowardennan Hotel at the northern end of the road along the eastern side of Loch Lomond—the B837—and the other from the southern end of Loch Dhu, off the B829, 6 miles west of Aberfoyle.

Because Ben Lomond is so popular it is in danger of becoming too much of a 'theme park', causing conservationists to wring their hands in despair as erosion worsens, but however many more generations of feet go tramping up, it will remain a splendid summit from which to view the Arrochar Alps, the Southern Highlands, and their famous loch. Even in the days of Gerard Manley Hopkins, when he was working from Glasgow in 1880, there was a threat:

What would the world be, once bereft
Of wet and wilderness?
Let them be left, wildness and wet;
Long live the weeds and the wilderness yet.

'Inversnaid' by Gerard Manley Hopkins

Inchmahome Priory

Take the A81southwest from Callander for 6 miles to Lake Menteith. (Weather dictates the running of the ferry, for which you pay; the priory on the island is open daily April–Sept and is free.) The Priory, now a romantic ruin, was founded for Augustinian monks in 1238 by Walter Comyn, 4th Earl of Menteith, and there may have been a Celtic monastery here before. Look out for the whimsical, weathered remains of the two figures of the 13th-century Earl and Countess of Menteith in the chapter house; they lie facing each other, their feet cosily resting on heraldic beasts with the Countess resting her hand on his shoulder.

In the choir is the grave of Robert Cunninghame Graham, the 'rebel laird' of the estate who died in Buenos Aires in 1936 aged 84, where he was known as 'Don Roberto'. This flamboyant character travelled extensively in South America, where he had a ranch, and in Spain and Morocco. He married a Chilean poetess, was imprisoned for 'illegal assembly' in 1887 (a Socialist demo in Trafalgar Square), was elected first president of the Scottish Labour party in 1888, and wrote many travel books, essays and short stories. He was a close friend of both Joseph Conrad and W.H. Hudson and his exotic tale *Mogreb-el-Acksa*, which tells of his attempt to reach the fobidden city of Tarouddant in Morocco, was claimed by Bernard Shaw as his inspiration for *Captain Brassbound's Conversion.*

Inchmahome was the refuge for Mary, Queen of Scots for three weeks in 1547, before she was sent off to France to grow up out of range of Henry VIII's 'Rough Wooing'. Needless to say there is now a Queen Mary's Bower, where she is supposed to have played.

Balquhidder: Rob Roy's Grave

The English ballad-singer's joy!
And Scotland has a thief as good,
An outlaw of as daring mood;
She has her brave Rob Roy.

'Rob Roy's Grave' by William Wordsworth

Balquhidder, about 10 miles north of Callander on Loch Voil, is the burial place of Rob Roy MacGregor. Liam Neeson's dashing portrayal of Rob Roy, filmed not so long ago, helped to revive the popularity of this colourful, Robin Hood-like character so romanticized by Walter Scott. Born in 1671 and so called for his red hair (from the

Gaelic *ruadh* (roy—red), he was the younger son of Lieutenant-Colonel Donald MacGregor of Glengyle, the clan chief. He fought under 'Bonnie Dundee' at Killiecrankie in 1689 when he was 18 and was known for his exceptionally long, almost simian, arms and skill with a broadsword. The Protestant MacGregors were notorious, extorting 'blackmail' (in its original meaning of protection money against depredation by free booters) in their territory in return for protection. In 1694, when their name was proscribed (not for the first time), Rob Roy took the name Campbell, having married a Mary Campbell the year before. For a while he lived honestly enough, becoming a prosperous cattle dealer under the protection of the Marquis of Montrose. He was accused of embezzlement in 1711, when a sum of £1,000 which he had borrowed from Montrose was stolen by his chief drover, a Macdonald. He was outlawed and so began his legendary exploits, depicted by Scott. He rallied the Clan Gregor to the Jacobite cause in 1715, submitted (after many adventures) to General Wade in 1725, converted to Catholicism and finally died in his bed in 1734. Legend has him visited on his deathbed by an enemy, for whom he insisted on being dressed in full armour, saying: 'It shall never be said that a foe saw Robert Roy MacGregor defenceless and unarmed.' After the man had left, Rob instructed a piper to play *Ha til me tulidh*—We Return No More—and died before the tune was finished. You can't miss his grave in Balquhidder churchyard: Clan Gregor have been unable to resist the temptation to do it up. The 'MacGregor Despite Them' refers to the proscription of the clan.

Crianlarich

The A84 north from Callander to Lochearnhead and then the A85 north and west take you to Crianlarich. This is all excellent walking and climbing country with good paths, often signed: all you need is a proper map and the right equipment.The village of Crianlarich is tucked into moorland about 12 miles southwest of Killin, isolated but by no means desolate. It has the somewhat incongruously urban-sounding title of 'railway junction', because this is where the lines from Oban and Fort William join up on their progress south. (The West Highland Line, from Glasgow to Mallaig, takes you through glorious scenery, and is worth travelling on for the sake of the journey itself.) The station is unmanned and rather ramshackle now, but in its midst, like an oasis in the desert, is a cosy café where travellers waiting for a connection sit contentedly munching delicious bacon butties and drinking hot coffee.

There are usually lots of people striding around Crianlarich in climbing boots and knapsacks—the 90-mile West Highland Way passes by on its way from Milngavie (pronounced Mull-guy) to Fort William and this is a favourite staging post. If you like a purpose to your walk, go a couple of miles on up the A82 and take the track just north of the school house at Castlebridge, across the River Fillan. The ruin here is that of St Fillan's Priory, associated with St Adamnan: Robert I brought St Fillan's arm here as a relic and founded an Augustinian priory in 1314. Or you can take a track east to Loch Dochart where there is the ruin on an island of a castle built by 'Black Duncan' Campbell of Glenorchy in the early 17th century and destroyed almost at once by his rivals, the Macnabs. For fans of James Hogg, 'the Ettrick Shepherd', Glen Dochart was the setting for his *Spectre of the Glen.*

Three road-routes also meet in Crianlarich: south to Loch Lomond, northwest to Oban and Fort William, or northeast to Pitlochry.

Tyndrum

Only 5 miles north of Crianlarich on the A82, Tyndrum nestles in a glacial valley at another junction of three routes, to the south, north and west. This is where the cattle drovers used to meet up on their way to markets at Falkirk and Crieff, a bleak-enough tryst. Tyndrum means 'The House on the Ridge'—i.e. the watershed between east and west. Some years ago this tiny settlement achieved a 'gold rush' status: extensive gold mining in the area led to speculation that this was about to become an important gold centre in Britain and some rather utilitarian accommodation was built. The gold fever seems to have died down, though you will still find the occasional loner, hopefully panning; the emphasis has shifted to tourism and some outsized hotels have been erected, to the detriment of the scenery. This is now a place to stop off en route to the western Highlands, or a centre for walkers and climbers. There are well over a dozen Munros within conquering distance; take a good map and stick to the accepted codes of practice and you can spend happy weeks in these hills. The **Clifton Coffee Shop**, by the Green Welly Shop, is a good place to refuel with fast food.

Where to Stay

expensive

Ben Doran Hotel, ✆ (01838) 400 373, and the **Royal Hotel**, ✆ (01838) 400 272, 🖷 200 453, both in Tyndrum, have similar standards of comfort and price.

moderate

Lake Hotel, Port of Menteith, ✆ (01877) 385 258, 🖷 385 671, is on the shore of Lake Menteith with a splendid conservatory restaurant overlooking the water. **Monachyle Mhor**, Balquhidder, ✆ (01877) 384 622, is a confortable pink-harled farmhouse with nice views and a relaxed family atmosphere. Its public bar is a lively centre of the local community.

Craigruie House, Balquhidder, ✆ (01877) 384 240, is a friendly Wolsey Lodge run by Sandra and Douglas Carter, a Victorian mansion deep in Rob Roy country with its grounds running down to Loch Voil and free fishing. Sandra is an excellent cook using local ingredients. Stalking and shooting can be arranged.

Creagan House, at Strathyre southeast of Balquhidder, ✆ (01877) 384 638, is a delightful old overgrown cottage, peaceful and welcoming with antique furniture and excellent food. **The Lodge House**, ✆ (01838) 300 276, on a knoll beside the road in Crianlarich, is very friendly and quite a good base for walkers.

cheap

The **Inverey Hotel**, in Tyndrum, ✆ (01838) 400 219, is a more basic option.

Eating Out

Braeval Old Mill, Aberfoyle, ✆ (01877) 382 711, is a converted mill just east of Aberfoyle, owned by Nick Nairn (of TV cooking fame) and his wife Fiona. Be sure to book. *Lunch and dinner Wed–Sat, lunch only Sun. Not cheap.*

Southwestern Highlands

Loch Lomond	80
Loch Lomond to Loch Fyne	83
Dunoon	85
West Loch Fyne	88
Inverary	88
Oban	92
Around Oban	93
Oban to Kintyre via Lochgilphead	94
Knapdale	97
Kintyre	99
Oban to Appin	102

The further west you go in the Highlands, the more beautiful, on the whole, the scenery becomes. The southwestern Highlands, for the purposes of this book, cover the area from Crianlarich and Tyndrum west to and around Oban, south round the Kintyre peninsula, and back to Crianlarich encompassing the Cowal peninsula and Loch Lomond.

Argyllshire, until recently embraced by Strathclyde, was where the ancient Dalriada Scots from Ireland settled and formed their powerful kingdom. Here, Columba landed to spread the Christianity St Ninian had introduced at Whithorn more than one and a half centuries earlier. As well as dozens of prehistoric burial mounds, stones and cairns, the coast is punctuated with the remains of fortresses and watchtowers, built to defend the land from invasion by sea.

The climate becomes milder the further west you go and supports gardens where exotic foreign plants thrive; many of these are open to the public. Some of the coastal scenery is as magnificent as you could hope for, though the further north you go the better it gets, partly because it becomes less and less populated. Inland, around Loch Lomond, the cities are too close to allow much solitude—the hills and glens well-trodden by hiking boots, but undeniably beautiful. Large areas are remote and wild still, with serpentine sea lochs eating into the land to form long peninsulas and narrow isthmuses. Moor, hill and forest are fringed by miles of beaches, with many islands lying off the coast like stray pieces of a jigsaw. Fishing, farming and tourism are the main industries in the region.

Loch Lomond

The A82 south from Crianlarich, through Glen Falloch and down the west side of Loch Lomond, takes you through some impressive mountainous scenery, but by the time you get to Balloch you are definitely in the urban hinterland of Glasgow.

Tourist Information

Balloch: Balloch Road, ✆ (01389) 742 306.

Loch Lomond

Oh, I'll tak the high road,
An you'll tak the low road,
An I'll be in Scotland afore ye
But me and my true Love will never meet again
On the bonnie, bonnie banks o' Loch Lomond.

The song 'Loch Lomond' was composed in Carlisle jail during the aftermath of Culloden by the Jacobite Donald MacDonell of Keppoch, awaiting a trial that ended in his brutal execution. The English were capricious in their distribution of justice: some prisoners were arbitrarily sent to the gallows, others were set free and told to walk home.

Argyll and the Southwestern Highlands

MacDonell, fairly sure of his fate, wrote that his spirit would return to Scotland on the 'high road', swinging on the gallows, faster than his living companions on the low road. (Some people sing the first two lines differently: 'You'll tak the high road'—the normal route—'And I'll tak the low road'—of death—but the first version is the original.)

Loch Lomond is the largest freshwater lake in Britain—24 miles from north to south—but only the third longest, after Lochs Awe and Ness, and the third deepest, after Lochs Morar and Ness. Its northern end is a long, thin neck, little more than an estuary for the River Falloch, widening to as much as 5 miles in the south. The **Inverarnan Drovers' Inn**, right up on the west side, before the river widens into the loch, is a wonderfully atmospheric 20th-century interpretation of an 18th-century inn—it was established in 1705. The rough rubble-walled exterior, with its gabled dormers and porch, sets the theme (though the original would have been harled, much smaller and the dormers and porch were 19th-century embellishments). Inside are low-lit rooms with bare floorboards pungent with the smell of wood smoke. Dusty curiosities adorn the walls and beams; in the hall are swords, shields and stuffed birds and bears. You can also stay here. **The Stagger Inn**, opposite, has good plain food and a shop.

At first the road is twisty and narrow, a nightmare in summer, but the newish stretch further south is better and gives excellent views of the loch with the hills on the far side dominated by Ben Lomond. There are tourist traps galore along this road, especially in the over-prettified estate-village of **Luss**, which even has a kilt shop and bagpipe works. A number of marinas offer all kinds of water activity and launching slips for your own boat.

A grand entrance on the main road heralds **Rossdhu House**, a classical mansion on the shores of the loch in an extensive landscaped park. It was built in 1773 for the Colquhourn family who have owned most of the land around here for 900 odd years. It is now an exclusive golf club attached to a 600-acre course which seems to have gone to the top of the league in a handful of years. The smartened-up ruins of the 15th-century castle decorate the 18th green, and the clan chapel, complete with chieftains' bones, presides over the game from some yew trees. The Loch Lomond Golf Club is not cheap, and attracts rich celebrities: Sean Connery, Clint Eastwood and Gerald Ford among them.

You can drive from Aberfeldy to the Inversnaid Hotel on the eastern shore of Loch Lomond, or up as far as the Rowardennan Hotel from the south. This is excellent walking country and includes one of the most popular routes up Ben Lomond. The best time to see the loch is in the early morning, before there is much traffic, when the mist clings to the glassy water as the sun rises over Ben Lomond. In the spring, bluebells carpet the ground under oak woods. Because of its accessibility from Glasgow, the loch is crowded with boats of all sorts in the summer; some say too many and that the washes from the speed boats will cause erosion. Even Queen Victoria noted the tourist traffic—large coaches with outside seats, full of tourists. She was reminded of Switzerland when she went cruising down the loch in 1869 and thought it magnificent—remarkably like Lake Lucerne, with truly alpine scenery. She and Princess Louise tried to sketch it but their steamer was too fast for success. Dr Johnson, on the other hand, visiting the loch 'in the rainy season', found nothing more than uncultivated ruggedness, but thought it would have been splendid in 'a happier climate' to own one of its islands.

The loch has more varieties of fish than any other in Scotland, including trout, salmon, sea trout, gigantic pike and freshwater herring, descended from sea herring trapped here after the last Ice Age. A number of cruise boats operate, weaving between the 30 or so small islands, some little more than rocks, scattered over the southern end. **Inch Cailleach** (Island of the Old Women) was the burial place of the fierce MacGregor clan. It belongs to Scottish Natural Heritage and has trails and woodland paths. Ruined **Lennox Castle**, on Inch Murrin (Isle of Spears), the largest island, was where the Duchess of Albany retired after James I had slaughtered her family in 1425.

Sports and Activities

Several companies offer cruises on the loch. Try **Sweeny's Cruises**, ✆ (01389) 752 376, or **Cruise Loch Lomond**, ✆ (01301) 702 636.

Loch Lomond ✆ (01389–)

Where to Stay

cheap

Loch Lomond Youth Hostel, ✆ 850 226, further south at Arden, must be Scotland's grandest youth hostel. It was one of a series of Baronial mansions built along the loch in the 19th century for rich Glasgow industrialists and even its porch is palatial. It has a ghost. There is another not so grand **youth hostel** at Rowardennan, ✆ (01360) 870 259, on the east side of Loch Lomond, which is well organized and more secluded.

The Cottage, Auchendennan, Arden, ✆ 850 287, is only a few minutes from popular Duck Bay and Loch Lomond, with just two bedrooms, and a quiet, secluded garden. **Loch Lomond Castle Lodge House**, Arden, ✆ 850 688, is an excellent budget family base, with a private beach and slipway, with boat and fishing facilities available. Secluded in the attractive grounds there are also well-equipped self-catering lodges, sleeping 4 to 6.

See also above, the **Drovers Inn** at Inverarnan.

Loch Lomond to Loch Fyne

About a third of the way south down Loch Lomond you can turn right on to the A83 and drive westwards around the head of Loch Long, through Glen Croe and Glen Kinglas to the head of Loch Fyne. **Tarbet**, meaning isthmus, particularly one over which a boat may be drawn, is where King Haakon IV's Vikings pulled 50 galleys across from Loch Long into Loch Lomond in 1263. From here they navigated the River Leven into the Firth of Clyde, and sailed down to Largs where, thanks to a bad equinoctial gale, many of the ships were wrecked and Haakon got his come-uppance from Alexander III. That was more or less the end of the Viking threat to Scotland.

Arrochar, at the head of Loch Long, where the Vikings began their 1½ mile haul, used to be a centre for cattle rustling. Robert Burns was unimpressed, writing that it was 'a land of savage hills, swept by savage rains, peopled by savage sheep, tended by savage people'. These days it is a picture-postcard holiday village with colourful hanging-baskets of flowers and trim B&Bs.

Immediately south of the Succoth turn-off, about a mile beyond Arrochar, there is an excellent path up **Ben Arthur**, 2,950ft (900m), known as the Cobbler because of its resemblance to a cobbler bent over his last. It is quite a scramble but not too rough underfoot and fairly easy to find your way. The summit is not for vertigo sufferers. There are other good climbs in the

Arrochar Alps, but the Cobbler seems to be the most popular. Ben Ime, Beinn Narnain, Ben Vane and Ben Vorlich march away to the northeast—all Munros, over 3,000ft (923m).

Doubling and doubling with laborious walk,
Who that has gained at length the wished-for height
This brief, this simple wayside call can slight
And rest not thankful?

William Wordsworth, 1803

The pass between Loch Long and Loch Fyne rises to 860ft (262m) and is called the **Rest and be Thankful**, after the inscription on a stone seat at the top. This was the military road built by William Caulfield over the pass between 1746 and 1748. According to Dr Johnson, who came this way in 1773, the milestones for the new road were removed by locals who said they would 'have no new miles'. In 1875 Queen Victoria, delighted as ever by the resemblance to Switzerland, descended from her coach and walked down the zigzag pass into Glen Croe.

The A814 from Arrochar skirts the eastern side of Loch Long. Towards Garelochhead, **Outside the Box**, ✆ (01436) 850 123, is a new residential centre for artists on a 50-acre site in Cove. It's open to the public on certain days and will present the work of resident artists each season.The first exhibition is scheduled for late October 2000.

The Cowal Peninsula

The A83, between the heads of Loch Long and Loch Fyne, cuts across the north of the Cowal Peninsula. It encompasses some gloriously high, wild places which earn it a place here, in spite of the more pacific areas to the south and southwest. It attracts many climbers, sailors and holidaymakers but, apart from some of the coastal resorts, is not too crowded. Cowal derives from Comhal, who was an ancient Dalriadic Scot. To get the best from Cowal you must walk or go by boat, but you can get an overview of what is on offer from your car.

The B828 south from the Rest and be Thankful takes you through dramatic Glen Mhoir along the River Goil, with the road dropping from 1,000ft (308m) to sea level in 3 miles, joining with the B839 down to Lochgoilhead. Unfortunately, the village is now dominated by the Drimsynie Leisure Centre, just to the west. Five miles down the west side of the loch takes you to **Carrick Castle**, a 14th-century ruin on a promontory in fjord-like Loch Goil. This was where the Campbells of Argyll kept their documents and their prisoners. A remote enough place in those days, the great shell of the keep is still aloof and impressive, even with the rash of water-sport enthusiasts nearby. James IV used it as a resting place when hunting wild boar in the area. Cowal is the last recorded place in Britain to have had indigenous wild boar. The 8th Earl of Argyll fortified the castle in 1681, in preparation for an attack by Cromwell which never came.

The road ends here and you can just see where the loch joins up with Loch Long to the south-east. The area within the triangle formed by the Rest and be Thankful, Loch Long and Loch Goil is known as **Argyll's Bowling Green**. A more unlikely name would be hard to find: measuring 8 miles by 4, it includes 10 major summits and is only accessible on foot. (In fact the name comes from *baile na greine*—sunny settlement.) You must retrace your route to 3 miles north of Lochgoilhead, where you can take the left fork and continue on the B839 west through Hell's Glen, a steep hanging valley running out to Loch Fyne.

Loch Fyne washes around the western curve of the Cowal Peninsula and is renowned for sea fishing, oysters and good sailing. The B839 joins the A815 south and you can drive down the eastern shore through a string of villages, with the Argyll Forest Park stretching away to the hinterland. Alternatively, keep on the A815 at Strachur and drive southeast down narrow Loch Eck, hedged in by steep, wooded slopes. Branch left at the Whistlefield Hotel and take the long way round, through Glen Finart to **Ardentinny**, a picturesque village with good beaches on Loch Long.

The road hugs the shore to Strone Point and back northwest along Holy Loch. Don't anticipate a spiritual experience here: until 1992 **Holy Loch** was the deep-water anchorage for the American submarine base, a teeming hive of activity closely guarded by security. The Americans have gone now. It is 'Holy' because of an incident in the 12th century when a ship, carrying earth from the Holy Land intended as sacred foundations for Glasgow Cathedral, foundered in a storm as it tried to round the headland into the sheltered Clyde. The name might also come from the church at Kilmun, on the north shore, founded in 1442 and dedicated to St Mundus, a 7th-century disciple of St Columba. Only the original tower survives.

The Younger Botanic Garden, Benmore (*open mid Mar–Oct daily; adm*) is barely 2 miles north of the head of Holy Loch on the A815. Planted in the last four decades of the 19th century and bought by the Younger family, famous for their ale, this garden was made over to the nation in 1928 and is now an offshoot of the Royal Botanic Garden in Edinburgh. It is really more of a park than a garden, with a splendid grass avenue of sequoias (giant Californian Wellingtonias) leading through to grounds that blaze with yellow, orange, flame and crimson azaleas in May and June. Its 250 species of rhododendron flower in succession from March to September and are thought by many to be one of the best collections in the world. It's an interesting and spectacular garden in which to wander among some of the largest trees in Britain.

Dunoon

Dunoon is a holiday base for the gregarious who intend to explore Cowal, and has long been the destination for generations of Glaswegians taking their summer break '*doon the watter*'. It was just a village until the early 19th century, when rich merchants built villas and developed it into a resort. The long, low sprawl of the town, washed by the Firth of Clyde, is backed by a crescent of blue-green tree-covered hills. It has a lively holiday resort atmosphere in summer, with its busy esplanade and rows of seaside boarding houses and hotels. In winter it goes into hibernation. Two ferry companies operate a service across the Clyde to Gourock—a 20-minute crossing. Dunoon stands on the threshold of fine walking and climbing country and also makes a good base for some idyllic sailing routes. For those who prefer to let someone else take the helm, there are also cruises on the Firth of Clyde in the summer.

Tourist Information

7 Alexandra Parade, ✆ (01369) 703 785.

Dunoon Castle

Only a trace remains of Dunoon Castle, on top of Castle Hill, dating from the 14th century. It was built on the site of an earlier fort, with a colourful history that kept it bouncing back and forth between English and Scottish hands like a ball in a game of catch. Edward I took it—Robert the Bruce snatched it back; Edward Balliol had a turn—to be ousted by Robert II. In 1471 the Earls of Argyll were made Honorary Keepers by James III, on condition they paid the Crown the fee of a red rose whenever demanded. When Queen Elizabeth II visited Dunoon in

1958 she was presented with a red rose without having to demand it. **Castle Buildings**, built in 1822 in the Gothic style with grandiose crenellations, has a museum.

Toward Castle, 8 miles south of Dunoon and just west of Toward Point, was the stronghold of the Lamont clan. In 1646 the bloodthirsty Campbells of Argyll surrounded the castle, captured a large number of the clan and dragged them off to Dunoon where they were hanged. In the words of a contemporary observer: the Campbells 'most barbarously, cruelly and inhumanly murdered several, young and old, yea, sucking children, some of them not one month old'. (The tree that served as the gallows was later felled and was said to gush blood from its roots.) Following this massacre the castle was deserted and fell into the ruins that are all that remain today. There is a Celtic cross memorial, erected in 1906 by descendants of the victims, in Tom-a-Mhoid Road, near Castle Hill.

The 2-mile **Ardnadam Heritage Trail** starts at Sandbank, a couple of miles northeast of the town. It is dotted with information boards telling you about the local flora and fauna and pointing out the site of an Iron-Age roundhouse.

Less than 4 miles north of Dunoon, beyond Hunter's Quay, **Lazaretto Point** was the quarantine station for servicemen fighting in the Napoleonic Wars. To explore the rest of the peninsula by car, take the B836 west from the head of Holy Loch to the head of Loch Striven and on to the A886. Here turn left and take the new road down the east side of Loch Riddon to **Colintraive**—meaning 'Strait of Swimming', from the time when the drovers used to swim their cattle across here. (In the recent past, people have tried to retrace the old drovers' routes with modern cattle. Among the many difficulties encountered was that of actually persuading the beasts to brave these deep passages of water.) A car ferry runs from Colintraive to Bute and there are splendid views across the Kyles of Bute to Tighnabruaich. You can get down to Strone Point but there is no road right up the western shore of Loch Striven.

Return to the head of Loch Riddon on the A886 and take the A8003 down its west side, high above the Kyles of Bute, with good views in all directions. **Tighnabruaich**—'house on the hill'—and **Kames** are two popular resorts looking across the Kyles to the Isle of Bute. A minor road runs on down to Ardlamont Point, the most southerly tip of the peninsula, rising to 205ft (63m). The waters of Loch Fyne, Kyles of Bute, Sound of Bute and Kilbrannan Sound meet in a flurry beyond the headland.

From Ardlamont, go north about 4 miles to Millhouse and then west a couple of miles to **Portavadie**, from where a ferry runs across to Tarbert on the Kintyre Peninsula. With deep water offshore, this area was chosen as an oil-platform construction site and £14 million was spent on ground preparation. An enormous dry dock was built but no one seemed to want oil platforms and the place stood unused. Eventually the sea-wall was breached, the dock flooded and the £14 million investment was washed away.

From Millhouse take the B8000 north through Kilfinan, a hamlet whose hotel has 16th-century vaults and whose church stands on a Celtic site. **Otter Ferry**, 3 miles to the north, takes its name from the Gaelic *oitir*—a sandbank (yachtsmen beware!). The sandbank sticks out more than a mile into Loch Fyne, prominent at low tide but easy for a boat to trip up on when it is submerged by the flood tide. The Norsemen who fought in the Battle of Glendaruel in 1100 beached their longships side by side on the sand bar, clambered ashore and marched over the pass into Glendaruel, 5 miles to the east. There they were slaughtered by the Scots who threw their bodies into the river—'ruel' is a corruption of the Gaelic for 'blood flowed'.

Sports and Activities

The **Cowal Highland Gathering**, which goes back 100 years, is an annual highlight, on the last Friday and Saturday in August. Over 150 pipe bands compete, drawing huge, convivial crowds. The World Highland Dancing Championships, at the same time, help to swell the throng.

Where to Stay

expensive

Creggans Inn, at Strachur on the shore of Loch Fyne, ✆ (01369) 860 279, 🖷 860 637, is a wonderful place: its food, friendliness and ambience are renowned. The late Sir Fitzroy Maclean, who died still active at the age of 85, revered writer, diplomat, MP, soldier, secret agent and model for James Bond, and his wife Lady Maclean, a well-known cookery writer, built up the reputation of this delightful 400-year-old inn on their estate, sticking to the hotel motto: 'good food and a warm welcome'. Understated elegance combine with true Highland hospitality and sublime food.

Ardentinny Hotel, ✆ (01369) 810 209, 🖷 810 241, dating from 1720, is a fine place to stay on Loch Long, on its own little spur jutting into the loch.

moderate

Kilfinan Hotel, Kilfinan, ✆ (01700) 821 201, 🖷 821 205, is a very comfortable old coaching inn which also serves exceptionally good food. **Cairndow Stagecoach Inn**, Cairndow, ✆ (01499) 600 286, 🖷 600 220, unusually for a historic coaching inn on Loch Fyne, has a sauna, solarium and multi-gym. Two of the rooms also have personal 'spa baths'.

cheap

The friendly **Cobbler Hotel**, Arrochar, ✆ (01301) 702 238, 🖷 702 353, is on the banks of Loch Long in 4 acres of attractive landscaped gardens. There's live entertainment every night, with accordion singers, dinner dances and bingo. **Ardluie Hotel**, Ardluie, ✆ (01301) 704 243, 🖷 704 268, is a cosy country house hotel actually on the bonnie, bonnie banks of Loch Lomond, with two restaurants and boat moorings.

Kames Hotel, by Tighnabruaich, ✆ (01700) 811 489, 🖷 811 283, with lovely views over the Kyles of Bute, is a good family hotel where dogs and children are welcome. There are fine real ales and malts, and good local seafood. **Colintraive Hotel**, Colintraive, ✆ (01700) 841 217, 🖷 is a cosy little hotel with large bedrooms and lovely views. The friendly staff will give you advice on local attractions.

Eating Out

The Oystercatcher, at Otter Ferry, ✆ (01700) 821 229, is a delightful pub renowned for its seafood, cooked as only the French know how, by French-born Alain and his wife Dorothy. They serve up delicious oysters, langoustine, scallops, mussels and salmon as well as an impressive range of steaks and game. Free moorings are available for people arriving by boat. It's best to book.

Chatters, 58 John Street, Dunoon, ✆ (01369) 706 402, serves excellent food. *Open Mon–Sat.* Also *see* **The Drover's Inn** and the **The Stagger Inn**, p.82.

West Loch Fyne

The A83 west from Arrochar on Loch Long, and the A819 south from Dalmally take you to Inveraray on the northwest shore of Loch Fyne. **Ardkinglas Woodland Garden** is on a hillside just beyond Cairndow with views over the loch (*open daily; adm*). It has one of the finest collections of conifers in the British Isles, including five 'champion trees', one of which is known as the 'mightiest conifer in Europe', dating back to 1790.

It is imperative that you stop off at **The Loch Fyne Oyster Bar**, ✆ (01499) 600 264, an excellent restaurant in an old farm building. Its founder is a food and wine buff and his influence has produced exceptional results—if in doubt try the seafood chowder. There is a shop attached, where they sell fresh and smoked sea food including oysters from the local beds, mussels, salmon and scampi. It's very popular so wise to book ahead. The adjacent **Tree Shop** specializes in selling specimen trees, indigenous Highland trees and shrubs. They also sell an extensive range of woodwork, basketwork, dried flowers and unusual gifts.

Inveraray

Inveraray is unusual in being one of the few planned Highland towns, and it's certainly the most gracious. The 18th-century town is built on a T-plan with the road north passing through an archway and the parish church on a mound dividing the main street. The tall, elegant, white terraced houses were designed by John Adam and Robert Mylne, now embellished with an overwhelming display of tartan and Highland-related souvenirs cramming the numerous tourist-traps. In South Main Street the architecture becomes distinctly more austere, lining the road with Robert Mylne's massive, three-storey tenements for the 'poorer labouring class', dating from 1775. Five blocks on each side are defined by huge crosswise chimney stacks and slate roofs above contrastingly small windows.

Old Inveraray was clustered round the former castle close to where the present one stands today, half a mile to the north, and was little more than a village. It was burnt in 1644 by Montrose, during his brief stint of brilliant military leadership. In 1741 work began on the new town in conjunction with the demolition and rebuilding of the castle by the 3rd Duke of Argyll. Understandably, the duke decided that his new castle deserved more privacy, so he planted the new town in its present, more attractive position. He employed Roger Morris and William Adam, both of whom died before the work was finished. John Adam, son of William, completed the job with the help of Robert Mylne. John Adam is thought to have been responsible for the Great Inn and it was here that Johnson and Boswell stayed during their tour in 1773. Johnson pronounced it 'not only commodious, but magnificent'. Boswell is more expansive: 'Dr Johnson owned tonight that he got as good a room and bed as at an English inn.' They 'supped well', and Johnson, who had refused to change his wet clothes, and whom Boswell had not seen drink any fermented liquor during their travels together, called for a gill of whisky, saying 'Come, let me know what it is that makes a Scotchman happy!' (He didn't drink all his dram, so Boswell finished it for him.)

Tourist Information

Front Street, ✆ (01499) 302 063.

The Town

The church on the island in the middle of the main street was built in 1798 with one side for Gaelic services and the other for English, in use until the 1950s; the Gaelic part is now the church hall. The Episcopal church, built in 1866, has a detached tower, built in 1914 with a peal of 10 bells, the second heaviest in the world, which are rung in memory of the Campbells who died in the First World War; a complete peal takes 4 hours to ring. This 126 foot (39m) granite tower, built by the 10th Duke of Argyll, gives fine views across Loch Fyne to Cowal, though it is rather an eyesore within the context of the rest of this stylish town.

Inveraray Jail (*open daily; adm*), in Church Square, is one of the best examples of reconstructed history in Scotland. In the 19th century courthouse and gaol which had fallen into dereliction, an excellent 'dark ride' has been created with the guides dressed as warders and prisoners, realistic waxwork models that talk, replica cells, an exhibition of tortures, and a court room where you can sit in and listen to the trial of a farmer accused of fraud. Like all such 'experiences', there is none of the authentic atmosphere of squalor and despair, but it makes a good springboard for the imagination.

Among other wet-weather pastimes in and around the town, there is a three-masted schooner, the *Arctic Penguin* (*open daily; adm*), with maritime displays and memorabilia.

Inveraray Castle

Inveraray Castle (*open 1st Sat in April–2nd Sun in Oct daily exc Fri; July and Aug daily; adm*) was built between 1741 and 1785 to replace a great tower house nearby, now demolished, home of the Earls and Dukes of Argyll since the 15th century. The Campbell clan has dominated the history of Scotland for centuries and became synonymous to some, notably the clan Donald, with 'enemy'. They transferred their allegiance from Balliol to Bruce at an opportune moment, and from then on became the lawkeepers and policemen for the government, involving amongst other things a relentless struggle to tame the lawless Lords of the Isles. They were amply rewarded for their loyalty to the crown, often with lands forfeited by the proud Macdonalds, who refused to be tamed. They were ruthless in their duties, seldom missing an opportunity to feather their nests, but there is no doubt that they helped to control the chaotic anarchy of *Gaidhealtachd*—Gaeldom. That it was a Campbell—Robert, of Glenlyon, a drunken bankrupt—who was chosen to implement the outrageous massacre of the Glencoe Macdonalds in 1692 (*see* pp.113–14), put the seal on the loathing that Clan Donald felt for Clan Campbell.

The present castle was designed by Roger Morris and Robert Mylne, with help from William, John and Robert Adam, though Vanbrugh is said to have had a say in the original conception. It stands four-square, greenish and imposing, in a dry moat surrounded by formal gardens, with some of the finest internal neoclassical decoration in Britain. It is perhaps unfortunate that the original proportions were tinkered with in 1877. (A century earlier, just after it was built, Dr Johnson had bemoaned the fact that it was 'too low' and wished it a storey higher.) Perhaps overawed by the prospect of his son's marriage to Queen Victoria's daughter in 1871, and a visit from the queen herself in 1875, the 8th Duke lost his head and commissioned the aggrandizement of his castle. The result was four witches' hats, perched on the four corner towers, and an additional floor with gabled dormers. The central hall soars to 90 feet and contains a magnificent collection of arms and armour. The castle also contains splendid Beauvais tapestries and fine paintings by Gainsborough, Batoni and Opie.

Boswell, ever the social mountaineer, dragged Dr Johnson here for a visit and was hurt when the duchess cut him dead, though it didn't prevent him from ogling the ladies' maids. Johnson was much struck by the grandeur and elegance of this princely seat: 'What I admire here, is the total defiance of expence [sic]).' When Queen Victoria first visited in 1847, the Marquess of Lorne, afterwards 9th Duke of Argyll, stood outside to greet her, aged two, 'a dear, white, fat, fair little fellow with reddish hair, but very delicate features'. When she returned, in 1875, Lorne was her son-in-law. It was during this visit that Queen Victoria visited Auchindrain.

Auchindrain

Auchindrain (*open April–Sept daily; adm*) is 5½ miles southwest of Inveraray on the A83. When the Duke of Argyll brought Queen Victoria here in 1875 he gave her a brief homily on the old system of 'village communities', on which the crofting townships were based. The people lived in a close-knit group and the farm was divided into pasture and arable. The pasture was held in common by all the families and the arable was divided by lot every year so each family had a turn at each plot of soil. When this practice was revised and families persuaded to divide the arable and hold it in perpetuity, Auchindrain remained the only communal tenancy township in Scotland to survive on its ancient site in the original form. Restoration began in 1963 and the whole village has been preserved, furnished and equipped in the style of the various periods through which it existed.

What you see in this open-air museum of an original West Highland township of great antiquity is much as it would have been when Queen Victoria saw it. It's been sanitized, of course, as all such reconstituted history must be, but each cottage, barn and farm building has been imaginatively restored. You should allow at least an hour to stroll around and inspect it all. There is the inevitable visitor centre, and demonstrations of the runrig or strip-farming methods prevalent until the end of the 18th century or even later in some places.

Furnace, a couple of miles further on, is an unhappy reminder of the troubled times that the 18th century brought. It is so called from the charcoal-burning smelting furnace founded by the Duke of Argyll to help the local economy. It was established here to make use of the trees felled by order of the Hanoverian government to deprive rebel Highlanders of somewhere to hide as they clung to the Jacobite cause.

Crarae Garden

Crarae Garden (*open daily; adm*), 10 miles south of Inveraray, is one of Scotland's most beautiful 'wild' gardens. Cumlodden estate was handed over to Captain (later Sir) George Campbell in 1926. His mother had already started planting exotic species in this wooded glen, encouraged by her nephew, Reginald Farrer, a well-known traveller and botanist, and by Sir James Stirling Maxwell of Pollok. Farrer had introduced unusual rhododendrons into Britain from trips to Kansu and Upper Burma, and with all this enthusiasm and expertise behind him, Crarae became George Campbell's lifelong interest. Trees had long been his passion; he started planting them at the age of 14. From 1926 he began to plant the banks of the Crarae Burn, cutting back the natural oak, birch, rowan, alder and haze and replacing them with exotics, protected from the prevailing southwesterly winds by periphery conifers. Although the climate and soil provide ideal conditions for rhododendrons, he was careful not to allow this genus to swamp others in which he was more interested. Gradually Sir George increased his plantings by taking in land on either side of the glen until, today, the garden covers some

40 acres. He preferred to plant groups of one species together, resulting in the spectacular drifts of colour both in spring, with the azaleas, and in autumn, when the decorative hardwoods turn. Around the Lodge there are lawns and borders, with Beinn Ghlas rising to the north, and views across Loch Fyne. The gardens lead you up the Crarae Burn, crossing and recrossing its tumbling water, through the banks dramatic with slabs of colour and texture: azaleas and rhododendrons, olearia, pittosporum, dogwood, sorbus, acers, eucryphia, eucalyptus and many, many more. It is always lovely, but early summer and autumn are most spectacular. A Neolithic chambered cairn, dating back some 4,500 years and once of considerable size, was excavated in the 1950s and is now a feature of the gardens.

The A83 takes you on down Loch Fyne to Lochgilphead. The A819 from Inveraray takes you north through Glen Aray to Dalmally and Loch Awe.

Loch Awe is well named, narrow and darkly brooding, dominated to the north by Ben Cruachan, 3,689ft (1,126m) and dotted with ancient remains. According to legend, there was a 'well of youth' in a corrie high on Ben Cruachan, guarded by the goddess Bheithir. Every day she bathed in the magic waters and one evening she forgot to replace the capstone to the well. All night the crystal water flowed down the hillside, flooding the valley, and in the morning—there was Loch Awe. Bheithir was banished and cursed with immortality by the irate gods; she is now Cailleach Bheithir, the winter hag of death and darkness and you hear her icy voice echoing round the chasms of Ben Cruachan on winter nights. Loch Awe is fed by the rivers Orchy and Strae to the north. Its outlet, the River Awe, runs through the Pass of Brander to Loch Etive and the sea. Electricity is generated at the Awe Barrage and at Cruachan Power Station, near the mouth of the River Awe, one of the largest freshwater lochs in Scotland, and renowned for its huge brown trout. Not so long ago, before there were sensible roads, Loch Awe was a major waterway for the area with regular steamer services and ferries.

Kilchurn Castle

Kilchurn Castle, best seen from a distance—sticking out into the north end of the loch on a peninsula, is a recently stabilized ruin dating back to 1440 when it was a five-storey tower-house built to guard Glen Orchy and Glen Strae. Badly damaged by the notorious MacGregors, it was rebuilt between 1614 and 1619, and later extended. During the Jacobite Rising it was garrisoned by Hanoverian troops with the consent of the anti-Jacobite Campbells who owned it. It was unroofed in 1775 and is now a picturesque shell, reflected in the waters of the loch with Ben Cruachan beyond, a scene painted by Turner and many others.

There are boat trips on the loch from the pier beside the Loch Awe Hotel, the huge Victorian pile you see from the road on the northwest tip of the loch. When the level of the loch is low, traces of several *crannogs*—man-made islands—can be seen, where early settlers built dwellings for protection against attack. Some of the islands were used as clan burial grounds, especially Inchail, where there is a 13th-century ruined chapel and several graves of the Macarthur clan. St Conan's Church, in Lochawe village west of Kilchurn, is a synthesis of architectural styles from ancient Roman to Norman, designed at the turn of the 20th century by an eccentric Campbell. At the mouth of the River Awe, on the A85, the Cruachan Power Station (*open daily; adm*) gives a guided tour deep into the side of Ben Cruachan, where you can see the works of the generating station which uses water from the Cruachan Reservoir above to power turbines supplying electricity. (It takes so much of this electricity to pump the water back up to the reservoir that the whole operation runs very fast in order to stand still.)

The Pass of Brander is a geological fault some four to six million years old, carved out by the receding Ice Age 10,000 years ago to form a gorge through which the River Awe squeezes itself into Loch Etive. In 1309 the Black Douglas, fighting for Robert the Bruce, vanquished John MacDougall of Lorne who, fighting for Edward II, had set up an ambush for Bruce's army in the Pass. As Bruce approached almost certain disaster, the Black Douglas led his men down from the summit of Ben Cruachan in a ferocious stampede, to slaughter the MacDougalls. The Pass was too narrow for more than one horseman at a time and the surviving MacDougalls fled in panic, impeding and killing each other in their frenzy to get over the bridge; many were drowned. John MacDougall escaped down the loch in his galley. You can drive all the way round the loch, though dense woods sometimes obscure the view, and continue south to Lochgilphead or north to Taynuilt (*Tigh an Uilt*—House by the Burn) and on to Oban.

Inveraray ✆ (01499–) ***Where to Stay***

expensive

The luxury **Ardanaiseig Hotel**, at Kilchrenan, ✆ (01866) 833 333, 🖷 833 222, is a memorable place to stay. Designed by William Burn in 1834 for Colonel Archibald Campbell, this Scots Baronial mansion overlooking Loch Awe and its islands from wooded grounds, still has a stately atmosphere, with antique furniture, log fires, lots of fresh flowers and every sort of comfort, as well as excellent food.

moderate

Argyll Hotel, Front Street, Inverary, ✆ 302 466, 🖷 302 389, was the Argyll Arms where Johnson and Boswell stayed, and where Johnson sampled whisky. Overlooking Loch Fyne, it has been well modernized since those days with the right blend of history and comfort. **Taychreggan**, Kilchrenan, ✆ (01866) 833 211, 🖷 833 244, is an old inn on the shore of Loch Awe, with comfortable rooms and excellent food.

moderate–cheap

Fernpoint Hotel, by the pier in Inveraray, ✆ 302 170, 🖷 302 366, is a Georgian house with a spiral stair and executive suites overlooking Loch Fyne. The public rooms are not that remarkable, but the food is varied and good. Alternatively, the recently refurbished **Loch Fyne Hotel**, Inveraray, ✆ 302 148, 🖷 302 348, has a relaxed and comfortable Highland atmosphere. **Bridge of Awe Lodge**, Taynuilt, ✆ (01866) 822 642, is a Wolsey Lodge which caters for fishermen. Comfortable and welcoming with good food. Book if you want dinner.

For self-catering, try **Braleckan House**, Inveraray, ✆ 500 662, a 19th-century building restored to make two peaceful and well-equipped houses on a family farm. **Killean Farmhouse**, Inverary, ✆ 302 474, does bed and breakfast.

Oban

Oban—The Little Bay—is the gateway to the isles, unashamedly a holiday resort in summer, when its streets seethe with visitors and traffic, but quiet and provincial in winter. Before the Victorians developed it into an important port and the principal town in Argyll, it was a mere hamlet with one inn. Now it is crammed with shops, hospitals and schools serving a wide area. Hotels, guest houses and neat villas offering bed and breakfast are numerous; cafés and restaurants are busy and there is a fairly lively night life offering discos, public *céilidhs* and other amusements. In spite of this, Oban remains truly West Highland and unspoilt.

Tourist Information

Argyll Square, ✆ (01631) 563 122.

The Town

The town rises steeply from a crescent-shaped bay, its main street fronting the harbour whence MacBrayne's ferries ply between Mull and the Inner and Outer Hebrides, and smaller ferries, fishing boats and pleasure craft come and go between the islands. The quays are thronged with people, cars and freight, loading and unloading from the ferries. High above the bustle stands **McCaig's Tower**, a large replica of the Colosseum built in 1897 at a cost of £5,000. A banker, McCaig erected it to give work to the many unemployed in the area and to create a museum and observation tower as a memorial to his family. It was never finished but remains a prominent landmark. Walk up here at sunset for views of the Morvern hills across the island-studded sea. The Catholic See of Argyll and the Western Isles has its well-attended cathedral, **St Columba's**, in the town overlooking the harbour. Although this area is predominantly Protestant, there are still communities left untouched by the Reformation.

The first National Mod was held here in 1892, and has often returned since. Because it is the main port for many of the islands, you will often hear Gaelic spoken on the pier or in the streets and shops. The Argyllshire Gathering in August is one of the major Highland Games and much less 'smart' than those around Royal Deeside.

Oban is a popular base for **scuba divers**, with air supplies in the town and good diving locations in the surrounding waters. The Sound of Mull is littered with wrecks, and the waters support a wealth of marine life beneath dramatic cliff scenery. The area is also ideal for sailing, offering some fairly challenging, but breathtakingly beautiful, stretches, especially south through the Firth of Lorne to the Sound of Jura, past the infamous Corryvreckan whirlpool (*see* p.230). There is plenty of wet-weather entertainment in the area: a **Sea Life Centre**; **Rare Breeds Farm**; and **Oban Distillery**, to name a few. A shed on the pier, between the MacBrayne's ticket office and the town, sells the most delicious fresh seafood snacks: baps generously filled with freshly cooked prawn or crab, still warm and outstandingly good.

Around Oban

Kerrera Island

From a point a couple of miles south of Oban on the Gallanach road, a foot ferry runs across to Kerrera, the 4-mile long island sheltering Oban from the worst of the southwesterly gales that rip up the Firth of Lorne. Alexander II came here in 1249 with a fleet to try to evict the Norsemen who held the island. He was taken ill and died in Horseshoe Bay. Kerrera was a droving station between Mull and the mainland, cattle having to swim across from its northern tip to the mainland. Gylen Castle is a ruin on the cliffs overlooking Port a' Chastell on the south coast. Built in 1582, this was the second stronghold of the MacDougalls after Dunollie, and was besieged and burnt by General Leslie and his Covenanters in 1647. It is currently being consolidated for its MacDougall owner. There is a monument to David

Hutcheson on the northern hammerhead; he masterminded the ferry services between Oban and the Hebrides before Caledonian MacBrayne got the monopoly. **Dunollie Castle**, the ruin on a promontory guarding the north entrance to Oban harbour, was the ancient stronghold of the MacDougall Lords of Lorne, one of the oldest clans in Scotland. **Ganavan Sands** is a good place to stretch your legs, but is not the place for a quiet day on the beach.

Oban ✆ (01631–) ***Where to Stay***

moderate

Manor House, Oban, ✆ 562 087, 🖷 563 053, was built for the Duke of Argyll in 1780 and was later the first bank in town. It is attractively furnished and decorated and the Scottish and French food is good. It's the best place to eat in Oban, even if you're not staying.

Clachan Beag, ✆ (01852) 300 381, looking down the Clachan Sound close to Seil Bridge, is a very comfortable Wolsey Lodge with a pretty garden, run by Colin and Jane Tindale. Colin is a keen sailor and can arrange outings in his boat.

cheap

Glenbervie Guest House, Dalriach Rd, Oban, ✆ 564 770, 🖷 566 723, a comfortable Victorian villa with good food, overlooks the bay, only 5 mins' walk from the town centre. **Lerags House**, by Oban, ✆/🖷 563 381, is a lovely Georgian country house on a tidal inlet on Loch Ferchan, only 10 mins' drive from Oban.

The Old Manse Guest House, Dalriach Road, Oban, ✆ 563 842, is a detached Victorian villa with wonderful sea views in a quiet area close enough to the town centre. *Closed Dec and Jan.*

The Falls of Lora Hotel, Connel Ferry, ✆ 710 483, 🖷 710 694, is a solid old building overlooking Loch Etive, with a log fire in the bar and a wide selection of malts. Some of its rooms are quite expensive.

The **Barriemore Hotel**, Corran Esplanade, Oban, ✆/🖷 566 356, is a friendly, restored Victorian hotel overlooking the bay. B&B only.

Oban ✆ (01631–) ***Eating Out***

The Boxtree, 108 George Street, ✆ 563 542, is a cheerful, good value bistro. **The Studio**, Craigard Road, ✆ 562 030, is reasonably priced and candlelit. *Open April–Oct 5–10pm.* **Onorio's**, on George Street, is famous for its fish and chips.

Oban to Kintyre via Lochgilphead

The A816 swoops south from Oban, flirting here and there with the sea, dipping and rising for 37 miles, with magnificent views as it kisses the coast. There are numerous side roads, tracks and footpaths, almost all of which are worth exploring. Walk up any of the glens to the east of the road and discover remote lochans hidden in the hills and wild moorland. Wherever you go to the west you will get to the sea and miles of empty beaches with sand, rocks and cliffs, and always those enchanting views of the islands.

About 6 miles south, at Kilninver, you can go west out to **Seil Island**, with its famous hump-backed 'bridge over the Atlantic' designed by Telford in 1792. Just over the bridge is *Tigh na Truish*—the House of the Trousers—where Highlanders who had been off the island in the days of proscription would change back into the forbidden tartan kilts. It is now an informal inn, ✆ (01852) 300 242, with a few rooms and very friendly atmosphere. Seil and its surrounding islands are known as the Slate Islands: slate was extracted as long ago as the 16th century and was an important industry, supporting the local population while creating some rather ugly blemishes. Easdale, just off the west coast, was particularly badly scarred, until a violent storm in 1881 flooded the quarries and hastened the decline and demise of the prosperous works.

An Cala Garden, on the island of Seil (*open April–Oct; adm*), is a coastal garden designed in the 1930s to be looked at as the foreground to a wonderful vista of sea and islands. It is laid out with meandering paths, streams, terraces, rockeries and formal beds, with ornamental trees and shrubs—an unexpected gem nestling amid the slate.

The National Trust for Scotland's **Arduaine Gardens** (*open all year; adm*) is about 20 miles south of Oban on the southwest side of Loch Melfort. It is most colourful in late spring and early summer with a blaze of rhododendrons and azaleas, but it is an all-season garden, with informal lawns and shrubberies and a wild woodland area. In the lower garden there are streams and ponds and lovely mixtures of texture and colour. Sheltered as they are from the strong winds that prevail around here, some of the ornamental trees and shrubs grow to a gigantic size.

About 30 miles south of Oban, around the little village of **Kilmartin**, history has left a remarkable detritus of cairns, standing stones and prehistoric remains. Throughout an area stretching 4 miles south to Dunadd, Stone and Bronze Age remains abound, many with information boards. Some of the cists have been reconstructed, with carvings on the walls, but they are far easier to understand and appreciate after a visit to the museum at **Kilmartin House** (*open daily; adm*), next to the church. The ticket lasts all day, so an overview obtained here can be followed up by a visit to the sites and then a return to the museum to study particular attractions in depth. As an excellent introduction to exploring some of the 150-plus prehistoric sites close by, this is a place worth making a detour to visit: even if you're not passionate about archaeology, Kilmartin House might well hook you. Start with the 12-projector audio-visual presentation on the Kilmartin Valley; much of the music for this is recorded on replica prehistoric instruments, such as the Bronze Age horn (over 2,500 years old) and the Pictish triple pipes, modelled on carvings in early Christian stones like the one from Ardchattan Priory. There's a large three-dimensional map of the various ancient sites (which light up at the touch of a button) with a time chart showing the world perspective and environmental changes over the past 13,000 years. Then come displays of artefacts and models from the first settlers (about 9,000 years ago) to the early historic period. Interestingly, some of the genuine artefacts are replicated, enabling you to see them as new. The hands-on exhibits include a quern stone for grinding corn, a flint axe and animal furs. Music from four listening posts brings it all to life: ringing rocks, pottery drums, cow horns, an Iron Age trumpet and monastic chanting.

At Ardfern there is a large marina, signed from the main road.

Dunadd Fort

Dunadd Fort to the west of the A816, 4 miles south of Kilmartin, is only special if you are fascinated by Scotland's ancient history, and the myths and uncertainties that surround it. Dunadd was the capital of the kingdom of Dalriada from the 6th to the 9th centuries, a powerful political centre and the headquarters of early missionaries, including St Columba, until Kenneth MacAlpine moved the capital to Pictland. A rocky hillock above a meandering river is all that is immediately obvious, but careful search will reveal a rock with carvings of a boar, some Ogham (ancient Irish) inscriptions (now protected by fibreglass) and... a footprint. Historians believe this to be the place where kings were crowned and that St Columba crowned Aidan here in 574, using the Stone of Destiny as the throne. The footprint is indisputable and only the most prosaic could resist the urge to stand in it and imagine those ancient ceremonies on this lofty site. In fact crowning didn't come in until much later, but the ceremony of enthronement was elaborate. In those days, *mormaers* owned their kingdoms and the High King was their overlord: King of Scots but not of Scotland. At the enthronement, each *mormaer* filled a shoe with earth from his kingdom and poured a little into this footprint, carved here on this rock at Dunadd. The King sat on the Stone of Destiny and put his foot over this cocktail of Scottish soil, thus establishing his overlordship. Archaeological findings include many brooches and intricate metal work, backing up the tradition that this was a royal residence.

It's about 5 miles south to Lochgilphead, but fun to branch off on the way, west to Crinan, along the B841 that follows the canal.

Where to Stay and Eating Out

moderate

Loch Melfort Hotel, at Arduaine, ✆/🖷 (01852) 200 214, has a reputation for comfort and good food. Philip Lewis, who runs it with his wife Ros, is an excellent and inventive cook using local shellfish and game. Yachtsmen of the yellow-wellie variety tend to stop off here for a civilized evening out, swapping Force Nine stories in the Chart Room Bar. The main house, built in 1900, gazes out across an island-speckled sea. The bedrooms are done up like guest rooms in a country house; rooms in the adjoining Cedar Wing have balconies and picture windows facing across the water.

Galley of Lorne, at Ardfern, ✆/🖷 (01852) 500 284, a traditional Highland inn on the shores of Loch Craignish, is comfortable and somewhat cheaper, with log fires, a good welcome from David and Susanna Garland and reasonably priced food. They serve meals on the terrace when possible, and offer a good range of malts. Dogs welcome.

Best of all is **Duntrune Castle**, near Kilmartin, with gourmet food and every comfort. Ring Andrew Malcolm, ✆ (01546) 510 271, or ✆ 0370 232 840. For self catering you couldn't do better than one of the six cottages around the castle on the Poltalloch Estate, ✆ (01546) 510 283, with names like Mother Brown's (the original castle lodge with windows placed to spot approaching carriages). Each cottage (sleeping 2–5) has been charmingly converted and equipped and people return year after year.

cheap

The **Culfail Hotel**, ✆ (01852) 200 274, is about 15 miles south of Oban on the A816. It's very popular with locals. *See* also above, *Tigh-an-Truish*, Isle of Seil.

In a converted barn at **Kilmartin House** you can try delicious local produce such as nettle or comfrey soup, squat lobsters, or crab claws, with heather ale or wines of bramble or silver birch. **The Cairn**, also in Kilmartin, is an excellent bistro/restaurant.

Knapdale

Kintyre and Knapdale run south from Lochgilphead like a giant lobster claw, with Knapdale just managing to cling onto the long pincer of Kintyre. This part of the west coast, on the Gulf Stream, is unbelievably lush in the summer. Autumn is glorious, with a wonderful range of colours shading the densely wooded hills. So too is spring, when the rhododendrons and azaleas are in bloom against the soft new green and the sparkle of water. Perhaps the best time of all, though, is November, when a light dusting of snow covers the last autumn leaves and the water shows steel-grey against hills etched in white. It is possible to drive most of the way round the coast of Knapdale from Lochgilphead and across its middle from Inverneil to Achahoish. Along the coast each mile opens up a fresh view to the islands of Jura and Islay in the west, or down through layers of hills to distant lochs and the sea.

Tourist Information

Lochgilphead: Lochnell Street, ✆ (01546) 602 344 (*open April–Oct*).

The Crinan Canal

The Crinan Canal slices through the top of Knapdale from Ardrishaig on Loch Gilp to Crinan on the west coast, cutting out the often treacherous passage round the Mull of Kintyre, once a severe hazard for the fishing fleets, commercial puffers and passenger craft that plied between the west coast and the more sheltered waters of the Clyde and Loch Fyne. The 9-mile stretch of canal—opened in 1801 with 15 locks, rising to 64ft (19½m)—was designed by Sir John Rennie, though Thomas Telford was called in to iron out a few teething troubles and got much of the credit. With the decline of the herring industry and the introduction of good road networks it lost most of its commercial traffic and is now mainly used by pleasure boats, saving the sailor 130 miles. Gliding down the canal in a small boat is a peaceful way to pass a fine day, though you have to work the lock gates yourself. In 1847 Queen Victoria sailed down the canal in a decorated barge drawn by horses ridden by postilions dressed in scarlet, on her way to the Western Isles: 'We glided along very smoothly and the views of the hills were very fine indeed; but the eleven locks we had to go through (a very curious process, first passing several by rising, and then others by going down) were tedious...'

It is fun to walk along the canal when there is traffic on the water, and watch the boats passing through the locks, not much more than 5 miles from the A816. **Crinan** itself is a pretty hamlet on a rocky peninsula with a sheltered harbour and the final, tidal gate between the canal and the open sea.

The left turn in Bellanoch, just before Crinan, and then right on to the B8025, takes you down the west side of Loch Sween and from anywhere along here your feet will take you to stretches of remote coast, with rocks, sand and cliffs, liberally dotted with prehistoric remains. The eastern road along Loch Sween goes past Castle Sween to Kilmory. **Castle Sween** is sadly best avoided if you are looking for ruins in fine scenery: it is surrounded by a huge caravan park. It was built to guard the entrance to Loch Sween from the eastern shore and some say it is the oldest stone castle on the Scottish mainland. Dating from the 11th century, it is a great sprawl of a ruin, Norman in style, with buttresses. Still visible are the old ovens, the well and the original drain and rubbish-chute in the wall of the round tower, down which everything, including sewage, was indiscriminately cast. The castle was a stronghold of the MacSweens who held the coast as far as Skipness. Robert the Bruce captured it in 1315 when the MacSweens sided with the English, and installed the McNeills of Argyll to maintain it, one of whom married a MacMillan. Thus Knapdale became MacMillan territory. The castle was destroyed in 1647 by Royalists, fighting for Charles I.

Two and a half miles on from Castle Sween, 13th-century **Kilmory Knap Chapel** is at the southern end of the peninsula. A glass roof protects the sculpted stones inside and the tall, very fine 15th-century **MacMillan's Cross**, elaborately carved with a crucified Christ on one side and a hunting scene on the other. It was probably made by monks from the monastery at Kilberry before the Reformation, after which masons were allowed to depict only 'Emblems of Mortality'—skulls, hourglasses, angels—with the result that many of the more elaborate embellishments died out. Unfortunately the track across to Loch Caolisport is private and has a locked gate, so you must go all the way back to the canal and down to Lochgilphead, to explore further south.

Lochgilphead

A couple of miles down the A816 from the Crinan turnoff, Lochgilphead, at the head of Loch Gilp, is a holiday resort as well as the shopping centre for the area, with plenty of shops down the wide main street that was once the market place. This was a fishing village until the Crinan Canal opened in 1801 and it became a popular stopping-off place for boats. Loch Gilp is an expanse of mudflats at low tide. The population expanded to supply services for people passing through the canal: a lunatic asylum and a poorhouse were built. Now it is a busy town and the regional headquarters. The Mid Argyll Show takes place here in August. **The Smiddy**, in Smithy Lane, is one of the best places to eat in Lochgilphead: a vegetarian 'bistro'-style establishment, with excellent home cooking.

Ardrishaig, a couple of miles south of Lochgilphead, stands at the southern end of the Crinan Canal. Passengers on the ferry from Glasgow used to transfer to a canal boat here for the journey up the canal to Crinan, where other ferries took them to Oban, Fort William and, after the Caledonian Canal opened in 1822, to Inverness. This was a thriving fishing village during the herring boom in the 19th century, providing work not only for people supplying the fishermen, but also for women gutting the fish.

Today Ardrishaig has a somewhat different character, its centre having been completely rebuilt in the 1970s. However, it has a pretty lighthouse and some old villas above. It is a good base for cycling and walking—the canal banks making a popular route for both purposes. The late John Smith, who led the Labour Party for a short time before his tragically early death in 1994, was brought up here.

To avoid the main road if you are going on down into Kintyre, take the B8024 a couple of miles south of Ardrishaig which follows the more scenic west-coast route.

At Achahoish, less than 5 miles from the turning, fork right, round the head of Loch Caolisport, pronounced and sometimes spelt—Killisport. Here is enchantment. Just over 3 miles along the road, overlooking a tiny bay, is **St Columba's Cave** behind the ruins of a 13th-century church and the tumbled stones of previous dwellings. There are in fact two caves in a cliff. The smaller is thought to have been a hermit's cell and the larger has an altar on a rock with crosses carved above. Strong local tradition holds that St Columba landed here on his way to Iona. There are a number of other places on the coast with similar claims and, given the frailty of his craft and the notorious weather conditions in these parts, there is no reason to suppose that he did not make several landfalls before he finally decided on Iona. Certainly there is a spirituality about this place that is almost tangible; and this is in spite of archaeological vandalism (a 19th-century laird cleaned out the cave and deposited a tip of debris from it outside). In 1959, when some of this tip was being restored to the cave, a sewing needle made from horn was discovered and the archaeologists moved in. A wealth of artefacts, including Viking weighing scales, was found, some of which dated back to 8000 BC.

Kilberry (about 12 miles down) has a splendid collection of 9th-and 10th-century stones gathered up from the surrounding area and housed under cover in a steading just north of the hamlet, signposted Kilberry Stones from the road. Marion Campbell, the archaeologist who collected the stones, used to live in Kilberry Castle, a brooding pile (medieval in origin, remodelled in the 19th century by David Bryce), which has belonged to the Campbells of Kilberry for centuries. The road takes you on southwards round Knapdale and up the west side of West Loch Tarbert.

Knapdale ✆ (01546–) ***Where to Stay and Eating Out***

expensive

Crinan Hotel, ✆ 830 261, 830 292, is renowned for its lovely position overlooking the sea towards the Sound of Jura—sunset over the islands is memorable—and for its comfort and excellent food, supplied daily by fishing boats that unload a short distance from the kitchen—people travel a long way to eat at **Loch 16**, its sublime seafood restaurant.

moderate

The **Tayvallich Inn**, ✆ 870 282, overlooking Loch Sween, specializes in delicious fresh seafood—sea-to-plate-fresh. The seafood platter is memorable, as are the mussels, the scallops, and the welcome. There is a tiny bar, and tables in a bay window or outside, weather permitting. Worth a detour.

Knock Cottage, at Lochgair, a little way up the west side of Loch Fyne, ✆ 886 331, is a Wolsey Lodge run by Mark and Nisa Reynolds in 10 acres of secluded wild gardens, loch and field with lovely views over the sheltered anchorage of Lochgair to Loch Fyne and the Cowal Hills. It is an old croft house with attractive modern additions, very cosy and friendly and the food is delicious.

For self-catering, the **Ormsary Estate Lodges**, Ormsary, near Loch Caolisport, ✆ (01880) 770 222, are 15 comfortably furnished and well-equipped lodges, sleeping 2–6, with lovely views to the west in one of the most beautiful locations in Kintyre.

North Beachmore Farm Restaurant, near Muasdale, signed off the A83, overlooking the Sound of Gigha, serves very good food. The roadside **Kilberry Inn**, ✆ (01880) 770 223, serves delicious food and has 2 cheap rooms. Worth a detour.

Kintyre

Tourist Information

Campbeltown: Mackinnon House, The Pier, ✆ (01586) 552 056.

Tarbert

An isthmus between East and West Loch Tarbert, straddled by the village of Tarbert, joins Kintyre to Knapdale. Here, in 1098, Malcolm Canmore struck a bargain with the Norwegian King, Magnus Barelegs, who was harassing him. He told Magnus he could claim any western island he could get to by boat with his rudder down. Magnus had his Viking henchmen tow him the mile across the isthmus in a boat—and claimed Kintyre as his. History doesn't relate the damage done to his rudder. Tarbert comes from *an tairbeart*—isthmus; there are several in Scotland. This one has an attractive bay with a backdrop of hills, popular with sailors, especially when regattas are held on Loch Fyne. It used to be a thriving ring-net herring-fishing port and still has a small fishing fleet, but tourism is the main source of income now, together with a bit of yacht- and boat-servicing. Tarbert Castle, above the village, was renovated by Robert the Bruce in 1325, but is now no more than a pile of stones with a good view.

The A83 zips down the west coast of Kintyre through villages and hamlets, most of which cater for summer visitors. The land and seascapes are similar to those of Knapdale, cut by wooded glens rising to hilly moorland.

Campbeltown

Campbeltown is 38 miles south of Tarbert at the head of Campbeltown Loch on the east coast, a haven for boats in a westerly gale and subject of that hopeful song: 'O Campbeltown Loch I wish you were whisky...' This is a holiday town and boating centre and, like most coastal settlements in these parts, was once an important herring port. Of its 34 distilleries, only two remain in business. Although less than 40 miles from Glasgow as the crow flies, Campbeltown is about 135 miles by road. Despite its Victorian appearance, it was founded in 1607. The 7th Earl of Argyll brought in Protestants from the Lowlands—mainly Ayrshire and Renfrewshire—in an attempt (known as the 'Plantation Policy') to pacify what was then rather a troublesome area. James IV had trouble here too and built Kilkerran Castle, now in ruins, in 1498 when he was desperately trying to bring the Lords of the Isles to heel. Rather sad is the Campeltown Cross, a truly splendid, intricately carved stone cross dating from 1380 and brought from Kilkivan near Machrihanish to be the market cross. It now stands on a roundabout. There is the usual Heritage Centre for a wet day (*open daily; adm*).

It would be a pity to visit Campbeltown and not venture out to the caves on **Davaar Island**, off the southeastern point of the loch. You walk the mile across a shingle spit—The Dhorlin—at low tide. It is marked by buoys and you must get the tides right (any local will tell you) or you will be cut off until the next low tide—you have about 6 hours, which is more than enough. The cave of most interest is on the eastern side of the island, not far along the path. In 1887 Archibald Mackinnon had a dream which inspired him to paint an El Greco-like Crucifixion here, secretly, on the rock, lit by a shaft of light that streams into the cave through an aperture. In 1934, when he was 80, he returned to the cave and restored the painting.

Machrihanish, 6 miles west of Campbeltown and fully exposed to the fury of Atlantic gales, is a holiday village with a hotel, golf course, campsite, sandy beaches, and a token airport. There are good walks across the moorland to the south and lovely coastal stretches, but beach-lounging can be breezy. **Southend**, 10 miles south of Campbeltown on the south coast, is another holiday village and nothing special: a golf course and sandy beaches with dunes covered in marram grass, useful for shelter from the wind. Nothing remains today of

Dunaverty Castle, which once stood on the vicious rocks here. Three hundred of Montrose's men, fighting the cause of Charles I, were besieged in the castle by the merciless Covenanter General, David Leslie. The Royalists, mostly Irish mercenaries, were forced by thirst to surrender and then shamefully massacred. **Sanda Island**, a couple of miles off the south coast from Southend, is where Robert the Bruce is said to have hidden in 1306 on his way back from Rathlin Island, spurred on towards Bannockburn by the spider. There is the ruin of a chapel dedicated to St Ninian, some crosses and a holy well, suggesting that he or his missionaries got to this area ahead of Columba.

Keil, a couple of miles west of Southend, has the ruin of a 13th-century chapel below the cliffs just before the point, built to honour St Columba, for this is yet another of the places where he is said to have first landed on his way to Iona. His 'footsteps' are 'burnt' into the rocky hump just past the ruins.

The Mull of Kintyre

The Mull of Kintyre, the southern tip of the peninsula, is a rocky extremity with a lighthouse and sheer cliffs, dramatic in westerly gales. You must walk the final 1.5 miles or so and it is particularly stirring on a fine, blustery day. Ireland is only about 13 miles away and when visibility is good you feel you could almost swim across. The Mull of Kintyre was put on the map by Paul McCartney, who owns a house here and wrote the popular song about the area.

The B842 takes you back along the east coast, a lovely drive up Kilbrannan Sound, with good walks in the hinterland. **Saddell Abbey and Castle**, about 13 miles north of Campbeltown, was a Cistercian abbey founded in 1160 by Somerled, King of Man and the Isles, with monks from Mellifont in Ireland. Somerled is thought to be buried here, and there is a grave slab bearing his effigy. Stones from the monastic buildings were used to build the castle in 1508, a typical tower house by the bay, burned by the English and subsequently rebuilt and extended. It is now owned by the Landmark Trust and available for holiday lets rather than open to the public on a daily basis. It has a pit prison, entered by a trapdoor in the entrance passage—not a cosy resting place for miscreants.

About 19 miles on, take the B8001, right, about 3 miles out to **Skipness Point**, where the ruins of a large 13th-century castle and chapel command the bay, built by the MacSweens to guard the Kilbrannan Sound. In 1537 the then châtelaine, Janet Douglas, Lady Glamis, was burnt for witchcraft, accused of poisoning her husband and plotting to kill King James V. He was in the process of ridding his kingdom of the Douglases, who had been a threat to his supremacy, and poor Janet had the misfortune to have been born a Douglas.

Tarbert ✆ (01880–) ***Where to Stay***

expensive

The comfortable **Stonefield Castle Hotel**, Tarbert, ✆ 820 836, stands in wooded grounds above Tarbert with stunning views of Loch Fyne. The food is good: the AA and the RAC have awarded Stonefield three stars and Egon Ronay agrees with them.

moderate

Skipness Castle, by Tarbert, ✆ 760 207, 760 208, is a modern house, built on the ruins of its Victorian predecessor which burned down in 1969, with spectacular views down to Kilbrannan Sound. It is nicely furnished and the food is good, with local ingredients from the estate (a working farm) and fresh from the sea. The **Columba Hotel**, Tarbert, ✆/🖷 820 808, is a comfortable place on the waterfront, with a gym and a sauna. The **Net Store** bar is very popular for visiting yachtsmen, as well as locals.

cheap

Tarbert Hotel, ✆ 820 264, 🖷 820 847, is right on the harbour front, popular for après-sailing gatherings and yarn-swapping. **West Loch Hotel**, ✆ 820 283, 🖷 820 930, is an attractive 18th-century former coaching inn just beyond Tarbert on the A83. Glorious views, good food and friendly. **Ardshiel Hotel**, Kilkerran Rd, Campbeltown, ✆ (01586) 552 133, is a comfortable, family-run hotel with palm trees growing outside. The traditional home cooking is served in a garden restaurant and there are 175 different malts for you to sample in front of the cosy open fire.

Tarbert ✆ (01880–) ***Eating Out***

The Anchorage, Tarbert, ✆ 820 881, is an excellent restaurant on the quay, especially for seafood. **The Whitehouse Old School Tearoom**, Kennacraig, near the ferry to Islay, has good home-made baking and snacks. *Open daily 10.30–7; closed Tues.*

Oban to Appin

It is a 7-mile ferry crossing from Oban to Achnacroish on **Lismore Island**, but the most popular route is from Port Appin, about 18 miles north off the A828. This crossing is only about a mile. Lying at the entrance to Loch Linnhe, between Morvern and the hammerhead of the Benderloch peninsula, Lismore is 10 miles long and only 1.5 miles wide, a limestone sliver overlaid with heather.

Because of its strategic position and its fertile soil it has always been an important place. Its Christian tradition goes back to St Moluag who, in the 6th century, is said to have cut off his finger and thrown it ashore in order to beat St Columba to claim the land. (They were rivals, one being a Pict and the other a Celt. This self-mutilating feat of foolhardy ambition is also claimed by the Irving clan, one of whose ancestors is said to have done the same with his hand—hence the red hand device on their crest— in order to be first ashore at what is now Irvine, in Ayrshire.) The pastoral staff of St Moluag is preserved in Bachuil House towards the north of the island. *Lios mor* means 'great garden' or 'enclosure'. When the Roman Church succeeded the Celtic church in 1200, Lismore became the centre of a bishopric, until 1507 when Luther stirred up the Reformation. The parish church incorporates the remains of the miniature cathedral and there is a ruined castle residence where the bishops lived at Achadun on the southwest end of the island. *The Book of the Dean of Lismore*, a 16th-century collection of Gaelic poetry, is in the National Library of Scotland, in Edinburgh.

Lady's Rock, off the southwest tip of the island in the Sound of Mull, is where in 1527 a MacLean of Duart marooned his discarded wife, a daughter of the Earl of Argyll. She was rescued by gallant men from Lismore and returned to her father who took dire revenge on the MacLeans.

Lismore suffered badly during 'the clearances' and the population dwindled from about 1,500 in 1775 to 600 by 1885. Today only about 140 people live here and you can still see the ruins of all the old croft houses, whose occupants subsisted on what they could get from the land, from the limeworks and from fishing.

Dunstaffnage Castle (*open April–Sept daily; Oct–Mar Sat–Wed; adm*) is 4 miles north of Oban just off the A85, on a massive crag guarding the entrance to Loch Etive. A splendid ruin, it seems to grow out of the rock with parts of it over 60ft (18½m) high and the walls more than 10ft (3m) thick, but its ancient glory is somewhat marred by a marine laboratory and housing developments. Its position, guarding both sea access to Loch Etive and Lorne, and the main route from the Lowlands to the Hebrides, made Dunstaffnage of vital strategic importance. The first fort was founded around the 1st century BC, and is said to have been a recruiting centre for soldiers to fight the Romans.

The present ruin dates from the 13th century and was built by the MacDougalls. Robert the Bruce captured it in 1309 and from then on it was usually in the hands of the Campbells of Argyll, who waged bitter battles against Macdonalds, Macleans and Camerons from here. Flora Macdonald was held prisoner here for a few days after helping Prince Charles in 1746. Tradition holds that the Stone of Destiny came here from Dunadd, staying until Kenneth Macalpine moved it to Scone in an attempt to draw together his kingdom of Picts and Scots. The Early Gothic chapel in the woods nearby is said to be of great architectural interest, with dog-toothed carving on its windows.

The Connel Bridge crosses the crooked finger of Loch Etive at the Falls of Lora, where sea and loch are in constant turmoil trying to pour in and out through a bottleneck over slabs of rock. Connel comes from *conghail*—tumultuous flood.

If you keep to the A85, along the south side of Loch Etive, you come to Taynuilt, after about 5 miles. **Bonawe Iron Furnace** (*open April–Sept daily 10–5; adm*) is signed from the village and is well worth the detour. The old iron ore smelter, of great importance during the Napoleonic wars, has been excellently preserved by Historic Scotland. It may not sound it, but it is fascinating for anyone interested in the industrial and related social history of the country. The Lorne Furnace Company was founded in 1753, using the plentiful and cheap supply of charcoal from surrounding oak and birch woods. Iron ore came in by boat and was processed into pig iron, with the River Awe providing power to drive the furnaces. This was an industrial community with cottages, a school, a laundry and everything needed to serve the workforce. Some of the buildings as well as the furnace can be seen.

Benderloch and Appin

Turn right just over the bridge and head along the northern shore of Loch Etive for about 5 miles to **Ardchattan Priory and Gardens** (*open April–Nov daily; adm*). The priory, founded by Duncan MacDougal, Lord of Lorne (who built the present Dunstaffnage), was for Valliscaulian monks. In 1309 Robert the Bruce summoned local chiefs here for a conference after he had captured Dunstaffnage, and it was one of the last parliaments to be held in Gaelic. After the Reformation the Campbells of Cawdor acquired the property and it remained with their descendants. The gardens are at their best between July and September, with shrub roses, herbaceous borders and potentillas. From Ardchattan, continue to Inveresragan and then north on the B845 to the A828.

Barcaldine Castle, an L-shaped fortalice overlooking Loch Creran, was built in 1609 by Duncan Campbell of Glenorchy and known as 'the black castle' because of its dark stones. It played a tragic part in the events that led up to the Massacre of Glencoe (*see* pp.113–14). The castle is privately owned and has recently been refurbished (*open to the public Easter–Sept*).

North again, you reach **Appin**, with its particularly satisfying combination of rugged hills and spectacular coast line. (*See* Ballachulish for the Appin Murder, p.111–12). **Port Appin**, on the flat, marshy peninsula off the southwest tip of Appin, is an attractive little place with a pier and lovely views across the islands of Loch Linnhe. The passenger ferry to Lismore runs from here. Linnhe Marine Water Sports Centre, at Lettershuna just to the east, is a family-run place with a variety of boats and courses.

Castle Stalker—*Caisteal Stalcair,* Castle of the Hunter—off Portnacroish, a few miles north, is a popular postcard/calendar picture on its small island at the mouth of Loch Laich (*open by appt. only April–Aug; adm to include boat:* ✆ *(01631) 730 234*). Former seat of the Stewarts of Appin, it dates back to about 1540 when it was built by Duncan Stewart of Appin for his kinsman, James IV, to protect the Stewart lands and to serve as a hunting lodge. It passed temporarily out of Stewart hands in the 17th century when its owner gave it to a neighbouring Campbell as payment for an eight-oared galley. It was forfeited after the Battle of Killiecrankie and garrisoned by Hanoverian troops during the '45 Jacobite rising. A small, grey tower house built over a pit prison, it has been well restored and you get a good view of it from the road.

Keep an eye out for the seals basking on the rocks around here: they flop down into the water if disturbed, and then pop up and stare balefully at intruders with their great, velvety eyes.

Port Appin ✆ (01631–) ***Where to Stay***

expensive

The **Isle of Eriska**, at Ledaig, ✆ 720 371, 🖷 720 531, *www.eriska-hotel.co.uk*, about 20 minutes' drive north of Oban, is situated on its own 300-acre island—connected to the mainland by a bridge. It has a swimming pool, gym, 9-hole golf course, tennis and clays, and wonderful wildlife—badgers are fed every evening at the door of the bar. Meals are plentiful and delicious, the staff are exceptionally friendly, and they have a fine selection of malts. **Airds Hotel**, in Port Appin, ✆ 730 236, 🖷 730 535, is an expensive, comfortable country house looking across to Lismore and Loch Linnhe. The family-home atmosphere is enhanced by gorgeous flower arrangements, comfortable furnishings and excellent food.

moderate

The excellent **Pierhouse**, ✆ 730 302, 🖷 730 400, is the old ferry inn at the end of the pier, where you can stay in a very reasonable room overlooking the sea and eat delicious seafood in the bistro-restaurant, bar or patio. **Kinlochlaich House Garden**, ✆ 730 342 (*open daily, except Sun in winter; adm*) is a marvellous garden centre and nursery in lovely surroundings with delightful cottages to let.

cheap

Lochside Cottage, Fasnacloich, Appin, ✆ 730 216, is a Wolsey Lodge run by Earle and Stella Broadbent, on the shore of Loch Baile Mhic Chailen, a peaceful, friendly cottage with good food. No smoking. **Fasadgh Guest House**, Port Appin, ✆ 730 374, is a modern bungalow on a croft in the village, with beautiful views across the water to Lismore and the Morvern hills.

Fort William 106
Fort William to Ballachulish 110
Ballachulish to Glencoe 113
The Rough Bounds 116
Fort William to Mallaig 116
Morar and Knoydart 119
Fort William to Moidart, Sunart and Ardnamurchan 121

Central West Highlands

Here is a Highland cornucopia: the highest hill with its skiing resort; the saddest glen still mourning its infamous massacre; the aptly named Rough Bounds; the many waymarkers on the Jacobite trail; glorious land- and seascapes; an enigmatic murder; poets and bards; saints and villains. The not too harsh climate tends to be damp, but when the sun shines, all else is forgotten. Away from the more popular areas around Fort William there are some truly remote corners where you might easily spend days without seeing a soul.

Fort William

North from Oban, Crianlarich or Callander, Fort William is a good centre from which to explore the central west Highlands. It is the southern entrance to the Caledonian Canal, tourist resort, shopping centre for the whole of this area and hub of several routes; it is also the northern end of the West Highland Way, the 95-mile hike from Milngavie in Glasgow. Not surprisingly, therefore, the town seethes with holidaymakers in summer and provides all the facilities needed for climbing, hiking and boating. It lies in the lee of Ben Nevis, Britain's highest mountain, 4,406ft (1,344m), a forbidding but seductive lump with several routes to the top, allowing for different levels of expertise and physical fitness.

Tourist Information

Cameron Square, ✆ (01397) 703 781.

History

The first fort was built by General Monk in 1655, an earth construction that proved to be of insufficient strength when put to the test by rebellious Highlanders later in the century. Rebuilt after 35 years, in stone, it was called after the new king, William of Orange, and withstood Jacobite attacks in 1715 and 1746. The scruffy settlement which grew up beside it was variously named: Maryburgh, after the wife of King William; Gordonsburgh, after its Gordon lairds in the 18th century; and Duncansburgh, after Sir Duncan Cameron of Fassifern, who owned it in the 19th century. Finally it reverted to the original name of the fort. (For Gaelic speakers it is still *An Gearasdan*—the Garrison.) The fort was demolished in the 19th century and a patch of grass edged with sections of stone rampart is all that remains today. It made way for the railway which used to run along the lochside to terminate in the centre of the town. (Later, this part of the line was replaced by the present dual carriageway. The new station was built near the site of the fort, together with Safeways, a drive-in Macdonalds and other modern essentials.) The small Victorian town that mushroomed around the railway is sturdy and busy rather than architecturally gracious. Its limits have spread beyond the streets of genteel gabled villas to suburbs of modern houses built to serve the various industries that have been developed on Fort William's doorstep.

The Town

The **West Highland Museum** in Cameron Square (*open July–Aug daily; Sept–June Mon–Sat, closed Sun; adm*) is one of the most rewarding ways of spending a few hours in the town, not just on a wet day. This is a traditional museum and carefully preserves traditional features such as its new display cases modelled on those of the 1890s, but with modern lighting. It is almost a 'museum of a museum', enhanced by modern technology with an amazingly wide range of exhibits in a series of well-laid-out rooms. The first thing to look for is the Ballachulish Goddess dating from 600 BC: a tall, graceful statue with quartz eyes, carved from black alder and found under 4ft of peat by Loch Leven. The best known exhibit is the 'anamorphic' portrait of Prince Charles, used in the days when loyal Jacobites toasted 'the king across the water'—a smear of paint on a tray, meaningless until you view its reflection on the side of a metal cylinder (or on the curved side of a wine glass if you were making a secret toast), when it is transformed into a recognizable portrait. (There are two more of these anamorphic paintings in the museum, both 'naughty pictures' for gentleman voyeurs.) Another highlight is the 'Black Gun of Misfortune', one of the four guns alleged to be *the* gun used in the Appin Murder (*see* p.111–12). This one, a long Spanish weapon, was found in a hollow tree near Lettermore not long after the murder and is most likely to be the true claimant to the dubious honour. There are Jacobite relics, Montrose's helmet, the re-erected interior of the governor of the fort's house, and more.

You can also pass a contented hour or so leaning over the rails beside the long ladder of locks that bring the **Caledonian Canal** down to the level of the sea and into Loch Linnhe at Corpach. The canal was opened in 1882 to allow vessels to avoid the Pentland Firth and marauding French privateers in the Napoleonic Wars. It is used now by fishing boats and pleasure craft and the gates are hydraulically operated, the water boiling through sluices until the level is equal either side. The eight locks at Banavie, Neptune's Staircase, rise 72ft in 500 yards, which presented Thomas Telford with an enormous problem when he built the canal. You can still see the original lock-keepers' houses, with bow windows that enabled the keepers to see the canal in both directions from inside. **Loch Linnhe** is always busy with pleasure boats in the summer and is fringed with moorings as well as a great many hotels and guest houses running some way out of the town. The northern suburbs are not attractive, rather dominated by a huge paper factory and lots of warehouses.

Inverlochy Castle, now a crumbling ruin at the mouth of the Lochy, has been stabilized by Historic Scotland. Its moat was filled by the river on which it stands, and its rectangle of curtain walls with four corner towers is thought to date from the 13th century, probably built by John Comyn of Badenoch. Later it passed to the Bruces and then to the Gordons of Huntly. It is likely that there was an earlier structure on this strategic site, sometimes connected with Banquo, Thane of Lochaber, thanks to Hector Boece. The historian, Boece, wrote a History of Scotland in 1527, inventing colourful stories to embroider an already colourful story. Holinshed used Boece as a primary source, and Shakespeare used Holinshed: hence the many legends that now flesh out the bare bones of fact. Also according to Boece, Inverlochy was once a prosperous, cosmopolitan city where King Achaius signed a treaty with Charlemagne in 790. Boece blames the Vikings for the lack of any surviving tangible evidence.

The **Battle of Inverlochy** in 1645 was the third of Montrose's great victories, before his defeat and execution. He had made a Christmas raid on his enemies, the Covenanting Campbells, at Inveraray and was marching his men back up the coast to the Great Glen. When they got to Fort Augustus (Kilchumein, in those days), he heard that the Earl of Argyll was behind him, garrisoned at Inverlochy with 3,000 men. He led his men back through the hills and descended on the Covenanters at dawn from above Inverlochy Castle. Argyll, with a dislocated shoulder, watched from a galley while the castle surrendered and 1,300 of his men were massacred as they fled. Montrose wrote to Charles I: 'I am in the fairest hopes of rendering this kingdom to your Majesty's obedience, and shall be able to come to your Majesty's assistance with a brave army.' History was to prove him wrong and within five years both Charles I and Montrose were dead, the latter having been executed for fighting for the cause of Charles II, who turned his back on his loyal subject in his hour of need.

Around Fort William

Aonach Mhor ski area, developed in 1989, is accessible off the A82, 7 miles northeast of the town. It has the only cablecar in Scotland—the Nevis Range gondola—and is now a popular and fast-expanding skiing resort. Although the weather is unpredictable there are some excellent runs for all standards of skier and the Corrie Dubh holds snow late in the season. The gondola runs daily throughout the year and gives access to a restaurant, bar and shops at 4,006 feet as well as lofty walks in the summer. There is also some of the most challenging rock climbing any expert could hope for.

From the summit of **Ben Nevis** on a clear day you can see Ben Lomond near Glasgow, the Cairngorms, the Cuillins in Skye and the Outer Hebrides. The tourist route to the top starts at Achintee Farm about a mile southeast of the town on the way into Glen Nevis. It is well signposted and well trodden. This was a pony trail in the last century, leading to the weather observatory at the top. In 1911 an Edinburgh motor dealer drove a 20-horsepower Model T Ford up here, taking five days. You are advised to allow about 7 hours to get there and back. 'Running the Ben', usually on the first Saturday in September, started in 1895, and about 500 runners compete. The record is 1 hour, 25 minutes, 34 seconds. A local octogenarian did it in 3 hours. For the less energetic, **Glen Nevis**, through which the Water of Nevis runs, circles the southwestern base of the Nevis range. The Glen gets better the further you go. It narrows dramatically and becomes less frequented; the scenery is almost primeval, with waterfalls and narrow gorges and tracks up into the hills at several points.

Fort William ✆ (01397–) ***Where to Stay***

expensive

Inverlochy Castle, Torlundy, 3 miles north of Fort William, ✆ 702 177, ✉ 702 953, *www.inverlochy.co.uk*, is so exclusive that it doesn't publish its prices, but everything is first class. Also *see* pp.107, 110 and 128.

moderate

The Grange, Grange Road, Fort William, ✆ 705 516, is a comfortable Victorian guest house overlooking Loch Linnhe where you will be well looked after by Joan and John Campbell. **Ashburn House**, Achintore Road, Fort William, ✆ 706 000, ✉ 702 953, is a modernized Victorian house on the shore of Loch Linnhe overlooking the Ardgour hills, yet only 5 minutes' walk from the town centre. Highly recommended, with good food, tasteful decor and comfortable rooms.

The **Moorings Hotel**, Banavie, Fort William, ✆ 772 797, ✉772 441, is a 4-star hotel a few minutes' drive from the town, beside Neptune's Staircase at the western end of the Caledonian Canal, with views of Ben Nevis and Aonach Mor. The rooms are comfortable with all the trimmings, and the food has won awards.

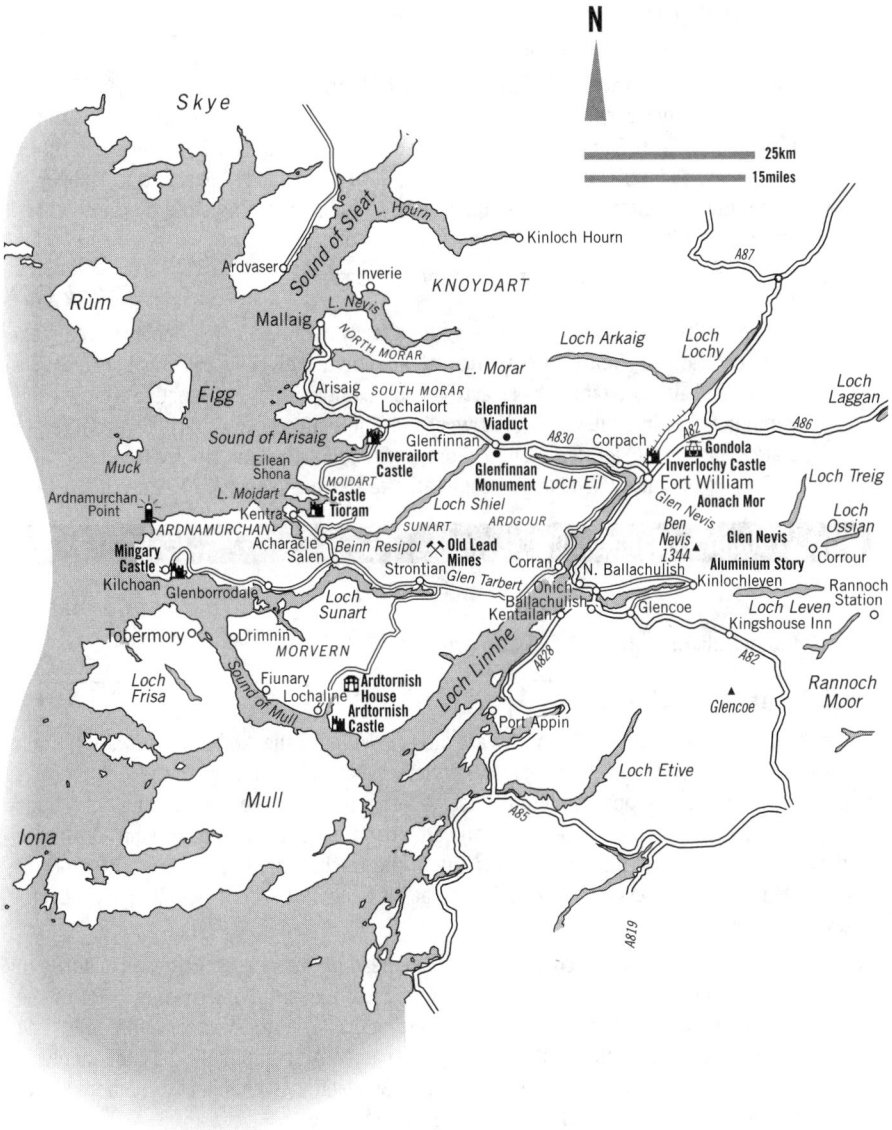
N
25km
15miles
Skye
Sound of Sleat
L. Hourn
Kinloch Hourn
Ardvaser
Inverie
KNOYDART
Rùm
Mallaig
L. Nevis
NORTH MORAR
L. Morar
Loch Arkaig
Loch Lochy
A87
Eigg
Arisaig
SOUTH MORAR
Lochailort
Glenfinnan Viaduct
Loch Laggan
A86
Sound of Arisaig
Glenfinnan
A830
Corpach
A82
Gondola
Inverlochy Castle
Muck
Eilean Shona
Inveraillort Castle
Glenfinnan Monument
Loch Eil
Fort William
Loch Treig
Ardnamurchan Point
L. Moidart
MOIDART
Castle Tioram
Kentra
Loch Shiel
SUNART
ARDGOUR
Aonach Mor
Glen Nevis
Ben Nevis 1344
Loch Ossian
ARDNAMURCHAN
Acharacle
Salen
Beinn Resipol
Old Lead Mines
Glen Nevis
Corrour
Mingary Castle
Kilchoan
Glenborrodale
Strontian
Glen Tarbert
Corran
N. Ballachulish
Aluminium Story
Kinlochleven
Rannoch Station
Loch Sunart
Onich
Ballachulish
Kentallan
Glencoe
Loch Leven
Kingshouse Inn
Tobermory
Drimnin
MORVERN
A828
A82
Loch Frisa
Sound of Mull
Fiunary
Lochaline
Ardtornish House
Ardtornish Castle
Loch Linnhe
Port Appin
Glencoe
Rannoch Moor
Loch Etive
Mull
Iona
A85
A819

cheap

If you want a Gaelic welcome, try Miss MacPhee, **Tangasdale**, Corpach, ✆ 772 591. The bungalow and setting are nothing special, but the hospitality and feeling of being in a Gaelic-speaking home make this an experience to savour. **Distillery House**, Nevisbridge, North Road, Fort William, is a 4-star guest house where you will get a warm welcome and dinner if you want it. **Calasona**, Onich, ✆ (01855) 821 291, is a very comfortable, clean, modern B&B run by a friendly young local couple, the Macalpins. The scenery is stunning.

Snowgoose Mountain Centre at Corpach, Fort William, ✆ 772 467, 🖷 772 411 has self-catering apartments in what was a smithy and forge before the building of the Caledonian Canal. They look over Upper Loch Linnhe and have been very well set up for family holidays. They sleep: 2–4, 6–8, and, in The Smiddy Lodge, up to 12 people. By no means isolated, with the steam train to Mallaig passing close by, these apartments make an ideal base for the area, and for skiers.

Fort William ✆ (01397–) ***Eating Out***

In Fort William, a very good place to go for a really memorable, reasonably priced meal is **The Crannog Seafood Restaurant** on Town Pier, ✆ 705 589. Located in a converted bait store which looks across Loch Linnhe, it has a distinctive red roof and veranda for eating outside in good weather. The seafood comes virtually from sea to plate. Langoustine, lobster, crab, scallops, etc. The food at **Inverlochy Castle,** ✆ 702 177, is exceptionally good and a real treat. *See* above and pp.107, 108 and 128.

Fort William to Ballachulish

Tourist Information

Ballachulish: ✆ (01855) 811 296 (*open April–Oct*).

Loch Linnhe to Loch Leven

After the strip of lochside hotels southwest of Fort William, the A82 zips you down Loch Linnhe about 7 miles to the Corran Narrows, where the already slim head of the loch narrows to a mere channel before opening into the sea. A ferry crosses to Ardgour, cutting out a huge loop for those heading west. Whenever you can, abandon your car, consult your Ordnance Survey map, and take off into the hills on any of the tracks marked. There is a network of tracks north from Loch Leven and Kinlochleven at the head of the loch, including old drovers' and military routes.

Kinlochleven sits somewhat incongruously at the head of Loch Leven below a backdrop of mountains. A settlement of three houses was transformed into a thriving town in 1904 by the founding of an aluminium works here—an interesting display at the Visitor Centre tells 'The Aluminium Story'. (A suggestion that the town be renamed Aluminiumville was not adopted.) Nearby there is a waterfall rated as one of the best in Scotland, descending past Mamore Lodge from the top of a cliff to drop 210ft (60m) into a hidden gorge.

At **North Ballachulish** (pronounced Balla-hoolish), 13 miles south of Fort William, a bridge spans the narrows between Lochs Linnhe and Leven where, not so long ago, a small car ferry used to slither and slide on the fast current. Many tales are told of this intrepid vessel's exploits, like the time it ran aground one Hogmanay because the skipper had swallowed some holly. Today you are over the bridge and away before you know it.

Highland Mystery World, billed as A Journey Beyond Belief (*open daily from 10; adm; ✆ (01855) 811 660*), is part of a tourist development on the site of the reclaimed slate quarry. This is a splendid 'virtual reality' experience, as fascinating for adults as for children. The ancient mysteries of the Highlands are brought to life by actors and special effects. Myth, legend and superstition are cleverly portrayed in five sections: Astromyth Theatre, Roots of Rannoch, Clootie Well, Viking Foodship (where you can eat), and Mysterymall. There is also an adventure playground, a crêche and a leisure centre with heated pool. A good day out.

Also in North Ballachulish is **Great Glen Fine Foods Confectionery Factory Visitor Centre** (*shop open Easter–Oct daily 9–5.30; rest of the year closed Sun; factory open Easter–Oct daily 10.15–5.15; rest of the year closed Sun, but not normally in production at weekends*). Here you can watch mouthwatering chocolates, fudges and pralines, etc. being made—and buy the end product.

The village of Ballachulish, a couple of miles to the east, grew up around Scotland's biggest slate quarry, still full of slate but no longer in use. The slate works have been landscaped and there is a large new hotel by the loch. Go on into Glencoe village and take the A82 into the famous glen.

The Appin Murder

Doubling back west towards Oban through South Ballachulish on the A828, you can contemplate one of Scotland's unsolved mysteries. In South Ballachulish there is a monument on a hillock just above the bridge. On it is inscribed: 'Erected in 1911 to the memory of James Stewart of Acharn, or James of the Glens, executed on this spot Nov. 8, 1752, for a crime of which he was not guilty.' The story behind it inspired Robert Louis Stevenson to embellish the truth in his novel *Kidnapped* and its sequel *Catriona*.

Colin Campbell of Glenure, known as the Red Fox, was factor and rent collector to several Jacobite estates which had been forfeited after Culloden. The Campbell clan had fought on the English side and were loathed as traitors by loyal Jacobites. On 14 May 1752, only six years after Culloden, when feelings were still raw and tempers high, Campbell crossed the ferry with three companions with the order to evict some Stewart tenants in Appin, in favour of some Campbells. This eviction order had been disputed by the staunchly Jacobite James Stewart. As well as three children of his own, he had staying with him his adventurer protégé Allan Breck—Allan the Pockmarked—who had fought for the English at Prestonpans and then changed sides and fought with the Jacobites at Culloden, for which he was now outlawed. Campbell and his companions rode from the ferry along the old road that cut across the hill to Kentallen. At about 5pm a shot rang out and put paid to Colin Campbell of Glenure. His companions set off for help, going south to Achindarroch and on to Acharn where they saw James Stewart busy on his land. On hearing the news, Stewart is alleged to have remarked: 'Whoever is the culprit, I shall be the victim.' He was prophetic. The prime suspect, Allan Breck the outlaw, had vanished.

The day after the murder James Stewart was arrested as an accessory and taken to Inveraray. He was tried before a jury of 15 that included eleven Campbells, presided over by their chief, the Duke of Argyll. James Stewart was taken to a hillock above the Ballachulish ferry on a wild November day and hanged, after a long and impassioned valedictory to his gathered clan, begging them not to seek vengeance. It was forbidden to cut down his body which hung in chains from the gallows for three years, guarded by soldiers to prevent the Stewarts taking it away for burial. At one point it fell from the chains but still the bitter sentence prevailed and the bones were wired together and rehung. When it fell again, in 1755, the bones were rescued and spirited away, thought to be buried lovingly among the Stewarts of Ardsheal in the graveyard at Keil. Some say that the name of the murderer is passed down from father to son by the Stewarts of Appin; if so, then at least one person today must know the truth. There are in existence four guns which were claimed to be the murder weapon: the most likely is the one in the museum at Fort William (*see* above). The rough stone on top of the memorial to James Stewart came from his farm at Acharn. Another memorial cairn, off a track in the woods above the road about a mile west of Ballachulish, marks the site of Campbell's murder. Further on at Duror, a traditional Lochaber bank barn stands close to the ruin of James Stewart's house at Acharn.

Where to Stay

moderate

Ballachulish House, Ballachulish, ✆ (01855) 811 266, ℻ 811 498 (*open all year*), was the home of the Stewarts of Ballachulish, rebuilt after it was burnt down by Hanoverian troops in 1746. As well as strong Jacobite connections, it had associations with the Glencoe massacre, and the Appin murder which was committed about a mile away. You walk into the hall and feel you have come to stay with friends, and when you leave you feel this even more so. Antique furniture and family photograph albums give a lived-in feeling; all the bedrooms (with en suite bathrooms) are like the best spare rooms in a private house. The food is excellent, with fresh local ingredients, and a good wine list. Guests help themselves to drinks in a 'trust' bar in the drawing room and the company is usually interesting.

Ardsheal House, Kentallen of Appin, ✆ (01631) 740 227, ℻ 740 342, a laird's house on a hill looking across Loch Linnhe towards Morvern. The original house was 16th century, destroyed by fire as reprisal for Culloden, and rebuilt around 1760 by Charles Stewart of Ardsheal, one of the Stewarts of Appin. Later extensions have obscured the 18th-century parts and the house now has the aura of a Victorian shooting lodge. Neil and Philippa Sutherland run it as their own home and you are greeted by the laird himself in his kilt and ushered in to sit by a roaring fire. The furniture and decoration fit the date of the house, with fireplaces made from local marble, and oak panelling and gleaming dark woodwork downstairs. There is a conservatory dining room overlooking the garden and a billiard room. The food is excellent, with local ingredients, home-baked bread, home-made jellies and jams, home-grown vegetables and fruit. A good selection of wines and malt whiskies is on offer and you can help yourself from a 'trust' bar. *Open Mar–Oct, or by prior arrangement.*

If you can muster 22 people, **Ardgour House**, by Fort William, ✆ (01413) 376 669, is a marvellous self-catering mansion sleeping 22. It was the former home of the MacLeans of Ardgour, a fine house in 6 acres of private garden with private fishing. There is a heated swimming pool, sauna, spa pool and billiard room.

Onich Hotel, Onich, ✆ (01855) 821 214, 821 484, overlooks Loch Linnhe and is one of the best of the many hotels on the A82. **The Lodge on the Loch**, Onich, ✆ (01855) 821 237, is a bit more expensive and also very nice.

Ballachulish to Glencoe

Although it is always awe-inspiring, Glencoe can show a benign face when the sun shines, especially if you get off the road and go into the hills. You will find creaming burns and falls, glistening rocks, hidden lochans and glens with surprise pockets of wild flowers and dramatic views. But when the weather closes in and cloud swirls down off the raw, steep-sided peaks slashed by white scars of cascading water, and the wind moans in the corries, an aura of doom and melancholy pervades the place. This is *Glen Coe*—the Glen of Weeping.

The Massacre of Glencoe

Everyone knows a version of the stirring story of the Massacre of Glencoe, unquestionably a hideous blemish on the honour of some members of the government of the day. When William and Mary succeeded James VII/II in 1689, the Jacobites posed a powerful threat to their stability. In an attempt to bring the rebellious clans in line it was decided that the chiefs must sign an oath of loyalty to the crown by 1 January 1692. The order was issued on pain of death and, after much hesitation, most of the chiefs obeyed, having received agreement from the exiled King James VII. MacIan of Glencoe was the chief of a small branch of Clan Donald and an obstinate old diehard. By the time he reluctantly conceded, it was too late. Starting off, he went the wrong way, to Fort William, where he learnt that the governor of the garrison was not empowered to take his oath. In filthy weather he then set off for Inveraray, but was delayed on the way by a blizzard and was stormbound at Barcaldine Castle (*see* p.103–4). He arrived after the deadline and the Sheriff, Campbell of Ardkinglas, was off duty nursing his New Year hangover. The oath was eventually sworn and accepted, but the delay was seized upon by the government as a pretext for dealing a short, sharp shock to Highland chiefs who might have had their fingers crossed while swearing their oaths. The Macdonalds of Glencoe were perfect scapegoats: not only was their loyalty to the Jacobite cause known to be extreme, but their numbers were small, their glen so enclosed that escape would be difficult, and their reputation among their neighbours as scoundrels was notorious. It was believed that their extermination, while being a lesson to some, would also be a relief to many.

The Secretary of State for Scotland, John Dalrymple, Master of Stair, masterminded the plan and it was endorsed by King William (who was not told, when the order was presented for his signature, that MacIan had eventually signed the oath, albeit late). Two companies of the Earl of Argyll's Regiment, recruited from the Campbell Clan, were ordered to Glencoe under the command of Robert Campbell of Glenlyon, an elderly alcoholic who had been forced into the army by bankruptcy caused partly by the depredations of the Glencoe Macdonalds. The Campbells moved into the glen on 1 February 1692; the Macdonalds, who had been evading their taxes, were obliged to accommodate them. The unwritten laws of hospitality by which all Highlanders were bound, ensured that the Campbells were safe among their enemies and well tended. In the harsh climate of mid-winter, the Campbells and Macdonalds cohabited in uneasy peace. Campbell of Glenlyon received his final order:

> *You are hereby ordered to fall upon the rebels the Macdonalds of Glencoe and put all to the sword under 70. See that this be put into execution without fear or favour, or you may expect to be dealt with as not one true to King or Government, nor a man fit to carry a commission in the King's service. Expecting you will not fail in the fulfilling hereof as you love yourself.*

At dawn on 13 February about 40 of the clan were slaughtered, including Maclan, his wife and two of his sons. Some believe that the Campbells were not as ruthless as portrayed; their military strategy did not go according to plan and quite a few Macdonalds managed to escape. Tradition has it that Glenlyon's piper played *People of This Glen* as a warning to the Macdonalds and that some of the Campbells passed oblique cautionary signals to their hosts concerning the danger of sleeping in the glen that night. The lasting disgrace of this massacre is the unforgivable betrayal of trust: guest vs. host. In the recriminations that followed, the massacre came to be represented as a Battle of the Clans—Campbells against Macdonalds, rivals since the beginning of time. In fact it was a cynical act of genocide in an attempt to enforce obedience to the law on a proud, independent, if roguish people. It failed and brought lasting dishonour and contempt upon its perpetrators. It is interesting that when Queen Victoria visited Glencoe in 1873, she wrote in her journal: 'The place itself is one which adds to the horror of the thought that such a thing could have been conceived and committed on innocent sleeping people. How and whither could they fly? Let me hope that William III knew nothing of it.'

The **Glencoe Folk Museum** (*open mid May–Sept Mon–Sat 10–5.30*), in the village tells the story of the massacre. The Massacre Memorial is a tall, slender Celtic cross where a small group of people meet on 13 February each year to honour the clan. The National Trust for Scotland have a **visitor centre** in the glen, set back to the left of the road as you drive east.

White Corries Ski Centre, a little further on, has the longest vertical descent in Scotland—2,600ft (793m) and plenty of challenging skiing on Meall a Bhuiridh, for those who aren't put off by capricious weather. Snow lingers long in Glencoe and the skiing season continues well into the spring. (*Ski Hotline: ✆ (09001) 654 658.*)

The Devil's Staircase is a zigzag track, part of the West Highland Way and former military route constructed by Caulfeild in the 1740s, climbing from Altnafeadth at the head of Glencoe, across a ridge and down to Kinlochleven. It is a steepish walk with views across the glen to Buachaille Etive Mor. The 17th-century **Kingshouse Inn**, on the left beyond the Pass, is said to be one of Scotland's oldest licensed inns. It was used as a barracks for the troops of George III after Culloden, hence its name, and has a colourful history. Dorothy Wordsworth wrote in her journal in 1803: 'Never did I see such a miserable, such a wretched place—long rooms with ranges of beds, no other furniture except benches, or perhaps one or two crazy chairs, the floors far dirtier than an ordinary house could be if it were never washed.' The supper, when it came, was 'a shoulder of mutton so hard that it was impossible to chew the little flesh that might have been scraped off the bones'. In spite of its isolation, Kingshouse received many visitors, being on the main route between Fort William and Glasgow and close to the drovers' route from Skye to the Falkirk Tryst; its tap room was notorious. At the turn of the 20th century, labourers working on the Black Water Reservoir used to drop in on their way to and from work; many who had imbibed too freely were lost and perished in the hills.

Rannoch Moor stretches away into the distance to the east beyond the Pass: a vast, swampy moonscape, unpopulated except by birds. It is bleak, even in summer. In the late 19th century an expedition to survey this most desolate of terrain prior to the construction of the West Highland Railway ended in disaster. A group of top railway executives set out over the moor in their best suits, got lost and separated from each other, and had to spend the night out in the bog. Some nearly died of exposure. The route eventually chosen for the West Highland Line across Rannoch Moor takes it from Rannoch Station to Tulloch via Lochs Ossian and Treig, far from human habitation and any road. Because of the boggy terrain the track was floated on a platform of timber piles and brushwood. You need a good map if you plan to walk through to the Grampians.

Loch Ossian is about 17 miles northeast of Glencoe, tucked into a valley surrounded by hills and inaccessible by public road. There is a **youth hostel** and the train stops at Corrour Station, but the energetic should attack it on foot. It is an easy 10-mile tramp from Black Corries Lodge, over the shoulder of Stob na Cruaiche, around the eastern end of the Blackwater Reservoir and along the railway.

Glencoe ✆ (01855–) ***Where to Stay***

moderate

The **Moor of Rannoch Hotel**, near Kinloch Rannoch, ✆/🖷 (01882) 633 238, is one of the best places in the area. The food is fantastic, eaten by a roaring fire in a panelled dining room, and the host and hostess very friendly.

cheap

Clachaig Inn, ✆ 811 252, 🖷 811 679, 2 miles east of Glencoe village, is an inexpensive hotel/ hostel which often seems to be full of dejected people sitting about 'waiting for the weather'. For 'outward-bounders' it is convenient and has all the facilities you want when hobbling in, soaking wet and freezing cold, after a day in the hills, but don't go here for peace and solitude. There is a resident warden who will advise on good walks and climbing in the glen. This is a centre for some of the most challenging mountaineering in Britain, much of it unsuitable for amateurs.

The **Kingshouse Hotel**, Glencoe ✆ 851 259, 🖷 259 216, now considerably altered from Dorothy Wordsworth's description (*see* above) provides excellent facilities for hikers, climbers and skiers, some of whom leave their backpacks to be transported on to their next staging post. It has a jolly, 'outward-bound' atmosphere that might put off anyone seeking solitude. Prices range from expensive to cheap. The **Glencoe Youth Hostel**, ✆ 811 219, is a marvellous base for walkers and climbers.

There are several good self-catering options: **Carefree Holidays Glencoe**, Clachaig, Glencoe, ✆ 811 679, have well-appointed chalets, sleeping 4–6, in lovely scenery, with the inn close by for extra snacks. **Invercoe Highland Holidays**, Invercoe, Glencoe, ✆ 811 210, have a choice of stone cottages, mobile homes or luxury lodges, sleeping 2–6.

The Rough Bounds

The Rough Bounds—*Garbh-chriochan*—is the name given from time immemorial to that southwestern corner of the Highlands, west of Fort William, between Loch Sunart in the south and Loch Hourn in the north. This was the heartland of the Lords of the Isles, accessed by sea and guarded at every headland by a fortress. Much of the interior is still reached only by the old hill tracks on which intruders were ambushed. It is said that when one of the Glengarry chiefs travelled into the Rough Bounds with his family, he packed his younger children into creels tied on to sturdy ponies; if one child weighed more than another, stones were used to even the balance.

At one time the whole of the *Garbh-chriochan* belonged to various branches of the Macdonald clan. Because of its inaccessibility, the area has been slow to change. Its people were largely Jacobite: Moidart and Morar remain mostly Catholic today, having clung to their faith in the face of great persecution in the 18th century. When a hardy old warrior who had been 'out' in the '45 was summoned to meet George III, he assured the king that he regretted nothing, although he added: 'What I did for the Prince, I would have done as heartily for your Majesty, if you had been in the Prince's place.'

Fort William to Mallaig

The **Jacobite Steam Railway** offers day trips from Fort William to Mallaig (*June–Sept Tues–Fri and Sun; adm; ✆ (01524) 73 2100*) west along Loch Eil, skirting Loch Nan Uamh where Prince Charles landed, and northwards along the gleaming Sands of Morar, with views west to the islands. The train stops at Glenfinnan. It is a fun day out, but if you want time and flexibility to explore and walk, take your car.

Whether you go by rail or road, this is one of the most beautiful routes in Scotland, in spite of heavy traffic to and from the busy port of Mallaig at the road's end. About 4 miles west of Loch Eil you come into **Glenfinnan** where three glens meet at the head of Loch Shiel against a layered backdrop of grape-blue hills.

Here, on bleak, swampy wasteland, stands **The Prince's Monument**, a gaunt column topped by a statue of the Prince, erected by Macdonald of Glenaladale in 1815. It commemorates the raising of Prince Charles' standard on 19 August 1745; the beginning of *Bliadhna Tearlach*—Charlie's Year.

The Jacobite Rising of '45

It is perhaps easier to recall the past if you turn your back on this 19th-century folly and look down the loch and up into the hills. When the Prince arrived here in the middle of the morning there was no one to greet him but two shepherds. Somewhat disconsolate, he took shelter in a nearby hut. After a while he was joined by about 150 Macdonalds

and by James Mor MacGregor, son of Rob Roy. (MacGregor was a double agent, acting as a spy for the Lord Advocate in Edinburgh, and at the same time pledging the allegiance of his clan to the Prince and bringing him the welcome news that the Camerons were already on their way.) It was crucial to the cause that Cameron of Locheil joined them, for he was a man whose great influence would sway the decisions of other clans. Though unenthusiastic about the uprising, this powerful chief was brave and loyal, declaring: 'I'll share the fate of my Prince.' Now, in the still afternoon, the waiting clans already committed to the young Prince heard the skirl of pipes. They turned to watch as Locheil marched down from the hills, leading 700 of his clansmen to join the Prince. (The well-known 'March of the Cameron Men' was composed by Mary Maxwell Campbell in 1829, to commemorate this event.) Locheil's action encouraged other clans to give their support and in the late afternoon a great red and white silken banner was unfurled. The Prince's father, who was the son and only male heir to James VII, was proclaimed King James of Britain, with Prince Charles Edward Stuart as his Regent.

Whatever misguided dream may have influenced this final Jacobite rising, it is tempting, when standing in this romantic setting, to forget its aftermath and feel staunchly Jacobite. When Queen Victoria came here in 1873, she revealed her strong sympathies for the Jacobite cause and noted: 'And here was I, the descendant of the Stewarts and of the very king whom Prince Charles sought to overthrow, sitting and walking about quite privately and peaceably.'

Glenfinnan

The **National Trust Visitor Centre** (*open April–Oct daily; adm*) has excellent maps showing the progress of the Prince's army throughout the Rising, tracing his wanderings after Culloden, out to the islands and finally back to Loch nan Uamh. The Glenfinnan Games are held every August on the nearest Saturday to the 19th, and are splendidly Highland and not too smart.

Trains still stop at **Glenfinnan Station**, including the tourists' steam train from Fort William. The building has been rescued from disuse by conversion into a museum with a 'diner' in a carriage in the siding.

The **Glenfinnan Viaduct**, carrying the railway across the glen, is an impressive landmark and a considerable engineering feat. When built (1897–1900) it was the longest, and first mass-concrete, viaduct in Britain. If you want a leg-stretch, a track under the viaduct leads through Glen Finnan and up the river into the hills. The Gothic-style **Catholic church** above Loch Shiel, built by the same Macdonald of Glenaladale who built the monument, must be the most beautifully sited Catholic church in Scotland, overlooking the loch with the hills behind. Inside there is another monument to the Prince.

Glenfinnan gets its name from St Finnan who came from Ireland to spread Christianity in its infancy. Climbing Ben Resipol from Loch Sunart he looked down upon Loch Shiel and saw a green island in the narrows where the loch turns west. Here he built a cell. The ruins of old foundations can still be seen on St Finnan's Isle, which became an important burial ground for the chiefs and clansmen of this region. It is still in use as a burial place and one of the most sacred places in the West Highlands. Islands were used for burials partly to protect the dead from predators such as wolves.

Halfway up the northern shore of Loch Shiel, inaccessible **Glenaladale** runs down from the hills to the north. The Macdonalds of Glenaladale no longer populate this remote glen: only the tumbled ruins of their crofts and shielings remain to bear witness to a loyal Jacobite clan. In 1772 Captain John Macdonald of Glenaladale took 300 of his Catholic clansmen to Prince Edward Island (now Canadian) where he had acquired some land. This was no cruel 'Clearance' but an expedient evacuation initiated by a Clanranald tacksman (small gentry) disillusioned by prospects in the West Highlands, and by the fact that Catholics in Scotland at this time were being forced into Protestant education, their freedom to worship limited, and their lives hedged by restrictions. Resettlement meant freedom and the chance of prosperity.

The road westwards twists through a bleak, unpeopled landscape, chasing the railway line and clattering under viaducts, with superb views westwards to the Small Isles. Between Borrodale and Arisaig it plunges into woodland, with banks of rhododendrons making it suddenly jungly, and riotously colourful in early summer.

Loch nan Uamh—pronounced 'naan ooa'—Loch of the Caves, to the west of the road beyond the head of Loch Ailort, is where Prince Charles arrived from Eriskay on 25 July 1745, at the start of his campaign to restore the Stuart throne, accompanied by only seven companions. These **Seven Men of Moidart** who had sailed from France with the Prince were: William Lord Tullibardine, the titular Duke of Atholl who had lost his title after the 1715 Rising; Sir Thomas Sheridan, Prince Charles's 70-year-old tutor; Aeneas Macdonald, a friend; John William O'Sullivan, a soldier of fortune who was later blamed bitterly by Lord George Murray for his part in the tragedy of Culloden; Sir John Macdonald, a lieutenant colonel in the Irish Brigade of the French army; Colonel Francis Strickland, whose father had gone to France with James VII in 1688; and the Reverend George Kelly, a clergyman who had refused to take the oath of allegiance to King William while James VII lived, and was thus banned from the church—a 'non-juror'. A cairn on a crag overlooking the loch beside the road (in the lay-by) commemorates the occasion, although nobody knows exactly where they landed. A year later, broken and defeated, the Prince embarked for France from this same place, leaving behind him many corpses, shattered hopes, vicious reprisals for generations to come, and the destruction of *Gaidhealtachd* (Gaeldom).

The knobbly, mottled sepia-grey hills of South Morar are rather gloomy though they offer unrivalled views across to Eigg and Rum. **Arisaig**, at the head of Loch nan Ceall about 7 miles west of the cairn, has a very sheltered anchorage and is a peaceful holiday village popular with 'white settlers' (the Scots' term for incomers—usually English). Yachts lie at anchor around the bay and a privately operated passenger ferry runs from Arisaig to the islands. In this largely Catholic area, the stark tower of the church of St Mary is a prominent landmark. Beside it stands the ruin of the medieval Kilmory church, and in its graveyard lies Alasdair MacMhaigstir, born about 1698, one of the greatest of the Gaelic poets, who took the Jacobite side in 1745 and was tutor/bard to the Prince.

Arisaig ✆ (01687–) ***Where to Stay***

expensive

Arisaig House, a few miles before the village, is now a comfortable hotel, ✆ 450 622, 🖷 450 626, *www.arisaighouse.co.uk*, with a splendid walled garden, terraces and fine wooded grounds. It was built in 1864 as the new mansion house for the estate and became one of the headquarters for the Special Operations Executive during the Second World War, where agents trained in the surrounding area before being dropped into occupied territory. A dour-looking country house from the outside, it is an elegant hotel within, with good food and expensive furnishings enlivened by touches of Art Deco.

moderate

Glenfinnan House Hotel, Glenfinnan, ✆/🖷 (01397) 722 235, is a Victorian mansion overlooking Loch Shiel and the monument. Real Highland hospitality here, with spontaneous *ceilidhs* and a piper, if you're lucky.

Borrodale House, in Arisaig, ✆ 450 229/238, is a large, restored farm house whose core dates back to about 1745 when it was possibly the home of the Macdonald of Borrodale who entertained Prince Charles. It was burnt down in 1746. Now a hotel with a pleasant atmosphere and friendly staff, it has large, attractive grounds from which there are good walks to the beach with its caves and magnificent views. **Arisaig Hotel**, ✆ 450 210, 🖷 450 310, dating from the early 18th century when the road ended here and Mallaig didn't exist, is near the jetty with a nice seating area outside from which to watch the bustle of the harbour. They do good bar meals and there's an above-average craft-and-book shop in an extension.

Woodend, Arisaig, ✆ 450 627, is a B&B in a simple Arts and Crafts type of cottage, run by Miss MacPherson. Inexpensive, quite old-fashioned but without ugly frills.

Old Library Lodge and Restaurant, Arisaig, ✆ 450 651, is a 200-year-old stable with a bistro atmosphere: you can sit outside to eat the excellent food, weather permitting. They also have accommodation.

The Prince's House, in Glenfinnan, ✆ (01397) 722 246, was an inn as long ago as 1658, although it has recently been done up. It is small, moderately priced and family-run, offering a warm welcome, comfortable rooms and 'gourmet' food with local ingredients, especially good seafood.

Glenfinnan Dining Car, ✆ (01397) 722 400, is an imaginative setting for excellent meals, snacks and refreshments—no licence, so take your own alcohol, and it is best to book.

Morar and Knoydart

Morar is the peninsula between the Sound of Arisaig to the south and Loch Nevis to the north. Loch Morar, cutting right across its heart, is the deepest freshwater loch in Europe—over 1,000ft (308m)—separated from the sea by only a few hundred yards over which the road and railway jostle for space. Its monster, Morag, is a rival to Nessie (the Loch Ness Monster): less famous but more sinister; her appearance is said to herald the death of a Clanranald Macdonald. It was beside this loch that Simon Fraser, 11th Lord Lovat, known as the Old Fox of the '45 (*see* Beauly, pp.174–5), was finally captured as he lay, so it is said, on two feather beds by the water's edge.

Tourist Information

Mallaig: ✆ (01687) 462 170 (*open all year; reduced hours in winter*).

Mallaig

About 10 miles north of Arisaig, Mallaig is the terminus for the railway and the road, and a busy fishing and ferry port. Unpretentious, it seems to say 'take me as you find me', and apart from a couple of attempts to entertain—Marine World and a Heritage Centre—it makes few concessions to the many tourists who find themselves waiting here for boats, trains and buses. The **Heritage Centre** (*open May–Sept daily; adm*) in a new building on the site of the old Railwaymen's Hostel, is of above-average interest, with exhibits about the people and history of the Rough Bounds, including videos and some fascinating old photographs. The **Marine World**, near the harbour (*open daily; adm*) has tanks of fish and sea creatures, and informative exhibits relating to the area.

Fishing boats pack into the harbour, bombarded by gulls and surrounded by all the clutter of their trade: fish-curing sheds, stacks of creels and fish boxes, piles of netting and gear. Mallaig deals mainly in prawns these days, most of them exported to Europe. One or two of the old fish-curing sheds survive, along with a quantity of modern replacements. Buying fresh fish is not as easy as it should be: the few outlets are usually 'just waiting on a load' or 'just sold out' or have 'plenty, if you don't mind frozen'. Your best bet is to try and chat up one of the boats.

Anyone who has read Gavin Maxwell's *Harpoon at a Venture* will recognise Mallaig as his mainland base where he struggled against the odds to establish a viable shark-fishing industry on the island of Soay just after the Second World War. It was in this harbour that he landed his first 'kill' in front of a large crowd of tourists—a 25-foot female basking shark, measuring 18 feet in circumference, caught off the Point of Sleat.

Caledonian MacBrayne have their office on the quay where you can buy ferry tickets. Ferries depart from Mallaig to Ardvaser in Skye, the Small Isles, and Castlebay and Lochboisdale in the Outer Isles. Ask around for a lift across Loch Nevis to Knoydart, or ring Bruce Watt, ✆ (01687) 462 320, who does the trip to Inverie three times a week.

Knoydart

One of Scotland's most isolated inhabited peninsulas, inaccessible by road, Knoydart is the northern extent of the Rough Bounds. This remote mountainous lump, washed by Loch Nevis (Heaven) to its south and Loch Hourn (Hell) to its north, thrusts westwards into the Sound of Sleat with a track across from its only village, Inverie, to Barrisdale on Loch Hourn, about 8 miles north. From here it is another 6 miles or so round the loch to the nearest road at Kinloch Hourn. The track from Inverie takes you through Glen Dulochan, between two Munros, of which Ladhar Beinn is the most westerly on the mainland. It's a good tramp on a fine day, but for shopping one must go to Mallaig, travelling by boat.

Knoydart's history is rather gloomy. It belonged to the Macdonells of Glengarry, large numbers of whom lived in the area until it was 'cleared' by Josephine Macdonell in 1853 and they were shipped to Nova Scotia in the wake of the potato famine. During the 20th century the land was sold repeatedly, none of its new owners staying for long. In 1948 squatters calling themselves the Seven Men of Knoydart tried to appropriate the land but were dispossessed by the then owner. Successive buyers with ulterior motives came, exploited, and departed. In 1992 the estate, much depleted by the selling of small packages of land for sporting interests, was bought by a Dundee-based jute company with plans for an activity centre and outdoor training establishment, which never got off the ground. With continuing financial problems, the

Inverie Estate has been on the market for some years, dogged by much speculation as to imminent sales which never quite come off. Inspired by recent events in Assynt and the Isle of Eigg, the residents (none of whom are descendants of Knoydart people) made a buy-out bid. It is too soon to know whether they will manage to bring prosperity to their lands.

Mallaig ✆ (01687–) ***Where to Stay***

moderate

West Highland Hotel, Mallaig, ✆ 462 210, 462 130, is a sprawling, traditional Highland hotel with panoramic views over the village. A lively, friendly place where freshly caught seafood is served every day without fail. **Morar Hotel**, ✆ 462 346, looks across the Silver Sands to the Inner Hebrides. Log fires and electric blankets keep guests warm, and the food is good home cooking. Local fishing can be arranged.

Pier House, Inverie, Knoydart, ✆ 462 347, is a guest house run by Dave and Jan Marriott. They have a tea room and restaurant with delicious food cooked by Dave—lobster and other seafood. (NB: Knoydart is not exactly crammed with places to eat and sleep.) **Doune Stone Lodge**, on the western tip of Knoydart, ✆ 462 667, is only accessible by sea and they collect you by boat from Mallaig. This is a custom-built lodge, not too many frills and an excellent base for outward bounders.

cheap

Western Isles Guest House, East Bay, Mallaig, ✆ 462 320, is a small quiet place not too far from the harbour. For a special, very reasonable B&B, go to Miss Teresa MacKenzie at **Achnaluin** nearby, ✆ 462 131, which is a proper old croft house, run by a local lady whose mother was born and died in the house. You can relax in a traditional Highland atmosphere and are looked after like one of the family.

Self-catering is a good alternative: try **Glashoille Holidays**, ✆ (01333) 360 251, a six-bedroom house sleeping ten people, in a glorious setting on the water. Or contact **Mrs Hayward**, Blynfield Farm, Stour Row, Shaftesbury, Dorset, SP7 0QP, ✆ (01747) 852 289. Her house is also on the water in Knoydart, with five rooms sleeping 11.

Sheena's Backpackers' Lodge, overlooking the harbour, is a splendid place with a covered timber veranda where you can while away the day on comfortable sofas and chairs, munching freshly cooked prawns, home-made scones and cakes. There are dormitory bedrooms.

The **Old Forge** is a splendid, friendly pub at Inverie, with an adjacent restaurant.

Fort William to Moidart, Sunart and Ardnamurchan

Tourist Information

Kilchoan: ✆ (01972) 510 222 (*open Easter–Oct*); **Strontian**: ✆ (01967) 402 131 (*open April–Oct*).

Loch Ailort to Loch Sunart

Travelling west from Fort William on the A830 to the head of Loch Ailort, take the A861 southwest through Moidart—from *midard,* heights of the sea spray. Like everywhere else in the Highlands, be prepared to get out of your car and walk. The road is all right for getting you from A to B and for a superficial overview, but to discover the true essence of the place, you must walk, climb and scramble; and you must take time to stop and talk to the slow, courteous, highly intelligent local people. Even today, the inhabitants of Moidart are mainly Catholic, living in peaceful harmony with their Protestant neighbours west of the River Sheil in Ardnamurchan.

Loch Ailort snakes its way out from Inverailort to the Sound of Arisaig. Approaching by boat can be a very tricky business, with fluky winds bouncing off the hills in all directions. **Inverailort Castle**, at the head of the loch, has at its core an elegant Georgian house, greatly impaired by subsequent Victorian additions and now in dire need of extensive repair and restoration. One room is still in use as the local post office. Like many other large houses in the area it played an important role in the activities of the Special Forces, later the Commandos, in the war. Its late owner, Mrs Francis Cameron-Head, was a devout Catholic, one of the last of an old school of eccentric Highland gentry (though actually of Irish birth). She kept open house here until she died and her table always had extra places set for unexpected visitors. She entertained parties of orphans and deprived children, keeping a firm eye on their activities, and was always deeply interested in other people's problems, social and economic. Her husband, who died many years before her, was a well-known Gaelic scholar. The spirit of the Cameron-Heads will live on here for many years.

Roshven House, overlooking the southern entrance to Loch Ailort stands derelict and has now been sold. In 1855 Professor Hugh Blackburn and his wife Jemima, one of the foremost illustrators of her day whom Ruskin pronounced the best artist he knew, set about restoring and rebuilding the plain Georgian house that survives at its core. The book *Jemima* by Rob Fairley gives an intriguing account of the life of Jemima Blackburn, reproducing many of her beautiful watercolours of the West Highlands and the birds and flowers to be found around Roshven. The new owner hopes to restore the house to its former glory. At present it is wrapped in scaffolding and the owner lives in a temporary dwelling close by.

This part of Moidart was accessible only by boat from Inverailort, or on foot, until 1966 when the road (A861) was built. The road turns south now and takes you down to Loch Moidart and eastwards along the loch to **Kinlochmoidart**. The house, recently restored to the highest standards, is available for extremely comfortable holiday lets (✆ (0990) 851 155). It was built between 1882 and 1884 for a wealthy businessman, Robert Stewart, who commissioned the fashionable Glasgow architect, William Leiper, to design him a baronial mansion. Its predecessor, the home of the Macdonalds of Kinlochmoidart, stood nearby until the 1980s. It was on this site, in an even earlier house (burnt down in 1746), that Prince Charles stayed for a week in August 1745 before going on to raise his standard in Glenfinnan. Here he waited while the clans were rallied to his cause, and it was here that his charm began to work on the chiefs who were reluctant to take part in the Rising. Traditionally, he sailed in through the north channel of Loch Moidart between Eilean Shona and the mainland and landed on the flat stretch of its northern shore. The **Seven Men of Moidart** mark this spot—five large beech trees, plus two saplings planted to replace the two blown down in gales.

The road then takes you inland about 6 miles to **Acharacle** (the 'ch' is guttural) where Loch Shiel narrows into its river and flows out under Shiel Bridge to the sea, or you can walk round the southern shore of Loch Moidart. St Adamnan mentions the River Shiel in his biography of

Columba, and describes how some of Columba's companions caught five salmon. Predicting a larger catch, he urged them to try again; they obeyed and caught a fish '*mirae magnitudinis*', of extraordinary size. Adamnan calls the Shiel '*fluvius piscosus*', a river abounding in fish. Acharacle is a scattered village very typical of many contemporary crofting settlements with a good mix of former thatched houses (many now relegated to barns), later gabled dwellings and modern bungalows. There is nothing twee about the genuine Highland vernacular style.

At Shiel Bridge a narrow road twists and turns out to the South Channel of Loch Moidart, to one of the most stirring, romantic ruins in Scotland. **Castle Tioram**—pronounced 'Chiram', meaning 'dry land'—stands high on a rocky islet overlooking Eilean Shona, reached on foot by causeway at low tide. This superbly defended stronghold of the 13th and 14th centuries was the seat of the Macdonalds of Clanranald. John of Islay, descended from Somerled, married his cousin Amie, who inherited Moidart, Arisaig and Knoydart from her father, one of Robert the Bruce's most faithful followers. Amie was divorced by John (who wished to marry a daughter of Robert II), and retired to Moidart, where she extended Castle Tioram to its present form in about 1353. Her son became the first Captain of Clanranald and the castle has always been associated with that clan. It was captured once by the cunning Campbells but swiftly retaken by the Clanranalds. In later sieges considerable damage was done and several cannon balls were found lodged in the walls in the 19th century. The castle was burnt in 1715 by its staunchly Jacobite chief, Allan Mor of Clanranald, to save it from falling into English hands. He stood on the wooded hill on the mainland opposite and watched Tioram burn before going off to fight at Sheriffmuir. (His other castle, Ormacleit in South Uist, also went up in flames on the night of Sheriffmuir, due to over-enthusiastic stoking of fires in the kitchen.) Workmen clearing the debris from the Tioram fire found a lump of metal with faint fragments of canvas or leather sticking to it, containing a number of solid silver Spanish dollars dating from the 17th century.

The Moidart people have a tradition that a murder of unusual atrocity was once committed in the dungeon and that the blood of the victim can never be wiped from the soil. To this day there's a constant oozing from the ground near the door, which turns a dark rusty colour on contact with the air and looks suspiciously like blood. Chemical analysis has proved that it isn't.

In 1984 these ancient walls became the setting for a gathering of Clanranald Macdonalds from all over the world. They were entertained by the present chieftain in the roofless banqueting hall, roasting whole lambs in the old hearth, and for a few hours the castle lived again, vibrant with pipe music, songs and laughter. The next day an open-air Mass was celebrated in the courtyard to rededicate the Clanranald banner, said to have survived Culloden. The ruin, at present reasonably well consolidated, was recently for sale. The Captain of Clanranald sent out the 'Fiery Cross' (two crossed sticks, charred at two ends and originally dipped in goat's blood—a traditional call to arms in the Highlands), in an attempt to persuade Macdonalds of Clanranald all over the world to buy it for the clan. He was outbid. The new owner, an enthusiastic businessman called Lex Brown, plans a sympathetic restoration of the castle with the interests of the Clanranalds at heart, but he has come up against problems with planning permission. At present his plans are 'awaiting judgement'.

Another road west from Acharacle goes out to Kentra Bay and Ardtoe, a sheltered, sandy haven that has been turned into a vast sea-water reserve for white-fish farming. South again across the eastern neck of Ardnamurchan, the road comes down to Salen on the north shore of Loch Sunart.

Loch Sunart

Loch Sunart is a perfect, safe anchorage for boats. There can be few more satisfying experiences than sailing out of this lovely loch early on a fine morning, the wind on your quarter, the sun on your back, watching the whole island-studded Minch open up ahead. **Strontian**—*sron-an-t Sidhean,* Point of the Fairies—at the head of the loch, caters well for visiting yachts with a well-stocked boat chandler. The rare mineral strontium, discovered in 1787, was so called because this is where it was found. (It was Sir Humphry Davy, the inventor of the miners' safety lamp, who realized its potential in the early 19th century: among other things, it gives fireworks their dazzle, and produces the isotope Strontium 90.) The Strontian Lead Mines, opened in 1722, were manned by French prisoners of war and provided bullets for the Napoleonic Wars.

It was just off Strontian, in Loch Sunart, that the Floating Church was anchored in 1843 during the 'Disruption', when the Free Church broke away from the Church of Scotland. The local laird refused members of the breakaway church land on which to build their new kirk so they bought an old ship on the Clyde, fitted it up as a suitable place of worship and towed it to Loch Sunart. For 30-odd years the congregation rowed out to their services without interference, protected by the freedom of the high seas.

Although some earlier buildings survive, the heart of Strontian is characterized by a 1960s development of houses, pleasantly sited round a central green. Don't be put off by the name of **Cozy Knits**, a short distance from the village centre. This 'workshop/tea-room' is well worth knowing about at the end of a strenuous walk—their food is excellent and the craft/bookshop with knitwear and tweeds is well worth a browse.

Heading westwards from Salen, the B8007 hugs the northern shore of Loch Sunart and finishes up at Ardnamurchan Point—Point of the Great Ocean. The rugged, wind-lashed peninsula of **Ardnamurchan**, familiar to west-coast yachtsmen as the most westerly point on the mainland of the British Isles, has a diverse landscape. The soil is poor, eroded by retreating ice in the last Ice Age, but manages to support trees to the east, giving way to heathery moorland presided over by the volcanic plug of Ben Hiant. Once well-populated, this area lost most of its inhabitants during the Highland Clearances. The ruins of many old crofting townships can still be seen, while a good number of surviving cottages have been gentrified or turned into holiday homes.

Northwest Ardnamurchan provides exceptional views across to the Small Isles and there are good sandy beaches. At Ardslingnish, about 8 miles from Salen, there is a tall pillar of red granite carved with a cross, thought to have been erected by St Columba in honour of the Irish saint, Ciaran, who died in 548. The ruin of **Mingary Castle**, another 8 miles on, was once the stronghold of the MacIans of Ardnamurchan, kinsmen of the Lords of the Isles. Dating from the 13th century, it stands on a rocky cliff from which its walls rise sheer on the seaward side, guarding the entrance to Loch Sunart and to the Sound of Mull. James IV came to Mingary to receive the homage of the Lords of the Isles in 1495, and was peeved by their lack of enthusiasm. The Campbells got their hands on the castle in the 1600s, but Alasdair Macdonald managed to capture it for Montrose in 1644. General Leslie took it back and it reverted to the Campbells; in 1745 it was garrisoned by government soldiers who built a barracks within the walls.

From **Kilchoan**, the largest settlement on the peninsula, a ferry runs across to Tobermory on Mull once a day.

Ardnamurchan Point, about 22 miles from Salen, is wild, heatherclad bedrock with a lighthouse at its tip. This listed building was designed in the 19th century by the Stevensons, the architects/engineers of most of the western seaboard's lighthouses. Ardnamurchan Lighthouse Trust opened an interactive display in the principal keeper's house in 1997. This includes relevant historical artefacts and a 'time capsule' showing a keeper's living quarters in the 1940s. The assistant keepers' cottages have been converted to holiday lets with a small café and gift shop in stables nearby.

This dramatic headland takes the full force of westerly gales and can present quite a challenge to small boats even in lighter winds. Johnson and Boswell, having waited for a fair wind to take them from Skye to Coll, finally embarked on a kelp boat. Dr Johnson did not have a happy voyage: 'We were doomed to experience, like others, the danger of trusting to the wind, which blew against us, in a short time, with such violence, that we, being no seasoned sailors, were willing to call it a tempest. I was sea-sick and lay down.' Boswell, having stayed on deck and flattered himself that he was a good sailor, became extremely anxious as the tempest increased and, as they rounded Ardnamurchan Point, changed direction and forced them to tack. It was on this trip that Boswell, anxious to help in the boat, was handed a rope and told to hang on to it until further notice. He did so, reflecting later that as the rope was fixed to the top of one of the masts, pulling it would have achieved nothing, the object having been to keep him out of the way and divert his fear by making him feel busy: 'Thus did I stand firm to my post, while the wind and rain beat upon me, always expecting a call to pull my rope.'

Morvern is the heel of this southwest corner, washed by Loch Sunart to the north, the Sound of Mull to the west and Loch Linnhe to the east. Sparsely populated, it clings to the mainland at Glen Tarbert, the 5-mile isthmus between Strontian and Inversanda. The largest granite quarry in Scotland is at Glensanda.

Lochaline, on the southern shore, means 'the beautiful loch' and so it is. It faces across the Sound of Mull to Fishnish Point, linked by a fairly frequent car ferry taking 15 minutes. Silica sand has been mined here since 1939 and is used for making optical glass.

Ardtornish House (*open April–31 Oct daily; adm*) is a striking landmark at the head of Loch Aline, a Victorian mansion designed by Alexander Ross in the late 19th century and described as 'a suburban villa afflicted with elephantiasis'. Set in a designed landscape, the lovely garden is full of unusual and exotic plants, shrubs and trees, and there are a number of interesting estate buildings.

Fiunary, 5 miles west of Lochaline, was the home of George Macleod, the left-wing Presbyterian who re-established a community on Iona in 1938. He was a controversial man, full of good intentions but not always tactful—he tried to introduce bishops into the kirk in the interests of church unity. He refused to use his title when he succeeded to a baronetcy in 1924, but chose the title Baron Macleod of Fiunary when created a life peer in 1967. The house—an old manse—is now falling into dereliction. There are good views across the Sound of Mull from this road, which peters out a few miles to the north at Drimnin.

You must walk to **Ardtornish Castle**, on a point a couple of miles east of Loch Aline. Built in 1340 and restored in 1910, it was for many years a stronghold of the Lords of the Isles. Its walls, which gave massive shelter and protection in the days when enemies stormed in from the sea, are nearly 10 feet thick. John, 1st Lord Macdonald of the Isles, died here in 1387 and it was his great-grandson the 4th Lord, also John, who received ambassadors from Edward IV of England here in 1462, and signed the Treaty of Ardtornish. This was a somewhat futile agreement to the effect that, if the Lords of the Isles consented to swear allegiance to Edward, they would get an English pension. It was also agreed that, in the event of England conquering Scotland, they would be given half the lands north of the Forth (the other half being promised to the Douglases). As the Lords of the Isles already held most of the land promised, this was hardly of much value, and when the English failed in their conquest, James IV was very quick to start dismantling the Lordship.

Where to Stay and Eating Out

expensive

Kilcamb Lodge, Strontian, ✆ (01967) 402 257, 🖷 402 041, overlooks Loch Sunart to the Morvern Hills and Ardnamurchan in an idyllic setting. This is a lovely place to stay: relaxed and friendly with a communal jigsaw for wet days and convivial company as well as excellent food.

Meall Mo Chridhe Country House, in Kilchoan, ✆/🖷 (01972) 510 238, was an 18th-century manse. An imposing country house above the village, it has recently been opened as an up-market guest house with excellent food—home-made bread, fresh seafood and game.

moderate

Cuildarroch, near Lochailort on the Road to the Isles, ✆ (01687) 470 232, 🖷 510 238, is a moderately priced Wolsey Lodge run by Gerald and Barbara Collins. There is a proper family-home atmosphere and excellent food. **Loch Sunart Hotel**, Strontian, ✆ (01967) 402 471, is a small 18th-century country house on the shore of the loch, marvellously situated for exploring Ardnamurchan. *Only open April–Oct.* **Feorag House**, Glenborrodale, Acharacle, ✆ (01972) 500 248, is also on the shore of Loch Sunart, offering a soothing haven of tranquillity and comfort.

Kinacarra Restaurant, Kinlochmoidart ✆ (01967) 431 238, is an unexpected bonus for such a remote place. Good home-cooked meals are served in what was once the village schoolroom by Frances and Angus MacLean, who look after you with warmth and gusto.

cheap

Clanranald Hotel, Acharacle, ✆ (01967) 431 202, no longer features in tourist brochures, but is still the place to go for if you want local atmosphere and Highland hospitality. It's a homely, slightly rundown hotel and bar with plenty of character and not too many frills. **Belmont**, in Acharacle, ✆ (01967) 431 266, is a very comfortable and reasonable B&B in a former manse.

See also self-catering in **Kinlochmoidart**. p.122.

The Great Glen—Fort William to Inverness 128
Lochaber 128
Invergarry to Kyle of Lochalsh—a Detour 135
Invergarry to Inverness 137
Fort Augustus 137
Loch Ness 139

Central Highlands

The Great Glen—Fort William to Inverness

The Great Glen—Glenmore Albin—*Gleann mor na-h Albin*—is that diagonal slash across the Highlands from Loch Linnhe in the southwest to Inverness and the Moray Firth in the northeast. It was carved out by receding ice in the last Ice Age, leaving a chain of lochs and rivers, now linked by the Caledonian Canal. Even before the canal, the Great Glen provided a route north as early as the time of St Columba. Although the route to Inverness is a well-worn trail, it offers many detours into less frequented glens and hills. As you go northeast the climate changes from the benign pearly dampness of the west to a more bracing easterly bite which can be diamond-hard and bright in winter.

Tourist Information

Spean Bridge: ✆ (01397) 712 576 (*open April–Oct*).

Lochaber

Lochaber, the region from Loch Leven to Glen Garry and out west to Moidart, has always been synonymous with the names Macdonald and Cameron. This territory, including the Nevis range and part of the Rough Bounds, was a seething turmoil of Jacobite unrest and has witnessed many a ferocious battle.

The A82 from Fort William follows one of General Wade's roads to Spean Bridge where several routes meet. To the west of the road on a large expanse of grazing land, you pass some rather unexpected ranch-style buildings, weathered now from their original sickly yellow with 'Great Glen Cattle Ranch' emblazoned on their walls. During the post-war years of hardship and shortage around 1946, Mr Joseph William Hobbs, an Englishman who had spent many years on ranches in Canada, decided to open a ranch in Scotland. He bought 10,000 acres here, revitalized what had been poor land and turned it into a highly successful Canadian-style ranch, producing 'beef in quantity'. It was a great success and he was given the Freedom of Fort William for his efforts. During his time here he lived at **Inverlochy Castle**, a baronial mansion built for the 3rd Lord Abinger in 1863, and now the very expensive **Inverlochy Castle Hotel** (✆ (01397) 702 177; *see* pp.107, 108 and 110).

It is not generally known that John Buchan's famous novel *John Macnab* is based on a true story connected with this place. An officer in the Cameron Highlanders, Captain James Brander-Dunbar of Pitgaveny near Elgin, together with some fellow officers, bet Lord Abinger that they could 'poach a stag, a salmon and a grouse' from his estate, undetected, and lay them at the door of Inverlochy Castle. By various means they carried out their objective and the *gralloch*—viscera—of the stag was delivered at breakfast the next day, on a silver dish from which the cover was removed by the butler. Proof of this story remains at Pitgaveny: the stag's head, labelled 'Poached in Inverlochy 1887'; a framed cheque made out to J. B. Dunbar, poacher; and a copy of Buchan's book signed 'To John Macnab from John Buchan'.

Spean Bridge Mill, ✆ (01397) 712 260 (*open daily*) has weaving demonstrations, a Clan Tartan Centre, a gift shop and a restaurant.

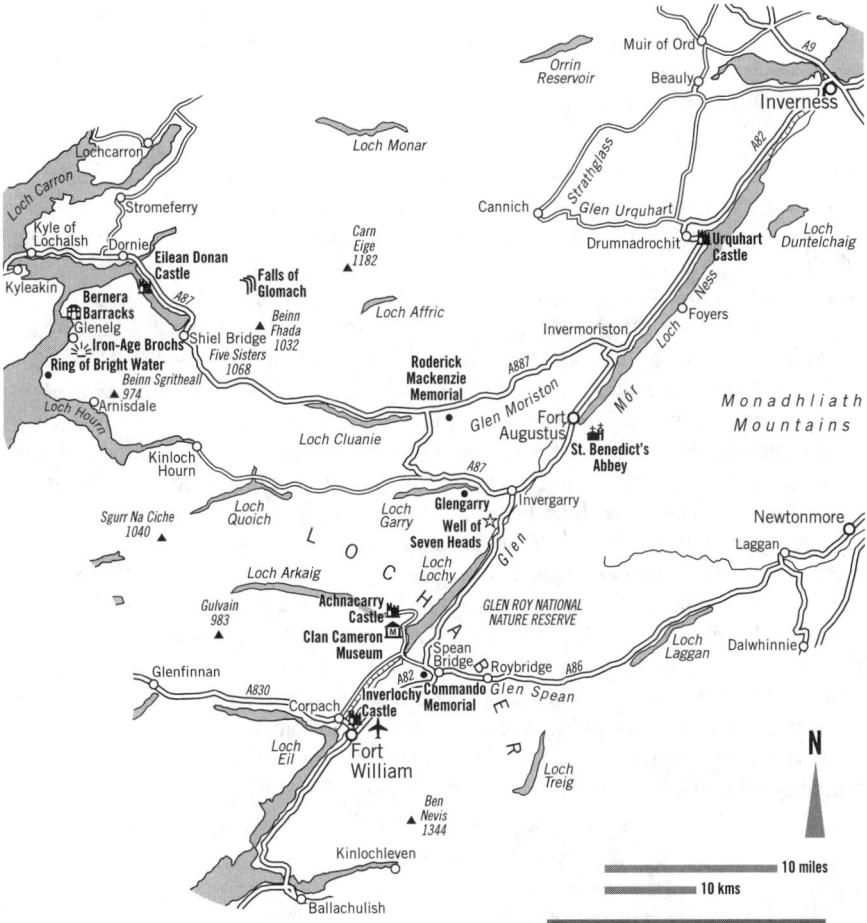

Central Highlands

Just northwest of Spean Bridge is the impressive **Commando Memorial** by Scott Sutherland, erected in 1952. A bronze group of commandos, high on a stone plinth, look out over their former training area in Lochaber and the Great Glen. To the northwest lies Achnacarry, home of the Camerons of Lochiel, which served as their headquarters during the Second World War. At **Highbridge**, a couple of miles west of Spean Bridge, one of General Wade's most remarkable bridges was built across the 100ft gorge of the River Spean. Most of the original structure is in ruins and a later metal bridge no longer spans the gap, but the site is spectacular: in summer the river seems little more than a stream, but when it is swollen with snow-melt and rain it is an awesome torrent. It was here that the first 'engagement' of the '45 occurred, and it is said that the outcome decided those of the chiefs who had not yet committed themselves.

Lowlanders Defeated at Highbridge

Two companies of the Royal Scots were on their way to Fort William as reinforcements at a time when it was known that local people were hatching mischief. The soldiers were mostly new recruits and as they approached the high bridge they heard bagpipes and discovered that 'a party of Highlanders' was in possession of the bridge. Macdonald of Keppoch, having heard of the march, had dispatched Macdonell of Tirandrish to set up an ambush here. The Highlanders numbered only about ten, but were sited cunningly to give the illusion of a larger force. The sound of the pipes skirled out from the high ground across the river, and Captain Scott, in command of the Royal Scots, sent his batman and a sergeant across the bridge to scout. The Highlanders disposed of the unfortunate pair and then leapt about brandishing their weapons and holding out their plaids between them, terrifying the raw recruits. Captain Scott, deeming it expedient to retire, turned his troops about and marched back the way they had come. As they hurried back up Loch Lochy between the hills and the water, their retreat was harried by the Highlanders, who fired down on them from above with just five old hunting guns between them. Keppoch had summoned more men to head them off and they were finally trapped at Laggan just south of Invergarry. With some soldiers dead and several wounded, Captain Scott, himself also wounded, was persuaded by Keppoch to surrender before there was a blood bath. His white gelding was dispatched to Prince Charles in Moidart, and Scott was imprisoned at Achnacarry. Here, Lochiel 'treated him more as a brother than an enemy and a prisoner', while Lady Locheil dressed his wounds herself. The wavering chiefs decided in favour of the prince. The affair is remembered in the pibroch 'The Rout of the Lowland Captain'.

And wild and high the 'Camerons' Gathering' rose,
The war-note of Lochiel, which Albynn's hills
Have heard, and heard, too, have her Saxon foes:
Now in the noon of night that pibroch thrills,
Savage and shrill! But with the breath that thrills
Their mountain pipe, so fill the mountaineers
With the fierce daring which instills
The stirring memory of a thousand years,
And Evans', Donald's fame rings in each clansman's ears.

From 'Childe Harold's Pilgrimage' by Lord Byron

The Clan Cameron Museum, at Achnacarry, off the B8005 at the southwest end of Loch Lochy (*open mid April–mid Oct daily afternoons only*), covers the history of this proud clan, described by General Wolfe as the 'bravest clan among them' in his description of Culloden. Though not one of the largest clans, the Camerons made up for their relatively small numbers by acts of chivalry and honour throughout history. They were always loyal to the Stewart cause. Donald, the 19th chief, known as 'the Gentle Lochiel', escaped to France with Prince Charles after Culloden, where he was conspicuously courageous; and his brother Alexander, Jesuit chaplain to the prince, was captured and died in a prison hulk on the Thames. Another brother, Archibald, doctor and ADC to the prince, also escaped to France, but returned, possibly to try and recover the Jacobite gold lost in Arisaig after a sea battle. He was captured and executed in 1753, the last man to die for the Jacobite cause.

Achnacarry Castle has been the home of the Camerons of Lochiel since the 1660s and the present house, designed by James Gillespie Graham, dates from 1802. The previous house was burnt down in reprisal for Gentle Lochiel's sympathies at Culloden; only an ivy covered stump of it survives, near the stables. A row of magnificent beech trees follows the line of the river at Achnacarry. It is said that Lochiel was planting a formal beech avenue here when news of Prince Charles' landing at Loch nan Uamh came to him. In a frantic rush to join the Prince, he heeled the young seedlings into a temporary trench intending to deal with them on his return. He never came back.

Five miles to the southwest off the B8004, **Erracht** lies tucked away up a track. This was the home of Alan Cameron of Erracht who, in 1793, raised the 79th Highlanders—the Cameron Highlanders, subsequently amalgamated and re-amalgamated to become what is now the Highlanders. A cairn was unveiled here in 1993 by Colonel Sir Donald Cameron of Lochiel. When the ceremony was over, a lone piper walked slowly away up towards the house playing the *Pibroch o' Donuil Dubh*, the haunting sound of his pipes receding until he was out of earshot.

Glen Roy leads off the A86 about 3 miles east of Spean Bridge at Roybridge. The River Roy tumbles through wooded gorges to meander at a more stately pace across the valley floor, bare hills rising on either side. Stop at the large observation car park some way along and look up the valley. A number of horizontal lines run across the upper hillside, each line exactly matched by one on the opposite side of the valley. These **Parallel Roads** mark the receding shoreline of an ice-lake in the late Ice Age, about 11,000 years ago, and are geologically famous because of their clarity. Among the scientists who puzzled over these scars was Charles Darwin. There are other parallel roads in this area, but this viewpoint is much the best. Several secret glens lie up beyond the end of the track and there are marvellous walks—take a proper map. Walk on up the Roy and then follow the track east to Loch Spey, where the Spey rises in the hills south of the Corrieyairack Pass very close to the source of the Roy.

The Corrieyarich Pass was an important military route and it was once possible to take a carriage through to Fort Augustus on Wade's road, today a track. Built to facilitate troop movements between the Highland forts, this route was used by Prince Charles in August 1745. General Cope was preparing to march his men through the pass on their way to Fort Augustus when he heard that the Prince, who now commanded a force of about 3,000 men, planned to ambush him there. Fully aware that it would be suicidal to attempt to force his way over this high, wild spot against men who knew every inch of it, Cope decided to abandon the plan.

The Prince meanwhile prepared his ambush and was thoroughly put out when Cope failed to materialize. All he got for his efforts was the capture of a few deserters from Cope's army, who told him of their general's change of plan.

From Roy Bridge the A86 winds through Glen Spean to Loch Laggan and into the Spey Valley, a lovely drive with the massive lumps of the Monadhliath (grey) Mountains to the north. About three-quarters of the way along Loch Laggan on its opposite shore, stands **Ardverikie House**, an astonishing pile which replaced an attractive shooting lodge where Queen Victoria had stayed with Prince Albert for about a month in 1847. They were looking for a Highland retreat and were much taken with the place, complete with murals by Landseer. Their host was Lord Abercorn, who had rented the house from Lord Henry Bentinck. The royal party stretched the capacity of the house so much that the Abercorn's four eldest children were moved out of their cosy nursery into rather cramped quarters in the home farm. Four-year-old Claud was so outraged by this that when he was presented to the Queen in his party kilt, he refused to bow and instead stood on his head, revealing the secret all Sassenachs long to know. He was suitably chastized and promised to apologize. But the Queen had not been amused and her expression so unnerved him that he stood on his head again and was banished for the duration. (In later life he became an MP and Lord of the Treasury, and in 1887 ADC to the Queen for ten years.) It rained continuously during the royal visit which is perhaps the reason they decided not to buy the house, which unfortunately burnt down in 1873.

From Kinlochlaggan you reach **Laggan**, a scattered settlement with two prominent churches, one a ruin with its tower preserved. There are no particular tourist attractions here but it is a good place for a base from which to explore the Monadhliath Mountains and for excellent walks to the west (over the Corrieyarich Pass) and to Glen Roy. This route runs through Strath Mashie into the Spey valley where the river, having gathered volume in its tumble from the hills, meanders over wide Strath Spey past Newtonmore (see p.172) and on down to the sea.

The Battle of the Shirts

On up the A82 from Spean Bridge, the road hugs Loch Lochy until the Caledonian Canal links it with Loch Oich at Laggan. This isthmus was the site of a famous battle—*Blar na Leine*—the Battle of the Shirts, fought between the Macdonalds and the Frasers in 1544. The Clanranald Macdonalds had rejected their legitimate chief Ranald in favour of a renowned leader, John of Moidart, and Ranald had been sent to his mother's kinsmen, the Frasers, to be brought up. When John was taken hostage by James V, Ranald reappeared to claim his heritage. He insulted his clan at Castle Tioram by rejecting the feast they had planned in his honour and announcing that 'a few hens would be amply sufficient to celebrate the event', thus earning for himself the name 'hen chief' and banishment by his people. This was too much for his protector, Lord Lovat, who with the help of Huntly descended on Loch Lochy, determined to take revenge. John of Moidart, recently escaped from captivity, enlisted the help of the Camerons and the Glengarry Macdonalds and prepared for battle. They assembled on the shore of a lochan beneath Ben Tigh and fed on oatmeal (a small quantity of which each man carried tied up in his plaid) mixed with water from the loch. Each man then drove a stick into the peat moss, a common practice before battle, how many had been slain being indicated by the number of sticks not retrieved afterwards. The battleground is now partly under water since Loch Lochy was raised several feet during the making of the canal. Here, 300 Frasers took on and were considerably outnumbered by John of Moidart and his men. Because it was an intensely hot July day, the men threw off their plaids, jackets and vests, and fought in their shirts which were knee-length 'tunics'. Lovat's son, the Master of Lovat, who had been left safely at home by his father, appeared on the scene and was killed almost immediately, fuelling the fury of the Frasers. Fighting chest-to-chest, the combatants were 'felled on each side like trees in a wood'. Ranald, the 'hen chief', fought like a hero but was killed by a dishonourable trick—his assailant crying out to him to beware of a man behind, and then killing him from behind when he spun round. Of the 1,000 men engaged, only 12 survived—all Macdonalds. The Frasers perished to a man, leaving the clan leaderless— fortunately 80 of the gentlemen's wives were pregnant at the time and each one, it is said, produced a male heir.

Further up the west side of Loch Oich, **Tobar nan Ceann** is the 'well of the heads' marked by a monument beside the road. An obelisk supports the bronze heads of seven men, held together by a dirk through their hair. Beyond, steps lead through a damp tunnel to a sinister well. Alasdair Macdonald, 12th chief of Keppoch, and his brother Ranald were murdered by their ambitious uncle Alastair Buidhe in 1663. For a while none of their kinsmen dared to avenge the murder, but the Keppoch Bard, Ian Lom Macdonell, poured forth such a torrent of invective against the murderers that Sir James Macdonald of Sleat felt obliged to do something. He dispatched Ian Lom up the valley of the Spean to Inverlair, west of Loch Laggan, where the murderer and his six sons were hiding. Justice was done. The seven men were beheaded and their heads were carried in a sack to Invergarry. Before presenting them to Macdonell of Invergarry (as a reproach for not having done the deed himself), Ian Lom washed them in the well on Loch Oich. The monument was erected by the 15th and last chief Macdonell of Glengarry in 1812. Inscribed in English, Gaelic, French and Latin are the words: 'this ample and summary vengeance'. The heads were buried in a little glade in Invergarry and the bodies at Inverlair. Some years ago the bodies were exhumed to prove the truth of the gory tale: seven headless skeletons were discovered, without coffins.

The ruin of old **Invergarry Castle** stands perched on a rock rising sheer from the waters of Loch Oich in what was a position of great strength. The rock is known as *Creag an Fhithich*—the Raven's Rock, which used to be the war-cry of the Macdonells of Glengarry whose stronghold this was. Tradition holds that the castle was created with stones passed from hand to hand by a chain of clansmen from Ben Tigh, some 7 miles away. Built in the early 17th century for the Macdonells of Glengarry, it was razed in 1654 by General Monk who reported that he had 'burned Glengaries new House' and that 'the remaining structure I order'd to be defaced by the pyoneers.' However, it was repaired by 1691 and described as 'ane extraordinary strong house. It is fortified and cannot be taken without great cannon.' At around this time, a detachment of red coats were sent from Inverness to take the recently rebuilt castle. Glengarry himself was at home, looking out from a castle window with his armourer. He waited till the column of invaders was nicely lined up, then told his armourer to fire through the window. He did so and picked off enough of the enemy, including their commander, to send them scurrying back to Inverness. In 1727 it was occupied briefly by an Englishman, Rawlinson, who was manager of the local iron smelter. The story of how he 'invented the kilt' is hotly denied by Scots purists. Rawlinson noticed the discomfort of his men working in the heat dressed in their 'breacan feile'—belted plaids, and suggested that they cut the cloth so that the upper portion could be removed leaving only the 'feile beag' or 'philibeg' or 'little kilt' that we know today. Those who refute this 'ridiculous' theory argue that the *feile beag* was worn long before Rawlinson was a gleam in his father's eye. Prince Charles stayed at the castle during his escape from Culloden in 1746 and it was blown up by Cumberland's forces in retaliation. It was never rebuilt and is now in danger of crumbling away .

Invergarry was built as an estate village in the 1860s by its new owner, Edward Ellice, who already owned Glen Quoich. Ellice, by the standard of many Victorian estate owners, was a good landlord, providing solid cottages, a school, hotel, cottage, hospital and church. They were picturesque buildings and they survive today, most with the Ellice monogram incorporated into their fabric. The **Glengarry Visitor Centre**, ✆ (01809) 501 424, on the site of the old inn by the Invergarry Hotel, has exhibitions of local and natural history, and up-to-date information on tourist attractions and facilities in the area.

Sports and Activities

Keen novice fishermen should contact **Fishing Scotland** at Roybridge, ✆ (01397) 712 812, where there is excellent fly fishing tuition in lovely scenery.

Where to Stay

expensive

Inverlochy Castle Hotel, ✆ (01397) 702 177, 🖷 702 953, *www.inverlochy.co.uk.* *See* pp.107, 108, 110 and 128.

Invergarry House, a forbidding Victorian pile overlooking Loch Oich in a lovely setting, was built as a baronial mansion between 1866 and 1869 by David Bryce. It is now **Glengarry Castle Hotel**, ✆ (01809) 501 254, 🖷 501 207, *www.glengarry.net*, its rather gloomy exterior belying a wonderfully comfortable and gracious inside, complete with stuffed birds and oil paintings. Some of the bedrooms—the 'superior' ones— have four-posters and sumptuous furnishings. There are a couple of 'de luxe' rooms, which are even grander. The food is good, the gardens pretty and the resident ghost has been seen quite recently. Run by David and Janetta MacCallum, the atmosphere is friendly and nothing is too much trouble for them. There is a tennis court and some rowing boats are available, enabling you to row down to Old Invergarry Castle or do some fishing on the loch. *Open Easter–early Nov.*

The Old Station, Spean Bridge, ✆ (01397) 712 535, is well worth a detour for exceptional seafood. The train still stops here. *Open April–Oct for dinner, 6.30–9.*

moderate

Old Pines, Spean Bridge, ✆ (01397) 712 324, 🖷 712 433, is a delightfully informal, family orientated home with excellent food and comfortable rooms catering for children (a babysitter is available).

Drumlaggan, at Balgowan just beyond Laggan, ✆/🖷 (01528) 544 242, is an idyllic 'retreat with a difference', conveniently placed between the ski slopes of Aviemore and Fort William. Will and Judy Carey offer hospitable and relaxed companionship while allowing you your own space. They're charming hosts and their detailed knowledge of the surrounding countryside is fascinating. Drumlaggan is just the place for walking or skiing holidays and the Careys can arrange transport. If you can't get a room here, the Careys will advise you where else to go in the area.

Invergarry Hotel, ✆ (01809) 501 206, 🖷 501 400, built in 1885, is picturesque and comfortable with a friendly atmosphere, well placed for a break en-route to Skye or Inverness. Locals frequent the bar, which has a good ambience.

Spean Bridge Mill (*see* above, p.128) has a restaurant.

cheap

Tomdoun Hotel, near Invergarry, ✆/🖷 (01809) 511 218, is a 19th-century coaching inn, unpretentious and very Highland, though it's for sale.

Invergarry to Kyle of Lochalsh—a Detour

At Invergarry the A87 takes you west to Kyle of Lochalsh, the stepping stone to Skye. This is an excellent, fairly new road along the north side of Loch Garry, over high moorland with sweeping views. It cuts through a wild, mountainous area which can only be explored on foot with a proper map—in the more popular areas it would be difficult to get lost, but in these more remote areas you can walk all day and not see a living soul. There are Munros galore, glens and waterfalls, secret lochans, and a number of good tracks.

Five miles west of Invergarry, a single-track road goes out to **Loch Hourn**, Loch of Hell. This, despite its name, is another glorious sea loch snaking out towards Skye, steep-sided and treacherous for sailors in certain winds. The road, which runs for miles through a landscape that was once an inspiration to the artist Landseer, is much bleaker since the damming of Loch Quoich by the Hydroelectric Board. It stops at Kinloch Hourn but there are a number of good walks including a track north through the hills to Glen Shiel. Another goes west, partly inland and partly following the north shore of Loch Hourn, right out to the mouth of the loch and well worth the effort. You can get scones and tea in the old farm steadings at Kinloch Hourn in the summer.

The A87 runs north of Loch Cluanie into Glen Shiel, dominated by the Five Sisters of Kintail that rear vertically on each side, a patchwork of grass, rock and scree, with glens slashed into the hillsides by rivers and burns.

At **Shiel Bridge**, on Loch Duich, 10 miles west of Cluanie, a narrow, twisting road branches off left and climbs over the **Mam Ratagan**—*mam* being Gaelic for Pass—the only way to Glenelg by land. This was the route taken by the drovers bringing cattle from Skye down to trysts at Falkirk and Crieff. The unfortunate beasts swam or were towed across the swirling channel from Kylerhea on precarious floats. This was also an important military route and when Johnson and Boswell travelled this way in 1773 soldiers were still working on it. The gaunt ruin of **Bernera Barracks**, built in 1722 and used until after 1790, lies north of Glenelg village. Boswell eyed Bernera as he shepherded Dr Johnson, who was in a bad mood that day, towards what proved to be very poor lodgings: 'I looked at them wishfully, as soldiers have always everything in the best order.' Poor Boswell: the inn (now gone) was not a success. 'The room was damp and dirty, with bare walls, and a variety of bad smells.' Their discomfort was eased somewhat by a local laird who, knowing the inn, sent them rum and sugar to help them through the ordeal.

Glenelg Candles is a modern, all-timber Scandanavian-style structure in the garden of Balcraggie House, almost worth a visit for the innovative building alone. A shop sells books, gifts, candles, etc. and there is a good café with excellent home baking.

Glen Beag runs east off a narrow road 2 miles south of Glenelg. Here you can see two of the most splendid examples of Iron Age brochs: **Dun Telve** and **Dun Troddan**, built to provide shelter and refuge for the chiefs, their people and their livestock. Their double walls are pierced by a single small entrance, easily defended, and honeycombed with galleries, in which the people lived, leaving the central enclosure for the animals. Dun Telve is the best preserved, over 10m in height, the bell-shaped outline very clear. At the end of the road a track leads to Dun Grugaig, an earlier fort, on the brink of a steep gorge.

Not far south of Glen Beag is **Sandaig**, with its islands; the house where Gavin Maxwell lived with his otters was on the beach below Upper Sandaig—it was burnt to the ground and its site is marked by an inscription set into a rock. In his well-known books, such as *Ring of Bright Water* and *The Rocks Remain*, Maxwell called the place Camusfeàrna (bay of the alders) in order to protect his privacy. His ashes were buried here and one hopes that his restless spirit has found peace at last in one of the most beautiful corners of the west coast. There are many genuine Camusfeàrnas in Scotland, causing some confusion. The rough road goes on down to Arnisdale and Glen Corran on Loch Hourn, 10 miles or so to the south.

Back on the A87, stop at Morvich, at the head of Loch Duich. From here you can walk about 7 miles to the truly spectacular **Falls of Glomach**, past a couple of smaller waterfalls by way of introduction. The 370ft (114m) torrent thunders down in two cascades over a projecting rock into a stomach-churningly deep chasm. The sides of the gorge are hung with lush green ferns and foliage and the air sparkles with moisture. Don't expect to be on your own here. There is a National Trust for Scotland visitor centre at Morvich with audio-visual exhibitions and information.

Eilean Donan Castle (*open Easter–Sept daily; adm*) is one of the most photographed castles in Scotland and familiar to anyone who has seen the film *Highlander*. Standing on a rocky island reached by a causeway in Loch Duich, it was built on the site of an ancient fort in 1230 by Alexander II who hoped to re-establish Scottish rule after the defeat of the Vikings at Largs. The castle became the seat of the MacKenzies, Earls of Seaforth but what you see today is modern—a loose 20th-century interpretation of a medieval castle, not entirely accurate but nonetheless attractive.

The old castle was garrisoned by Spanish troops and used as an administrative base in 1719, supporting one of the Jacobite attempts to regain the throne for the Stuarts; in reprisal it was bombarded by English warships whose efforts reduced it to a complete ruin. Thus it stood for 200 years, until its complete 'reproduction' was commissioned in the 1930s. It is dedicated as a war memorial to the Clan Macrae, who held the castle as constables to the Earl of Seaforth—the 'MacKenzie coat of mail'. Among other things housed in the castle there are some interesting Jacobite relics.

moderate

Loch Duich Hotel, at Dornie, near Kyle of Lochalsh, ✆ 555 213, 🖷 555 214, is a well-known landmark in a superb position overlooking Eilean Donan Castle and Skye. It's very comfortable and they serve good food.

Conchra House Hotel, ✆ 555 233, 🖷 555 433, at Ardelve overlooks Loch Duich and Eilean Donan. It was built in the 1760s as the home of the local constable, who was supposed to keep the peace after the second Jacobite rising. It later became the home of the Macraes of Conchra, and later of Eilean Donan, who extended it for use as a shooting lodge at the beginning of the 20th century. It has recently been refurbished and modernized and is now a 'country house' hotel. Adjacent farm cottages have also been done up to provide cosy self-catering places.

Mrs Margaret Cameron, Marabhaig, Glenelg, ✆ 522 327, runs an extremely efficient, clean, comfortable bed and breakfast with lovely views across to Kylerhea. **Duich House**, Letterfearn, Glenshiel, ✆/🖷 555 259, dating from 1830, is a Wolsey Lodge, near Eilean Donan, with stunning views. Cosy and friendly.

The **Glenelg Inn**, ✆ 522 273, is not the one Dr Johnson stayed in. It is a modern conversion of former stables and is an excellent place, cosy, and convivial. Many locals drink here.

cheap

Ratagan Youth Hostel, Glen Shiel, near Kyle, ✆ 511 243, is in a stunning position surrounded by Munros. The perfect base for climbers.

Invergarry to Inverness

Continuing from Invergarry, on up the A82, to Aberchalder, the canal connects Loch Oich with Loch Ness, 5 miles to the northeast at Fort Augustus.

Fort Augustus

Tourist Information

The Car Park, ✆ (01320) 366 367 (*open April–Oct*).

History

Fort Augustus, at the southern end of Loch Ness, is the halfway halt in the Great Glen, a popular tourist centre with an ancient history. This was a base for St Columba and the early missionaries when travelling from Iona to convert the east coast. Their names survive in the place names of churches, wells, hills, cemeteries and dwellings throughout the district. The Gaelic name *Cille-Chumein*, which the village of Fort Augustus bore for 1,300 years, and by which it is still known to Gaelic speakers, derives from St Cummein, a successor of Columba. He built a church here, among other things, whose ancient Celtic bell survived until 1559. The Dowager Lady Lovat, whose son and husband were killed in the Battle of the Shirts in

1554, came on a pilgrimage to the battlefield. On their return they took the bell, intending to put it in their own church near Beauly. A sudden storm got up in Loch Ness and the oarsmen threw the bell into the loch as a peace-offering to the spirit of the lake. The boat was saved and from then on people would take water from where the bell was thrown and use it for medicinal purposes. There is a pre-Christian crannog, **Cherry Island**—*Eilean Mhuirich* (Maurice's Islet)— about a mile up Loch Ness from the town. Occupied by the Frasers as a fort, it used to be much larger, but when the canal was made Loch Ness was raised by some 9 feet, submerging much of the remains. A chief of Glengarry came courting a Fraser here, it is said, when the Macdonalds and Frasers were having one of their deadly feuds. Stories vary as to exactly what happened, but he and his seven-strong bodyguard or 'tail' came to an untimely end. His body was flung into the water and those of his 'tail' were buried close by.

Fort Augustus marked the extremity of Fraser lands and was the setting for many territorial battles against the men of Lochaber. During the 18th century it was the hub of General Wade's road network, a fort having been built just behind what is now the Lovat Arms Hotel to protect the entrance to Loch Ness (part of the wall can still be seen). After 1715 the English garrisoned the fort in the hope of controlling the turbulent Highlanders, and when General Wade started work a much more substantial fort was built, on the same design as those at Ruthven, Bernera and Inversnaid. Traces of this can now be seen incorporated in the present abbey buildings: little remains but the dungeons and ancient bastions.

Wade named his new fort after William Augustus, Duke of Cumberland, a fat schoolboy of eight, son of George II, who was to go down in history as Butcher Cumberland. Jacobites gained control of the fort in 1745 until after Culloden, when the 'Butcher' took up residence and used it as a headquarters from which to wreak his atrocious revenge on the Highlands. From here he issued commands that were to tyrannize and destroy any fight that was left in a defeated people, including many who were innocent. Johnson and Boswell stayed with the Governor of the Fort during their tour in 1773, and it was still garrisoned when the Caledonian Canal was opened in 1822, with the ladder of locks now a focal point in the middle of the town. The fort was sold in 1867 to Lord Lovat, descendant of the 'Old Fox of the '45' who was imprisoned in the dungeons here before his execution in London. Lovat gave the fort to the Benedictines, who established a monastery and opened a boys' public school in 1878 and an abbey in 1882. The school closed in 1993, but the abbey lived on and was given a new lease of life thanks to the ingenuity of the monks. Very sadly this venture failed at the end of the 20th century and the abbey is now for sale—the monks gone—a heartbreaking loss for the large Catholic community here.

The Clansman Centre, beside the bridge over the canal (✆ *(01320) 366 444; open April–Oct daily; adm*), shows how the clans lived in the Highlands, and includes live presentations and a talk in a Highland turf house. You can even be photographed in authentic Highland costume. There are clothing and weapon demonstrations.

Fort Augustus ✆ (01320–) ***Where to Stay and Eating Out***

moderate

One of the nicest places to stay in this area is the **Old Pier House**, Fort Augustus, ✆ 366 418, 🖷 366 770, a Highland farmhouse on the shore of Loch Ness, built about a hundred years ago and extended. Mrs MacKenzie runs it as a ranch-style riding centre, as well as a very convivial place to stay. You can have dinner here if you want in the pine-furnished dining room—bring your own wine—and it is the sort of place where *céilidhs* develop spontaneously. The family is musical and they speak Gaelic as well as Italian, French and German. If you are lucky, daughter Sasha may be at home. She is well known in Europe and America as a Celtic harpist with a wonderful true voice. The small riding centre offers hill and forest rides for riders of all standards and ages. There are also boats available on the loch, fishing and mountain bikes for hire. As well as accommodation in the house, there is a log cabin with a veranda which would make an idyllic honeymoon retreat. *Open April–Halloween.*

The Lovat Arms, Fort Augustus, ✆ 366 206, is delightful and old fashioned, friendly and comfortable, with good food. Other good places to eat include **The Gondolier**, where you get upmarket Highland food; **The Bothy Bite**, in an old smithy, where they also do backpackers' accommodation; and **The Lock Inn**, beside the canal, which is popular with locals.

Loch Ness

Loch Ness is world famous, thanks to Nessie; it is also extremely beautiful. About 23 miles long, an average of a mile wide and reaching depths of 900ft (278m), it is so long and narrow that its steep wooded banks form a wind-funnel, causing surprisingly rough waters at times. Before General Wade got to work building roads in the region, Loch Ness was the main artery of communication between the east and west, and even after the roads Butcher Cumberland kept galleys to patrol the water.

The Loch Ness Monster

Feelings run high over Nessie—the Loch Ness Monster—known to the cognoscenti as Nessiteras Rhombopteryx. Sceptics may scoff, but St Adamnan records a sighting of her in his biography of St Columba, when they were sailing up the loch to convert Inverness. Columba, it seems, had a calming effect on her when she threatened one of his monks who was swimming across the mouth of the Ness to fetch Columba a boat. The monster appeared with 'one hideous roar' and made for the swimmer. Columba raised his hand, invoked the name of God and made the sign of the cross, saying: 'Thou shall go no further nor touch the man; go back with all speed.' The monster was terrified, according to Adamnan, and fled 'more quickly than if it had been pulled back with a rope...' and she has never been troublesome again. It must be remembered, however, that Adamnan was writing some hundred years after the event, and viewed St Columba through very rosy spectacles. Setting aside whisky-induced hallucinations, and wishful-thinking sightings, many eye-witness accounts of Nessie come from people whose honesty and integrity are beyond doubt. A 16th-century chronicle describes 'a terrible beast issuing out of the water early one morning about midsummer, knocking down trees and killing three men with its tail.' Curiously, considering how much traffic there used to be on the loch in the old days, almost all sightings have been recent. A monk who was organist at Westminster Cathedral saw her in 1973, and several monks at Fort Augustus Abbey have seen her. In 1961 thirty hotel guests saw two humps appear in an explosion of surf and cruise half a mile before sinking. Bertram Mills was sufficiently convinced to offer £20,000 to have Nessie delivered alive to his circus. However logical and phlegmatic one is, it is impossible to drive down Loch Ness without scanning its dark waters hopefully. Anyone who spends a night at anchor in a boat on the fringes of the loch will find themselves starting up in the darkness every time a ripple slaps the hull. (Anyone who has seen the film *Loch Ness* may have noticed a slip-up in the continuity department: scenes show this inland loch to be tidal.)

The A82 is the busy main road along the west side of Loch Ness, giving plenty of opportunity to view the loch but not many stopping places. The B862/852, part of it the original Wade road, is much less busy, very attractive, but with fewer views of the loch, some sections being inland. About 10 miles north of Fort Augustus, this road forks: the left branch goes to Foyers, where there is a splendid waterfall (except in drought) and attractive woodland walks. The origin of the hotel or 'Kingshouse' here is that of the 'General's Hut' mentioned by Dr Johnson in his journal. Such houses were established at intervals along the roads as they were being built, to house the officers in charge of the labouring troops. In 1773 this one was 'now a house of entertainment for passengers, and we found it not ill stocked with provisions.' From Inverfarigaig, about 3 miles northeast of Foyers, there are a number of excavated remains of burial chambers, forts and cairns, some in good condition, including a vitrified Iron Age fort at Ashie Moor, west of Loch Duntelchaig.

Glenmoriston

The A887 runs west through Glenmoriston, from Invermoriston, about 7 miles north of Fort Augustus and this was the route Johnson and Boswell took on their way to Skye. They stayed in the glen: Johnson distributed largesse to a party of soldiers who were mending the road, as a result of which they turned up at the inn, got drunk and 'left blood upon the spot and cursed whisky next morning'.

A cairn stands beside the road near Achlain in memory of a brave, loyal Jacobite, Roderick Mackenzie, a travelling merchant who had the dubious honour to be a Prince Charlie look-alike. He was shot by government troops who mistook him for the Prince, and had the presence of mind to cry out, as he died, 'Villains, you have murdered your Prince!' With great rejoicing the soldiers cut off his head, perhaps in expectation of the £30,000 reward offered for it, and took it to Fort Augustus. A Jacobite prisoner who was asked to identify the head carried the deception further by swearing that it was indeed the Prince, and Butcher Cumberland took it off to London in high glee, giving the Prince enough respite to enable him to reach safety.

The Seven Men of Glenmoriston—three Chisholms, two Macdonalds, a MacGregor and a Grant—swore an oath never to surrender to the English after Culloden. They made their home in a cave in the glen and waged continuous war on Hanoverians and against Highlanders who acted as guides and informers to the army. They evaded capture and did much damage to their enemies. On 29 July 1746 Prince Charles was brought to them in Glenmoriston and they hid and entertained him for three weeks until it was time for him to move on. When he said goodbye, he gave each man three guineas and shook his hand. Afterwards, Hugh Chisholm refrained from giving his right hand to any other person.

The A887 joins up with the A87 which runs between Invergarry and Kyle of Lochalsh.

About 7 miles up Loch Ness from Invermoriston on the A82, a simple modern cairn beside the road is a memorial to John Cobb, who was killed on the loch in 1952 trying to beat the world water speed record in his jet-propelled boat *Crusader*. Travelling at about 206mph, it is believed that his boat hit floating debris. It disintegrated in a great burst of spray. The memorial is inscribed in Gaelic: 'Honour to the brave and to the humble.'

Urquhart Castle

Urquhart Castle (*open daily; adm*) stands on the southern tip of Urquhart Bay, just south of Drumnadrochit. There is free parking off the road from which you get an excellent overview if you can't face the crowds. (It was crowded, too, in 1873, when Queen Victoria passed by, but those crowds were there to see their queen.) The castle is impressive—a jagged keep surrounded by crumbling walls which rise sheer from the water, against a backdrop of loch and hills. Built in the 12th century on the site of a vitrified Iron Age fort and frequently fought over, this was once one of the largest castles in Scotland, a motte and double bailey construction guarding the Great Glen. Edward I occupied it in 1296 and 1308; Robert I captured it in 1308 and it became a royal castle. But in 1509, when the Lords of the Isles were forever challenging the authority of the Crown, it was given to John Grant of Freuchie by James IV in the hope that it would help him to maintain peace. Covenanters and Jacobites tried to hold it in their turn and it was finally blown up in 1692 by government troops to save it from Jacobite hands. Romantics believe that Nessie lives in a subterranean cavern beneath the castle.

There are two Loch Ness Monster exhibitions at **Drumnadrochit**, just north of Castle Urquhart. You won't learn anything from either of them except that, despite all our modern technology, microchips, satellites, and robots taking holiday snapshots on Mars, Nessie remains an enigma.

From Drumnadrochit the A82 hugs the loch to Loch Dochfour where the River Ness runs in tandem with the canal to Inverness and the sea. The A831 runs westwards along Glen Urquhart to Strathglass. A mile or so along this road you can take an alternative, more attractive route northwards to Inverness on the A833, over wild moor and woodland. The A831 reaches Cannich before turning north and continuing through some lovely glens, best explored separately from Beauly.

Loch Ness ✆ (01456–) ***Where to Stay***

expensive

Knockie Lodge, ✆ 486 276, 486 389, just off the B862, is a rambling pile overlooking Loch Ness. Once a family home and now a very 'select' country house hotel, where you half-expect to find Jeeves, discreetly unpacking your luggage and laying out your dinner jacket. This is a perfect retreat for older travellers.

Polmaily House, Drumnadrochit, ✆ 450 343, 450 813, is a splendid and very comfortable country house hotel, with good food. Tennis, covered pool and riding.

moderate

Cluanie Inn, Glen Moriston, ✆ (01320) 340 238, 340 293, has been a beacon of hospitality for the best part of 200 years, an oasis in a remote, bleak landscape. It is the epitome of a wayside inn, with cosy rooms and reasonable food, and is the ideal base for a walking/climbing holiday. **Glenmoriston Arms Hotel**, Invermoriston, ✆ (01320) 351 206, 🖷 351 308, has a Highland atmosphere and is good value.

cheap

Drumnadrochit Hotel, ✆ 450 218, 🖷 450 793, is a hideous modern glass house, next door to the Monster Exhibition Centre, that looks like an ocean liner at night, but it's convenient and very good for monster-spotting. There's plenty of jolly entertainment for the gregarious in the evenings.

Foyers Bay Hotel, Lower Foyers, ✆ 486 624, 🖷 486 337, is small, quiet and friendly, with a garden and reasonable food. **Foyers Hotel**, ✆/🖷 486 216, is larger and more expensive. **Glenurquhart House Hotel**, ✆ 476 234, 🖷 476 286, is in a pleasant position in this lovely glen and offers true Highland hospitality. **The Old Parsonage** at Croachy, to the east of Loch Ness, ✆ (01808) 521 441, is a nice, family run B&B guest house.

For self-catering try **Mrs Mackintosh**, Achmony, Drumnadrochit, ✆ 450 357, who has a development of well-equipped, detached timber chalets, dotted around a 30-acre birch wood.

Kyle of Lochalsh 144
North of Kyle of Lochalsh 146
Ullapool 152
North of Ullapool 153

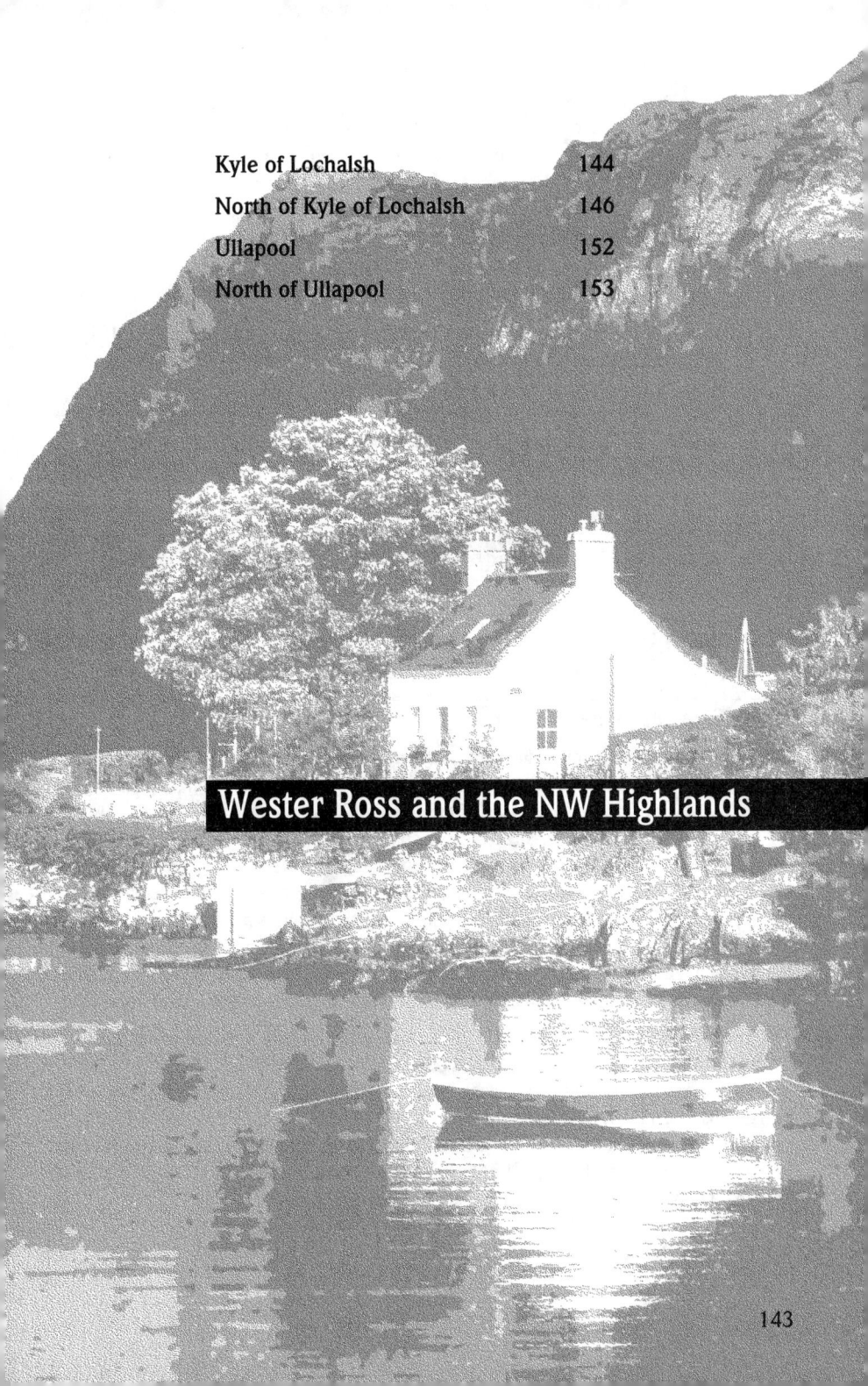

Wester Ross and the NW Highlands

This northwestern corner of Scotland, known as the Western Routes, offers the traveller a seaboard of unmatchable beauty, one of the few 'last wild places', once you abandon your car. There were virtually no roads in this area until General Wade's military roads were constructed in the first half of the 18th century. When the Highlands were devastated by the potato famine in the middle of the 19th century, Destitution Committees were set up to send supplies of meal and provisions to the starving Highlanders. Some of the 'Destitution Funds' collected were used to build access roads to remote communities, making it easier to send help and providing work for the people.

Even today, as in so much of the Highland hinterland, vast areas are totally inaccessible except on foot, and unlike other less remote places there are far fewer of the well-tramped byways festooned with cautionary notices. Your survival off-road here is up to your own common sense, equipment and experience. The climate is wild rather than harsh—mellow in the summer, gale-torn and often dramatic in the autumn and winter. The people are mainly crofters and fishermen, rapidly adding tourism to their economy.

Kyle of Lochalsh

Tourist Information

Kyle of Lochalsh: ✆ (01599) 534 276 (*open April–Oct*); **Gairloch**: Auchtercairn, ✆ (01445) 712 130.

Skye's Stepping Stone

Kyle of Lochalsh is the terminus for the railway from Inverness and the stepping stone to Skye. Until 1995 it was a bustling place, its car park crammed with vehicles waiting for the ferry across the Kyle, cheerful holidaymakers hanging about, stocking up in the shops. Now, with the new bridge marching across the narrow channel, not so many people linger here. The bridge has been a bone of contention since its inception. Many resent paying the rather exorbitant toll of £5.20 one way and have gone to great lengths to avoid doing so, resulting in some amusing stories. As foot passengers can cross free, farmers have been known to take their sheep to one side of the bridge, unload them, herd them across on foot, and transfer them to alternative lorries waiting on the other side. There have been demonstrations and ongoing enquiries into revising the toll, which has already been reduced for locals.

The bridge has a foot planted firmly on Eilean Ban, a tiny island in the Kyle where the writer Gavin Maxwell lived in the now derelict lighthouse cottages for the last 18 months of his life. There are plans for developing the island into some sort of memorial to Maxwell. However, suggestions for an interpretative centre based on his life and works, or for closed-circuit television to spy on otters here, with the island conserved as a wildlife haven, must have that eccentric recluse turning in his grave. One wonders if there is much in the way of wildlife left now that the bridge has brought traffic roaring overhead.

Cape Wrath
Sandwood Bay
Durness
Kinlochbervie
L. Inchard
A838
L. Laxford
Rhiconich
Eriboll
Handa I.
Laxford Bridge
Ben Hope 927
Handa Island Nature Reserve
Scourie
Loch Stack
Eddrachillis Bay
A894
Kylesku Bridge
A838
Pt. of Stoer
Loch Glencoul
Inverpolly National Nature Reserve
Drumbeg
Quinag 808
Eas-Coul Aulin
Loch Assynt
Enard Bay
Lochinver
Inchnadamph
Rubha Cóigeach
Inverkirkaig
Ardvreck Castle
Suilvern 731
Ben More Assynt 998
The Minch
Reiff
The Hydroponicum
Achiltibuie
A835
A837
Summer Is.
Ben Mor Coigach 743
Cromalt Hills
Priest Is.
I. Martin
Greenstone Pt.
Gruinard I.
Gruinard Bay
Little L. Broom
Ullapool
Rubha Reidh
Laide
L. Broom
Cove
Ewe
Inverewe Gardens
Dundonnell
Lael Forest
Ben Dearg 1081
Heritage Museum
Fionn Loch
An Teallach 1062
A832
Poolewe
Braemore
L. Gairloch
Gairloch
Loch Maree
Lochan Fada
Corrieshalloch Gorge
Loch Glascarnoch
Ben Wyvis 1046
Redpoint
A832
A835
Loch Fannich
L. Torridon
Lower Diabaig
Bein Eighe 1009
WESTER ROSS
Rona
Kinlochewe
A832
Loch Luichart
Garve
Dingwall
The Storr 719
Sound of Raasay
Inner Sound
Bein Eighe National Nature Reserve
Torridon
Achnasheen
Strathpeffer
Shieldaig
BEN-DAMPH FOREST
Muir of Ord
APPLECROSS FOREST
Applecross
Loch Damh
A890
Loch Monar
Raasay
Toscaig
Lochcarron
L. Carron
L. Kishorn
Stromeferry
Kyle of Lochalsh
Plockton
N
A87
Skye
Kyleakin
Broadford
Shiel Bridge
Beinn Sgritheall 974
10 miles
10 kms

Wester Ross

North of Kyle of Lochalsh

Keep to the left out of Kyle of Lochalsh and follow the road and railway to Plockton. There are lovely views west to Raasay and Skye and north to Applecross.

Plockton, in a sheltered appendix off the southwest of Loch Carron, was laid out as a planned Highland village in 1794. Once a working fishing village with attractive stone dwellings around its bay, it is now a picturesque tourist trap, much gentrified, its smart cottages gleaming with fresh paint, its pretty gardens adorned with velvet lawns, lush shrubs, birches and pines, even palm trees. Everything is neat and tidy in this 'holiday village'; the upturned fishing boats on the shore and the boats on moorings in the ba y seem to have been carefully arranged to create a pleasing composition for the dozens of artists who flock to capture it on canvas. There are craft shops and restaurants and lots of places to stay.

From here the road follows the southern shore of Loch Carron to the narrows at Stromeferry (no ferry now) and up to Strathcarron at the head of the loch. Look in at the **West Highland Dairy** at Dailfearn Achmore, near Stromeferry, where they make speciality cheese and dairy products from cow's, goat's and sheep's milk.

Applecross has no orchards: it is a mountainous lump to the west of Shieldaig, its village on a bay on the west coast. A road runs up its eastern side from Loch Kishorn to Loch Shieldaig, with one minor road running out to Applecross village and down to Toscaig in the southwest. The name comes from Aber-Crossan—the estuary of the Crossan, now the River Applecross. St Maelrubha founded a Celtic Christian community here in 673 which lasted for 200 years until the Vikings destroyed it. Maelrubha was Irish with Pictish blood, and his monastery was second only to that of Iona. He brought Christianity to much of the far north and legend has him buried here as well as in a number of other places including an island in Loch Maree, where he was a hermit for a while, and in Strathnaver. There are the remains of a 15th-century chapel which was part of the monastery, and part of a cross slab in the graveyard. Some fragments of elaborate stonework survive inside the present church, built in 1817.

A road that is little more than a track runs right round all but the southwest corner of the peninsula, and the views to the west from the marvellous sandy beaches are staggering. The road out to Applecross village from Tornapress at the head of Loch Kishorn is called *Bealach-nam-Ba*—Pass of the Cattle—a steep, narrow road with hairpin bends that make the adrenalin flow, rising to 2,053ft (625m). The scenery is almost alpine, fringed by cliffs and rock spurs, dotted with glinting lochans and burns with the distant hills of Skye in the west. Cattle were driven over this pass from Applecross en route for the lucrative markets on the east coast; records for 1794 tell of some 3,000 cattle leaving the district. In the 18th century there were three blacksmiths working full time to prepare the cattle for the long trek to market: their payment was the heads of all slaughtered cows. An excellent walk from Applecross village takes you northeast along the valley of the river, through Strath Maol Chaluim and then either left to Kenmore (about 8 miles) or right to Inverbain (about 7 miles).

Loch Torridon washes the northern shore of Applecross, with Ben Damph forest to its east, beyond Ben Shieldaig and Loch Damh. There are several good hills to climb including Beinn Damh, Meall a Chinn Deirg (a Munro) and An Ruadh Stac. This is wild, rugged terrain, and very beautiful. The 26,000 acre, Torridon Estate was acquired by the National Trust for Scotland in 1967. There is a visitor centre at the road junction at the head of Upper Loch

Torridon, with the inevitable audio-visual presentation on the area and a programme of guided walks and advice. There is also a deer museum set up by a local man who certainly knows his deer and spares you no details, both about the damage they do and the way they suffer at the hands of man. Mountains of sandstone, 750 million years old, dominate the whole of this region with their distinctive peaks of quartzite. Queen Victoria was impressed: 'Glen of Torridon opened upon us, with the dark mural precipices of that most extraordinary mountain Ben Liughach, which the people pronounce Liarach...The mountains here rise so abruptly from their base that they seem much higher than our Aberdeenshire mountains, although, excepting Ben Sleach (3,216 feet) and a few others, the hills are not of any remarkable height and the level of the country or land itself is barely a hundred feet above the sea, whereas Balmoral is eight hundred feet to begin with.' Liathach and Bein Eighe are two of the most popular peaks to climb and there are organized hikes.

The Bein Eighe National Nature Reserve (pronounced Ben Ay) lies northeast of Torridon—the first of its kind to be established for the preservation and study of the remains of the Caledonian Forest. Wildlife in the area includes deer, wild mountain goat, wild cat, pine marten and eagles. The ubiquitous visitor centre is at Aultroy Cottage just northwest of Kinlochewe, with more advice, an illuminated model of the district and details about the work done on the reserve.

Driving west along the northern shore of Loch Torridon you pass scattered crofting townships with sea views backed by massive hills. From Lower Diabaig a track continues further round the coast to a youth hostel and from here it is a glorious walk up the rocky, sandy coast to Redpoint. The A896 takes you northeast through magnificent Glen Torridon to join the A832 at Kinlochewe. The A832 to the northwest from Kinlochewe runs along the southern shore of **Loch Maree**, dominated by Slioch on its opposite side—another Munro. Loch Maree is 12 miles long. Its name is derived from St Maelrubha, the monk who founded the monastery at Applecross, who lived for a while as a hermit on Isle Maree, just to the east of the biggest of the islands in the loch. Some say he was buried here: there is certainly a burial ground. Queen Victoria paid her respects to Maelrubha—*see* below.

About 8 miles along is the **Loch Maree Hotel** (*see* p.151). Nothing seems to have changed since Queen Victoria stayed here for six days in 1877. She enjoyed it greatly ('A very nice little house, neatly furnished'), making daily excursions to paint several of her attractive water-colour sketches. The wasps were so bad that gauze netting was put over the open windows. They also had a fair amount of rain and 'the midges are dreadful, and you cannot stand for a moment without being stung'. Be warned (this was mid-September)—midges are not respectful of rank. On one of their outings, to Upper Loch Torridon, where the royal party picnicked and sketched, they passed 'a row of five or six wretched hovels, before which stood barelegged and very ill-clad children, and poor women literally squatting on the ground'. On the Sunday she was there, there being no kirk nearer than Gairloch or Kinlochewe, they read prayers in the hotel during the day, watched locals passing by on foot to church, and set out at tea time in a 'four-oared gig' to visit Eilean Maree. They landed and inspected the well whose waters were alleged to cure insanity, and hammered pennies into a tree, following an ancient (probably pagan) custom: this was a 'clootie well'—another pagan institution.

The A832 leaves Loch Maree soon after the hotel and heads westwards towards Gairloch. At **Kerrysdale**, about 10 miles beyond the hotel, the River Kerry dashes towards the sea through mossy glades and silver birches, with a few gnarled oaks and feathery rowans. Carpeting the dappled turf are a profusion of wild flowers: lousewort, milkwort, primroses, bluebells, wood anemones, orchids and many more.

Take the very minor cul-de-sac left from Kerrysdale, past the sheltered anchorage of Shieldaig and the bay at Badachro. This was once a large fishing station where curers bought herring, cod, ling, etc. from local fishermen. Now the community life is centred on a tiny, friendly shop-cum-post office. The road, built with money from the Destitution Fund, goes on to Redpoint. Heather-carpeted moorland runs down to rocky cliffs and crescents of red-gold sand, with views across to South Rona and Raasay, with Skye beyond. Sit for a while on the sheep-cropped turf above the cliffs. An otter swims in the sea and builds its cone of fish-remains; wheatears, ringed plovers, linnets and skylarks fill the air with song; colonies of seabirds mass on the rocks: cormorants, shags, gulls, terns, fulmars, gannets. An old man with piercing blue eyes sits on a rock sucking an empty pipe: 'You could never be bored here' he says: 'if you run out of things to do, you can just watch the weather.'

Back at Kerrysdale turn left to **Gairloch**, a well-developed holiday resort with sandy beaches and several hotels. The hub of the community seems to be the Wild Cat Stores, purveyors of fresh milk, fresh baps and local chat. Opposite is the award-winning **Gairloch Heritage Museum** (*open April–mid Oct Mon–Sat; 18 Oct–29 Oct Mon–Fri; or by appointment ✆ (01445) 712 287; adm*), easy to miss or pass by, thinking 'oh, another of those', but it's well worth a visit. In only a few rooms one can learn a great deal about life in the western Highlands. The exhibits range from Pictish stones and relics to Victoriana. There is a portable pulpit from the days when preachers from the Free Kirk had no church and preached to outdoor congregations in all weathers. In addition there is an old ice-making machine dating from before the days of electricity; stuffed birds and wild animals; an illicit still; spinning wheels with various wools and natural dyes; a wash house; a school room with Gaelic on the blackboard; a village store; a fisherman and his gear. The highlight is the replica of the inside of a croft house, imaginatively set up with press buttons to illuminate it, set the spinning wheel in motion and animate the old woman in front of the peat fire. She sings a haunting Gaelic lullaby to the baby, rocking in a cradle. An annexe contains interesting history displays and old photographs of the area. You could easily spend a couple of hours in here.

Around Loch Ewe

Poolewe, about 5 miles northeast of Gairloch, is built around a bridge where the mighty force of water from Loch Maree thrusts its way out into Loch Ewe, forming the pool that gave the place its name. Loch Ewe was an important naval base in the Second World War and there are still gun emplacements on its west side.

An attractive dead-end road along the west side of Loch Ewe goes out to **Cove** at the mouth of the loch, where there is a cave so deep and sheltered that it was once used as a place of worship by the Wee Frees, who dis-established themselves from the Church of Scotland during in the mid 19th century and found themselves without churches in which to worship. Their main bone of contention was their objection to the Patronage Act of 1712, which gave the local laird the right to appoint ministers regardless of the wishes of the congregation.

Inverewe Gardens (*visitor centre and shop open mid Mar–31 Oct daily 9.30–5.30; restaurant 10–5; guided garden walks mid April–mid Sept Mon–Fri at 1.30; dog owners should* *note that dogs aren't allowed in the garden, and there is no shade in the car park; adm*), half a mile north of Inverewe, is famous to horticulturists all over the world and for many is the principal reason for visiting this area. It was created by Osgood MacKenzie, son of the laird of Gairloch, a Victorian who spent much of his early life on the Continent. If you can find a copy of his book *A Hundred Years in the Highlands* you will never regret buying it. Not only does it give a vivid portrait of life in the Highlands in the last century but it also gives an account of how he established this remarkable garden. His mother, a splendid woman, bought him the land in 1862, and her job was to build the house. The 'policies' consisted of a peninsula—*am ploc,* The High Lump: a high bluff of Torridon sandstone jutting out into the sea, consisting mostly of sheep braes and peat hags, with a narrow strip of land down by the shore. This was to be the garden, Osgood's creation. There was virtually no soil, though in a few places 'peat and rotten rock jumbled up together, which we thought grand stuff in comparison with the rest'. They had to excavate masses of rock; the 'ploc' caught the full force of the prevailing southwesterly gales and was continually soused with salt spray. The vegetation consisted of heather, crowberry and two tiny bushes of dwarf willow about 3 feet high. Osgood, who was 'very young and perfectly ignorant of everything connected with forestry and gardening', learnt entirely by trial and error. There were few roads and soil was carried in wicker creels. He planted an outer windbreak of Corsican and Scots pine behind deer and rabbit-proof fences. 'For four or five years my poor peninsula looked miserable, and all who had prophesied evil of it, and they were many, said "I told you so".' Plants were introduced from all over the world and he was not ashamed to admit that many of these did far better than native stock. Now there are some 2,500 species in 50 acres of woodland, covering a steep hillside that juts into the loch, sheltered by hills behind. The garden lies only a little to the south of the latitude that runs through Cape Farewell in Greenland: it is the proximity of the Gulf Stream together with years of hard labour and acquired expertise that have been the key to the formation of this exotic, subtropical paradise. Osgood's daughter, Mairi T Nic Coinnich, inherited the garden when her father died in 1922; she made it over to the National Trust for Scotland in 1952.

Gruinard Bay

Gruinard about 11 miles north of Poolewe, has sandy beaches surrounded by hills and good views out to the Summer Isles. It is a magnificent spot with a campsite right on the beach at Mellon Udrigle. Gruinard Island, in the bay, has been much publicized over the years, and its story would make good subject matter for a spy thriller. In 1942 the Ministry of Defence wished to experiment with *Bacillus Anthracis* (anthrax) as a possible weapon of biological warfare. Some scientists from Porton Down in Wiltshire descended upon the island that winter and exploded six small bombs of anthrax. They then beat a hasty retreat, leaving a flock of sheep. The sheep died within days. The island was then sealed off with alarming notices warning the public not to go anywhere near it: Contaminated! It is said that anthrax spores can live on for a thousand years, but in 1987 a second team of scientists arrived, 'decontaminated' the soil, and, pronouncing it safe, restored it to its original owner.

A small sign beside the road at **Sand,** just to the east of Laide on the southwest corner of Gruinard Bay, points the way down a cliff path to two caves. The largest was a meeting place for hundreds of years and was used as a church by dis-established Presbyterians as late as 1843. The smaller cave was inhabited by an old woman and her girl companion in 1885. Families evicted from their crofts during the Clearances used to take shelter here. It is an idyllic place now, but must have been much less so for those unfortunate people huddled together inside with what they had saved of their possessions and livestock.

The A832 skirts Little Loch Broom (the Ardressie Falls about two-thirds of the way along are worth a look), and cuts across the moors. The road from Dundonnell, by Feithean, to Braemore Junction was another of the Destitution Roads built during the potato famine. Despite its gloomy origins, it's a lovely drive today.

Braemore Junction is at the confluence of the rivers Broom, Cuileig and Droma, known locally as 'The Valley of The Broom'. Stop at the large observation car park just before the A835 and look down into the junction of the three valleys, the steep wooded banks ablaze with colour in autumn. Less than a mile further on, a sign on the left marks the Corrieshalloch Gorge and the Falls of Measach, only a short walk from the road. An alternative approach on the A835, round the corner, has another car park and signs.

Corrieshalloch Gorge is unforgettable: a mile-long box canyon, 200ft (60m) deep and between 50ft and 150ft wide (15–46m), its sheer rock walls festooned with ferns and mosses, saxifrage, sorrel, tufts of grasses and wood-millet. Miraculously rooted wych elm, birch, hazel, sycamore, Norway maple and beech trees cling to its sides, as do goat-willow, bird-cherry and guelder-rose. There is an observation platform from which to view the Falls of Measach, a single cascade of 150ft (46m) that seems to hang in the air like smoke. For those who don't suffer from vertigo, there is a much better view from the suspension bridge that spans the gorge, erected in the 19th century by Sir John Fowler who also designed the famous Forth Railway Bridge. The deep pools below are rich in trout, and above the roar of the falls the angry 'pruk' of ravens can be heard from their nests on a ledge opposite the viewing platform.

The A832 takes you back down to the A832 at Gorstan and on to Dingwall and Inverness.

Sports and Activities

Applecross Peninsula Visitor Services, ✆ (01520) 744 262, offer half- or full-day guided tours of the area in a Land Rover.

Where to Stay and Eating Out

Kyle of Lochalsh ✆ (01599–)

moderate

Lochalsh Hotel, Kyle of Lochalsh, ✆ 534 202, 🖷 534 881, is an enlarged version of the original hotel here, overlooking the Kyle and the old ferry slipway. Now there is no longer a constant bustle around the jetty, this is a more peaceful place to stay than it used to be, though still close to the middle of the village.

moderate–cheap

Plockton Hotel, ✆ 544 274, 🖷 544 475, overlooking the water, in converted terraced houses, is cosy and good value. **Lochcarron Hotel**, ✆ (01520) 722 226, 🖷 722 612, also right on the water and slightly more expensive, has two 'lochside suites' and the hills behind. They serve lots of local seafood dishes. The **Kyle Hotel**, Main Street, ✆/🖷 534 932, is right on the road and very friendly.

For B&B try **Mrs Mackenzie**, at Duirinish near Plockton, ✆ 544 204, a working croft with outstanding views across the Sound of Raasay to Skye; you will get a warm welcome. **Craig Highland Farm**, Plockton, ✆ 544 205, offers B&B or self-catering in traditional stone cottages in glorious settings (2–6 people). There are seals, otters and a heronery on the doorstep, and a rare breeds conservation centre.

Off the Rails, ✆ 544 423, is a convenient and imaginative café/restaurant in the dark, timber-lined waiting room of Plockton Station. The **Seagreen Restaurant & Bookshop**, Plockton Road, Kyle of Lochalsh, ✆ 534 388, in the old village school, has a relaxed atmosphere, a license, and the food (seafood and vegetarian, no meat) is all made with local ingredients. There is a garden to sit in and traditional music. The bookshop is excellent, selling books of local interest, paintings and cards.

Next to the Kyle Craft and Model Shop, in the long station building (full of railway memorabilia), **The Seafood Restaurant** (which also sells crafts and cards) has delicious fresh fish depending on the weather, also good meat and vegetarian dishes.

At **Erbusaig**, near Plockton, **The Old Schoolhouse**, ✆ 534 369, serves excellent candlelit dinners to the strains of Beethoven. You can also stay here.

Gairloch ✆ (01445–)

expensive

Loch Torridon Hotel, ✆ 791 242, 🖷 791 296, is a baronial red sandstone mansion overlooking the loch, with friendly staff, tasteful rooms and the ambience of a shooting lodge—which it once was.

moderate

About 8 miles along is the **Loch Maree Hotel**, ✆ 760 288, 🖷 760 241, moderately priced and splendidly unspoilt. This is predominantly a fishing hotel and displays an impressive log of catches on the hall table. The **Shieldaig Lodge Hotel**, ✆ 741 250, is renowned for its excellent food and cellar as well as for its comfortable rooms and splendid situation.

Gairloch has plenty of choices. **Little Lodge** at North Erradale, ✆ 771 237, is a nicely furnished converted croft house with glorious views, good food and only three bedrooms. **Creag Mor Hotel**, ✆ 712 068, 🖷 712 044, is bigger and also comfortable, looking over the harbour. **Old Inn**, ✆ 712 006, 🖷 712 445, about the same size, is slightly cheaper. **Tigh An Eilean Hotel** (House of the Island), at Shieldaig, Strathcarron, ✆ (01520) 755 251, 🖷 755 321, is a small hotel, with sea views from most of the bedrooms and good food.

cheap

Badachro Inn, ✆ 741 255, is a whitewashed inn with a small garden on the edge of the bay. It has only two bedrooms, is friendly, unpretentious and very cheap. **Kerrysdale House**, ✆ 712 292, is small and cosy. **Applecross Hotel**, Applecross, ✆ (01520) 744 262, is a celestial inn, at the sea end of the Pass of the Cattle. Nothing pretentious here, just a warm welcome.

If you are more interested in location than luxury, drive about 10 miles to the end of the diminishing single-track road from Gairloch to Rubha Reidh. **Rua Reidh Lighthouse**, ✆ 771 263, has been converted into holiday accommodation and is a marvellous place to stay. You are allowed to take your own food if you prefer. It is ridiculously cheap, with a choice of double or bunk rooms, and a 4-bed family room with shower. The position is unbeatable: the beaches and cliffs along this peninsula are wonderful and virtually deserted.

Sand Hotel, ✆/🖷 731 385, *www.westhighlands.com*, has wonderful views of the ocean, a friendly atmosphere and access to hill walking, fishing and watersports. Its 9 rooms are all ensuite and it has a bistro.

Ullapool

Tourist Information

Ullapool: Argyle Street, ✆ (01854) 612 135 (*open all year*). **Lochinver**: Main Street, ✆ (01571) 844 330 (*open Easter–Oct*).

Ullapool is about 13 miles from the Corrieshalloch Gorge, another beautiful drive down the River Broom, with Lael Forest to the east and lumpy hills to the west across the valley. (If you are into trees, the Lael Forest Garden Trail has over 150 different species of trees and shrubs, all labelled.) There are good views across Loch Broom, fringed with beaches and picturesque picnic spots.

Herring fishing used to be the main activity here: successful fisheries elsewhere encouraged the British Fisheries Society to establish a number of new fishing settlements in the Highlands and Islands in the hope of bringing a measure of prosperity to these parts. Founded in 1788, Ullapool was the first of these and the town had grown rapidly by the beginning of the 19th century. But by 1830 herring stocks were dwindling and the industry was in decline. The railway never got there and in 1900 the enterprise was considered a 'dismal failure' and its carefully designed grid-plan town downgraded to a 'dreary fishing village'. Then the road improved and, when east-coast trawlers discovered Ullapool's excellent deep-water anchorage and sheltered harbour in the 1920s, the town was regenerated. It became a popular rendezvous for the factory ships of Eastern Europe and Russia, and today you see them out at anchor in the bay.

After the boats came the tourists, and Ullapool is now a thriving holiday resort and the ferry terminus for boats to Stornoway in Lewis. Freshly painted houses line the sea front in an original curving terrace. At one end they look down on a jumble of quays and slipways cluttered with small boats and fishing gear, creels, spars, nets and fish boxes. Many of the buildings date from the 18th-century birth of the town, and they were lucky to have Thomas Telford for a while as Surveyor of Buildings.

Ullapool Museum and Visitor Centre (*open daily except Sun; adm*) in West Argyle Street has recently had a face lift. In a converted church, grade A listed, designed by Telford in 1829, it charts the development of the fishing industry and tells about life in the area from the arrival of the earliest settlers. 'The People of the Loch' is a good audio-visual presentation which you can watch from the old kirk pews.

There is a good range of shops, restaurants, cafes, bars and accommodation. The tourist office will arrange sea fishing and boating cruises, or you can hang about on the quay and ask someone off one of the boats. Across the loch at Lagaidh, Glasgow's Hunterian Museum has excavated a 1st millennium BC vitrified fort, an early AD broch, and remains of a 12th-century motte and bailey castle.

Local boats regularly visit the Summer Isles in season; or you could try **Summer Queen Cruises** from Ullapool, ✆ (01854) 612 472.

Ullapool ✆ (01854–) ***Where to Stay***

expensive

Altnaharrie Inn, near Ullapool, ✆ 633 230, is an old drovers' inn on the shores of Loch Broom, reached by private boat which you ring up for from Ullapool. Small and very select, its bedrooms are pretty and the food is sublime. It is the only place in Scotland to have been awarded two well deserved Michelin stars.

moderate

Tanglewood House, Ullapool, ✆/🖷 612 059, is a Wolsey Lodge perched up in the heather above Loch Broom, with panoramic views. Anne Holloway, the owner, is an innovative cook, and there is a 9-hole golf course close by. No smoking. **Morefield Hotel**, Ullapool, ✆ 612 161, 612 171, is also good for gourmets.

cheap

The Céilidh Place, Ullapool, ✆ 612 103, is a mildly eccentric, rather unexpected sort of Arts Centre where you can stay, eat wonderful seafood, and sometimes listen to live jazz, classical and folk music in the clubhouse opposite. The accommodation ranges from moderately priced, cosy bedrooms to a bunkhouse, from £10. There is a large, comfortable residents' sitting room, with a beamed ceiling and a 'trust' bar. You can browse among masses of books and games and make your own tea or coffee in an annexe kitchen. There is also a coffee shop and a bookshop.

Don't be put off by the name of the **Four Seasons Travel Lodge**, Garve Road, Ullapool, ✆ 612 905, 🖷 612 674. It's a rambling place only 5 minutes from the middle of Ullapool, right on the shore of Loch Broom, with lawns going down to the pebble beach and views to gladden the most sluggish heart. This is an excellent family base and they welcome dogs.

Brae Guest House, Shore Street, Ullapool, ✆ 612 421, is right on a busy corner in the middle of town, but it's cheerful and offers good Highland hospitality. **Ardureck Guest House**, North Road, Morefield near Ullapool, ✆ 612 028, is an excellent place overlooking Loch Broom, but it hasn't got a licensed bar. For a good B&B in the area, try **Mrs MacLeod**, Dornie House, Achiltibuie, ✆ 622 271, who has two bedrooms in a modern bungalow, with idyllic views across the water to the islands. *Open Mar–Oct.*

North of Ullapool

North of Ullapool you can be fairly sure that any track you take to the west will have a pot of gold at the end of it. The main road—A835/837—gives you a foretaste, but push west wherever you can and whenever you have time. About 7 miles beyond Ullapool, turn left off the A835 at Drumrunie. A narrow single track winds out through a wild landscape of hills and lochs to the Coigeach peninsula—you must walk the last couple of miles to Rubha Coigeach for windswept, uninterrupted views across the Minch to the Outer Isles. Down the western side of the peninsula is **Achiltibuie**, remote but not unpopulated because it has become a favourite spot for family holidays, based at the Summer Isles Hotel or one of the several good self-catering establishments or bed and breakfasts in the area. There is everything from walking and climbing, to fishing, boating, lovely beaches and trips to the Summer Isles, just to the west. Well-known but interesting is the **Summer Isles Garden of the Future**, or **Hydroponicum** (*open daily Easter–end Sept 10–6; adm*) near the hotel. Created by Robert Irvine, it has 'hi-tech soil-less growing houses'—an amazing place with three distinct climates emulating those of Hampshire, Bordeaux and the Canaries. Strawberries are picked fresh every day from April to October and bananas flourish. Figs, lemons, passion fruit, vines, vegetables, flowers and herbs all grow luxuriantly in greenhouses with liquid feed but without soil. The 90-minute tour is particularly instructive on solar energy. At the Lilypond Café you can sample the produce, much of it delicious. You don't have to tour the Hydroponicum to use the café (✆ (01854) 622 202).

Three miles to the north is the **Achiltibuie Smokehouse** (*open May–Sept daily except Sun; Oct–April weekdays*), where fish and meat are cured and there is a retail shop.

The sixteen or so **Summer Isles** are scattered out across the mouth of Loch Broom. They were put on the map by Sir Frank Fraser Darling, a learned ecologist who farmed the largest island, Tanera Mor, for five years during the Second World War and wrote about his experiences in *Island Farm.* Darling was a champion of the 'wholeness and interdependence' of the natural world and spent much of his life studying and writing about deer, sheep, birds, fisheries, agriculture and crofting. He also wrote the definitive *Natural History of the Highlands and Islands.* Both books are worth getting hold of.

118 people lived on Tanera Mor in 1881; by 1931 it was uninhabited. Today some of the cottages have been done up as holiday lets. Groups of self-sufficiency dreamers have tried to settle permanently, but none have lasted. Priest Island and Isle Martin are bird sanctuaries, owned by the RSPB.

The Inverpolly National Nature Reserve spreads across the northeast of the Coigeach peninsula, distinguished by the great lumps of Cul Beag, Stac Pollaidh and Stac Mor. The silhouette of Stac Pollaidh with its dramatic jagged ridge is familiar from photographs. The red sandstone is eroding alarmingly and several of its pinnacles have been lost in recent years—you can see chips and chunks scattered down the hillside. Stac Mor is the highest of these three and the views from the summit are stunning, but Stac Pollaidh is the most satisfying climb. There are several ways up, the shortest being a steep scramble from the car park at the bridge over the burn coming down from Coire Gorm, 5 miles along the road from Drumrunie. The path up the grassy hillside to below the summit is steep and earthy. From here you can explore the fantastic pinnacles but watch out for loose scree.

Ledmore is less than 8 miles beyond Drumrunie, where the A835 joins the A837. To the southeast the road runs 30 miles back to Bonar Bridge, through Strath Oykel. **Inchnadamph** at the head of Loch Assynt is about 5 miles north of Ledmore, along a passageway through the hills.

Assynt

There's a tortuous but spectacular drive to Loch Assynt and the north via the very minor road up the coast, starting from the Coigeach peninsula. Turn right at Badagyle beyond Loch Badagyle and twist your way up to **Lochinver** at the head of Loch Inver, with Stac Polly, Cul

Mor and Suilven towering to the east and an ever-changing seascape to the west. Lochinver is a large-ish village, holiday resort, working fishing port and the only place of any size between Ullapool and Scourie. Even in this remote place there is a visitor centre—quite a good one, with information about the local wildlife. Close by are several pleasant sandy coves. Cruises run from the village in the summer with a chance to see some of the many birds and seal colonies around the coast. The **West Highland Stoneware Potteries**, ✆ (01571) 844 376, in Lochinver, is a marvellous place to visit. A working pottery, it has a shop, and some of the seconds are true bargains. They also have a place in North Road, Ullapool. This is a popular centre for fishermen and climbers. Suilven—the Sugar Loaf—(2,399ft, 738m) was called the Pillar Mountain by the Vikings and the Grey Castle by the Gaels. The climb is a fairly serious scramble over not too difficult ground, easy to navigate and taking about 8 hours for the round trip. Start from the parking area at the end of the road east from Lochinver, walk through the grounds of Glencanisp Lodge and go left when you reach Loch Druin Suardalain. A good stalkers' track runs east to the hill through lochans and rocks and from there on the way is obvious. If you don't want to climb, walk out from Inverkirkaig, a couple of miles south of Lochinver, to the Inverkirkaig Falls along the signed track.

Loch Assynt, dark and mysterious in its bowl of hills, holds memories of betrayal. **Ardvreck Castle**, a jagged fang of a ruin three storeys high, stands on a turf-covered rocky peninsula on the northeast shore. It dates from the 15th century and was owned by the Macleods who had held the Assynt lands since the 13th century. It was never a big building, the lack of roads making it difficult to maintain a large establishment. There are conflicting stories about what happened here in 1650. James Graham, Marquis of Montrose, fighting for the cause of Charles II, fled here after his defeat at the Battle of Carbisdale, near Bonar Bridge. One story is that he threw himself on the mercy of the Macleod laird who responded by selling him to the government for £20,000 and 400 bolls of meal—which turned out to be sour. Others say that Macleod found him and captured him honourably.

Whatever the truth, Montrose was imprisoned in this grim fortress before being taken to Edinburgh, tied back-to-front on his horse, where he was hung and disembowelled, without trial. Maybe he was incarcerated in one of the two semi-dungeons still existing. (It was not until over 200 years later that a tomb and monument were erected for him, at St Giles in Edinburgh.) Charles II, for whom he had given up everything, had by now settled his affairs with his lords and chose not to intervene. In the words of a biographer, Montrose 'presents a standard of honesty, generosity and decent dealing which is conspicuously absent in 17th-century Scottish politics. Companions fought and died for him and enemies marvelled at the courage with which he met his execution.'

In caves near **Inchnadamph**, 2 miles south of Ardvreck, archaeologists have found evidence of occupation by early man going back at least 11,000 years, including carefully buried skeletons, charred bones and stones. They also found the bones of arctic animals: reindeer, bear, lynx and arctic fox.

Unless you are really pushed for time, take the coast road north from Lochinver (the B869). It's about 35 miles at a snail's pace, rather than 4 quick miles on the A894, and is really stunning. At **Kylesku**, by Unapool, a bridge whips you across the narrows where Lochs Glendhu and Glencoul flow into Loch Cairnbawn and out to Eddrachillis Bay and the Atlantic. A tiny ferry used to be the only way north from here, holding up traffic for hours in the holiday season and giving time to wander and wonder. The old jetty is still a hive of activity with a very nice old inn perched above it and chalked notices saying when fresh prawns and langoustine will be for sale. It's a favourite meeting place for seals.

Boats run from Unapool, down Loch Glencoul to see **Eas-Coul-Aulin**, Britain's highest waterfall at 658 feet (202m), four times the height of Niagara and higher than the Falls of Glomach in Kintail though far less well known. Sometimes called 'The Maiden's Tresses', for obvious reasons, its Gaelic name means 'The splendid waterfall of Glencoul' and very splendid it is too, thundering down in staggers of glistening tresses splintered by the rocks. It is possible to walk out to it along a track that leaves the A894 3 miles short of Unapool, past Loch Gainmhich under the northern flank of Glas Gheinn. However, it is quite tricky to find and the boat trip is fun, with occasional glimpses of minke whales if you are lucky.

For a decent walk, take the stalkers' track west, about 4 miles north of Inchnadamph—there is a car park on the right—and aim for Quinag. Walk across the moor to the foot of the southeast ridge of Spidean Conich and climb the edge of the escarpment. From here you can get to the summit of Quinag and explore its Y-shaped crests, with amazing views of the west coast.

Scourie

Scourie is about 8 miles north on the A894, a sheltered village within the arms of Scourie Bay with sandy beaches and rock pools, slightly spoiled by a camping ground overlooking the bay. The mild climate supports several varieties of orchid and an Atlantic palm. It is a trout fisherman's haven but there is much else for the outward bounder to do. Boats run from Tarbet to **Handa Island**, north of the bay, a 760-acre lump of Torridon sandstone and moorland, with 400ft guano-splashed cliffs—an ornithologists' paradise. A variety of sea birds congregate on Handa, including razorbills, guillemots, kittiwakes and skua—watch out for the skua who dive bomb intruders remorselessly. Puffins dig their burrows in the turf and can be seen strutting about guarding their offspring in summer. This is a Scottish Wildlife Trust sanctuary, uninhabited except by a warden. A self-governing community of some 12 families lived here off potatoes, fish and seabirds until the potato famine in 1847, when they were forced to emigrate to Canada. They had their own queen, the oldest widow in the community, who reigned supreme even over mainland royalty, and the men met each morning to settle the day's business. Boats run intermittently to **Tarbet** until 4pm and there's also a postbus from Scourie.

The road north from Scourie joins the A838 at Laxford Bridge, another centre for fishermen. An alternative route goes southeast to Lairg through rocky hills that tower menacingly over the road with sharp turns and blind summits. On a sunny day the sparkling waters of Lochs More, Merkland and Shin make this a magic drive, but on a grey, sullen day of mist and rain it can be melancholy.

Rhiconich, 4 miles north of Laxford Bridge at the head of Loch Inchard, is where the fish lorries turn off to **Kinlochbervie**, now one of Scotland's main fishing ports. As long ago as 1840, the minister of Eddrachillis remarked on the excellence of the harbours along this coast and pronounced: 'they are sufficient to afford safe anchorage to the whole naval and mercantile shipping of Great Britain.' Lorries arrive at this benighted spot to collect the catches of the trawlers. It is fun to watch the boats come in after weeks at sea and unload on the teeming quays, where sometimes you can buy a bag of fish from an obliging skipper. Once loaded, the lorries set off in the evening to drive to Aberdeen for the early morning market. Many of the fishermen come from the east and set off home late on Friday night, returning at crack of dawn on Monday. Strong currents around the northern headland make swimming extremely dangerous here: beware.

Drive on past Kinlochbervie to Sheigra where a signpost marks the start of the 4½ mile walk out to **Sandwood Bay**, a 7-mile sweep of empty sand dunes and dramatic rock stacks believed by some to be the most beautiful beach in Scotland, although it's not safe for swimming. Sandwood's ghost has been experienced too often to be a myth. He is a bearded seaman with a peaked cap and brass buttons on his coat, thought to have been the victim of one of the many shipwrecks on this treacherous coast. Leaving no footprints in the sand, he threatened two local men who were collecting driftwood, and appeared to some men from Kinlochbervie who were looking for stray sheep. He made his presence felt to campers near Sandwood cottage, now untenanted, and on one occasion a visitor to the cottage was woken in the night by 'a thick blackness' that pressed down on him. His most recent appearance was not so long ago when he passed a honeymoon couple on the path and vanished when they greeted him. There was once a settlement here, evacuated after the potato famine, and it is possible that the mortal remains of the sailor lie in the old burial ground now obliterated by sand. A great many people say they get a feeling of oppressive doom here. On a sunny day it is glorious.

From Rhiconich the 15-mile drive north to Durness is through a bleak wilderness of rock-strewn glens, forbidding hills and dark, sombre lochs.

Sports and Activities

Laxford Cruises, ✆ (01971) 502 251, offer daily excursions around Loch Laxford, starting from Fanagmor, 6 miles north of Scourie (*Easter–Oct only*).

Where to Stay and Eating Out

expensive

Inver Lodge Hotel, Lochinver, ✆ (01571) 844 496, 🖷 844 395, is modern, luxurious and in a perfectly lovely position, but it lacks any traditional character. The food is excellent.

expensive–moderate

Summer Isles Hotel, Achiltibuie, ✆ (01854) 622 282, 🖷 622 251, is wonderfully remote and in a spectacular setting overlooking the Summer Isles and the Hebrides beyond. Its rooms are country-house-style and comfortable and there is a 'trust bar' in the lounge. There's also a log cabin annexe with rooms on to a veranda. The excellent meals are enhanced by the nearby smokehouse and the Hydroponicum, which provides fresh fruit and vegetables, its own dairy products, veal, quails, duck, fish, etc. *Open April–Oct.*

The Albannach, Lochinver, ✆ (01571) 844 407, 🖷 844 285, is a friendly place with imaginative furnishings, flagstones and rugs, tartan and cane, wood-lined ceilings in the older bedrooms, four-poster beds and Victoriana. Good locally produced food is served in a cosy restaurant.

moderate

Inchnadamph Hotel, Loch Assynt, ✆ (01571) 822 202, 🖷 822 203, was a coaching inn 200 years ago. Known as the 'Angler's Retreat', it is a genuine Highland fishing establishment where homely comfort is more important than double glazing (though that is being installed). It went through a bad patch a few years ago but is now in the capable hands of three generations of the Archibald and Harding families who know how to make you (and your pets) feel welcome. There is free fishing for salmon, grilse and brown trout, trophies of which hang on the walls in abundance.

Kylesku Hotel, ✆ (01971) 502 231, 🖷 502 313, is a cottage-style inn overlooking the old ferry ramp and Loch Glendhu with Suilven, Quinaig and Ben More Assynt beckoning from the distance. The rooms are cosy and pretty, and delicious fresh seafood caught in the hotel's boat is served daily. **Scourie Hotel,** ✆ (01971) 502 396, 🖷 502 423, is popular with fishermen whose trophies adorn the walls, caught in one of the 250 lochs the hotel has rights to. It is built round an old keep disguised now by weatherboard. The décor is unpretentious.

Kinlochbervie Hotel, ✆ (01971) 521 275, 🖷 521 438, rebuilt after the well-remembered old inn was burnt down in the 1960s, overlooks the village, loch and harbour with panoramic views out to sea and is well equipped for family holidays. The bedrooms are comfortable and there is a snug upstairs sitting room where it is easy to snooze away a wet day. The food is excellent and the atmosphere friendly. This is a good stopping off place for refreshment after the walk out to Sandwood Bay.

Old School Hotel, Inshegra, Kinlochbervie, ✆ (01971) 521 383, is really a restaurant that grew in the old school house, looking out across Inshegra. The schoolroom is the dining room with school memorabilia as decoration. Good plain food is served with plenty of seafood fresh from the loch. The cheerfully furnished and comfortable bedrooms are in an annexe at the back beside a burn.

cheap

Lochinver House Travel Lodge, ✆ (01571) 844 270, 🖷 844 483, a large unpretentious place overlooking the harbour, has not too many frills but a good friendly atmosphere, and is very reasonable.

The very best place to go for B&B is to **Mr and Mrs MacLeod,** Dornie House, Achiltibue, ✆ (01854) 622 271, whose modern bungalow has such stunning views and who give such a warm welcome that you have to drag yourself away. Breakfast supreme. *Open Easter–Oct.*

The **Riverside Bistro,** Lochinver, ✆ (01571) 844 356, will give you a good choice of excellent homely food.

At the **Lilypond Café,** ✆ (01854) 622 202, in the Hydroponicum, you can sample the produce, much of it delicious. You don't have to tour the Hydroponicum to use the café.

Tarbet, where you catch the boat for Handa, has a marvellous **café/bistro** (call ✆ (01971) 502 251 for opening times), with delicious, fresh seafood: lobster, crab, prawns, etc, inexpensive and worth a detour.

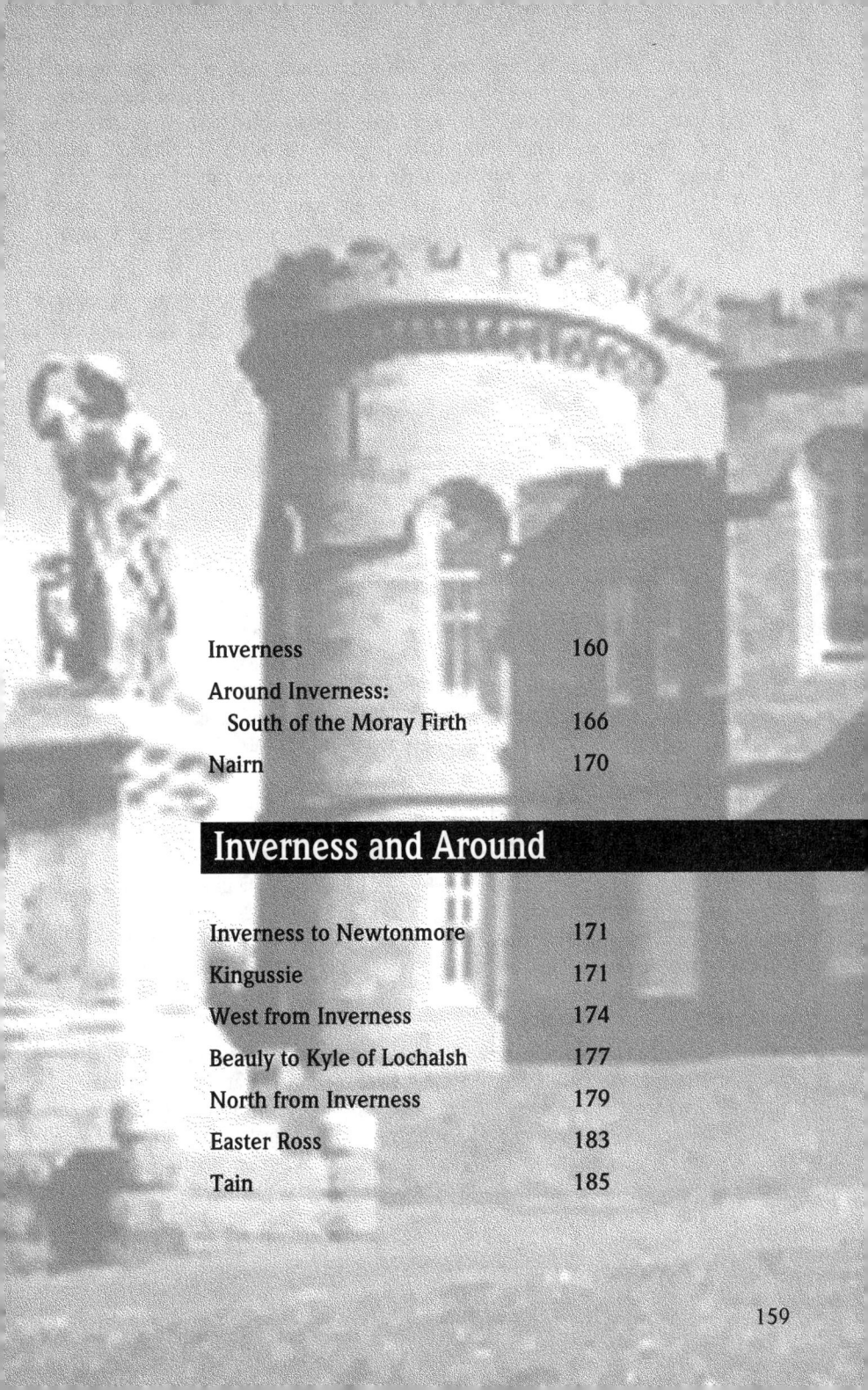

Inverness 160

Around Inverness:
South of the Moray Firth 166

Nairn 170

Inverness and Around

Inverness to Newtonmore 171

Kingussie 171

West from Inverness 174

Beauly to Kyle of Lochalsh 177

North from Inverness 179

Easter Ross 183

Tain 185

With the capital of the Highlands at its heart, this area is more populated and prosperous than its northern and western neighbours. Large sporting estates attract southern and foreign visitors; there is good skiing from Aviemore, and infinite scope for climbers and walkers, both in the hills and in the fertile straths; historic castles and battle sites bear witness to a violent history. Hard winters give way to frequently hot summers; snow lies all year in north-facing corries. There is some good farmland here, but the economy is turning more and more to tourism.

Inverness

As the capital of the Highlands and the junction of many routes, Inverness—from *Inbhir:* 'mouth' of the River Ness—is a good place from which to explore the north of Scotland. The river flows through the heart of the town, the original settlement having grown up 5,000 years ago at the first place where people could ford it at low tide, the sea and hills forcing travellers from all directions to pass through a bottleneck. Being also the navigable limit of the Moray Firth, with a good sheltered harbour at the river mouth, Inverness became the focal point of trade routes. Trade brought prosperity and the threat of attack. From early times Inverness was of strategic importance—whoever controlled the ford controlled the Northern Highlands.

History

Traces of ancient forts, castles and garrisons scattered in and around the town bear witness to thousands of years of struggle to gain and hold this vital area. The early population probably lived in small farming and fishing communities dotted around the coast and in the river valleys, adjacent to a hill fort where they and their livestock could seek refuge in times of danger. The most impressive of these is on Craig Phadraig, the small hill just west of the town, which still has the remains of a 4th-century vitrified fort.

St Columba is recorded by his biographer, St Adamnan, as having visited and converted the Pictish King Brude in a castle somewhere near the River Ness in AD 565. This could have been the one on Craig Phadraig—the old Gaelic name for which was *Larach an tigh mhor*: 'site of the great house'—which was still used in Brude's time. But Craig Phadraig was bleak and windswept and the fort was partially ruined by the 6th century. It is more likely that Brude's stronghold stood on Castle Hill, where the castle stands today, less dominant strategically than Craig Phadraig but nevertheless a defensive site. (According to St Adamnan, Columba's first task was to get past the king's druids, which he did by singing Psalm 46, 'God is our Refuge and our Strength', so loud that the druids gave way.)

Macbeth arrived on the scene four and a half centuries later, disposed of King Duncan and took the Crown of Scotland. His stronghold was almost certainly at the eastern end of the Crown, still referred to as Auldcastle. Historical fact and poetic fiction have become so inextricably interwoven around the story of Macbeth and his bloodstained journey to the throne that there are several different claims for the setting of King Duncan's murder in 1039. The most reliable sources say the deed was not done in Macbeth's castle in Inverness but in a house near Elgin, though it was the one at Auldcastle that Malcolm Canmore destroyed in revenge. A new castle was built on Castle Hill in the 12th century and was much abused in subsequent years. The English occupied it in the War of Independence and Robert the Bruce destroyed it.

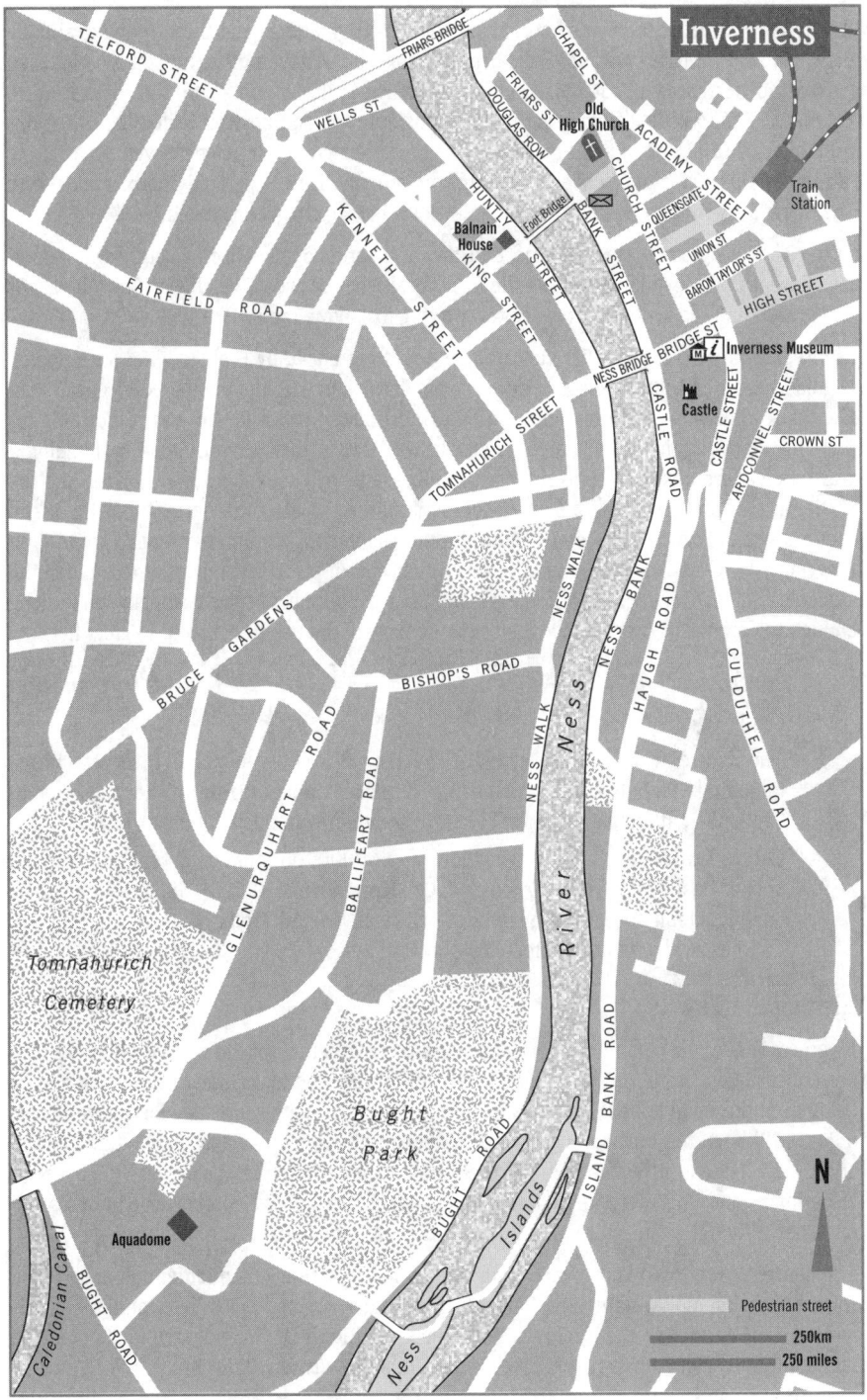
Inverness
TELFORD STREET
FRIARS BRIDGE
WELLS ST
CHAPEL ST
FRIARS ST
DOUGLAS ROW
Old High Church
ACADEMY STREET
Train Station
QUEENSGATE
CHURCH STREET
BANK STREET
Ness Bridge
HUNTLY STREET
KING STREET
KENNETH STREET
Balnain House
UNION ST
BARON TAYLOR'S ST
HIGH STREET
FAIRFIELD ROAD
NESS BRIDGE
BRIDGE ST
Inverness Museum
Castle
CASTLE ROAD
CASTLE STREET
ARDCONNEL STREET
CROWN ST
TOMNAHURICH STREET
NESS WALK
NESS BANK
HAUGH ROAD
CULDUTHEL ROAD
BRUCE GARDENS
BISHOP'S ROAD
GLENURQUHART ROAD
BALLIFEARY ROAD
River Ness
Tomnahurich Cemetery
Bught Park
BUGHT ROAD
Islands
ISLAND BANK ROAD
Aquadome
Caledonian Canal
BUGHT ROAD
Ness
N
Pedestrian street
250km
250 miles

Its successor became the focus for conflict between Highlanders and those trying to subdue their wild ways. Mary, Queen of Scots hanged its rebellious governor from the ramparts when he refused her entry in 1562. Jacobites occupied it in 1715 and 1745 and blew it up in February 1746 to keep it from government hands. Johnson and Boswell visited the site of this ruin on Castle Hill, mistaking it for Macbeth's castle, which didn't deter Boswell from having 'a romantick satisfaction in seeing Dr Johnson actually in it. It perfectly corresponds with Shakspear's description, which Sir Joshua Reynolds has so happily illustrated.'

In the Middle Ages Inverness developed further as a port and ship-building centre with important European trade links. It became the focus for clashes between the chiefs of the Highlands and Islands and the Scottish Crown, forever trying to subdue them.

Mary, Queen of Scots came here in 1563, and was entranced by Highland life. She adopted Highland dress and forced some of her courtiers into plaids, hastily purchased locally. When General Monk was the Commander in Scotland under Cromwell, he was responsible for building a fortress, the Citadel, a polygonal artillery fort, in the harbour. Stone for building it was removed from various ruins such as the abbeys at Fortrose, Beauly, and Kinloss, and the castle on Ormond Hill. It was demolished and obliterated after the Restoration. In Queen Victoria's time Inverness became the hub of the Highlands, with its converging routes and new railway. Grand new Highland mansions on sporting estates mushroomed under the Queen's influence. She visited Inverness several times, but only in transit, stopping off for long enough to approve its charms and receive the homage of the people gathered to greet her.

Inverness ✆ (01463–) ***Tourist Information***

Castle Wynd, ✆ 234 353.

The centre will provide details of the many lively events that Inverness hosts, including **The Northern Meeting Piping Competition** in Eden Court in September, attracting the finest pipers who gather to compete for prestigious awards.

Guide Friday, at the railway station, ✆ 224 000, do tours on an open-top double decker bus. *Tours May–early Oct daily*. **Ken White**, ✆ 223 168, does personally conducted mini bus tours, including Loch Ness; **Tartan Taxis**, ✆ 233 033/713 555, do tours over a wide area, including one to Skye.

Visiting the Town

Inverness is now the communications and administrative centre for the north of Scotland. The present castle on Castle Hill was built in the 19th century and looks brand new, its bare walls rising from the small hill exactly like a toy fort. It houses the law courts and local government offices. Although not outstandingly beautiful, parts of Inverness have a certain sturdy charm and the riverside is attractive. Perhaps the best view is from the bridge below Bridge Street. Fishermen stand thigh-deep in the fast-flowing river, flanked by well-proportioned houses and churches. When the sun shines, which it often does, it is a curiously Continental scene.

The centre of the town is compact, with the Station Square in the middle, dominated by a splendid war memorial statue of a Cameron Highlander, erected in 1893 to mark the centenary of the Camerons—the local regiment. There are the usual chain department stores in a hideous indoor shopping complex. Like so many other towns, Inverness has sacrificed most of its character to Mammon and you must search beyond its modern veneer to find traces of a more gracious past.

Inverness Museum (*open Mon–Sat 9–5; closed local holidays*) in Castle Wynd, between the castle and the town hall, has displays of social and natural history, archaeology, the culture of the Highlands and Jacobite relics. There are often exhibitions, talks and slide shows. The Art Gallery includes interesting views of Old Inverness.

St Andrew's Cathedral is south of the Ness Bridge, an imposing, pinkish building on the banks of the river. Consecrated in 1869, it was the first cathedral to be built in Britain after the Reformation. Designed by the architect Alexander Ross, it has two great towers which somehow never got their intended spires. The elaborate interior includes five gold icons, presented by the Tsar of Russia. **Eden Court**, beyond the cathedral, is a glass edifice built in 1976, incorporating the 19th-century house of Bishop Eden. Inside is an 800-seat multipurpose theatre, conference centre, art gallery and an excellent restaurant. Ambitious programmes are laid on throughout the year, including art exhibitions and the latest films. Up-river from Eden Court, **Ness Islands** form a public park spread over a series of small islands in the river. They are linked by several footbridges, with views down the river towards the town.

Art. TM, 20 Bank Street, ✆ (01463) 712 240, is a newish and very trendy art gallery, worth a visit. **Bught Floral Hall and Visitor Centre**, Bught Lane, ✆ (01463) 222 755, is for horticultural enthusiasts—an indoor tropical garden (*open daily; adm*). **Castle Garrison**, 3 Connel Court, ✆ (01463) 243 363, has live shows depicting life during the last Jacobite rising (*open Easter–Nov Mon–Sat; adm*).

Tomnahurich—Hill of the Yews, sometimes called Hill of the Fairies—is the small, boat-shaped hillock to the southwest. Two wandering fiddlers, Thomas and Farquhar, were lured to Tomnahurich by the Fairy Queen, to play for a night's dancing. In the morning they found the town and its people strangely altered and everyone laughing at them. The 'night' had lasted a hundred years. They crept into a church for refuge—and crumbled into dust. Tomnahurich is now the town's cemetery, with many elaborate monuments clinging to the steep, wooded slopes, and a splendid viewing point from the top. Below lie the environs of Inverness, with neat villas, well-kept gardens and an air of solid respectability.

The northern entrance to the **Caledonian Canal** is in the western suburbs. The canal was constructed in the 19th century by Thomas Telford, a considerable feat of engineering, linking Loch Ness, Loch Oich and Loch Lochy to form a 65-mile waterway between the east and west coasts. Before its construction, large vessels had to circumnavigate Scotland via the Pentland Firth, a hazardous slog not only because of the harsh conditions but also because of marauding privateers. The canal is still used by fishing boats but nowadays is mostly the haunt of pleasure craft, being a perfect way for sailors to explore the Great Glen.

Like a wise old sentinel guarding the town, 19th-century **Cameron Barracks** stands on Knockentinnel—the Rallying Hill— a high ridge above Millburn Road on the eastern edge of Inverness. It was from here that many a brave young Cameron Highlander walked out, newly trained, ready to give his life so that his Highland home should remain free. The Camerons amalgamated with the Seaforth Highlanders in the early 1960s, to become The Queen's Own Highlanders. They then amalgamated wih the Gordon Highlanders and these three famous regiments are now known as the Highlanders.

Shopping

You can watch kilts being made by hand at the **Kiltmaker Visitor Centre**, 4–9 Huntly Streeet. The **Pringle Woollen Mill**, at Holm Mills, Dores Road, is a 200-year-old weaving mill with a large mill shop, a tartan centre and a restaurant (*open daily*).

Inverness ✆ (01463–)

Sports and Activities

Balnain House, in Huntly Street, ✆ 715 757 (*open Mon–Sat; summer Sun too*) is a splendid Highland music centre with performances and classes and the opportunity to join in music sessions. There is a fun café/bar in the basement with good food, and live music in the summer. There are lectures throughout the year, not all on music.

Cabin cruisers can be hired from the marinas located just down from the entrance, and passenger cruises run in the summer. One of the best is **Caley Cruisers** in Canal Road, ✆ 236 328, with a fleet of 50 cruise boats, each sleeping between 2 and 8 people, with all canal charges included in the rent. Or try **Jacobite Cruises**, ✆ 233 999, who run steamer cruises on Loch Ness.

Inverness Aquadome, in Bught Park, ✆ 667 500, has everything a swimmer could possibly want, toddler or professional. The adventure zone with flumes, whirlpools, vortex and cyclone is not for the faintheatred (*open daily; adm*). There is also an impressive **Sports Centre** in Bught Park, ✆ 667 505, offering pretty well everything in the way of games, fitness classes, martial arts, etc.

Moray Firth Dolphin Cruises, Shore Street Quay, ✆ 717 900, run dolphin-spotting cruises (*Mar–Oct daily*).

Inverness ✆ (01463–)

Where to Stay

expensive

Bunchrew House Hotel, Bunchrew, ✆ 234 917, 🖷 710 260, *www.bunchrew-inverness.co.uk*, on the south side of the Beauly Firth about 5 miles west of Inverness, is a Victorian mansion with a late-Georgian core in 15 acres of attractive garden. It has turrets and towers, is comfortable, full of atmosphere and peaceful, and the food is good. **Culloden House Hotel**, 3 miles east of Inverness, ✆ 790 461, 🖷 792 181, is a Georgian mansion built round a Jacobean castle near the battlefield. Bought by an American millionaire who traces his roots back to the time of Robert the Bruce, the hotel has four-poster beds, Adam-style décor, posh bathrooms and elegant public rooms. Staying here is an extravagance—and worth every penny.

Kilravock Castle Hotel, ✆/🖷 (01667) 493 258, is perfect if you are a non-smoking, abstemious Christian in search of an historical setting. The emphasis is on God: grace before meals, Bible readings and comment at breakfast and dinner; no drink—though naughty guests have been known to smuggle bottles of the devil's brew into their bedrooms and smoke up the chimney. Country-house bedrooms in a wing of the castle are cheap; those in the castle proper cost a little more but are still reasonable.

Dunain Park, ✆ 230 512, 🖷 224 532, on the road to Fort William, is a quiet but very convivial mansion-house hotel, with a small swimming pool and excellent food.

Kingsmills Hotel, Culcabock Road, ✆ 237 166, 🖷 225 208, just off the A9, is modern but first class, with comfortable rooms and good food. **Culduthel Lodge**, 14 Culduthel Road, ✆/🖷 240 089, is an elegant Georgian mansion overlooking the River Ness, with every possible comfort including a decanter of sherry to greet you.

moderate

The Station Hotel, ✆ 231 926, 🖷 710 705, is wonderfully traditional and comfortable, with an air of genteel respectability, and a foyer straight out of an Agatha Christie novel, but it's quite expensive and the food is unexciting. Fishing enthusiasts should try the **Grouse and Trout**, at Flichity Farr, in Strathnairn, east of Loch Ness, on the old route to Fort Augustus, ✆/🖷 (01808) 521 314, a converted farm steading, with exposed beams and stonework, acclaimed by fishermen. Mr and Mrs Thornton offer cosy comfort and warm hospitality and the food is excellent.

Brae Ness Hotel, Ness Bank, ✆ 712 266, 🖷 231 732, is a Georgian house on the banks of the River Ness, with much of its original character unspoilt by modernization. Family-run and good value. **Inchberry House**, Lentran, 5 miles from Inverness on the A862, ✆ 831 342, is a Victorian farmhouse, overlooking the Beauly Firth. Friendly and comfortable, and the menu includes their own home-reared beef.

Moyness House Hotel, 6 Bruce Gardens, ✆ 233 836, is a 5-star guest house, elegantly furnished in nice grounds, once the home of the writer Neil Gunn. **The Mapel Court Hotel**, 12 Ness Walk, ✆ 230 330, 🖷 237 700, beside the river in attractive surroundings, is only a few minutes from the town centre, and serves good food.

cheap

Glenruidh House, Old Edinburgh Road, ✆ 226 499, just outside the city centre, has nice views and a cosy atmosphere. The **Columba Hotel**, Ness Walk, ✆ 231 391, 🖷 715 526, looks over the river up to the castle. It takes bus parties and offers live Scottish entertainment most nights. **Felstead**, Ness Bank, ✆ 231 634, opposite Eden Court, is a family-run guest house which is good value and friendly.

For B&B try **Taigh na Teile**, 6 Island Bank Road, ✆ 222 842, which is good value; breakfasts are first class.

Inverness ✆ (01463–) ***Eating Out***

Dunain Park, *see* above, also offers excellent food and is not too pricey. **Café One**, ✆ 226 200, in Castle Street, has a good reputation, and booking is advisable.

La Riviera, part of the Glen Moriston Hotel, Ness Bank, ✆ 223 777, is one of the upmarket favourites, on the river, with an Italian slant. **River Café**, 10 Bank Street, ✆ 714 884, is a smallish place with an excellent fishy menu, though it also does local dishes of a stodgier kind. **Riva**, in Ness Walk, ✆ 237 377, serves delicious Italian food, pastries and coffee.

The Castle Restaurant, by the main tourist centre, is a really good café with excellent simple food. **Blue**, opposite the old Safeways behind the Forty Five Botham in Rose Street, is a 'groovy' nightclub (*open Thurs–Sun*).

Inverness to Nairn

The south side of the Moray Firth is low-lying open farmland with views across to the Black Isle and the hills of Easter Ross, often snow-capped. This is a gentle landscape compared with the ruggedness more commonly associated with the Highlands, but its soil is as stained with Highland blood as any in Scotland.

Culloden

Taking the back roads, east of the A96, Culloden lies about 5 miles east of Inverness. Brown tourism signs point the way.

The excellent **visitor centre** on the edge of the battlefield (✆ *(01463) 790 607; open daily except Jan; adm for audio-visual and cottage; site open all year; free*) has an audio-visual show with details of the battle which took place here on 16 April 1746, when Prince Charles Edward Stuart and his 5,000 exhausted, starving and ill-equipped Highlanders were defeated by the Duke of Cumberland, son of George II, and his 9,000 well-trained and well-equipped troops. 1,200 Highlanders fell; a large number were butchered by order of the Duke as they lay wounded; others, and their families, were later rounded up, slaughtered, persecuted or exiled. Accounts of the Prince's reaction to the failure of his dreams vary: some say he tried to rally his Highlanders; some, that he had to be held back from galloping forward to a hero's death; other accounts are less flattering. Whatever the truth, he was led away and hidden by loyal Highlanders for five months, with a price of £30,000 on his head, until he returned to the Continent in a French frigate, to live out the rest of his life in wretched, debauched exile.

The history of events leading up to the Battle of Culloden is well known. Many a Highlander who 'was out' with the Prince, followed his heart, not his head. It is said that there were more Scots fighting for the government at Culloden than there were fighting for the Prince. That it was an ill-advised and disastrously ill-managed battle is certain, as is the fact that it spelt the demise of a whole way of life and a social system that had endured for centuries.

On the battlefield plaques tell which clan fought where and how the battle progressed. There are clan graves: communal burial sites with simple headstones bearing clan names, and a memorial cairn erected in 1881. On the edge of the bleak site is the Well of the Dead, where wounded Highlanders were slain as they drank water in desperation to revive themselves. A single stone bears the inscription: 'The English were buried here'. The flat stone beyond the visitor centre is called the Cumberland Stone, thought to have been the vantage point from which the Duke viewed the battle. Try to picture it as it was then: 'a very cold, rainy morning...' the well-fed Redcoats, in perfect control; the Highlanders already dispirited, hungry and exhausted. The advance of the Redcoats was described by an eyewitness: 'It resembled a deep and sullen river, while the Prince's army might be compared to a streamlet running among stones, whose noise sufficiently showed its shallowness.'

The old cottage outside the visitor centre (included in your ticket) is the only building to have survived. Still inhabited at the beginning of the 20th century, it is now a folk museum, restored as an 18th-century bothy with authentic furnishings. Taped music and Gaelic add a poignant touch. It is said that 30 Highlanders were burnt alive nearby, after the battle.

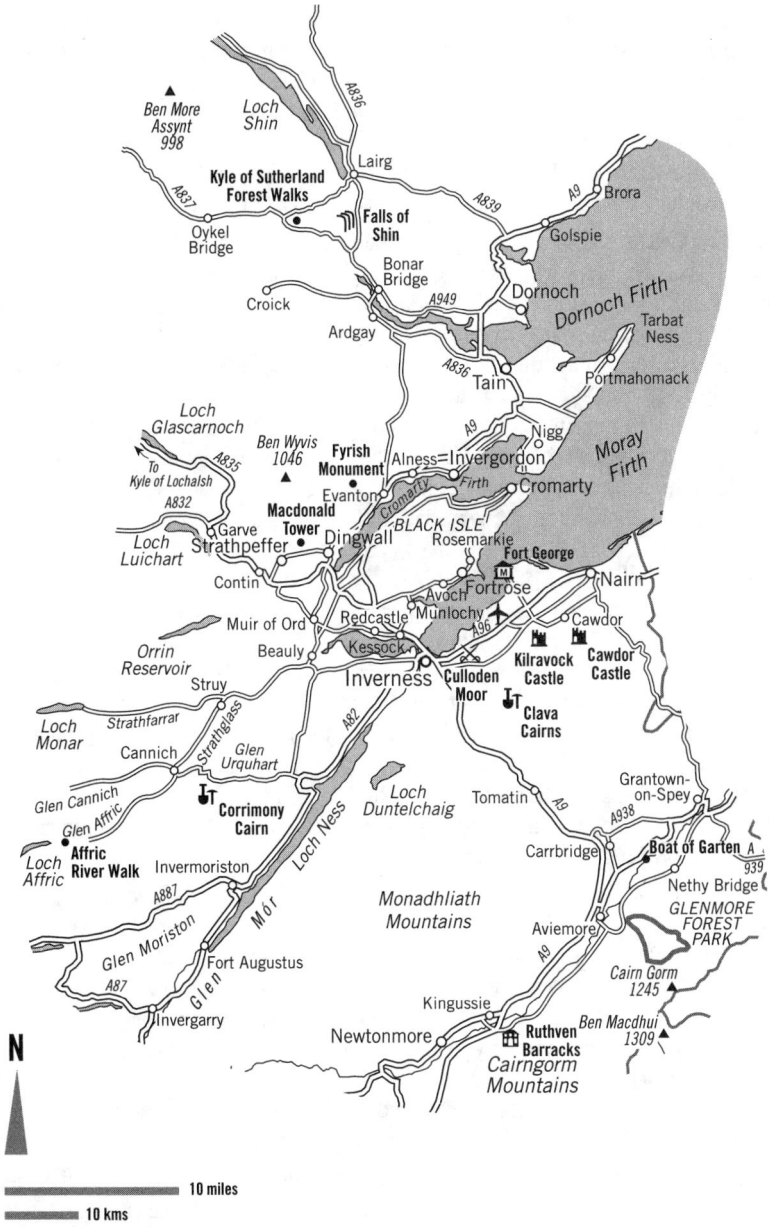

Inverness and Around

Culloden House Hotel, 3 miles east of Inverness, is a Georgian mansion built round a Jacobean castle near the battlefield (*see* above, 'Where to Stay'). Prince Charles spent the night before the battle in a house on this site. It was the home of Duncan Forbes, the Lord President, one of Scotland's most trusted judges. His canny diplomacy dissuaded many north-eastern Jacobites from taking part in the '45 and, although he supported the government, he advocated leniency for the rebels after the battle. Some 30 or so Highlanders took refuge here afterwards, to be slaughtered by Cumberland's men. A mound marks the burial ground; no heather grows there now, it being a hater of chalk and calcified bones. Culloden House was destroyed by fire soon after the battle and replaced in 1772 by the present mansion.

The Clava Cairns, signed a mile east of Culloden, are a remarkable Stone Age and Bronze Age burial site, possibly dating from 2000 BC. Three large burial cairns in a glade of beech trees take you back to the prehistoric rituals that would have accompanied the internment of those farmers and herdsmen so many years ago. Two of the cairns have passages leading into them; the third has curious stone strips radiating from it like the spokes of a wheel. Each is surrounded by a circle of standing stones, some inscribed with cup-and-ring symbols. Excavations revealed traces of cremated human bones, pottery and other remains: memorials of people who were alive nearly 4,000 years ago. A line through the two graves with passages points exactly to the spot where the sun sets at midwinter, and the geometrical accuracy with which the cairns are laid out suggests a sophisticated knowledge of mathematics and astronomy.

Kilravock Castle

Kilravock Castle—pronounced Kilrawk—(*grounds open Mon–Sat; house open end April–Sept Wed afternoons; adm*) is 5 miles northeast of Culloden, keeping to the back roads. In 1190 a Norman called Rose came north, married into a local family, and settled on these lands; Kilravock has been the home of the Rose chiefs ever since. In 1460 they were authorized by the Lord of the Isles to build a tower and the result was the massive stone keep on a steep drop over the River Nairn. In the 17th century a four-storey mansion was added, with further additions in the 18th century. Since then it has been preserved almost intact because its owners never had enough money to alter it. Mary, Queen of Scots was entertained in the original keep in 1562, during her Highland tour that year.

Among its relics the castle has two reminders of Culloden—a punch bowl and a pair of leather thigh boots. Rose of Kilravock entertained Prince Charles before the battle and offered him punch from this bowl. He was not a Jacobite, but the Prince had called on him and no true Highlander refuses hospitality. Shortly afterwards Cumberland appeared, flushed with the celebration of his 25th birthday and exhilarated with anticipation of the battle: 'I hear, Sir, you have been entertaining my cousin!' Rose explained, and was excused. Cumberland, for some inexplicable reason, left his boots behind. There is something wonderfully ironic about the relics left by the two men: Prince Charles, merry and charismatic, who later drowned his failure in alcohol; and Butcher Cumberland, all 18 stone of him, brash, gross and cruel in his jackboots.

The gardens and grounds are attractive, especially in spring. Prince Charles walked here with his host and watched young trees being planted; he remarked on the contrast between this peaceful scene and the commotion that was going on all around, as preparations were being made for the battle. Some of the beautiful old trees growing here today could be the ones he watched being planted. Kilravock is now an hotel, *see* above, 'Where to Stay'.

Cawdor

Cawdor (pronounced Cawder), 8 miles northeast of Culloden, is familiar to anyone who has read or seen Shakespeare's *Macbeth*, although 11th-century Macbeth was dead long before this place came into being. **Cawdor Castle** (*open May–2nd Sun in Oct daily; adm*) was originally named Calder, home of the Thanes of Calder. It dates from 1372 when William Calder built the central tower, probably replacing an older building which might have been more familiar to Macbeth. That would have been Old Calder, a Norman 'moatstead' not far north of the present castle. The Campbells of Argyll acquired the castle in 1510, one of them having abducted and married a Calder heiress.

Protected by a gully on one side and a dry moat on the other, the castle is entered over a drawbridge. Domestic buildings were added in the 16th century and later remodelled; inside, it feels like a living home rather than a museum, probably because the Cawdors still live here. Among the things to see are Flemish tapestries, paintings, weapons, household equipment and family heirlooms. Carbon dating has confirmed that the scrap of an ancient tree, railed off in the basement, is older than the castle, thus authenticating an old story. The original founder, Thane William, was granted a licence to build himself a fortress. He was told in a dream to load a donkey with panniers of gold and build a castle wherever it stopped. He obeyed and the donkey stopped for a rest in the shade of a holly tree, round which William built his castle. Don't resist buying the official guide written by a previous Lord Cawdor: irreverent descriptions of ancestors and heirlooms add humour to an otherwise fairly standard collection of memorabilia. Outside, as well as a walled garden, ablaze with colour in the summer, there is a charming, less formal 19th-century garden and a maze. There are riverside and woodland walks, a nine-hole mini-golf course, putting green and picnic spots, as well as a licensed restaurant and souvenir shop.

In a conservation area, Cawdor village, straggling round the castle grounds, is not at all typical of the rest of the Highlands: its peaceful cosiness matches that of the castle. The church is 17th-century, built in thanksgiving by the 12th Lord Cawdor after he survived a shipwreck.

Fort George

Fort George (*open daily; adm*), about 8 miles northwest of Cawdor on the B9006, on a windswept promontory jutting out into the Moray Firth, is the most unspoilt example of an artillery fort in Europe. Built between 1748 and 1769 to replace 'Old' Fort George in Inverness which was destroyed by Prince Charles in 1746, it is a classic 18th-century fortress. The defences include the traditional outer works: ravelin, ditch, bastion and rampart, designed by William Skinnor who in his day was the leading expert on artillery fortification. The government contractor was John Adam, oldest son of architect William Adam, and brother of Robert and James, both of whom spent years as overseers of the work.

Passing through the forbidding fortifications, one is brought to a delighted standstill by the mellow pink sandstone garrison buildings, their impeccable proportions mercifully unscarred by later 'improvement'.

The fort was built to house a garrison large enough to overawe Jacobite support in the Highlands, but by the time it was complete the Jacobite threat was finally dead, so it has never had a history of conflict. It became a base where a long series of regiments was mustered and equipped before embarking for service in America, the West Indies, the Middle East, India and

South Africa. In 1881, when each British infantry regiment was allocated its own territorial recruiting area and home base, Fort George became the depot for the Seaforth Highlanders. Generations of Highland soldiers trained there for colonial service, for two world wars and for modern Cold War campaigns. The regiments of the garrison change every two or three years and they have the privilege of living in barracks that are the oldest in the world still occupied by a battalion of British infantry.

The Regimental Museum of The Highlanders (The Queen's Own Highlanders' Collection) is in the Fort (*open April–Sept daily; Oct–Mar Mon–Sat; donations welcome*). It contains a fascinating display of the story of an unrivalled Highland regiment whose battle honours blaze through the pages of history.

Nairn

Nairn, almost 9 miles east of Fort George, is a seaside holiday town, sometimes called the Brighton of the North. On the mouth of the River Nairn, it has sandy beaches along the Moray Firth, two golf courses and a reputation for a high average of annual sunshine. In Victorian times a Dr Grigor put Nairn on the map by recommending it to his patients as 'one of the healthiest spots in Britain'.

Tourist Information

62 King Street, ✆ (01667) 452 753 (*open April–Oct*).

The Town

Imposing houses built by retired Victorian empire-builders and trim villas with neat gardens give it an aura of old-fashioned gentility. The town lays on plenty of entertainment in the summer, including Highland Games, a Holiday Week, Vintage Car Rally, Fairground Fortnight and Farmers Show. There is a Performing Arts Guild, a Repertory Theatre and a Fishertown Museum. Even so, you won't die of excitement in Nairn. **36 High Street** looks comparatively modern, but it encases a much older building which was the townhouse of the Roses of Kilravock. The Duke of Cumberland stayed here the night Prince Charles dined with the Roses at Kilravock (*see* p.168).

Nairn ✆ (01667–) ***Where to Stay and Eating Out***

expensive–moderate

Geddes House, ✆ 452 241, 🖷 456 707, a small mansion in a typical Highland estate 3 miles outside Nairn, is a lovely place to stay. Elizabeth Mackintosh-Walker, who runs and owns it with her husband Jamie, is a keen and talented cook, and they both know how to make you feel comfortable and at home. **Clifton House** in Seafield Street, Nairn, ✆ 453 119, 🖷 452 836, is a large town house transformed into a stylish hotel with that certain something that makes people return. It's not cheap but worth every penny, from the excellent food to the fresh flowers and the thoughtful attention of the staff.

The Longhouse, on the corner of Harbour Street, Nairn, is a good, inexpensive, unpretentious restaurant. *Open Thurs–Saturday and Sun lunch.*

Inverness to Newtonmore

Tourist Information

Aviemore: Grampian Road, ✆ (01479) 810 363; **Kingussie**: King Street, ✆ (01540) 661 297 (*open May–Sept*).

Inverness to Aviemore

The A9, part dual carriageway and part frustrating, even dangerous, single carriageway, speeds you south from Inverness. To the southwest lie the massive Monadhliath Mountains; to the southeast, Strathspey and the Grampians. **Moy**, about 12 miles south of Inverness, has long been the home of the chief of the clan Mackintosh, though Moy Hall, where Prince Charles stayed on 16 February 1746, no longer stands. Lord Loudoun, in command of the government forces in Inverness, led 1,500 men to capture the Prince. Mackintosh heard of this attack and, though no Jacobite himself, warned the Prince, who escaped wearing a highland bonnet over his nightcap. The chief's wife, 'Colonel' Anne Mackintosh, who was an ardent Jacobite, dispatched five loyal men to ambush the army. They fired their guns and made such a din shouting battle cries that Loudoun's men panicked and ran. This was 'The Rout of Moy.' The old house burnt down and was replaced by a very grand pile which had to be abandoned because of dry rot in the 20th century. The present Moy Hall was built in the 1950s.

For a lovely walk, turn right at Findhorn Bridge, a mile south of **Tomatin**. Drive for about 5 miles up the River Findhorn and abandon your car when the road becomes a track. This will take you up the river into the very heart of the hills, remote and beautiful. You can follow any of the tributaries of the Findhorn and find waterfalls, lochans, birds and wild flowers.

At **Carrbridge**, 24 miles from Inverness and bypassed by the A9, is the Landmark Visitor Centre, with well-presented Highland history and a fairly predictable Adventure Park.

Aviemore, about 7 miles south of Carrbridge, is a thriving tourist centre and dormitory for the Cairngorm ski resort, teeming with energetic skiers and walkers. It used to be no more than a railway station on the main line to Inverness, without even a pub. In the 1960s, it was chosen as the Highland's first 'designer resort' and some rather hideous structures were built.

If you are gregarious and looking for action, then the **Aviemore Mountain Resort** is just the place for you. It has every sort of accommodation, cafés and restaurants, bistros and bars, gift shops, craft shops, souvenir stalls, amusement arcades and discos, cinemas, a dry-ski slope and an ice rink. There are controversial plans for a funicular railway and for extensive expansion of the town. Throughout the year, the town is a kaleidoscope of anoraks and knapsacks, psychedelic skiing clothes, or shorts and t-shirts in all shapes and sizes. The skiing is centred on **Cairngorm**, to the southeast, with about 30 runs spread over two valleys. It is short on black runs, but challenging enough for most people who don't mind capricious weather; it can be Arctic on the higher pistes. (Ski hotline, ✆ (01479) 861 261/✆ 09001 654 655.)

Kingussie

By-passed by the A9, Kingussie (pronounced Kin-you-see, with no pause in the middle) is another tourist resort about 13 miles on from Aviemore, but with a very different, more peaceful atmosphere. Perhaps this is because it is thought to have been founded by

St Columba: a church dedicated to him, of which only parts of the burial ground remain, once stood at the west of the town. The Duke of Gordon founded the present town, selling off plots of land in 1799. It was intended as a centre of woollen manufacture, but failed to prosper.

The Highland Folk Museum merits a detour to Kingussie and to Newtonmore (✆ *(01540) 661 307; open May–Aug Mon–Fri 10.30–5.30, last admissions Kingussie 4.30, N'more 3.30; Sat and Sun 1–5, last admissions Kingussie 4, N'more 3.30; April, Sept, Oct Mon–Fri guided tours only, Kingussie 10.30–4.30 hourly, N'more 11 and 2 only; adm*). It was founded in Iona in the 1930s and later moved here under the control of the universities of Glasgow, Edinburgh, St Andrews and Aberdeen. Beautifully arranged, both inside and out, it includes an authentic black-house, built by a Lewisman as a replica of his childhood home, a clack mill (named for its 'clacking' noise)' and many other exhibits of farming and domestic life, including a salmon smokehouse. Both locations are outstanding.

The gaunt shell of **Ruthven Barracks** (pronounced by some to rhyme with driven), stands on a hillock east of the A9. Originally a 12th-century Norman motte on the site of a stronghold of the Wolf of Badenoch (the notorious son of Robert II), it was built after the 1715 Jacobite uprising to discourage further rebellion. General Wade extended it in 1734 and added the stables on the west side to accommodate a troop of dragoons. Prince Charles captured it from a handful of government troops, and it was here that some 1,500 survivors from Culloden assembled to await their Prince. They waited in vain until the message came that the cause was dead and they must now fend for themselves. The following day Lord George Murray sat down in the barracks and wrote a long, bitter letter to the Prince, resentfully listing all the blunders that had contributed to their defeat. He blamed Colonel John William O'Sullivan, the plausible Irishman whom the Prince had trusted 'with the most escential things in regard to your operations', who had 'committed gross Blunders on many occasions.' It is a sad letter, written in the searing pain of defeat, lashing out with many understandable grievances and concluding with his resignation. Prince Charles never forgave him. Before disbanding to return to their homes, most of which had been razed, the loyal Highlanders blew up Ruthven to save it from the enemy. It remains, nonetheless, an important and dramatic landmark.

Newtonmore is a popular Highland holiday village which always seems to have bunting hanging along its one main street, full of hotels, guest houses, B&Bs, craft shops and tea rooms, Newtonmore has a certain charm, and a convenient 24-hour garage/shop. **Waltzing Waters**, at Newtonmore, ✆ (01540) 673 752, is an elaborate water, light, music production which is experienced in a seated theatre. Thousands of dazzling patterns of moving water, synchronized with music—very spectacular. *Open Feb–early Dec daily; adm.*

Sports and Activities

The Strathspey Clansman on the **Strathspey Steam Railway** runs between Aviemore and Boat of Garten (*mid April–Oct*). On Wednesdays in high summer you can have luncheon in a restaurant car that was once in the Flying Scotsman. They also have Enthusiasts days and other special events.

There is plenty to do around Aviemore: **Loch Insh Watersports Centre** includes a boat house and reasonable restaurant (built by the owner out of telegraph poles), and pleasing accommodation. **Rothiemurchus Visitor Centre** features everyday life on a working Highland estate; and you can hire mountain bikes (maps, rucksacks and waterproofs, etc. provided); **Cairngorm Reindeer Centre** at Glenmore (*open daily; adm with guided tours among the reindeer*); **Loch Morlich Water Sports; Kincraig Highland Wildlife Park**, a children's paradise: wolves, lynx, otters, arctic fox, bears, etc. You can drive around and watch the animals being fed. Weekends and holidays have themed events, with talks and activities (*open daily; adm*); also at Kincraig, on the B9152, **Leault Farm**, ✆ (01540) 651 310, has demonstrations by working sheepdogs—up to 8 dogs working as a team, each with its personal set of commands (*demonstrations Sun–Fri taking about 45mins; adm*); and much else besides.

Kingussie ✆ (01540–) ***Where to Stay and Eating Out***

expensive

Duke of Gordon Hotel, Newtonmore Road, Kingussie, ✆ 661 302, 🖷 661 989, has just been restored at vast expense, and you are piped into dinner. Queen Victoria mentions it in her diary. **Auchendean Lodge**, at Nethybridge, ✆/🖷 (01479) 851 347, *www. auchendean.com*, has seven rooms and an excellent restaurant, with a chef who takes infinite pains with every detail. Local chanterelles, wild venison from the west coast, their own wild strawberries, are all recommended and the kilted host will advise you on the best malt to choose from their extensive list.

moderate

The Cross, ✆ 661 166, 🖷 661 080, on the outskirts of Kingussie, is an excellent (though not cheap) restaurant with charming rooms in a converted tweed mill. *Open Mar–Nov. Closed Tues.* **Columba House Hotel**, ✆ 661 402, 🖷 661 652, next door to the Folk Museum, is a very nice 19th-century former manse in pretty gardens with croquet and a putting green. The atmosphere is homely, the food good, the rooms comfortable. This is splendid for a skiing holiday as well as for summer breaks. **Scots House Hotel**, in Kingussie, ✆ 661 351, 🖷 661 111, is small and family-run, with excellent service and good food.

Dalrachney Lodge Hotel, Carrbridge, ✆ (01479) 841 252, 🖷 841 383, is in nice grounds, comfortable and friendly. **The Boathouse**, Kincraig, ✆ 651 394, is a good place to eat. *Open April–Oct.* **Corrour House**, Aviemore, ✆/🖷 (01479) 810 220, is a delightful country house hotel, very friendly and extremely good value.

Opposite the garage in Newtonmore—and don't let this put you off—is the **Eagle View Guest House**, ✆ 673 675. This is a splendid place to stay: the owners are friendly and have recently redecorated, the rooms are comfortable and the food good.

The **Old Bridge Inn**, in Aviemore, will give you a good meal.

cheap

The **Osprey Hotel**, Ruthven Road, Kingussie, ✆/🖷 661 510, is good value in a pleasant setting, and the food is first class. **Fairwinds Hotel**, Carrbridge, ✆/🖷 (01479) 841 240, was a Victorian manse, in 7 acres of attractive gardens, and is extremely good value.

You will be well looked after at the following guest houses: **Avondale House**, Newtonmore Road, Kingussie, ✆ 661 731; The **Hermitage Guest House**, Spey Street, Kingussie, ✆ 662 137; **Homewood Lodge**, Newtonmore Road, Kingussie,

✆ 661 507. For B&B try: **Glengarry**, East Terrace, Kingussie, ✆ 661 386; **Rowan House**, Homewood, Newtonmore Road, Kingussie, ✆ 662 153; and **The Aspens**, Spey Bridge, Newtonmore, ✆ 673 264.

West from Inverness

Beauly

Beauly is 10 miles west of Inverness at the mouth of the River Beauly, which is fed by several rivers including the Glass, the Affric and the Cannich, all of which start their lives high in the hills to the southwest. The surrounding landscape is gentle, rich farmland and wooded hills.

This is Lovat country. The Lovats came to Britain with the Normans and it was their French influence that inspired the name Beauly—*Beau Lieu.* (Romantics prefer to attribute the name to Mary, Queen of Scots who, fresh from her French château, exclaimed: '*Ah, quelle beau lieu.*') The Lovats named their home Beaufort Castle, no doubt with the same French influence. The town was developed in 1840 by Thomas Fraser of Strichen, Lord Lovat, and a monument in the centre of the square erected in 1905 commemorates the Lovat Scouts, a special unit raised by Simon Joseph, 16th Lord Lovat in 1900 to serve in the Boer War. The Lovat Scouts became famous for their service in harsh conditions. The recruits were Highlanders who had been born and bred to survive and work in tough surroundings: men who had been stalkers, keepers or ghillies, in harmony with nature. In many ways they were the forerunners of today's SAS.

Beauly straggles along a main street that widens into a market square, attractive in spite of being a main-road village. It has deservedly won the 'Scotland in Bloom' prize for large villages for six successive years as well as the 'Britain in Bloom' prize in 1995. Its charm is enhanced by Beauly Priory at the north end of the square beyond the old cross. Founded in 1230 for Valliscaulian monks from Burgundy, only the well-kept ruin of the church survives, but in the south wall there are three fine triangular windows embellished with trefoils, once part of the original building. The Reformation spelt its demise as a priory and in the 1650s Cromwell's soldiers removed some of the masonry to build a fort in Inverness. Among the memorials here, is one to the Fraser of Lovat who was killed in the Battle of the Shirts (*see* pp.132–3).

Perhaps the most colourful member of this family was Simon, Lord Lovat, born in about 1667. His many notorious escapades included the attempted abduction of an heiress and his subsequent marriage by force to her mother, a deed that left him convicted of high treason and outlawed. Having come into the title by devious means he became a Jacobite agent, involved in conveying false information to the enemy. Outlawed once more, he turned government man and received a full pardon. Swearing loyalty to the Crown, however, he sent his son to fight for Prince Charles in 1745. He was beheaded, finally, in London, having conducted his own defence, and met his end with humorous dignity. 'You'll get that nasty head of yours chopped off, you ugly old Scotch dog,' taunted a Cockney woman in the crowd. 'I believe I shall, you ugly old English bitch,' he replied. Hogarth painted a portrait of him in hideous old age, just before he was helped up the steps to the scaffold—racked by gout, bloated and villainous, with satanic eyebrows and a cruel mouth. Known as 'The Old Fox of the '45', he was indisputably a rogue, traitor and hypocrite. He was also, if contemporary reports are to be believed, intelligent, witty and charming.

A small **Lovat Memorial Garden** has recently been planted, behind the bank in Beauly. The large, Victorian Catholic church is well attended, the Catholic Lovats having attracted a large Catholic following in the area. **Beaufort Castle**, at Kiltarlity nearby, is Victorian baronial, rebuilt in 1937 and sold after the death in 1995 of *'Shimi'*—Gaelic for Simon, the previous Lord Lovat. He had made over his estates to his son, Simon Fraser, the Master of Lovat, to try to combat death duties. Unfortunately, his son could not cope with such a responsibility and a vast fortune slipped through his fingers. Both he and his brother died prematurely in 1994, within weeks of each other, their father following them to the grave a year later—a broken man.

In 1990 a sponsored 'Poethon' was organized to raise money to establish a Writers' Centre, **Moniack Mhor**, in steadings on the Moniack estate. For 24 hours, at various venues, 144 people recited contemporary poetry from memory, with the help of such celebrated poets as James Fenton and Wendy Cope. They raised a lot of money and the centre is now a going concern, tucked away up on the moors with inspiring views.

Straths Glass, Farrar, Cannich and Affric

Beauly is at the junction of several routes. The A862 takes you back to Inverness along the south side of the firth with good views northwards to the Black Isle. The A833 takes you south (past Beaufort Castle) to Milton in Glen Urquhart, a pretty drive not much frequented. For a good day out, take the A831 southwest to Cannich. The road runs along the River Beauly and then the Glass, where fishermen in waders stand thigh-deep in swirling waters surrounded by lichen-hung woods and gravelly islands. To the east there is a ridge of high ground stretching down to the Aird country of Lovat, while the three lovely glens of Affric, Cannich and Farrar converge from the west. Strathglass was one of the places that suffered most in the Clearances. In the first three decades of the 19th century Elizabeth Chisholm of Strathglass, acting for her sick husband, managed to clear the land of virtually all the people whose roots had been embedded there for centuries.

At **Kilmorack**, 2 miles from Beauly, there are the remains of two Iron Age forts. Further on, at **Aigas**, there are hydroelectric dams where visitors can watch salmon being 'lifted' on their way upstream to breed.

At **Struy** you can go west into Strath Farrar and follow the River Farrar up to Loch Monar. From here you can walk up into the hills along any of the many tracks and you won't be jostled off the path by herds of hikers, nor distracted by endless notices telling you how to behave and equip yourself.

For an interesting detour, take the left turn over the River Glass at Struy, and head back up the east side of the Beauly on the very minor **Eskadale** road. The peaceful little chapel of St Mary's was once the main Catholic centre for this area. In its graveyard is a memorial to an almost-forgotten episode in Scotland's history: the graves of the 'Sobieski Stuarts'. These two brothers, John Sobieski Stolberg Stuart and Charles Edward Stuart, conned Victorian society into accepting them as grandsons of Prince Charles Edward Stuart. They claimed that their father, Lieutenant Thomas Allen, Royal Navy, was the legitimate son of Prince Charles by Louise of Stolberg. They called themselves Counts d'Albanie and fought for Napoleon at Waterloo. It was fashionable to support their pretensions and many did, including Lord Lovat, who established them at Eilean Aigas House, where they kept deerhounds, wrote several collections of poetry and invented tartans with which to impress their gullible friends. They also 'discovered' the *Vestiarium Scoticum*, an 'ancient' work on clan tartans with a provenance as unlikely as Macpherson's Ossian (*see The Sobieski Stuarts* by H. Beveridge, 1909).

You can keep to the east side of Strathglass on the small road down to Cannich, but if you cross back to the A831, stop off at the Holy Well of St Ignatius, beside the road at **Glassburn**, where there is an intriguing old headstone in a modern cairn, with engravings that include references to St Columba (563), St Bean (1015), and St Margaret (1070), as well as to Pope Leo XIII. There is also a poem which could be the rallying hymn of the Temperance League:

Water bright water, pure water for me,
the drink of the wise, the wine of the free...

At Cannich, 17 miles southwest of Beauly, the A831 returns eastwards through beautiful Glen Urquhart to Loch Ness (*see* pp.139–40). Three miles to the southeast (2 miles by foot), the **Corrimony Cairn** is a Stone- and Bronze-Age burial chamber, its passage still roofed, surrounded by a stone circle. The Glass meets up with the Cannich and the Affric here, with two more glens that, like Strath Farrar, should be explored on foot. The scenery is gentler than that of the western Highlands but just as beautiful, enhanced rather than spoiled by the hydro-electric schemes that have changed the landscape. Steep, pine-clad rocks rise from peaty lochs in moss-green valleys where gnarled old trees are encrusted with silvery lichens. If you have time to explore only one glen, then **Affric** is the most beautiful, though there's no guarantee of solitude. Drive to the car park about 2 miles before Affric Lodge and leave your car. Take the track past the lodge and around Loch Affric. The track to the north of the loch is more scenic. At its western end, follow the river to Alltbeithe, about 10 miles from the car park, where there is a youth hostel. Ten miles or so further on is Loch Duich on the west coast.

Shopping

Campbells of Beauly, ✆ (01463) 782 239 (*open Mon–Sat 9–1 and 2–5.30, Thurs 9–1 only*) at the southern end of the square, is internationally renowned for top-quality tweeds, woollens, tartans and every possible Highland accessory, ready to wear or bespoke, served with great charm and efficiency by the Campbell family.

Beauly ✆ (01463–) **Where to Stay and Eating Out**

expensive

Mullardoch House Hotel, in Glen Cannich, ✆/🖷 (01456) 415 460, is a sporting lodge in a peaceful, Highland setting with 11 Munros on the doorstep, and good food.

moderate

For something different, **Aigas Field Centre**, ✆ 782 443, 🖷 782 097, is a Victorian-Gothic mansion with a relaxed, friendly atmosphere on a working estate in magnificent surroundings. There are optional field study programmes. The **Priory Hotel**, The Square, Beauly, ✆ 782 309, 🖷 782 531, is attractive, well run and comfortable.

Mains of Aigas, ✆ 782 423, in Strathglass, has a choice of 5 self-catering apartments (sleeping 4–6) in converted farm buildings which have been beautifully refurbished and equipped. It's in a lovely position, with its own golf course beside the River Beauly. **Tomich Holidays**, near Beauly, ✆ (01456) 415 332, have cottages and chalets sleeping 4–6.

Moniack Castle Winery and Wine Bar, ✆ 831 080 (*open Mon–Fri*) is an excellent staging post about 4 miles southeast of Beauly. Here, their own home-produced country wines, meads and a variety of delicious jellies are served in the castle's converted outbuildings. The food is excellent and the wine, jams, and chutneys make excellent gifts.

cheap

The **Lovat Arms**, Beauly, ✆ 782 313, 782 862, in the main street, is comfortable, informal and very good value, with nice food. **Brockies Lodge Hotel**, Kiltarlity, near Beauly, ✆ 741 257, 741 258, is good value and caters for children. For friendly B&B try **Kerrow House**, Cannich, ✆ (01456) 415 243; **Wester Moniack Farmhouse**, Kirkhill, ✆ 831 237; or **Broomhill**, Kiltarlity, ✆ 741 447.

Ardgowan Lodge Guest House, Wester Phoineas, near Beauly, ✆ 741 745, is part of a Victorian coach house and stables in 2 acres of secluded garden. Comfortable, and good food.

Beauly to Kyle of Lochalsh

Tourist Information

Strathpeffer: in the square, (✆ (01997) 421 415 (*open Easter–late Nov*).

Muir of Ord and Contin

Muir of Ord lies north of Beauly on the A862. Muirs (moors) provided large areas of unfenced land for the assembling of cattle and sheep, and this one, being at the confluence of several routes, was the largest tryst in the north of the country in the 19th century. Beasts that had travelled this far over soft ground were shod at Muir of Ord for the hard surfaces of the routes to the southern markets. A straggling village grew up to serve the needs of the drovers, but today little of the colour and bustle that must have characterized the place survives. For those interested in archaeology, quite a few chambered cairns and ancient remains can be found in the vicinity, but on the whole the agricultural landscape is tame and unremarkable. **Gilchrist**, or Kilchrist, on the outskirts of Muir of Ord, witnessed a nasty scene in 1603 when the Macdonells of Glengarry locked some Mackenzies in the parish church and torched them.

Contin, about 8 miles northwest on the A832 on the west side of the River Blackwater, has an old coaching inn from which passengers used to depart on the tortuous journey west to Poolewe and Ullapool after the roads were built in the 18th century. Telford built the first bridge here, which was later swept away by flood water. Dealers used to come up from England to the Contin Horse Fair to buy sturdy Highland ponies for work in the coal mines. Fair days were festive occasions, drawing people from far afield to jostle and gossip over braziers, amongst the peddlers' stalls and animal pens.

Strathpeffer

Before going on west, visit Strathpeffer, a couple of miles northeast on the A834, a famous spa town until the First World War. The springs were used as early as 1770, and visitors, including foreign royalty, came from overseas to take the sulphur and chalybeate waters. In 1819 Dr Thomas Morrison pronounced these the most efficacious in Britain: they were analysed and found to contain more hydrogen than any other. The small Pump Room (now derelict) was built in 1859, and villas, hotels and hospitals sprung up around it. In 1885 a railway station was built to serve the ailing visitors arriving by train on a branch line from Dingwall (now dismantled). The station is now a craft centre. After the First World War the popularity of the spa declined, though Strathpeffer remained a holiday resort. Lying in a sheltered dip in wooded hills with houses and hotels rising in neat terraces from its heart, the town is now a holiday centre whose gently refined atmosphere has won it the title 'Harrogate of the North', with a preponderance of coach tours.

There is a **Water Sampling Pavilion** on the site of the old bath house, where visitors can hold their noses and drink the revolting water (*Easter–end Oct; free*). There are **Highland Games** in August with all the traditional events such as tossing the caber, putting the shot, piping and dancing, and drinking. The village is dormant in the winter, but you can get good snacks in the licensed **Spar Tearooms** through the Spar shop in the square (*open till 3pm*).

The **Eagle Stone** stands 3 foot tall on a hillock to the east of the town, reached by a well-signed lane near Eaglestone House. It is a Pictish symbol stone with an engraved eagle and a horseshoe and was the subject of one of the Brahan Seer's prophecies (*see* p.43–4). If the stone should fall three times, he said, then ships would tie up to it. Setting aside a mighty tidal wave, this seems improbable at first, but the seer had uncanny prescience. It is said that the stone has already fallen twice (it's now cemented into place) and that on the second occasion the Cromarty Firth flooded up to the old county buildings in Dingwall. The stone is only 4 miles to the west and the River Peffery runs very close by on its way to the firth, though way down in the valley.

A couple of miles due east of the symbol stone—a nice walk along the ridge called Druim Chat, meaning 'cat's back'—there is a well-preserved vitrified fort, **Knockfarrel**, one in a line of three great Pictish defence sites, the other two being at Craig Phadraig in Inverness and Ord Hill in Kessock. You can see the foundations clearly—a vast place, extending to some 810ft (250m). This is believed to have been a stronghold of Fingal and his warriors.

More fact than legend was the clan battle between the Macdonalds and the Mackenzies in 1429 at Kinellan, just southwest of Strathpeffer. Margaret Macdonald, daughter of the Lord of the Isles, had been sent to the 6th Chief of the Mackenzies to be his wife, though they had not met. When she arrived she was found to be blind in one eye, so her furious bridegroom-to-be returned her to her family accompanied by a groom, a horse and a dog, all blind in one eye. The Macdonalds swiftly sought their revenge for such an insult, but they lost the battle.

Climbing **Ben Wyvis**, the great bulk to the north of Strathpeffer, takes about 5 hours. Start from the bridge over the Allt a' Bhealaich Mhoir near Garbat on the A835 Dingwall–Ullapool road. There is a signed path to start you off but you will need a map. Bear left above the forest and go up the west ridge of An Cabar. This takes you to the extraordinary Glas Leathad Mor, a soft carpet of moss stretching for about one and a half miles to the summit. It is wonderful walking, and also some of the most unusual mountain terrain in Scotland.

Back in Contin, head west on the A832 a couple of miles to the **Rogie Falls**, well signposted and only a short walk from the car park. You won't be alone here but it is usually possible to find a reasonably secluded spot for a picnic amongst the birches, rowans and gnarled oaks, with bracken, heather and mossy crags for carpet and table. There is a suspension bridge over the river where you can, with luck, watch salmon trying to leap the falls: they often reach astonishing heights. There is a salmon ladder at the side for the ones that don't manage.

expensive–moderate

More of a private house than a hotel, **The Dower House** at Highfield, a mile out of Muir of Ord, ✆/🖷 (01463) 870 090, *www.thedowerhouse.co.uk*, is a marvellous place to stay, winner of the AA's 'Best New Incomers for Scotland Award'. Converted to its present 'cottage' style in 1800, the Aitchisons run it as a guest house where you can relax in front of log fires and feel at home. The food is first class—worth a detour even if you can't get a room.

Coul House Hotel, Contin, by Strathpeffer, ✆ 421 487, 🖷 421 945, is a large, secluded country house in an attractive setting, elegantly furnished and comfortable, with good food and candlelit dinners. **Ord House Hotel**, Muir of Ord, ✆/🖷 (01463) 870 492, is a delightful 17th-century laird's house in 50 acres of garden and woodland. The **Achilty Hotel**, Contin, ✆ 421 355, 🖷 421 923, is comfortable and has good food and beamed ceilings, stone walls, log fires and lots of atmosphere.

moderate

Ben Wyvis Hotel, in Strathpeffer, ✆ 421 323, 🖷 421 228, has the air of a spa hotel—comfortable and large. Much smaller and cheaper, but good value, are: **Brunstane Lodge Hotel**, Golf Course Road, Strathpeffer, ✆/🖷 421 261; and the **Richmond Hotel**, Church Brae, Strathpeffer, ✆ 421 300.

For a cosy guest house try **Dunraven Lodge**, Golf Course Road, Strathpeffer, ✆ 421 210, or the **Garden Guest House**, Garden House Brae, Strathpeffer, ✆ 421 242 (smoking allowed in the garden). For high class B&B try **Mrs Cameron**, White Lodge, Strathpeffer, ✆ 421 730, or **Craigvar**, The Square, Strathpeffer, ✆ 421 622 (with a four poster bed!).

North from Inverness

The Black Isle

Although not actually an island, being securely tied to the mainland by the 5-mile isthmus between Beauly and the River Conan, the Black Isle was once sufficiently sea-girt to feel like one. Until 1982 the narrow neck of water between the Beauly and Moray Firths was crossed in a small car ferry which slithered over the turbulent currents between two queues of cars: a half-mile voyage necessitating as much as an hour's wait. The alternative was to drive all the way round the Beauly Firth. Now, with a link to Inverness via the Kessock Bridge, there is no ferry journey to give an impression of insularity. You are over the bridge and across the peninsula on the fast A9 without noticing, and the island feeling has gone. But things change slowly and the scattered communities retain much of their separateness. The first settlers arrived about 5,000 years ago and started leaving traces of their habitation about 1000 BC. There are still plenty of ancient remains: chambered cairns, duns and Pictish stones dotted around. No one is quite sure about the 'Black': some say it is because the climate is milder, and that frost and snow are rare, leaving the land 'black' when all around it is white. Others say the name is derived from St Duthus, or Duthac (*dubh*—black) who was born in Tain around the year 1000 and did a lot of missionary work in the area.

About 45 miles of coastline strung together by attractive fishing villages enclose a district of rolling farmland interspersed with forestry and moor, with no significant heights. The Black Isle is unlike anywhere else in the Highlands and has its own, soft, sing-song dialect. When the elegant, award-winning bridge was opened by the Queen Mother, opinions were divided. Locals can nip into Inverness in a matter of minutes now, but their quiet countryside has been opened up as a dormitory for the town, and offers easy pickings for itinerant vandals.

Munlochy Bay, about 3 miles up a twisting minor road from the first turning right north of the bridge, is vibrant with the cackle of geese in winter, targets for sportsmen who like to see wildfowl at the end of their guns. Ask in the village for the 'Clootie Well'. This one is not so well known as the one near Culloden, but over the years petitioners have turned the hedgerow into an extraordinary collage of filthy rags of all materials, including plastic. The origins are pagan, the superstition still strong; no one dares to remove the offerings for fear of supernatural reprisals. The **Black Isle Wildlife Park and Country Park**, ✆ (01463) 731 656, is on your way to Munlochy, at the Croft, Drumsmittal (*open Mar–Nov daily 10–6; adm*). There is nothing too unusual here, and for those who hate to see wild animals in captivity (Highland wild cat) it's not the place—but during spring and summer you can watch chicks pecking their way out of their eggs.

Avoch (pronounced Orch or Och, with a guttural 'ch'), another 3 miles east on the A832, is a picturesque fishing village with a small harbour, and miles of bracing walks along tidal sandflats with good views across the firth. About a mile to the south on Ormond Hill, is the ruin of the castle in which Sir Andrew Murray, or de Moravia, lived. From this stronghold he raised the north against Edward I, while William Wallace was busy raising the south. He was killed as a result of wounds at the Battle of Stirling Bridge in 1297. He shared responsibility with Wallace for Scotland's victory over the English, but his death deprived him of most of the credit.

Fortrose, a couple of miles on, is a pleasant, no-nonsense resort town with the strong feel of an island community. Between it and **Rosemarkie**, a mile to the north, the flat, tapering nose of Channonry Ness, ending in Channonry Point, protrudes into the Moray Firth, sheltering Fortrose and balancing Rosemarkie on its bridge. Rosemarkie's first church was built by St Moluag in the 6th century, together with a school, and it is said that he is buried beneath the Pictish stone in the churchyard. In the 12th century King David I authorized the building of a great cathedral, of which only the sandstone ruins remain on a well-kept green in Fortrose. There are memorials here to Lord Seaforth and his family, confirming the Brahan Seer's prophecy about the downfall of the House of Seaforth (*see* p.44). In 1880 a hoard of silver coins was dug up from the green, dating from the reign of Robert III. Cromwell recycled much of the fabric of the cathedral to build a fort in Inverness. **Channonry Ness** has a golf course, caravan park and lighthouse; the beaches are popular in summer, with golden sands and rock pools. It also has a memorial cairn to the Brahan Seer, who is alleged to have been burnt here in a barrel of tar. This is where witches were burnt, so it would have been a likely spot for the demise of *Coinneach Odhar*, whose prophesies have proved uncannily accurate.

Groam House Museum (*✆ (01381) 620 961; open May–Sept Mon–Sat 10–5, Sun 2–4.30; Oct–April Sat and Sun 2–4; Easter week 2–4.30; adm*) in Rosemarkie, has local and archaeological exhibits: carved stones found in the vicinity of the church, indicating the importance of Rosemarkie in early Christian times; fragments of cross-slabs and gravestones and a particularly fine Pictish slab, all well laid out and explained. There are audio-visual shows and the curator is very knowledgeable—a good place to learn the little that is known about those illusive Picts.

Cromarty

Cromarty, on the northeastern tip of the Black Isle, about 23 miles from the Kessock Bridge, is sheltered by the great headland of the South Sutor at the mouth of the Cromarty Firth. This picturesque, 18th-century fishing town was once an important port with a magnificent natural harbour and was a Royal Burgh for several centuries. Some of its old merchants' houses are important examples of domestic architecture for the period, and rows of terraced cottages stand gable-end-on to the street, hunched against the wind, forming 'rope walks' where fisherwomen stretched out new ropes from the town's rope factory. A number of old buildings that were in danger of dereliction have been rescued and reused in an imaginative way: the old rope works has been converted into housing; the old brewery has become a small residential conference centre; fishermen's cottages and the old manse have been modernized. Escaping later development, Cromarty was designated a 'conservation area', with the result that its picture-postcard prettiness is almost too good to be true.

Sir Thomas Urquhart was one of Cromarty's more endearing lairds in the 17th century, and an ardent Royalist. Knighted by Charles I, he fought for him at Worcester in 1641 and was imprisoned as a result. He tried to bribe his way out of prison by offering Cromwell the first complete Universal Language which reads as well backwards as forwards, and wrote reams of good prose and bad poetry. He was said to have died of an uncontrollable fit of laughter when he heard of the Restoration of Charles II in 1660.

Cromarty was bought in 1772 by George Ross, some of whose descendants still live here. Ross made his money as an army agent who supplied uniforms and advanced pay, always with a commission. He built the harbour, founded a cloth factory, a rope factory, a nail and spade factory, a brewery and a lace industry. He imported Highlanders to work for him and built them a Gaelic chapel. George Ross also built Cromarty house in 1772, which now stands in its own private grounds to the east, on the site of Cromarty Castle, built to watch over pilgrims coming to St Duthas. The town was on the main coastal route north from Inverness (which included ferry links across the firths) and it thrived until the decline of the fishing industry. Trade and population dwindled further with the establishment of a road and rail network bypassing this eastern outpost.

Cromarty Courthouse (✆ *(01381) 600 418; open April–Oct daily 10–5; Nov, Dec and Mar daily 12–4; Jan and Feb by arrangement; adm*) is one of the town's successful restorations of an old building and it has won several well-deserved awards. It is an '18th-century experience', with a courtroom scene and animated models. From here you can hire a 'walkman tour of Cromarty' narrated by Hugh Miller himself .

Hugh Miller's Cottage (✆ *(01381) 600 245; open May–Sept daily 11–1 and 2–5, Sun 2–5; adm*) in Church Street, is a nostalgic journey into the past. The long, low, thatched cottage with crow-stepped gables, its tiny upper windows half-buried in the eaves, was built in 1711 by the great-grandfather of Hugh Miller (1802–56). Hugh rose from simple beginnings as a stonemason and poet to become a famous palaeontologist, naturalist and journalist. He was also a radical theologian. Working at the same time as Darwin, he expounded his own God-centered theories of evolution and argued that evolution was not a gradual but a sudden change. As with Darwin, his work with fossils cast serious doubts on the accuracy of the Bible as history. Among much else, he wrote about the Brahan Seer in *Scenes and Legends of the North of Scotland.* Torn apart with doubt, he shot himself on Christmas Eve 1856, having recorded 'a fearful dream'. Restored by the National Trust for Scotland, the cottage contains a museum devoted to collections of his writings, personal belongings, geological specimens and such endearing memorabilia as the wooden chair in which his mother sat to nurse him.

The North and South Sutors guarding the entrance to the Cromarty Firth were once two giant cobblers (*souter* is the Scots word for shoemaker) who protected the Black Isle from pirates. Perhaps they slept whilst on duty: they were turned to stone. In the First World War the Cromarty Firth provided a sheltered harbour for half the North Sea fleet, the other half using Scapa Flow in Orkney. Charles II landed somewhere near here on his way to be crowned at Scone in 1650. The view north to the modern constructions of the oil installations at Nigg is a splendid contrast to the picturesque elegance of the old 18th-century town.

The B9163 takes you westwards along the firth and on round the perimeter of the Black Isle. To complete a circular tour, a one-track road skirts the northern shore of the Beauly Firth, 10 miles back to the Kessock Bridge. It hugs the shore for the last stretch, where tidal flats are rich in wildfowl, backed by blue-grey hills to the north with traces of snow even in late summer. The ruined castle (private, but visible from the road) behind a wall at the western end of the firth is **Redcastle,** one of Scotland's architectural tragedies. Until it was abandoned in the 1950s, Redcastle is reputed to have been one of the oldest continuously inhabited strongholds in Scotland. A castle called Edradour was known to have stood here for many years before William the Lion strengthened it in 1179. It passed through several hands until it was annexed by the Crown after the fall from power of the notorious Douglas family. The Mackenzies held it for 200 years from 1570. According to legend, they resorted to sorcery and human sacrifices in a vain attempt to save the land from a cattle plague, and were subsequently cursed. The present castle was built for Rory Mackenzie in 1641 and this 'new strong house of Redcastle' was besieged by Covenanting troops who 'brunt the castle to ashes, with all the good furnitur'. It was quickly repaired and the estate was sold by the Mackenzies in 1790. A gutted skeleton today, its rose-red shell rises from a wilderness behind an ivy-clad wall. Less than 50 years ago it was a splendid lived-in castle with well-tended gardens: the present owners have resisted all attempts to save it.

North Kessock straggles along the shore, its core of attractive fishermen's cottages fringed by much new development.

Cromarty ✆ (01381–) ***Where to Stay and Eating Out***

moderate

Cromarty Arms Inn, ✆ 600 230, ▣ 230 861, is a reasonable place to stay, simple and full of character. **North Kessock Hotel**, ✆/▣ (01463) 731 208, is an inexpensive, old-fashioned inn overlooking the ferry terminal (no longer in use except as a slipway), with views across the Beauly Firth to Inverness. A listed building, it has only a few rooms and a genuine Highland atmosphere. The food is first class, imaginative, unfussy and not expensive. The **Royal Hotel**, Marine Terrace, Cromarty, ✆ 600 217, ▣ 600 813, is a splendidly friendly place on the harbour, and very good value.

For B&B try **Craigiewood**, North Kessock, ✆ (01463) 731 628; or **Braelangwell House**, at Balblair, ✆ 610 353, a comfortable Georgian house in 50 acres of woodland and garden, with facilities for children.

Florence's Tearoom, on the corner of Church Street in Cromarty, does excellent teas with home baking and delicious cakes and biscuits. *Open Thurs and Sat–Mon.* If it's shut, try **Binnie's**, opposite. **Thistles**, Church Street, Cromarty, ✆ 600 471, serves excellent food. *Closed Sun evening and Mon lunch.*

cheap

Royal Hotel, Fortrose, ✆ 620 326, is a splendid black and white turreted, old town-centre hotel.

Easter Ross

Dingwall

At the junction of several main routes on the southwestern corner of the Cromarty Firth, Dingwall's name is derived from the Norse *thing* (parliament or council) and *volle* (place). For Queen Victoria, who stopped here several times in her royal train, it was set 'in a glen, with hills rising above it, extremely pretty and it reminds me of Switzerland [her ultimate accolade].' Pretty isn't quite the right word for Dingwall today. It is a Highland market town, with an early 18th-century town house and tollbooth and an ancient mercat cross. It is possible that Macbeth was born here in the castle that once stood in Castle Street, of which only a handful of stones remain. Robert the Bruce's wife is said to have been a prisoner here during his exile, and it was the hereditary home of the Earls of Ross in the 13th and 14th centuries. It is hard to believe that Dingwall was a thriving port before the waterway at the mouth of the River Peffery silted up—cutting off deep-water access to the Cromarty Firth. The canal at the end of Ferry Road was built by Telford in an attempt to cut through the encroaching mudflats. It was always an important livestock market and even today you may hear a few exchanges in Gaelic around the market square on Wednesdays. The Dingwall Highland Gathering is in July.

Not many people stop to read war memorials these days, but spare a moment for the one in the Station Square, in the form of an intricate rustic cross. It was first erected in Fontaine Notre Dame in France by members of the Seaforth Highlanders, in honour of their comrades who fell at the Battle of Cambrai. The original remained in France for six years, its inscription composed by the villagers: 'Mort Pour La Patrie, 4ème Les Seaforth Highlanders, Honneur aux Hommes, Mobilisés dans cet village pour la Bataille de Cambrai 1917.' In 1924 the Seaforth Reunion Club brought the cross home to Scottish soil, and thus it stands today, its wood recently replaced but the inscription original.

The Town House (1730; *open Easter–Sept; adm*) is a museum with a special exhibition about General Sir Hector Macdonald (1853–1903). Known as 'Fighting Mac', Hector was a brave, tragic man who rose from the ranks to become a Major General; almost unheard of in those days. He distinguished himself through many acts of conspicuous bravery, until the Battle of Omdurman, in 1898, when he and 'his black brigade performed prodigies of valour' and won the day. Fêted as a public hero, with honours of all kinds lavished upon him, he attained the rank of Major General KCB and was finally posted to Ceylon. While here 'grave charges affecting his moral character were made against him'. It is almost certain that these charges were totally unfounded and arose from jealous tongues—being a man of the people, he treated his servants and house-boys as members of the family, unlike many others in his position. It was confidently expected that his court martial in 1903 would result in a complete and honourable acquittal but he shot himself before it could take place. Deeply shocked by this appalling smear against their beloved Hero of Omdurman, the local people erected an impressive monument to him on Mitchell Hill, a battlemented **tower** that is a landmark for miles.

Dingwall to Bonar Bridge

The surprising Indian temple on the hill above Evanton, known as the **Fyrish Monument**, is a folly erected by General Sir Hector Munro (1726–1805) as a philanthropic gesture to provide work to the unemployed in the area. It is modelled on the gateway to Negapatam, an Indian town captured by Sir Hector in 1781. Although it is clearly seen from the road, it is much more fun close to, and not an exacting climb.

Because it is potentially dangerous, you aren't encouraged to go to the **Black Rock Gorge** at Evanton, about 6 miles north of Dingwall on the back road, so there are no signposts to it. Go through the village and take the left turn just after the bridge. Take the third track to the left about 1½ miles down Glen Glass, and you will find a magnificent 2-mile chasm, with sheer sides up to 200ft deep and so narrow that in places it would almost be possible to jump across. At this point it might be wise to chain and padlock your children and dogs. The River Glass tumbles on its way far below and it isn't too difficult to catch the quick flash of a water sprite, darting through the mossy chasm in the sparkling air.

If you are going northwest and don't want to explore the Tain peninsula, by far the most scenic route from the south is on the A836, starting a couple of miles on from Evanton. This road goes up over the windswept, heathery moors and then zigzags down through dramatic ravines to the Dornoch Firth: stop at the Stone Viewpoint, at Struie, about 10 miles up the road, for panoramic views over the Kyles of Sutherland. There is a view indicator and a board explaining the glacial action that created this lovely land and seascape.

Dingwall ✆ (01349–) ***Where to Stay***

expensive–moderate

Kinkell House, Easter Kinkell, ✆ 861 270, 🖷 865 902, is close to Dingwall and very comfortable. The **Novar Arms Hotel**, Evanton, ✆ 830 210, 🖷 830 739, is cheaper and also comfortable.

moderate

Tulloch Castle Hotel, Dingwall, ✆ 861 325, 🖷 863 993, will give you a warm welcome and good value. Friendly staff.

cheap

Black Rock Bunkhouse/Hostel, Evanton, near Dingwall, ✆ 830 917, is good value, with camping ground and linen hire, a pub close by, and a bus stop.

The Tain Peninsula

Although the exploitation of North Sea oil has inevitably changed the character of the hammerhead peninsula jutting eastwards between Nigg Bay and Tain, it has enough attractions to make it worthy of attention.

The A9 bypasses **Invergordon**, 14 miles northeast of Dingwall, and unless you have a reason to stop off, don't bother. It is a busy industrial centre on the western tip of Nigg Bay, dominated by the surrealistic constructions built for the oil industry. The Cromarty Firth is one of the finest deep-water anchorages in the world and is now one of the most important European centres for the repair and maintenance of the exploration rigs. Although not a town to visit for an outing, there is something curiously striking about some of the giant skeletons whose fragile-looking girders are built to withstand the full force of a North Sea gale.

Don't let the A9 sweep you past the B9165 turning to **Fearn**, off to the east in the midst of rich farmland, where cottages with pretty gardens are grouped around a green. Fearn Abbey was founded in the 13th century and its restored nave and choir are still used as the parish church. The first martyr of the Scottish Reformation, Patrick Hamilton (1498–1528), was titular abbot here. He was of royal descent through an illegitimate granddaughter of James II, and educated in Paris and Louvain, where he came under the influence of Lutheran theology. Converted to Protestantism, he married and returned to St Andrews where he was arrested and tried for heresy by Archbishop James Beaton. He was burnt at the stake in St Andrews in 1528 (there is an impression of his face on the stone wall nearby, left there when his soul flew out of the flames). This martyrdom was one of the sparks that kindled the Scottish Reformation.

Portmahomack, about 7 miles north of Fearn on the B9165, sprawls upwards around a sheltered harbour. At **Tarbat Ness**, on the northern tip of the peninsula, one of the highest lighthouses in Britain warns ships of the dangerous sandbanks threatening the entrance to the Dornoch Firth. The Norsemen called them Gizzen Briggs and were among their earliest victims. The views are stupendous and there are sometimes seals basking on the rocks below. You can walk for miles along the shore or on the red sandstone clifftops. At **Shandwick**, about 10 miles down the east coast, people have found interesting fossils in the bay and its caves. The 9ft (3m) stone cross-slab above the village was erected in memory of one of three Norse princes who were shipwrecked on a reef here, while chasing an Earl of Ross who had abused his wife—their sister.

Tain

Tain, on the south side of the Dornoch Firth, 11 miles north of Invergordon, takes its name, like Dingwall, from the Norse word *thing*—a meeting place or parliament. Of more historic than aesthetic interest, it has a pleasant east-coast sturdiness, its red-sandstone buildings sheltered by hills to the west as they gaze across the Dornoch Firth and its acres of sandflats at low tide.

Malcolm Canmore granted it royal status in the 11th century, probably because St Duthus, or Duthac, was born here in about 1000. He died in Ireland towards the end of the century and his remains were brought back here to be interred in St Duthus Chapel, now an overgrown ruin in the cemetery between the 18-hole golf course and the sea. It was built on the site of his birth as a 'prayer cell', with a resident hermit guarding the sacred relics which were believed to work miracles. Hundreds, maybe thousands, of people made pilgrimages here.

Like other sacred places, this was a place of sanctuary for fugitives. Elizabeth de Burgh, wife of Robert the Bruce; his daughter by his first wife, Marjory, who was to become mother to Robert II; and Isabella Countess of Buchan, whose family, the Macduffs, held the hereditary right to crown the kings of Alba, together took refuge here when fleeing to Orkney while Bruce was in exile. The sacred right of sanctuary was violated by the Earl of Ross, who took them prisoner and handed them over to the English in 1307—an act Scotland did not forget. The chapel was torched by a smuggler, McNeill of Creich, in 1427, to destroy an enemy he had chased inside.

St Duthus Collegiate Church was built in 1360 on the site of an earlier church, traces of which can be seen in the chapter house. It is now a show place and memorial, no longer used for worship. After the chapel was burnt, the relics of St Duthus were brought here (they disappeared in 1560) and this became the focus for pilgrims. Among them was James IV, seeking absolution for having been instrumental in his father's death. He made the pilgrimage every year for 20 years, but not entirely from religious fervour: he liked to keep in touch with his people all over Scotland and had established his favourite mistress, Janet Kennedy, in Darnaway Castle in Morayshire. Look out particularly for the stained-glass windows showing Malcolm Canmore and Queen Margaret bestowing a royal charter on the town; and an assembly of the Scottish parliament adopting John Knox's Confessions of Faith in 1560.

Tain and District Museum (*open Easter–Sept Mon–Sat; donation box*), in Castle Brae off the High Street, was founded as an exhibition for the visit of the Queen Mother in 1966 and became permanent. It has relics, manuscripts, photographs, archaeological remains and 18th- and 19th-century displays of social history. There is also information on St Duthus and on the patronage of James IV, though not of 'Flaming' Janet. **Tain Through Time** (*open April–Oct 10–6; ring ✆ (01862) 894 089 for winter openings; adm*) offers a 'sound and light' show, guides in costume, audio-visual shows, live acting, artefacts and documents, all giving an excellent interpretation of Tain and its history. There is also a tour of the historic sites of the town using a personal CD player. **The Tolbooth** is 16th century, rebuilt in 1707, the year of the Act of Union. It is a striking building with a tall, castellated keep, a conical spire and angle turrets. Its bell is the original curfew bell of 1616.

North of the town is the **Glenmorangie Distillery**, founded in 1843. The A9 takes you a couple of miles west from Tain and then sweeps across a grand causeway-bridge over the Dornoch Firth, considerably shortening the distance north. The route to the west is the A836, past Bonar Bridge along the southern shore of the Dornoch Firth.

Croick Church

Turn left at Ardgay (pronounced Ardguy, as in Fawkes) 14 miles west of Tain, just before Bonar Bridge at the head of the Firth and you won't regret a 10-mile detour up Strath Carron, a wide valley bordered by hills, bracken and lichen-hung birches. Little Croick Church lies at the end in a walled churchyard surrounded by a scattering of wind-bent trees in a pocket of desolate moorland—one of the most poignant places in Scotland. Nowhere tells the story of the Clearances so eloquently. In the spring of 1845, families who had been evicted from their crofts in Glencalvie by the Duke of Sutherland's agents intent on clearing the land for lucrative sheep, had nowhere to go. They camped here in an improvised shelter against the church wall, made from rugs and plaids stretched over poles. The memorials they scratched on the diamond panes of this simple kirk can still be read today: 'Glencalvie people was in the church here May 24 1845...' 'Glencalvie people the wicked generation...' Inside, the kirk is plain, with unadorned walls, an iron stove, benches and table and a big pulpit. An interesting display board shows an assortment of contemporary newspaper cuttings from *The Times*. You can walk on up the track from the end of the road, for miles into the hills.

Bonar Bridge

Bonar Bridge, about 5 miles beyond Struie and a mile north of Ardgay, is so called after the bridge that spans the Kyle of Sutherland, a replacement of Thomas Telford's, built in 1813. Once a staging post on the A9, when this was the only route north, it is now a backwater hoping for tourists. In the 14th century an iron foundry was established here which consumed all the timber in the area in its rapacious smelters. James IV ordered more trees to be planted, some of which can still be seen among the ubiquitous pines of the Forestry Commission. A ferry bridged the Kyle until a tragedy in 1809: too many passengers were allowed to board the ferry, against the wishes of the sheriff, Mr MacCulloch. It was a calm night, but the boat was unevenly laden and it capsized, drowning over 70 people, including the sheriff.

Around Bonar Bridge

The Kyle of Sutherland separates Easter Ross from Sutherland: the River Shin runs into it from the north and the lovely Oykel runs in from the rugged hills in the northwest. After the rather tame landscape of the Black Isle and the Tain Peninsula, you are back in truly Highland scenery, with walks and climbs all around and not too many people other than fishermen, who always prefer to be on their own. The roads aren't crowded, and once you step away from them you can walk for miles and not see a soul.

About a mile past Ardgay, heading up the west side of the Kyle of Sutherland, turn left up a track to the site of the Battle of Carbisdale in 1650. You can also get to it past the school further on in Culrain. This was one of Charles II of England's least honourable legacies. He had encouraged James Graham, 1st Marquis of Montrose, to go to Scotland to try to win the Crown for him without having to sign the Covenant. Montrose, who had previously been a Covenanter himself, gathered up a little army and was defeated here at Carbisdale on 27 April. He escaped and was given refuge by Macleod of Assynt, but was then betrayed—opinions differ as to by whom—captured and taken to Edinburgh. But Charles had by now signed the Covenant and found it expedient not to intervene when his loyal subject was condemned to death and hanged at the Mercat Cross in May (*see* p.155).

The massive neo-Gothic pile that towers over the road just to the north is **Carbisdale Castle**, nothing to do with Montrose, but an early 20th-century peace offering to the dowager Duchess of Sutherland after an ugly battle with her stepchildren over her husband's will, which landed her with a 6-week jail sentence. It is now a youth hostel, but a youth hostel with a difference. Gracious slumming here and you don't have to earn your keep (✆ (01549) 421 232).

Lairg is a road junction with the railway close by, not particularly exciting but a useful centre for fishing holidays and for stocking up the picnic box. At the southeast end of Loch Shin, it straddles the River Shin, serving several outlying crofting communities as well as tourists. It is also the sheep market for the area. Not far down the Shin, the **Falls of Shin** are impressive but too popular, complete with car park, café and gift shop. The **Falls of Shin Coffee Shop** is above average and their food is excellent and unfussy.

The A839 goes west from Lairg to Inchnadamph on Loch Assynt and the northwest. It joins up with the A837 from Invershin, a prettier route through Strath Oykell. Just after the roads join, turn north up Glen Cassley to look at the impressive waterfall, with an old graveyard below. Over-enthusiastic planting of conifers all around here spoils what must once have been glorious open views.

Back to the A9 causeway over the Dornoch Firth, Dornoch (*see* pp.190–2) lies out on the northeastern side of the firth, bypassed by the main road.

Shopping

In Tain, **Aldie Water Mill**, ✆ (01862) 893 786, is a restored mill with an above average craft shop selling some unusual and good stuff (*open daily 10–5, seasonally; ring for dates*). You can visit the **Highland Fine Cheeses Factory** during working hours, see how cheese is made, and sample it.

Tain ✆ (01862–) **Where to Stay and Eating Out**

expensive

Glenmorangie House, Cadboll, Fearn, ✆ 871 671, 🖷 871 625, is the best place in the area if money is not a problem. **Morangie House Hotel**, Tain, ✆ 892 281, 🖷 892 872, is a little cheaper and very comfortable. It serves excellent food, with lots of choice, at reasonable prices.

expensive–moderate

Mansfield House, Tain, ✆ 892 052, 🖷 892 260, is a baronial-style Victorian country house in nice grounds with eight good golf courses within half an hour's drive. The elegant rooms are furnished with antique furniture; some have jacuzzis. Good food.

Oykel Bridge Hotel, Rosehall, near Lairg, ✆ (01549) 441 218, 🖷 441 384, is a charming, pretty place by the river with a secluded, colourful garden. It caters mainly for fishermen, with all the facilities required at the end of a day's fishing. Quiet and relaxing it has an impressive standing stone in the garden, rescued from the river and installed to add character. The dining room has an excellent central table where guests can help themselves to the delicious locally produced food. This is a very convenient as well as comfortable base within easy reach of all the activities this area has to offer.

Mounteagle, Fearn, ✆ 832 213, is an Edwardian farmhouse with lovely views, within a few hundred yards of a major stopping-off point for migratory waterfowl. Its charming hosts, Prue and John Douglas-Menzies, are enthusiastic fishermen, gardeners and beekeepers and much of the delicious food served here is grown or caught by themselves. This is a real home-from-home, and excellent value. Book well ahead.

cheap

Golfview House, 13 Knockbreck Road, Tain, ✆ 892 856, is a friendly guest house. For somewhere a bit different, try **Mrs Munro**, Corvost, Ardgay, ✆ (01863) 755 317, on the road to Croick Church. Up a track in a somewhat ramshackle farm steading, you may be greeted by a displaying peacock, a French partridge or an ancient and rather decrepit stag. Not many frills here (the rooms aren't ensuite), but a warm welcome and excellent supper and breakfast.

The Oyster Catcher, in Portmahomack, ✆ 871 560, is a splendid café with cheerful murals and a great atmostphere. *Open all year except Feb daily 11–6 and 7–8.30. Closed Mon.* Also *see* **Falls of Shin Coffee Shop**, p.187.

Sutherland and Caithness

Dornoch 190

Dornoch to John o'Groats 192

Helmsdale 194

Dunbeath 197

Wick 199

John o'Groats to Cape Wrath 202

Thurso 203

Sutherland was named by the Vikings as the land to the south of Caithness—an indication of the degree to which the two northern counties of Scotland were colonized by the Norsemen in the past. As you go north you will notice fewer Gaelic-derived names and more with Nordic origins. In the last couple of centuries, the fortunes of many of the villages and small towns along the coast rose and fell with the herring industry. The settlements along this coast reflect the hardship of the lives of the people who lived there, with little sign of frivolous embellishment. Nevertheless, many of the harbours are attractive, if somewhat changed from the days when they were packed out with fishing boats. The Flow Country is the name given to all the peatlands of Caithness and Sutherland, about 150,000 acres, just over half the total area of these counties. If you have time, explore these great tracts of wasteland along the glens of the rivers that run down to the sea from the south. This distinctive landscape is awesome in a melancholy way and certainly not unattractive when the sun shines.

Dornoch

Dornoch, a Royal Burgh, is delightfully unexpected. Tucked away above the Dornoch Firth, it is remote enough to have hung on to an old-world dignity and has managed to remain unspoilt in spite of the new road bridge making it more accessible. A higgledy-piggledy town with an attractive central square, it is a holiday resort and a golfing centre. On the same latitude as Hudson Bay and Alaska, it has the most northerly first-class golf course in the world and many say it is the finest in Scotland—its links were played on in medieval times when the monks from St Andrews used to come here for their recreation.

Excavations have dated settlements in the area at least as far back as 1000 BC. There is thought to have been a community of Celtic monks long before David I referred to a monastery here in 1140. Like several other places, Dornoch claims to be the place where the last witch in Scotland was burned in 1722, and there is a Witch's Stone to commemorate the occasion in a private garden in Carnaig Street. Some say Janet Horne was convicted of having turned her daughter into a pony and ridden her to a witches' meeting where she had arranged for the Devil to shoe her. During her trial she became muddled and misquoted the Lord's Prayer in Gaelic, thus signing her own death warrant. She was tarred, feathered and burnt at the stake; history doesn't relate what happened to her daughter—the pony.

Tourist Information

The Square, ✆ (01862) 810 400. *Open all year.*

The Town

Dornoch Cathedral dates from 1224. St Gilbert of Moray was Bishop of Caithness in 1222. Worried by the murders of two of his predecessors, he decided to move his seat into an area where he could look for protection from his kinsman, the Earl of Sutherland. The cathedral he built must be the most cosy in the country: small and cruciform, with a remarkable inner glow from colourful windows that illuminate its mellow raw-stone walls. Gilbert died in 1245, the last Scotsman to be canonized before the Reformation. The cathedral was burnt in a clan

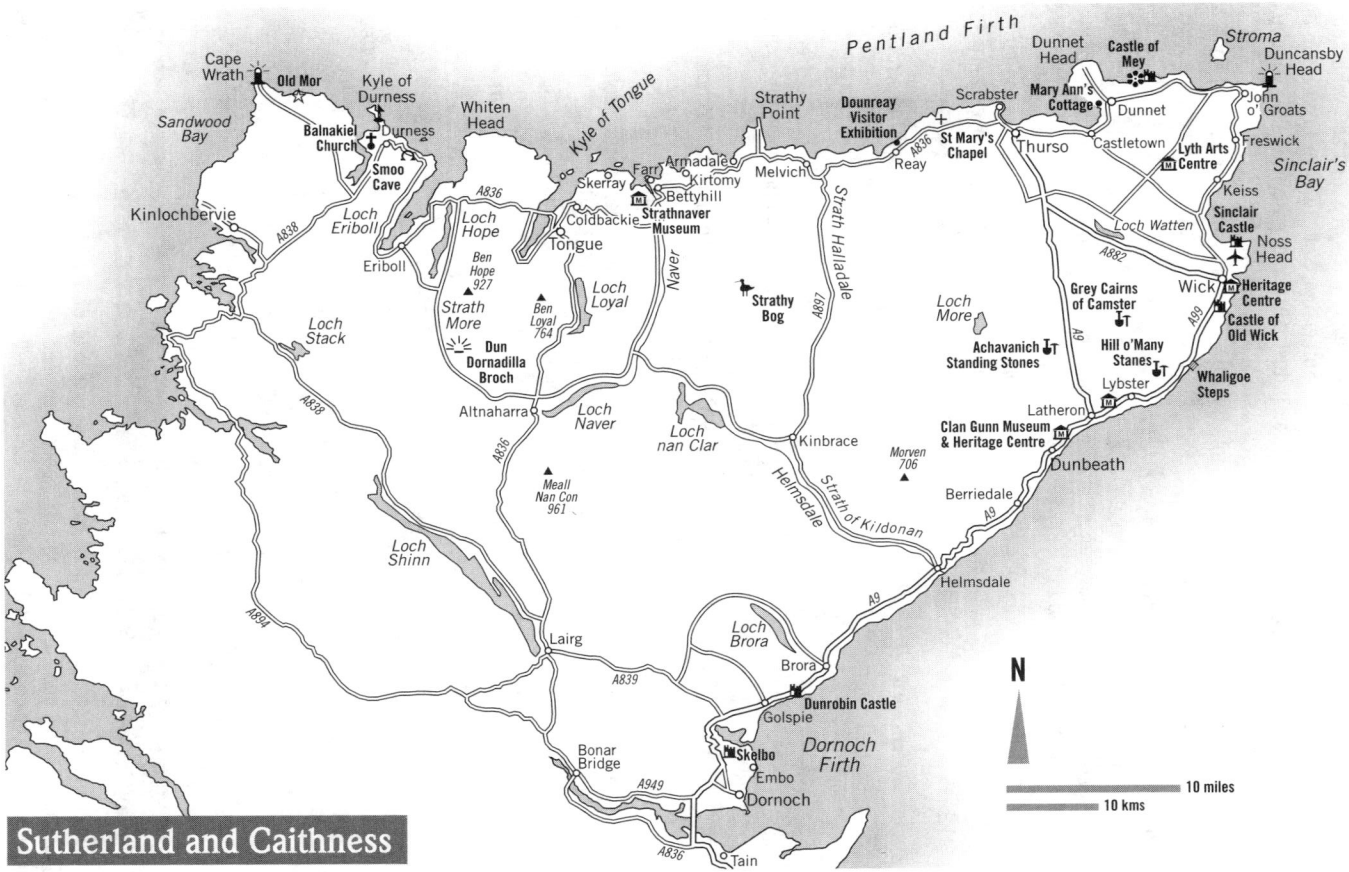

Sutherland and Caithness

dispute between the Murrays and Mackays in 1570 with only the tower and spire surviving. It was restored in 1616 and further restored in 1835 by the Duchess of Sutherland, with unfortunate results. The remains of a number of Earls of Sutherland, from 1248 to 1766, lie in the transept. When Andrew Carnegie, the great industrialist and philanthropist, bought a Highland estate at Skibo in 1897, he endowed the stained-glass windows in the north wall. In 1924, to celebrate its 700th anniversary, much of the Victorian work was stripped away to reveal the original 13th-century stonework and thus it stands today as the main parish church.

The Craft Centre and Town Jail (*open daily, except winter weekends; free; adm for jail*) has the usual reconstructed jail exhibits, and demonstrations of weaving tartan and kilt making. Leave it for a wet day. It has recently changed hands and the new owner has not yet revealed his plans for the future.

Dornoch is flanked by miles of clean sand, ideal for holidays today but not so good for the evicted crofters of the last century who, during the Clearances, were moved here and expected to farm the infertile dune land. Small wonder so many of them had to emigrate.

Dornoch ✆ (01862–) ***Where to Stay***

expensive

Skibo Castle, ✆ 894 600, 894 601, *www.carnegieclub.co.uk*, is an extremely expensive private sports club and hotel. Membership, which includes other clubs, does not cover meals and accommodation.

Dornoch Castle, ✆ 810 216, 810 981, opposite the cathedral, is a splendid 16th-century fortified tower which used to be the bishop's palace. It is now a good place to stay with traditional bedrooms full of character. Its restaurant is one of the best in the area and the cellar is good. There is a sunny terrace, a nice garden, and a bar with original panelling overlooking the Square. The **Royal Golf Hotel**, 1st Tee, Dornoch, ✆ 810 283, 810 923, overlooks the golf course, with splendid views all round. Good food and friendly.

moderate

Inistore Guest House, Castle Street, ✆ 811 263, above the 2 Quail Restaurant, is central, small and relaxed. For B&B try **Highfield House**, Evelix Road, ✆ 810 909, which is very comfortable.

cheap

The recently refurbished **Eagle Hotel**, Castle St, ✆ 810 008, 811 355, is typical of Dornoch itself: peaceful and attractive. Not annoyingly busy, it's cosy and friendly, with a couple of family rooms. **Trevose Guest House**, Dornoch, ✆ 810 269, is an attractive old stone cottage with a colourful garden, looking on to beautiful Cathedral Square. *Open Mar–Oct.*

Dornorch to John o 'Groats

Embo, about 3 miles north along the sands, was one of the villages set up during the Clearances to house crofters who had been displaced from their homes by the Duke of Sutherland. The cottages of the original hamlet were built in 1830, their gable-ends facing the sea; the area is now a gigantic caravan park and holiday resort with yachting and water-skiing facilities. The New Statistical Account of 1845 states:

> *The people here are rather above the middle size. They are in general well made and handsome, and the women comely. On the whole they are a moral and religious people; industrious, peaceable and respectful of their superiors... poaching and illicit distillation are now scarcely known among them.*

There are two Stone Age burial chambers dating from 2000 BC at the entrance to the caravan site. When they were excavated it was discovered that two later cist tombs had been built into the originals. A battle was fought near here against the Danes during which Sir Richard de Moravia, the brother of the founder of Dornoch Cathedral, was killed. A large stone near the village commemorates this event.

On a grassy mound on the shore of Loch Fleet, a couple of miles further north, stands the scant ruin of 14th-century **Skelbo Castle**. It was here, in an earlier wooden castle in 1290, that emissaries of Edward I waited to greet the little Princess Margaret, Maid of Norway, whose marriage to Edward's son was to solve the problem of sovereignty in Scotland. Whether it would have done so or not was never to be known, for it was here that they heard of the child's death, caused by sea sickness on the voyage. This triggered off the Scottish Wars of Independence and Edward's ruthless 'hammering' of the Scots.

The A9 hugs the coast through a string of small towns and villages, each with an 'east coast' austerity and the uncompromising stoicism that characterizes the inhabitants of this harsh climate. Whenever you can, dive west into the moors and hills and discover the bleak majesty of this forsaken land, with its poignant memorials to a time when today's tumbled ruins were townships teeming with life. It is bleak and, in its own way, beautiful.

Golspie

Golspie, 9 miles north of Dornoch, is the farming centre for the area and has a good golf course. 17th-century St Andrew's Church has a splendid old canopied pulpit, fine panelled walls and carvings. You cannot forget the Clearances around here, not only because one of the main perpetrators, the first Duke of Sutherland, lived nearby at Dunrobin Castle. A 30-foot-high red-sandstone statue, depicting him as a hero draped in a toga, towers over the landscape from its 70-foot plinth, high on Ben Vraggie (*Beinn a'Bhragaidh*) to the west of Golspie, his back to the lands he cleared of people. This statue has been the cause of much dispute recently; some would like to see it torn down and smashed—the Highland Clearances being an emotive subject (*see* 'The Clearances', p.38). The Duke of Sutherland's name is synonymous with terrible events, though in fact it was his wife who authorized the atrocities perpetrated by his agents. By the 1820s the Sutherland estates covered one and a half million acres, 'an area unequalled in the British Empire'. The first Duke, whose statue rises so dominantly from Ben Vraggie, was blamed for his harshness to crofters, but praised for sponsoring many social improvements in the area. The truth lies somewhere in the middle and the blame rests mainly with his unscrupulous agents: James Loch, William Young and Patrick Sellar. They were given a free hand to implement 'improvements' to the estate. Climb to the top of Ben Vraggie and read the inscription cut into the base of the statue. It was erected a year after the Duke's death, in 1834 and its fulsome eulogy to a 'judicious, kind and liberal landlord...' is somewhat ironic.

Dunrobin Castle

Dunrobin Castle (*open Easter–Oct daily; adm; for variable opening hours call ✆ (01480) 633 177*) stands on a natural terrace overlooking the sea, a mile north of Golspie. Built as a great square keep in 1275 by Robert, Earl of Sutherland, on the site of an ancient broch, it was redesigned and extensively rebuilt in the romantic Gothic style between1845 and 1850, by Sir Charles Barry, who also designed the Houses of Parliament in London. Queen Victoria stayed here in 1872; the description in her *Highland Journal* is worth reading. This huge extravaganza rises above formal gardens, its towers and turrets a flamboyant pastiche of French and Scottish architecture. Many of the rooms reflect the hand of the architect Sir Robert Lorimer, a leading light in the Scottish Arts and Crafts movement, who made quite a few improvements during the First World War. The castle contains some fine paintings, including two Canalettos, magnificent furniture, tapestries and other heirlooms. A summerhouse in the park has been turned into a museum, with archaeological exhibits, Victoriana, crafts and natural history including a zoo's worth of stuffed animals. There is a café/restaurant in the castle.

Brora

Five miles up the coast from Golspie, **Brora** is a tourist resort and small industrial town with some of the best salmon fishing in the country. Its older part is built on the south side of the river, dating mainly from the 18th century. This was an important port as early as the 16th century, used for trading vessels as well as for fishing, though there is little to see of the harbour now, due to silting. The *Statistical Account of 1793* records that 'the sea and even the very shore here abounds with excellent fish'. It was from here that the first emigrants to New Zealand left the north of Scotland. Brora tweed is famous throughout the world and large quantities of cloth, yarn and rugs are exported by Hunters of Brora, mainly to America. Visit their mill (*✆ (01408) 623 500; open daily Mon–Sat 9–6, Sun 10–4*) and, if you are a compulsive shopper, lock up your credit card.

The surrounding district is littered with hill forts and Pictish brochs, the best being about 3 miles north between the road and the sea, with domed chambers in its walls and outworkings. Two headless skeletons were excavated from the site in 1880.

If you take the minor road west out of Brora, you get a good look at Sutherland's unique landscape. The road follows the river, past Loch Brora, where you will probably pass frustrated salmon fishermen in season, and down Dunrobin Glen back to Golspie. There are several good tracks north across the moors from this road.

Helmsdale

Helmsdale, 10 miles north of Brora, is a fishing and holiday town where the main road and railway part company. You have to search for the remains of 15th-century Helmsdale Castle, on a plateau above the natural harbour. It was within these innocent-looking walls in 1567 that Isobel Sinclair poisoned the Earl and Countess of Sutherland, so that her son might inherit the earldom. The plot failed, though, because her son drank the poison by mistake and died with them. The castle was rebuilt in the early 19th century by the Duke of Sutherland—him on the Monument. It was he who, having evicted the crofters from his lands, tried to make amends by resettling them. Helmsdale was devised as a fishing/farming community, the crofters being divided into those who would work the smallholdings attached to the village and those who would fish. Few of the families had any knowledge of the sea or the tradition of fishing, so fishermen from such established fishing ports as Fraserburgh were encouraged to move here to set an example. The east coast herring boom was just starting and the Duke provided an extensive harbour and well-equipped curing sheds, the best on this coast, and boats came from all over the country—upwards of 200 packed into the harbour. The life of fishermen in those days was a hard one, vividly depicted in the novels of Neil Gunn. The *New Statistical Account* has an interesting description of a typical day during July, August and September when the herring were running. The boats usually left between five and seven o'clock in the afternoon and shot their nets about dusk. Thus they drifted, east or west, until about three o'clock in the morning, when all hands hauled in the nets over the stern and disengaged the fish from the meshes. Returning to shore, they landed the catch for the women to gut and pack into barrels with salt. Then they spread their nets out to dry until the afternoon, and returned to their homes for refreshment and a few hours' rest before starting again. This went on for five nights a week, every week; sometimes they got no sleep at all.

There was a bad slump at the end of the 19th century when the local fishermen found they couldn't compete with the larger boats and the advanced gear of their competitors, but they recovered in the 1930s. Today the harbour has a resident fleet and the town's major industry is processing lobster, crab, scallop and prawn.

Timespan Heritage Centre (*open April–mid Oct Mon–Sat 9.30–5, Sun 2–5; July and Aug till 6; last admission 1 hour before closing; call ✆ (01431) 821 327, for out of season opening times; adm*), signed off the main road into the village, is a good example of its type. It traces the history of man in the Kildonan area from the stone circles, cairns and brochs of prehistory, through Norse invasion, the Clearances, herring fishing, gold rush and crofting, to the present day. Film and animated tableaux stir the imagination and are extremely effective, though young children might find some of the displays rather scary. There is a café.

Even if you don't want a meal, find room for a snack so you can look in at **La Mirage**, opposite Timespan. The lady in charge is a Barbara Cartland fan who models herself on the writer and has created a sort of 'Cartlandesque' boudoir from which to run her café, all decked out in pink, with a fake palm tree in the middle and acres of photographs of celebrities. Nothing could be more delightfully incongruous in this down-to-earth seaport.

Brora ✆ (01408–) ***Where to Stay***

expensive

The **Links Hotel**, Golf Road, Brora, ✆ 621 252, 🖷 621 181, is a traditional Edwardian hotel overlooking the Dornoch Firth and the golf course. From here you can visit the Royal Marine Hotel's leisure club. The **Royal Marine Hotel**, Golf Road, Brora, ✆ 621 252, 🖷 621 181, is a country house hotel, near the golf course and affiliated to the Links Hotel, which has its own leisure club, indoor swimming pool and conference rooms.

moderate

Navidale House Hotel, in Helmsdale, ✆ (01431) 821 258, 🖷 821 531, is a splendid fishing hotel overlooking the sea, with a reputation for its seafood. **The Factor's**

House, Berriedale, ✆ (01593) 751 280, 751 251, about 10 miles north of Helmsdale, is a Wolsey Lodge run to the usual high standards by Robert and Davina Howden. It's a proper family house in a sporting estate, 300ft above the sea with wonderful views. It's comfortable and friendly and the food is good, with plenty of local ingredients.

cheap

For B&B try **Alistair Fortune**, Glenaveron, Golf Road, Brora, ✆ 621 601 (non-smoking), or **Tigh Fada**, 18 Golf Road, Brora, ✆ 621 332 (also non-smoking).

Rogart Railway Carriage, Rogart Station, south of Golspie, ✆ 641 343, is an unusual hostel in old sleepers, with 16 berths in eight two-berth compartments. Handy for rail travellers.

The **Sutherland Arms**, Golspie, ✆ 633 234, once a coaching inn, is very good value with a friendly atmosphere.

Around Helmsdale

The River Helmsdale, one of the most renowned salmon rivers in Scotland, flows through the Strath of Kildonan, erstwhile territory of Clan Gunn. Its population in 1811 was 1,574; 20 years later it had fallen to 257. Gold has occasionally been found in burns that feed the Helmsdale, giving rise to periodic gold fever. **Baile an Or** (gold field), about 8 miles up the glen from Helmsdale, grew into a gold-rush shanty town after a good yield from the Kildonan Burn in 1869, but great expectations yielded little lasting treasure. You will find details in the Timespan Heritage Centre.

The Ord of Caithness is the coastal pass from Sutherland into Caithness. Before the road was improved it was one of the most nerve-racking drives in the country, with seaward precipices so terrifying that 'whenever any of the landed proprietors entered the county, a troop of their tenants assembled on the border and drew the carriage themselves over the hill, a distance of two miles, that nothing might be trusted in such a scene to the discretion of quadrupeds'. The Rev Donald Sage, whose fascinating memoir *Memorabilia Domestica* describes this area in detail, including first-hand experiences of the Highland Clearances, wrote in 1825:

> *The old road over this promontory—the same identically which William, Earl of Caithness, nearly four centuries ago, had passed with his gallant band, clad in green, to the fatal battle of Flodden—was really dangerous. It lay within a foot, and stretched along the very edge, without any protecting buttress, of a precipice 800ft above the sea.*

They say that no superstitious Sinclair—the clan of the Earl of Caithness—has crossed the Ord on a Monday, since that Monday in 1513 when the Earl led his men this way to fight for James IV at Flodden, from which not one of them returned.

There is a broch at Ousdale, a couple of miles beyond the Ord, where the A9 runs inland for a while. Take the track out to the old hamlet of **Badbea**, 2 miles east on the cliffs. Crofters from Ousdale took refuge here during the Clearances and stories are told of the beasts and children having to be tethered to prevent them being blown into the sea.

Dunbeath

Dunbeath, 6 miles to the north, was another of the east coast ports that shared in the herring boom. The local laird built the harbour in 1800 and by the middle of the century there were about 90 boats based here. The writer Neil Gunn was born here in 1891 in a house built by his seaman father, and several of his books reflect his strong association with this area. *Morning Tide* depicts his upbringing; *The Silver Darlings* is based on the profession of his forefathers; while *Highland River* is a brilliant portrayal of life around Dunbeath Water.

With 14th-century origins, spectacular **Dunbeath Castle** is visible from the road on a steep rock south of the harbour. Though captured by Montrose in 1650, it was occupied for centuries, almost uninterrupted, by Sinclairs. The Dunbeath Highland Games are held in July.

The Clan Gunn Museum and Heritage Centre (*open July–Aug daily; June–Sept Mon–Sat; adm*) is at Latheron, 3 miles beyond Dunbeath, in a converted 18th-century church. It tells the story of this ancient clan from its Norse origins, and illustrates its links with America before Columbus. In the churchyard there is a small hut which was used as a watch house against grave robbers. It was customary for someone to keep watch for 14 days after a funeral to prevent body snatching.

Christianity is believed to have been brought to Latheron by St Ninian early in the 5th century. The ruined pre-Reformation chapel of St Mary has doors less than 4 feet high. In 1699 the minister was suspended by the Presbytery when he admitted that he had not administered the sacraments or catechized anyone for 16 years and that he had danced, or as he put it, 'gone up and down the room' at a wedding. In 1734 the minister was suspended for nine months because he 'slit a man's ear for stealing'. From here up to Clyth Ness the coast is strikingly picturesque, with high cliffs and rocky ledges sticking out into the sea—quite dangerous. The name of some of the coves—the Whaler, the Frenchman—are grim reminders of ships that foundered here in days gone by.

The A895 runs due north from here to Thurso across desolate moorland. A considerable length of this road was laid out in one day in the 18th century, under the command of a local laird, Sir John Sinclair. He used every able man and beast and stone in the district. About 6 miles up the road is the **Achavanich Standing Stone Circle**, a ritual site in the form of an unusual truncated oval, thought to have once contained up to 60 stones. Less than a mile to the west is **Rangag Broch**, dating from 150 BC, once 40 or 50 feet high.

In **Lybster**, 4 miles north of Latheron, turn off the broad thoroughfare, flanked by sturdy, dignified houses, and go down to the harbour, scooped out of rock to provide a perfect haven for the large fishing fleet that plied the waters here in the 19th century. For centuries this district was the most sparsely populated part of Latheron parish, inhabited by only a small number of scattered crofters.

In 1810 the local laird built a wooden pier within the small creek at the mouth of the Reisgill Burn to allow his tenants to supplement their income by fishing. The project was successful and the pier was replaced in 1833 with the present stone one. The harbour is very attractive, with steep grassy banks forming a sheltered bowl, covered with primroses in spring. By 1840 Lybster was the third-largest fishing station in Scotland, with upwards of 200 boats working out of the harbour until the slump in the herring industry towards the end of the century. Many men resorted to their crofts and endured such hardship that they were forced to emigrate. The fleet is now reduced to a few lobster boats and a number of pleasure craft, but the atmosphere is still very much that of a fishing community.

About a mile east of Lybster, on the A9, take the minor road north up the Clyth Burn, signed to **Grey Cairns of Camster**, about 5 dead-straight miles over the moor. In this remote spot, easy to miss in the mist if there aren't cars already parked there, are two spectacular restored Neolithic monuments, including what has been described as the most outstanding long (200ft) horned cairn in the country, dating back to about 3800 BC.

On the right are two beehive-shaped chambers, incorporated at a later date into the huge elongated mound of piled stones with horns at either end. The corbelled, drystone roofs cover the hidden chambers which you can crawl into through very low narrow tunnels—not for the claustrophobic. The other chamber is on the left: a single, smoothly rounded cairn with an entrance tunnel.

The cairns are approached by duckboard walkways over the bog, and explanation boards tell you all about them. Human and animal remains were excavated and it is intriguing to ponder on what sort of men these were, to have been such efficient builders nearly 6,000 years ago. The climate was milder and better in those days and the soil more fertile, enabling those early farmers to cultivate wheat and raise cattle and sheep.

A couple of miles to the east, reached up a short road signed off the A9, the **Hill o'Many Stanes** is an early Bronze Age site which has puzzled the archaeologists for years. What you see is an area of small standing stones apparently dotted at random over the heather. In fact it is not as random as it appears and was a ribbed fan, each rib containing about eight or more stones, numbering some 200 in all, and thought once to have been about 600.

It could have been a ritual site for burials, like other henges, or some form of astronomical calculator, lined up with the sun, stars and moon, for calculating the farming cycle. Whatever its purpose, it is eerie to stand on this lonely, windswept moor trying to picture those early settlers, once surprisingly numerous in this northern corner of the British Isles.

About 8 miles north on the A9 from Lybster, past a church on a sharp bend, you come into the unsigned hamlet of **Whaligoe**. A staggered crossroads has a left turn marked to an alpine nursery. Almost opposite, flanked by a telephone kiosk and a letterbox, a small road goes past a row of terraced cottages to a house with a high stone wall, where you can park.

A flight of 365 recently restored stone steps zigzags steeply down the cliff to the old harbour, long gone but once used by fishing fleets to moor and unload their catches, among the cheerful bustle and raucous banter of the fishermen and the teams of women working at the gutting. The fishermen used these steps to get to their boats, and lives were lost in their use.

This is a magical place now, the deep cleft in the sheer cliffs providing a sheltered bay with ink-dark water, wild flowers and no people. In some places, to secure their boats from being dashed to pieces against the rocks in storms and high tides, the fishermen hung them by ropes on hooks fixed in the rock, where they were safely suspended until the weather improved.

> *Certainly Wick in itself possesses no beauty: bare grey shores, grim grey houses, grim grey sea; not even the greenness of a tree... In Wick I have never heard anyone greet his neighbour with the usual 'Fine day' or 'Good morning'. Both come shaking their heads, and both say, 'Breezy, breezy!' And such is the atrocious climate that the remark is almost invariably justified by the fact. The streets are full of highland fishers, lubberly, stupid, inconceivably lazy and heavy to move. You bruise against them, tumble over them, elbow them against the wall- and all to no purpose; they will not budge; and you are forced to leave the pavement every step.*

So wrote Robert Louis Stevenson to his mother in 1868. By contrast, Elin Burritt, an American traveller, wrote in 1864, that it was 'a brave little city by the Norse Sea, which may not only be called the Wick but the candle of Northern Scotland... the great metropolis of Fishdom.'

Wick, so called from the Viking word *vik* meaning 'bay or creek', is a substantially built seaport and tourist centre, stretching round the sweep of Wick Bay, 15 miles northeast of Lybster. There is a harbour, airport and railway terminal. Norse pirates were drawn to Wick by the shelter of its bay at the mouth of the river and by the magnet of the rich farmland beckoning from the west. Created a Royal Burgh in 1140, it had the exclusive right to trade abroad, being nearer Europe than Thurso, which had the better harbour. It was only properly developed in the 19th century by the British Fisheries Society, which commissioned Telford to design a model village at Pulteneytown, south of the river, named after its director Sir William Pulteney, who had taken the name of the Pulteney heiress he married. It is difficult to believe now that 1,122 herring boats once plied from the complex of three harbour basins, before the decline of the herring stock and the development of vast factory ships. At the height of the boom, 3,800 fishermen were employed and about 4,000 people had related jobs such as curing. None of the boats was more than 30 foot long, all undecked and unprotected against wind and waves. The sight of the fleet putting to sea in the late afternoon was memorable.

> *About this time [5pm] may be seen hundreds of stalwart fishermen, clad characteristically in northwester, fearnought jackets and high fishing boots, with kit across the back containing refreshment for the night. In an hour or two the expanse of ocean is studded with a thousand tiny barks, each under canvas and the guidance of the weather-beaten and experienced skipper, bounding along in the direction of the fishing ground.*

Thus wrote the poet James Thomson in 1849. In 1845 the *New Statistical Account* took a grimmer look at the fishing boom: 'The herring fishing has increased wealth, but also wickedness. No care is taken of the 10,000 young strangers of both sexes who are crowded together with the inhabitants within the narrow limits of Wick during the six weeks of the fishery, when they are exposed to drink and every other temptation...There is great consumption of spirits, there being 22 public houses in Wick and 23 in Pulteneytown...Seminaries of Satan and Balial.' If the fishing was successful, the report continues, not less than 500 gallons of whisky were consumed in a day. Wick today is a shadow of its former self, but white fish trawlers still use the harbour. On the morning of 19th August 1848 a gale from the southeast struck Wick just as the fleet was heading homewards. Forty one boats were lost, most of them within a few yards of the harbour.

Tourist Information

Wick: Whitechapel Road, ✆ (01955) 602 596 (*open all year*); **John o' Groats**: County Road, ✆ (01955) 611 373 (*open April–Oct*).

The Town

The **Heritage Museum** (*open June–Sept Mon–Sat*) near the harbour, tells the fishing story of Wick. Its collection includes a fishing boat, working lighthouse, kippering kilns, blacksmith's shop, coopering shop and fishing gear. When the herring industry declined, Wick established the **Caithness Glass Factory** (*visitor centre open Mon–Sat 9–5; Easter–Dec also Sun 11–5; glassmaking all year Mon–Fri 9–4.30; ✆ (01955) 602 286*) to offer alternative employment for the fishermen. On the north side of the town, in the Airport Industrial Estate, visitors can watch craftsmen fashioning molten glass, shaping it and engraving it. It is interesting that in this land so full of echoes of Norse occupation, the designs of the glass are distinctively Scandinavian.

Around Wick

To the south of the town, perched on a peninsula between two precipitous cliffs, with a ditch protecting it from the mainland, **Oldwick Castle** was probably the resort of St Rognvald and other Norse dignitaries when they visited the mainland from Orkney. Rognvald made a pact with God that he would build a great cathedral in honour of his uncle, St Magnus, if he should win the Earldom on Orkney, and St Magnus Cathedral in Kirkwall was the result. Known to seamen as the 'Auld Man o'Wick', this three-storey ruin had no water supply and so was unable to withstand long sieges. It was abandoned in the 16th century.

Take time to walk along the cliffs and appreciate the spectacularly shaped rocks. **Brig o' Trams** is a natural rock arch, and there is splendid rock sculpture at **Noss Head**, a glorious 3-mile walk north to the lighthouse. From the point, it is less than half a mile west to **Sinclair** and **Girnigoe Castles**, the dramatic ruins of two separate castles on a precipitous promontory looking north over Sinclair's Bay. As you walk across a field to reach them, they seem to grow out of the horizontally layered cliff. William Sinclair, 2nd Earl of Orkney, built Girnigoe having surrendered his earldom of Orkney to the crown in 1472. The tower was four storeys high with a courtyard beyond, great ditches making it virtually impregnable from the land. The 5th Earl built Sinclair Castle nearby in 1606, a pseudo-Renaissance palace which hastened his bankruptcy. The Sinclairs lived in the two castles as one dwelling, constantly attacked by ambitious rivals. Ghosts lurk in the walls: in 1570 the 4th Earl, suspecting his son of plotting to kill him, imprisoned him in the dungeons for seven years till he died of 'famine and vermine'.

The great sandy sweep of Sinclair's Bay leads north along a coastline believed to be among the earliest inhabited in Scotland. Excavations have revealed that Middle Stone Age man existed here in large numbers on the fertile hinterland, living a primitive life long after more advanced cultures—New Stone Age and Iron Age—were flourishing in other parts of the country.

Lyth Arts Centre (✆ *(01955) 641 270; open July and Aug daily; adm*), about 4 miles inland, off the A9 halfway round the bay, is an unexpected venture in a Victorian village school in the middle of nowhere. For the two months they are open they exhibit the work of artists and performers from many countries, some of great merit, and there is a permanent collection of Scottish work. Live performances are presented throughout the year: drama, dance and all types of music. There is a café open whenever the centre is open.

On the northern point of the bay, at **Keiss**, a tall slender tower on top of the cliff is all that remains of **Keiss Castle**, home of William Sinclair, founder of the first Baptist church in Scotland. A couple of miles further on, the scant ruin of 12th-century **Bucholie Castle** was the stronghold of Sweyn Aslefson, a Norse pirate featured in the old Norse sagas. A 10th-century Viking settlement is still in the process of being excavated a mile further on at **Freswick.**

John o' Groats

Although it is neither the most northerly nor the most easterly tip of Britain, John o' Groats, about 12 miles north of Wick, is loosely accepted as the northeastern extremity, linked diagonally to Land's End, 876 miles away in the southwest—which is also in fact neither the most southerly nor the most westerly tip of the country. Stop on the summit of the final curve of moorland and look across. It is a bleak, scattered village, washed by the Pentland Firth whose islands sometimes appear so close you could almost jump the gap. It is an awe-inspiring vista—the edge of the world. But it has to be said that John o' Groats itself is often a disappointment to tourists—little more than an uninspiring coach and car park, a few ugly buildings containing souvenirs, snacks and woollens, a rather overpriced 'craft community', and a flat, dreary landscape, though the Tourist Information Centre is good. Much of John o' Groats has recently been bought by Kevin Leech, a rich Englishman who has ambitious 'plans' for improvement. Whatever these may be, he could hardly make the place much worse.

The small settlement, given over to supplying the needs of dozens of expectant tourists, got its curious name from a Dutchman, Jan de Groot, who established a ferry link with the newly acquired islands of Orkney in 1496, under the rule of James IV. There are several explanations for the octagonal house with eight doors that he built, no longer standing but represented by the octagonal tower on the hotel which is believed to stand on the same site. One explanation is that he wanted to provide shelter from every point of the fierce wind for his waiting passengers. Another theory is that when his eight sons squabbled over who should take precedence at the dinner table, he decided to settle the dispute by having an octagonal table and eight doors, so that each son had his own entrance and everyone sat at the head of the table. It is said that Jan charged such extortionate rates for his ferry that he was ordered by magistrates to fix the fare at four pence—a small silver coin that became a 'groat'.

Duncansby Head

Duncansby Head is Scotland's real northeastern corner, a couple of miles east of John o' Groats, and much more satisfying. You can drive out to the lighthouse and then walk along the cliffs to see dramatic stacks and rock formations. Many different species of seabird throng the headland, and in clear weather the only limit to the view over the Pentland Firth is the keenness of your eye. The 12-knot tide rip here is a notorious hazard to shipping: over 400 wrecks have been recorded in the last 150 years alone. Once you get away from the blemishes of tourism, this coastline is perfect for anyone who likes wild and lonely places, birds and wild flowers and exhilarating extremes of weather.

Wick ✆ (01955–) ***Where to Stay***

expensive

Ackergill Tower, near Wick, ✆ 603 556, 🖷 602 140, is the place to go around here if you can afford it, with a great position and true Highland atmosphere.

moderate

Dunbeath Hotel, Dunbeath, ✆ (01593) 731 208, 🖷 731 242, is an excellent place from which to explore the area, with extremely comfortable rooms in a traditional-style building and good food. Enquire about the special rates. **John o' Groats House Hotel**, ✆ 611 203, 🖷 611 408, has recently had a complete overhaul by its new owner, and is now reasonably comfortable with friendly staff.

cheap

Norseman Hotel, Riverside, Wick, ✆ 603 344, 🖷 605 456, is rather large, but it's right on the water and has a friendly atmosphere. **Queen's Hotel**, 16 Francis Street, Wick, ✆ 602 992, is solid, respectable and dependable.

Wellington Guest House, High Street, Wick, ✆ 603 287, is very much in the heart of things, lively and not very sophisticated, but with good hospitality. **Seaview Hotel**, John O'Groats, ✆/🖷 611 220, is not a beautiful building and has few frills, but the view is very fine. Dogs welcome.

John o' Groats to Cape Wrath

This is an edge-of-the-world highway. The 'blanket bog' to the south has been a bone of contention between conservationists and foresters. The distinctive peatland is a fragile, living surface of floating peat with heather and sedges growing over a carpet of sphagnum mosses, supporting an amazing concentration of rare wildlife. The forestry tycoons have already 'reclaimed' 16 per cent of the Flow Country, proud to have made productive use of such a 'dreary wasteland'. The conservationists argue that this is the largest (in Europe), oldest and least disturbed blanket bog in the world. Its depth, up to 20 feet, and age, mean that it holds within its soggy bosom important data for meteorological historians. Among the threatened victims of its population are 55 species of birds related to Arctic tundra, including 70 per cent of Britain's greenshanks, meadow pipits, red-throated divers, peregrines and merlins. Among the many plants which could be lost to the forests is the rare insect-eating sundew.

Very different and equally rewarding are the side-tracks to the north off the A836. Each one unfolds a new, wild view of the Pentland Firth, from cliff tops and from sandy beaches, from sheltered bays and gale-lashed headlands. Spare a thought for the Roman fleet of Agricola, which supplied the advancing legions as they tried to conquer Scotland. They battled their way round from the east coast and triumphantly reported that Britain was indeed an island.

Tourist Information

Bettyhill: Clachan, ✆ (01641) 521 342 (*open April–Sept*).

John o'Groats to Thurso

Castle of Mey, 7 miles west of John o' Groats, was built around the middle of the 16th century for the 4th Earl of Caithness and remained in the family until 1889. It was bought in 1956 by one of Britain's best-loved public figures, Queen Elizabeth, the Queen Mother, whose age keeps pace with that of the century. Turrets of the castle can be glimpsed from the road, sheltered by trees at the end of no-entry drives. The gardens are open on certain days in the summer in aid of charity, and are well worth a visit for their unexpected lack of grandeur. There is a charming chaos, lots of weeds, not much in the way of landscaping and few choice blooms. Given the climate, this isn't surprising..

Dunnet Head, 9 miles further on, is the most northerly point of Scotland's mainland, a sheer promontory of red sandstone, with a lighthouse 300 feet (91m) above the sea. Walking out to the point (although it is possible to drive), you're surrounded by pink thrift laced with tormentil, trefoils, wild thyme, yellow saxifrage, purple butterwort and dozens of other species of wild flowers. There are puffins here: endearing birds with their comic tuxedo garb and vivid striped beaks, burrowing in the turf. The village of Dunnet is a scattering of houses on the vast sweep of Dunnet Bay. Signed on the way towards the point is **Mary Ann's Cottage** (*open June–Sept Tues–Sun pm; adm*). Mary Ann Calder lived here until she moved to a nursing home at the age of 93 in 1990, and the cottage and croft have been preserved as they were when worked by Mary Ann and her husband, James. The buildings are an aid to interpreting the past, pre-improvement community system of crofting and show how innovations and more modern concepts replaced the old.

The tower of the white church behind the hotel, with its saddle-backed roof, dates from the 14th century, a pre-Reformation survivor that confirms the comforting continuity of a place that seems to have changed little over the years. The fishing is good around here, in sea, river and loch. A halibut weighing 210lbs (93kg) was caught here with rod and line in 1975. Intrepid surfers also brave the waves.

Thurso

The name of Thurso, 20 miles west of John o' Groats, stems from the Norse *Thorsa* meaning River of the God Thor, and the town is perhaps more interesting as a flag on the Scottish map than as a tourist attraction. It used to be the main trading port for Scandinavia and was granted the status Burgh of Barony in 1633, which gave it the right to trade within Scotland. As an important Viking stronghold, it reached its zenith in the 11th century under Thorfinn, who defeated King Duncan's nephew in 1040 in a mighty battle here. In 1158 the body of murdered Earl Rognvald was brought here, probably to a chapel on the site of St Peter's Church. It is now the largest town north of Inverness, with elegant 18th-century houses built of brown sandstone around a central square, and a long, narrow harbour. Sir John Sinclair of Ulbster, related to the Sinclair Earls of Caithness, was born in Thurso Castle in 1754 and was instrumental in the building of the present town. He was a noted agriculturist and a keen 'improver' and was one of the few landlords in this area who saw the enormous potential of Cheviot sheep and yet desired nothing more than the protection of his tenants. He was also a prime mover in the publication of James Macpherson's Ossianic collection in 1807—inspiring Samuel Johnson's contempt.

Riverside, ✆ (01847) 892 371 (*open April–Oct*).

The Town

St Peter's Church, near the harbour, dates from the 12th or 13th century, and stands on the site of the chapel where Earl Rognvald's murdered body was brought. Most of what survives dates from the 16th and later centuries—some of the original stone can be seen in the curious choir, a semi-circular apse within a square end. The church was used for worship until 1862.

Thurso Castle, the Victorian Gothic ruin on the east side of the river, was built for Sir John Sinclair in 1872 and lived in by Sinclairs until it was demolished in 1952. **Harald Tower**, just over a mile along the coast to the northeast, was built in 1780 to replace a previously demolished chapel which had served as a burial place for the Sinclairs and contained the grave of Harald, Earl of Caithness, a mighty war lord who ruled over half Caithness and Orkney and was killed in battle nearby in 1196.

Thurso ✆ (01847–) ***Where to Stay***

expensive

For somewhere special to stay near Thurso, try **Forss Country House Hotel**, ✆ 861 201/2, 🖷 861 301, built as a private house in 1810 in 20 acres of woodland only 100 yards from falls of the River Forss. The immediate garden is very pretty and when conditions are right you can watch salmon leaping in the river. The hotel, run by the MacGregor family, has a comfortable, welcoming feel to it and the food is first class. Breakfast is served in a conservatory full of plants overlooking the garden, and there are well over 100 malt whiskies to sample in the bar. As well as the spacious, elegant rooms in the house there are lodges in the garden with five more rooms, offering more privacy and flexibility for fishermen.

moderate

Castle Arms Hotel, Mey, ✆/🖷 851 244 (formerly the Berriedale Hotel), was a 19th-century coaching inn and is now a comfortable hotel within sight of the Castle of Mey. They are proud of their royal neighbour and have a Royal Gallery with a unique collection of photographs of her and her family, copies of which can be bought. One of the bedrooms actually looks across at the castle. The local shop is round the back.

cheap

Ormlie House Hotel, Ormlie Road, Thurso, ✆ 892 733, is a sturdy, old-fashioned place with comfortable rooms and friendly service. For a nice B&B, go to **Mrs Falconer**, Murray House, 1 Campbell Street, Thurso, ✆ 895 759, a traditional old stone house where you can be sure of a welcome and a comfortable night.

Scrabster

Scrabster, a mile to the northwest along the bay, is the terminal for the car ferry to Stromness in Orkney. The *St Ola* runs daily (except Sundays in winter), linking with a day-excursion tour on Mondays, Fridays and Saturdays from April to October. It is an invigorating nearly 2-hour trip on a fine day. It is likely that Scrabster was a powerful Viking stronghold in the 12th century. A castle was built to house the bishop in 1223, and remained the bishop's palace until the abolition of episcopacy.

At Crosskirk, overlooking Crosskirk Bay, 5 miles or so west of Thurso, signed off the main road, **St Mary's Chapel** is about half a mile's walk across turf on low cliffs. This simple little roofless kirk dates from the 12th century, its chancel containing three Gunn memorials accessed from the nave by a small doorway. Remote and peaceful in a walled churchyard, the place has a timeless serenity.

The **Dounreay Nuclear Power Station**, about 7 miles on along the cliffs, was established in 1954, bringing temporary prosperity to Thurso, with a workforce of 2,000. Its closure in 1994 brought hardship to many who had settled within commuting distance of the works, and relief to the anti-nuclear brigade. Work is now in progress to 'decommission' the three reactors and associated plant, a £500 million, 10-year operation ensuring local employment for the duration; meanwhile non-nuclear activities for the plant are being investigated for the future. An exhibition (*open June–Sept daily*) gives an insight into Dounreay's role in British science.

About 6 miles west, the A897 branches off south back to Helmsdale through Strath Halladale and Strath of Kildonan. Continue west along the main road a few miles and turn north to **Strathy Point** where the sea has carved fabulous arches and caverns in the cliffs. The coast from here to Bettyhill is wonderfully diverse, with sheltered sandy beaches, as at Armadale Bay, and sea-eroded cliffs, as between Ardmore and Kirtomy. On Farr Point, **Borve Castle** stands in ruins, a former stronghold of the Clan Mackay, destroyed by the Earl of Sutherland in 1515.

Bettyhill

Bettyhill on the shore of Torrisdale Bay at the mouth of the River Naver is said by some to be named after a local woman Betty Cnocan, who kept an inn at the top of the hill, rather than after the Duchess of Sutherland who was responsible for so much of the anguish this village commemorates. The people of Strathnaver were cleared to Bettyhill and told to rebuild their lives by fishing and cultivating wind-torn land on the infertile coast.

Strathnaver Museum (*open April–31 Oct Mon–Sat, for winter visits call ✆ (01641) 521 330; adm*) is in what was once the large church of the parish of Farr. If you only have the time and inclination for one museum in the far north, let it be this one. The story of the Clearances is poignantly told by children, on simple posters, in a building in which it is likely the minister may have read out eviction notices to his congregation from the imposing hooded pulpit. There is a lot else to see, including old photographs, a bothy room with a box bed, and a Clan MacKay room. In a description of the Battle of Druim na Coup in 1431, when the MacKays cut down their Sutherland rivals to a man, the sad end came when Angus Dhu MacKay came back to survey the scene of his victory and was killed by the arrow of the last dying Sutherland. Also in the museum is an exhibition about Rob Donn, or Doun, born of humble origins in Strathmore in 1715, and illiterate, who became one of Scotland's leading Gaelic poets (*see* Balnakeil, where he is buried, p.208).

Next to the museum, **The Old Nick Tearoom** is a welcome if unsophisticated place for a snack. There is also a useful Tourist Information Centre, and a craft shop upstairs.

To get some idea of how those crofting families must have suffered, go through the village and take the little road south signed to **Achanlochy** by the bridge over the River Naver. About a mile along there is a cairn in a gravel pit with Achanlochy written on it. Walk up the slope to the site of one of the cleared hamlets, well explained on an information board. From this hillock you can picture how it would have been, living in Strathnaver before 1819. Bettyhill is referred to in Gaelic as *am bl'ran odhar*—the grey place, or the little dun-coloured field—in contrast to the lush, green, sheltered land of the Strath from which its people were evicted.

Also along this road, just before Achanlochy up on the left, is a remarkable Neolithic chambered burial cairn, a great mound of tumbled stones 75 yards long with its entrance running in from the north. One of the three burial chambers, now unroofed, is fairly easy to get into and you can see the method of construction with huge stone slabs set vertically with flat-laid drystone walling. The B873 runs south through Strathnaver where many croft houses went up in flames during those troubled times, and where people died of exposure, huddled against the ruins of their homes.

Invernaver National Nature Reserve, around the mouth of the River Naver, has the finest collection of mountain and coastal plants in the north. Among the rarer birds that breed here are greenshank, ring ouzel and twite. On the edge of the reserve, on a plateau, is **Baile Marghair**, once a Neolithic community, with graves, hut circles and a broch.

Tongue

Tongue, about 10 miles on from Bettyhill, is on the eastern shore of the Kyle of Tongue, with Ben Hope and Ben Loyal to the south. When Borve Castle, along the coast, was destroyed by the Gordons of Sutherland in 1554, the Mackays adopted Tongue as their stronghold. Here they remained until Donald Mackay espoused the cause of Charles I and republican troops garrisoned the town.

A new mansion, the **House of Tongue**, was built in 1678, with a wing added by a later Mackay, 3rd Lord Reay, who also built the first road fit for a horse-drawn carriage in this area, to take him to church. This is the house on the shore to the east of the causeway, with an impressive steading. The clan Mackay was not so loyal to the Stuarts a century later. Sad to tell, when a sloop called the *Prince Charles*—formerly HMS *Hazard*, captured by the Jacobites—was on its way to Inverness carrying French gold to boost the Prince's funds in March 1746, it was spotted by some naval ships and chased up the coast and into the Pentland Firth. Hoping to evade the English by sailing into the shallow Kyle of Tongue, it foundered on a sandbank within gunshot of HMS *Sheerness*. In the ensuing battle the *Prince Charles* was destroyed. The crew escaped hoping to carry the gold overland to Inverness but anti-Jacobite Mackays followed them, captured them and locked them in the boathouse that still stands near House of Tongue. Sensing their imminent defeat the fugitives threw the gold into a loch but most of it was recovered. Prince Charles had sent 1,500 of his men north to collect the gold, thus significantly depleting his army for the fateful battle. Stories are still told of the occasional piece of gold turning up, in particular about the one which emerged firmly wedged into a cow's hoof.

The name Tongue is Norse and the ruin of **Castle Varrich** which stares down on the village from a rocky hill was a Norse stronghold in the 11th century. Nothing much is known about it, but it is a nice walk from the village with a profusion of wild flowers including gentians in season and good views of the Kyle. The road crosses the middle of the Kyle on a causeway and at low tide the whole long, shallow inlet seems almost to dry out to shiny sand. **Coldbackie Bay** is lovely for bathing and picnics.

There are good walks out along the coast to **Whiten Head**—or Kennageal—at the tip of the peninsula between Tongue and Loch Eriboll, with caves under the cliffs where Atlantic grey seals play. This peninsula is a wilderness of moor, rock and hill, beautiful in sunshine but awesome in storm.

If you want a good day's walk, head up either **Ben Hope** (a Munro) or **Ben Loyal**. Hope is quicker, about 5 hours and not too challenging, but it needs good navigation. Start at the cowshed a couple of miles south of the head of Loch Hope, where a path goes up the bank of a burn. There is a choice of ascents: the northern one, up the main burn, has a tricky bit, with an alternative path through the gully if you can't face it. There are wonderful views from the top, with Strath More laid out below you and the Pentland Firth lashing away to the north.

Ben Loyal takes longer, about 7 hours, and is best done from the north where there is a path and you miss the bog that spoils the shorter approach from the east. Begin at the start of a private road to Ribigill Farm, 1½ miles south of Tongue on the old road. The farm track goes south over the moor to Cunside Cottage (near which is a chambered cairn called Jeremy's Grave, marked on the map as Uaigh Dhiarmaid). The track becomes a path and takes you up the burn where you climb steep turf and heather to reach the first summit, and, if you have the energy, the others beyond. It's fairly obvious once you start.

A couple of miles before you reach Loch Eriboll on the A838, a road runs south down **Loch Hope** towards Altnaharra and the road southwards. Ten miles down, on the Strathmore River, there is the ruin of a broch—**Dun Dornadilla**—well placed to guard the glen and provide shelter in times of attack. You can't go inside but there is an impressive large triangular lintel above the doorway.

Loch Eriboll runs parallel with the Kyle of Tongue, a deep sea loch running some 10 miles inland and the subject of one of the prophesies of the Brahan Seer early in the 17th century. He named Loch Eriboll as a place where a war would end one day. In 1945, at the end of the Second World War, German submarines came into the loch to surrender. Servicemen stationed here during the war to protect convoys passing through the Pentland Firth nicknamed it Loch 'Orrible. After the First World War, land on the west side of the loch was allocated to the repatriated heroes to give them a chance to start a new life. One look at the inhospitable landscape will explain why they were less than delighted with the munificence of this gesture.

There are the remains of several ancient settlements around here. About a mile north of Laid School on the west side of the loch, there is a souterrain, complete and untouched, with curved steps leading down to a round chamber. You need a torch for this earth house, which floods after heavy rain. Look for two cairns in a bracken-infested lay-by on the right just past a fish farm in a bay; the souterrain is towards the loch from here.

Smoo Cave is signposted from the road just before Durness, down a steep, stepped path with a grassy slope opposite festooned with the names of visitors of all nationalities picked out in pebbles on the turf. The vast limestone cavern has three compartments formed by continuous erosion. The outer chamber is 200ft (61m) long and 120ft (37m) high, its glistening, floodlit walls hung with ferns and lichen, with holes in the roof and access to the inner chamber over a bridge. Here the Alt Smoo River thunders down from the cliffs into the cave in an awe-inspiring 70-foot waterfall which fills the cave with spray. You can get into the third chamber by boat when there isn't too much water. Walter Scott came here in 1814 and wrote one of the best descriptions of it in his diary.

Durness, 6 miles west of Loch Eriboll, is the gateway to Cape Wrath, the top lefthand corner of Scotland. Perched on the coast, built to withstand the fury of the elements, it is a small reprovisioning base for exploring this area and has an excellent Tourist Information Centre. It was a Pictish settlement in about 400 BC and has been farmland ever since, bought by the Sutherlands in 1829. When attempts were made to clear it in 1841, over 300 crofters protested vociferously until troops of the 53rd Regiment were ordered to move in from Edinburgh. Some of the land was cleared, but Durine and Sangomore were reprieved, giving inspiration to others who had hitherto accepted their fate. There are crofting communities all around, with the Kyle of Durness cutting off road access to the Cape. (Seasonal tourist information, ✆ (01971) 511 259.)

Balnakeil Craft Village (*mostly open from Easter and closed by end Oct; some shops closed Sun*) is in a ghastly former Ministry of Defence Early Warning Station camp along the road heading west from Durness to the golf course. It is a 'community co-operative of crafts' where a group, mostly of incomers, sell their predictable, not always homemade stuff. Embroidery, stone, leather, pottery, wool, enamel, basketry-ware, screen prints and paintings can all be found. 'For Sale' notices seem numerous, and 'Gone out—back in an hour' suggest little trade. A rather depressing place but there are a couple of coffee shops and if you persevere you may even find bargains.

Durness Old Church, not far on along the same road, dates from 1619, an ivy-clad, roofless shell on the site of at least two older churches. Just inside the entrance on the left is a recessed tomb dated 1623 and well preserved. Among the elaborate carvings both on it and on a plaque above are a skull and crossbones with the hopeful inscription 'Memento Mori'. The epitaph reads: 'Donald Macmurchow hier lyis lo, vas il to his freind, var to his fo. True to his maister in veird and vo.' (*var*— worse, *veird*— prosperity). This is said to be the grave of a notorious highwayman, who hoped to buy his way into the afterlife by making substantial contributions to the building of the church and his tomb. One of the previous churches on this site appears in records in the Vatican as having contributed to one of the Crusades in the 12th century.

In the kirkyard there is a monument to Rob Donn, born in 1715, one of the greatest Gaelic poets whose work has been compared to that of Burns. Of humble origins, he was illiterate, but Gaelic poetry was an oral art and he had the gift. Cattle drover and notorious poacher, he composed and recited his poetry for all occasions. Although Gaelic poetry loses its lyrical magic in translation, much of his was translated and endures today. He wrote about ordinary people living ordinary lives and was always invited to celebrations—if he was not, he composed rude comments in verses which spread like wildfire, such as '*the men who caused no dissension...*

So far as anyone knew
Nor did they perform one act
that the world calls grace
but they were reared and they grew.
A sweep of life passed over them
And in the end they died.

'The Rispond Misers Poem', by Rob Donn
(misers meaning merely 'miserable people')

The Summer Palace for the bishops of Caithness was where the substantial Balnakeil Farmhouse now stands, opposite the church. One of the best walks in the area begins here, out round the bay to Fair Aird—Far Out Head—through dunes and over springy turf, carpeted with wild flowers in spring, where you should also see puffins. The far end of the bay is good for hardy swimmers.

Further on round the corner, the Durness Golf Course is the most northerly in mainland Britain with perhaps the most glorious surroundings. One hole includes a shot 'over the Atlantic' and the club rule is that players give way to anglers on Loch Lanlish.

Cape Wrath

A ferry runs across the Kyle of Durness in the summer, weather and conditions permitting, ✆ (01971) 511 376, and connects with a minibus out to the cape, ✆ (01971) 511 287/343. Officially, it runs from 9.30am and makes about 8 trips a day, but as it can't run at low tide the timetable is flexible; the round trip takes about 2 hours.

The Clo Mor Cliffs are the highest in Britain—523 feet high (161m), with veins of rich pink pegmatite running through the gneiss. The lighthouse on the point was built by Robert Louis Stevenson's father. It is an outlandish place—compelling in its end-of-the-world, wild loneliness—and a paradise for ornithologists. (The name Wrath—pronounced Raath—comes not from the often furious seas around the cape, but from the Viking word *hvarf*, which means 'turning point'.)

To the north lies the island of North Rona, with Stack Skerry and Skule Skerry further east. Turn your back on the great fort-like lighthouse and look across the bleak moor—the Parbh—that stretches away to the south. Wolves once roamed here in great numbers: an eerie thought as the mist comes creeping in over the desolate wasteland and you look around to make sure the minibus hasn't left without you. You can walk on round the coast to Sandwood Bay, only about 6 miles as the crow flies but over difficult, slow terrain with several rivers to be forded, taking up to 6½ hours, with no track. It is then 4½ miles further to the nearest road. Sandwood is lovely and worth visiting, (*see* p.157) but you are better off walking out from the south and retracing your steps (9 miles the round trip).

Tongue ✆ (01847–) ***Where to Stay***

moderate

The **Melvich Hotel**, ✆ (01641) 531 206, 🖷 531 347, in Melvich, is a country-house hotel, very comfortable with peat fires in the sitting rooms and friendly staff. It has its own brown trout lochs and access to salmon fishing as well as being well situated for beaches, walking, stalking, bird-watching and botanizing.

Borgie Lodge Hotel, Skerray, near Tongue, ✆/🖷 (01641) 521 332, lies in a secluded glen on the banks of the River Borgie and was the factor's house. The owners, Peter and Jacqui MacGregor, have managed to retain the 19th-century character of the house, with original panelled rooms, stag's antlers, tartan carpets, sporting prints and crackling log fires. They have fishing rights on the rivers Borgie and Halladale and boats for wild brown trout on the hotel's 20 hill lochs. Peter can supply all the tackle and tuition you may need.

The nicest place to stay in Tongue is the **Tongue Hotel**, ✆ 611 206, 611 345, recently refurbished without loss of its well-known Victorian charm and style. Built in 1880 as a hunting lodge for the Duke of Sutherland, it lies at the foot of Ben Loyal overlooking the Kyle of Tongue. Stuffed birds and animals greet you in the hall. There is a good number of books lying around, and the bedrooms are splendidly old fashioned with original doors and fireplaces, some with good views over the Kyle. One of them is haunted by a friendly ghost who was last seen three years ago; you are not told which room until you leave. People come back here over and over again, remembering happy childhood holidays, and are rarely disappointed.

Ben Loyal Hotel, Tongue, ✆ 611 216, 611 212, is just down from the Tongue Hotel with the same views. It lacks the old-world atmosphere of the above but is comfortable and prettily furnished. It has a range of accommodation from 'superior' to 'bungalow annexe', and they are relaxed and friendly.

Cape Wrath Hotel, ✆ (01971) 511 212, 511 313, overlooks the Kyle of Durness and faces the setting sun. Built in 1820 as a sporting lodge on the Sutherland estate, it's well equipped and comfortable. It has an old-fashioned feeling and if you stray into the kitchen you are likely to find fresh home-made bread cooling on wire racks and the friendly staff busy preparing meals that are entirely home-cooked. The dining room in which you eat these delicious meals is splendidly situated overlooking the Kyle with Mr Briggs' fishing prints around the walls. The hotel can arrange fishing on a number of lochs.

For somewhere to stay inland, **Altnaharra Hotel**, ✆/ (01549) 411 222, is a real Highland hotel, very conveniently placed en route north, 21 miles beyond Lairg and 17 miles south of Tongue in a sheltered situation. They have been catering for fishermen since 1800 and are called 'The Sportsman's Retreat.' It is a comfortable place to stay and worth stopping off at for a meal, even if you aren't a fisherman.

cheap

The **Sheiling Guest House**, Melvich, ✆ (01641) 531 256, is comfortable and friendly, with good views and excellent breakfasts. **Cloisters**, Church Holme, Talmine (near Tongue), ✆ 601 286, is a delightful B&B in a great setting. **Port-Na-Con**, near Durness, ✆ (01971) 511 367, is a very comfortable guest house, with good food, especially seafood.

Islands of the Clyde 215
Great Cumbrae 215
Arran and Holy Island 216
Bute 220
Inner Hebrides 223
Gigha 223
Islay 225
Jura 229
Colonsay and Oronsay 230
Mull 232
Iona 238
Coll and Tiree 242
The Small Isles 245
Rum 245
Eigg 246
Canna 247
Muck 248

Islands

Scotland's islands add greatly to its charm; each one has its own character, 'entire of itself': a native of Eriskay feels homesick living a mile away across the water in South Uist. About 130 of these 790 islands are inhabited. This book deals only with those served by public transport; for the rest you need your own boat, and a good knowledge of seamanship and navigation. Until recently, almost untouched by the distractions of an increasingly materialistic world, islanders tended to build their lives around God and the Church—a church that varies, depending on the island, from staunch Roman Catholic to extreme Presbyterian. With improved communications, younger generations are more in tune with the modern world and less prepared to subscribe to the old values which made their ancestors a 'race apart'.

The islands can be divided into four main groups: the islands of the Clyde, the Inner Hebrides, the Outer Hebrides—all lying to the west—and the Northern Isles.

History

First known to be populated around 3800 BC, many of the islands are rich in archaeological sites, many of which have yet to be dug. Mesolithic man gave way to Neolithic, who came in boats made of animal hide, bringing skills and culture and leaving burial cairns as evidence of his existence. Gaelic immigrants from Europe arrived with Celtic arts; building brochs and stone circles, practising a Druid religion and worshipping nature gods, until the first Christian missionaries from Ireland landed early in the 6th century. Norsemen took a number of the islands over at the end of the 8th century and remained until the defeat of King Haakon by Alexander III at Largs in 1263. Haakon's son, Magnus IV, realized that the Viking era in the Western Isles was over, and he signed the Treaty of Perth in 1266, ceding them to the Scottish Crown in return for an annual fee.

Stronger than the authority of the Crown was the Lordship of the Isles: chiefs who were as powerful as kings, paying no heed to a government which ruled from the lowlands of mainland Scotland. A succession of Stewart kings tried to whip in the arrogant clans of the Western Isles, but they clung to their own traditions and loyalties. A patriarchal clan system existed, with every member of the clan family being independent and equal in status, looking to their chief for guidance and justice but not for oppressive authority. This was the foundation of the proud independence that still endures in the Hebrides today; a classless pride that has survived even the suppression of the clans after Culloden and, in the 19th century, the appalling depopulation caused by the Highland Clearances.

The outer islands to the south of Benbecula rejected the Reformation, following the inclination of their chiefs, their faith kept alive by Gaelic-speaking monks who came over from Ireland. These islands remain almost entirely Catholic. Those north of Benbecula, as well as Skye, Mull and most of the inner isles, embraced the Reformed Church with such enthusiasm that visitors today must be careful not to offend their Sabbatarianism.

Most island families have their own croft, or smallholding, their tenancy carefully controlled by the Crofters Commission enacted in 1886 as a result of public indignation after the Clearances (*see* Napier, etc. p.41–2). But crofting is a hard life. With only a few acres, poor markets and expensive freight, few can exist solely on its returns. Crofting is therefore usually an ancillary occupation, undertaken in the evening in summer, during weekends and on spare days off from more lucrative employment such as building, fishing and work in public service.

Inner Hebrides and the Islands of the Clyde

Most of the old croft houses have been replaced by more comfortable modern ones, but some are still occupied. In the original reed-thatched 'black houses', squat and shaggy like crouching sheep, the byre was usually part of the dwelling; the thick stone walls were rounded at the corners to withstand the wind and the peat fire raised on a platform in the middle of the room, its smoke escaping through a hole in the roof. Black houses are mostly folk museums now, restored and authentic in design, but misleadingly cosy in atmosphere. No museum would want to replicate the reality: the vermin, the pervading damp, the smell from the animals and the heavy pall of smoke, all of which contributed to the poor health of many of the people.

Electricity transformed living conditions and later it brought television, which has all but finished off the *céilidh* tradition. In the old days, when a crofting township was similar to a sophisticated and successful commune, the day's work was done on a cooperative basis. In the evenings, communities gathered together round the fire in one of the black houses, to listen to music and poetry and to tell the old sagas. Attempts have been made to capture some of this ancient folklore and put it down on paper, but this isn't the same: it was a living thing, passed on orally from generation to generation, embroidered and altered year by year.

Gaelic is still the first language for most people in the Outer Hebrides, but an influx of non-Gaelic speakers means that the children of today are growing up speaking English for preference. There has been a recent revival of enthusiasm for Gaelic and the *gaidhealtachd* ('gaeldom'), especially in Skye, where the Gaelic College, **Sabhal Mor Ostaig,** has proved highly successful. Opinions are divided about the wisdom of trying to resuscitate a dying language that never belonged to the classroom.

People who go to the islands for holidays enjoy outdoor life: walking, climbing, bird-watching, wild flowers, boating, fishing and shooting. Whatever the weather—and it is often good—each day is an adventure. Walk 5 miles to an isolated beach, collect driftwood and make a fire using dried heather twigs as kindling. Cook sausages or fresh-caught mackerel and wash them down with peat-coloured water from a burn. Collect mussels from rocks below the high tide and rake cockles out of the white sand; pick wild mushrooms from the grassy hillsides. You can even have a quick swim—diving into deep icy water as clear as glass.

Although Skye, being more accessible, has a much more modern culture than the outer islands, only in its capital, Portree, and Stornoway in Lewis, will you find many shops, and these are mainly general stores which stock most things from boots to butter. There are a few craft/souvenir/post-card shops, weavers, and a post office here and there, but people for whom 'shopping' is an integral part of a holiday tend to stay on the mainland. Because of deeply held religious beliefs, most businesses are closed on Sundays and there is no scheduled public transport. In the Presbyterian islands, hotel bars, pubs and restaurants also close, though some hotels are open to non-residents for meals. A few B&B landladies and self-catering proprietors prefer guests not to arrive or depart on Sundays, so it is worth checking to avoid giving offence.

For public entertainment there may be a local *céilidh* in a village hall to mark a particular occasion, or spontaneously erupting in a hotel bar; and there are Games in the summer on the larger islands. Otherwise, evenings are spent in front of a peat fire with a book, or the television if there is one, or, if you are lucky, in the pub listening to the tales of local people who can still tell much of the old folklore, and who will often make music for you.

The Islands of the Clyde

Great Cumbrae, Arran, Holy Island and Bute make up the cluster of islands tucked between the Firth of the Clyde and the peninsula of Kintyre, known as the Islands of the Clyde.

Great Cumbrae

Although it wouldn't thank you for saying so, Great Cumbrae is so close to the Ayrshire mainland that it hardly counts as an island. The island is less than 4 miles in length and 2 in width, with a 12-mile coastal road round it—ideal for bicycling. The highest point is 416ft (127m).

Because of its proximity to Glasgow, a great many people go to Cumbrae in the summer, so don't expect isolation: the beaches are packed on a fine day. Watersports are popular and the Scottish National Watersports Centre, based in Largs, caters for all kinds of aquatic activities. Windsurfing is good off Millport beach.

Getting There

The roll-on roll-off ferry runs every 15 minutes from Largs, taking just a few minutes.

Tourist Information

Largs: ✆ (01475) 673 765; **Millport**: ✆ (01475) 530 753 (*open April–Oct*).

Millport

Millport has a wonderfully old-fashioned sea-front holiday atmosphere. It straggles around a wide bay looking south across the Tan to Little Cumbrae, which was maintained as a deer forest by Robert II and Robert III, who both used the now-ruined 14th-century castle as their royal residence. The Victorian Gothic Episcopal collegiate church, consecrated in 1876 as the **Cathedral of the Isles**, is the smallest cathedral in Britain, seating 100 people. Its founder, George Frederick Boyle, later the Earl of Glasgow, had been involved in the Oxford Movement during the late 1840s and the cathedral was his attempt to revive the Episcopal Church in Scotland, complete with 'bells and smells'. The theological college that went with it was closed in 1885 and its buildings are now a retreat centre and cheap, basic holiday accommodation, ✆ (01475) 530 353. In the 19th century the minister in the parish kirk, Rev James Adam, used to pray for 'Great and Little Cumbrae and the adjacent islands of Great Britain and Ireland'.

Millport ✆ (01475–) — *Where to Stay and Eating Out*

There are quite a few hotels, guest houses, B&Bs and self-catering places. It's a popular resort and you should book well ahead. Or you can take a day trip from the mainland.

The Royal George Hotel, ✆ 530 301, is in a fine position overlooking the bay. Another good possibility is **Millerston Guest House**, ✆ 530 840.

For self-catering, **Mrs Luckie**, ✆ (01324) 551 570, has a selection of flats on the seafront in Millport, in a house built by her family in 1794 (sleeping 2–10). **Mrs Elliott**, ✆ 530 040, has a modernized cottage and runs Sailaway Sea School.

The Ritz Café in Millport is a wonderful, unpretentious 1950s-style place, run by Italian Scots since 1906. Food, served on Formica tables, is of the 'mushy peas and vinegar' type and they have won awards for their ice cream.

Arran and Holy Island

The miracle of Arran—Gaelic for 'peaked island'— is that it has clung to its character despite the thousands of holidaymakers attracted every year by its beauty. It is slightly larger than the Isle of Wight, about 20 miles across and 56 miles in circumference. Often described as 'Scotland in miniature', it is divided in two by the Highland Line that splits the mainland from northeast to southwest. The northern half is rough and hilly, its highest hill being the granite Goat Fell; the southern half is gentler. Because of the complexity of its geology, Arran is a popular place for university field studies. Although hotels, guest houses and chalet settlements ring the island, it is possible to roam inland for miles and feel surprisingly remote.

Arran was inhabited by Neolithic farmers, as its ancient stones and burial cairns prove. Since then its lovely landscape and mild climate have been put to many uses. The Irish Scots came over and settled in the early 6th century, making Arran part of the Kingdom of Dalriada. The Vikings sacked it in 797 and it was claimed by Magnus Barelegs in 1098. Somerled, Lord of the Isles, of Norse descent himself, annexed it and it became part of the Kingdom of Scotland in the Treaty of Perth in 1266. In the 1650s it was occupied by Cromwellian troops who were massacred for their pains. The Clearances took their toll in the 19th century when enclosed sheep farms drove out one third of the population and killed off Gaelic culture.

The main village and ferry terminal is Brodick (Norse *Breidr vic*—broad bay) with a population of about 1,000. The other ferry terminal is at Lochranza in the north of the island, with crossings to Claonaig. There is so much to do here that it would be easier to list what is not available. Sea sports include: swimming, sailing, windsurfing, water skiing, sub-aqua diving and fishing. Land sports include: golf, riding, pony trekking, tennis, squash, bowling and—of course—walking and climbing. Time spent birdwatching will reward you with sightings of rare species, and the flora and fauna of the island are diverse.

Getting There

Ferries run between Ardrossan and Brodick (with train connections to Glasgow Central) about 6 times a day, 4 times on Sundays, taking 55 minutes. 10 sailings a day run between Claonaig and Lochranza, taking half an hour, with bus links to Brodick. ✆ (01475) 650 100/000.

For details of the Holy Isle Ferry Service, ring ✆ (01770) 600 998, or 600 349. These numbers also cover self-drive boat hire for sea angling, mackerel fishing trips and sea angling charters.

Tourist Information

Brodick: The Pier, ✆ (01770) 302 140/302 401

Brodick

Brodick is a large resort-village with plenty of hotels and other accommodation. It spreads around the great sandy sweep of Brodick Bay, overlooked by Brodick Castle with the hills in the background. Old Brodick is below the castle: New Brodick developed during the 19th century as increasing tonnages meant that new facilities would be needed to cope with the new steamers in the Clyde.

Brodick Castle (*open 1 April (or Good Friday if earlier) –30 June and 1 Sept–31 Oct daily 11–4.30, last adm 4; 1 July–31 Aug daily 11–5, last adm 4.30; reception centre and shop 10–5; restaurant 11–5; garden and country park all year daily 9.30–sunset; adm*) stands high on the north side of the bay. In 1503 James IV gave it, with the Earldom of Arran, to his cousin James, Lord Hamilton. There was probably once a Viking fort on the site, and remains of previous strongholds may be incorporated into the present castle, which occupies a good strategic position. 'Bruce's Room' and the link with Robert the Bruce must be a reconstruction, as the castle was completely demolished in 1455 and again in 1544. This rather splendid red sandstone fortress is a mixture of Scottish Baronial and Gothic Revival: tall and formidable, set in gorgeous gardens. The oldest section visible from outside is the gaunt east tower, built in 1588 by the 2nd Earl of Arran, guardian to Mary, Queen of Scots. Cromwell's troops occupied the castle following the execution of the 1st Duke of Hamilton, and the death in battle of his heir, the 2nd Duke, and were responsible for extensive fortification and extensions. The 10th Duke was largely responsible for the castle's appearance today, planned by James Gillespie Graham in the mid 19th century. The interior is neo-Jacobean (1840s) and contains a lot of treasures, including all that is left of the fabulous collection of William Beckford of Fonthill, in Wiltshire, whose daughter, Susan Euphemia, married the 10th Duke. Beckford, hounded from society for having been caught in flagrante with a young boy, used his vast fortune and energy collecting treasures from all over the world. A good guide book gives details of the objects on display, and the gardens are exotic enough to appear in *Vathek*—Beckford's masterpiece of oriental extravagance. The gardens were rescued and replanted by the Duchess of Montrose, daughter of the 12th Duke who inherited the castle in 1895, with the help of her son-in-law, JPT Boscawen of Tresco Abbey, which is why many of the trees and plants came from Tresco. The gardens are now in the care of The National Trust for Scotland and the mild Gulf Stream climate supports rare foreign species.

Isle of Arran Heritage Centre (*open April–Oct daily 10.30–4.30; adm*) is in an 18th-century croft-farm at Rosaburn on the edge of Brodick, with smithy, cottage and stable block. There is plenty of splendid nostalgia here, covering the way of life of the islanders over many centuries—kettle on hob, iron bedstead under the eaves, old tools and equipment.

The road round the island only loses the sea occasionally, while the String Road cuts through the middle from Brodick to Blackwaterfoot. Another road cuts through Glen Scorrodale from Lamlash to Lagg Inn.

Goat Fell, 2,866ft (874m), north of Brodick, which dominates Arran, is best attacked on a clear day. There are a number of ways up, some well-trodden, and the view from the top makes it worthwhile. Some say the name comes from *geit-fjall*, Norse for goat mountain, others that it was *gaoith bheinn*—Gaelic for windy mountain. Whichever is correct, you won't see goats, though you might see golden eagles gliding on air currents in a corrie below you, and you will certainly feel the wind. One way is to start opposite the car park at Cladach on the north side of Brodick Bay. You can't miss the well signed stony track, which turns into a path through woods, heads up the glen of the Cnoacan Burn and traverses the moorland to the eastern ridge of Goat Fell. Here it joins another path, from Corrie, and goes quite steeply up to the top. If you start from Corrie, it's a bit quicker. Allow about 5 hours there and back.

Corrie is about 6 miles north of Brodick, with white cottages, trim colourful gardens, a harbour, quay and beach—a picturesque village popular with artists. There are plenty of nice walks up into the glens that cut into the hinterland like spokes of a wheel. **Glen Sannox**, a couple of miles north, hides some delightful, secret places where heather, lichens, mosses and alpine willow grow, as well as rare flowers. The **Fallen Rocks**, a couple of miles along a coastal track, are thought to be the relics of a land-slip in the Palaeozoic Age, which sent these massive boulders, some as big as houses, tumbling to the beach. Rock climbers like this area, and Sannox also has a nine-hole golf course.

Lochranza, possibly from loch of the *chaoruinn* (rowan), lies 2 miles southwest of the northern headland, Cock of Arran, and is the chief settlement at the north end of the island. 13th-century **Lochranza Castle** is a romantic three-storey L-plan ruin on the tidal flats, backed by the hills, with a pit prison in the vaulted basement. It is said to have been a staging post for Robert the Bruce in 1307 when he was returning from his encounter with the spider on Rathlin Island, to liberate Scotland from the clutches of Edward II. **The Isle of Arran Distillery** (*open April–Oct 10–5, ✆ (01770) 830 264*) is 'Scotland's Newest Distillery'.

Heading south from Lochranza down the west side of the island, the road clings to the sea with hills tumbling down almost to the beach. Steep-sided **Glen Catocol** runs inland up into the hills through beech, oak and larch, chestnut and fir, on carpets of vivid green ferns. **Thunderguy**, 5 miles south of Lochranza, gets its strange name from *tor-na-gaoith*—hill of the wind. Two miles further south, **Pirnmill** is derived from the bobbin mill that was here in the days when linen was an important industry in the island. The mill has now been converted into holiday flats. **Glen Iorsa** runs northeast through marshy bog land, hemmed in by barren hills. It is a great tract of lonely, waterlogged moor, lying below frowning crags, cut by steep ravines and lochans. The southwest corner of the island is rich in prehistoric remains. These include **Auchgallon Stone Circle**, 15 red sandstone blocks which once encircled a cairn; the **Farm Road Stone Circle**, close by; the **Machrie Standing Stones**, slim, primeval monoliths whose mysterious purpose is still unknown, and the **Kilmory Cairns**, at Lagg Inn.

It was at **King's Caves** at Drumadoon, Blackwaterfoot, that Robert the Bruce is said to have sheltered when returning to free Scotland from the English. Legend brings the 3rd-century warrior-poet, Fingal (Fionn) MacCumhail here, father of Ossian and leader of the Feinn, who feature in the old sagas. There are rock carvings of animals and typical Pictish hunting scenes in the caves. A lovely 10-mile drive (or walk) goes up Glen Scorrodale from Sliddery, along Sliddery Water to Lamlash Bay,

Kildonan, 6 miles east of Sliddery, is a sprawling farming village with two hotels, a sandy beach and **Kildonan Castle**, a ruined keep on a rocky plateau protected by a precipitous cliff on the seaward side and a ravine on the north. There are views from here of **Pladda Island Lighthouse** and **Ailsa Craig**, which rises like an iceberg 13 miles out to sea. Look for a colony of Atlantic grey seals along the shore towards Bennan Head to the west. Unafraid and curious, they come quite close to the shore to inspect passers by. The mysterious carcass of a large sea creature, discovered here in 1981, baffled experts for some time until it was identified, with great disappointment, as a gigantic basking shark. Before the headland, a winding path used by smugglers in the 18th century hugs the cliffs and leads to the road above.

Whiting Bay, 5 miles north of Kildonan, is a popular holiday village. Here, shops and hotels jostle with holiday cottages along the waterfront. There is a craft shop which specializes in leather, pottery and wood carving, and there is an 18-hole golf course with splendid views across the Firth of Clyde to the Ayrshire hills. **Glen Ashdale Falls** are signposted from the south end of the village, up a steep, wooded glen to where crystal water cascades down on to glistening rocks. **The Giant's Graves** (signposted) is a stone circle traditionally associated with Fionn MacCumhail.

Lamlash, 3 miles south of Brodick on Lamlash Bay, which is almost blocked at the mouth by Holy Island, completes the circular tour of the island. The bay provides a wonderfully safe anchorage, now a yachtsman's haven, and has given shelter to many an important traveller. King Haakon and his fleet took refuge here before their defeat in the Battle of Largs in 1263, and in 1548 the ship carrying five-year-old Mary, Queen of Scots to France from Dumbarton sheltered here. Lamlash has annual sea angling competitions, renowned throughout Scotland.

Holy Island

Holy Island, a mile offshore, provides excellent shelter for the bay. An Early Christian and medieval monastery was established here. The 6th-century St Molaise went into retreat in a cave on the western shore at the base of Mullach Mor. Viking inscriptions in the cave are said to date from the 13th century, graffiti scratched by King Haakon's fleet while they waited for the weather. It was the same bad weather that was to prove their undoing, for the Scots deliberately kept them waiting for their battle until they were completely demoralised by seasickness. There is the ruin of a 14th-century monastery and a chapel on the island and the ghost of a farmer's wife, murdered by her husband after she had presented him with his fifteenth daughter. The Buddhist monks from Samye Ling, in Eskdalemuir in the Borders, bought the island in 1992, and have developed it into a retreat and meditation centre. Work is still in progress, but much has already been achieved. For further details, ✆ (01387) 373 232.

Arran ✆ (01770–) ***Shopping***

Arran Aromatics, ✆ 302 595, a mile north of Brodick (*open daily 9.30–5.30*) produce specialist body-care products from natural ingredients. **Arran Provisions**, the Old Mill, in Lamlash sells Arran's unique blends of mustard, delicious jams, jellies, sauces and chutneys, and a Dunlop cheese made at the Creamery in Kilmory.

Arran ✆ (01770–) ***Sports and Activities***

Flying Fever, 2 Coastguard House, Kildonan, ✆ 820 292, offers hang-gliding and para-gliding with tuition, courses and cheap accommodation.

Arran ✆ (01770–) ***Where to Stay***

expensive

Kilmichael Country House Hotel, Brodick, ✆ 302 219, is worth spending a bit more on. An attractive house, it has won de luxe awards, and the food is excellent. Even if you don't stay here, try to eat here at least once.

moderate

Kinloch Hotel, overlooking the sea at Blackwaterfoot, ✆ 860 444, 🖷 860 447, is a comfortable modern eyesore with good food, indoor pool, solarium, sauna and squash court. **Auchrannie Country House Hotel**, Brodick, ✆ 302 234, 🖷 302 812, *www.auchrannie.co.uk*, a Scottish mansion in 10 acres, is very good value, with a grand leisure complex including a 20m indoor swimming pool, a sauna, and beauty and health treatments like aromatherapy. This is also one of the best places to eat, either in the bistro bar or the dining room.

The Lagg Hotel, Lagg, ✆ 870 255, is an 18th-century coaching inn on the river with a nice atmosphere, reasonable food and pleasant terraced gardens. **Apple Lodge**, Lochranza, ✆ 830 229, was the village manse and has been smartened up. The food is fine if you like everything well embellished.

cheap

Catacol Bay Hotel, on the shore at Catacol, ✆ 830 231, 🖷 830 350, is good value and fairly basic, except for the food, which is exceptional. There's also live music, and a week-long folk festival in early June. More like a family home than a hotel. **Butt Lodge Hotel**, Lochranza, ✆ 830 240, has good sea views. **Corrie Hotel**, ✆ 810 273, beside the sea, is very good value and easy-going, with a lively bar frequented by locals.

Arran ✆ (01770–) ***Eating Out***

Creelers, ✆ 302 810, at Home Farm, a mile north of Brodick, has memorable seafood. You should book. *Only open mid Mar–Oct.* **Carraig Mhor**, at Lamlash, ✆ 600 453, is on the seafront and the food is excellent, particularly the seafood.

Bute

Bute is another holiday island too close to the mainland for seekers of seclusion, though it does have one or two lonely corners, mostly in the northwest. It is 15 miles long and from 3 to 5 miles wide, with the Highland Line almost cutting it in two across Loch Fad.

Rothesay is the main town with bright lights and tourist traps, a little run-down though great efforts are being made to revive it. Its Victorian public lavatories are a sight in themselves. The **Kyles of Bute** are the narrow straits separating the island from the mainland in the northwest and northeast. Sailors are at an advantage, having access to a number of secret bays populated only by seals and sea birds. There is plenty to do in Bute, especially for the gregarious: swimming, sailing, golf, bird-watching, walking bicycling and night life.

Getting There

A roll-on, roll-off car ferry runs frequently from Wemyss Bay to Rothesay, taking half an hour. There is also a ferry from Colintraive in Argyll, taking five minutes to cross the Kyles of Bute to Rhubodach, where the drovers used to swim their cattle across. Planes fly from Glasgow.

Tourist Information

Rothesay: 15 Victoria Street, ✆ (01700) 502 151.

Rothesay

Bute Museum (*open April–Sept Mon–Sat 10.30–4.30, Sun 2.30–4.30*) covers the island's history, archaeology and natural history. The **Winter Garden** is a Grade-A listed building, built on to an existing bandstand in 1924. Its circular cast-iron and glass structure with a domed roof has been restored and is a multi-purpose building with cinema and a restaurant.

St Mary's Chapel is a smattering of ruins in the grounds of Rothesay's High Kirk. It was the medieval parish church and served as a cathedral of the Isles in the 17th century. One of the tombs is thought to be that of Marjory, first wife of Walter the High Steward, father of Robert II and founder of the Stewart/Stuart dynasty.

Rothesay Castle (*open all year; closed Thurs and Fri pm and Sun am; adm*) is one of the finest surviving medieval castles in Scotland, dating from the late 12th century, though its origins are thought to go back to 1098. It was the seat of the Marquises of Bute (*see* Mount Stuart below), an almost circular 'castle of enclosure' with high curtain walls and drum towers (of which only one remains), surrounded by a moat. It's hard to understand why it was built where it is. 19th-century experts dismissed its strategic position as 'wretchedly deficient', arguing that it showed 'very little in favour of the military knowledge that erected it—even the gate is neither flanked nor machicolated'. In the old days the sea came closer to it than it does now and it could have been mined or bombarded from almost any angle: it was besieged and captured by Vikings in spite of the defenders pouring molten lead and pitch on them from the battlements. King Haakon occupied it before the Battle of Largs. Robert the Bruce captured it in 1313 and it was his great-great-grandson who was first created Duke of Rothesay, a title held by the present Prince of Wales. The castle was used as a headquarters when both James IV and James V tried with little success to subdue the arrogant Lords of the Isles. Cromwell battered it badly during the Civil War and it was burned by Argyll during the Monmouth Rebellion in 1685. It remained a ruin until restoration finally began in the 19th century.

Mount Stuart

Mount Stuart (*open May–Sept Mon, Wed and Fri–Sun; winter by prior arrangment; adm; ✆ (01700) 503 877*), 5 miles south of Rothesay, only opened to the public in 1995, so has not yet become as familiar as many other stately homes and is a remarkable monument to what money, determination and persistence can achieve. John Patrick Crichton-Stuart, born at Mount Stuart in 1847, inherited the title 3rd Marquess of Bute six months later, together with 110,000 acres and one of the largest private fortunes of his time. He converted to Catholicism when he was 21 and was the inspiration for Disraeli's *Lothair*, in which a wealthy nobleman juggles the merits of Catholicism and Anglicanism. The Butes were of royal descent, from Robert II, whose son John Stewart became Keeper of Rothesay Castle and was granted lands on the island. The castle was the family's first home, followed by a house which still survives as the Bute estate office in the High Street.

The first house at Mount Stuart was built in 1719 and was gradually decaying when the 3rd Marquess came of age in 1869. He started with repairs, vitally needed because of extensive dry rot, and then gradually made plans for rebuilding. A new chapel with painted decorations, like a miniature basilica, was designed for the first floor of the north wing. A new entrance hall was added and Lord Bute, who was fond of exotic animals, installed a colony of beavers in the grounds and set wallabies grazing on the lawns. He spent more than £2,000 a year, no mean sum in those days, until 1877 when a fire gutted the central block. This gave him the excuse he needed to stop tinkering about and build a new house, and in 1878 the architect Robert Rowand Anderson finally drew up the designs for him.

Lord Bute took a very active interest in the progress of his new venture; many of the papers, letters and plans survive, both at Mount Stuart and in Edinburgh University Library. It was a long-drawn-out procedure, with orders and counter-orders, and Lord Bute overseeing every step. When his architect once commiserated with him over a delay, he replied: 'Why should I hurry over what is my chief pleasure? I have comparatively little interest in a thing after it is finished.' Money was no object: when choosing between marble and granite for some pillars, on being told granite would cost £20,000 more, he remarked: 'true, but that's not the point. The question is which will look best.' Completed in 1891, the hall was a triumph, with 12 windows illustrating the constellations filling the room with rich, flickering colour and showing off the Gothic elevations of green, white, buff and grey Italian marble. Lord Bute was an enthusiastic Wagnerian and it could be that he was influenced by the rich contrasts of scenery in *Parsifal*, which deeply moved him. Much remained to be done when he died in 1900 and although further drawings were commissioned and schemes discussed, nothing more came of them until, by his widow's death in 1932, the house was seen as a liability. In 1920 the 4th Marquess had advertised it for sale 'conditional to its complete demolition and removal by the Purchaser. Suitable for re-erection as a Hotel-Hydro, Restaurant, Casino or Public Building, etc'. Fortunately no one showed an interest and the house survived until John, the 6th Marquess, began full-scale renovation and restoration in 1983. Ten years later he died and his family decided that as it had been his intention to open the house to the public they should honour his wishes. Hence the chance to enjoy this magnificent creation today.

There are 300 acres of designed landscape and 18th-century woodland, created by the 3rd Earl between 1725 and 1778. A major project is under way in a large octagonal glass pavilion in the kitchen garden, an attempt to create a 'microcosm' of mountain and rainforest from Borneo and Papua New Guinea. There is a giftshop and tearoom where you can get light lunches and snacks, and an adventure play area with a huge Doll's Play House.

Other Sights

St Blane's Chapel, on the southern peninsula, just off the road, is a roofless 12th-century ruin with a carved Romanesque chancel arch, dedicated to St Blane who was born on Bute in the 6th century and founded a monastery close by. **Ascog Hall Fernery and Garden**, at Ascog, is a splendid sunken Victorian Fern House, fully restored in 1986, brimming with sub-tropical species. **Kames Castle** (private, but clearly seen from the road between Port Bannatyne and Ettrick Bay) dates back to the 14th century, with a house added in 1799. The home of the Bannatyne family, it was restored by David Bryce. It passed to a nephew, Henry Home, later Lord Kames, in 1780 and later to the Earls of Bute.

Events and Activities

There is plenty of organized jollity in the summer: a **Jazz Festival** in May, a **Folk Festival** in July and the **Bute Highland Games** in August. There are angling competitions, a bowling tournament, three golf courses, tennis, riding, fishing and water sports of all kinds.

Bute ✆ (01700–) ***Where to Stay and Eating Out***

moderate

St Blane's Hotel, Kilchattan Bay, ✆/🖷 831 224, is on the water's edge, with six moorings for visiting yachtsmen. They run a courtesy bus, but you should take your car if you want to explore. Pets welcome. **Ardyne Private Hotel**, 38 Mountstuart

Road, Rothesay, ✆ 502 052, 🖷 505 129, is on the seafront, with spectacular views across the Kyles of Bute. A good family base (and special rates for children).

Ardmory House Hotel and Restaurant, Ardmory Road, Ardbeg, ✆ 502 346, 🖷 505 596, overlooks the Clyde, and has a restaurant open to non-residents. **Kingarth Hotel and Restaurant**, Kingarth, ✆/🖷 831 662, is a comfortable, country inn-style hotel overlooking Kilchattan Bay, with good food. **Cannon House Hotel**, Battery Place, Rothesay, ✆ 502 819, is a pretty Georgian town house near the harbour with views over the bay to the hills and good food. Sailing available on a 40ft yacht.

For self-catering, **Ardencraig House**, High Craigmore, Rothesay, ✆ 504 550, is a newly done up Palladian mansion with five luxury apartments (sleeping 2–6) and seven chalets in the grounds (sleeping 4–6). **Mrs J. Hardy**, Kames Castle, Port Bannatyne, ✆ 504 500, has six Victorian cottages in a private estate on Kames Bay, near the castle (sleeping 2–9).

cheap

New Farm, Mount Stuart, ✆ 831 646, is a delightfully cosy little cottage. Mrs Carole Howard is justly proud of her home-baked bread, traditional Scottish breakfasts and dinners cooked with home-grown herbs and vegetables. **Mrs Watson** runs Ascog House, Ascog (on the coast southeast of Rothesay near Mount Stuart House), ✆ 503 372, one of the best B&Bs, in a 250-year-old farmhouse, secluded and very friendly with log fires for rainy days. **Bayview Hotel**, Rothesay, ✆ 505 411, looks over Rothesay Bay and is cheap and cheerful, and only a 10-minute walk from the pier.

The Commodore, 12 Battery Place, Rothesay, ✆ 502 178, on the seafront near the town centre, is an attractive building with comfortable well-equipped bedrooms and free coarse fishing. In the grounds there's a small, modernized self-catering cottage.

The **West End** in Gallowgate, Rothesay, ✆ 503 596, has won well-deserved awards for its fish and chips.

The Inner Hebrides

Gigha, Islay, Jura, Colonsay and Oronsay, Mull and Iona, Coll and Tiree make up the Inner Hebrides, with Rum, Eigg, Canna and Muck making up the Small Isles

Gigha

Pronounced with hard g at the beginning, silent g in the middle—Ge'a—Gigha's name is said to come from *Gudey*—Norse for God's Isle—and indeed this subtropical island is an earthly Garden of Eden. On the other hand, the name could come from the Norse *gja-ey*—cleft island. Although it is only 56 miles from Glasgow and 3 miles from the mainland, this low-lying, fertile piece of land, 7 miles long by a mile wide, has managed to retain its island character. It is firmly on the tourist map, but even that has not broken its magic spell.

Getting There

Flights from Glasgow to Campbeltown, twice daily on weekdays, and taxi from Campbeltown—25 miles, to the ferry terminus at Tayinloan, is one way of travelling. Or drive to Tayinloan where you are encouraged to leave your car and hire a bicycle, rather than clutter the one road on the island. The ferry, which will take cars if you insist, runs hourly in the summer (less in winter) and takes about 20 minutes.

Tourist Information

Campbeltown: West Highland and Islands Tourist Board, The Pier, ✆ (01586) 552 056. Or talk to the McSporran family, in the shop at Ardminish.

Visiting the Island

Gigha has changed hands often in the recent past—14 owners in 200 years—and is dependent on the whims of its owner/landlord. Islands like this can suffer dreadfully from being bought and sold as business ventures and toys for tycoons, but Gigha somehow manages to blossom in spite of having had to endure its share of speculators. Perhaps the most influential of these 'white settler' lairds was Colonel Sir James Horlick, whose malted beverages lulled the world to sleep and made him a fortune. He bought Gigha in 1944 and lived there till his death in 1972, indulging his passion for gardening.

Achamore Gardens (*open daily; adm*) was the result. Thanks to the balmy Gulf Stream giving an almost frost-free climate, as well as the acidic soil, the already established trees and, of course, the Horlick fortune, these 50 acres are a riot of rhododendrons, azaleas and camellias in early summer, along with many rarer exotic plants, shrubs and trees. Achamore is a vivid focal point in a wonderful island sea-scape.

The **Achamore creamery**, recently revived and supplied by local Ayrshire cattle, produces a very good cheese; previously, the milk—some half a million gallons a year—had to be sent off to Campbeltown every day. There is also a fish farm on the estate.

The village is **Ardminish**, where everything happens. Perhaps the most celebrated of Gigha's 120 residents is Seumas McSporran, a sturdy figure with a genial smile almost as wide as his face. He has lived here for all but two years of his life and until recently held some 14 or 15 jobs. 'I had to consult a list to keep up to date with them.' They included: shopkeeper, bicycle hirer, gas agent, sub-postmaster, postman, registrar, Pearl Assurance agent, coastguard, special constable, fireman, ambulance driver, taxi driver and undertaker. He had a uniform or outfit to go with each job. His shop, a family concern, stocks everything you might need, and they can also get things from the mainland for you, ✆ (01583) 505 251.

The ruined medieval parish church is at **Kilchattan**, with intricately carved late medieval grave slabs in the burial ground. Nearby is the 'ogham stone', brought from Ireland in pre-Christian times, with an indecipherable inscription on it. There are quite a few archaeological sites: cairns, standing stones, forts and duns. A Viking grave was found in 1849 at East Tarbert Bay, in which was an ornate portable scales with decorated pans and weights. King Haakon stopped off here on his way to defeat at the Battle of Largs, probably sheltering from the awful weather which made his men so seasick that they hadn't a chance against the hardy locals.

Gigha ✆ (01583–) ***Where to Stay***

moderate

The Gigha Hotel, ✆ 505 254, 🖷 505 244, is a perfect honeymoon retreat, almost ranch-style, in the original 1789 inn. It's not a bit grand, with a cosy lounge and cheerful bar in which to pick up local gossip. It's in a lovely position, the food is good, and they will arrange golf on the nine-hole course just north of Ardminish and skippered fishing boat hire for sea angling or trips round the island from Ardminish Bay. The hotel also operates four self-catering cottages, including **Ardailly House**, and Seumas McSporran, needless to say, offers accommodation in **Post Office House**, ✆ 505 251.

Islay

Islay (pronounced Eyela), 15 miles off the west coast of Argyll and only 23 miles north of Northern Ireland, is the most southerly of the Inner Hebrides, and one of the largest of the islands, 25 miles long and 19 miles across—246 square miles. Its landscape is very varied, from hilly moorland traversed by burns, to sheltered woods and fertile farmland, with a rugged coastline giving way to open sweeps of beach. A favourite holiday island for birdwatchers, naturalists, photographers and artists, it also has much to interest archaeologists, having been inhabited since Neolithic times. Excellent trout and salmon fishing can be found on the rivers Duich and Sorn and on well-stocked lochs such as Gorm, Torrabus and Ballygrant. Boats can be hired locally for sea fishing, too. Warmed by the Gulf Stream (so they say—the sea isn't quite Mediterranean), miles of sandy beaches offer swimming and sunbathing, and the surf is sometimes good. The 18-hole golf course at Machrie is well known.

Perhaps best known for its distinctive peaty malt whisky, Islay has a number of distilleries, such as Laphroaig, Lagavulin, Ardbeg and Bowmore, that scent the air with the pungent smell of smouldering peat. Now and then islanders tangle with conservationists who insist that the special Duich Moss peat, essential for the flavour of Islay whisky, should be preserved for Greenland white-fronted geese. At a stormy meeting not so long ago, the islanders, furious at Green interference, argued that whisky was more vital to their survival than 'any bloody goose'. The distilleries welcome visitors.

Apart from whisky, agriculture is the main industry. Tourism is a growth industry with 45,000 summer visitors coming in on the ferries and 11,000 by air. So far they haven't managed to spoil the island. In 1831 the population was 15,000; it now stands at 4,000.

Historically, Islay was the administrative capital of the Lords of the Isles, and therefore of prime importance until the forfeiture of the Lordship in 1493. There was a military and naval base at Dunivaig on the south coast and the civil headquarters were on two small islands on Loch Finlaggan. These were the centres of power for an administration which, at its zenith in the early 15th century, ruled all the islands off the west coast and almost the entire western seaboard from Cape Wrath to the Mull of Kintyre.

Martin Martin, whose *Description of the Western Isles of Scotland*, published in 1703, encouraged Dr Johnson to make his tour, describes 'Ila' in great detail, and it doesn't seem to have changed all that much in the intervening 300 years.

Getting There

Ferries cross from Kennacraig to Port Askaig, taking 2 hours, and from Kennacraig to Port Ellen, taking just over 2 hours. Western Ferries, ✆ (01496) 840 681.

Flights go daily from Campbeltown, Monday to Friday, and twice daily from Glasgow, Monday to Saturday. British Airways, ✆ 0345 222 111.

Tourist Information

Campbeltown: The Pier, ✆ (01586) 552 056; **Bowmore**: The Square, ✆ (01496) 810 254. *Both open all year.*

Festivals

The 2-week Islay **Folk Festival** is at the end of May/early June, ✆ (01496) 302 413.

Visiting the Island

Port Ellen is the ferry arrival point at the south end of the island; its distillery, built in 1815, dominates the skyline above Leodamus Bay, but is now no longer in operation. It's an attractive little place with terraced houses round the harbour and a laid-back atmosphere. A road runs round the coast northeastwards for about 10 miles and then gives way to a track. Three familiar names grace this road—Laphroaig, Lagavulin and Ardbeg— and an amusing story is told about them. John Campbell of Ardmore, a relative of the laird and previous Chamberlain to the Duke of Inveraray, died in 1860 and his body was returned to Islay for burial in the family plot at Kidalton. It was carried, as was the custom, in relays along the road, with frequent stops to rest along the way. With the three distilleries so handy it was easy to get flasks refilled for toasts to the deceased and for refreshment. When the cortège reached the cemetery they realised they were without the coffin. Hurrying back, they discovered it lying peacefully on the road between Lagavulin and Ardbeg.

Dunyvaig Castle is the 14th-century ruin on the cliff 3½ miles to the east of Port Ellen. It was the stronghold of the Macdonalds of Islay when the Lords of the Isles were dominant and considered themselves above the authority of the crown. They had an excellent vantage point here from which to keep an eye on invaders from the south. Dunnyvaig was their military and naval headquarters.

Kidalton Crosses, beside ruined Kidalton Chapel, about four miles on up the road, is an important survival of Celtic art: an Early-Christian wheel cross over 7ft high, probably dating from the 9th century, carved from a single block of locally quarried stone. It's the finest example of its kind outside Iona, and its carvings looking incredibly fresh after nearly 2,000 years. The front depicts the story of Abraham and Isaac; Daniel and a lion; and the Virgin and Child guarded by angels. One of the raised bosses on the back is a bird's nest with three eggs, symbolizing the Blessed Trinity. Somehow it escaped the Viking raids which so devastated the Celtic Church in the west. In the 1890s the remains of a Viking ritual killing were found under the cross—a rather nasty ceremony that involved 'spread-eagling' the 'blood eagle' (lungs) and holding them up before burial. There was an Early Christian chapel and a monastery here, too, before the present Kidalton Chapel was built by the Lords of the Isles in the 14th century. It is roofless but substantial, and there are some late-medieval grave slabs inside.

Claggain Bay, a couple of miles north of the Kidalton Crosses and chapel, is sandy, with rocky pools, against a backdrop of **Beinn Bheigeir**, the highest hill on the island, standing at 1,612ft (496m). The road peters out after Claggain Bay but there are lovely walks further on along the coast, or west into the hinterland.

The **Oa Peninsula** (pronounced 'Oh'), 5 miles southwest of Port Ellen, was the rugged haunt of smugglers and illicit whisky distillers, who made cunning use of its sheer cliffs honeycombed with caves. The only road goes down to the Mull in the southwest; otherwise most of it is accessible only by foot. Good bird watching here. The American Monument—an obelisk in memory of two American ships which sank here at the end of the First World War—is signed off the road to the Mull of Oa, about a mile's walk uphill. The setting is spectacular, and if you brave it in a storm you can understand how the ships were wrecked. **Machrie**, on Laggan Bay northwest of the Oa, has a well-known 18-hole golf course on the machair, and the airport. The River Laggan runs into the north of the bay and Martin Martin records: 'I was told by the Natives that the Brion of Ila, a famous Judge, is, according to his own Desire, buried standing on the Brink of the River Laggan; having in his right Hand a Spear, such as they use to dart at the Salmon.'

Bowmore, about 9 miles north of Port Ellen, was the old capital and administrative centre of the island, built by Daniel Campbell the Younger in 1768 on the site of monastic lands. It is one of the earliest of Scotland's planned villages, introduced by wealthy 'improvers' in the 18th century. A delightful feature of the village is the **round church**, built as the parish church in 1769. It is of Italian design and so shaped to deprive the devil of any corners in which to lurk. Bowmore Distillery, established in 1779, claims to be the oldest legal distillery on Islay and is still privately owned.

The Rhinns of Islay project westwards like a great hammer-head with wonderful walks and views and excellent fishing. **Port Charlotte** is a pretty village half way down the southeastern edge of the hammer with a **Museum of Islay Life** in a converted church (*open April–Sept daily; Oct–Mar Mon–Fri; adm*). There are quite good displays here on local history, as well as the usual array of traditional artefacts and some 16th-century carved stones. There is also an excellent wildlife information and field centre which is good for all ages and very hands-on, with guided tours, ✆ (01496) 850 288.

Ellister, south of Port Charlotte, is a wildfowl sanctuary, and **Loch Gruinart** to the north is an RSPB reserve. Here, in 1598, at the head of the loch, was fought the Battle of Traigh Gruinart—one of the last great clan battles, between the Macleans of Duart and the Macdonalds. The Macleans had invaded Islay intending to capture the castle of Gorm, in Loch Gorm, but the Macdonalds defeated them, slaying 380 of the 400 who landed, including the Maclean chief. From **Portnahaven**, at the southwest tip of the Rhinns, the green coast of Ireland is only spitting distance away.

Inland from the head of Loch Indaal, **Loch Finlaggan,** with its ruins on an islet, was the administrative capital of the Lords of the Isles. It is difficult to picture how it must have been in those medieval days, looking at its peaceful isolation now. Dean Donald Munro, writing in 1549, describes how the 14 members of the Council of the Isles, which met on the small Eilean na Comhairle—Council Isle—at Finlaggan: 'decernit, decreitit and gave suits furth upon all debaitable matters according to the laws made by Renald McSomharkle (Reginald, son of Somerled) callit in his time King of the Occident Isles. In thair time thair was great peace and welth in the Iles throw the ministration of Justice.' On Eilean Mor, linked to the Council Isle by a causeway, there are the remains of a chapel and over 20 buildings, many of which date from the time of the Lordship. Writing nearly 300 years ago, Martin Martin writes of Loch Finlaggan and the Court of the great Mack-Donald, where he had his residence, his house and chapel, while his guards, called *Lucht-taeh*, 'kept Guard on the lake-side nearest to the Isle'. He tells of how the Judge got an eleventh share of any sum in debate. And he tells of 'a big Stone of seven

Foot square, in which there was a deep Impression made to receive the Feet of Mack-Donald; for he was crown'd King of the Isles standing in this Stone, and swore that he would continue his Vassals in the possession of their lands, and do exact Justice to all his Subjects' (*see* Dunadd Fort, p.95–6) He then describes the anointing by the Bishop of Argyle and seven priests, and all the ritual of kingmaking. The 14 chiefs who were summoned here to the council meetings came from all over the Kingdom of the Isles, many in coracles, each with his 'tail'—henchmen from the clan. They were proud men, settling their disputes and problems independently of the Scottish Parliament, usually with wisdom and justice, and often bloodshed. There is no doubt that, in spite of the efforts of the Crown to undermine their strength, the Lords of the Isles ruled with effect. There is a visitor centre here, illustrating some of the intriguing history of those times and displaying archaeological remains unearthed by recent diggings.

Port Askaig is the other ferry terminal for the mainland and for Jura, a ramshackle little place in a steep-sided bay with views across the narrow Sound of Islay to Jura, less than a mile away. The hinterland to the north and west is a network of rivers and burns, virtually without roads.

Islay ✆ (01496–) ***Where to Stay***

Nothing is too expensive and all is much the same in standard: what you may miss in glamour you will certainly gain in Highland hospitality, warmth and friendliness.

moderate

Bridgend Hotel, ✆ 810 212, 810 960, at the head of Loch Indaal, has a nice garden. The **Harbour Inn**, Bowmore, ✆ 810 330, 810 990, overlooking Loch Indaal, is a bit cheaper and also serves very good food. Book ahead if you want to eat here. **Port Askaig Hotel**, ✆/ 840 295, is on the Sound of Islay with good views of Jura. **Port Charlotte Hotel**, ✆ 850 360, 850 361, in the main street, is Victorian, with a conservatory and a garden going down on to the sandy beach.

Kilmeny Farmhouse, at Ballygrant, near Loch Finlaggan, ✆ 840 668, is a cosy little place with good views, where you are treated as part of the family. Run by Blair and Margaret Rozga, it has won deluxe awards and serves excellent food. No smoking. **Glenegedale House**, by Port Ellen, ✆ 302 147, a 17th-century farmhouse, near the airport and golf course, looking across Laggan Bay to the Atlantic, is a bit cheaper.

For self-catering, **Kilchoman House** by Bruichladdich, ✆ 850 382, has five cottages in 40 acres of farmland near a sandy beach. There is a separate restaurant.

cheap

At **The Kennels**, Ballygrant, ✆ 840 237, some way off the main road in quiet woodland, you will be plied with home-baked hospitality. **Ballygrant Inn**, ✆ 840 277, in Ballygrant, is a comfortable, family-run place in 2½ acres of woodland. The food is good and the rooms are made cosy with log stoves.

Islay ✆ (01496–) ***Eating Out***

The **Harbour Inn** and **Port Charlotte Hotel**, *see* above, are both good bets. **Kilchoman House**, ✆ 850 382, is also very good. Book in advance. The **Croft Kitchen**, Port Charlotte, ✆ 850 230, is a coffee/gift shop by day and a restaurant by night. Booking essential. *Open Mar–Oct.* **The Old Granary**, Kintra Farm, ✆ 302

051, is a converted barn which serves good basic (and cheap) food. *Open May–Aug.* There's a good campsite too, and a hostel and B&B in the farmhouse. **Ballygrant Inn**, ✆ 840 277, does reasonable pub meals, with curry as a house special. **The Machrie**, Port Ellen, ✆ 302 310, serves good food and is not expensive.

Jura

Just off the northeast coast of Islay, Jura has very little tourist accommodation and is far less frequented, though more beautiful—some 27 miles long, 5 to 6 miles wide and sparsely populated. Silver and white sandy beaches give way to rugged shingle, teeming with wildfowl. Loch Tarbert almost cuts Jura in two from the west. The three Paps (or 'bosoms') of Jura rear up at the south end of the island—the highest is 2,576ft (793m). Their distinctive outlines are as familiar to sailors as the Cuillins of Skye, and serve as a landmark for miles. A single-track road runs south from the ferry and then some way up the east coast. Most of the island is only accessible on foot. The west coast—private land—has some amazing caves, some of which have been adapted for temporary use by shepherds, and, in recent years, by a young woman artist.

Wild and rugged, Jura is famous for its red deer, some 5,000 of them, which are keenly stalked by the owners and guests of the sporting estates of which the island is comprised. Martin Martin recorded in the 18th century that 'the hills ordinarily have about three hundred Deer grazing on them, which are not to be hunted by any, without the Steward's Licence.' The name Jura comes from the Norse word *dyr-ey*—deer island—though Martin Martin was told by 'natives' that it comes from Dih and Rah—two Norse brothers who fought and killed each other and whose ashes are buried in urns under two 7ft stones 60 yards apart at Knock-Cronm.

One hundred and fifty years ago Jura had about 1,000 inhabitants; now there are less than 200. With only one hotel and limited bed and breakfast accommodation, tourism is very low key, mainly geared for day visitors from Islay. The sportsmen who pay large sums for their pursuits aren't too keen on seeing hikers in their gun sights. Most of the locals work on their crofts, or for the Forestry Commission, as estate workers or in the distillery.

Getting There

There is no direct link with the mainland. A car ferry runs frequently from Port Askaig on Islay to Feolin on Jura, a 10-minute crossing; fewer ferries on Sundays.

Tourist Information

Campbeltown: The Pier, ✆ (01586) 55205.

History

In the 19th century Jura was the stepping stone for drovers taking cattle from Islay and Colonsay to the mainland markets, with two to three thousand head of cattle crossing every year.

Archaeological remains show that Jura was inhabited as long ago as 7000 BC. There is a Neolithic burial cairn south of Strone Farm and no fewer than seven Bronze Age standing stone sites in the southeast. Of the several Iron Age forts and duns, the best is An Dunan, on Lowlandman's Bay. Martin Martin recorded that this island was the most 'wholesome' place in all Scotland, due to its position, the height of its hills and 'by the fresh Breezes of Wind that come from 'em to purify the air'. The inhabitants, he said, were less prone to: 'Gout, Agues,

Sciatica, Convulsions, Vapours, Palsies, Surfeits, Lethargies, Megrims, Consumptions, Rickets, Pains of the Stomach or Coughs.' Apparently, few women died in childbirth. He was told of one man, Gillouir Mack-Crain, who lived 180 years. The natives were 'very well proportioned, being generally black of Complexion, and free from bodily Imperfections'.

The Island

One of Jura's most infamous features is the **Corryvreckan Whirlpool**, in the strait between its northern point and Scarba. Notorious to west-coast sailors, it can be both lion and lamb. Flood tides meet around a steep pyramid rock, 15 feet below the surface, causing the whirlpool, whose noise has been heard up to 10 miles away. Roaring like an express train, its mighty maw has been known to suck down whole boats, but at slack tide it can be approached by sea, its satin-smooth water ruffled by tiny eddies that pull gently at a boat without harm.

In May 1946 George Orwell, born Eric Blair, rented Barnhill, an abandoned farmhouse at the end of a 5-mile, heavily rutted track from Ardlussa where his landlady Margaret Fletcher lived. Over a period of summer visits, he wrote *Nineteen Eighty-Four* here, fighting the tuberculosis that was to kill him, and was contented in his rather morose way. He was a competent boatman, but on one occasion he misread the tide table and capsized in the Corryvreckan with his three-year-old adopted son Richard and a couple of friends. Miraculously, no one was drowned and they were rescued, unscathed, from a rock by some lobster fishermen.

Craighouse, the only village, on the southeast coast looking out across the Sound of Jura to Knapdale and Kintyre, has the island's only hotel and the distillery.

Jura House Gardens is an oasis on the southern shore (*open all year; adm*). Its large walled garden was established in the middle of the last century to exploit the natural features and beauty of the area; thanks to the mild climate exotic Australasian plants are grown. Everything is organically produced, and there is an attractive walk through woodland to the shore at Ardfin.

Where to Stay

Jura Hotel, Craighouse, ✆ (01496) 820 243, 820 249 (the only one), is all you could wish for: relaxed, friendly, in a lovely setting and with good local food. It's very reasonably priced and often fully booked.

Colonsay and Oronsay

These two tiny islands, joined at low tide, lie 10 miles west of Jura, 25 miles from the mainland. **Colonsay** is about 8 miles long and up to 3 miles across, while **Oronsay** is little more than 2 miles in any direction. To the west, way out to sea, the only thing between here and Canada is Dubh Artach Lighthouse. The landscape is made up of craggy hills, woods and a rocky coastline broken by silver sands. The name Colonsay comes from St Colomba who landed here on his way to Scotland from Ireland. Legend has it that when he could still see the land from which he had been exiled, he pressed on to Iona—whether from repugnance or homesickness is not related. (It is also said that he banished snakes from the two islands, as he did on Iona.) The Gaelic name is *Eilean Tarsuing*—cross-lying island, which indeed it is. Oronsay's name might stem from St Oran, a disciple of St Columba, or from the Norse *orfiris-ey*—ebb-tide island, though it is when the tide ebbs that it stops being an island. The strand linking the two can submerge rapidly in the flood tide, so apprise yourself of the tide table and try to choose a spring tide if you are wanting to spend time exploring the Priory. Colonsay seems to have a little of every type of landscape: machair, woodland, cultivated woodland, both rocky and sandy beaches, cliffs, moorland and pasture.

Getting There

There are three boats a week from Oban (*Mon, Wed and Fri*), taking 2½ hours. On Wednesdays from April to September there is a sailing from Kennacraig via Islay allowing a 6-hour day visit before the boat returns in the late afternoon. A tour bus meets this boat and takes visitors round the island.

Ferry Information: Caledonian MacBrayne, Gourock, ✆ (01990) 650 000.

Tourist Information

Oban: Argyll Square, ✆ (01631) 563 122. *Open all year.*

Around the Islands

Kiloran Bay, in the northwest of Colonsay, is probably the most unspoilt beach in all the islands. After a strong westerly wind there are rollers good enough for surfing, though it can be dangerous. Both islands have higher than average sunshine, comparable with Tiree which holds the record for Scotland, and the annual rainfall is half that of the Argyll mainland. Frost and snow are rare. Over 500 species of wild flowers can be found including rare purple orchids, sea samphire, marsh helleborine, a burnet rose unique to Colonsay and the very rare orchid, *Spiranthes romanzoffiana.* Bluebells and primroses bloom in the woods in spring, wild irises flower in damp corners, harebells nod on the sand dunes, and purple thrift clings to the rocks. Over 150 bird species have been recorded. Wild goats flourish at Balnahard and on Oronsay, thought to be descended from survivors of a wreck of the Spanish Armada in 1588, carried on the ship to provide provisions for the fleet. If you are lucky you may see otters.

Archaeological remains point to early settlement in both islands. On Colonsay, Fingal's Limpet Hammers are standing stones at Kilchattan; Dun Eibhinn, behind Scalasaig, is an Iron Age fort, later occupied by the MacDuffies or MacFies of Colonsay until they were deposed as the ruling families by the MacNeills in 1701. There are Mesolithic sites at Loch Staosnaig, locally known as Queen's Bay.

Oronsay has Mesolithic shell mounds dating from before 4000 BC, giving one of the earliest records of human settlement in Scotland. Dun Domhnuill is an Iron Age fort on top of a rocky mound, well sited for defence. The stabilized ruins of Oronsay Priory and cloisters date from 1330–50, founded by Augustinian monks under the patronage of the Lords of the Isles; masonry within the circular wall which encloses the ruins dates from the 6th century. Here, until about 1500, was one of the workshops where the monks produced the intricately carved grave-slabs and crosses that can be found all over the Highlands and Islands. The Oronsay Cross is a good example, and there are about 30 other carved stones within the Prior's House dating from the 15th and 16th centuries. There is a prostrate sanctuary cross halfway over the Strand.

In 1841 these two islands had a population of 979; now it is about 100, and they have become a holiday haven away from it all. Although self-catering cottages are fast out-numbering those of residents, they have not yet spoiled the tranquillity.

Colonsay House, in a sheltered niche of woodland north of Loch Fada, was built by Malcolm MacNeill in 1722, probably with the stones of Kiloran Abbey, which once stood here, and it was enlarged in the 18th century. The estate was bought in 1904 by Donald Smith, Lord Strathcona and Mount Royal, a Forres man who made his fortune in Canada with the Hudson's Bay and Canadian Pacific Companies. He used the natural contours, rocks and streams to create the attractive gardens and woods which you are allowed to visit, with large palm trees, eucalyptus, mimosa and many rare, tender shrubs that flourish in the mild climate as well as the rhododendrons, azaleas and meconopsis that thrive in these parts. The house has now been converted into holiday flats.

According to Martin Martin, when the 'natives' of Colonsay went across to the Priory, it was their custom to make a tour 'sunways' about the church before they 'entered upon any kind of business.' While he was here, his landlord borrowed a Bible from him in order to fan the face of a sick relative with the holy pages. Three doses of this treatment appear to have cured the patient. There is a primitive and challenging 18-hole golf course on the west coast.

Shopping

Virago, adjacent to the Colonsay hotel, is an interesting bookshop with new and second hand books on Scottish and west Highland themes. They can often get out-of-print books for you, and sell coffee and crafts too.

Colonsay ✆ (01951–) ***Where to Stay***

The Isle of Colonsay Hotel, Kiloran, ✆ 200 316, is small, family run and friendly, and the food is excellent, using local ingredients whenever possible, such as oysters, mussels and other seafood, honey, fresh milk, cream and butter from a Jersey herd. They also have self-catering chalets and they run wild flower courses.

The Colonsay Estate arranges self-catering, ✆ 200 312. **Mr and Mrs Lawson**, ✆ 200 315, run one of the best guesthouses, **Seaview**, and also have a self-catering studio flat sleeping 2.

Mull

Mull—'Isle of the Cool, High Bends'—is the second largest of the Inner Hebrides after Skye, and merits a whole book to itself. Shaped like a caricature of the British Isles, its southwestern peninsula kicks skittishly upwards. Encircled by 300 miles of rugged coastline, it is deeply cut by lochs, with many wooded hills and secret corners, some easily reached by coastal roads, others only on foot. Mull's western seaboard is sprinkled with islands: **Iona**, **Inch Kenneth**, **Ulva**, **Staffa** and, further west, the **Treshnish Isles** with **Coll** and **Tiree** beyond. There are plenty of boat trips to the islands and some of the hotels charter their own boats. In addition, local men will take you fishing or sightseeing, which is much the most fun way to get about. The whole coast is a sailor's paradise: Loch Na Keal, Loch Scridain, Loch Buie and Loch Spelve are deep sea lochs which penetrate far inland and provide sheltered anchorages. The hinterland is a mass of hills, dominated by **Ben More**, 3,169ft (966m), in the west, its scree-covered flanks the result of a volcano which exploded some 60 million years ago. Students come from far afield to study the interesting geology, and archaeologists come to study the large number of prehistoric sites: cairns, standing stones, vitrified forts, duns and brochs. There are some fine castles and an ancient pilgrim track across the Ross of Mull, used by pilgrims to Iona. Johnson and Boswell came to Mull during their tour of the Hebrides. Johnson lamented the lack of trees, attributing this to local idleness, but applauded the French wine he was given.

In 1821 the population was 10,600. Until fairly recently there was a steady decline but it now seems to have stabilized at about 2,400. With fishing, farming, tourism and building to employ them, fewer young people are seeking the bright lights of the mainland and there are also many English and mainland Scottish incomers who prefer insular peace and beauty to the scramble of the cities. There is not always perfect harmony between the 'white settlers' and the 'natives'.

There are more red deer than people: over 3,000 roam the island, and smaller fallow deer can be seen in the woods around Gruline and Salen. Polecats, weasels, stoats, mink, feral ferrets and otters also share the island. Wild white goats can be seen from Grass Point down to the Ross of Mull.

Martin Martin recorded: 'the Natives are accustom'd to take a large Dose of Aquavitae [whisky] as a Corrective, when the Season is very moist, and then they are very careful to chew a piece of Charmel-Root, finding it to be aromatick; especially when they intend to have a drinking-bout, for they say this in some measure prevents drunkenness.'

Getting There and Getting Around

Car ferries run frequently from Oban to Craignure in about 40 minutes; Oban to Tobermory takes under 2 hours, and Lochaline to Fishnish, a quarter of an hour. A car ferry from Kilchoan to Tobermory takes half an hour. For details contact Caledonian MacBrayne, ✆ (01475) 650 100. Ask about the various 'Rover' and 'Multi-stop' tickets which are much cheaper if you are island-hopping.

There is an **airfield** on the island. Charter flights can be arranged from Glasgow. You can hire **cars** easily. Most roads are single track with passing places.

Inter-island cruises in high-speed charter boats to Staffa, the Treshnish Isles, Coll, Eigg and Muck, can be booked from Richard and Judy Fairbairns, Dervaig, ✆ (01688) 400 223; or Turus Mara, ✆ (01688) 400 242. You need to be well prepared for quick weather changes and take seasick pills if you have an uneasy stomach: the slow Atlantic swell has been known to disturb even hardened mariners. You might see whales and dolphins.

Tourist Information

Craignure: The Pier, ✆ (01680) 812 377 (*open all year*); **Tobermory**: Main Street, ✆ (01688) 302 182 (*open April–Oct*); **Oban**: Argyll Square, ✆ (01631) 563 122 (*open all year*).

Tobermory

Tobermory—'the Well of St Mary'—is an unexpected gem, with one of the most sheltered harbours in Scotland tucked in behind a headland. Founded as a fishing village in 1789 on the site of an earlier Christian settlement, tall Georgian houses line the harbour, washed in strong poster-paint colours, with long, narrow windows and gabled dormers. You won't find too many tartan souvenirs here: stacks of lobster creels, business-like tackle shops and pubs show where priorities lie. Some people who live in remote Morvern and Ardnamurchan on the mainland go across to Tobermory to do their shopping, it being their nearest metropolis.

Mull Museum (*open Easter–mid Oct Mon–Sat; adm*), in an old baker's shop, is a concession to one of Mull's main industries—tourism. Here you can get a good overview of the history of the island, and of the wrecked galleon *Florencia*, part of the Spanish Armada and still a focus of interest today. The ship sought shelter here in a storm in 1588. Always hospitable, the islanders treated the Spaniards with courtesy, restocking their stores and entertaining them in grand style. But Scotsmen are thrifty as well as hospitable and when rumours spread that the *Florencia* was about to depart without having paid its dues, a local man, Donald Maclean, went aboard to remonstrate. He was locked up in the ship's cell but managed to escape. In retaliation he blew up the ship, together with the hoard of gold and treasure it was alleged to have been carrying. So far only a few coins and cannon have been rescued, but the search continues. Divers should note, however, that the wreck is protected and it is forbidden to dive in its area. Tobermory has a nine-hole golf course on the northern tip of the island owned by the Western Isles Hotel. Spectacular views down the Sound of Mull are apt to distract players.

West from Tobermory, the B8073 passes the three-in-one Mishnish Lochs where there is good trout fishing. Snake Pass, beyond the last one, is the home of many adders and the start of a nice walk out to Loch Frisa. On the hill down into Dervaig there is a cemetery at Kilmore, with some of the oldest gravestones on Mull. Film buffs may recognize this as one of the locations for *Where Eight Bells Toll.*

Mull Little Theatre, ✆ (01688) 400 377, in Dervaig, 5 miles from Tobermory, featured in the *Guinness Book of Records* as the smallest professional theatre in Britain, with 37 seats, but it has recently lost that accolade by providing six extra seats. Six times a week from Easter to October, two or more actors from visiting professional companies stage really excellent and varied productions which should be booked well in advance. Amateur productions are staged in the winter. The theatre stands in the grounds of **Druimnacroish Country House Hotel** (*see* below), where you can get dinner before and after the show, and lunch before matinées.

The **Old Byre Heritage Centre**, a mile beyond Dervaig (*open Easter–mid Oct daily; adm*) is a typical crofting museum with tableaux showing life at the time of the Clearances: family and animals living together in a black house with a central fire, and people busy about their daily lives. A half-hour video illustrates further what life was like.

The west coast road gives views out to the scattering of islands that enhance the wonderful seascapes, especially when seen against a setting sun. There are good sandy beaches, the one at **Calgary Bay** being particularly notable. Calgary was once a prosperous crofting community, but its people were evicted and made their way across the Atlantic, trekked across Canada and established a town in the Northwest Territory in 1884. Nostalgic and homesick, they called their new town after their old home.

Boats run from Dervaig or Ulva to the **Treshnish Isles** and to **Staffa** when the weather is fair. A new landing stage on Staffa makes access easier in rough weather, and some cruises allow you an hour ashore. You can go into **Fingal's Cave** by boat, or walk into it along a platform around its edge. This huge, cathedral-like cavern is made up of columns of basalt, similar in geology to Ireland's Giant's Causeway, some hexagonal, truncated at different levels like organ pipes. The formation inspired Mendelssohn in 1829 to write the *Hebrides* overture. Should there be a swell and you feel a little nervous, Queen Victoria would have sympathized. During her cruise of the west coast in the royal yacht *Victoria and Albert* in 1847, they anchored off Staffa and the royal party were rowed into the cave in an open rowing boat: 'the effect was splendid, like a great entrance into a vaulted hall: it looked almost awful as we entered and the barge heaved up and down on the swell of the sea. It is very high, but not longer than 227 feet, and narrower than I expected, being only 40 feet wide. The sea is immensely deep in the cave. The rocks, under water, were all colours—pink, blue, and green—which had a most beautiful effect. It was the first time the British standard with a Queen of Britain, and her husband and children, had ever entered Fingal's Cave, and the men gave three cheers, which sounded very impressive there.' Only an hour later, the sea was such that they would not have been able to enter the cave—and they had not a life-jacket between them.

Cruises which include **Lunga** in the Treshnish Isles are especially good during the nesting season. You are advised not to linger too long over the puffins at the start of your tour: they are so bewitching you may never see the rest of the island. They sit about, scratching, chatting to each other and popping in and out of their burrows, an arm's length from you. There are also kittiwakes, razorbills, shags and guillemots, and lots of black rabbits.

The island of **Ulva** will be familiar to anyone who knows the poem *Lord Ullin's Daughter*, which tells the sad tale of her eloping to join her lover, 'The Chief of Ulva's Isle', and of how she drowned in the ferry as she fled her father's wrath. Lord Ullin stands helpless on the shore:

'Come back! Come back!' he cried in grief,
Across the stormy water,
'And I'll forgive your Highland chief,
My daughter! Oh, my daughter!'
'Twas vain: the loud waves lashed the shore
Return or aid preventing.
The waters wild went o'er his child,
And he was left lamenting.

'Lord Ullin's Daughter' by Thomas Campbell (1777–1844)

On a calm day these waters look innocent enough, but Lord Ullin's daughter was not the only one to perish here. Among many others was 'the young Laird of Col' who, having treated Dr Johnson to warm Highland hospitality in 1773, perished in the passage between Ulva and Inch Kenneth a year later. A ferry runs all day in summer, ✆ (01688) 500 226. Ulva has an Interpretative Centre (information boards) and a tea room.

A couple of miles before the Ulva ferry, look for the Eas Forss, a waterfall that cascades over the cliff into a pool and then under a rock, arching into the sea.

You can walk across a causeway to the even smaller island of **Gometra**, where there is a very secure natural harbour, haven for sailors caught in a storm.

The walks and views all down the west coast are good. Much of the coastline is columnar basalt with sandy bays and rocky coves, seals, guillemots, oystercatchers and herons. Wild flowers are abundant: orchids, bright pink thrift, yellow irises and many more.

The best way to climb **Ben More** (3,450ft, 1,050m) is from the southern shore of Loch na Keal, from the bridge over the Abhainn na h-Uamha. You more or less follow your nose across the moor and up, reaching An Gearna first and then on up the steeper slope of Ben More, where it's truly magnificent. To make a round trip, go on across to A' Chioch and then down the Abhainn na h-Gearna which has lovely pools and waterfalls to cool yourself in and a 'natural' bridge.

Where the B8035 turns south, inland across the Ardmeanach peninsula, look out across the entrance to Loch na Keal to **Inch Kenneth**, named after one of St Columba's followers. It served Iona as a granary and was the burial place for Highland chiefs when the weather was too wild for the crossing to Iona. A ruined chapel and a number of carved slabs and crosses remain. Johnson and Boswell were here in 1773 as guests of Sir Allan Maclean and his two daughters, one of whom was to marry young Col, who was on his way to see her when he drowned the following year. Dr Johnson was pleasantly surprised by the civilized conditions of the Maclean household in comparison to some of his other Highland experiences. It was here that he expounded on the evils of drink: 'in proportion as drinking makes a man different from what he is before he has drunk, it is bad: because it has so far affected his reason.' Boswell found some human bones here which he buried in a shallow grave, applauded by Johnson who could not assist because of his squeamish nature. The island was bought by Lord Redesdale, father of the Mitford sisters, and Unity Mitford took refuge here after her association with Hitler and the Nazis. The rather strange, elongated appearance of the present house is the result of their 'improvements'.

The southwestern end of Mull's **Ardmeanach Peninsula** is owned by the National Trust for Scotland. Leave the B8035 where it turns southeast and take the track to Balmeanach Farm. A path from here goes out to the cliffs and, after less than a mile, descends steeply on to the beach. **MacKinnon's Cave** is most impressive and may be the one visited by Johnson. His escort forgot to take a flare and had to go and find one: be warned—and don't go in on a rising tide. You can walk right round the coast from here, but it is quite a hike. Alternatively take the track from the southeastern corner of the peninsular, back west to **Burgh** on the headland. **MacCulloch's Tree** is signposted. John MacCulloch was the naturalist and geologist who discovered the tree in 1819. Sixty million years ago, between sporadic outbursts of lava and in a warm, humid climate, soils developed here and supported a substantial flora of oak, hazel, maidenhair and magnolia trees. This one had been overwhelmed by lava and is still vertical, about 40 foot high and 6 foot wide. Most of the trunk was replaced by lava, so that what you see today is really just a cast of the tree. Sadly, though well protected now, what little remained of the actual tree was mostly removed by fossil collectors, but the thought of its antiquity is awesome.

The **Ross of Mull** is the southwestern headland of the island, and the scenery is gentler. Almost attached to its tip, the tidal island of **Erraid** is where, in Robert Louis Stevenson's *Kidnapped,* David Balfour and Alan Breck were shipwrecked in the brig Covenant before setting off to witness the Appin Murder (*see* p.111–12). Stevenson's uncle, Alan, was engineer to the Commissioners of Northern Lights and looked after the lighthouses in this area. The island is now inhabited by members of the Findhorn Foundation, who sometimes seem to find communicating with non-members rather difficult.

Uisken on the south coast, reached by the road from Bunessan, is a lovely beach with lonely crofts, mostly ruined—another victim of the Clearances.

Bunessan has the Isle of Mull Wine Company, which makes Isle of Mull Vermouth and 'The Mull Riveter'—a blend of their own vermouth and bitters with vodka. Here also is the **Isle of**

Mull Angora Rabbit Farm (✆ *(01681) 700 507; open Easter–Oct daily except Sat; adm*) where there are clipping and spinning demonstrations, an angora shop, tea and snacks.

At **Pennyghael** on the northeast shore of the peninsula, head south through Glen Leidle to **Carsaig**, a lovely spot with a massive, beautifully constructed old pier, no longer used by ferries. There is an interesting old laird's house (privately owned) and the Inniemore School of Painting, a residential summer painting school established in 1967 in a Victorian lodge. Leave your car here and walk the 3 miles southwest along the coast to Malcolm's Point. Here are the **Carsaig Arches**, a famous geological freak which left a natural jagged archway carved through the rock.

From the head of Loch Scridain the A849 goes back inland to the east coast through Glen More. About 17 miles on from Bunnessan, take the track south to Lochbuie, about 4 miles, for a lovely walk along Loch Airdeglais through Gleann Chaiginn Mhoir. Or you can drive, crossing the bridge over the Lussa River at Ardura, and running along past Loch Spelve and Loch Uisg. Moy Castle, the ruin at the head of Loch Buie, was the ancestral home of the MacLaines of Lochbuie. It was later replaced by an elegant Georgian mansion which still stands, somewhat down at heel, nearby. There are several caves along the western shore of Loch Buie, one of which is called Lord Lovat's Cave, though no one seems to know the story behind this.

Duart Castle

Duart Castle (*open May–Sept daily; adm*) is about 5 miles northeast of the head of Loch Spelve, an impressive fortress on a headland guarding the approach to the Sound of Mull and clearly seen from the Oban ferry as it passes Lady's Rock, off Lismore Lighthouse at the head of Loch Linnhe. In the 16th century a Maclaine of Lochbuie, disenchanted by his wife, tethered her to this rock. Taking pity on her, some passing fishermen released her and she fled to her father, Campbell of Inveraray. This irate chief invited the Maclaine to stay on the pretext of commiserating with him on the loss of his wife. After dinner the 'deceased' wife confronted her husband and her relatives set about him with broadswords. Home of the 28th chief of the Clan Maclean, the castle dates from the 12th century and is one of the oldest inhabited castles in Scotland. The massive enclosure would have contained timber buildings, to which has been added a great tower house and later works. Probably built by descendants of Somerled, it passed to the Lords of the Isles and then by marriage, around 1367, to the Macleans. It was besieged by Campbells in 1691 and garrisoned by Commonwealth forces until the Restoration, when it was restored to the Macleans. But their Stuart sympathies led to its forfeiture and it became a government barracks from 1741 to 1748. It was then allowed to rot until it was bought back and restored by the then Maclean chief, Sir Fitzroy, in 1911. He was a gallant Hussar Colonel who had ridden with the Light Brigade in the Crimea and died at the age of 100, affectionately known as Old Man A Hundred.

As well as the keep, visitors can see the cell where prisoners from the Spanish galleon *Florencia* were held after it had been sunk in Tobermory in 1588 by Donald Maclean. There are relics of the Maclean family in the main hall, with many of the gifts presented to the late Chief during his world tours—he was, among other things Chief Scout and Lord Chamberlain. There is also an exhibition of scouting throughout the Commonwealth, in the old staff rooms at the top of the castle.

Just south of Duart, the road to **Grass Point**, on Lochdon, was the old drovers' road for cattle and sheep from the Outer Isles, bound for mainland markets. It was also the landing point for pilgrims going to Iona. The seal on one of the rocks round the bay is of rather a different species to those living in the waters round Mull. It was the handiwork of the sculptor, poet and writer, the late Lionel Leslie. First cousin of Winston Churchill, he and his wife Barbara came to live in the old drovers' inn here after the last war, building it up from a ruin with their own hands. Boatloads of visitors came over from Oban in the summer to have tea, buy local crafts and listen to the sculptor's fascinating stories. Even in his mid-eighties his wit was as sharp as the stone he could no longer see to carve. There were also bas reliefs of a deer, an eagle, fighting swans and horses on the walls of a roofless byre beside the house, in lasting memory of a great artist and a great man. (The house has now been done up for holiday lets.)

Torosay Castle (*open mid April–mid Oct daily; adm*) is a mile west as the crow flies across Duart Bay. Designed in 1856 by David Bryce, with all the Scottish Baronial embellishments so beloved by the Victorians, it has 11 acres of terraced Italian-style gardens with a statue walk and water garden laid out by Sir Robert Lorimer. Although the castle has none of the history of Duart, its endearing informality and random collections make it a fun visit. As well as wildlife paintings by Thorburn, Landseer and Peter Scott, and portraits by Poynter, de Lazlo, Sargent and Carlos Sancha, there is a wealth of memorabilia belonging to the Guthries, who own the castle. There are numerous hunting trophies including the enormous head of a prehistoric Irish elk, archives, a library and huge family scrapbooks going back 100 years. In the high season boats run from Oban direct to Torosay. A miniature railway runs the mile and a half from Craignure Pier to the castle—the only passenger train service in the Hebrides.

The roofless, ruined church by the cemetery at **Salen** is unlikely to be restored. A wicked Maclean of Duart was buried here many years ago with the consequence that the roof blew off. Three times they put it back and three times it blew away, unable to settle over the remains of such a villain. The 1st-century statue of the Virgin Mary that used to be in this church has sadly been stolen. **Aros Castle**, just across Salen Bay, dates from the 14th century and was one of the strongholds of the Lords of the Isles.

Events and Activities

There is a **Drama Festival** in March, a **Music Festival** in April, **Tobermory Highland Game**s in July and also Children's Highland Games. **West Highland Yachting Week** takes place in early August; **Salen Show**, including a dog show, is in August and there is a car rally in October.

Wet- or dry-fly **trout fishing** is available in Mishnish Lochs, Loch Tor and Loch Frisa. Licences, tackle and bait can be obtained from Brown's Ironmongers, Tobermory High Street, or the National Forestry Commission's office at the south end of Loch Frisa.

Iona

An I mo chridhe, I mo grîdh
An îte guth manaich bidh geum bî
Ach mun tig an saoghal gu cruch
Bidh I mar a bha

In Iona of my heart, Iona of my love,
In the place of monks' voices will be lowing of cattle
But ere the world shall come to an end
Iona shall be as it was.

St Columba's Prophecy

No one can visit Mull without making a pilgrimage to the 'cradle of Christianity', though in fact St Ninian was spreading the word nearly 150 years before St Columba founded his church on Iona in 563. 1997 was the 1,400th anniversary of Columba's death and it was celebrated in many ways both on and off the island with a fair amount of interdenominational rivalry, which would have amused that wise founder of the One True Faith.

Getting There

The passenger ferry from Fionnphort on Mull takes 5 minutes. There is also a Sacred Isles Cruise on certain days in the summer, sailing from Oban via Staffa to Iona. This allows you 2½ hours on Iona before the return journey.

History

Columba, whose name comes from the Gaelic *Colum Cille* meaning 'Dove of the Church', was born in Donegal in Ireland in AD 521, of royal descent. He was exiled, possibly for having indulged in a spot of plagiarism while transcribing a rare text belonging to his mentor, and may even have been excommunicated. Although Iona claims to have been his first landfall, there are several other places on the western seaboard with similar claims. Given the inhospitability of the Atlantic and the small, probably leaky boat crammed with a dozen monks, it is most unlikely that they sailed directly across from Derry to Iona. Their most likely route would have been within the lee of Islay and Jura, and the chances are that they stopped off several times, to shelter, to take on provisions, and maybe even to explore. Eventually, however, they did land on Iona, and stayed—some say because it was the first place from which Columba could no longer see Ireland.

Here was a man born to lead and to fight with all the romantic dreams and ideals of a Celt; a man steeped in religious learning, burning with missionary zeal, banished from his beloved homeland, leaving scandal and disgrace in his wake. His biographer, St Adamnan, was ninth abbot of Iona some 80 years after Columba's death, and he seems to have viewed his subject through rose-tinted spectacles. With only apocryphal evidence, we have to draw on our imaginations to try to see the man through what he created and what he left behind.

Archaeological excavations revealed occupation by farming communities as far back as 3500 BC, and a formation of standing stones on Mull are thought to be waymarks for pilgrims to Iona, indicating a site of pre-Christian worship or ritual. One of Columba's great strengths was that he was tolerant of the pagan rituals that had preceded him. Those first converts hedged their bets, as can be seen on ancient crosses that combine Christian symbols with pagan, and Columba was careful with his new broom until he had established confidence in his One God and was able to lay down rules for living a godly life.

Iona was a productive island, surrounded by waters full of fish, strategically situated on the sea routes between Ireland and Scotland and along the west coast. The monks grew crops, mainly barley, on the machair where the soil was a fertile mix of peat and sand. They raised cattle and poultry and lived off bread, eggs, fish, meat and dairy products. They used seals for oil, skins and food, and were skilled craftsmen with metal, glass, wood and leather. They slept in single cells in a timber monastery and ate communally in a refectory. It was a simple, hardworking life combining the daily struggle to exist with their vocational life of prayer, study and evangelism. They spoke Latin and Gaelic, chanted psalms, copied and illuminated manuscripts.

Paganism was not their only enemy. The voracious Vikings were a constant menace, raiding, pillaging and murdering, until, in 807, the Abbot and his monks escaped to Kells in Ireland, leaving a tiny community behind to keep the faith alive.

Iona was by now a renowned Holy Island and an important burial place for kings: 48 Scottish, 8 Norwegian and 4 Irish rulers are traditionally believed to be interred here. Among the Scottish kings were Kenneth MacAlpine, Macbeth and Duncan, whom he murdered. Over the centuries, in spite of the Vikings, the various buildings were consolidated. In 1200 Reginald, son of Somerled, Lord of the Isles, founded a Benedictine community, and in 1507 the abbey church became the cathedral for the bishropric of the Isles. The Reformation brought to an end the monastic life founded by Columba, and Protestantism seems to have been adopted without too much of a struggle of conscience. Plainchant no longer rose from the cloisters and the cathedral fell into disrepair; spiritual needs were supplied by a series of ministers, disrupted now and then by secret visits from deposed Catholic priests; secular life went on the same. In the 1630s attempts were made to restore the Cathedral of the Isles, in conjunction with Charles I's hopes to reintroduce Catholic elements into the new church, but by the end of the 18th century the monastic buildings were ruinous.

The potato famine of 1846 took its toll, and in 1847 98 people, one-fifth of the community, emigrated. The remaining islanders managed to keep going and by the end of that century Iona was a popular destination for day trippers in yachts and steamers, and for holidaymakers who stayed in one of the two hotels or in local houses. The locals were not slow to see the potential profit from pious pilgrims and tourism—the sale of guide books, souvenirs and craftwork proliferated. In 1899 the Iona Cathedral Trust was founded and repair work began, proceeding spasmodically as funds were raised, and the first service was held in the partly restored cathedral. Once this and its satellite buildings were more or less functioning, thoughts turned to the monastic ruins.

In 1938 George Macleod, a Presbyterian socialist who had renounced an inherited title (later to accept one bestowed by the State), settled a new community on the island and began the rebuilding of the monastery. He believed that the church needed to get closer to the lives of ordinary people and that practical and spiritual work in a community would be good training for people with vocations for public service of any sort. Thus the Iona Community was born. George Macleod spoke no Gaelic, nor did the majority of his followers; they were not Gaels and had no cultural ties with their adopted home. There could never be full integration, although the natural courtesy of the islanders forbade outward animosity towards the zealous incomers.

Visiting the Island

When Johnson and Boswell came here in 1773, Johnson was deeply moved by the atmosphere: 'that man is little to be envied whose piety would not grow warmer among the ruins of Iona'.

Today he may have felt differently. Opinions differ: for some, the sanctity of the restored abbey has been erased by the zeal of Iona Abbey Limited, and they find it hard to kneel and say a prayer among the hugging and hand-holding and happy clappery of the community, despite its commendable focus on world-wide issues. Instead they find their peace in St Oran's Chapel and in the *Reilig OdrÓn*—the ancient burial ground—and in the remoter parts of the island. Mammon rules within the precincts, and even a ferryman has been known to ram a visiting boat, innocently trespassing on his commercial berth. But with under three hours, day visitors haven't time to disrupt the real Iona. When the last boat leaves at about 5.30pm, the native islanders emerge and get on with their real lives.

There is a well-stocked, licensed Spar shop selling delicious home-made bread, run by a local family, who also run the only pub and an excellent restaurant. There is an up-market Craft Shop; a tourist trap souvenir shop called Finlay Ross, which sells good books; and a marvellous little pottery with pieces that mirror the exceptional colours of the Iona land and sea. And there is a tiny bookshop with a tiny doorway, across the road from the Columba Hotel, selling, when it is open which isn't often, everything from rare books to tatty paperbacks.

Iona is special, in spite of all the trappings and communal bonhomie. Walk away from the designer Holy Place and climb the small hill, Dun I, to the north of the abbey. Look down on the restored buildings where so much attention has been paid to the fabric that they forgot to restore the Holy Spirit; on the postcard and booklet stalls; on the trails of people with strap-hung cameras, chattering and munching. Stay very quiet and listen: you may catch a faint echo of ironic laughter and feel a charismatic presence beside you. St Columba was known to have had a well developed sense of humour.

Where to Stay

Mull

expensive

Druimnacroish Country House Hotel, Dervaig, ✆/🖷 (01688) 400 274, in a converted watermill, has what its name implies—a country-house atmosphere and excellent service. The bedrooms are quite pretty and nicely furnished and the decor is rather 'thespian'-inspired (*see* Mull Little Theatre, above).

Ardfenaig House, near Bunessan at the head of Loch Caol, has a self-catering lodge in 15 acres of grounds, sleeping 6. Open all year. Contact the manager, Peter Halcrow, ✆ (01681) 700 436. **Killiechronan House**, Killiechronan, ✆ (01680) 300 403, is a former estate house at the head of the loch, comfortable with good food.

moderate

The Western Isles Hotel, Tobermory, ✆ (01688) 302 012, 🖷 302 297, is a massive Victorian pile, high above Tobermory with stunning views and an old-world charm. This is a great place to stay, where they really understand about Highland hospitality. It has a wonderful large conservatory overlooking the harbour and bay and serves great food.

Tiroran House, on the north shore of Loch Scridain, ✆ (01681) 705 232, 🖷 705 240, is a remote and enchanting Wolsey Lodge, run by Colin and Jane Tindal. Cosy and hospitable, with a nice garden and good food. **Ardachy House Hotel**, Uisken,

✆/🖷 (01681) 700 505, is small and cosy, overlooking the sands of Ardalanish. **Assapol House Hotel,** Bunessan, ✆ (01681) 700 258, 🖷 700 445, is a family-run country house on the loch, very comfortable and good food.

Pennyghael Hotel, Pennyghael, ✆ (01681) 704 288, is in a spectacular setting by the loch, informal and family-run, with good home-cooking. **Ulva House Hotel**, Strongarbh, Tobermory, ✆/🖷 (01688) 302 044, is a Victorian house with sea views, excellent food, garden, log fires, and Land Rover expeditions to see otters, eagles, etc.

cheap

Tobermory Hotel, ✆ (01688) 302 091, 🖷 302 254, right on the waterfront, is a jolly place, full of character where people swap stories of near-shipwreck and Force Nine gales. **Craignure Inn**, Craignure, ✆ (01680) 812 305, is a 17th-century inn on the water, renowned for its lively bar and friendly staff. **Ardbeg House Hotel**, Dervaig, ✆ (01688) 400 254, is a Victorian country house in a nice setting, homely and full of character. **Bellachroy Hotel**, Dervaig, ✆ (01688) 400 314, dates from the 16th century when it was a droving inn. Cheap and cheerful, and very friendly.

Calgary Farmhouse and Dovecote Restaurant, ✆ (01688) 400 256, is a good place for a meal, and you can also stay. **The Puffer Aground**, ✆ (01680) 300 389, is a good café in Salen. For a really lively evening, go to the **Mishnish** in Tobermory, an excellent pub, with great atmosphere. **The Green Barn**, Tobermory, part of the farm where they make Mull cheddar, is a splendid glass barn where you can get good farmhouse food. *Open May–Sept Mon–Fri 10–4.*

Iona

Argyll Hotel, Iona, ✆ (01681) 700 334, 🖷 700 510, is right on the water, built in 1868 as the inn, with 15 cosy bedrooms en suite, though some of the baths are so small you have to ablute in sections. The food is excellent. **St Columba Hotel**, Iona, ✆ (01681) 700 304, 🖷 700 688, is on rising ground north of the village, half a mile from the jetty, and has plenty of mod cons. **Finlay Ross**, the souvenir shop on Iona, ✆ (01681) 700 357, does a good bed and breakfast.

Or there is **The Abbey**, on Iona, ✆ (01681) 700 404, which offers full board from March to December, very cheap and pretty spartan which is good for the soul—monkish food and no licence. Visitors are expected to take part in the day-to-day activities of the community. They also do week-long courses.

Coll and Tiree

Coll and Tiree, less than 11 miles off the northwest of Mull, are low-lying islands which look barren from the sea until you step ashore and discover green fields surrounded by an almost continuous string of deserted white beaches, home to lots of different sea birds, seals and otters. Strong winds, very shallow soil and free-ranging sheep keep them treeless, hence the deceptively barren look from afar. Because there are no proper hills to attract rain clouds, these islands have an exceptionally high record of sunshine, but for the same reason there is little shelter from the persistent and battering wind. A number of the old-style cottages survive, with rounded corners to withstand the gales, and humpy thatched or tar-felted roofs.

Getting There and Getting Around

There is a boat from Oban, daily except Thursdays and Sundays, taking 3 hours to Coll, 4½ hours to Tiree. Boats also run from Tobermory. There are one to two flights to Tiree from Glasgow (*daily except Sun*), and from Barra (*Tues–Thurs*).

You can hire a car to meet you at the ferry or you can hire a bicycle which is the best way to get about, except for the wind.

Tourist Information

Local knowledge is far the best. For practical information before you go:

Oban: Argyll Square, ✆ (01631) 563 122.

Coll

Coll is an endearing fish shape, 13 miles long and 3 miles wide, with a population of about 150, down from as many as 1,450 before the Clearances. The low terrain is surrounded by wonderful sandy beaches, azure water and rocky coves, backed by machair strewn with wild flowers in spring. Johnson and Boswell spent some days on Coll, as bad weather forced them to seek shelter here en route to Mull from Skye. Dr Johnson, recovering from seasickness and glad to make a landfall anywhere, described it well: 'one continued rock, of a surface much diversified with protuberances, and covered with a thin layer of soil.' Later, and still stormbound, he remarked: 'it would require great resignation to live in one of these islands if you were shut up here, your thoughts would torment you: you would think of Edinburgh or London and that you could not be there.' By the fifth day of their enforced stay, he said: 'I want to be on the mainland and go on with existence. This is a waste of life.'

Two standing stones at **Totronald** called *Na Sgeulachan*—the Tellers of Tales—are thought to be part of a pagan temple, and traces of prehistoric forts and duns scatter the island. During the Norse occupation of the islands, Coll was the headquarters of Earl Gilli, brother-in-law to Sigurd, ruler of Orkney and the Hebrides in 1000. By the end of the 13th century it belonged to the MacDougalls of Lorne, from whom it was taken by Robert the Bruce. It passed to a second son of the Macleans of Duart in the early 1400s and remained in their ownership until 1856, when Hugh, last Maclean laird of Coll, was forced to sell his estates to pay for his extravagant lifestyle. It was bought by John Stuart of Glenbuckie, factor to the Duke of Argyll, and his ruthlessly efficient farming methods resulted in mass emigration to Canada and Australia by the unfortunate crofters unable to afford his inflated rents. Traces of their abandoned croft houses can still be seen at the northern end of the island. The population includes quite a few incomers—'white settlers'—and holiday home owners. The island is known for its trout-filled lochs. Sea fishing is also good, and local fishermen will take visitors out in their boats. Walking, bicycling, swimming, birdwatching, botany and relaxation are the chief occupations for visitors. There is a nine-hole golf course at **Arinagour**. This village has the main concentration of Coll's population, a trim place which lies around the western shore of Loch Eatharna, with little cottages and gardens. **Breachacha Castle,** at the southern end of the island, is now used as the headquarters for an adventure training school. The later (new) castle dates from 1750 and was described by Dr Johnson as 'a tradesman's box' and by Boswell as 'a neat gentleman's house'. It was heightened and baronialized in the mid 19th century but is now almost beyond hope of restoration.

Coll's economy depends mainly on farming, commercial fishing and tourism. There is a small factory in Arinagour where a range of herbal skin-care products is made.

Coll ✆ (01879–) ***Where to Stay***

Isle of Coll Hotel, at the head of Arinagour Bay overlooking the Treshnish Isles, ✆ 230 334, 🖷 230 317, has a jolly, Hebridean atmosphere. **Tigh-na-Mara**, also looking over the bay, ✆/🖷 230 354, is modern and a bit cheaper. **Achamore**, ✆ 230 430, is a very cheap, comfortable guest house in a splendid setting.

For B&B, **Tigh Solas,** at Arinagour, ✆ 230 333, is a modern box but cheap and very friendly. For self-catering there is one chalet and three flats in **Arinagour**, ✆ 230 373, and a house, a bungalow and a bothy, ✆ 230 339.

Tiree

Tiree, southwest of Coll, is about 12 miles long, 7 miles at its widest, dwindling to less than a mile at its narrowest. The resident population of about 800 (4,450 before the Clearances) swells almost to 19th-century proportions during the tourist season. Much more fertile than Coll, its name comes from *Tir-iodh*—Land of Corn—dating from the days when it supplied corn to Iona. It is so low and flat that it has the Gaelic nickname *Tir fo Thuinn*—Land Below the Waves. The highest hill, **Ben Hynish**, is a 480ft (148m) pimple, topped with a prominent 'golf ball' radar station for tracking aircraft. Tiree shares with Coll a reputation for glorious beaches, abundant wild flowers and birds (it used to be famous for its snipe before much of the ground was drained), as well as a high average of sunshine. This, with its magnificent Atlantic rollers, has earned it the title 'Hawaii of the North'. Windsurfers come from all over Britain to compete in Tiree where the clean, gently sloping beaches are first rate in all directions of wind. **Wave Classic** is a major event every October, during which world-class windsurfing can be watched. There is a nine-hole golf course, popular with the island's phenomenal population of hares.

A standing stone near Balinoe is thought to have been part of a Druid temple. Many of the island names are Viking in origin, from the 400 years of Norse occupation (*c.* 890–1266). Among the many ancient remains scattered over Tiree is **Dun Mor Broch** on Vaul Bay on the north coast. A well-preserved ruin, it is one of the tall, hollow towers probably built for refuge from Norse and other invaders. It is 30ft (9m) in diameter, its walls as much as 13ft (4m) thick. **Gott Bay** is a 3½-mile crescent of sand, backed by rich machair carpeted with wild flowers. The ferry docks at **Scarnish**, the main township on Gott Bay, and there are a number of crofting townships dotted around, many with restored thatched cottages. **Hynish**, in the south, has a small dry dock, flooded by an elaborate system of fresh water from springs. Skerryvore Museum, in the old signal tower at Hynish, tells the story of the construction of the famous Skerryvore Lighthouse, visible through a telescope, built by the father of Robert Louis Stevenson. There is a young people's outdoor training centre based in the lighthouse cottages. On the north shore of Balephetrish, *Clac Ğ Choire*—Stone of the Corrie—is a large, granite boulder perched on a rocky base, a relic from the Ice Age. Decorated with intriguing prehistoric carvings, it is known locally as the Ringing Stone because of the metallic note it produces when struck. It is said that when *Clac Ğ Choire* shatters, Tiree will sink below the waves.

Views are marvellous all round the coast, especially those eastwards to the Treshnish Islands, with the aircraft-carrier-shaped *Bac Mor*—The Dutchman's Cap. One of the best places to see the birdlife is under the sheer cliffs below Carnan Mor in the south. Look for the distinctive greenstone on the beaches, found also in Iona.

Tiree ✆ (01879–) ***Where to Stay***

Scarnish Hotel, ✆ 220 308, ✉ 220 410, and **Tiree Lodge**, ✆ 220 353, are both on Gott Bay.

Balephetrish Guest House, ✆ 220 549, is a pebble-dashed croft house overlooking Balephetrish Bay on the north coast. **Kirkapol House**, Gott Bay, ✆ 220 729, is a converted Victorian church on the beach, with great character and very friendly. **Tiree Lodge Hotel**, ✆ 220 368, is also friendly and comfortable.

Self-catering is by far the best bet and you can buy essential basic stores on the island. For the perfect honeymoon (it only sleeps two), **Kenovay Thatched Cottage**, is a restored croft-bothy in the middle of the island and 10 minutes from beaches, ✆ (01505) 690 662. **Lighthouse View,** Scarnish, ✆ (01828) 670 626/✆ (0141) 778 1405, sleeps eight.

The Small Isles

Getting There

Caledonian MacBrayne, ✆ (01475) 650 100, runs a service to all four islands, not every day and not on Sundays. Ring for schedules. **Murdo Grant**, ✆ (01687) 546 224, runs regular cruises from Arisaig (*Easter and May–Sept; less frequently out of season*). His boat, MV *Shearwater*, is fast and comfortable and takes 130 people. He will also charter.

Tourist Information

For practical details, contact the Highlands of Scotland Tourist Board, Aviemore, ✆ (0990) 143 070.

Rum

Rum is an island shaped like a squashed diamond, rising to a series of peaks; an unmistakable landmark for sailors, 8 miles west of Sleat in Skye. The peaks of the Rum Cuillins reach 2,000ft (610m) and contain some semi-precious stones as well as rocks similar to those found on the moon. These hills are the first to be hit by Atlantic depressions which deposit an annual rainfall of 90 inches. Inhabited since the Mesolithic Age, Rum was later held by the Clanranald Macdonalds until the 15th century. They exchanged it for Maclean of Coll's 'great galley' which turned out to have rotten timbers. The population of over 400 was reduced to one family in 1826 to make way for one sheep farm of 8,000 sheep. It was bought by the 2nd Marquess of Salisbury in 1845, deer were introduced and it became a private sporting estate. It was bought in 1879 by John Bullough, a self-made Lancashire textile machinery manufacturer and his son George built Kinloch House. The organization now known as Scottish Natural Heritage acquired it from his widow in 1957 and it is now an 'outdoor laboratory' dedicated to discovering how the Hebrides can best support their wildlife.

The name Rum is thought to come from the Greek *rhombos*, referring to its rhomboid shape. The 'h' that sometimes creeps into its spelling was added by the Bulloughs, hoping to give the name a Gaelic flavour, not realizing that 'r' is never aspirated in Gaelic. (Some say that another reason for the 'h' was George Bullough's wish to disassociate his island from the alcoholic drink.) Rum's chief interest is its wildlife, and special permission must be obtained from the Scottish Natural Heritage warden to visit most places.

The half-wild golden-brown ponies are said to be descended from survivors of a Spanish galleon, part of the Armada, which was wrecked off these coasts in 1588. There are also wild goats, golden eagles, plenty of red deer and a prodigious colony of Manx shearwaters which nest in underground burrows in the south of the island. There are also rare alpine plants.

The red sandstone castle that looks across the bay is **Kinloch Castle**, built in 1901 by the Bulloughs. It is said they offered extra wages to employees to work in kilts, despite the fact that Rum is notorious for its midges. The castle is now an hotel/hostel, *see* below. It has the atmosphere of a baronial seat and most of the original furnishings survive intact, if a little jaded. One of its features is the extremely rare electric 'orchestrarian', a Heath Robinson contraption tucked under the stairs, whose parts represent a full orchestra, activated by a vast library of pre-set cylinders each programmed with a well-known tune. All the working components can be seen in action in a huge glass chamber in the hall. The conducted tours of this amazing time-warp are well worth doing. The guide is full of amusing gossip about past visitors, including Edward VII in amorous pursuit of the mistress of the house.

Eigg

The poet Hugh MacDiarmid wrote: 'if I have to choose among the Hebrides, I choose Eigg.' However, that fiery Scottish nationalist might not have said the same today.

Seven miles off Morar on the mainland, 7 miles by 5 in dimensions, Eigg is shaped like an upturned boat or a crouching lion, its name derived from the Gaelic for 'notch', referring to the deep divide between the massive Sgurr in the south, and the rest of the island. In 1844 Hugh Miller (*see* Cromarty pp.181–2) came to the island with John Swanson, the Free Kirk minister for the Small Isles. Swanson was preaching and Miller had gone along for the ride with his geologist's implements. To his surprise, he discovered that the Sgurr of Eigg, 'a veritable Giant's Causeway, columnar from end to end, rested on the fossilized remains of a prostrate forest'. This was at a time when his deep religious convictions were battling with his study of fossils, which led to doubts about the credibility of the creation story in the Bible.

Eigg is a magical isle surrounded by clear, sparkling water. Its recent history of bitter politics has not detracted one bit from its beauty, though there is a rather run-down feeling about the place. Settled since prehistoric times, it has remains going back to Iron Age forts, a 6th-century Christian church, Viking burial mounds and the site of a Macdonald burial ground. This was a base for the Lords of the Isles and their Clanranald descendants, who were not above acts of piracy in the surrounding seas.

In 1828 the debt-ridden Clanranalds sold Eigg, along with most of their other territories in the western Highlands and Islands. The new owner, Hugh MacPherson, was a professor of archaeology, and there followed a succession of industrial tycoons, one of whom created an Italianate lodge and garden in the late 1920s. Because of its great beauty and comparative remoteness,

Eigg has always attracted 'white settlers'. Its decline from a true Hebridean island was no different to that of any other: incoming Victorians clearing out the people and using it for sport.

In recent decades the story of the island's ownership has become something of a soap opera. English incomers and escapers from the mainland now outnumber the islanders, who have mostly been too courteous to protest against what became a state of open warfare with the proprietors. The penultimate landlord, a flamboyant philanthropic vegetarian called Keith Schellenberg, was loathed by the incomers who transformed him into a symbol of the cruel and hated 'Laird'. The priceless vintage cars he had imported to keep safe from mainland vandalism were torched and a vindictive war waged on Schellenberg by the media. Eventually he sold up and departed, to be replaced by a fire-eating German artist known as Maruma. Hailed as their saviour by the white settlers, the absentee Maruma turned out to be full of empty promises and financially unsound. The community's determination to become masters of their own destiny strengthened. Fundraising proceeded in earnest, supported by extensive publicity. They have now bought the island for themselves, with the help of generous donations and the pledge of considerable sums of public money. It will be interesting to see how their self-government gets on.

Walking up around the bay from the little harbour in the southeast, you come upon the ancient burial ground at Kildonan Church. This is the resting place of the Macdonalds of Clanranald, whose chieftain owned Eigg until the 1820s. A broken Celtic cross, a scattering of grave stones and a roofless ruin are all that remain.

An aura of tragedy still hangs over *Uamh Fhraing*, a cave southwest of the pier, easily reached by a path from Galmisdale—take a torch. In 1577 some Macleods were forced to shelter from a storm on Eigg. Owing to constant feuding over disputed land, the Macdonalds were not welcoming. The Macleods left and returned later to take revenge. The Macdonalds took shelter in this cave and the landing party found only an old woman, whose life they spared. But as they were putting out to sea they saw a scout, sent from the cave to see if they had gone. They rushed back, found the cave and lit a fire at its mouth, suffocating all 398 inhabitants—the entire population of the island. Sir Walter Scott is said to have found bones here in 1814 and taken a souvenir away with him. Several reliable people have seen ghosts in the vicinity.

Palm trees and flame trees thrive on the almost subtropical climate of the garden surrounding the lodge. The 'Musical Sands' on the Bay of Laig are well worth a visit, so called because they make a curious keening sound in certain conditions. Cattle wander on the beach and the views across to Rum are glorious on a clear day.

Canna

Sometimes called the Garden of the Hebrides, Canna lies less than 5 miles off the west coast of Rum and is actually two islands, joined to Sanday in the southeast by a causeway. Together, they are shaped like a hand gun, measuring 5 miles by 1, with a grassy plateau sloping in stepped terraces down to the sea, sliced off by cliffs to the north. The highest point is only 690ft (212m) above sea level. Magnetic Hill, 458ft (141m) in the north, is so called because of its magnetic rock that can distort the true readings of a ship's compass. Martin Martin put this to the test: 'I laid the Compas on the stony Ground near it, and the Needle went often round with great Swiftness, and instead of settling towards the North, as usual, it settled here due East.'

Canna was an early Christian settlement, and there are still the remains of a Celtic nunnery with one of the three oldest Celtic church structures identified in Scotland. The island was part of the land attached to the Benedictine monastery of Iona, and has a weathered cross and a well, said to have curative powers. The Clanranald Macdonalds held the island until debts forced them to sell to Hector MacNeill in the 1820s. He evicted 200 islanders, in arrears with their rent after the decline of the kelp industry. A family of Glasgow shipbuilders called Thom bought it in 1881; they built the pier and Tighard House. In 1938 the island was bought by the late John Lorne Campbell and his wife Margaret Fay Shaw. They were both learned scholars of Gaelic literature and music and they built up an impressive archive which they shared hospitably with any interested visitor. They instigated agricultural improvements and planted woodland; having no heirs, they gave the island to the National Trust for Scotland in 1981. An application to the Heritage Lottery Fund to help with the creation of a centre for Gaelic culture and learning is currently under consideration; meanwhile, a tiny fragile Hebridean community survives here, but only just.

Muck

About 7 miles south of Rum, Muck is the smallest of the Small Isles, its name derived from the Gaelic *muc mara*—sea pig or porpoise. It is a pretty little green island with lovely sandy beaches. The Macleans of Ardnamurchan owned the island until the end of the 18th century, the last laird running into debt due to an over-extended family and his excesses during his post as Deputy Lieutenant of the Tower of London. The Clanranald Macdonalds rescued him, in return for Muck, which they had to sell off in their turn to pay off their own debts. Poverty in the 19th century drove many of the islanders to emigrate. A sea captain called Thomas Swinburne bought it in 1854, developed the fishing, introduced sheep, built Gallanach House and sold it in 1879 to Lawrence Thompson MacEwan, who already owned Eigg. He introduced cows and exported cheese. His heir, William MacEwan, planted the first trees in 1922 and created a model island unit, carried on today by his son Lawrence and 25 residents.

Where to Stay

Kinloch Castle, ✆ (01687) 462 037, is an hotel/hostel, with a price range reflected by the range of accommodation—from faded grandeur to student dormitories. The hostel section is in the old servants' quarters.

The inhabitants of Eigg are in the process of making decisions about an effective balance between tourism, private enterprise, public subsidy and their desire to get away from it all. Sue Kirk, ✆ (01687) 482 405, can organize or recommend accommodation. Tourist information centres will have up-to-date details.

The National Trust for Scotland has a guest house on Canna—members get priority. Apply to 5 Charlotte Square, Edinburgh EH2 4DU, ✆ (0131) 226 5922. There is no shop on the island.

The Estate Office on Muck can arrange self-catering cottages and camping, ✆ (01687) 462 365.

Kyleakin and the Sleat Peninsula 253
The Cuillins 256
Portree 256
Trotternish 257
Waternish 259
Duirinish 261
Raasay 262

Skye

Latha dhomh air Sgùrr a' Ghreadaidh,
Na mo sheasamh air an roinn aird eagaich.
Ag amharc sìos air Coire 'n Uaigneis
Troimh bharcadh a' cheò mun chairt orm,
Ann am bristeadh an t-siabain
Dhealraich aiteal òir air sgiathan
Iolaire dol searchad shìos ann
Ri taobh nam ballachan cliathaich;
Is dhomhsa thar glòir gach ianlaith
Aiteal òir an eòin Sgitheanaich.
Thionndaidh me, 's a tuath 's an iarthuath
Bha Minginis 'na bòidhche shianta
Agus Bràcadal uaine;
Diùirinis is Tròndairnis bhuaipe.
Dhiùchd dhomh bòidhche an t-sair Eilein,
Dhiùchd ach thàinig sian a' pheileir:
Ciamar a chumas an gaol seo
Greim air creig dheighe 'n t-saoghail?

I was one day on Sgurr á Greadaidh,
standing on the high notched knife-edge,
looking down on the Corrie of Solitude,
through the mist surging around me,
in a breaking of the drift
a glimmer of gold shone on the wings
of an eagle passing down below
beside the flanking walls;
and to me above the glory of all birds
the golden glimmer of the Skye bird.
I turned, and north and north-west
there was Minginis in her enchanted beauty,
and green Bracadale
Diuirinis and Trondairnis beyond.
The beauty of the great Island rose before me;
it rose, but the bullet whizzed:
how will this love keep its hold
on the icy rock of the world?

from 'An Cuilithionn—The Cuillin—1939' by Skye's greatest contemporary poet, the late Sorley MacLean (Somhairle Macgill-Eain)

Skye is *An t-Eilean Sgiatheanach*—The Winged Island—*sgiath* meaning 'wing' in Gaelic, referring to the winged promontories of Trotternish in the northeast and Duirinish and Waternish in the northwest. On the map Skye looks more like a great, misshapen lobster claw than a flying bird, its pincers being its lumpy peninsulas separated by fjord-like inlets, surrounded by many islands. Its silhouette is dominated by the Cuillins, a massive range of black, pointed peaks, and by Macleod's Tables, the two, distinctive flat-topped hills further north.

The island contains extraordinary volcanic features such as the Quiraing and the Old Man of Storr. Among the many archaeological remains that testify to prehistoric settlements are two particularly fine examples of brochs: Dun Ardtreck, near Carbost, and Dun Beag, just west of Bracadale, both well built with square-sided facing stones.

Skye is one of the most popular of the Western Isles; though tourism has had a significant impact on it, it has not yet spoiled it. The opening in 1996 of the new government-sponsored and privately funded road bridge between Kyle of Lochalsh and Kyleakin has improved communications dramatically, but not without a great public furore. Whether this will provide an incentive for opening a Bonnie Prince Charlie Theme Park is another issue. Meanwhile this elegant half-mile link, the longest single-span bridge outside Australia, does not detract from the scenery as much as some of its opponents would have you believe.

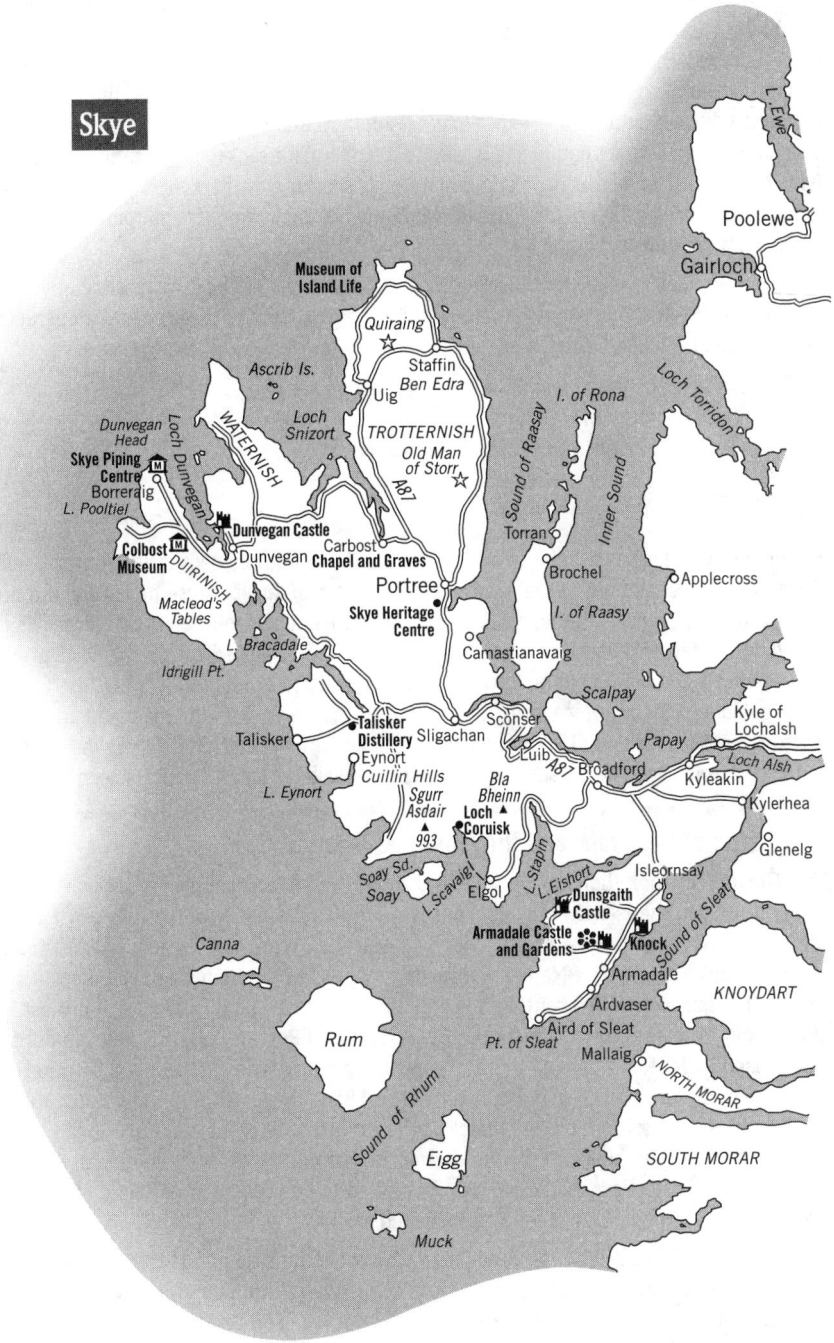
L. Ewe
Poolewe
Gairloch
Loch Torridon
Museum of Island Life
Quiraing
Staffin
Ben Edra
Uig
Ascrib Is.
Loch Snizort
TROTTERNISH
Old Man of Storr
A87
WATERNISH
Dunvegan Head
Loch Dunvegan
Skye Piping Centre
Borreraig
L. Pooltiel
Dunvegan Castle
Colbost Museum
Dunvegan
Carbost
Chapel and Graves
DUIRINISH
Macleod's Tables
L. Bracadale
Idrigill Pt.
Portree
Skye Heritage Centre
Sound of Raasay
I. of Rona
Inner Sound
Torran
Brochel
I. of Raasy
Applecross
Camastianavaig
Scalpay
Sconser
Talisker
Talisker Distillery
Sligachan
Eynort
Cuillin Hills
L. Eynort
Sgurr Asdair
993
Bla Bheinn
Loch Coruisk
Luib
A87
Broadford
Papay
Kyle of Lochalsh
Loch Alsh
Kyleakin
Kylerhea
Glenelg
Isleornsay
Soay Sd.
Soay
L. Scavaig
Elgol
L. Slapin
L. Eishort
Dunsgaith Castle
Armadale Castle and Gardens
Knock
Sound of Sleat
Canna
Armadale
Ardvaser
KNOYDART
Rum
Pt. of Sleat
Aird of Sleat
Mallaig
NORTH MORAR
Sound of Rhum
Eigg
SOUTH MORAR
Muck

Off the main roads on the island, there are still rural communities relatively untouched by the influx of knapsacks and campers. Gaelic is no longer the first language for the majority of the inhabitants, though it is still spoken and road signs are bilingual. Spirited attempts are being made to revive the old language, and Sabhal mor Ostaig, the Gaelic College in Sleat, is flourishing. Gaelic playgroups are opening all over the island and Gaelic folk music and other elements of the culture are experiencing an incredible revival. But *Gaidhealtachd*—Gaeldom—is an abstract notion and is hard to pin down: it needs to be a free spirit, growing of its own accord. The increasing influx of non-Gaelic speaking 'white settlers' is diffusing the old culture, fashioning a kind of 'designer Gaeldom', which may be pretty and romantic, but is not *Gaidhealtachd* in its old guise.

Portree is the chief village on the island, a lively and expanding centre, particularly busy in summer. There is an excellent Heritage Centre, an Arts Centre, theatre shows, opera, traditional music, Highland Games, and some good accommodation and eating places.

Speed bonnie boat, like a bird on the wing,
'Onward' the sailors cry;
Carry the lad that's born to be king
Over the sea to Skye.

from the 'Skye Boat Song' by H.E.Boulton

Bonnie Prince Charlie has a lot to answer for on Skye, not only because the outcome of his Rising was the beginning of the death of *Gaidhealtachd,* but because he left behind him a miasma of emotive romanticism giving rise to an international neo-Jacobite cult for seeking out the various sites marking the events of *Bliadhna Tearlach*—The Year of Charlie. During his escape after Culloden he hid on Skye, having arrived from the Outer Isles disguised as Flora Macdonald's maid, and it was from Skye that he escaped back to the mainland and exile in France. The island is dotted with caves that he is said to have hidden in, rocks that he sat on, huts that he sheltered in and several places where he bid his faithful subjects goodbye.

The Battle of the Braes and the Glendale Martyrs

The Clearances took their toll in Skye as elsewhere: 30,000 people are thought to have emigrated from the island between 1840 and 1888. The Battle of the Braes in 1882, and the consequent protest of the 'Glendale Martyrs', were very largely responsible for the Crofters' Act (*see* The Napier Commission pp. 41–2), which established security of tenure at a fair, controlled rent, and is still effective today. The battle was a protest by the people of several townships of the Braes, south of Portree, against their landlord, Lord Macdonald, for depriving them of essential grazing land. Encouraged by other rent strikes, and by the successful Irish Land Act of 1881, they withheld their rents, tore up the resulting eviction orders and attacked the unfortunate officers commanded to serve them. Fifty Glasgow policemen were drafted in, baton charges were met with hails of stones, and arrests were made. No one was killed but a great deal of public interest was aroused and the paparazzi of the day swarmed in.

Meanwhile, encouraged by the Braes men, those of Glendale and Husabost near Dunvegan followed suit. The authorities, sensing a revolutionary situation and with lessons learned from Ireland, were anxious to appease. The token arrest of five

Glendale men was made. They spent two months in prison and emerged as triumphant heroes, known ever since as the Glendale Martyrs. Gladstone hastily set up the Napier Commission, many of whose commissioners, such as Donald Cameron of Lochiel and Sir Kenneth Mackenzie of Gairloch, were sympathetic to the crofters' cause. The objective was an investigation of recent events relating to land ownership in the Highlands and Islands, and the thorough and shocking report which the Commission produced resulted in the Crofters' Holdings Act.

Getting There and Around

Apart from the toll bridge between Kyle of Lochalsh and Kyleakin, there is a daily ½hr **ferry** service from Mallaig to Armadale, for which it is essential to book; and a limited, summer service for the short, picturesque crossing from Glenelg to Kylerhea. There is a regular ferry service between Uig and the Outer Isles. Caledonian MacBrayne, ✆ (01475) 650 100.

Trains run from Inverness to Kyle of Lochalsh—the Kyle Line, one of the most scenic in Britain. Even better is the West Highland Line, from Glasgow to Mallaig, connecting with the ferry to Armadale. Skye-ways Citylink Travel coaches, ✆ (01599) 534 328, operate from/to Kyle of Lochalsh.

Once on the island, there is a limited bus service serving most areas, and you can hire cars in Broadford and Portree. Broadford has a 24-hour petrol station.

Tourist Information

Portree: Meal House, ✆ (01478) 612 137; **Broadford**: ✆ (01471) 822 361 (*open May–Sept*).

Kyleakin and the Sleat Peninsula

Kyleakin, until recently a busy ferry terminus, with crowded shops, queues of traffic and lots of visitors hanging about, is now something of a backwater: a cluster of unremarkable buildings and a large, useful slipway. The small harbour is overlooked by **Castle Maol** (or Moil, or Dunnakyne), a jagged double-toothed fragment of a ruin on a knoll; familiar from postcards. This 12th-century relic was once a Mackinnon stronghold. Kyleakin and Dunakin are said to be so named after King Haakon, who sheltered here with his fleet while on his way south. A story is told of one of the castle's earliest inmates, Saucy Mary, a Norwegian princess, who somehow managed to stretch a barrier across the Kyle in order to levy tolls from passing ships.

The new bridge whips you away westward; after about 2 miles a turning left leads over moorland, through Glen Arroch to Kylerhea, pronounced Kyle-ray, where the ferry runs to Glenelg from just below the Old Ferry Inn. A couple of miles past this turning, the A851 leads south to the **Sleat Peninsula**, pronounced 'slate', formerly Macdonald territory.

Isleornsay overlooks the Sound of Sleat on the east coast of the peninsula, reached across 9 miles of heather-carpeted moor. Once the commercial centre for the island, called *Eilean Iarmain*, this attractive group of buildings includes a hotel, shop, small art gallery, *céilidh* hall and whisky centre, as well as the old sea-flushing lavatory—now a dovecot. There's a lighthouse and a ruined chapel, dedicated to the Columban monk Oran, on the Isle of Ornsay, just offshore.

Sabhal Mor Ostaig—big barn of Ostaig—is the Gaelic college, in a former Macdonald home farm near Isleornay. Founded by Iain Nobel, it runs popular and successful courses on the Gaelic language, music and culture. **Castle Camus** or **Knock Castle**, 3 miles further on, overlooking Knock Bay, is an overgrown ruin on a rocky peninsula, once held by the Macdonalds on condition they were always ready to receive the king or one of his representatives. Keep an eye open for the *glaisrig* who haunts this ruin—a female sprite who accepts libations of milk.

Armadale Castle, another 3 miles south, was built by James Gillespie Graham in 1815, with additions by David Bryce in 1856. Gutted, partly demolished, and left as a 'sculptured ruin', it stands today as a centrepiece for the restored gardens. The earliest part survives as the **Clan Donald Centre** (*open April–Oct daily; adm*), with a Museum of the Isles exhibition, telling the story of Clan Donald and the Lords of the Isles, enhanced by suitably stirring sound-effects. The former coach house and stable block has won awards for its restoration and conversion into a well-stocked book and gift shop, along with an excellent restaurant. The Clan Donald library is in the former gardener's house up the road, with Macdonald archives and a study centre. The lovely grounds, with a mature arboretum, are open to the public all year.

Armadale Pier, the ferry terminal for the summer boat to Mallaig, is unexpectedly well served for such an end-of-the-road place. There is a seafood takeaway, a Craft Shop, a Batik Shop and **Sleat Trading**—a smart tourist trap with an excellent secondhand book section stocking a good selection of out-of-print books relating to Scotland. If you are looking for an edition they don't have in stock, leave your name and they can often find it for you, even years later.

The road continues for another 5 miles to **Aird of Sleat** with glorious views across the sound. A couple of miles' walk takes you to the lighthouse on the southern tip of the peninsula, where there is a sandy beach and more good views. Returning on the same road, the narrow, twisting lane to the west, a mile north of Armadale, runs 5 miles through woodland and moor, past lochans and mossy glades among silver birches, out to the west coast of Sleat.

Tiny settlements cluster round coves and sandy beaches. **Dunsgaith Castle**, about 2 miles north of Tarskavaig, is one of the oldest fortified headlands in the Hebrides, the Macdonalds' home until the late 16th century. Little remains now except stacks of stones on a rock 40ft (12m) high, overlooking Loch Eishort. Celtic legend tells of Scathac the Wise, Queen of Skye in the Dark Ages, who held court here and preached the arts of peace and war to Cuchullin, an Ossianic hero. Cuchullin went back to Ireland to practise his newly learned arts, leaving his beautiful, impregnated wife Bragela weeping in vain at Dunsgaith on 'The Isle of Mist'.

Another 2 miles north at **Ord**, the views to the Cuillins across Loch Eishort and southwest to the Isle of Rum are magnificent. From here it is 15 miles to **Broadford**, the track rejoining the main road a couple of miles short of Isleornsay. This straggling settlement is a busy, useful place on a crossroads, with hospital, hotels and eating places, shops, bank, garage and a baker who makes delicious bread and cakes. There is also, somewhat incongruously, **Skye Serpentarium** (*open Easter–Oct daily; adm*). Here, in suitably 'natural' surroundings, is a collection of the smaller reptiles such as snakes, lizards, frogs and tortoises; and they also give a home to abandoned or illegally imported reptiles.

Fourteen miles to the southwest is **Elgol**, a scattered village with more splendid views. From here you can get a boat across Loch Scavaig to **Loch Coruisk** (*coire uish*—cauldron of water), one of Skye's special places, painted by Turner and understandably a popular destination for Victorian tourist steamers. The *Bella Jane* makes the trip from April to October and it is essential to book (✆ *0800 731 3089; 7.30–10am or 7.30–10pm*). The excursion takes over an hour, with a stop that allows you time to walk across ice-smooth rocks to the inland loch, long, deep and dark, reaching northwestwards into the foothills of the Cuillins which fence it round with steep, uncompromising security. In the evening the sun goes down behind the hills sending up great shafts of colour refracted by the proximity of the hills. Sir Walter Scott wrote of it, in *The Lord of the Isles:*

A scene so rude, so wild as this,
Yet so sublime in barrenness
Ne'er did my wandering footsteps press...

...For all is rocks at random thrown,
Black waves, bare crags and banks of stone,
As if were here denied
The summer sun, the spring's sweet dew,
That clothe with many a varied hue
The bleakest mountainside.

For the energetic, another route to Coruisk is along the Camasunary track, which starts at Kilmarie, about 3 miles before Elgol. It is a relatively easy walk, taking a good 2 hours over stony ground through bracken and heather with just one tricky bit known as 'The Bad Step'.

It is from this Camasunary track that non-serious climbers should climb *Bla Bheinn*—**Blaven**—considered by some to be the finest mountain in Skye, partly because it is isolated from the other Cuillpin peaks so that you get a wonderful view of them, as well as of the whole area. It is a 6 to 7 hour walk/climb and though you need a map the way is simple. You cross the moor on the track from just south of Kilmarie until you get to the cairn above Camasunary, where you take the right fork across the hillside to the foot of the ridge. Another cairn, on a rock, marks the path up the ridge to the top.

Anyone fortunate enough to be exploring by boat should put into the perfect natural harbour on the island of **Soay**, off the entrance to Loch Scavaig. The remains of a primitive shark factory can still be seen on the quay, established after the Second World War by the author Gavin Maxwell. His subsequent book, *Harpoon at a Venture,* is a compelling read about the days when sharks and whales were so plentiful in the Minch that at times the water seemed to be black with them. The factory folded after a few years due to financial difficulties. The impractical Maxwell had forgotten that in order to produce a sufficient quantity of the valuable fish-oil, he must first land a mountain of dead sharks on Soay. Had he devised a means of processing these carcasses efficiently, he might have been successful; instead he was left with putrid flesh and a tank full of maggots.

Continuing north from Broadford, the road follows the east coast, looping around long inlets, up and down hills. In a thatched cottage at **Luib**, 7 miles northwest on Loch Ainort, there is a Folk Museum (*open April–Oct daily; adm*), a loose late 20th-century interpretation of a croft house 100 years ago, with an 'on the trail of Bonnie Prince Charlie' exhibition. Among predictable domestic artefacts there are interesting newspaper clippings relating to the Braes and Glendale incidents in the 19th century (*see* p.252–3). From Luib, there is an easy 4-mile walk due south following the river along Strath Mor between the rounded peaks of the red Cuillins to the isolated 'black Cuillin'—Blaven (*see* above for the easy way up).

The Cuillins

Thar lochan fala clann nan daoine,
thar breòiteachd blàir is strì an aonaich,
thar bochdainn caithimh fiabhrais amhghair,
thar anocothrom eucoir ainneart ànraidh,
thar truaighe eu-dochas gamhlas cuilbheart,
thar coint is truaillidheachd, gu furachair,
gu treunmhor chithear an Cuilithionn
'S e 'g éirigh air taobh eile duilghe.

Beyond the lochs of the blood
of the children of men,
beyond the frailty of plain and the labour of
the mountain,
beyond poverty, consumption, fever agony,
beyond hardship, wrong, tyranny, distress,
beyond misery, despair, hatred, treachery,
beyond guilt and defilement; watchful
heroic, the Cuillin is seen
rising on the other side of sorrow.

the final lyric from 'The Cuillin' by Sorley MacLean

Cú Chulainn was a Celtic hero who according to tradition visited Skye from Ireland to learn martial arts and from whom the name for the Cuillins was thought to have derived. Other derivations include *cuilionn*, a Celtic word for 'wilderness' and a Nordic word, *kjollen*, meaning 'keel-shaped ridge'.

The Cuillins attract serious mountaineers from afar and should only be tackled by people who know what they are doing: they have claimed many lives over the years and make no concessions to ill-equipped amateurs. The Red Cuillins to the east are weathered and eroded into symmetrical cones, while the tougher, rougher Black Cuillins have withstood erosion and, according to John MacCulloch the geologist, writing in 1824, have 'a nutmeg-grater-like surface in contact with which the human body may almost defy the laws of gravity'. (MacCulloch, in fact, didn't manage to climb the Cuillins, partly perhaps because he tried to do so on a horse.) The main semi-circular ridge, with spurs intersected by deep and often sheer corries, includes some 20 Munros.

Surrounded by the sound of cascading water, these hills reign supreme, looking as if they have been dragged upwards from the earth by their Creator. Whether capped with snow, their lower slopes mottled and smeared like camouflage jackets, elusive and eerie in mist, or shrouded by swirling cloud, or brilliant against a postcard-blue sky, they always present a challenge.

The road north up the east coast, 9 miles from Sligachan to Portree, runs through empty Glen Varragil: bleak moorland forestry plantations, rivers and burns. Just south of Portree the B883 road goes out to the **Braes**, overlooking the Sound of Raasay, scene of the Battle of Braes, *see* p.252, and home of the late Sorley MacLean whose evocative poetry lives on to prove that the *Gaidhealtachd* is not yet dead.

Portree

Portree is a busy little tourist resort, lively and attractive, built round a natural harbour with houses rising steeply from the water's edge, neat and brightly painted. The name is derived from *Port righ*—King's Port—after a visit by James V during a Hebridean tour in 1540. During the summer bus excursions run from the town to many of Skye's beauty spots.

Coming into Portree from the south you pass the **Skye Heritage Centre** (*open daily; adm to exhibition*) with its **Aros Experience**, one of the best of these many ventures, with an excellent exhibition, a good restaurant and a shop. The exhibition, which starts with an audio-visual show, takes you through graphic representations of the Jacobite rising, with life-like tableaux. There is also a chance to hear Gaelic concerts here on Thursdays—ask at the desk for details.

It was in a room in what is now the **Royal Hotel** in Portree that Prince Charles (aka Betty Burke) took his leave of Flora Macdonald. He repaid her the half-crown she had lent him, gave her a miniature of himself, and declared: 'For all that has happened, I hope, Madam, we shall meet in St James yet.' He bowed, kissed her hand and departed—a fugitive with a bundle of clean shirts, a wrapped-up chicken, a bottle of whisky and a bottle of brandy tied at his waist, and a £30,000 reward on his head.

Trotternish

Geographically part of the Quiraing, or Trotternish Ridge, **the Old Man of Storr**, about 7 miles north of Portree to the west of the road, is another of those landmarks familiar from postcards. The easiest route is through the forestry along maintained paths, rather than up the steep grassy slopes to the south. At over 180ft (55m) high and 40ft (12m) in diameter, the Old Man is the tallest of a group of mighty towers and pinnacles of basaltic rock, a great weathered stack, undercut and pointed at the top like a giant fir cone.

In 1891 on the shore below the Old Man of Storr, a hoard of treasure was unearthed; a remarkable collection of silver neck rings, brooches, bracelets and beaten ingots, together with many 10th-century coins, some from Samarkand. It is believed they must have been hidden there by a Norseman, who presumably came to an untimely end before he could claim them or bequeath them to an heir. You can see them in the Antiquities part of the Royal Museum of Scotland, in Edinburgh. There is good trout fishing in the **Storr Lochs**, from bank or boat.

The road twists and turns up the east coast of Trotternish with staggering views across the islands of Rona and Raasay to Applecross, Torridon and Dundonnel on the mainland; to the south lie the Cuillins and to the west, the Quairaing ridge. Stop at the car park at **Loch Mealt**, 7 miles north of the Old Man of Storr, where the road comes to the brink of the cliff. The loch drains in a sheer 300ft (92m) white cascade, plummeting into the cobalt sea. **Kilt Rock**, north of Loch Mealt, is so called because of its vertical columns of basalt on horizontal stripes of grey and white oolite, like the pleats and pattern of a kilt.

The **Quiraing** is 2 miles west of Staffin. Park by the burial ground or in the lay-by at the top of the hill and approach it across the moor. The last bit is quite a scramble up scree, through a steep, narrow gorge flanked by great pillars of basaltic rock, like a surreal Gothic cathedral. At the top there is a plateau of emerald-green grass, as big as a football pitch; a magical place with panoramic views. Cattle used to be driven up here for safety during raids in the old days—they must have been as nimble as mountain goats.

Flodigarry, about 3 miles north of Staffin, is where Flora Macdonald lived for eight years, after her marriage to Captain Allan Macdonald of Kingsburgh in 1751. Six of her seven children were born in the pretty cottage which is now an annexe to the hotel, remodelled in a late 20th-century interpretation of 'traditional'.

Duntulm Castle is a jagged ruin less than 5 miles to the west. The castle, with a water gate, stands in an easily defended position on a precipitous cliff; today it is much eroded and at risk of further collapse. Built on the site of an earlier fortress, it became the stronghold of the Macdonalds of Sleat from the 16th century (although only their principal residence from 1616) under the authority of James VI, during his attempts to discipline the Hebridean chiefs. Sir Donald Gorm Macdonald was ordered to maintain his fortress in good condition, to restrict his household to six gentlemen, to limit his consumption of wine to four tuns (1,008 gallons) a year and to produce three of his kinsmen annually as surety for his good behaviour.

The family left the castle after a nursemaid carelessly dropped the chief's infant son into the sea whilst holding him out of a window to look at the boats. The nursemaid was punished for her carelessness by being cast adrift in an open boat full of holes.

A story is told of Hugh Macdonald, the heir of another chief, who hired a hit man to speed up his inheritance. Unfortunately his written instructions got muddled and the assassin received an invitation to dinner, while the instructions for the murder were delivered to the chief. Hugh found himself incarcerated in the vaults of the castle he had coveted with only salt beef to eat and nothing to drink. It is said that many years later a skeleton was unearthed here, clutching an empty water pitcher.

One of Scotland's most popular heroines, Flora Macdonald, is buried below a large, white Celtic cross in the windswept churchyard at **Kilmuir**, a couple of miles further south. The cross is a replacement of the original which was a victim of souvenir-hunters. On it, an inscription gives a quotation by Dr Johnson, who visited her and her family during his Hebridean tour in 1773: 'Flora Macdonald, a name that will be mentioned in history, and if courage and fidelity be virtues, mentioned with honour.' In his journal he went on to describe her as 'a woman of middle stature, soft features, gentle manners and elegant presence', which is admirably portrayed in the painting of her by Alan Ramsay, showing a woman with large eyes and a calm, fine-boned face of classic Scottish beauty. They say her shroud is the sheet on which Prince Charles slept when he was hidden at Kingsburgh House.

As is well known, Flora smuggled the Prince, disguised as her maid Betty Burke, from Loch Uskavagh in Benbecula to Skye, and was instrumental in ensuring his safe sojourn until his departure from Portree. It was a brave venture and he was no easy conspirator, striding about with manly vigour, hitching up his skirts and presenting his unshaven cheek for the embrace of his hostess at Kingsburgh. For her act of courage Flora was briefly imprisoned. She then lived with her family in North Carolina for some years before returning to Kingsburgh for the last decade of her life, dying at the age of 68. From the churchyard you can look westwards across the entrance of Loch Snizort, where Flora and the Prince approached Skye on their daring voyage from the Outer Isles.

The Skye Museum of Island Life (*open April–Oct Mon–Sat; adm*) is close to the churchyard, and one of the best of its kind. Two thatched cottages (one unusually large) and a byre have been restored and a number of new buildings constructed in recent years, to show life in a mid 19th-century crofting township, complete with the usual domestic artefacts and some interesting documents and photographs. The land stretching away to the south is known as the Granary of Skye and was once a loch until drained in the 19th century.

Ruinous **Monkstadt House**, 4 miles south of Kilmuir, succeeded Duntulm as the Macdonald seat before they built Armadale Castle. A plain 18th-century laird's house, it was the home, in 1746, of Sir Alexander Macdonald, who supported the Hanoverian cause. Flora and the Prince landed here while the house was occupied by Hanoverian troops, but fortunately Macdonald was away ingratiating himself with the Duke of Cumberland in Fort Augustus and they were met by his wife Lady Margaret, who was a staunch Jacobite. The Prince hid in the grounds where he was served by Macdonald of Kingsburgh who brought him food and wine under the noses of the redcoats.

Sir Alexander is reputed to have made a fast buck by shipping Highlanders to the Caribbean as slaves. In fact, he seems to have been reasonably honest, if naïve, and only sanctioned the removal of undesirables, such as thieves, from his lands. It is said that Macleod of Dunvegan was much more deeply and dishonourably involved in this nasty practice.

Uig Bay, 3 miles to the south, lies at the foot of a green amphitheatre of hills, a long pier cutting across it like an out-flung arm. The village of Uig is busy with ferry traffic at certain times of day, for this is the terminal for the steamer to the Outer Isles. If you are lucky one of the fishing boats that use the pier may have berthed with a load of scampi and may agree to sell you a bagfull, scooped up from a great pile on its deck. Boil these for just a few moments and eat them while still warm, accompanied by a slice of locally baked brown bread from the village shop.

At Borve, 11 miles south of Uig, take the right turn (west) to **Skeabost**, at the head of **Loch Snizort Beag**. Below the bypassed stone bridge, the river branches round an island, now reached by a timber footbridge. This was the site of an ancient Christian settlement, probably founded by St Columba whose name it bears. It was the burial ground for the Bishops of the Isles, from at least 1079 (except for about 60 years when it was transferred to St Germains on the Isle of Man) until the bishopric moved to the Benedictine Monastery of Iona in 1498 after the eclipse of its patrons, the Lords of the Isles. The small cruciform church dates from the 13th century and the 16th-century mortuary chapel is said to contain the remains of 28 Nicolson chiefs. There are some important medieval gravestones carved with effigies; information plaques give some of the history of the site.

Annait is the site of the oldest Christian settlement in these parts. The walls and foundations of a small chapel and the monks' cells are scattered across a green promontory between two deep gullies. In this wild and lonely place the only sounds are the piping of skylarks, the chatter of running water and the wind.

Waternish

At **Trumpan** is the consolidated ruin of Cille Chonain, a church with an unholy history. In 1597, when the Macleods were attending a service here, they were attacked by their bitter enemies, the Macdonalds of South Uist, who set fire to the church and burnt virtually the entire congregation. One woman, cutting off a breast in order to escape through a narrow slit-window, managed to get away and warn the remainder of the Macleod clan, who arrived with their Fairy Flag and massacred the Macdonalds as they returned to their boats. No wonder, really, that exasperated monarchs like James VI kept trying to subdue the clans.

From the road south towards Dunvegan, the outline of **Macleod's Tables** dominates the horizon 10 miles away to the southwest. It is said that when Alasdair Crottach Macleod went to the court of King James V at Holyrood in Edinburgh in the 16th century, he was asked somewhat patronisingly whether he was impressed by the grandeur of the palace. He replied that he saw nothing to compare for grandeur with his own domain in Skye. When the King then visited Skye in 1540, trying to rally support from the Hebridean clans, Macleod gave an open air banquet for him on the lower of the two 'tables', lit by his kilted clansmen each holding aloft a flaming torch. 'My family candlesticks', he told the King, with a casual sweep of his hand.

Dunvegan

Dunvegan Castle (✆ *(01470) 521 206; open summer 10–5.30; winter 11–4; boat trips, shops and restaurant summer only; adm*), 5 miles southwest of the Fairy Bridge, is the seat, since about 1200, of the Macleods, who can trace their lineage back 30 generations to Norse origins. Standing on a rock, this massive castle has evolved over the centuries with Georgian and Victorian additions which do little to soften its austere appearance. Today it is approached by a bridge over a ravine which once formed a dry moat. In the old days the only way in was from the sea through a water-gate on the rocks.

When Johnson and Boswell came to stay, the Doctor slept in the 15th-century Fairy Tower and remarked in his diary that his hostess, Lady Macleod, newly come to Dunvegan after many years in England, 'knew all the arts of southern elegance and all the modes of English economy'. They stayed for some time and experienced some strong winds. Sir Walter Scott stayed in the same room in 1814.

The castle contains family heirlooms, pictures, arms, original furnishings, documents and relics. One of these, Rory Mor's Horn, was shown to Dr Johnson: 'an ox's horn, hollowed so as to hold perhaps two quarts, which the heir of Macleod was expected to swallow at one draught, as a test of his manhood, before he was permitted to bear arms, or could claim a seat among the men.' This initiation rite is still practised, the quantity to be quaffed being a bottle and a half of claret: the present chief managed to down his in 1 minute 57 seconds in 1965.

Displayed above a marquetry table is the castle's *pièce de résistance*: **the Fairy Flag**, a frail scrap of faded and worn silk, shot with gold thread and marked with crimson 'elf spots'. Legend tells of the Macleod who fell in love with a fairy, hundreds of years ago. The lovers were forced to part (at the Fairy Bridge, to the north) and the fairy left the flag as a coverlet for their child. This flag had the power to save the Macleod Clan from destruction three times, but only if waved in a genuine crisis. It has been used twice: once at Trumpan, helping the Macleods to massacre the marauding Macdonalds of South Uist, and once during a famine caused by cattle plague. Less romantically, it was subjected to modern tests that dated it to between AD 400 and AD 700 and suggested Middle Eastern origins; perhaps an early Macleod went on one of the Crusades. The Gardens are both formal and informal, with attractive walks.

Boat cruises run from the jetty below the castle to the little islands where seals bask on the rocks. In August the Gala Day and the Dunvegan Show are held here. Look out for the craft shop just outside Dunvegan village, near the pier. A few miles on past the castle there are seal colonies and swans sit on the lochs, and, at Claigan, a path leads to lovely coral beaches.

Duirinish

The Duirinish Peninsula, topped by Macleod's Tables, stretches away west of Loch Dunvegan. Macleod's Maidens, only visible if you walk or go by sea, are off the southern tip 8 miles south of Dunvegan. These three basalt stacks are named after the wife and daughters of a Macleod, who drowned here in a shipwreck. Don't be put off by the Tourist Route signs that lead you round the peninsula—it is not awash with picnic sites and caravans yet.

At **Colbost** there is another Folk Museum (*open Easter–Oct Mon–Sat; adm*), a restored 'black house', complete with peat fire in the middle of the room and all the 19th-century bric-à-brac typical of such places. There is also an illicit whisky still, once common all over the Highlands, though this one is certainly not an original. Three miles to the west at Glendale—home of the Martyrs, *see* pp.252–3—is an old watermill by the shore with a thatched roof.

This road is of particular interest to piping enthusiasts. **The MacCrimmon Piping Heritage Centre** at Borreraig is a tribute to the MacCrimmons, hereditary pipers to the Macleods of Dunvegan and leading pipers and pipe teachers through the 17th and 18th centuries. One of them, Padruig Og, founded a piping school here which closed in about 1770, its scant remains marked by a cairn on the headland. The Piping Museum, in the old school, ✆ (01470) 511 316, is open at varying times all year, except on Mondays, and gives piping tuition; you can also hear wonderful recordings of *piobaireachd.*

Carry on west to Loch Pooltiel, with its sheltered anchorage, and then to Neist Point, the most westerly point in Skye. Park at the top if you want to walk down to the lighthouse—unmanned these days.

About 8 miles south on the main road from Dunvegan, look carefully up to the left as you drop down into Bracadale. **Dun Beag** (always accessible) is one of the best brochs in Skye. It seems to grow out of the hillside and would be easy to miss though only a few minutes' climb away, over springy turf and stones. Once 40 or 50ft (12–15m) high, this 2,000-year-old relic was used as a refuge by farmers, herdsmen and their families. Its double walls were braced by a honeycomb of chambers and galleries with cells in which the people took refuge, linked by passage and stairways. The animals would have been driven into the inner enclosure and there are also traces of outbuildings.

A detour west from Drynoch takes you to **Talisker**, home of Skye's malt whisky, with daily tours on weekdays. Johnson and Boswell stayed at Talisker House, at the foot of Preshal Mor, home of Colonel Macleod who had been granted indefinite leave due to 'this time of universal peace' (Napoleon being barely 4 years old). Johnson found Talisker rather gloomy:

> *Talisker is the place beyond all that I have seen, from which the gay and the jovial seem utterly excluded: and from where the hermit might expect to grow old in meditation, without possibility of disturbance or interruption.*
> *It is situated very near the sea, but upon a coast where no vessel lands but when it is driven by a tempest on the rocks.*

Johnson also recorded the sad story of the young man who lost his dog in the night and found only its carcass in the morning with two replete eagles close by. This is a good base for exploring the Cuillins and there is a camp site and a hostel here.

Raasay

Coille Ratharsair 'na ciùine
ri taobh na Clàraich gu mùirneach,
siubhal uaine an ùrlair
th' aig a' Chuilithionn ris na sùghan.

The wood of Raasay in its gentleness,
joyful beside the Clarach,
the green variation on the pibroch theme
that the Cuillin makes with the waves.

'The Woods of Raasay' by Sorley MacLean (born in Raasay, 1911)

The island of Raasay, reached by ferry from Sconser (daily except Sundays, ✆ (01478) 660 226), is 13 miles long and about 3 miles at its widest, with the smaller island of Rona just off its northern shore and the lump of Scalpay to the south. Within the lee of the Skye and Applecross hills, it is sheltered and relatively fertile and was one of the hiding places of the fugitive Prince Charles who spent a couple of days and a night in a 'mean, low hut' here, in a downpour, in July 1746.

Dr Johnson visited the island during his tour of the Hebrides with the faithful Boswell and was lavishly entertained at **Raasay House**, 'a neat, modern fabrick', built by his hosts the Macleods out of the shell of the old house that was ravaged in 1746. They were greeted on the lawn in front of the house by a large number of visiting gentry, having negotiated a difficult landing stage which Johnson decided had been deliberately kept thus in order to deter invaders. The Macleods had three sons and ten daughters and the visitors were entertained with dancing and 'Erse' songs. Amazingly, 'six and thirty people sat down to two tables in the same room for supper'. Allowing for the large family, their tutor and guests, this still points to a considerable household. Johnson was delighted with the 'general air of festivity, nor did ever fairies trip with greater alacrity. More gentleness of manners, or a more pleasing appearance of domestick society, is not found in the most polished countries.'

As their stay on the island continued, however, he found the lack of intellectual stimulation irksome and was impatient to get on with his tour. Boswell recorded that, though Macleod of Raasay's lands didn't yield much revenue, he was such a good landlord that 'in the present rage for emigration, not a man has left his estate'. A hundred fighting men had left Raasay to join Prince Charles' army and 'all but about fourteen' returned home. In retribution for their loyalty to the Jacobite cause, the island suffered badly.

About a month after Culloden a party of sailors, marines and militia, under a Lieutenant Dalrymple, methodically burned and pillaged everything in sight, including the laird's house and most of the other houses on the island, and wantonly slaughtered all the animals they could find. The sight of these depredations greatly distressed Prince Charles and he swore that one day he would have the burnt turf cottages replaced with proper stone houses. Having arrived at dawn, he departed on the evening of the following day, deciding that Raasay had nothing to offer as a place of refuge. With dogged determination, the islanders managed to rebuild their lives and recover their former existence until the salt tax was imposed, preventing the export of fish—their main livelihood.

In 1843 the last resident chief became bankrupt and was forced to sell up and emigrate to Tasmania. From then on the island passed through the hands of a succession of self-interested owners wanting a sporting estate. It was eventually compulsorily purchased in 1979 for £135,000 from a Dr Green, who had paid less than £8,000 for it. He was an absentee landlord who let the place fall into wrack and ruin. Raasay House, almost beyond hope, was rescued and is now the **Raasay Outdoor Centre**.

Castle Brochel—*Caisteal Bhrochail*—(always accessible) is a ruin on a rock on the eastern shore overlooking a bay with the hills of Torridon massing on the eastern horizon. It was once the stronghold of the Macleods of Raasay and the danger notices are fully justified. Boswell, exploring this ruin, discovered that it contained a privy—a convenience that was sadly lacking in Raasay House where they were staying. He pointed this out to their host: 'You take very good care of one end of a man, but not of the other.'

There are two carved crosses within easy walking distance of Raasay House and a ruined medieval chapel dedicated to St Moluag of Lismore, standing beside an 18th-century chapel in an enclosed burial ground. There are the remains of a broch at Dun Borodale. A nice walk up the Inverarish Burn takes you to the flat-topped, volcano-like Dun Caan, upon which Boswell and his companions danced a Highland Fling while he was being shown the island on a 24-mile hike.

Shopping and Events

In June, **Portree** is the setting for Skye Week, with every sort of Scottish entertainment both indoors and out. The Portree Show takes place in July; the Skye Highland Games in early August; the Portree Folk Festival in mid-August; and the Portree Fiddlers' Rally in September.

The Skye Woollen Mill usually has excellent cashmere and lambswool products at reduced prices and they have a coffee shop. Fishermen should visit **North West Fishermen**, down by the pier, for fishing tackle, flies and fishing permits. **The Gathering Hall** has splendid Friday night 'gatherings', very lively and a good place for a 'crack' with locals.

Where to Stay and Eating Out

Sleat Peninsula

expensive

Kinloch Lodge Hotel, ✆ (01471) 833 214, 🖷 833 277, is on the northeast corner of the Sleat Peninsula overlooking Loch na Dal. It was a former tacksman's house converted into a Macdonald lodge in the 1870s, and is now the home of Lord and Lady Macdonald. An attractive, white building, it has marvellous views across to Knoydart on the mainland and west to the Cuillins. Lord Macdonald is High Chief of Clan Macdonald and Lady Macdonald is well known as Claire Macdonald the cookery writer. Her numerous books are to be found in many a gourmet kitchen throughout Britain. Everything served at Kinloch is home-made, from the breakfast scones to the after-dinner fudge. Family portraits and antiques add an ancestral touch to the house's homely atmosphere.

Hotel Eilean Iarmain, Isleornsay, ✆ (01471) 833 332, 🖷 833 275, is traditional 'Highland' with sporting trophies, tartan galore and suitable prints, right on the water with good views over the Sound of Sleat. It is owned by Sir Iain Nobel, a self-taught Gaelic-speaking 'white settler' and entrepreneur, who has done much to foster the revival of Gaelic and who encourages his staff and his guests to speak Gaelic, if they can. It has been known for visitors to mug up a few words in the hope of 'one on the house'. The food is excellent, both in the restaurant and the bar.

moderate

Dunollie Hotel, Broadford, ✆ (01471) 822 253, 822 060, in the middle of Broadford, is large, with cheerful staff and atmosphere. The **White Heather Hotel**, Kyleakin, ✆ (01599) 534 577, is right on the harbour, run by a local family, with all the islanders' warmth and friendliness. **The Ardvasar Hotel**, in Ardvasar, ✆ (01471) 844 223, is a nice old hotel, simple and reasonably priced. *Open Mar–Dec.*

cheap

The Picture House, Broadford, ✆ (01471) 822 531, is a guest house with wonderful views across the water.

Mrs B. La Trobe's house in Fiordham Ord, Sleat, ✆ (01471) 855 226, is one of the best B&Bs in Skye, where the sea laps below the dining room whose picture windows look west to the setting sun, and the Highland hospitality is magnificent. Non-residents can dine here: take your own wine.

The **Seagull Restaurant**, just south of Broadford on the main road, is a good place to eat, and popular with the locals. *Open April–Oct 5–10pm and for Sunday lunch.*

The Cuillins

moderate–cheap

Sligachan Hotel, ✆ (01478) 650 204, 650 207, is a famous hotel at the head of Loch Sligachan, 5 miles west of Sconser, on the junction of the east and west routes to the north, popular with anyone planning to climb the Cuillins, as well as with fishermen. It is splendidly easy-going and traditional; H. V. Morton visited it in the late 1920s in a raging storm: 'in spite of its hot baths, its aquatints and its garage, it was spiritually a mountain hut: the only place of warmth and shelter in the abomination of desolation.' The hotel knows how to pamper people who come in cold and hungry.

Portree

moderate

Viewfield House Hotel, on the outskirts of Portree, ✆ (01478) 612 217, is a Victorian country house in 20 acres of garden and woodland. Run by the family for whom it has always been home, it retains the atmosphere of a relaxing, comfortable family establishment, surrounded by pictures, furniture and heirlooms that have been there since the house was built. **Royal Hotel**, Bank Street, ✆ (01478) 612 525, 613 198, is not quite what it was in the days when Prince Charles took his leave of Flora Macdonald in one of its parlours, but some of the atmosphere of history clings to the walls of the older part.

Flodigarry Country House Hotel, ✆ (01470) 552 203, 552 301, has won awards for food, service and comfort. A 19th-century shooting lodge in secluded grounds beneath the Quiraing, with views across to the mainland, it has cosy bedrooms, a bar with Moorish-style decor in the converted billiard room, and a splendid conservatory.

The **Rosedale Hotel**, Beaumont Crescent, ✆ (01478) 613 131, 🖷 612 531, is comfortable and serves good food. The **Bosville Hotel**, ✆ (01478) 612 846, is friendly and comfortable; the Chandlery Seafood Restaurant has views over the harbour.

cheap

The Isles Inn, Somerled Square, ✆ (01478) 612 129, is central and friendly. **The Kings Haven**, Portree, ✆ (01478) 612 290, is a restored Georgian house overlooking the harbour. The atmosphere is relaxed and the rooms are comfortable.

One of the best self-catering places in Skye is at **Braes**, high above the Narrows of Raasay, south of Portree. This is a truly cosy converted croft house, sleeping 6 or 7, looking across to Raasay and the mainland. Because it is also a much-loved home to the owners it contains all the comfortable extras of family life. Contact Mrs J.D. Bengough, White Lodge, Sidbury, Devon, EX10 0SB, ✆ (01395) 597 214.

The Lower Deck, on the harbour in Portree, ✆ (01478) 613 611, serves delicious seafood. *Open April–Oct 11am–10pm.*

Trotternish

expensive–moderate

Skeabost House Hotel, ✆ (01470) 532 202, 🖷 532 454, is a large, comfortable Victorian lodge, built in 1870, which offers salmon fishing and serves very decent lunches.

moderate

Duntulm Castle Hotel, ✆ (01470) 552 213, 🖷 552 292, is gloriously situated in the old inn near the castle. They also have five self-catering cottages, all with wonderful sea-views, sleeping from 4 to 8, ranging in price and quality from cosy chalet to luxury bungalow.

Uig Hotel, ✆ (01470) 542 205, is an old coaching inn on the hill overlooking Uig Bay and the ferry terminal. It has plenty of character, comfortable rooms and is very friendly. The breakfasts are especially good, making it a useful stopover for an early ferry. The **Ferry Inn**, Uig, ✆ (01470) 542 242, is a bit cheaper and equally friendly.

Duirinish

expensive

The Three Chimneys, Colbost, 5 miles west of Dunvegan, ✆ (01470) 511 258, is a first class restaurant, worth every penny. They also have 6 luxurious rooms.

moderate

Neist Point lighthouse (*see* above, p.261)—unmanned these days—has cottages available as holiday lets; ✆ (01470) 511 200.

Kinlochfollart, by Dunvegan, ✆ (01470) 521 470, 🖷 521 740, is a restored former manse on the shore of Loch Dunvegan, run as a Wolsey Lodge by Donald and Rosemary MacLeod who make you feel at home in an informal, relaxed family atmosphere. Good home cooking with local ingredients. No smoking. **Talisker House**, ✆ (01478) 640 245, 🖷 640 214, the remote, elegant country house where Johnson and Boswell stayed, is now an up-market Wolsey Lodge in a wonderful position, extremely comfortable and relaxing with excellent food. *Open Feb–Oct.* Book well ahead. **Harlosh House**, about 5 miles south of Dunvegan, ✆ (01470) 521 367, does supper only to a very high standard, especially seafood. **Atholl House Hotel**, Dunvegan, ✆ (01470) 521 219, is another option.

The Tables Hotel and Restaurant, ✆ (01470) 521 404, is a small friendly hotel with panoramic views over MacLeod's Tables and Loch Dunvegan. They also have a self-catering cottage at Waternish.

cheap

Mrs Flora Cumming, Eilean Dubh, Edinbane, ✆ (01470) 582 218, has one of the best B&Bs in Skye: it is so welcoming and hospitable it is like going to stay with an old friend, and you will find yourself extremely reluctant to leave.

The licensed **Macleod's Tables Restaurant Bistro**, ✆ (01470) 521 310/521 206, serves everything from snacks to full meals. Ring for evening bookings. There are holiday cottages available all year; for details ring the Estate Office, ✆ (01470) 521 206.

Isle of Raasay

Isle of Raasay Hotel, ✆/🖷 (01478) 660 222, is very good value (*open all year*); as is **Churchton House**, also on Raasay, ✆ (01478) 660 260, a guest house with a friendly atmosphere. For B&B there is **Mrs Mackay**, 6 Ostaig Park, Raasay, ✆ (01478) 660 207, who serves dinner. *Open all year.*

Lewis and Harris 270

Lewis 272

Harris 277

Berneray 282

North Uist 282

Benbecula 285

South Uist 287

The Outer Isles

Eriskay 292

Barra 293

St Kilda 295

From the lone shieling on the misty island
Mountains divide us, and a waste of seas
Yet still the blood is strong, the heart is Highland
And we, in dreams, behold the Hebrides.

Canadian Boat Song

Of all Scotland's islands, the Outer Isles seem to evoke the deepest nostalgia, and their exiles suffer the strongest pangs of homesickness. The distinctive tang of peat smoke, the Gaelic, the wild flowers on the machair, the cry of the curlew, the fundamental faith, the humour—these and many other characteristics cast an unbreakable spell. The Outer Hebrides run about 130 miles from the Butt of Lewis in the north to Barra Head in the south. The main islands include Lewis and Harris, Berneray, North Uist, Benbecula, South Uist, Eriskay and Barra. About 29,000 people live here—mostly bilingual gaels. An aerial photograph reveals a land broken up by a vast number of lochs and lochans, which once provided waterways throughout the islands. The climate is unpredictable. Gaelic still lives and tourists should note that all road signs are now in Gaelic, except in Benbecula. They are often difficult to translate into the more familiar Anglicized version, but the Western Isles Tourist Board have published an excellent booklet with all the names in both English and Gaelic. The tourist brochures will show you white beaches, aquamarine seas and azure skies. It can be like this, but even when the gale-force winds invade these islands are still marvellous.

Getting There

by sea

Caledonian MacBrayne, The Ferry Terminal, Gourock, PA19 1QP, ✆ (01475) 650 100, holds the monopoly for ferries to the Outer Isles, and for some of the inter-island services. Ask about Island Hopscotch, and Island Rover fares.

Ullapool–Stornoway on Lewis (2½hrs);
Uig on Skye–Tarbert on Harris (1½hrs);
Uig on Skye–Lochmaddy on North Uist (1½hrs);
Oban/Mallaig–Lochboisdale on South Uist/Castlebay on Barra (Oban–Castlebay 5hrs Mallaig–Castlebay 3½hrs; 1½hrs on to Lochboisdale);
Otternish/Newton Ferry on North Uist–Leverburgh on Harris (1hr).

Timings vary day to day and are seasonal.

by air

British Airways Express, St Andrew's Drive, Glasgow Airport, Paisley, PA3 2TG, ✆ 0345 222 111:

Glasgow/Inverness–Stornoway (*Mon–Sat up to three times daily*);
Glasgow–Barra/Benbecula (*Mon–Sat; flights to Barra also Sun in high summer*).
They also run inter-island flights between Stornoway, Benbecula and Barra.

by rail

Trains go to Oban, Mallaig and Kyle. For Ullapool, you can go to Inverness by train and link with a bus. For details, ring national rail enquiries, ✆ 0345 484 950.

Outer Hebrides

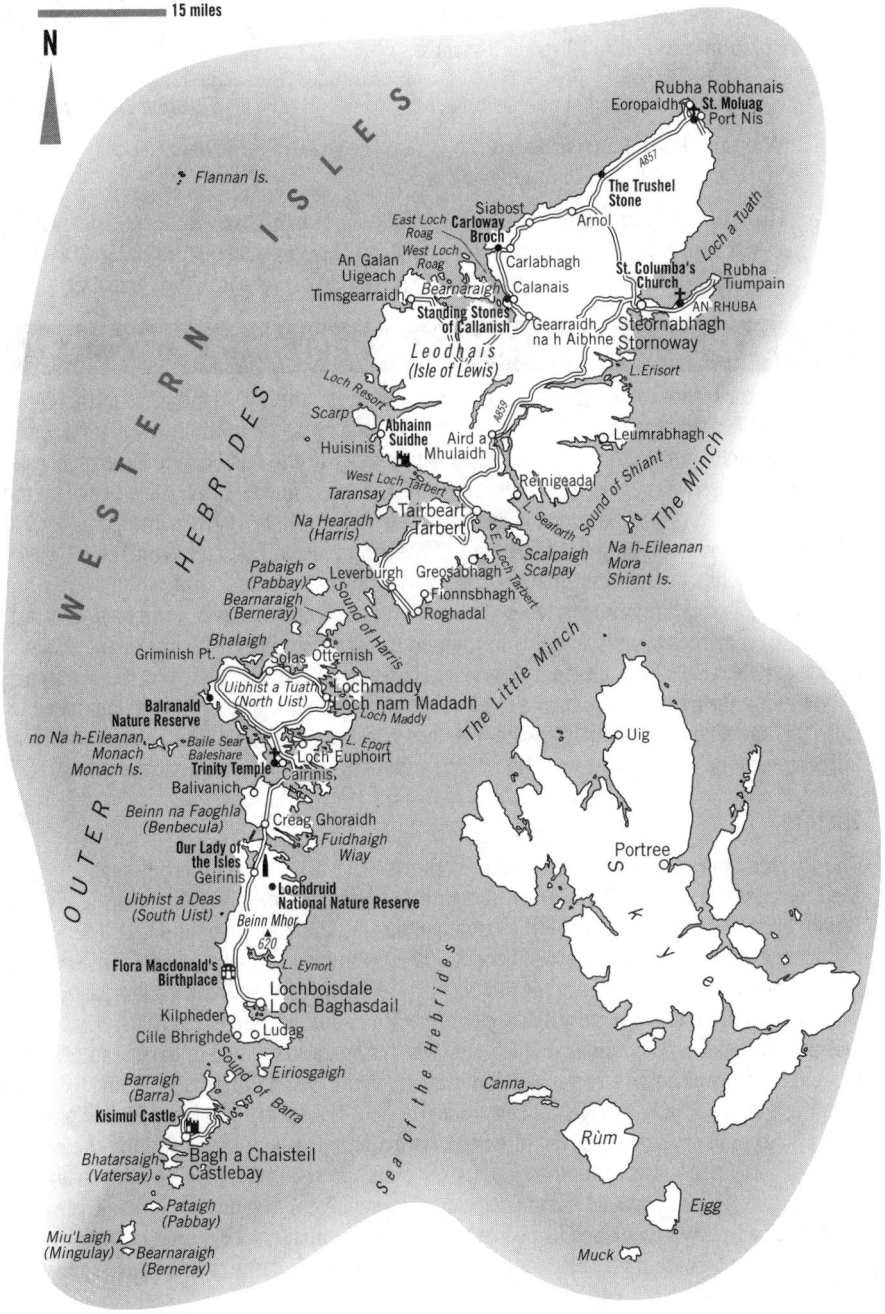

by road

Scottish Citylink Coaches, ✆ 0990 505 050, and **Skye-ways Express Coaches**, ✆ (01599) 534 238, run services to Ullapool, Uig, Oban and Mallaig which all connect where possible with ferries. **Macdonald Coaches**, ✆ (01851) 706 267/820 367, runs services to Ullapool/Inverness.

Tourist Information

Western Isles Tourist Board, 26 Cromwell Street, Stornoway, Isle of Lewis HS1 2DD, ✆ (01851) 703 088. *Open all year.*

Harris: Pier Road, Tarbert, ✆ (01859) 502 011; **North Uist**: Pier Road, Lochmaddy, ✆ (01876) 500 321; **South Uist**: Pier Road, Lochboisdale, ✆ (01878) 700 286; **Barra**: Main Street, Castlebay, ✆ (01871) 810 336 (*open early April–mid Oct*).

Lewis (*Leodhas*) and Harris (*Hearadh*)

Lewis and Harris are joined to form the largest and most northerly land mass in the Outer Hebrides—Siamese twins with two separate identities. Lewis, the northern two-thirds of this island, has mountains in the southwest, undulating moor in the middle, hundreds of lochs—especially in the southeast—green fertile croftland and many fine beaches. Aline Lodge, at the head of Loch Seaforth, marks the boundary between the two lands. Harris is divided into north and south by a narrow isthmus at Tarbert (*Tairbeart*), between East and West Loch Tarbert. North Harris has outstanding mountain scenery and the west coast of South Harris has machair and vast white sandy beaches. The east coast of South Harris is a complete contrast, with a rugged, rocky landscape cut by numerous inlets studded with rocks and islands. Although geographically one island, Lewis and Harris are effectively divided by the high range of hills along their border, the moors of Lewis giving way to the hills of Harris, dominated by Clisham, the highest mountain in the Western Isles at 2,600ft (800m). Although not as impressive as the mainland Munros, these hills and their glens offer wonderful walks.

History

The early history of Lewis includes that of Harris. The first settlers were thought to be a Mediterranean race, megalithic Stone Age or early Bronze Age, who colonized the west of Britain by sea and built the Callanish Standing Stones in the 2nd millennium BC. Then came migrating Celts from central Europe in about 500 BC who built brochs, of which Carloway is a prime example. Norse invaders in the 9th century are thought to have married into island families and given their blood to the original clans: the Morrisons, Nicolsons and MacAulays. But it was the Macleods who dominated much of Lewis' history, also reputed to have been of Norse descent, and it was between two Macleod brothers that Lewis and Harris were divided at an unknown date: Torquil Macleod got Lewis and Tormod, Harris. In 1598 James VI had plans to 'plant policy and civilization in the hitherto most barbarous Isle of Lewis and to develop the extraordinarily rich resources of the same for the public good and the King's profit'. He agreed a contract with some Lowland 'Gentlemen Adventurers', who, in return for financial rewards, were to invade Lewis and teach its people 'religion and humanity by deporting them or exterminating them'. These men sailed for Stornoway and took the castle, but the Macleods were too strong for them and after several attempts to gain supremacy the Lowlanders were forced to withdraw. In 1607, after a third colonizing attempt was made, Stornoway was granted status as a Burgh of Barony. Lord Kintail, Chief of the Clan MacKenzie, now bought the right to Lewis from the 'Gentlemen Adventurers', and there ensued a battle for power between the MacKenzies and the Macleods which, after a considerable struggle, the MacKenzies finally won. In 1623 the MacKenzie chief was created Earl of Seaforth and asked Charles I to make Stornoway a Royal Burgh. The King, seeing profit for the Crown from the fishing industry, was willing, but the Convention of Royal Burghs of Scotland were not so keen, seeing a threat to the Royal Burghs of Tain and Inverness. Cromwell had a grudge against the Earl of Seaforth and punished him by destroying Stornoway Castle (near today's ferry terminal) in 1653.

After Culloden in 1746, Prince Charles hoped to find a boat in Stornoway to take him back to France. The Rev John Macaulay, Church of Scotland minister in South Uist and grandfather of the historian Lord Macaulay, a lonely Protestant among Papists, had discovered his intentions and sent an urgent message to his father, the Rev Aulay MacAulay, Minister of Harris. MacAulay led a party of armed men to the island of Scalpay where the Prince was hiding, but was sternly repulsed by the Prince's host, Donald Campbell, who, though no Jacobite, was deeply aware of the obligations of Highland hospitality. MacAulay and his troop fled in shame. When the islanders heard of Prince Charles' presence, however, they did not wish to tangle with the Government despite being sympathetic to his cause. They indicated that, although they would not betray him, they would prefer him not to linger on their island. They refused to lend him a boat or even a pilot and he was forced to retreat south to the Uists and Benbecula.

In 1844 the Mackenzies sold Lewis to Sir James Matheson who built Lews Castle in Stornoway and tried to create a viable economy including an unsuccessful attempt to extract tar from peat. His activities included afforestation, new houses, gas and water works and an improved harbour in Stornoway. He tried to help his tenants after the potato famine in 1845 by providing work on road and quay building, drainage and land improvement. He established a regular shipping service to the mainland and was responsible for the building of about 150 miles of roads.

Lord Leverhulme, founder of Lever Brothers, bought Lewis and Harris in 1918 and spent close to a million pounds trying to redeem the islanders from poverty and create wealth through enterprise and the exploitation of the natural resources of the sea. He financed fishing boats, a cannery and ice factory, roads, bridges and even a light railway. He created a chain of retail fish shops—MacFisheries—with the ambition of controlling the fishing industry from the time the fish left the sea until it arrived on the table. Stornoway was to become the main town of the West Highlands—the 'Venice of the North'.

But there was a strong desire by islanders returning from the First World War to control their own lands, particularly as there was land settlement taking place elsewhere in the Highlands. They preferred the idea of possessing their own crofts to Lord Leverhulme's expensive 'improvements'. Land raids began in 1919. Lord Leverhulme stopped all his island operations in 1920, but the Secretary of State for Scotland reminded him that unless he resumed his schemes the government would no longer be justified in stalling the islanders' claims for land. Agreements and disagreements ensued until economic recession and the decline of the herring market landed Lord Leverhulme in financial difficulties and he was forced to withdraw his interests from Lewis. This brought about drastic unemployment and hardship and the emigration of over a thousand men to America. He turned his attention to Harris and transformed the small village of Obbe into a busy harbour town, renamed Leverburgh, with a number of ambitious projects for public works. With his death in 1925, enthusiasm dwindled and died and Leverburgh reverted to the sleepy village it is today.

The economy of the two islands is based on crofting, fishing and Harris Tweed, supplemented by increasing investment in tourism. There is still a flourishing network of tweed weavers throughout both Lewis and Harris. Under the Harris Tweed Act, the cloth is only 'Harris Tweed' if it has been handwoven by the islanders in their homes in the islands and finished in the islands, and it must comply with the quality requirements in the regulations which apply to the famous Orb trade mark.

Controversial plans to form huge quarries in the hills for rock infill are under discussion. They could provide much-needed employment but could bring less welcome developments: a rash of unattractive housing estates, a severe threat to fragile road networks, damage to the environment, and disruption of tranquillity.

The islanders speak different Gaelic dialects. Local children are brought up speaking Gaelic at home, but a growing number of 'white settlers' means that English is more and more the language of the playground at school and at social events.

Lewis (*Leodhas*)

> *The Island of Lewis is so call'd from Leog, which in the Irish Language signifies Water, lying on the Surface of the Ground; which is very proper to this Island, because of the great number of fresh-water Lakes that abound in it.*
>
> Martin Martin, writing in 1716.

Lewis has some spectacular prehistoric remains including the 4,000-year-old Standing Stones at Callanish, and 2,000-year-old Carloway Broch. Lord Leverhulme took over the island in 1918, *see* p.271. Perhaps his greatest weakness was to fail to appreciate the inborn pride of the islanders, for whom owning their own land was far more important than wealth. Since the 1843 Disruption the people of Lewis have been staunch members of the Free Church, and nowhere else have the 'Wee Frees' exerted more influence.

Stornoway

Stornoway (*Sternabhagh*), the only town in the Outer Isles, is on the east coast and is where 8,000 of Lewis's population of 20,159 live. It houses the headquarters of the Western Isles Council—*Comhairle nan Eilean*—which struggles to bolster Gaelic culture but which lost £23 million of public money in the early 1990s, having invested in the Bank of Credit and Commerce International before its notorious collapse.

Stornoway is the terminal for Caledonian MacBrayne's ferry service to Ullapool, and its airport links the island with Barra, Inverness, Benbecula and Glasgow. It's a sturdy, unglamorous town with adequate shops for basic needs, a swimming pool, a college, a museum and a small Arts Centre. When Lord Leverhulme was forced to give up his attempts to boost the economy of Lewis, he offered to give the island to the people, having lost a considerable sum of money trying to establish a strong fishing industry, but, much as they valued land ownership, pride forced them to refuse his gift. Stornoway Town Council, however, accepted the land of the Stornoway Parish, including croftland, the town itself, Lews Castle and grounds. The

Stornoway Trust was formed, a unique form of land ownership in the Highlands at the time. It is administered by elected trustees so that the crofters are at the same time their own landlords and tenants of the Stornoway Trust, which is democratically administered by themselves. Unfortunately their track record in managing and improving the land left to them, particularly the policies of Lews Castle, has been deplorable.

The busy harbour, with fishing boats and all the clutter of the waterfront, is the focus of the town, crowned by **Lews Castle** whose once-attractive wooded grounds (*open to the public*) are now devastated by needless neglect. A future use for the castle has been under discussion for some time; meanwhile it lies empty.

The Wreck of the Iolaire

On New Year's Eve 1918 a troop ship, *Iolaire*, left Kyle of Lochalsh with 284 naval ratings on board, returning to their homes on Lewis after the First World War. A gale blew up from the south in the small hours of New Year's Day. The *Iolaire* hit Holm Rock at the entrance to Stornoway harbour and sank; 205 men died, affecting almost every family on the island. Most of the 79 survivors owed their lives to John Macleod who jumped into the sea with a heaving line and swam ashore with it. Anchoring himself to rocks on the beach, he pulled a hawser across from the ship, giving the survivors a hand-hold along which to guide themselves to the beach.

Western Isles Museum—*Museum nan Eilean*—(*open April–Oct Mon–Sat; Sept–Mar Mon–Fri*), at the top of Francis Street, has collections of artefacts, photographs and exhibits of archaeological and historical interest with a focus on the social history of the Western Isles. To get full benefit from the museum you must be prepared to spend time reading the many wall hangings, nicely displayed but rather indigestible if you have limited time. There are plenty of hands-on activities, workshops and Activity Days.

The award-winning **An Lanntair Art Gallery** (*open Mon–Sat*) is in the former Town Hall at the opposite end of Francis Street. Lively and innovative, the gallery has local, national and international exhibitions, event programmes, a café and a small book, craft and souvenir shop. The exhibitions are changed every month; the events range from traditional and classical to jazz and rock, with plenty of emphasis on aspects of Gaelic culture.

Lewis Loom Centre (*open Mon–Sat; adm*), in an old grainstore overlooking the inner harbour in Bayhead, the extension of Cromwell Street, is an excellent place to learn about the Harris Tweed industry. A guided tour taking between 30 and 40 minutes leads you through the traditional methods of carding, spinning, warping and waulking, all by hand, with plant-dyed wools and weaving. There is a shop selling tweeds, jackets, hats, bags, etc.

Beyond Stornoway

About 3 miles south of the town on the edge of **Arnish Moor**, a cairn commemorates the night Prince Charles spent here while trying to negotiate for a boat during his fugitive days after Culloden. When Donald Macleod, one of his three companions, went ahead into Stornoway to make enquiries, he found a number of nervous, armed Mackenzies who had heard that the Prince was arriving with an army of 500 Highlanders.

East of Stornoway, past the airport, a narrow neck of land connects **Point** (*an Rubha*) to the rest of Lewis. It is also called the Eye (or *Ui*) Peninsula, after a Norse word meaning narrow ford or isthmus. The 14th-century **St Columba's Church**, at the western end of Point, is the burial ground of the Macleod chiefs. There are some fine carvings in the church, which was last used in 1828.

North of Stornoway, **Back** (*am Bac*) and **North Tolsta** (*Tolastadh*) have fertile croft land, steep cliffs and large expanses of white beach, unique for the east coast of the Western Isles. At the end of the road is Lord Leverhulme's 'bridge to nowhere', the beginning of the road he hoped to build between Tolsta and Ness to complete the coastal road.

The Butt of Lewis (*Rubha Robhanais*) is a bleak headland on the northern tip of the island, 27 miles from Stornoway by road, topped by a lighthouse. This is a birdwatcher's dreamland: shag, cormorant, puffin, razorbill, guillemot, tern, curlew, kittiwake, fulmar, gull, oystercatcher, plover, redshank and greenshank are just a few of the birds you might see here.

The Ness (*Nis*) district just to the south has a hotel, a tearoom (open in summer only), and a football and social club. There are good beaches here, particularly the one near the harbour at Port Nis. On the road out to the lighthouse, the old *feannagan*, or inappropriately named lazy beds, can be seen clearly, an old and difficult method of agriculture practised throughout the islands until relatively recently and still sometimes in evidence. There was nothing lazy about the hard work that went into digging these strips and fertilizing them with seaweed carted laboriously from the shore in heavy creels.

At **Europie** (*Eoropaidh*), the hamlet southwest of the lighthouse, is the restored 12th-century **St Moluag's Chapel**, known as Teamphull Mholuidh and built on the site of an early Christian chapel. The key for this charming little place is obtainable from the shop. Episcopal services are held occasionally and there is a strong feeling of the simple, uncomplicated faith that keeps such a remote church alive. About 10 miles down the A857, the 20ft (12m) monolith, the **Trushel Stone** (*Clach an Truiseil*), is the largest single stone in Scotland, a relic from prehistoric settlers. There is a primal aura around this site, as there is at the burial cairn within a stone circle surrounded by bleak moorland at **Steinacleit**, about a mile away.

Arnol, about 8 miles further on, has the **Black House Museum** (*open Mon–Sat; adm*) in an authentic, restored black house dating from 1870 and inhabited by a local family until 1964. It is perhaps the best example of its kind, particularly if you can persuade the curator to turn off the electric lighting so that it is seen as it was when occupied. The original furniture, made mostly from driftwood, has been preserved and a peat fire burns all day on the floor in the middle of the main room, with no hole in the roof to allow the smoke to escape. This black house is considerably longer than those seen on other islands, with a large enclosure for animals at one end, a living room and a sizeable bedroom with box beds. There are also extensive store rooms. The double-thickness stone walls are only a few feet high, with an inner cavity of rubble for insulation; the sod and reed-thatched roof, tied with ropes over timber beams, descends to the inner edge of the walls, allowing an external walkway for roof maintenance.

At **Bragar**, little more than a mile beyond Arnol, look for a gateway, set back and at right angles to the road, topped by the massive jaw bone of an 85ft (24½m) blue whale that was washed ashore in the bay in 1920, the harpoon that killed it still embedded in the bone. So impressive was the corpse that a blacksmith in Stornoway was commissioned to create this archway which soon became a landmark.

Shawbost Folk Museum (*Siabost*) in a converted church (*open Mon–Sat; donation box*) is a couple of miles further on and very easy to miss. It stands beside the school and in front of a factory-type building; the windows are covered in corrugated sheeting and a blue sign on the wall looks like a church board until you are close enough to read 'Museum'. Started by local schoolchildren, the museum is a splendidly random collection of artefacts, most of them donated by members of the community. The exhibits are laid out on tables, reminiscent of the white elephant stall at a village fête, with delightfully naive hand-written labels; to the provenance of a 'miner's lamp' remarkably similar to those sold by Habitat in the 1970s, is added the comment that the owner 'had no idea where it came from'.

Don't miss **L for Leather**, just beyond the museum on the same side of the road, a small cottage identified by piles of netting and buoys in the garden and the name painted on the gable end. Pick your way round to the door and discover Kenny Stephen perched in a dentist's chair in a trim, flower-bedecked workshop surrounded by the bags and belts he creates from leather collected from all over the world.

Shawbost Norse Mill and Kiln (*always accessible*) is signed not far beyond Shawbost to the right, with a car park and short walk over a brae. These two small thatched buildings illustrate how barley was processed into meal at a time when this was a crucial part of crofting life. The grain was dried in kilns like the one you see and then milled in the water-driven mill. The buildings were restored with assistance from local schoolchildren who helped to set up the museum.

Between Shawbost and Carloway (*Carlabhagh*) there are two good sheltered beaches at **Dalbeg** (*Dail Beag*) and **Dalmore** (*Dail Mor*), down two turnings off the A857.

In **Carloway**, 5 miles southwest of Shawbost, drive out to the parking place at the end of the Gearrannan road. Just round the corner a cobbled road twists down to a cluster of traditional black houses—the fishing settlement of Gearrannan—restored by the Gearrannan Trust. One is the Gatliff Trust Hostel, pretty basic with a very cosy living room; one is an amenity centre and a third is lived in.

Carloway Broch (*always accessible*), on a small hill signed to the right, a couple of miles beyond the village, is the best-preserved broch in the Hebrides. Its only rival for age and quality of preservation is Mousa Broch in Shetland. Part of its circular double-thickness drystone wall rises to about 30ft (9m), close to its original height, with a honeycomb of galleries and stairs in the cavity. An information board illustrates the probable construction of the makeshift shelters erected inside the enclosure in times of trouble. These 2,000-year-old brochs, of which the ruins of hundreds lie scattered around the coastline of Scotland, are thought to have been built to provide refuge for communities and their animals from invaders. The one small entrance in the tapered structure was easy to defend.

Callanish Standing Stones

Callanish (*Calanais*) Standing Stones (*always accessible*) are well signed, about 6 miles south of Carloway overlooking Loch Roag. A path leads up from the car park to the stones and, unlike at Stonehenge, there are no restrictions to access through a gate in the surrounding fence, although visitors are encouraged to look at the stones from an encircling path. Erected about 4,000 years ago, they rank in importance with Stonehenge, and form one of the most complete prehistoric sites in Britain.

The 47 surviving stones are said to depict a Celtic wheel-cross (not easy to define) with a burial cairn at the centre, approached from the north and south by avenues of pillars. Traces of cremated bones were found in the cairn. The central pillar casts its shadow along the entrance passage into the grave only at sunset on the days of the equinox. As with other standing stones, speculation about their purpose favours some sort of astrological observatory and they are also thought to be linked to rituals that included human sacrifice. This dramatic place conjures up in the imagination the burial of some priest-king with elaborate pre-Christian ceremony and ghostly figures flitting among the monoliths; whatever their true function, the atmosphere here is primal.

Beyond the car park, a mini **Museum and Visitor Centre** (*open Mon–Sat; adm*) has an audio-visual show and displays of information about the site. There is a scant, predictable souvenir shop and a café where you can get filling meals and excellent home-made soup. The fairly recently opened building is carefully designed to be out of sight from the stones. Very modern in concept, it is rather like a child's kit-construction of a jumbo-sized 'traditional' island dwelling.

Far more atmospheric and very easy to miss, because the tourist signs point you to the Historic Scotland-owned Visitor Centre, is a converted **Black House Café** and gift shop diagonally opposite the stones. You can reach it on foot from the main car park, having viewed the stones, or drive round to it on a badly signed road about half a mile north of the main turning. Inside the authentic-looking building there is a cosy tea-room with home baking, and quite expensive tweedy and woollen garments and craft-type souvenirs.

On a clear day the **Flannan Islands Lighthouse** can be seen 15 miles to the west. On 15 December 1900 a passing ship signalled to Oban that the Flannan light wasn't working. A supply boat was already on its way there, on a routine trip, but was delayed for a further 11 days by storm. By the time it arrived, all three of the lighthouse-keepers had vanished without trace. As in the *Marie Celeste*, a meal was laid on the table; nothing except an overturned chair indicated alarm. Many stories were subsequently concocted, each worthy of a gripping Alastair Maclean adventure, but the truth will never be known.

After Callanish the B8011 branches southwest at **Garynahine** (*Gearraidh Na H-Aibhne*) for **Great Bernera** (*Bearnaraigh*) and **Uig**. The island of Bernera is reached by a 'bridge over the Atlantic' built in 1953. The men of Bernera were agitators in the period leading to the 1886 crofters' revolt, when they marched with their grievances to the landlord, Sir James Matheson, in his castle in Stornoway. **Bosta Beach** on the northern tip is well worth a visit. Go on down the B8011 and explore the district around Uig which has some of the most beautiful scenery in the islands. The famous **Lewis Chessmen**, made of walrus ivory, were dug up (by a cow they say) in 1831 in the sands of **Ardroil** (*Eadar Dha Fhadhail*) a few miles south of Gallan Head. Of 12th-century Norse origin, they are thought to have been buried here by nuns living in a Benedictine convent at Brenish at the end of the road, to save them from theft by invaders. Replicas can be bought all over the islands. The original chessmen are divided between the British Museum and the Scottish National Museum.

This is grand walking country—along the coast to the Uig Hills and south to the hills of Harris. Heading south from Stornoway the road runs through the 'Lochs' area, and a detour east on the B8060 leads down to Lemreway (*Leumrabhagh*). The land is split by deep sea lochs and many lochans surrounded by heathery hills.

moderate

The Royal Hotel, ✆ 702 109, 🖷 702 142, is probably the best hotel in Stornoway. Otherwise book into the comfortable and very friendly **Hebridean Guest House**, ✆ 702 268, overlooking the golf course at Bayhead. **Park Guesthouse**, in James Street, ✆ 702 485, is another nice place to stay, with excellent food.

One of the nicest places to stay on Lewis is **Baile-Na-Cille**, ✆ 672 242, at Timsgarry overlooking Uig Sands. Richard and Joanna Gollin offer easy, friendly hospitality in their converted 18th-century manse. Set menu dinners of good home cooking are served at communal tables where guests quickly make friends and swap adventures. Helpings are generous (the soups are meals in themselves), and one seldom has room for the cheese and fruit. Family pets lie on favourite chairs, homework is struggled with at the centre of activity, and sheep are sternly repulsed from Richard's proposed tennis court.

Eshcol Guest House, Callanish, ✆ 621 357, is on the west side of the island with superb views and the standing stones in the background. Highly recommended for its food, friendliness and dependability. **Doune Braes Hotel**, Carloway, ✆ 643 252, 🖷 643 435, also on the west side, always provides a warm welcome, and the staff are helpful with their local knowledge.

Galson Farm Guest House, South Galson, ✆ 850 492, is a restored 18th-century farm house with sea views and a warm welcome. They also have an excellent bunkhouse. Alternatively try **Angus and Catherine MacIver**, Whitehaven, Loch Street, Barvas, ✆ 840 253; or **Mrs C. Mackay**, Blackburn, 109 Newmarket, Stornoway, ✆ 705 232, where you will get a truly Hebridean welcome and (in the latter) a good breakfast.

For B&B, try **Mrs Margaret Fraser**, Seaside Villa, Back, ✆ 820 208, overlooking the picturesque bay with a sandy beach, this cosy little cottage serves up excellent home-cooking. *Open Mar–Oct.*

For self-catering, the **Garenin Residential Blackhouse**, 3 Garenin, near Carloway, is a converted thatched blackhouse, sleeping up to 16, with wonderful Atlantic views.

Tigh Mealros, ✆ 621 333, at Garynahine, is a very good eating place with excellent seafood. BYOB. **The Copper Kettle**, ✆ 710 592, an all-day eatery at Dalbeg, signed off the main road, is part tea-room with home-baked goodies and part restaurant. This unexpected haven serves up very good food and it is wise to book for evening meals. Sunsets are spectacular from here.

Harris (*Na Hearadh*)

The boundary between Harris and Lewis runs between Loch Resort and Loch Seaforth with Harris itself being further split into north and south by the narrow isthmus at Tarbert, between West and East Loch Tarbert. This relatively small 'island' contains a kaleidoscopic variety of scenery: mountains, moorland, lunar rockscapes, sandy beaches and, on the southeast coast, myriad rocky or sandy inlets backed by heather-strewn crags.

History

The early history of Harris, with a population today of about 2,200 people, is similar to that of Lewis until it was given a separate identity in Norse times when the one landmass was divided between two Macleod sons. The Macleods held Harris for 500 years, subservient to the Lords of the Isles, with fewer battles for supremacy than were fought in Lewis. Around the time of the 1745 Rising, the chief, Norman Macleod, bankrupt by gambling and improvidence, raised the rents of his impoverished tenants. The probability of mass emigration was deflected by his grandson, General Norman Macleod, who inherited the property in 1772 together with a vast debt, and sold it to his kinsman Captain Alexander Macleod in 1779.

Captain Alexander was an enlightened landlord. He promoted the fishing industry, improving existing facilities and building more; he imported east coast fishermen to teach the islanders, lent money for boats and equipment, and provided cottages and land, rent free. He established a spinning factory, built a school and an inn, and constructed roads. In 1834 his grandson sold Harris to the Earl of Dunmore who, in 1868, sold North Harris to the Scotts.

The Earl's mother, the Dowager Countess of Dunmore, is said to have been the founder of the Harris Tweed industry. She bought a length of the island-created tweed in 1842 and was so delighted with it that she introduced it to her aristocratic friends. Within a short time Harris Tweed was the 'in' thing for sportsmen, their wives and gamekeepers all over the country.

When Lord Leverhulme, who had bought Lewis and Harris in 1918, pulled out of Lewis in 1923 he concentrated his energies on Harris. He started to develop Obbe as a fishing station, renaming it Leverburgh, bought a Norwegian whaling station at Bunavoneadar, built a spinning mill and started on an ambitious road-building programme. Although his schemes had far more support from the islanders than they had had in Lewis, none flourished and they died with him in 1925. The estates and various developments were subsequently sold for a fraction of the amount Leverhulme had invested in them. Today, Harris' economy, like that of Lewis, is based on crofting, fishing, tweed and, increasingly, tourism.

Visiting the Island

Tarbert (*An Tairbeart*) is the main village, at the head of East Loch Tarbert, with the Tourist Information Centre, a few shops—mostly souvenirs—and the ferry port linking Harris with Uig on Skye and Lochmaddy on North Uist. It is an attractive, down-to-earth place; a good base for fishermen in pursuit of salmon, sea trout and trout, and for sea fishing too.

Scalpay (*Scalpaigh*), the island at the entrance to East Loch Tarbert, was where the fugitive Prince Charles stayed for four days with his three companions, as guests of the tenant Donald Campbell, hoping to arrange a boat from Stornoway. It was here that the only recorded attempt was made to betray the Prince for the £30,000 reward offered for his capture, by Aulay Macaulay who was minister in Harris. Donald Campbell's house stood where the Free Church Manse stands today.

The footpath east from the Tarbert–Scalpay road was until recently the only access by land to the small village of Rhenigidale (*Reinigeadal*). The new road down from Maaruig makes life easier for this small community.

When weather permits, boat cruises run from Tarbert to the **Shiant Islands**, 12 miles to the east, wild and cliff-lined with a natural sea-arch and a huge colony of puffins as well as other sea birds. Compton Mackenzie did some of his writing here. The Shiants are overrun by a colony of black rats, virtually extinct elsewhere.

The road to Stornoway from Tarbert runs through heather-carpeted rocky hills sliced by burns, and bleak moorland. The B887 goes west off the A859 to **Bunavoneadar** (*Bun Abhainn Eadarra*), where you can see the remains of the Norwegian whaling station which Lord Leverhulme tried unsuccessfully to regenerate. All that is left is the tall, red chimney from the oil-extraction plant and a few desolate ruins. Whales were plentiful in these waters but, as with Gavin Maxwell and his shark fishery on Soay, there were insurmountable problems: isolation from a capricious market, lack of processing and preserving facilities, hazardous weather and fishing-grounds and a dwindling demand for whale products.

About 8 miles further on, salmon jostle in the sea waiting to jump up the falls where **Loch Leosaidh** disgorges down a series of rock slabs into the sea below **Amhuinnsuidhe Castle** (difficult to pronounce—approximately 'Aven-soyr' or 'Aven-soy-rr'). If you are lucky you will see the fish making their heroic leaps from pool to pool, against almost impossible odds, in their journey to their spawning grounds. The road runs right past the front door of the castle just beyond the falls; understandably the owners are trying to get it diverted. Amhuinnsuidhe is a Victorian shooting lodge built in 1868 for the Earl of Dunmore; today it is a private home and is not open to the public. Writer James Barrie began his novel *Mary Rose* here.

There is a lovely walk starting up the track to the power station just before you come down to the salmon leap and castle. Park at the power station and walk up the track to the dam, round the reservoir and the loch beyond into a dramatic 'hidden' glen.

Hushinish (*Huisinis*), another 6 miles on from the castle, has a sheltered sandy beach at the head of the bay. The island of **Scarp**, a massive lump of sheer rock north of Hushinish Point, is best known as the proposed recipient of a very advanced method of postal delivery in 1934—the dream-child of the German rocket scientist Gerhardt Zucher. Mail and emergency medicines were to be fired at it in a rocket. A special stamp was issued, coveted by philatelists, and the first rocket was launched, loaded with 30,000 letters. Alas, it exploded, as rockets tend to, destroying the mail and the dream.

The east coast route down South Harris, called the Golden Road, is a tortuous single track through a bleak, stony landscape enhanced by wonderful remote rocky inlets and the clustered cottages of small communities. Tiny parcels of land were painstakingly cultivated and nurtured here by people evicted from the fertile west coast, expected to try and make a living from fishing. Many of their descendants are weavers and, around **Plocrapool** (*Plocrabol*), there are a number of places where you can watch them weaving Harris Tweed on looms in their houses. A good one to visit, where you can buy reasonably priced tweed and woollens, is run by the Campbell family, signed off the road in Plocrapool. They usually have a good stock of sweaters, socks and stockings, as well as wonderful tweeds.

St Clement's Church, at Rodel (*Roghadal*), on the northern headland of Loch Rodel (*always accessible*) is the finest pre-Reformation church in the Western Isles, its cruciform design thought to have been influenced by that of Iona Abbey. The present building, probably built on the site of a former church, dates from the mid 16th century. With the coming of the Reformation soon after its completion, it was in fact hardly used for worship. Frequently restored, most recently in 1873, it is now being repaired by Historic Scotland, though some of the walls and the greater part of the tower are original. You can climb to the top of the tower on a series of stairs and ladders. Of the two medieval tombs inside, the most magnificent is that of Alasdair Crottach, the Macleod chief from Dunvegan who entertained James V on MacLeod's Tables (*see* p.260) and died in 1548. A pointed surround and a recessed arch behind the recumbent stone effigy are decorated with elaborate carvings, unrivalled in the Hebrides. These depict the Macleod coat of arms, a birlinn (galley), animals and various saints and religious scenes. Walk round the outside to the east face of the tower. There is a worn carving of St Clement above the window and below him, to the right, a *sheila-na-gig*—a 'fallen angel' woman with flowing hair and skirts lifted to display her private parts, a common device originating from Ireland, thought to distract the evil spirits that followed worshippers into church. Most unfortunately some hideous public lavatories have slipped past the watchful eye of conservationists and landed up just below this otherwise wonderful building.

The attractive, secluded 18th-century harbour at Rodel is overlooked by various derelict buildings including the **Rodel Hotel**, closed, dilapidated and almost beyond renovation, with a notice on the wall recording a visit by Queen Elizabeth II in 1956. The house was built by Captain Alexander Macleod in 1785 when he returned rich from India and bought Harris. He built the harbour and established a fishing station here with ancillary buildings, as part of his plan to develop the potential of the island. In an attached, unprepossessing Victorian extension, there is a bar which still opens regularly and in which you will find a truly Hebridean atmosphere. The imminent ruin of the Rodel Hotel and the lack of concern for its historic setting is one of the tragedies of the Outer Isles.

Leverburgh

Leverburgh (*An T-ob/Tob*), on the south coast about 3 miles northwest of Rodel, was developed from the small settlement of Obbe by Lord Leverhulme after his plans for Stornoway had collapsed. He put a great deal of money into improving the harbour, building a large pier, houses, kippering sheds, roads and lighthouses. But he died a year after the local fishing industry began to flourish and with him died the drive and energy needed to keep things going. It isn't much of a place to linger in: a few rather dismal souvenir shops, a café above the general store which opens too late for arrivals off the first ferry wanting breakfast, and closes too early for passengers waiting for the last boat off the island. (The car ferry from here to North Uist and Berneray only has slot-machine beverages and chocolates; if you arrive in Leverburgh on the first boat you will be lucky if you find anyone serving breakfast south of Tarbert.)

Wonderful sandy beaches fringe the west coast, including **Luskintyre Beach** (*Losgaintir*), one of the most beautiful you could ever hope to find, sheltered and empty against a backdrop of hills. It looks out westwards to the island of **Taransay**, inhabited until 1974 and currently the base for a laughable experiment organized by the BBC, whereby a random mix of volunteers live there for a year (2000) to see if they can be self-sufficient. At the time of writing they have already proved themselves to be unworthy. Park at the end of the road and walk on round the dunes to the north.

Harris ✆ (01859–) ***Where to Stay***

expensive

Scarista House, ✆ 550 238, is a Georgian manse just off the road at Scarista, a comfortable guest house with peat fires, antique furniture, a good library, and a reputation endorsed by those who go back for a second stay. Non-residents can eat here (must book) and the set-menu dinner is excellent with an extensive wine list. They also have self-catering accommodation in the grounds. No chance of a drop-in breakfast off the ferry from North Uist.

Ardvourlie Castle, ✆ 502 307, on the northwest shore of Loch Seaforth, about 11 miles north of Tarbert on the A859, was a Victorian shooting lodge and is now a guest house owned by the Martins, who will make you very welcome. Deceptively gaunt in appearance, it has period furnishings and marvellous ancestral bathrooms. The atmosphere is relaxing and friendly and people return time and again. The restored library has a grand piano, and the dining room, with place settings that include beautiful glass, is lit by gas and oil lamps.

expensive–moderate

The Harris Hotel, in Tarbert, ✆ 502 154, 🖷 502 281, is large by island standards, sprawling and easy-going. Not all the 26 bedrooms are en suite but it is cosy and welcoming and the staff are prepared to put themselves out for you if you arrive at inconvenient times (e.g. off the early ferry from North Uist wanting a late breakfast). **Leachin House**, just along the north shore of West Loch Tarbert, ✆/🖷 502 157, is a comfortable and welcoming Victorian house run as a Wolsey Lodge. The food is superb.

moderate

Carminish Guest House, Strond, Leverburgh, ✆ 520 400, is a modern house in a fine situation with views over the Carminish Islands and the Sound of Harris. This is a good base from which to explore the glorious southwestern corner of Harris. Good food, friendly owners and smokers' lounge.

cheap

Allan Cottage Guest House, Tarbert, ✆ 502 146, is a splendid place, once the Harris telephone exchange, now renovated and transformed into a cosy guest house with very good food.

For a really good B&B, try **Mrs Flora Morrison**, Tigh na Mara, at East Tarbert, ✆ 502 270, who has a modern house with lovely views, spotlessly clean, 5 minutes' walk from the ferry. Flora gives her guests every attention and is proud of her home baking and hearty meals. **Mrs Corinne Miller**, Minchview House, Tarbert, ✆ 502 140, runs a friendly B&B with views from each room across the Minch to Skye. *Open April–Oct.* Or try **Mrs Christina Morrison**, Dunard, Tarbert, ✆ 502 340/502 493, in a 19th-century house where you will get 21st-century comfort and a great welcome.

Am Bothan Bunkhouse, Leverburgh, ✆ 520 251, is a bunkhouse with a difference, with its own very special brand of hospitality. There's a dormitory with futons, family bunkrooms, cosy living rooms and plenty of atmospere, as well as views over the Sound of Harris.

For self-catering try **Angus Macleod**, Tarbert, ✆ 502 364, who runs 4 well-equipped cottages overlooking Tarbert and East Loch Larbert (sleeping 4–6); or **Mrs Margaret Mackay**, 4 West Tarbert, ✆ 502 361, whose cottage overlooks the sea (sleeping 5).

First Fruits Tearoom, in Tarbert by the pier, does excellent teas.

Berneray (*Eilean Bhearnaraigh*)

This small, peaceful island lies to the south of Harris, just off the northern shore of North Uist, accessible by car ferry from Leverburgh in Harris and by a new causeway from Otternish in North Uist. About 8 miles in circumference with a population of about 130, engaged mainly in crofting, lobster fishing and knitting, it is low-lying with 3 miles of sandy beach on the west coast. The name comes from the Norse: *Bjorn's Isle*. At **Ruisgarry**, a group of surviving traditional thatched houses have been designated a conservation area. For some years this was the favoured retreat of the Prince of Wales who came here to play at crofting.

Berneray✆ (01876–) ***Where to Stay***

Donald MacKillip, Burnside Croft, ✆ 540 235, does B&B and will share his crofting activities if desired. **Mrs MacAskill**, Morven, ✆ 540 230, has a modern, well-equipped croft house overlooking the sea, sleeping 8 for self-catering.

North Uist (*Uibhist a Tuath*)

The island of North Uist, between Harris and Benbecula (to which it is linked by a causeway), is about 17 miles long and 13 miles wide. It encompasses a great deal of water—so much so that half the total area is submerged. Wild peat moors and myriad lochs and lochans cover the island's eastern side and centre, while to the north and west there is farm land, with some splendid sandy beaches. Loch Eport almost cuts the island in two from the east. Of the few, insignificant hills, Eaval is the highest at 1,138ft (347m), a wedge shape, dominant over its low-lying surroundings. Grimsay is the tidal island in the southeast, linked to both North Uist and Benbecula by causeway and a centre for the fishing industry, mainly lobster.

Getting There

The main village in North Uist is Lochmaddy, the terminal for car ferries from Uig in Skye and Tarbert in Harris. A car ferry also runs from Newtonferry (Otternish) to Leverburgh in Harris. Balivanich Airport across the causeway in Benbecula provides an air link with Glasgow, Stornoway and Barra.

Tourist Information

Lochmaddy: Pier Road, ✆ (01876) 500 321. *Open early April–mid Oct.*

History

As with the other islands, prehistoric remains tell of ancient settlers, and the Nordic colonists bequeathed many Norse place names—Uist is derived from the Norse *I-vist*, an abode or indwelling. The Macdonalds of Sleat, descendants of Somerled, held the island from 1495 until 1855. The early 19th-century kelp boom encouraged more settlers than the poor land could support; by the time the market slumped the population had risen to 5,000. This slump, and the subsequent clearance of the land by Lord Macdonald to make way for more lucrative sheep, forced over 1,000 islanders from their lands and caused violent confrontation between crofters and the police.

The population is now about 1,800, with an economy based on crofting and fishing—mainly for shell-fish—fish farming, tweed, knitwear and tourism. The island is as firmly Presbyterian as its northern neighbours, in contrast to the strong Catholicism of the south.

Lochmaddy

Lochmaddy (*Loch na Madadh*) is the island port, a sprawling village with a sheltered harbour, busy when the boats come in. Some say the three rocks at the harbour entrance look like crouching dogs—the port's name comes from the Gaelic for dog, *madadh*—but you need a good imagination to see it. There is a new **Museum and Arts Centre** (*open Mon–Sat; adm*), near the pier in the former inn, Taigh Chearsabhagh, with exhibitions of local history and activity workshops, a shop and café. The court house, hospital, church, a few shops, and a bank make up most of the rest of the village. The **Tourist Information Centre** is beside the harbour. Walk out to the 'Sea-Sky' chamber at Sponish, close by. In a small stone beehive there is an intriguing camera obscura giving a fresh look at the sea and sky (*always accessible*).

Around the Island

A road circles the island through a series of crofting and fishing townships. Peat bogs flank the road with rows of neatly stacked peat bricks waiting to be transported to the houses. Travelling anti-clockwise, about 3 miles west of Lochmaddy there are three standing stones on the slope of **Blashaval** (*Blathaisbhal*). These are the 'Three False Men', said to be three men from Skye who were turned to stone by a witch as punishment for deserting their wives; another explanation is that they represent three spies who were caught and buried alive.

Five miles west of Lochmaddy, a small road goes north to **Newton Ferry** (*Port Nan Long*). In a loch on the right of this road just before its end, is a well-preserved fortress, **Dun-an-Sticir**, reached by a causeway and occupied as late as 1601 by Hugh Macdonald, descendant of the Macdonalds of Sleat.

Back on the circular road, **Eilean-an-Tighe** is a rocky islet in Loch-nan-Geireann, 2 miles west. It was the site of a Neolithic potters' workshop, the oldest to be excavated in western Europe. The pottery found here was of a very high quality, better than that of later times, and there was so much of it that the factory must have supplied a large area.

In **Sollas** (*Solas*), 3 miles west, a medieval settlement is being excavated. This district was the scene of one of the episodes of the Clearances. In 1849 Lord Macdonald, 4th Baron of the Isles, was faced with debts of around £200,000. Among other schemes to find money to pay off his creditors he decided to evict some 600 crofters from the overcrowded, uneconomic area around Sollas and rent the land to sheep farmers from the south. Since the potato famine in 1846 the people had been living well below subsistence level, but they loved their land and resisted eviction physically. There were some unfortunate and much publicized skirmishes with the Sheriff's officers and the police. Eventually the crofters were forced to give in, but for various reasons there was a three-year delay before they were shipped off to Canada—in a frigate carrying smallpox germs below decks.

Vallay (*Bhalaigh*), pronounced Varlie, is a tidal island at the entrance to a wide shallow bay running north and west from Sollas. What was once a large Edwardian house stands sadly crumbling above the sand, a resting place only for birds and dead animals. There are also the remains of an earlier house and outbuildings as well as a litter of antiquities—duns, standing stones and chapel ruins. You can walk out to Vallay at low tide but watch out for the flood tide; it fills the channels fast, cutting off the unwary. The road south across the moor from here is called the Committee Road, built in the 19th century as a famine relief scheme, to provide a short cut to the west coast.

Scolpaig Tower, on a small island in a loch just off the road about 3 miles to the west, is a 'folly' built in the 19th century from the ruins of a dun. At **Hosta**, about 4 miles on round the coast, a footpath leads 2 miles east across the moor to a chambered cairn on **Clettraval**, built when birchwood copses grew here. Later, an Iron Age fort was built over it, and pottery excavated here was found to be the same as that made in the workshop at Eilean-an-Tighe.

At **Balranald** (*Baile Raghaill*), stretching out to the most westerly tip of the island at **Aird an Runair**, there is an RSPB reserve, supporting one of the highest densities of breeding waders in Britain. Altogether 183 species of bird have been recorded on the reserve. Visitors are asked to report to the RSPB cottage on arrival.

Unival is a hill north of the road, 6 miles southeast of Huna. Walk across the moor up its eastern flank, on the west side of Loch Huna, to a chambered burial cairn with a small cist. A couple of miles further down, the road forks south to the right and northeast to the left. The left-hand road completes the circuit of the island and takes in two of its best treasures.

Pobull Fhinn

Two miles along this road back to Lochmaddy, a track to the right is signposted to Langass Lodge Hotel. Park at the hotel and take the footpath up behind it, a 10-minute walk up through heather, bracken and bog-myrtle. On the hillside is an oval of standing stones—Pobull Fhinn, Finn's People. This is a memorable prehistoric site, its mysticism enhanced by its remoteness. In such a place, hundreds of years before Christ, an annual ritual might have included the ceremonial sacrifice of the 'king'.

Barpa Langass

Less than a mile northeast on the main road, on the shoulder of **Ben Langass**, Barpa Langass is a large mound of stones shaped like a squashed beehive, obviously man-made. This well-preserved chambered burial cairn is the tomb of a chieftain, thought to date from about 1000 BC. Visitors are asked not to crawl through the tunnel into the cairn, both for their own safety and for the preservation of the site. Great stone slabs line the interior and there are traces of where other cells may have led off the main chamber.

From here it is about 6 miles on to Lochmaddy to complete the circuit of the island. Going back southwest to the fork, **Carinish** (*Carinis*), where there are some interesting remains, is 2 miles down the road to the south.

Teampull-na-Trionaid (Trinity Temple) is a ruin on top of a knoll on the Carinish promontory at the southern end of the island. A large building with a detached side chapel reached by a vaulted passage, this church was founded by Beathag (Beatrice), daughter of Somerled, Lord of the Isles, in about 1203 on the site of an earlier church, and was regarded as an important seat of learning for priests in medieval times, similar to the one on Iona. There are interesting grave stones here.

The last battle to be fought in Scotland using just swords and bows and arrows was the Battle of Carinish, in 1601 between the Macdonalds of Uist and the Macleods of Harris. The cause of the battle appears to have been the insulting behaviour of one of the Macdonalds, who divorced his Macleod wife and sent her home. The Macleods descended on Carinish in a frenzy of rage and all but two of them were killed in the battle that ensued. **Feith-na-Fala** (The Field of Blood) marks the site of the battle, just north of the Carinish Inn.

Sports and Activities

Uist Outdoor Centre, on the outskirts of Lochmaddy, ✆ (01876) 500 480, is an adventure training establishment where groups or individuals can enjoy sub-aqua diving, watersports of all kinds, climbing, walking, wildlife watching, environmental and field studies. The accommodation is in bunk rooms, with 2 bath/shower rooms for 20 people.

North Uist ✆ (01876–) ***Where to Stay***

moderate

Lochmaddy Hotel, ✆ 500 331, 🖷 500 210, is a comfortable, old-established fishing hotel, traditional and friendly, with good food. **Langass Lodge Hotel**, ✆ 580 285, 🖷 580 385, is a converted shooting lodge overlooking Loch Langass, a cosy, remote and peaceful haven (recently done up), with first-class food, especially the seafood.

Sealladh Traigh, Claddach Kirkibost, ✆ 580 248, is a modern guest house overlooking the sea, with good home cooking and a warm welcome from Mr and Mrs Quarm. **Carinish Inn**, Carinish, ✆ 580 673, is modern and comfortable.

cheap

Stag Lodge, Lochmaddy, ✆ 500 364, is another friendly guest house which is comfortable and handy for the ferry. **Temple View Hotel**, also at Carinish, ✆ 580 676, 🖷 580 682, is a traditional, hospitable island house.

For self catering, **Mrs MacDonald**, ✆ 510 342, has a big modern house near the reserve, sleeping 15. **Angus Dingwall**, Smithy Croft, Lochmaddy, ✆ 500 391, has a modernized holiday cottage with nice views, sleeping 4–6. **Peter and Morag Murray**, Bayhead, ✆ 510 379, have a house which sleeps 4. **Alasdair Seale**, ✆ (0131) 447 9911, has a house which sleeps 6–7.

For B&B try **Mrs Alina Morrison**, Old Bank House, Lochmaddy, ✆ 500 275/324, overlooking the ferry terminal; or **Mrs Sandra MacIntosh**, 1 Grenitote, Sollas, ✆ 560 288, 10 minutes from the Otternish ferry amidst miles of sandy beaches and sea views; or **Mrs Norma Shepherd**, Struan House, Sollas, ✆ 560 282, who has a modern house with more glorious views, and 4 star treatment.

Benbecula (*Beinn Na Faoghla*)

Benbecula, its name derived from the Gaelic *beinn a'bhfaodhla*—mountain of the fords—is about 5 miles long by 8 miles wide, linked to the south of North Uist by a succession of causeways, built in 1960. The low-tide route across North Ford by foot is dangerous for those who don't know the path; locals tell hair-raising stories of lost travellers and quick-sands. Rocky bays and inlets surround the causeway, washed by the ever-changing tides. The 'mountain' is

Rueval, a rounded hillock only 409ft (126m) high, giving a good view of the otherwise flat, waterlogged island. To the west there is fertile machair and sandy beaches, some of which seem to trap more than their share of rotting seaweed. The main road cuts through the middle, with minor roads off to the east, and a circular road runs round the west coast to the airport at **Balivanich**, with air links to Glasgow, Stornoway and Barra.

The population of about 1,800 is dominated by army personnel and their dependants, who are stationed at Balivanich to work on the missile range in South Uist. This army base, considerably reduced these days, has provided a boost to the economy and, ugly though it is, will be sadly missed if it is ever closed. The Presbyterianism of the north and the Catholicism of the south meet in Benbecula in roughly equal strength, and without animosity.

The history of the island is that of its neighbours, recorded in a few prehistoric remains and predominantly Norse place-names. It was part of the patrimony of the Macdonalds of Clanranald from the 13th century until 1839 when they were forced to sell their lands to pay impatient creditors. Colonel Gordon of Cluny bought the island, together with South Uist, Eriskay and Barra, and his family owned it for just over a hundred years, during which time hundreds were ruthlessly cleared from their homes and sent abroad to places like Nova Scotia. The northern part of the island was then sold to the Air Ministry and the remainder to a London businessman.

At **Nunton**, 2 miles south of Balivanich, there is a ruined 14th-century chapel which belonged to a nunnery whose inmates were brutally massacred when the building was destroyed during the Reformation. Stones from the nunnery are said to have been used to build the large farmhouse by the road, the 18th-century former home of the Macdonalds of Clanranald, Nunton. This L-plan building, with a pavilion on each side of its courtyard entrance, succeeded Ormiclate Castle on South Uist as Clanranald's residence after the Benbecula branch of these Macdonalds inherited the chieftainship. **Borve Castle**, a gaunt ruined keep near the road 4 miles south of Balivanich, was another Clanranald stronghold and scene of many a bloody skirmish. The scant remains of the castle chapel can still be seen nearby. This was a centre for Gaelic culture in the 15th and 16th centuries.

In 1988 a new secondary school and community centre was built at **Liniclate** (*Lionacleit*) on the southern end of the island. It is an impressive place with a swimming pool, sports facilities, restaurant, library and museum, serving children throughout the islands, some of whom previously had to board on the mainland for their education. Open to the public, one of the rare bones of contention between Presbyterians and Catholics was over its Sunday opening. There is a restaurant, andf good *céilidhs* and events in the theatre in the summer.

Wiay (*Fuidhaigh Wiay*), an island off the southeast tip of Benbecula, is a bird sanctuary for a variety of wild-fowl including snipe, duck, geese and swans.

It was from **Rossinish** on Benbecula's northeast corner that Prince Charles sailed 'over the sea to Skye' disguised as gawky Betty Burke, the servant of Flora Macdonald.

Shopping and Activities

D. MacGillivray and Co, at Balivanich, ✆ (01870) 602 525, opposite the high, cone-shaped water tank at the airport, is well worth a visit. Inside an unpretentious building is an Aladdin's cave of tweed and woollen products, usually including some fantastic bargains, as well as an excellent selection of books, both new and second-hand. It's the sort of place you pop into for a quick look and stagger out a little while later laden with parcels.

There is a 9-hole golf course, a mile north of Balivanich on the B892.

Benbecula ✆ (01870–) ***Where to Stay and Eating Out***

The hotels and guest houses are all inexpensive and friendly with not much to put between them in standard. Try the **Dark Island Hotel**, at Liniclate, ✆ 603 030, 🖷 602 347; or **Creagorry Hotel**, at Creagorry, ✆ 602 024, 603 108, where the public bar is a popular meeting place for locals.

Mrs Gretta Campbell, 5 Torlum, ✆ 603 235, will give you a warm welcome in her guest house. **Mrs Emma MacDonald**, ✆ 602 965, has a splendid B&B at Muir of Aird, and will do dinner.

For self-catering, **Mrs Esther MacDonald**, ✆ 602 536, has a traditional thatched croft house at Gramsdale, sleeping 2–4. **Mrs Morag Macintosh**, ✆ 602 239, has a well-equipped, modernized house overlooking South Ford, sleeping 8.

Stepping Stones, ✆ 603 377, at Balivanich, is a restaurant/café, run by chef brothers Ewan and Alan Maclean, who make the most of local ingredients, especially fish.

South Uist (*Uibhist a Deas*)

A straight causeway links Benbecula with South Uist, less than half a mile across South Ford. At low tide here there is usually at least one figure stooped over the sand, scooping up the cockles that lurk just below the surface. There is a knack to this: you look for the tiny holes and dig in fast—a kitchen spoon is the best tool.

South Uist is about 20 miles long and 8 miles wide at its widest point—a land area of 141 square miles, with hills and long sea lochs to the east, silvery shell-sand and machair to the west, with peat bog and moorland in between, studded by more than 190 freshwater lochs with excellent trout and sea-trout fishing. Beinn Mhor, less than halfway down in the east, is the highest peak at 2,034ft (626m).

The island suffered badly from the Clearances in the 19th century, in the hands of Colonel Gordon of Cluny, who bought it in 1838, along with Benbecula, Eriskay and Barra, from the Macdonalds of Clanranald who, after the failure of the kelp industry, had squandered what was left of their patrimony in riotous living in the south. Between 1841 and 1861 the population fell from 7,300 to 5,300 as townships were cleared for sheep; many islanders emigrated to North America.

The present population of about 2,200 live in crofting townships scattered throughout the island, linked by a network of one-track lanes radiating from the main, north–south road which varies from single track to short stretches of EEC-funded double-track carriageway. These random lengths of fast highway terminate abruptly, often without obvious warning, and can be extremely dangerous. Since the middle of the 20th century the economy has been dominated by the army missile range on the northwestern corner of the island, the closure of which is periodically discussed. Other sources of income include crofting, fishing—mainly for lobsters and crabs—fish-farming and seaweed, as well as maintenance of public services and building.

A roadside shrine to the Virgin Mary, just south of the causeway from Benbecula, is a reminder that you have left the Presbyterian north and are on the threshold of the Catholic south. The first road to the east, a mile south of the causeway, goes out 2 miles to **Loch Carnan**, a beautiful fjord-type sea loch with a pier for large boats.

Three miles to the south, the main road becomes a causeway and crosses **Loch Bee**, one of the largest swan reserves in Britain. The area of marshland to the east is a nature reserve, the breeding ground of many wildfowl including greylag geese. The hill to the left, just south of Loch Bee, is another named Rueval, crested by a futuristic contraption which is an army range head. Rocket targets can sometimes be seen off the west coast and the muffled bang of firing can be heard. Rising from the western slope of Rueval, seen clearly from the road, is a simple statue of **Our Lady of the Isles**, carved from white granite by Hew Lorimer. The clean-cut purity of the Madonna, holding her child high on her shoulder, enshrines the deep faith that exists in these islands. It was erected in 1957 by the local community.

The next road east, a mile south, runs 4 miles out to **Loch Skipport** (*Loch Sgioport*), another fjord-like sea loch where there is a deep-water anchorage, a salmon farm and the skeleton of a pier which used to be the principal ferry stop for the island. The **Loch Druidibeg National Nature Reserve**, just to the south, provides an ideal habitat for many species of waterfowl.

Less than 2 miles further south on the main road, beyond the road west to Drimisdale (*Dreumasdal*), there is a small loch with an island and a ruined castle. A submerged causeway runs out to the island. Beware! Some of its wobbly stones have been known to topple the unwary into the dark peaty water of the loch. The ruin was once **Caisteal Bheagram**, a 16th-century keep that was, in its heyday, a Clanranald stronghold. Some years ago the present Captain of Clanranald tried to map out the original layout of the castle and discovered that its foundations cover almost all the island.

A mile south, a side road runs west a mile to **Howmore** (*Tobha Mor*), the most important religious site in the Outer Hebrides, with a history that goes back over a thousand years to the dawn of Christianity in the Western Isles. There was probably a monastery and a collegiate church here in medieval times. Substantial fragments of two churches, dedicated to Mary and Columba, and three chapels survive. The *Book of Clanranald*, compiled by the MacMhuirichs, the hereditary poets and genealogists to the Clanranalds, records that several members of the ruling family of Clanranald were buried here between 1500 and 1700, and a number of grave stones and wheel-cross monuments adorn the enclosure (some modern). One of the surviving chapels is called *Caibeal Chlann 'ic Ailean*—Clanranald's Chapel—built in 1574 for the Clanranald chief, Iain Muideartach, who 'left funds to erect a chapel at Howmore where his body was buried'. It was from this chapel that the Clanranald Stone disappeared in 1990, a heavy armorial panel bearing the arms of Clanranald. Because the islanders don't fence off or lock up their historic treasures, this 16th-century stone was lying on the ground near the ruins and was stolen by two young men who coveted it for their London flat. Five years later one of the young men died, some say cursed by the removal of the stone, and his father discovered it propped up in his son's living room. Sensing its importance he contacted the British Museum, who contacted the National Museum of Scotland in Edinburgh. Amidst great rejoicing the stone was returned in June 1995, not to Howmore but to the small museum at Kildonan (*see* below) where it is now protected from thieves, vandals and the elements. The symbols depicted on the stone are: a birlinn (galley), a fist holding a Celtic cross, a castle, a lion rampant and a bird on a thistle. A network of one-track roads and tracks west of the main road meander through the machair, linking small townships and isolated dwellings. Some of the tracks lead across dunes to the beach.

Ormiclate Castle (*Ormacleit*) (*always accessible*), a couple of miles or so to the south of Howmore, between the main road and the sea, is a roofless shell attached to a later farmhouse, now restored. Farm cottages and buildings, some derelict, surround the ruin. The castle, finished in 1704, was built by Allan Macdonald of Clanranald, whose wife Penelope had spurned their humble dwelling, declaring that 'even her father's hens were better housed'. Only eleven years later, in 1715, Ormiclate was accidentally burnt down, on the eve of the Battle of Sheriffmuir in which the chief was killed (*see* Castle Tioram, p.123).

Hecla, 1,988ft (606m), and **Beinn Mhor**, 2,034ft (620m), rise to the east of the main road, from which they can be approached over a wasteland of bog. The summits can be dangerous in high winds, especially the sharp serrated edge of Beinn Mhor, with vertiginous drops off the east side. East of Hecla is **Usinish lighthouse**, no longer manned. When the writer Gavin Maxwell was trying to make a go of shark fishing, the lighthouse keeper here was an enthusiastic informant as to when there were sharks in the area. Usinish was one of the places where they used to congregate in large numbers. **Nicolson's Leap**, just south of Usinish Point, is said to be the place where a Nicolson leapt the 50ft (15m) chasm on to the rock stack, escaping revenge from a Clanranald chief. Having been found in bed with Clanranald's wife, Nicolson took their baby son as a hostage. He tried to bargain from the top of the stack and when he failed to do a deal, he leapt into the sea, still holding the baby in his arms. So they say.

To the south, **Loch Eynort** (*Loch Aineoirt*) is another sea loch. Martin Martin writes: 'it reaches several Miles Westward, having a narrow Entry, which makes a violent current, and within this Entry there's a Rock, upon which there was staved to pieces a Frigot of Cromwell's, which he sent there to subdue the Natives.' This is a good starting point for walks over the remote moorland between Lochs Eynort and Skipport. Beinn Mhor can also be reached from here, as can Glen Corodale, about 4 miles northeast of the end of the road. This wild country north of Loch Eynort, among the hills and glens surrounding Beinn Mhor and Hecla, was where Prince Charles took refuge for a while in a shieling, hiding in a cave when discovery seemed likely. The cave is not the one marked on the map, easily visible above a group of ruined houses by a burn. The true one is difficult to find, up on the rock face. This whole area is only accessible on foot or by boat.

Bornish, west of the main road about a mile south of the Loch Eynort turning, is a straggle of dwellings with a church. Gaunt and rectangular on the outside, this charming church has a raw, unfaced stone interior with a large crucifix against a rich red cloth behind the altar as the focal point. A homely lady chapel with a lace backdrop, simple stations of the cross and the steady, ruby glow of the sanctuary lamp give a warm, lived-in feeling. The road runs out west to **Rubha Ardvule**, surrounded by slabs of flat rock—a good viewpoint, particularly during Atlantic gales. Archaeologists are excavating the dun you can see to the left.

Kildonan Museum (*open June–Sept daily; adm*), beside the main road a couple of miles to the south, has been restored, with a Lottery grant and public subscription. Housed within an extension of the old Kildonan school, the museum contains displays ranging from archaeological finds to crafts, local artefacts, photographs and history. A café and some attractive landscaping enhance this imaginative project. The archaeological department of Sheffield University has been working on the island for many years and the results of their research will become a frequently updated feature of the museum.

Half a mile south, a road west is signed to Milton (*Gearraidh Bhailteas*) where a cairn marks **Flora Macdonald's birthplace** (she was born in 1722). Flora's father was a Clanranald tacksman. She was tending her brother's cattle at a shieling about 3 miles from here when the Prince was brought to her in need of help.

Askernish (*Aisgernis*), a mile south, has a nine-hole golf course on the machair where players dodge sheep and plovers' nests among the dunes. The South Uist Games take place on the golf course in July, usually followed by a dance or a concert in the church hall. Everyone on the island turns out for the games, where, as well as piping, dancing and all the traditional sports, there are jovial gatherings of spectators among the parked cars and in the beer tent.

Daliburgh (*Dalabrog*) is a village on the crossroads west of Lochboisdale. There are three shops (general stores) and a post office, a small hospital, an old people's home and the Borrodale Hotel. A road to the west leads to the Catholic parish church of St Peter's, a large, simple building dating from the 1860s, weathered and unadorned, the priest's house attached. This is the living heart of the island, filled to capacity for Sunday Mass and well attended throughout the week, as indeed are the other churches that support it to the north and south. The Church of Scotland kirk and manse stand prominently on the crossroads. Northwest of St Peter's lies what must be one of the most beautiful, remote burial grounds in the country, on the edge of the machair overlooking the Atlantic.

The road east from Daliburgh goes 3 miles to the 'port' of **Lochboisdale** (*Loch Baghasdail*), with an excellent tourist information centre, hotel, bank, police station and harbour. A row of newly constructed shops await proprietors. The village is at its busiest when the Caledonian MacBrayne ferries are arriving or departing, turning the quay into a bustling place with a babble of Gaelic voices. A few visiting yachts anchor in the two small bays either side of the pier in the summer. Looming over Loch Boisdale's northern shore is Ben Kenneth (*Beinn Ruigh Choinnich*). There is a challenging race to its summit every year for the young men of the area, who may take whichever route they choose.

A mile south of Daliburgh, a small road runs about 2 miles west to Kilpheder (*Cille Pheadair*), from where a track leads out to the machair to an Iron Age Pictish wheel house. This communal dwelling with a central hearth, from which cells radiate like the spokes of a wheel, had elaborate drainage systems and storage places sunken deep into the floor.

Two miles south of Daliburgh, a road runs east for 2 miles through **South Lochboisdale** (*Taobh A Deas Loch Baghasdail*). From the parking bay at the end of the road, a map is needed to follow a faint track over hills and moor, along Lochs Kerrsinish, Marulaig and Moreef, a total of 5 miles southwest to Bun Struth, a loch joined to the sea by a narrow passage of sheer rock, surrounded by hills. It is inaccessible except by boat or on foot, inhabited only by sheep, birds and the ghosts of the people who once lived in the now-ruined croft houses that lie scattered over the area. When the tide is out, the loch is higher than the sea, draining over a shelf of rock in the entrance passage, marooning boats until the next tide, which swirls in through the passage, fast and tricky to navigate. Golden eagles can sometimes be seen, gliding on the air currents above the hills to the north of Loch Marulaig.

All this southeastern foot of the island is good walking country; sheep-tracks serve as paths and the best route must be chosen by careful observation of the boggy terrain ahead. Views from the summits of the hills are spectacular; on a clear day you can see Ardnamurchan Point on the mainland as well as Skye and the Small Isles, Barra and Eriskay. When Skye looks so close you could almost touch it, and when its rocks glint, it usually means rain.

The road out to the west, opposite that to South Lochboisdale, leads to a white shell-sand beach with the gloomy remains of a once-flourishing seaweed factory. A few years ago any islander could cut seaweed—a laborious job—and sell it to this factory, where it was processed into alginates for use in a large number of products ranging from soap to beer and cosmetics. Now, any seaweed that is harvested is collected in lorries and shipped to factories on the mainland. If you see a small boat chugging at snail's pace through the water with a vast, dark patch behind it, it is towing a floating island of seaweed, contained within a long rope, to the nearest beach from which it will be lifted. The white beach runs for miles in great sweeps of sand where keen eyes will spot tiny pink cowrie shells. The wide fringe of machair is famous for its carpet of wild flowers in the summer.

Opposite the seaweed factory there is a small conical island called **Orosay**, accessible at low tide, with good views. In westerly gales, spray has been known to break over its top.

The road south climbs to the modern wedge-shaped church at **Garrynamonie** (*Gearraidh Na Monadh*), built in 1963 and rather bizarre in its setting. Its stations of the cross were designed by a priest from Barra, Father Calum McNeil, and it has an enamelled mosaic behind the side altar. Here, as in the other churches, you can hear Mass in Gaelic. Opposite the church is the old school, now disused. This is where Fredrick Rea, a young Englishman, was sent as head-master at the end of the 19th century, the first Catholic schoolmaster since the suppression of Catholicism. He spoke no Gaelic. The students acted as his interpreters and each child arrived at school carrying peat for the fire, often having walked several miles in bare feet. His recently reprinted book, *A School in South Uist,* tells of his life here.

Ludag is a couple of miles east along the south coast and ferries run from the pier here to Eriskay (cars) and Barra (passengers only). A sandy bay beyond, at South Glendale, dries out at low tide, and the sheltered, turf-covered rocks around make it an excellent picnic spot. Southeast of Glendale, along the rocky shore and below the water, lies part of the wreck of the *Politician*, imortalized as the *Cabinet Minister* by Compton Mackenzie in his book *Whisky Galore.* The true story was only slightly embroidered in the novel. The ship was carrying 20,000 cases of whisky to America in 1941 at a time when whisky was scarce in the islands. Magnetic minerals in the rocks distorted the compass readings and she went off course, riding over Hartamul, the rock at the entrance to the Sound of Eriskay and finishing up against the cliff. The islanders made a valiant attempt to 'rescue' the whisky, thwarted by the bureaucracy of the Customs and Excise Department, and not a few families still own a much-valued 'Polly Bottle'. Stories are still told, with a twinkle and a knowing shake of the head, of animals reeling down the road, and of bottles dug up on the machair that had been buried for years. Recently one of the bottles went up for auction and fetched nearly £100.

South Uist is littered with places where Prince Charles is said to have sheltered. He certainly hid for a time in the jagged ruined castle on Calvay Island, at the entrance to Loch Boisdale, clearly seen from the ferry.

Shopping

At Iochdar, near the causeway to Benbecula, there is a **jewellery** workshop and gift shop with wrought-silver craft work, pottery, books and the usual range of gifts. Should you have an urgent need for a passport photograph, they also provide this service. **Salar Fish Farm Shop and Smokehouse**, on Loch Carnan, ✆ (01870) 610 324, sells delicious smoked salmon and more. Good for presents.

South Uist ✆ (01878–)

Where to Stay

moderate–cheap

Lochboisdale Hotel, ✆ 700 332, 🖷 700 367, stands in a prominent position overlooking the harbour, a Victorian fishing hotel, very much in that character still, with some appreciated concessions to modernity. With extensive fishing rights it has long been popular with anglers, the results of whose endeavours are displayed in the entrance porch. Groups of them gather before dinner in the lounge bar and discuss the dimensions of 'one that got away'. It has comfortable bedrooms and excellent food.

The **Pollachar Inn** (*Pol A Charra*), ✆ 700 215, is 5 miles south of Daliburgh, overlooking one of the most beautiful views in Scotland. Much of the character of the old Hebridean bar, once a favourite haunt for locals, was lost when the building was enlarged and altered, but the hotel offers comfortable, inexpensive accommodation. You can sit outside and enjoy your drink overlooking an ancient standing stone and the Sound of Eriskay, across to the hills of Barra.

Orasay Inn, near Loch Carnan, ✆ (01870) 610 298, 🖷 610 390, is small, modern and comfortable, with good food, and special rates for longer stays. **Anglers Retreat**, Iochdar, ✆ (01870) 610 325, is a small, modern B&B on a croft, catering especially for fishermen, birdwatchers and hillwalkers. It is inexpensive and friendly, and they do dinner. *Open Mar–Dec.* **Borrodale Hotel**, ✆ 700 444, 🖷 700 446, opposite the kirk at the hub of Daliburgh, is busy and cheerful, with 12 of its 14 rooms en suite. It will arrange free golf, and is a good place to hear live Scottish music from local or visiting musicians. *Open all year.*

Clan Ranald, ✆ 700 263 is a comfortable guest house at Garryhallie, just north of Daliburgh, where you can be sure of a warm welcome from Mr and Mrs MacDonald. **The Shieling**, almost next door, ✆ 700 504, run by Mrs Katie Peteranna, is a bit cheaper and equally friendly and cosy.

Mrs Flora MacInnes, Sealladh Mara, in South Lochboisdale, ✆ 700 580, has one of the best B&B houses on the island. It overlooks the loch, is comfortable, very reasonable and exudes warm hospitality.

Tobha Mor, Howmore (Gatliff Trust), is a newly renovated black house, run by the SYHA, sleeping 17. No telephone, no bookings: just turn up.

Eriskay (*Eiriosgaigh*)

From the Norse *Eiriks-ey*—Eric's Island—Eriskay is a mere 2½ by 1½ miles in size with a community of about 200, largely Catholic. It shares its history with the other Hebridean islands, the MacNeils of Barra owning it until 1758 when they sold it to the Macdonalds of

Clanranald. When Colonel Gordon of Cluny bought it in 1838, with South Uist, Barra and Benbecula, he offered some of the Uist crofters holdings in Eriskay where the land was too poor even for sheep. With the choice between this meagre allotment and emigration, many of them chose the former and managed to subsist on scant crops and potatoes grown in lazy beds. The economy is based on fishing and crofting. Eriskay ponies are the last survivors of a small, native Scottish breed used to carry seaweed and peat, and are sadly almost extinct. The island has invented its own unique pattern for hand-knitted sweaters.

A car ferry runs from Ludag in South Uist but as the road is a scant 2 miles long it is hardly worth taking a car. The ferry crosses the mile-wide sound to **Haun** (*Haunn*), a smiling village of white cottages with roofs of bright blue, pink, green and red, sheltered by hills. St Michael's Church, perched high above the harbour, is the heart of the island, built in 1903 by Father Allan MacDonald, who wrote down the folklore and many of the songs of the Hebrides, and was a distinguished poet and scholar. The plinth of the altar is the prow of a lifeboat, the focal point for a community whose existence has always been influenced by the sea. The ship's bell outside the church was rescued from the *Derflinger*, one of the German fleet that sank in Scapa Flow in 1919. There is a village shop, a primary school and a post office. There is also **Am Politician** at Baile, ✆ (01878) 720 246, the only bar on the island, which serves good seafood meals; named after the Whisky Galore ship.

Just beyond the village on the western shore there is a crescent of sand called Prince Charlie's Bay. This was where the prince landed from France on 23 July 1745 and where he spent his first night on Scottish soil. The black house he stayed in was pulled down in 1902. Its smoky interior drove him out into the fresh air several times during the night. It was a simple place like the others of its kind, with cupboard beds, hens running over the earthen floor and wooden trunks holding the family possessions. The pink convolvulus called Prince Charlie's rose, in the machair round the bay, is said to have been introduced here from a seed dropped from his shoe, though it can now be found elsewhere on the mainland. Ben Scrien is the highest hill—610ft (186m).

The Stack Islands lie just off the southern tip of Eriskay, only accessible by boat; there is a rocky creek on the east side of the main island that offers safe shelter in calm weather. From here it is a scramble up the precipitous cliff to the Weaver's Castle at the top. A notorious Macneil lived here, much feared as a wrecker and pirate. He built the castle as a stronghold, and stole a girl from a shieling in South Uist to be his wife and the mother of a large number of sure-footed children.

Where to Stay

Mrs Marion Campbell, ✆ (01878) 720 274/720 236, has a chalet with two bedrooms, sleeping 4, for self catering.

Barra (*Barraigh*)

Barra, 4 miles south of South Uist at the nearest point, is partly fringed by a number of smaller islands, including Vatersay, Sandray, Parbay and Mingulay to its south, all of which were once inhabited. Eight miles long by 4–5 miles wide, Barra is encircled by a 12-mile road with an arm running north to the airport and Scurrival Point. It has a predominantly Catholic population of about 1,300.

Beaches and machair, croftland and a hilly interior make up this compact haven of an island, which took its name from St Barr (Finbarr) of Cork who converted its people to Christianity. The seascapes have inspired many artists, writers and musicians. The history of the island echoes that of the other islands, told by its prehistoric remains, Norse names and a medieval castle. When it was bought by Colonel Gordon of Cluny in 1838, he offered to sell it to the government as a penal colony. His offer was turned down. Later, the Clearances led to massive emigration.

No one arriving in the ferry forgets their first sight of **Castlebay** (*Bagh A Chaisteil*). **Kisimul Castle** (*open May–Sept Wed all day and Sat pm; adm; check with the tourist office*) stands on a rock in the middle of the harbour. Some claim that it dates from 1060 and is one of Scotland's oldest castles, but there is no firm evidence that it existed before the 15th century. It is a splendid sight in any weather, but most romantic when silhouetted against a half-dark sky on a summer night. The Macneils acquired the castle as a reward for fighting with Robert the Bruce at Bannockburn. The clan was famous for its lawlessness, piracy and arrogance. A clansman from Barra is said to have declared, 'The reason there was no Macneil on Noah's Ark is that the Macneil had a boat of his own.' Traditionally, a Macneil clansman used to scale the tower daily and proclaim: 'Macneil has dined: Kings, Princes and others of the earth may now dine.' Martin Martin tried to gain admittance to the castle during his visit to Barra but the Macneil and his wife were away and their retainers refused to let him in, being 'very apprehensive of some Design I might have in viewing the Fort, and thereby to expose it to the Conquest of a foreign Power; of which I suppos'e there was no great cause of fear.'

Kisimul was virtually destroyed by fire at the end of the 18th century and remained in ruins until the 45th Macneil chief, returning from his adopted homeland in America in 1937, bought it and restored it to its present condition.

Neat shops and houses line the road that climbs from the harbour in Castlebay, overlooked by Heaval, Barra's highest hill—1,260ft (388m). High on Heaval's southern shoulder stands a statue of the Blessed Virgin, her child on her shoulder, holding a star. This sculpture was carved from Carrara marble and erected in 1954 to celebrate the Marian Year, and in memory of the 58 men from Barra who died in the Second World War, mostly in the Atlantic convoys. This and the large church, Our Lady, Star of the Sea, which also overlooks Castlebay, are symbols of the deep faith of the people of these islands.

Martin Martin had another disappointment when he tried to see a wooden statue of St Barr, kept on the altar of one of the churches. The locals hid it whenever he tried to view it, 'lest I might take occasion to ridicule their Superstition, as some Protestants have done formerly'.

The Isle of **Vatersay** (*Bhatarsaigh*), just off the south coast of Barra, has a population of about 70. Until 1990 cattle destined for the market had to swim across the Sound of Vatersay to meet the ferry in Barra, but when a prize bull, Bernie, was drowned in 1986, the ensuing outcry forced the Government's hand and a long-awaited causeway was built. The other islands, now uninhabited, are only accessible by private boat.

Going clockwise 2 miles west from Castlebay, the standing stones beside the road past the Isle of Barra Hotel are said to mark the grave of a Norse pirate. **Dun Bharpa** is a large chambered cairn surrounded by standing stones, on the eastern side of Beinn Mhartainn, reached from the end of the road through Craigston.

On the eastern side of the peninsula at the north end of the island, the 2 square miles of white cockle-shell strand is **Traigh Mhor**, where the plane comes droning in like a bumble-bee, to touch down on the firm sand when the tide permits. The house overlooking this impressive strand was the home of Compton Mackenzie, the writer who settled in Barra in 1928 and caught the spirit of the Hebrides more perceptively than most. He attracted a lively community of writers and Gaelic scholars when he lived here and is buried in the graveyard at Eoligarry (*Eolaigearraidh*), just to the north. Here among the ruins of a chapel are burial slabs said to have arrived from Iona as ballast in an ancient galley.

Another well-known name can be seen in the cemetery; that of John MacPherson, better known to lovers of Gaeldom as 'The Coddy', who died here on his native island in 1955. *Tales from Barra*, recorded in both Gaelic and English, and recently republished, is a collection of folk tales told by the Coddy in his inimitable voice—a delight for exiled Scots all over the world. A grassy mound is all that remains of Eoligarry House, a three-storey Georgian house built by the Macneils after Kisimul Castle burned down in 1795. It was a substantial ruin until not so long ago.

Boats run from Castlebay in the summer (✆ (01871) 810 223) to the island of **Mingulay**, deserted since 1912 but enchanting, with a sandy beach and sad ruins, including a graveyard. The famous Mingulay Boat Song—a *céilidh* favourite—tells of the women waiting at the harbour 'since break of day' for their fishermen who never return.

Barra ✆ (01871–) ***Where to Stay***

moderate

In Castlebay, **Castlebay Hotel**, ✆ 810 223, 🖷 810 455, and the slightly smaller **Craigard Hotel**, ✆ 810 200, 🖷 810 726, are good value and comfortable. You will get a great taste of Hebridean hospitality wherever you stay. The **Isle of Barra Hotel**, Tangasdale Beach, ✆ 810 383, 🖷 810 385, is modern, and has a glorious setting on the beach, but it somehow lacks the local atmosphere of its neighbours in Castlebay.

One of the nicest guest houses in Castlebay is **Tigh-Na-Mara**, ✆ 810 304, 2-minutes' walk from the ferry. (*Tigh-Na-Mara* means house-by-the-sea.) It has 5 en-suite bedrooms with a TV and tea-making facilities in each, and lots of pictures on the walls of the Prince of Wales who actually paid Mrs Maclean a visit here a few years ago.

For self-catering, try **Mrs Mary Flora MacLeod**, ✆ 890 384, who has two well-equipped modern houses at Bruernish, Northbay, each sleeping 4–8; or **Mrs Diana Savory**, Northbay House, Balnabodach, ✆ 890 255, sleeping 4 in a former school.

For B&B try **Mrs Anne MacNeil**, Grianamul, Castlebay, ✆ 810 416, near the ferry terminal, where you will be well looked after.

St Kilda

St Kilda, consisting of four islands and a few great rock stacks, is the most westerly of the British Isles apart from Rockall. This lonely archipelago is owned by the National Trust for Scotland and partly occupied by a small detachment of gunners who man a missile-tracking station, with a nature reserve managed by Scottish Natural Heritage.

There are a number of cruises to St Kilda but passengers are only able to land when weather permits, which isn't very often. The best approach is via the NTS, ✆ (01631) 570 000, who may be able to arrange for you to join a working party. Private yachts are frequently unable to find safe shelter for long enough to anchor and go ashore.

Hirta

The main island, on which the people used to live, is called Hirta, possibly derived from the old Norse for shepherd—*hirt*. The origin of the name St Kilda is disputed—there was no saint of that name. Kilda may have come from Hirta, which the islanders actually pronounced Hilta.

Essential reading for anyone planning a visit is *The Life and Death of St Kilda* by Tom Steel, and *An Island called Hirta* by Mary Harman. Recent archaeological work uncovered an ancient stone building thought to date from the Bronze Age, and it is thought that further research may reveal occupation for up to 3,500 years. There is the site of a pre-Viking settlement at Glen Bay but no written record until a visit by Dean Monro in 1549, who described 'a simple, poor people, scarse learnit in aney religion'. 150 years later Martin Martin wrote of a population 'happier than the generality of mankind, as being the almost only people in the world who feel the swetness of true liberty'. He spoke too soon: subsequent history is one of decline brought about by isolation in a world increasingly obsessed by centralization and conformity. A small, patriarchal, strongly Presbyterian society subsisted, paying rent to their landlords, the Macleods of Harris and Dunvegan, with meat, feathers and oil from seabirds. (Martin Martin calculated that 180 islanders ate about 226,000 birds each year.) Pulpit-thumping ministers held them in an iron grip, regulating their lives and driving them to the kirk on pain of everlasting damnation, often to the detriment of essential work on the land. They were frequently cut off by storms. Except for 1727, when a smallpox epidemic increased the death rate, the population of about 200 in the 18th and 19th centuries remained fairly constant, kept in check by puerperal fever. The men were the Parliament, meeting daily to discuss the day's work, often using up precious daylight hours in their lengthy debate.

In 1834 the first tourist boat landed on Hirta. The introduction of money and visitors from the 'sophisticated' mainland reduced the islanders' self-reliance and made them dissatisfied: many of the younger ones left to seek their fortunes on the mainland. In 1930 the few remaining able-bodied members of the community, attracted by the lure of the outside world and dragged down by continuous hardship, persuaded the older ones to evacuate to the mainland.

Some of the houses at Village Bay have been preserved, as have their cleits—beehive-shaped cells of rough stone that served as larders and storerooms. The careful design of these cleits allowed air and wind to circulate inside and preserve the meat of the sea birds; it also kept clothes and gear dry.

A visit to this gale-torn outpost fills one with a curious melancholy, that a community could have existed here for so long, beset by worries, and then ultimately sail away and abandon its roots forever.

Orkney 299
Mainland Orkney 300
Kirkwall 300
Islands South of the Mainland 305
Islands North of the Mainland 307
Shetland 311
Mainland 314
Fair Isle 320

The Northern Isles

Although separated by 60 miles or so of wild ocean, and very different in character, Orkney and Shetland have a common history and tend to be bracketed together. Norsemen called them the 'Nordereys'. Orkney, on foundations of old red sandstone, has fertile farmland, while Shetland has poorer soil and relies on the sea for its economy. The poet Hugh MacDiarmid wrote: 'It is indeed impossible to eke out a decent living in Shetland by crofting alone. That is the difference between Orkney and Shetland: the Orcadian is a farmer with a boat, the Shetlander is a fisherman with a croft.'

Both groups—about 70 Orkney islands and 100 Shetland islands—were inhabited in the Stone Age. The Picts colonized them in the 1st century AD and were subjected to continual harassment from the Vikings for centuries, until the Norse King Harold Harfagri annexed them in 875. When Harold succeeded to the throne of Norway in about 860, large parts of his kingdom didn't recognize the authority of the Crown. Harold was in love with a Princess Gyda, daughter of one of the rebel 'kings', and she refused to marry him until he had conquered all Norway. He vowed that he would not cut his hair or his beard until he had done this. He claimed his bride 10 years later.

All the dispossessed jarls, or minor kings, took refuge in Orkney and Shetland and proceeded to harass Norway with wild Viking raids. King Harold, exasperated, collected up a fleet and sailed down to put an end to their antics. He landed at what is now Haraldswick in Unst, Shetland, and declared all the islands to be a 'Jarldom'. The Norse occupation of these islands is recorded in romantic, stirring sagas, handed down over the centuries. The Orkneyinga Saga is one of the best known.

By the 13th century, although still ultimately under Norse rule, the islands were presided over by Scots earls. It wasn't until Princess Margaret of Norway and Denmark became betrothed to James III of Scotland in 1468, that her father, King Christian I, pledged the islands to Scotland as part of her dowry. They were formally annexed in 1472 and ever since then they have been part of Scotland.

Norse place names still predominate, and the people of these northern islands are a blend of Norse and Scots, very different in character to the dreamy Celts of the Hebrides. They are extremely friendly, extrovert and stolid, industrious and mainly Presbyterian.

Their accent is singsong; the old 'Norn' language (partly old Norse, partly Icelandic) disappeared during the 18th century although some phrases have remained, and when the islanders talk among themselves they use many words more akin to Norwegian than English.

The coming of the oil boom struck hard at established roots, bringing innovations that were not always popular, and making Shetland relatively rich compared to the rest of Scotland. On the whole, however, the islanders have managed to retain their old way of life and things have settled down.

Orkney

Orkney lies 6 miles off the north coast of Scotland, separated from the mainland by the Pentland Firth with its notoriously treacherous fast tides. On the same latitude as St Petersburg, the island group extends 53 miles from north to south and about 23 miles from west to east. Oslo is closer than London. Nineteen of the 70 islands are inhabited. Orkney means 'seal islands', the *ey* being Norse for islands: no one talks of 'the Orkneys', just Orkney. First impressions are of emerald green plateaux of turf above sheer rock cliffs and sandy beaches washed by sparkling sea; fertile farmland with large farmhouses, many producing Orkney cheese, and more cattle than sheep. Inland there is less of the lush farmland and more wild heathland. Apart from Hoy, nothing is higher than 900ft (278m). A great dome of clear sky sheds an ethereal greenish light, and sunsets in May and June are fantastic; at midsummer the sun is above the horizon for 18 hours and it is possible to read a book outside all night. This midsummer twilight is called 'Grimlins' from the Norse word *grimla*, to glimmer or twinkle.

Birdwatching is almost compulsive. One in six of all seabirds breeding in Britain nests in Orkney. The long-eared owl is an endearing resident; its 'ears' are elongated feathers and have nothing to do with hearing; its low, moaning hoot is an eerie sound at night. There are short-eared owls, which hunt by day over the moors; red-throated divers, so graceful until they come on to land; razorbills with their fascinating courtship displays and refusal to build nests; puffins, whose brightly coloured bills are a weapon and a spade with which to dig their burrows.

For **botanists** the wild flowers are a joy: tiny *Primula scotica*, a survivor from the last Ice Age; grass of Parnassus, whose honey-scented white flowers litter the marshland; bog pimpernel, oysterplant, bog asphodel and many, many more. For general **naturalists** there is the unique Orkney vole to look out for, a sweet little round ball of fur. There are otters—Kirkwall must be just about the only town to display a red triangular road sign reading: 'Otters Crossing 100yds'.

Fishermen leave Orkney with enough fishing stories to keep them happy till they return. Brown trout are the best in Britain and fishing is free, thanks to Norse law. Sea angling is also good. **Watersports** enthusiasts will find perfect waters for **sub-aqua** diving, especially wreck-diving around Scapa Flow. For **archaeologists** there are more prehistoric remains than anywhere else in Scotland, some in a remarkable state of preservation: brochs, standing stones, burial cairns—an average of three sites per square mile.

It is beyond the scope of this book to describe each of the many hundreds of historic sites and antiquities that pepper Orkney: we have included a very small selection. The Orkney Tourist Board in Kirkwall has a good selection of guides, including *The Orkney Guide Book*, *The History of Orkney*, and *Ancient Monuments of Orkney*, as well as booklets on specific sites.

Getting There

P&O Scottish Ferries, ✆ (01856) 850 655, run from Aberdeen to Stromness, taking 8hrs, and must be booked in advance. They also run from Scrabster to Stromness, taking 1hr 45 mins; this route should also be booked in advance. Ferries run from Stromness on to Shetland departing once a week and taking 8hrs. They produce a brochure detailing special offers.

John o' Groats Ferries, ✆ (01955) 611 353, take 40–45 mins from John o' Groats to Burwick on South Ronaldsay, passengers and bicycles only (*1 May–30 Sept daily*).

British Regional Airways operates the route from Aberdeen to Orkney, and **Loganair** operates all the others (from Edinburgh, Glasgow, Inverness and Wick), with connections from London, Birmingham and Manchester. There is also a service from Shetland to Orkney (*Mon–Sat*). There are no flights to Orkney on Sundays. There is a short 'Airbridge' flight from Wick to Kirkwall and inter-island services; ✆ (01856) 872 494. (The shortest flight, between Westray and Papa Westray, takes only a minute in good conditions.)

There are **rail** links to Thurso, by Scrabster, from all over the country, to connect with ferries, or to Aberdeen or Wick to connect with flights/ferries. Call national rail enquiries: ✆ 0345 484 950.

Scottish Citylink, ✆ 0990 505 050, have coaches to the various ferries and airports from all major UK cities, sometimes with overnight stops in Glasgow, Edinburgh or Inverness. The **Orkney bus**, ✆ (01955) 611 353, links Inverness and Kirkwall, via the John o' Groats ferry (*1 May–7 Sept daily*).

Tourist Information

Orkney Tourist Board: 6 Broad Street, Kirkwall KW15 1NX, ✆ (01856) 872 856.

Mainland Orkney

When an Orcadian talks of the Mainland, he means Mainland Orkney—the big island. (The mainland of Scotland is 'the sooth'.)

Kirkwall

Kirkwall is the capital of Orkney and one of the earliest established Norse trading towns. It is referred to in *The Orkneyinga Saga* as Kirkjuvagr—Church-bay-of-the-Vikings—indicating that the Norsemen found an Early Christian church here when they arrived. It is an ideal centre from which to explore these fascinating islands.

The Ba' Game

Kirkwall has its own unique 'Ba' Game' dating from Norse times, loosely described as football. It is played on Christmas Day and New Year's Day, between the 'trsuppies' and 'trsdoonies' and often involves as many as 150 men from either end of the town. If the ball finishes up in the harbour it is victory for the 'trsuppies'; if it reaches the goal at the old castle, then the 'trsdoonies' win. The game can last all day.

St Magnus Cathedral (*open Mon–Sat; only open for worship on Sun*) dominates the town, though it is not in fact as large as its clever proportions suggest. This cruciform building, founded in 1137, was built up of alternating stripes of local red sandstone and yellow stone and looks more continental than Scottish. St Magnus, who was murdered in 1116 and whose canonization may have been more political than spiritual, was the uncle of Jarl Rognvald Kilson, the founder of the cathedral. The bones of both these men now lie beneath the columns of the central bay of the choir. They were discovered during repair work in the 20th century, hidden in chests. The cathedral has been carefully restored; the rose window is

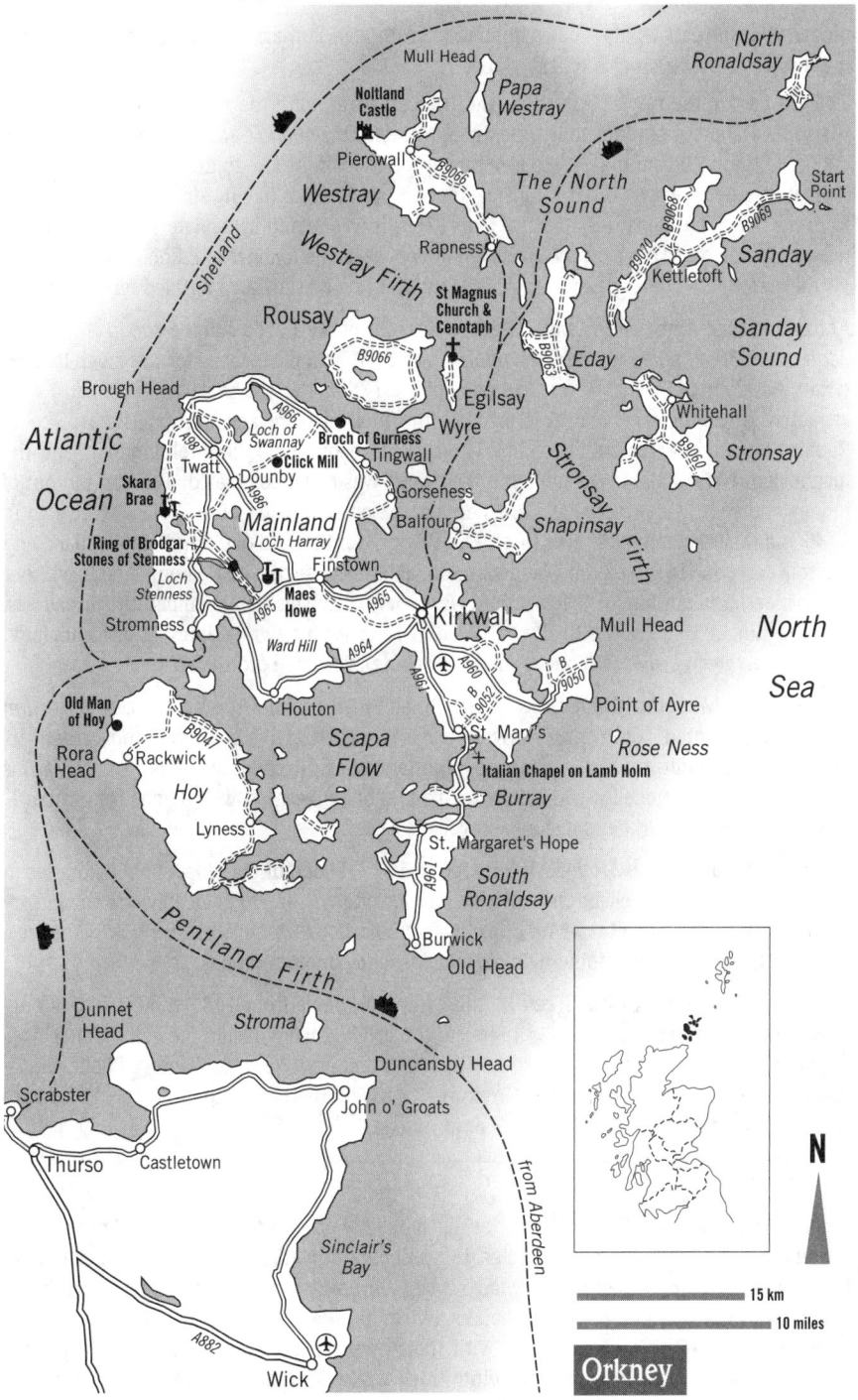
North Ronaldsay
Mull Head
Papa Westray
Noltland Castle
Pierowall
B9066
Westray
The North Sound
Start Point
B9068
B9069
B9070
Sanday
Kettletoft
Shetland
Westray Firth
Rapness
St Magnus Church & Cenotaph
Rousay
B9066
B9063
Eday
Sanday Sound
Brough Head
Egilsay
Whitehall
Atlantic Ocean
A966
Loch of Swannay
Broch of Gurness
Wyre
B9050
Stronsay
A987
Click Mill
Tingwall
Twatt
Stronsay Firth
Skara Brae
Dounby
A986
Gorseness
Mainland
Balfour
Shapinsay
Ring of Brodgar
Stones of Stenness
Loch Harray
Finstown
Loch Stenness
Maes Howe
A965
Kirkwall
Stromness
Mull Head
North Sea
Ward Hill
A964
A960
B9052
B9050
Point of Ayre
Houton
Old Man of Hoy
St. Mary's
Rose Ness
B9047
Rora Head
Rackwick
Scapa Flow
Italian Chapel on Lamb Holm
Hoy
Burray
Lyness
St. Margaret's Hope
A961
South Ronaldsay
Pentland Firth
Burwick
Old Head
Dunnet Head
Stroma
Duncansby Head
Scrabster
John o' Groats
Thurso
Castletown
from Aberdeen
Sinclair's Bay
A882
Wick
N
15 km
10 miles
Orkney

modern but the east window dates from 1511. Although St Magnus is still called a cathedral, the services are Church of Scotland.

The old part of the town clusters around the cathedral, with the ruin of the 12th-century **Bishop's Palace** next door to it (*open daily except Fri pm and Sat in winter; adm*). It was built for Bishop William the Old, to give him accommodation close to the splendid new cathedral. It was here that poor old King Haakon of Norway died, having struggled back this far from his defeat by Alexander III at Largs in 1263. It was rebuilt in the late 15th century and restored in the mid 16th century by Bishop Robert Reid, the founder of Edinburgh University. Further work was done by Earl Patrick Stewart who saw it as his own fortified residence.

Across the road from the Bishop's Palace is the ruin of the **Earl's Palace** (*open April–Sept Mon–Sat 9.30–7, Sun 2–7; closed winter; adm*), built by forced labour for the much-loathed tyrant, Earl Patrick Stewart at the beginning of the 17th century. The palace is L-shaped with attractive angle-turrets, once described as 'the most mature and accomplished piece of Renaissance architecture in Scotland'. The carved decorations, the oriel windows and the magnificent Great Hall are splendid, but the design was never completed. The Earl ran out of money and shortly afterwards was arrested for treason. The slates of the palace were sold in 1745 and it has been roofless ever since. Earl Patrick was Steward of Orkney and Shetland and entirely corrupt. He forced the islanders to do 'all sorts of servile and painful labour without either meat, drink or hire'. His final crime was to try to save his skin by implicating his adolescent illegitimate son. He was finally executed in 1615 for his awful crimes against humanity, having been given a week's reprieve so that he could learn the Lord's Prayer.

The Orkney Museum, Tankerness House, Broad Street (*open Mon–Sat and Sun pm; adm*) is in a well-restored 16th-century townhouse with an attractive courtyard and garden. Its oldest part was built in 1574 by the first Protestant priest, Archdeacon Gilbert Fulzie, as his residence. It was remodelled in 1820 by the Baikies of Tankerness, who owned it from 1641. Over 4,000 years of Orkney's history are well displayed.

Orkney Library (*open Mon–Sat*), founded in 1683, is one of the oldest public libraries in Scotland and has an excellent Orkney Room for anyone wanting to go deeply into the history of the islands. **The Wireless Museum**, near the harbour (*open April–Sept; adm*), gives a fascinating history of early domestic radio and wartime communications.

The **Mercat Cross** on Kirk Green by the cathedral, dates from 1621 though it was only moved here in 1762. The Cross is a replica, the original being inside the cathedral. This is where the 'Ba' is thrown up, to start the Christmas and New Year 'Ba-Games'. Public proclamations were always made from the Cross and it was also used as the town pillory. Kirk Green is the venue for the annual St Magnus Fair in August.

Stromness

Stromness, about 17 miles west of Kirkwall, is the only other proper town in Orkney and the terminal for the car ferry from Scrabster. It is a delightful place, full of charm and character, reminiscent of a Norwegian fishing village. Many of the narrow, twisting streets are cobbled and paved, tightly packed with stone houses, two and three storeys in height, often with gable ends to the street or harbour, many with their own landing stages. Because of the wild weather, windows are small, set deep into thick walls. A number of the houses have been converted to shops, retaining their traditional character. Yards and gardens lead off the streets down alleyways and there are often attractive vistas through to the waterfront.

Stromness has a long history of catering for the needs of passing ships. From the 17th to the 19th centuries Britain's various wars made the English Channel a dangerous place for trading vessels and most of them chose to take the route round the north of Scotland, despite the risk of encountering privateers. The Hudson's Bay Company did much of their recruiting in Stromness from about 1702 and appointed a Stromness merchant, David Geddes, as their local agent in 1791. By this time Orcadians comprised three-quarters of the company's workforce in Canada, and their ships used Stromness as a port for provisions and water until the early 1900s. Captain Cook, the great navigator, used the port, and his ships *Discovery* and *Resolution* called in on their return from the South Seas after their captain had been clubbed and stabbed to death in Hawaii in 1779.

From the 1770s whaling ships from Dundee and Hull, looking for young men skilled in small boats, took on crew from Stromness and engaged local merchants, establishing a link with the whaling industry until after 1900. Walter Scott immortalized John Gow, an 18th-century pirate from Stromness, in his book *The Pirate.*

The **Pier Arts Centre** (*open Tues–Sun*) occupies a well-restored 18th-century building and has an excellent collection of 20th-century paintings. **Stromness Natural History Museum** (*open Mon–Sat; May–Sept also Sun; adm*) has collections of birds, fossils, shells and butterflies. There are exhibitions covering whaling, fishing, the Hudson' Bay Company, Scapa Flow and the German fleet.

Scapa Flow

Scapa Flow is a great inlet to the south of Mainland, surrounded by protective islands. This perfect deep-water anchorage, up to 10 miles wide, was adopted as the main base of the Grand Fleet in 1912. At the end of the First World War the German Navy sailed their fleet into Scapa, having surrendered. Then, on 21 July 1919 on the order of Rear Admiral Ludwig von Reuter whose pride balked at the shame of surrender, the whole fleet of 74 warships was scuttled. A party of schoolchildren, on a trip round the Flow, witnessed this dramatic event. At the beginning of the Second World War a German U-boat crept through the defences and sank the *Royal Oak*, after which the Churchill Barriers were erected, making the anchorage almost impregnable. Today, sculptural wrecks break the water in violent contrast to the peaceful, lovely scenery. Most of the wrecks have been salvaged, but seven warships and four destroyers remain on the bottom, giving great scope for wreck diving. Good supplies of air can be obtained locally.

In 1916 a German U-boat managed to cross Scapa Flow in spite of blockades and sail north to lay mines off Birsay. One of these was hit by *HMS Hampshire* which was carrying General Kitchener on his way to Russia at the age of 66. He was killed, together with all but 12 of the ship's company, and there is a memorial to him at Marwick Head, overlooking the place where the warship went down.

Brough of Birsay is a tidal island reached by a causeway which is open for about 2 hours at low tide. There are the remains of a Viking village here and a Romanesque church, St Magnus, built in 1064 and rebuilt in 1664 and 1760, where St Magnus' body was taken after his murder in 1116, to be interred later in the cathedral. This is a good place for 'wave-watching'.

Back across the causeway to the village of Birsay, there is a huge palace built by Earl Patrick Stewart, with very fine stonework. At the farm house close by there is a double water mill with both over- and under-shot wheels, still intact but definitely in need of some careful restoration, and a third which is the last water mill for meal in Orkney. There have been mills here since Viking times. Walk northeast along the footpath to **Skipi Geo**, a former fisherman's cove with a restored turf-roofed hut and two of the cleets they used for hauling up the boats in winter. (There are more of these huts at **Sandgeo** a couple of miles south of Marwick Head.) A few hundred yards beyond Skip Geo there is a huge whalebone like a gigantic sculptured bird. A little further on, **Longaglebe Geo** is a wonderful 700ft (200m) gorge eroded by the sea. In early summer the cliffs are covered in richly coloured wild flowers and nesting birds.

Maes Howe

Maes Howe (*open April–Sept daily 9.30–6.30, last adm 6; Oct–Mar daily 9.30–4.30, last adm 4, Sun 2–4.30; adm*) is 10 miles west of Kirkwall, just off the main road to Stromness. This huge Stone Age burial cairn is unquestionably the most outstanding in Britain. The passage into the cairn, made of huge single slabs of stone, is so aligned that a shaft of sunlight pierces its 36ft (11m) length into the chamber on only one day of the year, that of the winter solstice. Burial cells lead off the main chamber which has massive stone buttresses in each corner.

When Maes Howe was first excavated in 1861 the cells were found to be empty, and this fact, together with runic Viking inscriptions on the walls, misled archaeologists into thinking the tomb was Norse. Then it became obvious that the structure dates back to many centuries before that, probably to around 3500 BC. The Vikings came much later, sacking the tombs and leaving their graffiti on the walls. In fact the graffiti are just as fascinating as the much older cairn. There are references to treasure and to the Crusades, and a collection of sex slogans that are as modern as any today: 'Thorny was bedded, Helgi says so', reads one; 'Ingigerd is the best of them all', says another. There is an excellent guidebook on sale at the site. Beside the car park is **Tormiston Mill**, a restored 19th-century water mill with a very obliging restaurant where they will make up sandwiches for you. There is also a craft centre.

The Ring of Brodgar

The Ring of Brodgar (*always accessible*) is on the narrow neck of land between Harray and Stenness Lochs, 4 miles northwest of Maes Howe. From the original 60 stones, 36 remain. They are precisely set, being 6 degrees apart, with a surrounding ditch cut from bedrock, as much as 9ft (2.75m) deep and 27ft (8m) wide, crossed by two causeways. These stones date from about 1560 BC and are believed to be some sort of lunar observatory, a splendid reminder that Stone Age man may have been primitive but he certainly wasn't stupid. Try to see these stones at dawn or dusk to get the full benefit of the weird light and the shadows they cast.

The Stones of Stenness

The Stone of Stenness (*always accessible*) date from around the 3rd millennium BC, only four stones remaining of the original circle. Excavations uncovered an almost square setting of horizontal stones, scattered with fragments of cremated bones, charcoal and shards of pottery, indicating that this must have been some sort of cremation and burial site. The two outlying stones, the Barnhouse and the Watch Stone, were probably associated with this circle, as must have been the many cists and cairns that have been unearthed in this area.

Skara Brae

Skara Brae (*open April–Sept 9.30–6.30, last adm 6; Oct–Mar 9.30–4.30, last adm 4; adm*) is 5 miles northwest of the Stones of Stenness, on the west coast and on the southern arm of the sandy sweep of the **Bay of Skaill**. This was a Stone Age settlement, hit by a massive storm that buried it in sand for about 4,000 years. Another storm then blew away some of the sand to reveal the village. It is unique, giving an insight into the whole way of life of those prehistoric tribes, rather than just revealing a burial cairn which tells only a fraction of their story. Careful excavation has uncovered about six of the original ten single-roomed houses, a workshop with covered passages from one to another, and a communal paved courtyard. Lack of wood meant they used stone for their furniture, and the old bed platforms, cupboards, hearths, fish tanks and tables can still be seen, as well as a fascinating collection of tools and implements. Recent progress in carbon-dating means that more and more information is coming to light about those mysterious settlers, and there is an excellent guide book with up-to-date findings. Midden (rubbish heap) excavations have revealed that the inhabitants of this earliest-known fishing village in Scotland were also farmers. A small museum gives more details of the site.

While you are at Skara Brae, you should visit **Skaill House** (*open 1 April–30 Sept daily; adm*), overlooking the lovely Bay of Skaill and only 300 metres from the Neolithic village. It is one of the most complete 17th-century mansion houses in Orkney, surrounded by lawns and gardens. Built in the 1620s for Bishop George Graham, it has been added to by successive lairds ever since, culminating in the north tower and wing which give it such a distinctive profile today. Inside the beautifully restored rooms, including the Bishop's rather cosy bedroom, you can see such things as Captain Cook's dinner service, and other memorabilia.

Orkney's only surviving **Click Mill** (*always accessible*) is beyond Dounby about 8 miles northeast of Skara Brae. It is a horizontal water wheel, built in about 1800 from an earlier design and so called from the noise it makes as it turns. It is preserved in working order although the pool has been drained. A couple of miles to the south, **Corrigall Farm Museum** (*open Mar–Oct daily; adm*) is an excellent re-creation of a mid 19th-century farmstead with all the buildings, implements and household artefacts as well as the native livestock.

On the wild, windswept headland at **Gurness**, 5 miles northeast of the Click Mill, there is one of the best preserved brochs in Orkney (*open daily; adm*) dating from about the 1st century BC. A booklet describes the complicated layout of the site. Built as a broch, it was occupied by Picts and then by Vikings, who added to the original structure. It includes domestic buildings, Norse longhouses and a well.

Islands South of Mainland

Lamb Holm

Lamb Holm is linked by a mile of causeway south of the Mainland. When the Churchill Barriers were erected at the beginning of the Second World War (*see* above), 1,700 men worked on them including Italian POWs. Homesick for their warm, Catholic land, these Italians created the **Italian Chapel** out of two Nissen huts on Lamb Holm in their spare time. It is a miracle of faith with its cast-concrete altar and altar rail, delicate wrought-iron tracery, and plasterboard painted to resemble bricks and marble. Domenico Chioccetti, who painted the frescoes, including a Madonna and Child behind the altar, returned in 1960 to restore his work. He died in 1999. On the 50th anniversary of the chapel's completion a group of the original Italian prisoners came back to commemorate their work, known locally as 'The Miracle of Camp 60'. **Burray**, linked to Lamb Holm by a causeway to the south, has a **Fossil Centre** (*open April–Sept; adm*) with fossilized fish over 300 million years old. There is a cafe at the museum.

South Ronaldsay

South Ronaldsay, joined by causeway to Burray, has a picturesque village on its north coast, **St Margaret's Hope**, the third largest in Orkney—with a poignant memory. In 1290 the seven-year-old Princess Margaret, Maid of Norway, died of sea sickness in the ship bringing her from Norway to marry Prince Edward of England and unite their countries. The ship bearing the wasted body of the little princess put in to St Margaret's Hope. It is a picturesque place in a sheltered bay, with houses dating from the 17th century. In the 19th century it was a busy fishing port. The **Tomb of the Eagles**, on the southeast toe of South Ronaldsay, is so named because of the many sea-eagle claws found in the Stone Age chambered tomb which you can crawl into. Call at Liddle Farm first (*adm*). Mr Simison, the farmer who found and excavated the tomb, will usher you along a wonderful cliff-top walk to see it, and will tell you all about it. He will also show you, on a different site in the same field, an equally fascinating Stone Age house complete with oven and cooking facilities. Back in the delightfully amateur 'museum' in the farm house, his daughter will let you hold 5,000-year-old tools, skulls and claws.

Hoy

Hoy (Norse '*Haey*'—High Island), the largest island after Mainland, about 3 miles south of Stromness, is the only one that is not flat, and has scenery much more like Shetland. Its hills give a good backdrop to views over the flat green farmland that characterizes the landscape wherever you are in these islands. Ward Hill rises to 1,500ft (460m).

The Old Man of Hoy is a familiar outline, a towering pinnacle of horizontally layered rock, sandstone on basalt, 450ft (138m) high on a promontory above the sea off the northwest coast. It is a favourite challenge to serious rock climbers; the first successful climb was in 1966, by a three-man team led by Chris Bonnington. Legend, however, tells of an elderly local who swarmed to the top for a bet, with no climbing aids, and, having left his pipe on the summit, went back to retrieve it. A marked footpath takes you out to the Old Man from **Rackwick**, with one or two quite steep bits, taking about 90 minutes. Rackwick itself is well worth seeing, with a beautiful bay surrounded by cliffs, and attractive, scattered cottages, done up in traditional style with old stone roofs.

The Dwarfie Stane is the only example of a rock-cut tomb in Britain, a huge rectangular red-sandstone boulder, hollowed out for a body about 5,000 years ago. It has a beautifully fitting carved block for a door and you can crawl inside. In Walter Scott's *The Pirate*, it was the favourite residence of 'Trolld', a dwarf from Norse legend. There is a Persian inscription among the graffiti carved in 1850 by the somewhat eccentric Major William Mouncey who had been a spy in Afghanistan and Persia and who spent several nights in this tomb in Persian dress.

St John's Head, not far north of the Old Man of Hoy, is part of a 1140ft (350m) vertical cliff, teeming with seabirds and rare plants. Just off the main road south, clearly visible, is a white-washed gravestone—**Betty Corrigall's Grave**. Left pregnant and deserted by a visiting sailor in the 19th century, this young girl from Lyness committed suicide. By law she was not allowed to be buried in hallowed ground, and she was buried in this lonely spot on the parish boundary.

Melsetter House, on the south coast (*not open to the public but visible from the road*), was built on to an older house in 1896 by the famous Arts and Crafts architect W. R. Lethaby. New and old have been kept distinct, but the scale and materials blend nicely into the Orkney landscape. The earlier part was looted by Jacobites in 1745.

Islands North of Mainland

Shapinsay

Shapinsay guards the entrance to Kirkwall harbour and it was from Elwick Bay that King Haakon sailed south in 1263 to his ignominious defeat at Largs. Earlier still, in AD 84, it is said that one of Agricola's galleys was wrecked at Grucula on the west coast. **Balfour Castle** in the southwest corner was designed by David Bryce in 1848 for a Colonel Balfour and his son, who did much to improve the farming methods on the island. You get a good view of this imposing pile, with its turrets, towers and battlements, from the ferry from Kirkwall. It is run as a private hotel (*see* p.310). The Tourist Board can also arrange guided tours of the castle and Victorian gardens on Sundays and Wednesdays. Much of the interior is unchanged from when it was created by 30 Italian craftsmen 150 years ago. At **Burroughston** there is a reconstructed broch, with illustrated explanations of its features. Shapinsay's Lairobell Farm goat's cheese is particularly tasty, in spite of its maker's struggles with EC bureaucracy, and is worth seeking out.

Washington Irving

In 1760 a family called Irving emigrated from Quholm in the northeastern corner of the island. They sided with the rebels in the American Revolution and made their fortune. Washington Irving, born in 1783, became America's first internationally renowned writer. He returned to Britain and struck up a friendship with Sir Walter Scott, who persuaded him to go back to America and write a number of best-selling essays and tales, including adaptations of *Rip Van Winkle* and *The Legend of Sleepy Hollow*. His most prodigious work was a five-volume biography of George Washington.

Rousay

Rousay, a couple of miles northeast of Mainland, has a burial cairn at **Midhowe** on the west coast. This cairn has a chamber 76ft (23m) long by 7ft (2m) wide, with 24 burial cells leading off it, in which the remains of 25 human bodies were found, earning it the name 'The Great Ship of Death'. Another tomb on the island, **Taversoe Tuick**, is unusual because it is two-storied. One tomb sits on top of the other, each with its own entrance passage. The Jacobean-style mansion, **Trumland House**, at the south end of the island, was built by David Bryce in 1876 for General Sir Frederick William Traill-Burroughs. Known locally as 'the Little General' and 'the worst landlord in Orkney', Burroughs made life impossible for his crofting tenants and caused much unrest and hatred. In contrast, in the 1930s, Walter Grant lived here and used his considerable wealth and resources to employ leading archaeologists to excavate many of the important prehistoric sites.

Wyre, a mile southeast of Rousay, has the ruin of a 12th-century stone castle, one of the oldest square keeps in Scotland, known as **Cubbie Roo's Castle** and probably the stronghold of a Norse robber baron. There is also a ruined 12th-century chapel, **St Mary's**.

Egilsay

Egilsay is 2 miles east of Rousay. **St Magnus Cenotaph** marks the site of the murder of Jarl Magnus in 1116. The ruin of **St Magnus' Church** dominates this small, low-lying island, with a tall, tapering round tower at the west end. This design is of Irish origin, indicating close contact between Ireland and Orkney during Viking times. It was probably built in the 12th century and its walls still stand to their full height. The tower, at nearly 50ft (15m), was once taller and seems to beckon from all around. Magnus was killed on the order of his rival Earl Haakon who wanted sole power over Orkney. Egilsay has a large proportion of incomers in its small population.

On **Eday**, 4 miles to the east of Egilsay, there are chambered tombs and an Iron Age-dwelling that was once a roundhouse with radial divisions inside.

Westray

Westray, 7 miles north of Rousay, is one of the most Orcadian in atmosphere, having fewer resident incomers. The formidable ruin of **Noltland Castle** at its north end was built in 1560 by Gilbert Balfour, who was implicated in the murder of Cardinal Beaton and served his punishment on a French galley beside John Knox. He was later Master of the Household for Mary, Queen of Scots. Its design is Z-plan with all-round visibility and an extravagant provision of gun loops. It was burned by Covenanters in 1650.

Southwest of Noup Head, 'The Gentleman's Cave' was a refuge for a number of Orkney lairds who supported the Jacobite cause in 1745. Tradition links the cave to Noltland Castle by an underground tunnel. It is tricky to get to and you should seek local advice before trying.

Papa Westray

Papa Westray, 2 miles off the northeast tip of Westray, is so called from the hermits who lived in the cells here. This island was part of an important Norse family estate in the 11th and 12th centuries and archaeologists discovered the remains of Neolithic settlements which have provided valuable clues to the lifestyle of those ancient inhabitants, including the earliest standing dwelling-house in northwest Europe, dating from 3500 BC.

North Ronaldsay

North Ronaldsay is the most northerly island of Orkney, 15 miles east of Papa Westray and 32 miles northeast of Kirkwall. It is surrounded by a sea dyke designed to keep the unique breed of sheep off the grass, so that they feed from the rich seaweed on the shore. The meat of these small, sturdy animals has a distinctive flavour as a result.

Sanday, south of North Ronaldsay, has sandy beaches and fertile farmland dotted with large, stone 19th-century farmhouses.

Events

St Magnus Festival in Kirkwall, towards the end of June, is a week of music, drama and art, rapidly growing in popularity and attracting companies from many countries. The standard is high and it is wise to book well in advance, both for performances and for accommodation. For two weeks in July there is a **Craftsmen's Guild** in Kirkwall, with demonstrations of local craftwork. Stromness has a **Folk Festival** in May and a **Shopping Week** in July.

Kirkwall

moderate

Ayre Hotel, on the harbour front, ✆ 873 001, 🖷 876 289, is 200 years old and a good place to stay if you want to be in Kirkwall, at the upper end of moderately priced. Roy and Moira Dennison look after you well and so do their helpful staff. Ask for a room overlooking over the sea. **Kirkwall Hotel**, also overlooking the harbour, ✆ 872 232, 🖷 872 812, is a large, French-roofed stone building of 1890. It's comfortable (and cheaper) and has a good restaurant—especially for seafood. **West End Hotel**, in Main Street, ✆ 872 368, 🖷 876 181, built in 1824, has more character and is smaller (but a bit pricier). The lounge bar is a good place to experience local atmosphere.

Foveran Hotel, St Ola, ✆ 872 389, 🖷 876 430, is only 2 miles out of Kirkwall, with stunning views of Scapa Flow. Built in Scandinavian style in 34 acres, it is a good bet if you want peace. They have an excellent menu—particularly the seafood, again—and Bobby and Ivy Corsie, the hosts, will advise you on the best places to explore.

moderate–cheap

For a good B&B in Kirkwall, with wonderful cooking, try **Mrs Flett**, Briarlea, 10 Dundas Crescent, ✆ 872 747. The 19th-century stone town house has a large walled garden, and Mrs Flett is a splendid hostess. Alternatively try **Mrs Forsyth**, 21 Willowburn Road, Kirkwall, ✆ 874 020, whose house is very homely.

For self-catering try **Mr Gray**, Terrawinz, St Ola, ✆ 874 590, who has two apartments in Kirkwall, sleeping 4; or **Mrs Currie**, 1 Dundas Crescent, Kirkwall, ✆ 873 541, who has a house in a walled garden overlooking the Earl's Palace, sleeping 6; or **Mr Work**, ✆ 873 235, who has a cottage and a stables, both sleeping 4.

Stromness

If you want to stay in Stromness, **The Stromness Hotel**, ✆ 850 298, 🖷 850 610, is probably your safest bet, a traditional stone-built hotel overlooking the harbour and Scapa Flow. Handy for the ferry, it is reasonably priced and has good food. The **Ferry Inn**, John Street, ✆ 850 280, is cheap and unpretentious with a strong nautical flavour. For B&B, try **Mrs Strachan**, Sinclair View, 5 Franklin Road. ✆ 850 199, where you will be well looked after and comfortable.

The Hamnavoe Restaurant in Graham Street has very reasonable, delicious and imaginative food, especially the seafood, in a nice dining room with an open fire.

Birsay

Barony, is a fairly basic but cheap and friendly place to stay, ✆ 721 327.

Stenness

Standing Stones Hotel, on the shore of Loch Stenness, ✆ 850 449, 🖷 851 262, is a very reasonably priced fishing hotel in a lovely position, congenial and comfortable though the 'modern' decor leaves much to be desired. You can get boats and ghillies and the brownies are a good size—2–3 kgs is not unusual. Stenness has several B&Bs: **Mr Savory**, Mill of Eyrland, ✆ 850 136, lives in a comfortable converted mill with a lovely garden. For self-catering, **Mrs Francis**, Outbrecks, ✆ 851 223, has a charming old Orkney stone cottage with wonderful views, sleeping 4. **Mrs Macleod**, Lochend, ✆ 851 003, has a first floor flat overlooking Stenness and Harray Lochs, sleeping 4.

Skara Brae

The nicest place to stay for peace and hospitality is with **Mrs Anderson**, Rickla, ✆ (01756) 761 575, a first class B&B. For self-catering stay in the **Old Kirk**, ✆ 771 570, in a splendid setting, sleeping 8.

South Ronaldsay

Creel Inn and Restaurant in Front Road, St Margaret's Hope, ✆ 831 311, serves up some of the finest food in Orkney, and you can stay here as well. * FANTASTIC

Shapinsay

Balfour Castle, ✆ 711 282, is run as an expensive private hotel for up to 12 people. It is an imposing pile, with its turrets, towers and battlements. Much of the interior is unchanged from when it was created by 30 Italian craftsmen 150 years ago. *See* above, p.307. **Mrs Wallace**, ✆ 711 256, does a cosy B&B and dinner. Very cheap.

Rousay

The **hotel** on the island has glorious views, ✆ 821 325. For **self-catering** for 3 people call ✆ 821 252.

Westray

Cleaton House, in Cleaton, ✆ (01857) 677 508, 🖷 677 442, is an attractive Victorian manse, now a small, comfortable, inexpensive hotel, with lovely views, friendly staff and good food.

Papa Westray

Beltane House Hotel, ✆ (01857) 644 267, is in recently converted terraced cottages, small, cosy, very friendly and they will collect you from the boat or plane. The food is homely and the community shop is next door.

North Ronaldsay

You can stay on the island in very cheap solar- and wind-powered accommodation, ✆ (01857) 633 200.

Sanday

There are two cheap hotels on Sanday: **Belsair Hotel**, ✆ (01857) 600 206, and **Kettletoft Hotel**, ✆ (01857) 600 217. For B&B try **Mrs Flett**, ✆ (01857) 600 467. For self-catering, **Mrs Thomson**, ✆ (01857) 600 339, has a farmhouse on a working farm with lovely views, sleeping 6; **Mrs Towrie**, ✆ (01857) 600 347, has a modern bungalow, sleeping 6.

Shetland

According to Tacitus, when the Romans sailed round the north coast of Scotland and found Britain was an island, they 'discovered and subdued' Orkney but they 'left Shetland alone because of the wild seas that lay between them'. He called Shetland *Thule*, that mythical island which the ancients believed lay on the edge of the world.

Sixty miles north of Orkney and halfway to Norway, Shetland is extreme, dramatic and magical enough for *Ultima Thule* to seem entirely appropriate—not just one island but 100, of which 15 are continuously inhabited. An archipelago of outstanding beauty, the perfect place for peace and solitude. In spite of being on the same latitude as Greenland, the climate is mild because of the Gulf Stream, with plenty of summer sunshine and less rain than the Western Isles (but more than its fair share of wind). Like Orkney, Shetland has long summer nights, the 'simmer dim' twilight of midsummer adding a touch of timelessness to holidays. The name Shetland is derived from the Norse word *hjaltland*, meaning Highland. Locals talk about Shetland, never the Shetlands, and when they talk about Mainland they are referring to the principal island.

The terrain is mostly peat bog and rough highland hillside, carpeted with heather and turf and dotted with small lochs—not green and fertile as it is in Orkney. Ronas Hill to the northwest of Mainland is the highest point at 1,475ft (454m), and nowhere is more than 3 miles from the sea. The narrow roads deter caravans and coaches. There is wonderful cliff scenery with long winding inlets called 'voes', battered into arches, fissures and jagged stacks, eroded by wind and sea into sculpture for giants; rock-scapes as dramatic as that of the more famous Fingal's Cave. Few trees survive the gale-force winds that lash these islands.

Dairy farming and vegetable crops thrive in the south and central Mainland, and sheep-farming is important, including the black and brown Shetland sheep. The Shetland cabbage is salt resistant and grown as a fodder crop. Knitwear from the islands is world famous. In the old days the wool was plucked, or 'roo'ed', from the sheep's neck by hand, being too fine for shears, but this is no longer common except with some show animals. A true Shetland shawl should be so fine it can be pulled through a wedding ring. The colours of the land- and sea-scapes enhanced by the extraordinary clarity of light must have had a strong influence on the natural shades used in the knitwear, particularly those in the Fair Isle designs. Shetland ponies—not strictly wild, as they are all owned—roam over the hills and common grazings. Originally mini draught horses on the crofts, they were then bred for work in coal mines, with 'as much strength as possible and as near the ground as can be got'. The skeleton of one found in the middle of Jarlshof Broch was smaller than the modern breed. Their tail hair was used as fishing line and it was illegal to steal hair from another man's horse.

Peat cutting is still an important part of life and you will see intricately built peat stacks along the lonely roads, transported to the houses in decrepit old cars these days, instead of in pony panniers. The old life of crofting, fishing and knitting was greatly changed when the oil boom hit Shetland, but the oil depots are well confined to the Sullom Voe area on Mainland. They have not spoiled the rest of the islands and have brought a new prosperity. In fact it is easy to spend a holiday in Shetland and never catch a glimpse of the oil industry. If you do take a trip along Sullom Voe, you will see that the installations don't even break the skyline.

In these islands you can experience the sensation of being the only human being in a world of birds, animals and flowers, just as it must have been thousands of years ago, the melody of myriad bird-songs harmonizing with the ever-restless sea. For **ornithologists** there are huge colonies of birds, both northern and migrant. Among the hundreds of species to be seen is the **Shetland wren**—the 'stinkie'—even smaller than her more common cousin. Fair Isle, halfway to Orkney, has an observation station and is a famous staging post for migrants. With such a variety, Shetland is a twitcher's paradise.

For **botanists** the wild flowers are marvellous: there are around 500 species of plants to discover. Because much of the pasture land is untreated, many that have become rare elsewhere have survived, including the rather hideous large Australian daisy. You can also find arctic flowers, the American mondey flower and the tiny blue caucasus from Asia Minor in Shetland. For **naturalists** there are vast quantities of seals to watch, basking on the rocks, known locally as 'selkies' (too many of them, from the fishermen's point of view, due to culling restrictions). Otters can be seen around small rocks and skerries in the remoter coastal areas. Whales, killer whales, sharks, dolphins and porpoises can all be seen off the coast.

Trout fishing is excellent in the lochs, of which there are more than 300, with brownies up to 8lbs (3½kg), and there are some salmon (including escapees from salmon farms). Sea trout can be caught, spinning from beaches or where a burn enters the sea (but not on Sundays). Char can be caught on the Loch of Girlsta. Fishing permits can be bought from the Tourist Office in Lerwick, where you can also get details about boats and local associations. **Sea angling** is first class and fishermen catch cod, halibut, tusk and many other white fish. Porbeagle shark of up to 450lbs (200kg) have been caught in local waters and the current European record of a 226.8lb (103kg) skate is held by Shetland. There is a staggering wealth of prehistoric remains for **archaeologists** and some of the most glorious **walking** in Scotland. Ask at the Tourist Office for the series of books by Peter Guy on walking in Shetland.

Getting There

British Airways Express, ✆ 0345 222 111, operates 5 flights a day from Aberdeen on weekdays and a reduced service at weekends. They also run services from Glasgow, Edinburgh and Inverness and Orkney, as well as all other major UK airports. London is about 3 hours from Shetland by air. Flights connect with those from and to many UK and international airports. Sumburgh Airport is 25 miles from Lerwick and there is a connecting bus service as well as taxis. Self-drive cars can be hired at the airport. There are a range of special fares with substantial savings if booked in advance. They also offer special rates in conjunction with local hotels.

P&O Scottish Ferries, PO Box 5, Jamieson's Quay, Aberdeen AB9 8DL, ✆ (01224) 572 615, operate almost daily between Aberdeen and Lerwick. Twice weekly during the summer the boat goes via Orkney. Departure from Aberdeen and from Lerwick is usually 6pm, to arrive at 8am the next day.

Getting Around

Loganair runs a regular inter-island service from Tingwall Airport, Lerwick, to the islands of Foula, Fair Isle, Papa Stour and Out Skerries, and from Sumburgh Airport to Unst. A frequent passenger and drive on/drive off **car ferry** links most of the islands with the Shetland Mainland; passenger fares are very cheap. Some of the ferries can be very busy at peak times and advance booking is recommended. Full details of schedules and fares are obtainable from the Tourist Information Centre in Lerwick.

20km
15miles

N

Muckle Flugga Lighthouse
Haroldswick
A968
Unst
Fetlar
B9088
A968
Yell
B9081
Ulsta
Ronas Hill
A970
Esha Ness
The Drongs
Dore Holm
Sullom
Sullom Voe
Toft
B9076
Brae
Housay
Out Skerries
Atlantic Ocean
Muckle Roe
Papa Stour
Sandness
B9071
A970
Whalsey
B9075
Mainland
A971
B9071
Reawick
Whiteness
Bressay
Bressay Sound
Lerwick
Noss
North Sea
Foula
Scalloway
Burra
A970
Sandwick
Mousa
Mousa Broch
St. Ninian's
B9122
Croft Museum
Southvoe
Grutness
Sumburgh
Jarlshof
Sumburgh Head
Fair Isle

With 500 miles of roads, personal transport is the best way of exploring Shetland, either in your own car, or a hire car. Bicycles can also be hired.

Tourist Information

Lerwick: Market Cross, Shetland ZE1 0LU, ✆ (01595) 693 434. Shetland Events Hotline, ✆ (01595) 694 200. Wildlife Tours, ✆ (01950) 422 483.

Festivals and Activities

Up-Helly-Aa is held in Lerwick on the last Tuesday in January and is a survival from Viking days. This pagan fire festival used to mark the end of Yuletide and symbolize a desire for the sun to appear again after the long winter nights. A Viking galley is carried to a park in the centre of the town amidst a forest of blazing torches and set alight while 'The Norseman's Home' is sung as a funeral dirge. In the old days blazing barrels of tar were rolled through the streets and carried to the tops of the hills.

Nowadays there is a strong contemporary culture based on the past but looking towards the future. Because they were such good seamen, Shetlanders were vulnerable to press gangs: the fiddle tune 'Jack is yet alive' was composed for a Shetlander who had been press-ganged, served his time and returned to a family who had written him off long ago. **Fiddle music** is still very popular throughout the islands. Fiddling and dancing at Islesburgh Community Centre in Lerwick provide lively entertainment (*Wed evenings in summer*), and the **Shetland Folk Festival** is a must for music-lovers (*April*), as is the Shetland Accordion and Fiddle Festival (*Oct*).

Mainland

Mainland is by far the biggest of the islands, its chief town being Lerwick, Britain's most northerly town, so called from the Norse *leir-vik* meaning 'muddy shore'. Looking over sheltered Bressay Sound, Lerwick has always been a refuge for seafarers, and was a stopping-off port for Norsemen; King Haakon reprovisioned his fleet here on the way to his defeat at Largs in 1263.

Lerwick

Lerwick has always been important for fishing: the home waters are productive and it lies on the edge of the valuable northern fishing fields. Dutch fishing fleets were based here in the 17th century and by the 18th century the export of salt fish was thriving. In the 17th century the town became important as a base for the British Navy. Fort Charlotte was built in 1665 to protect the Sound of Bressay from the Dutch. Today, despite its geographical isolation, Lerwick is a lot more up-to-date than some towns in the Highland region of Scotland. Sometimes the Sound is busy with vessels of all kinds and nationalities, the crews of which amble around the town adding a cosmopolitan touch with their different languages. (It is said that many Norwegians come here for bargain shopping, away from their own exorbitant prices.)

The buildings that grew up round the port were sturdy and compact, designed to withstand violent storms; some of them were the town houses of Shetland's lairds, who succeeded the Norsemen and found winter conditions rather bleak in the surrounding countryside. Now, the old houses are interspersed with a sprawl of characterless modern buildings.

The *Dim Riv* is a replica Norse longship, over 40ft (12m) long, which takes visitors on trips round the harbour in the summer. The harbour is a lively, bustling place with a picturesque waterfront and charmingly haphazard, flagstoned Commercial Street, straggling up behind. This is the main shopping centre of the town and the steep, narrow lanes around it are said to cover a network of secret tunnels and passages used by smugglers in the past. Boat trips run from Victoria Pier and cruise round the coast in the summer. Look out for the distinctive Shetland sailing dinghy, a local design with the elegant double-prow, echoing the Viking longboats. These can be seen in most of the harbours around Shetland and are raced in local regattas.

Fort Charlotte (*open daily*), built by Cromwellian troops, was partly burned by the Dutch in 1673. It was repaired and restored in 1781 and garrisoned during the Napoleonic wars. It is the only Cromwellian military building still intact in Scotland. The **Town Hall**, above Commercial Street in Hillend, is a Victorian Gothic building, partly resembling a church with tower and rose window, four corner turrets, a central oriel window and stained-glass windows on the upper floor. These enclose the main hall and depict the history of Shetland, beginning with the Scandanavian conquest in 870. There are full-length figures of Norway's King Harald Harfagri, the conqueror of the islands, and Rognvald, Jarl of More, to whom Harald offered the first earldom. The windows cover all the main events in Shetland's story and include one of the Maid of Norway who died at sea nearby.

Shetland Museum (*open Mon–Sat*), opposite the town hall, is well worth a visit. It has four galleries devoted to the history of man in Shetland from prehistoric times to the present. Look for the Papil Stone, dating from the 7th century, showing a procession of 'papas' or priests, one of whom rides a horse. Other exhibits include the history of Shetland knitting and the history of the islands' marine and fishing past. There are also replicas of the treasure found on St Ninian's Isle. **Bod of Gremista Museum** (*open June–mid Sept Wed–Sun; adm*) has fishing displays. **Up Helly Aa Exhibition** (*open mid May–mid Sept Tues, Fri and Sat; adm*) has a replica galley and exhibits related to the festival. **Tangwick Haa Museum**, Eshaness, North Mainland (*open May–Sept Mon–Fri 1–5, Sat and Sun 11–7*) is not to be missed: a former laird's house, renovated as a museum with the old interiors. There are microfilm census records here.

Around Lerwick

In July and August you can visit the excavations at **Old Scatness Broch**, South Mainland, one of the best Iron-Age villages (*daily guided tours of work in progress*). **Quendale Watermill**, South Mainland (*open May–Sept; adm*) is a restored 'overshot' watermill. **Shetland Crofthouse Museum**, Southvoe (*open May–Sept; adm*) is a good example of a thatched crofthouse, dating from 1870.

Clickhimin Broch (*always accessible*) is on the western outskirts of the town on an island in a loch, reached by a causeway. It is 65ft (20m) in diameter, its walls 18ft (5½m) thick and 15ft (4½m) high, on a massive stone platform. Excavations on the site suggest that it may have been a late Bronze-Age settlement.

A frequent car ferry crosses to the island of **Bressay** just east of Lerwick, and from here a boat crosses the 200 yards (185m) to the bird sanctuary on **Noss** (*open mid May–Aug Tues–Sun except Thurs; adm*). Among the many birds to be seen on Noss are a colony of gannets—the great yellow-headed Solon geese whose vertical dives are a joy to watch, plummeting into the water from tremendous heights to catch unwary fish.

Scalloway

Scalloway is Mainland's other town, in an attractive bay 7 miles west of Lerwick. It was the capital until 200 years ago and is still an important fishing port. Much older than Lerwick, it retains a quiet, old-fashioned atmosphere. There is a small local **museum** in the middle of the town which has, among other things, a detailed history of the Shetland Bus. During the Second World War, small Norwegian fishing boats crossed to Nazi-occupied Norway to carry out sabotage or to land secret agents and bring back refugees. 'To take the Shetland Bus' meant to escape from Norway. *The Shetland Bus* by David Howarth gives a vivid account of these brave operations. **Lunna House** in northeast Mainland, now a guest house, was the original headquarters of this Norwegian resistance movement before it was transferred to Scalloway

Scalloway Castle (*always accessible*) dominates the town, a forbidding ruin built in 1600 by Earl Patrick Stewart, the notorious despot who tyrannized the Northern Isles until he was executed (*see* pp.302). Built in medieval style, the roofless shell with corner turrets and gables stands on a narrow promontory by the water. The Earl is said to have hung his victims from an iron ring in one of the chimneys. The castle was, not surprisingly, left to rot after Stewart's death. Scalloway is at the southern end of the agricultural valley of **Tingwall**, so called after the site of the old Norse parliament, or *thing*, at the northern end of Tingwall Loch, reached by stepping stones. There are bridges across to the islands of **Tronda** and **Burra** just to the south.

South of Lerwick

Mousa Broch (*open daily; free, with fee for ferry*), on Mousa Island, is one of Shetland's principal archaeological treasures, accessible by boat, weather permitting, from Sandwick, 11 miles south of Lerwick. Mousa Island, a mile offshore, is inhabited only by sheep and ponies and its broch is the best preserved in existence. It is eerie to climb its steps and know that you are walking in the 2,000-year-old footsteps of its Pictish builders. Over 50ft (15m) in diameter, 45ft (14m) high, with walls that taper from 12ft (3½m) to 7ft (2m) in thickness, this was one of the smaller of the brochs and probably one of the latest. Galleries honeycomb the double walls, and stairways lead to a parapet around the top. It illustrates clearly how the builders tapered the walls inwards to within about 10ft (3m) of the top and then sloped them outwards, making it impossible for invaders to climb to the top.

Mousa appears romantically in two of the old sagas. In 1150 the Norwegian Prince Erland abducted a famous beauty and held her in the broch until her son, a Jarl, unable to storm the impregnable fortress, had to consent to their marriage. Another saga tells of a young man called Bjorn, who brought Thora, whom he had seduced, to Mousa in 900, where they set up home together. There are late-night boat trips to watch the storm petrels which nest in the broch (call Tom Jamieson, ✆ (01950) 431 367). Mousa is privately owned and camping is not allowed without permission.

St Ninian's Isle is 4 miles southwest of Sandwick, off the west coast of Mainland. You can walk to it along a white crescent of sand, called a 'tombolo', that forms a causeway. Here there are the foundations of a 12th-century chapel buried by sand for many hundreds of years. In 1958 Aberdeen University began excavating the site and discovered not only the foundations of the chapel but also a Bronze Age burial ground and the remains of a pre-Norse church. Under a stone slab in the chapel nave they found a hoard of 8th-century Celtic silver, now in the Royal Museum of Scotland in Edinburgh, with a replica collection in the museum in

Lerwick. It is believed that this wonderful cache was buried by the monks who lived here, probably during a threat of Viking invasion. It includes silver bowls, delicate brooches and a Communion spoon.

Shetland Croft Museum (*open May–Sept daily; adm*) is at Boddam on the east coast of Mainland, 5 miles south of Sandwick. The museum is a restored croft house, typical of the mid 19th century, with its original driftwood furniture and all the domestic utensils. The restored **Quendale Mill** is a 19th-century watermill several miles away.

The modern, clean-cut airport buildings at **Sumburgh**, on the southern tip of Mainland, 27 miles south of Lerwick, present a remarkable contrast to the antiquity and character of Jarlshof, nearby.

Jarlshof (*site always accessible; visitor centre open April–Sept daily; adm*) was a name invented by Sir Walter Scott in *The Pirate*. He visited the island in 1814, was impressed by the 'laird's hall', and wrote his story round it. He was not to know how misleading this name was to prove because it was not until 1905 that a violent storm revealed to archaeologists that the site had been occupied for over 3,000 years, by seven distinct civilizations of which the Norse Jarls were by far the most recent. Some of the artefacts dug from the site are exhibited, with a good ground plan and audio-visual interpretations.

The remains of these village settlements, from Bronze Age to Viking, are sprawled over a low green promontory by the sea. The first house dates from the early or middle part of the second millennium BC. It would be impossible to sort out the various ages and purposes of the conglomeration of stones without the excellent explanations and the guide book. The Bronze-Age huts include stalls and a metal workshop; the Iron-Age settlement has two earth houses and a broch. The three 8th-century wheel-houses are thought to be family dwellings consisting of a number of individual recesses separated as if by the spokes of a wheel, with a central hearth. A confusion of long-houses is all that is left of the Norse occupation. It was the now-ruined medieval farmhouse that Sir Walter used as the setting for his book.

Sumburgh Head is a solid mass of birds (and twitchers in season). Hundreds of thousands of guillemots, puffins, gulls, razor-bills and terns crowd the cliffs and stacks below the lighthouse, despite the expansion of the airport into one of the busiest in Scotland. You get excellent views of Fair Isle from here.

North of Lerwick

At **Sandness**, about 25 miles northwest of Lerwick, watermills have been restored to show something of Shetland's heritage. There is also Jamieson's traditional woollen mill. Boats run from West Burrafirth nearby to **Papa Stour**, a couple of miles off the coast. The boats go four times a week and day trips are possible on Fridays and Saturdays. The sea caves are said by some to be the finest in Britain and you will need to hire a boat locally to see them properly. The scent from the wild flowers on Papa Stour was said to be so strong that fishermen could fix their position from it if caught in fog out at sea.

Lunna is about 18 miles north of Lerwick as the crow flies, out on the east coast. When Lunna House was the original headquarters of the Norwegian Resistance, the barns and outhouses were used as an arsenal. **Lunna Kirk** is one of the oldest Shetland churches still in use. Built in 1753, it is a charming old building with a leper squint through which lepers could listen to the service and receive Communion without infecting the rest of the congregation.

At **Brae** about 23 miles north of Lerwick, a narrow neck of land called **Mavis Grind** prevents the northwest corner of Mainland from being an island. You can stand on this 'anchor cable' of land and throw stones one way into the Atlantic and the other way into the North Sea.

Sullom Voe Oil Terminal (pronounced Soolem), with its complex of buildings and jetties, occupies the peninsula of Calback Ness 7 miles northeast of Brae, joined to Mainland by reclaimed land. The terminal is tucked away so discreetly that you are hardly aware of it, though you cannot miss the ugly buildings that house the oil workers—somehow incongruous set against the bleak landscape. **Firth**, nearby, was built to house the oilmen. **Toft** is 4 miles east of Sullom Voe and from here the car ferry crosses to **Yell**, 3 miles to the northeast.

This northern part of Mainland is dominated by **Ronas Hill**, Shetland's highest point, 1,475ft (454m) high, 10 miles north of Brae and well worth climbing just to sample the marvellous views. **Eshaness**, on the coast 15 miles northwest of Brae, has precipitous cliffs and breath-taking views of the **Drongs**, a collection of weird stacks carved by the force of the ocean. These stacks include a huge natural arch call the **Dore Holm**.

Islands North of Mainland

The island of **Yell**, to the north, is mostly peat moor. It was described by Eric Linklater as 'dull and dark and one large peat bog'. Although the second-largest of the Shetland islands, it has suffered from depopulation and can be rather depressing but it is one of the best places in Britain to see otters.

A minister of the kirk once said: 'Yell is Hell, but Unst—Oh! Unst!' **Unst** is Britain's most northerly island, with **Muckle Flugga** lighthouse on a rock just off its tip. The lighthouse was built by Robert Louis Stevenson's father, and while he was designing and building it, his son stayed on Unst dreaming up the story of *Treasure Island.* Unst supports a number of Shetland ponies and it has wonderful cliff scenery. Until recently, philatelists could get a special frank on their letters at Britain's most northerly post office in **Haroldswick**, in northeast Unst, where Harald Harfagri landed from Norway to subdue the troublesome dispossessed Viking jarls. The last postmistress has now retired and a replacement is being sought.

Fetlar, east of Yell and much smaller, derives its name from the Norn name for 'fat land', and is the most fertile of the islands, supporting a large number of birds. Snowy owls bred on Fetlar until 1975, when the resident male died. Now, although they no longer breed here, hopeful visiting females can sometimes be seen. They have a buzzard-like flight and distinctive white plumage. Another of Fetlar's rare visitors is the red-necked phalarope which spins round on the water, stirring up insects with its long, needle-like beak. The miniature curlew-like whimbrel, usually a coastal migrant, nests on Fetlar and can be seen combing the shore for molluscs and worms, prodding with its long curved beak.

Whalsey, a couple of miles off northeast Mainland, is important for fishing and fish processing. On the pier there is a 17th-century Hanseatic trading booth. The Hanseatic League merchants came from northern Germany to Shetland to trade, buying fish and salting it for export, until salt tax was introduced in 1712. The traders set up booths like this one, from which they offered fine cloth, fishing tackle, exotic foods, tobacco, fruit and gin at a farthing a pint, in exchange for fish, butter, wool and fish oil. It is intriguing to look at this quiet, peaceful place and try to picture what it must have been like when the merchants haggled and bartered from their booths.

Whalsey has two prehistoric sites: the **Standing Stones**, at Yoxie, and the **Benie Hoose**, thought to have been the dwelling for the Druid priests who were responsible for the ceremonies performed at the standing stones.

Foula, 27 miles west of Mainland, has dramatic cliff scenery and a colony of skuas. Still inhabited, it is often cut off in bad weather. This was the last place where Norn was spoken as a first language, in the 19th century.

Lerwick

Kveldsro House Hotel, ✆ 692 195, 🖷 696 595, tucked away in the old town overlooking the harbour, is luxurious and serves good food. However, **Lerwick Hotel**, ✆ 692 166, 🖷 694 419, *www.shetland/hotels@mes.co.uk*, is the best place to stay in the town, at the upper end of the moderate range in price. A purpose-built construction with wonderful views over Brei Wick bay and Bressay, it is comfortable inside and the food is excellent.

Breiview Guest House, 40 Kantersted Rd, ✆ 695 956, is a cheap, modern house, very clean and spacious, 20 minutes' walk from the town centre with a sandy beach nearby. **Alderlodge Guest House**, 6 Clairmont Place, ✆ 695 705, is a sturdy, stonebuilt house with large, cheap comfortable rooms (each with its own fridge). Wholesome Scottish food is served.

Scalloway

The **Scalloway Hotel**, ✆ 880 444, 🖷 880 445, in the main street, is moderately priced and very friendly. **Broch Guest House**, ✆ 880 767, in Upper Scalloway, and **Hildasay Guest House**, ✆ 880 822, nearby, are very reasonable places to stay; the latter will arrange trout fishing for you.

Jarlshof

Sumburgh Hotel, ✆ (01950) 460 201, 🖷 460 394, is an old manor house, near the airport and Jarlshof, with wonderful views and a friendly atmosphere. Good value.

Walls

Burrastow House, ✆ 809 307, 🖷 809 213, 2 miles from Walls, overlooks Vaila Sound on Shetland's most westerly point and is much the best place to stay. This 18th-century 'Haa' house is small, extremely comfortable and fairly expensive, run by the laird and his wife like a well-appointed private house, with gourmet food made from local produce. The view from the Tester bed must be the best view from any bed in Scotland, and from the terrace you can see seals, and watch otters fishing. A ghillie and boat are available for fishermen in this idyllic place which is the ultimate 'away from it all' location in Britain. Its advertising photograph doesn't do it justice.

Brae

Busta House Hotel, ✆ (01806) 522 506,🖷 522 588, is a large country house in a nice garden, overlooking Busta Voe, fairly expensive, but with good food and 120 different malt whiskies.

Buness House, in Baltasound, ✆ (01957) 711 315, 711 815, is a listed 17th-century house, very nicely done-up. Run by David and Jennifer Edmondston, it is a good value Wolsey Lodge, with good food and glorious views. **Baltasound Hotel**, ✆ (01957) 711 334, is Britain's most northerly hotel.

Fair Isle

Only 3 miles by 1½, the 'Far Isle' of the Vikings, halfway between Orkney and Shetland, is a buffer between the North Sea and the Atlantic. It must be the most gale-battered island in Britain, presenting a tough challenge to the 60-odd people who live there. The bird population is enormous, preserved by the warden of the Observatory where data is collected and analysed. Over 300 species have been recorded; as well as supporting resident colonies, it is a regular staging post for many migratory birds. Although bleak, Fair Isle is magnificent, with needle-sharp rocks pounded by ferocious seas and sheer cliffs topped by green turf and some of the 240 species of wild flowers that thrive here.

Getting There

Fair Isle is 24 miles southwest of Sumburgh and boats run to it from Grutness Pier near Sumburgh Airport, taking 2 hours (*Tues, Thurs and Sat*). These aren't day trips: they involve a three-day stay on the island before the next boat back. For bookings, ring J. Stout, ✆ (01595) 760 222. Alternatively you can fly from Tingwall, taking 25 minutes (*Mon, Wed and Fri; May–Oct also Sat*), and from Sumburgh (*May–Oct Sat only*).

A Fair Isle Yarn

In 1588 *El Gran Grifon*, flagship of the transport squadron of the Spanish Armada, was wrecked on Fair Isle. The 17 households, already barely subsisting, took in, housed and fed the 300 survivors who stayed for 6 weeks. In 1984 a delegation of Spaniards in full conquistador regalia dedicated an iron cross in the island's kirkyard to the 50 men who lost their lives. Legend has it that these Spaniards taught the islanders how to knit their intricate patterns, but that is hotly denied, though it is easy to see that there could have been some Moorish influence on designs that date back to Viking times. There is an island co-operative of men and women who work machines and hand finish 200 orders of Fair Isle jerseys, scarves, hats and gloves a year, each jersey taking seven hours to finish by hand. Handspinning, weaving and dyeing have also been revived in recent years, and workshops and demonstrations are organized by arrangement.

Fair Isle ✆ (01595–)

Where to Stay

Paying guests can stay in the summer at **The Observatory**, ✆ 760 258, at first glance an unappealing place but more than compensated for by the friendly crofting community atmosphere. Warm and cosy inside, it provides a variety of reasonably priced and cheap accommodation and is an excellent base for an outdoor holiday.

There are also two B&Bs which do full board very inexpensively, both of which offer all the friendly hospitality of the islands. **Mrs Riddiford**, at Schoolton, ✆ 760 250, and **Mrs Stout**, at Barkland, ✆ 760 247.

The Gaelic *clann* means offspring, family, stock, race, derived from Latin *planta*—meaning 'sprout' or 'scion'.

When Robert the Bruce released Scotland from the English yoke in 1314, he opened the field for tremendous power struggles between the leading clans. Some became too powerful, others sank into obscurity. Many families, too weak to survive alone, sought the protection of stronger neighbours; some of these took the name of their adopted chief, others retained their own names. Thus many clans have 'septs' and dependants. Clans amalgamated for strength: the Clan Chattan Confederation consisted of a large number of clans who joined forces under Mackintosh hegemony. The chiefs of the Highland clans ruled with total disregard for the authority of the Crown, as did the powerful Border families. The final Jacobite rebellion (1745–56), resulted in the death of the old clan system. (*See* also 'Clans and Tartans', p.36.)

Today, although all that is left is the clan name, many still live in the area traditionally associated with their clan, and there remains a pride and sense of loyalty so strong that people come from all over the world to visit the land of their ancestors. This is a list of the main clans and families, with the address (where there is one) of the clan secretary, or clan centre, who will send more information if required. Names not included will be those of septs, or clan branches. Anyone seriously seeking their roots should get hold of *The Clan Almanac*, by Charles Maclean, published by Lochar, a comprehensive little book which lists, among other things, the septs and dependants of the main clans. Mac and Mc mean son of, as of course does any name ending in son.

Anderson: son of Andrew, Highland version MacAndrew. They came from Badenoch and their motto is 'Stand Sure'. In the 15th century they were part of the Clan Chattan Confederation. Clan Chattan Secretary, Dyunmaglash, Westhill, Inverness-shire.

Armstrong: the original, armour-bearer to a King of Scots, saved his king, fallen in a battle, by lifting him on to his horse. He was given land as a reward and named Strong-arm. They were Borderers and their motto *Invictus maneo* means 'I remain unvanquished'. Clan Secretary, Brieryshaw, Langholm, Dumfriesshire.

Baird: from an old Scots word meaning sumptuous dress. They came from Aberdeenshire and their motto *Dominus fecit* means 'The Lord made'.

Barclay: derived from the Berkeley family who came over with William the Conqueror. They settled in Aberdeenshire and Kincardineshire and their motto *Aut agere aut mori* means 'Either action or death'.

Blair: from Gaelic *blar*—field, battlefield; motto: *Amo Probos*—'I love the righteous'. An ancient family, one branch having roots in Renfrew, Ayr and Wigtown; and another in Perth, Fife and Angus. The Barony of Blair, in Ayrshire, was granted by William the Lion in the 12th century. When the two

branches competed for chieftainship, James VI settled the dispute by appointing the oldest man in either family to be chief. Thus the honour alternates, depending upon seniority. Clan Secretary, 15 Brompton Terrace, Perth.

Brodie: from their Norman ancestor, de Brothie. They settled in Morayshire and their motto is 'Unite'. Clan Secretary, Brodie Castle, Forres, Moray.

Bruce: from the French town Brix—Adam de Brus came over with William the Conqueror. They lived in Annandale, Clackmannan and Elgin, and their motto, *Fuimus*, means 'We have been'. Robert the Bruce won independence for Scotland at the Battle of Bannockburn in 1314; Thomas Bruce, 7th Earl of Elgin and 11th Earl of Kincardine (1766–1841), rescued the decorated sculptures on the Parthenon from vandalism and installed them in the British Museum.

Buchanan: from Gaelic *mac-a-Chanonaich*—son of the canon. They lived around Loch Lomond and their motto is *Clarior hinc honos*—'Brighter hence the honour'. Clan secretary, Brechin Robb, 24 George Square, Glasgow.

Cameron: from Gaelic *cam-shron*—crooked nose. They lived in Northern Argyll and Locheil. Their mottos, translated from Gaelic, are: 'Unite'; 'For King and Country'; and 'Sons of the hounds come here and get flesh'. The Cameron Highlanders, now amalgamated with the Seaforth Highlanders to become the Queen's Own Highlanders, were raised by Sir Alan Cameron in 1793. Their Clan Centre is at Aberchalder, Loch Eil, and the new Clan Cameron Museum is at Achnacarry. Clan Secretary, 78 Milton Road West, Edinburgh.

Campbell: from Gaelic *cam-beul*—crooked mouth. They came from Argyll, Cawdor, Loudoun and Breadalbane. Their various mottos are: 'Forget not'; 'Follow me'; 'Be mindful'; 'I byde my tyme'. The Duke of Argyll is their chief and the clan centre is Inverary Castle, Argyll.

Chisholm: means a water meadow which produces milk good for cheese-making. They lived in Roxburghshire and Berwickshire and later moved to Inverness-shire. Their motto *Feros ferio*, means 'I am fierce with the fierce'. Clan Secretary, 21 Blytheswood Square, Glasgow.

Colquhoun (pronounced *k'hoon*): the name comes from the Barony, in Dunbartonshire and they lived around Loch Lomond. Their motto, *Si je puis*—'If I can', was said by one of their ancestors, to James I, when ordered to capture Dumbarton Castle. (He did.)

Cumming: the name derives from the herb cumin, which is the clan's emblem. Cummings come from Roxburghshire, Buchan, Badenoch and Altyre and their motto is 'Courage'. The Comyns came to Scotland during the reign of Malcolm Canmore in the 11th century, and it was Sir John Comyn—'The Red Comyn', who was murdered by Robert the Bruce in order to gain the Crown. Clan Secretary, House of Altyre, Forres.

Douglas: from Gaelic *dubh glais*—black water. They lived in Lanarkshire, Galloway, Dumfriesshire and Angus and were as powerful as kings in the Middle Ages. Their motto, *Jamais arrière*, means 'Never behind'. Archibald Douglas became known as Bell-the-cat, from his undertaking to kill the much-despised favourites of James III. Sir James Douglas was killed in 1330 while honouring his promise to take Robert the Bruce's heart to the Holy Land.

Drummond: derived from Drymen, near Stirling. They came from Perthshire and their motto is 'Gang (go) warily'.

Duncan: more properly Clan Donnachaidh—Brown Warriors. They came from Atholl and Lundie in Fife and their motto is *Disce parti*—'Learn to suffer'. Donnaichaidh Clan Secretary, 127 Rose Street, South Lane, Edinburgh.

Elliot (there are different spellings): probably derived from Old English *Aelfwald*—Elf Ruler, which became the Christian name Elward. They were one of the strongest of the Border families and their mottos are *Soyez sage*—'Be wise', and *Fortiter et Recte*—'With Strength and Right'. Clan Secretary, Redheugh, Newcastleton, Roxburghshire.

Erskine: from the Barony of Erskine in Renfrewshire. They lived around Alloa and their motto is *Je pense plus*—'I think more'. John Erskine, 11th Earl of Mar, was known as Bobbing John during the Jacobite rebellions because he kept changing sides.

Farquharson: the Gaelic *fearchar* means dear one, and they came from Aberdeenshire and Invercauld. Their motto is *Fide et Fortitudine*—'By Fidelity and Fortitude'. They were part of the Clan Chattan Confederation. Clan Chattan Secretary, Dyunmaglash, Westhill, Inverness-shire.

Ferguson: Fergus founded the Scottish kingdom of Dalriada, and they inhabited the lands of Argyll, Perthshire, Dumfries, Galloway and Raith. Their motto is *Dulcius ex asperis*—'Sweeter after difficulties'. They are one of the oldest clans. Clan Secretary, Pendle Cottage, Dunigoyne, Glasgow.

Forbes: from Gaelic *forba*—field or district. They were powerful in Aberdeenshire and their motto is 'Grace me guide'. Clan Secretary, Balforbes, Lonach, Donside, Aberdeenshire.

Fraser: of Norman derivation, from *fraises*—strawberry flowers. Originally they were in East Lothian, then Aberdeenshire. Their motto is *Je suis prest*—'I am ready'. Clan Secretary, Balblair House, Beauly, Black Isle, Ross-shire.

Gordon: from Gordon in Berwickshire, where they settled, as Anglo-Normans, in the 12th century. They became very powerful in the northeast in Strathbogie, Deeside and around Aberdeen, and their chief was called Cock of the North. Their mottos are *Animo non Astutia*—'By Courage, not Craft'; and *Bydand*—'Remaining'. Clan Secretary, Harlaw House, Harlaw Hill, Prestonpans, East Lothian.

Graham: Anglo-Saxon origin—*graeg ham*, meaning grey home. William de Graham came to Scotland with David I, who gave him lands, and the family became prominent in the Wars of Independence. Their lands included those north of Glasgow, Loch Katrine, part of Perthshire, and around Dundee and Montrose. Their motto is *Ne Oublie*—'Do not forget'. Among their greatest ancestors were Montrose, that gallant Royalist, and Graham of Claverhouse (Bonnie Dundee), hero of Killiecrankie in 1689. Clan Secretary, 23 Ardmillan Terrace, Edinburgh.

Grant: derived from the French *grand*—'great'. Their origins are disputed: some say the first Grant was a Nottinghamshire squire married into an Inverness-shire family, some that they are descended from Kenneth MacAlpine, some that they are descended from MacGregors. Their lands were Strathspey, Rothiemurchas, Glen Moriston and Loch Ness and their motto is 'Stand fast'. Clan Secretary, 18 Great Stewart Street, Edinburgh.

Gunn: possibly from Gunni, in the Norse sagas, or from Gaelic *guineach*, meaning fierce, or of Pictish descent. Their lands were in Caithness and Sutherland and their motto is *Aut Pax Aut Bellum*—'Either Peace or War'. Clan Secretary, 22 Muirhouse Gardens, Edinburgh.

Hamilton: derived from Hameldone, meaning crooked hill', in England, whence came Walter Fitz-Gilbert to lands in Renfrewshire and Arran during the Wars of Independence. Their motto is 'Through'. Patrick Hamilton (1498–1528), was the proto-martyr of the Scottish Reformation. Clan Secretary, Lennoxlove, Haddington, East Lothian.

Hay: derived from La Haye, in Normandy, which stemmed from *haie*, meaning hedge. Their lands were Aberdeenshire and Tweedale and their motto is *Serva jugum*—'Keep the yoke'. Clan Secretary, 12 St Peter's Place, Edinburgh. Clan Centre, Delgatie Castle, Turriff, Grampian.

Henderson: in Gaelic, this clan is MacEanraig, anglicized as MacKendrick. Their lands were Caithness and Glencoe and their motto is *Sola Virtus nobilitat*—'Virtue alone ennobles'.

Home (pronounced Hume): derived from Gaelic *uamh*—cave. Their lands were the Borders and their motto is 'A Home, a Home!' Among their scions were David Hume, the great philosopher of the Scottish Enlightenment, and Sir Alec Douglas-Home, Prime Minister of Britain.

Innes: meaning 'greens'. Innes was a town in Morayshire for which the family received a royal charter in the 12th century. Their motto is *Be traist*—'Be faithful'. Clan Secretary, 35 East Claremont Street, Edinburgh.

Johnstone: derived from John's *toun*—homestead; the Gaelic for John is Iain, giving MacIain. There are various spellings, but Johnson is uncommon in Scotland. They were a powerful Border family and also had lands in Aberdeenshire. Their mottos are *Numquam non paratus*—'Never unprepared', and 'Light thieves all'.

Keith: from the town of Keith in Banffshire. Their lands stretched from East Lothian to Caithness and they held the hereditary office of Great Marischal of Scotland from the 12th to the 18th centuries. Their motto is *Veritas vincit*—'Truth conquers'. Clan Secretary, North Dykes, Kilbirnie, Ayrshire.

Kennedy: from Gaelic *ceann éitigh*—grim-headed—or possibly from *ceann dubh*—black-headed. Their lands were in Ayrshire, Lochaber and Skye and their motto is *Avise la Fin*—'Consider the end'. The seat of their chief, the Marquess of Ailas, is Culzean Castle.

Kerr: pronounced *kar*, the name is derived from the Norse *kjarr* meaning 'brushwood'. They were an Anglo-Norman family who came to Scotland in the 12th century. Their lands were Roxburghshire and their motto is *Sero sed serio*—'Late but in earnest'. Legend has the Kerrs left-handed so they reversed the spiral of their staircases to allow space for the left sword-arm.

Lamont: derived from Lawman, Lawgiver; MacKeracher is the Highland version. Their lands were in Argyll and Cowal and their motto is *Nec parcas nec spernas*—'Neither spare nor dispose'. Clan Secretary, 17 Broomhall Loan, Edinburgh.

Leslie: taken from the barony of Leslie in Aberdeenshire which they adopted in the reign of William the Lion. Their motto is 'Grip fast'.

Lindsay: Lindsey means Linden (lime tree) Island. They came to Scotland with David I and became very powerful, with lands in the Borders and in Angus. Their motto is *Endure Fort*—'Endure with Strength'. Clan Secretary, 112 Corsebar Road, Paisley.

Livingstone: from Livingstone in West Lothian where they held land, as well as in the Trossachs and Lorne. Their motto is *Si je puis*—'If I can'. Clan Secretary, Bachuil, Isle of Lismore, Oban, Argyll.

Logan or **MacLennan**: Logan is in Lothian, with MacLennan as the Highland version. Their lands were in Lothian, Berwickshire and Easter Ross, and their motto is 'The Ridge of Tears'.

MacAlister: son of Alasdair, Gaelic for Alexander, who was descended from the great Somerled. Their lands were Kintyre, Arran and Bute, and their motto is *Fortiter*—'Boldly'. Clan Centre, Glenbarr Abbey, Kintyre, Strathclyde.

MacAlpin: Alpins claim descent from 9th-century King Alpin, and Dunstaffnage was their traditional home, though the race had no land. Their motto is *Cuimhnich bas Ailpein*—'Remember the death of Alpin'.

MacArthur: the MacArthurs were the senior branch of the Campbell clan, taking their name from Arthur Campbell in the 14th century. Their lands were Argyll, Cowal and Skye and their mottos are *Fide et Opera*—'By Fidelity and Work' and *Eisd! O eisd!*—'Listen! O listen!' Clan Secretary, 14 Hill Park Road, Edinburgh.

MacAulay: son of Olaf, who was King of Man and the Isles in the 13th century. Their lands were Dunbartonshire, Isle of Lewis, Sutherland and Ross. Their motto is *Dulce Periculum*—'Danger is sweet'. Clan Secretary, Cameron Loch Lomond Ltd, Alexandria, Dumbartonshire.

MacBean: son of Beathan, or from the Gaelic *bian*—fair skin—or from King Donald Ban, from whom they claim descent. Donald Ban was the son of Duncan, murdered by Macbeth. Their lands were in Inverness-shire and their motto is 'Touch not the cat bot (without) a targe (shield)'. At Culloden, gallant Gillies MacBean breached a gap in a wall with his enormous body and killed 14 Hanoverians before he was himself slain.

MacBeth: derived from the Gaelic for 'Son of Life'. Their lands were in Morayshire and Perthshire and their most famous ancestor, King MacBeth (1040–57), was very different from Shakespeare's character: a wise, generous, pious ruler, the last of the Gaelic kings.

MacCallum: *calaman* is Gaelic for dove, implying a disciple of St Columba whose emblem was the Dove of Peace. Their lands were in Argyll, and their mottos are *In ardua petit*—'He has tried difficult things', and *Deus refugium nostrum*—'God is our refuge'.

Macdonald: *Dòmhnall* is Gaelic for world ruler. Donald of Islay was grandson of Somerled, Lord of the Isles and Ragnhildis, daughter of King Olaf of Man. Clan Donald was the largest and most powerful of the clans, with a number of branches, reigning supreme in the northwest Highlands and Islands. There are a variety of spellings, including MacDonnell. (Mac was not used in the surname until the 16th century.) It is the commonest Mac name in Scotland. The main branches were: Sleat in Skye, Clanranald in Moidart, Glengarry, Keppoch in Lochaber, and Glencoe. They were staunch Jacobites and Royalists, fiercely claiming their position on the right wing of any battle, given them by Robert the Bruce at Bannockburn and still held at Culloden. Their mottos include: *Per mare per terras*—'By land and by sea'; *Fraoch eilean*—'The heathery isle'; 'My hope is constant in thee'; *Dh'aindeoin co'theireadh e*—'Gainsay who dare'; *Creag an fitheach*—'the Raven's Rock'; and *Dia's naomh Aindrea*—'God and St Andrew'. Clan Centre, Armadale Castle, Sleat, Skye. Clan Secretary, Ceadach, 39 Redford Road, Edinburgh.

MacDougal: from the Gaelic *dubh gall,* meaning 'dark stranger'. Their lands were Lorne, and their motto is *Buaidh no bàs*—'To conquer or die'. They fought against Robert the Bruce, and with the Hanoverians at Culloden. Clan Secretary, Dunollie Castle, Oban, Argyll.

MacDuff: from the Gaelic *mac dubh*—son of the dark one. Their lands were in Fife, Lothian, Strathbran and Strathbogie, and their motto is *Deus juvat*—'God assists'. The MacDuffs spawned a number of other clans: a MacDuff earl was known as *Mac an tòiseach*—son of the chief, which became MacIntosh, for example. Clan Secretary, 5 Sidlaw Road, Glasgow.

MacEwan: son of Ewan, who flourished in the 13th century. Their lands were Cowal, Lennox and Galloway, and their motto is *Reviresco*—'I grow strong'.

MacFarlane: son of Partholon, whose father, Sear, took over Ireland after the Flood. Their lands were around Loch Lomond, Tarbert and Arrochar, and their motto is *Loch Sloigh*—'Loch Sloy'.

MacFie: derived from the Gaelic *Dubhsìth*, meaning 'peaceful dark one', the MacFies are a branch of the Clan Alpine. Their lands were Colonsay, and their motto is *pro rege*—'for the king'. Clan Secretary, 120 Cockburn Crescent, Balerno, Midlothian.

MacGillivray: *gille breth* is Gaelic for 'servant of judgement' and the clan belonged to the Clan Chattan Confederation. Their lands were in Mull, Lochaber and Morven, and later in Inverness-shire. Their motto is Dunmaghlas, the name of the chief's castle. MacGillivray of Dunmaglass led the Clan Chattan at Culloden. Clan Secretary, Dunlichty, 7 Cramond Park, Edinburgh.

MacGregor: *Grioghair* is Gaelic for Gregory, and they claim descent from Griogar, son of 8th-century King Alpin. Some prefer to claim Pope Gregory the Great as their forefather. Whatever the truth, they all claim royal descent. Their lands were in Argyll and Perthshire and their motto is *S'rìoghail mo drèam*—'Royal is my race'. Their name was first proscribed 'under pain of death' after a blood-thirsty massacre of the Colquhouns in 1603, and again by William III. Many changed their names. Clan Secretary, 14 Lockharton Avenue, Edinburgh.

MacInnes: *aontaghais* is Gaelic for 'unique choice' and they were an ancient Celtic clan. Their lands were Morven and Ardnamurchan, and their motto is *Irid Ghibht dhe Agus an Righ*—'Through the Grace of God and the King'. Clan Secretary, 35 East Claremont Street, Edinburgh.

MacIntosh: *see* **Mackintosh** and **MacDuff**.

MacIntyre: *an-t-saor* is Gaelic for 'son of a carpenter' and the clan is said to have taken this name from one who chopped off his thumb to stop a leak in a Macdonald chief's galley. Their lands were Kintyre, Glenoe and Badenoch and they were part of the Clan Chattan Confederation. Their motto is *Per ardua*—'Through difficulties'. Clan Chattan Secretary, Dyunmaglash, Westhill, Inverness-shire.

MacKenzie: *coinnich* is Gaelic for 'fair' or 'bright' and was a popular Celtic forename, anglicized as Kenneth. MacKenzie lands were in Ross and Cromarty and the Isle of Lewis. Their mottos include *Luceo no uro*—'I shine, not burn'; *Tulach Ard*—'The High Hillock'; and *Cuidich 'n righ*—'Save the King'. Traditionally they provided most of the men in the Seaforth Highlanders, now amalgamated with the Cameron Highlanders to form The Queen's Own Highlanders. Clan Secretary, 1b Downie Place, Musselburgh, Midlothian.

MacKinnon: Kinnon derives from 13th-century Fingan, and the MacKinnons were the family of St Columba, part of the Clan Alpin. Their lands were Iona and North Mull, then Skye and Arran, and their mottos are *Audentes fortuna iuvat*—'Fortune favours the brave'; and *Cùimhnich bas Ailpein*—'Remember the death of Alpin'. Clan Secretary, 222 Darnley Street, Pollockshiels, Glasgow.

MacKintosh: *toiseach* is Gaelic for 'tribal leader' or thane, and the clan descended from the MacDuffs, originally the leading family of the Clan Chattan Confederation. Their lands were Inverness-shire and their motto is 'Touch not the cat bot (without) a glove'. Brave, beautiful, Jacobite Lady Anne MacKintosh, known as Colonel Anne, masterminded the Rout of Moy, ousting 1,500 of Cumberland's troops with a mere five men. Clan Secretary, Moy Hall, Moy, Inverness-shire.

MacLachlan: Lachlan was a Celtic forename derived from Lochlann, the Gaelic for Norway, and the clan claims descent from Niall of the Nine Hostages, High King of Ireland, who won land in Argyllshire. They later spread to Lochaber, Perthshire and Stirlingshire. Their motto is *Fortis et Fidis*—'Brave and Trusty'. MacLachlan of MacLachlan, Prince Charles' ADC, died at Culloden in 1746. Clan Secretary, Tigh-na-Croft, Enochdhu, Blairgowrie, Angus.

MacLaine of Lochbuie: *gille Eoin* is Gaelic for 'servant of John',„and they claim descent from Lachlans and MacLeans. Their lands were Lochbuie, and their motto is *Vincere vel mori*—'conquer or die'.

MacLaren: from the Gaelic, 'son of Lawrence'. Their lands were Strathearn and Balquhidder, and their motto is 'The Boar's Rock'. Clan Secretary, 1 Inverleith Place, Edinburgh.

Maclean: *gille Eoin* is Gaelic for 'servant of John', and they claim descent from the Kings of Dalriada. Their lands were Morvern, Mull, Coll and Tiree, and their mottos are *Bas no Beatha*—'death or life'; and *Fear eile airson Eachairn*—'Another for Hector'. Clan Secretary, 12 Elie Street, Glasgow.

Macleod: *liotr* was old Norse for 'ugly'; *leod* was Saxon for 'prince.' They claim descent from Olaf the Black, King of Man and the Islands in the 13th century, and their lands were Skye, Lewis and Harris. 'Hold fast' is their motto. Clan Secretary, 38 Ravelston Gardens, Edinburgh.

MacMillan: *maoilein* means 'bald one', meaning tonsured and therefore priest, so their origins were ecclesiastical. Their lands were Lochaber, Argyll and Galloway, and their motto is *Miseris succurrere disco*—'I learn to succor the distressed'. John MacMillan (1670–1753), founded the Reformed Presbyterian Church. Clan Centre, Finlaystone, Langbank, Renfrewshire. Clan Secretary, 21 Huntley Gardens, Edinburgh.

MacNab: from *aba* meaning 'abbot', the MacNabs are descended from the Abbot of Glendochart, in the time of David I. Their lands were Glendochart and Loch Tay and their motto is *Timor omnis abesto*—'Let fear be far from all'. Raeburn's magnificent painting of *The MacNab* was of the 12th chief, Francis (1734–1816), a remarkable eccentric, described by one as 'a herculean Highlander'. Clan Secretary, Finlarig, Killin, Perthshire.

MacNaughton/MacNachtan: *neachdainn* is Gaelic for 'pure one' and they can be traced back to Pictish royalty. Their lands were Strathtay, Lewis and Argyll, and their motto is 'I hope in God'. The Clan Centre is at Dunderaive Castle, near Inveraray. Clan Secretary, 2 Douglas Crescent, Edinburgh.

MacNeil: descended from the O'Neills who were High Kings of Ireland. Their lands were Barra, Gigha, Knapdale and Colonsay, and their motto is *Vincere vel mori*—'To conquer or die'. Clan Secretary, 34 Craigleith Hill Avenue, Edinburgh.

MacNicol or **Nicholson**: sons of Nicol. They can trace their ancestry back to the dark ages. The clan's lands were Sutherland, Skye and Argyll, and their motto is *Sgorra Bhreac*—Skorrybreck.

MacPherson: *phearsain* was Gaelic for 'parson'. They were part of the Clan Chattan Confederation and trace their ancestry to Ferchar, King of Lorne, who died in 697. Staunch Jacobites, they arrived too late for the Battle of Culloden. Their land was Badenoch and their motto is 'Touch not the cat bot (without) a glove'. Clan Secretary, 39 Swanson Avenue, Edinburgh.

MacQuarrie: *guardhre* is Gaelic for 'noble one' and they trace their roots to the Clan Alpine and Saint Columba's family. Their lands were Ulva, and their motto, *An t-arm breac dearg*, means 'the red tartaned army'.

MacQueen: from the Norse *sweyne*, or Gaelic *siubhne*, meaning 'good going'. They were strong members of the Clan Chattan Confederation, with close Macdonald connections. Their lands were Skye, Lewis, Argyll and Lanarkshire, and their motto is 'Constant and faithful'. Clan Chattan Secretary, Dyunmaglash, Westhill, Inverness-shire.

MacRae: means 'son of grace', probably of ecclesiastical origin. Known as the 'Wild MacRaes' and also as 'MacKenzies Coat of Mail,' they were hereditary Constables of Eilan Donan Castle for the MacKenzies of Kintail, now restored by one of their descendants. Their lands were Beauly and Kintail, and their motto is *Fortitudine*—'With Fortitude'. Clan Secretary, 6 Gardiners Crescent, Edinburgh.

Malcolm: followers of St Columba. Their lands were in Argyll, Fife, Lochore and Dumfriesshire. Their motto was *Deus refugium nostrum*—'God is our refuge', and is now *In ardua petit*—'He aims at difficult things'. Clan Secretary, Duntrune Castle, Kilmelford, Lochgilphead, Argyll.

Matheson: *math-ghamhainn* is Gaelic for 'bear' and, traditionally, the Clan of the Bear helped Kenneth MacAlpin against the Picts in 843. Their lands were Lochalsh and Sutherland, and their motto is *Fac et Spera*—'Do and hope'. Clan Secretary, Burnside, Duirnish, Kyle of Lochalsh, Ross-shire.

Maxwell: from Maxwell on the River Tweed, derived from Maccus's Wiel, they were a powerful Border family descended either from 11th-century Maccus, King of Man and the Isles, or from Norman settlers. Their lands were in Nithsdale, and their motto is *Reviresco*—'I flourish again'.

Menzies (correctly pronounced *mingiz*): from Mesnières in Normandy. Although of Anglo-Norman origin they became Gaelicized. Their lands were Atholl, Weem, Aberfeldy and Glendochart, and their mottos are *Vil God I Zal*—'Will God I shall'; and *Geal 'us dearg a suas*—'Up with the white and red'. Clan Secretary, 1 Belford Pl, Edinburgh. Clan Museum, Castle Menzies, Aberfeldy, Tayside.

Moncreiffe: from Gaelic *monadh craobhe*—tree on the moor, descended from Maldred, brother of King Duncan. Their lands were in Perthshire and their lairds were traditionally archers of the sovereign's bodyguard. Clan Secretary, Easter Moncreiffe, Perthshire.

Montgomery: from Montgomerie, in Normandy, the family are descended from Anglo-Norman Robert de Montgomery, who came to Scotland in the 12th century. Their lands were Eglinton, Ardrossan and Kintyre, and their motto is *Gardez bien*—'Look well'. Clan Secretary, c/o P.O. Box 6, Saltcoats, Ayrshire.

Morrison: *gille Mhoire* is Gaelic for 'servant of Mary', presumably of ecclesiastical origin, and they trace their ancestors to the MacLeods of Dunvegan in 13th century. Their lands were Lewis, Sutherland, Skye and Harris. Hebridean Morrisons are well-known pipers today. Clan Secretary, Ruchdi, by Loch Maddy, Isle of North Uist.

Munro: from the Gaelic *Rothach*—man from Ro, thought to be from the River Roe in Ireland. Their lands were in Easter Ross, their motto is 'Dread God' and their war-cry, 'Castle Foulis Ablaze!', refers to the beacon that used to be lit on the chief's castle to summon the clan to arms. They were Whigs, supporting the Government against the Jacobites.

Murray: from Moray, the place name meaning 'settlement by the sea'. They are descended from Pictish Mormaers, with lands in Morayshire and Perthshire. Their motto is *Tout pret*—'All ready'. Andrew Murray, who died in 1338, was Regent of Scotland; Lord George Murray was a Jacobite general, believed by some to have been a traitor at Culloden. Clan Secretary, 204 Bruntsfield Place, Edinburgh.

Napier: descended from the ancient earls of Lennox; legend has it that one, having been particularly brave in battle, was ordered by his King to change his name to 'Nae peer'! Their lands were Gosford, Fife and Midlothian, and their mottos are *Sans tache*—'Without stain'; and *To vincula frange*—'To break bones'.

Ogilvie: from Brythonic *ocel fa*—'high plain'. Ogilvie Earls of Airlie descend directly from the Earls of Angus, and were granted lands in Angus by William the Lion. Their motto is *A fin*—'To the finish'. St John Ogilvie (1579–1615), was a Scottish Jesuit martyr, canonized in 1976.

Ramsay: meaning 'wild-garlic island'. The family is descended from an Anglo-Norman, Simund de Ramesie, who was granted lands in Lothian by David I. Their lands were Dalhousie and Perthshire, and their motto is *Ora et labor*—'Pray and work'.

Robertson: the eponymous Robert was Robert Riabhach (Grizzled Robert) Duncanson, 4th Chief of Clan Donnachaidh, and the Robertsons of Struan are one of the earliest known families in Scotland. Struan was their land, and their mottos are: *Virtutis Gloria Merces*—'Glory is the reward of valour'; and *Garg'n uair dhuis gear*—'Fierce when raised'. Clan Secretary, 29 Lauriston Gardens, Edinburgh.

Rose: descended from the Norman family de Rose and first recorded in Scotland in the reign of Alexander II. Their lands were Strathnairn and Ross-shire, and their motto is 'Constant and true'. Clan Secretary, Kilravock Castle, Nairnshire.

Ross: the Gaelic *ros* means 'headland'; Brythonic *ros* means 'moor'. They are descended from Fearchar Mac-an-t-Sagairt of Applecross, created Earl of Ross in 1234. Their lands were Ross-shire, Ayrshire and Renfrewshire, and their motto is *Spem successus alit*—'Success nourishes hope'. Clan Secretary, 57 Barnton Park View, Edinburgh.

Scott: the Scoti were the Irish tribe who gave Scotland its name. The family descend from Uchtred, *filius Scoti*—'son of a Scot'—in the 12th century, and were one of the most powerful Border families. Their lands were in the Borders and Fife and one of their best-known scions is Sir Walter, the 19th-century writer.

Scrymgeour: from French *eskermisor*—sword-fencer or skirmisher. Their ancestor Alexander 'Schyrmeschar' was royal banner-bearer, hanged by Edward I in 1306. Their lands were in Argyll and Fife, and their motto is 'Dissipate'. Clan Secretary, 21 Braid Farm Road, Edinburgh.

Shaw: possibly derived from the Gaelic *seaghdha*—pithy. Principal members of the Clan Chattan Confederation, they were probably descended from 14th-century Shaw Macduff, founder of the MacIntosh clan. Their land was Strathspey, and their motto is *Fide et Fortitudine*—'By Fidelity and Fortitude'. Clan Secretary, Tordarroch House, Tordarroch, Inverness-shire.

Sinclair: from the French St Clair sur Elle, in Normandy, whence came William de Sancto Claro in the 12th century, receiving the barony of Roslin. Their lands were in Midlothian, Orkney and Caithness, and they were jarls of Orkney in the 14th century. Their motto is 'Commit thy work to God'. Clan Secretary, 2 Shandon Road, Edinburgh.

Skene: from Skene in Aberdeenshire, they are descended from Robertsons of Struan. Their lands were in Aberdeenshire, granted by the king in 11th century. Their motto is *Virtutis regia merces*—'A palace the reward of bravery'.

Stewart: derived from High Steward. Walter Fitz-Allan, an Anglo-Norman, came to Scotland in the 12th century and was given land and the greatest office in the realm—Steward of Scotland. The family provided Scotland with 14 sovereigns, five of whom also reigned in England. Stuart was the French form of the name, adopted in England. Their lands were Renfrewshire, Teviotdale, Lauderdale, Appin and Ardshiel, and their motto is *Virescit vulnere virtus*—'Courage grows strong at a wound'. Probably the best-known Stuart was the one who never got to the throne, Prince Charles Edward (1720–88). Clan Secretary, 48 Castle Street, Edinburgh.

Sutherland: Sudrland was the Norman name for Sutherland, to the south of Caithness. The clan is descended from early inhabitants of Sutherland, which was granted to them in 1228. Clan Secretary, Dunrobin Castle, Golspie, Sutherland.

Urquhart: derived from Brythonic *air cairdean*—at the woods, the name of the district where the family originated. William of Urquhart was hereditary sheriff of Cromarty during the reign of Robert the Bruce. Their lands were in Ross-shire and Inverness-shire and their motto is 'Mean, speak and do well'. Thomas Urquart (1611–60), who claimed descent from Adam, was a brilliant translator of Rabelais and is said to have died of laughter, on hearing of the Restoration. Clan Secretary, Bigram, Port of Monteith, Stirlingshire.

Wallace: derived from Wallenses, the mediaeval word for the Welsh who peopled Strathclyde, from whom the Wallaces are descended. Their lands were Ayrshire and Renfrewshire, and their motto is *Pro Libertate*—'For Liberty'. William Wallace fought for Scottish independence, paving the way for Robert the Bruce.

Scottish Monarchs

Kenneth Macalpine: 843–58
Donald: 858–62
Constantine I: 862–77
Aed: 877–8
Eochaid and Giric (joint kingship): 878–89
Donald II: 889–900
Constantine II: 900–43
Malcolm I: 943–54
Indulf: 954–62
Dubh: 962–6
Culen: 966–71
Kenneth II: 971–95
Constantine III: 995–7
Kenneth III: 997–1005
Malcolm II: 1005–34
Duncan I: 1034–40
Macbeth: 1040–57
Lulach: 1058
Malcolm III, Canmore: 1058–93
Donald III Bane: 1093–4 (six months)
Duncan II: 1094 (six months)
Donald III Bane: 1094–7
Edgar: 1097–1107
Alexander I: 1107–24
David I: 1124–53
Malcolm IV, the Maiden: 1153–65
William I, the Lion: 1165–1214
Alexander II: 1214–49
Alexander III: 1249–86
Margaret, Maid of Norway: 1286–90
John Balliol: 1292–6
Interregnum: 1296–1306
Robert I (the Bruce): 1306–29
David II: 1329–71

Stewarts

Robert II: 1371–90
Robert III: 1390–1406
James I: 1406–37
James II: 1437–60
James III: 1460–88
James IV: 1488–1513
James V: 1513–42
Mary: 1542–67
James VI/I: 1567–1625
Charles I: 1625–49
The Commonwealth: 1649–60
Charles II: 1660–85
James VII/II: 1685–8
William and Mary: 1689–94
William (alone): 1694–1702
Anne: 1702–1714

Hanoverians

George I: 1714–27
George II: 1727–60
George III: 1760–1820
George IV: 1820–30
William II/IV: 1830–7

Saxe-Coburg-Gotha

Victoria: 1837–1901
Edward I/VII: 1901–10

Windsors

George V: 1910–36
Edward II/VIII: 1936
George VI: 1936–52
Elizabeth I/II: 1952–

83 Defeat of Picts at battle of Mons Graupius by Roman Agricola.
141–2 Building of Antonine Wall.
397 Founding of Christian church at Whithorn by St Ninian.
410 Departure of Romans from Britain.
500 Invasion of Scotland by Irish Scots, settlement of Dalriada.
563 Landing of St Columba in Iona, conversion of Picts to Christianity begins.
794 Invasion of Hebrides by Norsemen.
844–60 Kenneth Macalpine unites Picts and Scots.
1034 Whole of Scotland united into one kingdom under Duncan I.
1040 Duncan I murdered by Macbeth who is in turn murdered by Malcolm Canmore.
1057–93 Anglicizing of Scotland under Queen Margaret.
1102 Western Isles granted to Magnus of Orkney.
1124–53 David I founds many abbeys and burghs, grants land to Normans.
1174 William the Lion forced to acknowledge supremacy of Henry II.
1214 Alexander II, Golden Age of Scottish history.
1263 Battle of Largs, defeat by Alexander III of King Haakon of Norway. Annexation of the Hebrides.
1286 Death of Alexander III, succeeded by Margaret of Norway.
1290 Death of Maid of Norway at sea on her way to Scotland.
1291 Edward I arbitrates between Robert the Bruce and John Balliol. Balliol gets crown.
1296 Balliol renounces his crown in favour of Edward I. Scottish nobility agree to treaty of mutual assistance with Philip IV of France—the beginning of the Auld Alliance.
1297–8 William Wallace stirs up resistance, defeats Edward at Stirling Bridge, and is defeated at Falkirk. Goes into hiding.
1305 Capture and execution of William Wallace.
1306 Robert the Bruce slays John Comyn and is crowned at Scone.
1307 Edward I dies.
1314 Battle of Bannockburn, Bruce defeats English.
1320 Declaration of Arbroath.
1326 First Scottish Parliament at Cambuskenneth.
1328 By treaty of Edinburgh England recognizes Robert the Bruce as king of independent Scotland
1346 Battle of Neville's Cross. David II taken prisoner by English.
1371 Robert Stewart crowned Robert II, first Stewart King.
1406 James I captured, Duke of Albany becomes guardian of Scotland.
1414 Foundation of St Andrews, Scotland's first university.
1450–5 Struggle for supremacy between Stewarts and Douglases. Douglases crushed by James II.
1469 Orkney and Shetland pledged to James III as part of dowry of his wife, Margaret of Denmark.
1476 Overthrow of Lords of the Isles.
1488 James III defeated and killed by rebels at Sauchieburn.
1491 Perkin Warbeck claims English throne, encouraged by James IV.
1503 James IV marries Margaret Tudor, daughter of Henry VII.
1513 Battle of Flodden, death of James IV.
1528 Burning of Patrick Hamilton, proto–martyr of Reformation.
1538 Marriage of James V to Marie de Guise-Lorraine.
1542 Defeat of Scots at Solway Moss, death of James V, accession of his infant daughter, Mary.
1544 Rough Wooing, devastation of Lowland Scotland by Henry VIII.

1554 Regency of Marie de Guise.
1557 Signing of first Protestant Covenant.
1558 Marriage of Mary to Dauphin of France, later Francis II.
1559 John Knox returns to Scotland. Reformers destroy the abbey church at Scone.
1561 Mary, Queen of Scots returns to Scotland.
1565 Marriage of Mary to Darnley. Moray's rebellion is suppressed.
1566 Murder of Rizzio. Birth of James VI.
1567 Murder of Darnley, marriage of Mary to Bothwell; defeat, imprisonment and abdication.
1568 Mary escapes to England and is imprisoned by Elizabeth.
1570 Moray is assassinated and Lennox becomes regent of Scotland.
1582 James VI is abducted in the Ruthven raid.
1587 Mary, Queen of Scots is executed.
1603 Accession of James VI to English throne making him James VI/I (VI of Scotland, I of England). Establishment of Episcopacy in Scotland.
1637 Riots of Edinburgh against Charles I's new prayer book.
1638 Signing of National Covenant to uphold Presbyterian worship.
1643 Signing of Solemn League and Covenant recognized by English Parliament.
1645 Battle of Philiphaugh. Defeat of Royalist Montrose by Covenanters under Leslie.
1646 Charles surrenders to the Scots.
1647 The Scots give Charles to the English.
1649 Execution of Charles I, Charles II proclaimed King in Scotland.
1650 Signing of Covenants by Charles II. Invasion of Scotland by Cromwell.
1660 Restoration of Monarchy.
1662 Renunciation of Covenants by Charles II and re-establishment of Episcopacy.
1666 Start of the Killing Times, persecution of Covenanters.
1688 James VII/II tries to restore Catholicism. He is deposed in favour of William and Mary.
1689 Highlanders, under Claverhouse, Bonnie Dundee, defeat King's army at Killiecrankie.
1692 Massacre of Glencoe.
1695 Bank of Scotland founded and Company of Scotland established to colonize Darien coast.
1699 Darien colony evacuated.
***c.* 1700–*c.* 1800** The Age of Enlightenment
1707 Union of Parliaments.
1715 Rebellion in favour of the Old Pretender.
1736 The Porteous Riots: Scots rebel against English domination.
1745/6 Final Jacobite rebellion. Defeat of Prince Charles Edward Stuart at Battle of Culloden. Repression of Highlands. Soon followed by the beginning of the Highland Clearances.
1760 Carron Ironworks starts production.
1845/6 Irish potato famine spreads to Scotland causing starvation and terrible hardship.
1947 Founding of Edinburgh International Festival, putting Scotland back on the cultural map.

Chronology

1970s North Sea oil industry developed.
1979 Scotland rejects devolution in a referendum.
1997 Referendum again. Scots vote by 74% for a Scottish Parliament.
1999 First Edinburgh Parliament.

Aber mouth of: confluence of (rivers)
Advocate barrister
Aird point, promontory
Allt stream
Aros dwelling
Athole brose delicious drink of whisky, honey, oatmeal and cream
Auch a field
Auld old
Aye yes
Bairn child
Bal town, home
Ban fair
Bannock oatmeal pancake/scone
Bap bread roll
Bard poet
Barr crest
Beag small
Bealach, balloch mountain pass
Bean woman
Ben, beinn mountain
Bhlair plain
Blether talk nonsense
Bogle frightening ghost
Bothy rough hut
Brae hill
Branks bridle, halter
Braw fine
Breeks trousers
Bridie pie with filling of meat, onions, vegetables, etc.
Brig bridge
Broch prehistoric round stone tower with hollow walls, enclosing cell-like galleries, and stairways
Burn stream
Byre barn
Cailleach old woman
Cairn stone monument
Cam crooked
Canny prudent
Caolas firth
Capercailie wood-grouse
Car curve
Ceann head
Céilidh informal social gathering, often with spontaneous singing, music, story telling, etc.
Chanter double-reeded pipe
Cil church
Clach stone
Cladach beach
Clarty dirty
Claymore sword
Cleg horsefly
Cnoc hillock
Collie sheepdog, wood
Corbie crow
Corrie hollow
Crack conversation
Craig rock
Crannog small man-made island dating from Iron Age. Stones piled on wooden base with easily defended single dwelling on top, often reached by a sunken causeway
Creel pannier-type basket, also lobster pot
Crowdie soft cheese
Cuddy donkey
Cul recess
Cutty short (cutty sark, short petticoat; cutty stool, stool of repentance)
Dal field
Dalr valley
Damph deer, steer
Daunder saunter
Ding knock, beat
Doo dove
Doo'cot dovecot
Dour dry, humourless
Douse sweet, gentle
Dram one-eighth fluid ounce/ generous tot of whisky
Dreich dreary, boring

Drochit bridge
Dross coal dust
Drove road tracks used for herding cattle or sheep to market
Druim, drum ridge
Dubh dark, black
Dun hillfort
Dyke wall of stones or turf
Dysart hermit's retreat, desert
Eaglais church
Eas waterfall, gorge
Eilean island
Ey island
Factor land agent, usually of private estate
Fada long
Fail rock
Fank sheepfold
Fash trouble, upset: 'dinna fash yersel'
Fear man
Feu feudal tenure of land with rent paid in kind or money
Fey susceptible to supernatural influence
Fillebeg kilt
Fionn gleaming, white
Firth wide mouth of river, estuary
Flit remove, move house
Fou full (of drink)
Fraoch heather
Gearr short
Geodha chasm
Gil ravine
Glass grey
Glen valley
Gleo mist
Gobha blacksmith
Gorm blue, green
Gowk fool
Greet cry
Harling rough-cast facing to walls
Haver talk nonsense
Heugh hillock
Hog unshorn lamb
Hogmanay New Year's Eve
Holm low ground by river, islet in river
Hope bay
How burial mound
Howe low-lying ground, hollow
Howff meeting place, refuge, burial ground
Howk dig
Ilk same, of that ilk—surname
Inch island
Inver mouth of river
Kail cabbage
Kailyard cabbage patch, back yard
Keek peep
Kelpie water-sprite, water-horse
Ken know
Kenspeckle easily recognizable, conspicuous
Kil burial place, church
Kin head (of loch, river)
Kirk church
Knock, knowe knoll, hillock
Kye cattle
Kyle strait, narrow channel between two points of land
Lag, laggan hollow, dip
Laird owner of estate
Land tenement
Larach site of ruin
Larig, learg mountain pass
Law round hill
Leana plain
Liath grey
Links dunes
Linn, linne pool
Lis garden on site of fortress
Loan lane

Glossary

Loch, lochan	lake, small lake
Lug	ear
Lum	chimney
Machair	sand-peat lowland bordering seashore
Maol	bare headland
Manse	minister's house (ecclesiastical)
March	boundary
Meikle	large
Mon	moor
Mor	great
Moy	plain
Muc, muic	sow
Muckle	large
Mull	promontory
Neeps	turnips (English swedes)
Neuk	nose
Ob, oba, oban	bay
Ochter	high
Pit	dip
Plenishing	furniture, domestic equipment
Ploy	activity
Poke	bag
Policies	grounds within an estate
Poll	pool
Provost	mayor
Puddock	frog
Quaich	shallow, two-handled drinking bowl
Rath	fort
Reek	smoke
Reidh	smooth
Rig	ridge
Ross	peninsula
Ru, rhu, row, rubha	point
Sark	shift, shirt
Scunner	dislike
Selkie	seal
Sgeir, skerry	sea, rock
Sgor, scuir, sgurr	sharp rock
Sheiling	hut for summer pasture
Shinty	hockey
Siccar	certain
Siller	silver (money)
Slochd	hollow, grave
Sonsie	bonnie
Soutar	cobbler
Spittal	hospice
Stob	stake, point
Strath	broad valley
Strone	nose, promontory
Struan, struth	stream
Swither	vacillate
Syne	ago
Tarbert, tarbet	isthmus
Tassie	cup
Thing	parliament, council
Thole	endure
Thrang	thronged
Thrawn	awkward
Tigh	house
Tir	land
Tobar	well
Tocher	dowry
Tod	fox
Toom	empty
Tom	hillock
Torr	hill
Tow	rope
Tulloch, tilly, tully	knoll
Uachdar	upper, high
Uamh	cave
Uig	sheltered bay
Uisge, esk	water
Uisge beatha	water of life (whisky)
Unco	strange, very
Usquebaugh	whisky
Vennel	alley
Voe	narrow bay, fiord
Wean	child
Weems	caves
Whinn	gorse
Wick, vik	bay
Wight	strong
Wynd	alley
Yett	gate

Non-fiction

A Century of the Scottish People, 1830–1950.

Beveridge, H., *The Sobieski Stuarts.*

Boswell, James, *Journal of a Tour to the Hebrides* and **Johnson, Samuel**, *A Journey to the Western Islands.* Can be obtained in one volume and should be read together.

Bray, Elizabeth, *The Discovery of the Hebrides.*

Cameron, A.D., *Go Listen to the Crofters.* Napier Commission & Crofting, a century ago.

Daiches, David, *A Companion to Scottish Culture.*

(ed) **Duff, David**, *Queen Victoria's Highland Journal.*

Fraser, Antonia, *Mary, Queen of Scots.*

Grant, Elizabeth, *Memoirs of a Highland Lady.*

Grant, I. F., *Highland Folk Ways.*

Haldane, A. R. B., *The Drove Roads of Scotland.*

Harris, Paul, *Scotland: An Anthology.* Delightful, idiosycratic literary collection.

Haswell-Smith, Hamish, *Scottish Islands.*

Keay, John, *Highland Drove.* An account of droving cattle today using the old methods and routes. Good descriptions.

Linklater, Eric, *The Prince in the Heather.* Prince Charlie's escape after Culloden.

Maclean, Alasdair, *A Macdonald for the Prince.* The story of Neil MacEachen, native of Uist and father of Napoleon's Marshal Macdonald.

Mackenzie, Alexander, *The Prophecies of the Brahn Seer.*

Mackenzie, Osgood, *A Hundred Years in the Highlands.*

Maclean, Calum I., *The Highlands.* Charming reminiscenses, reprinted to include an introduction by his brother Sorley, the poet, with outstanding photographs by his nephew, Cailean.

Maclean, Fitzroy, *A Concise History of Scotland*; and *Bonnie Prince Charlie* (beautifully written and entirely unbiased).

Madders, Mike and Welstead, Julia, *Where to Watch Birds in Scotland* (Helm). Useful book for birdwatchers.

Martin, M., *A Description of the Western Islands of Scotland.* James Thin reprinted a facsimile of this 1716 gem.

Maxwell, Gavin, *Harpoon at a Venture; Ring of Bright Water; The Rocks Remain; and Raven Seek Thy Brother.* All describe Maxwell's fascinating life in the Western Highlands.

Mitchell, Ian, *Isles of the West.*

Moncreiffe of that Ilk, Sir Iain, *The Highland Clans.* Not quite so readable but an erudite book of great value.

Further Reading

Morton, H. V., *In Search of Scotland*, and *In Scotland Again.* Written in 1929 and 1933 and are as fresh and readable today as then.

Murray, W. H., *The Islands of Western Scotland.*

Prebble, John, *The Lion in the North.*

Scott, Walter, *Tales of a Grandfather.* The history of Scotland as told to his young grandson.

Smout, T. C., *A History of the Scottish People 1560–1830.*

Steel, Tom, *Scotland's Story;* and *The Life and Death of St Kilda.*

Wallace, Ian, *Reflections on Scotland.* A traveller's scrap-book, by the Scottish singer.

Wigan, Michael, *Scottish Highland Estate: Preserving an Environment.*

Novels

Banks, Iain, *The Crow Road.*

Buchan, John, *John Macnab, The Thirty-Nine Steps*, etc,

Crichton Smith, Iain, *Consider the Lilies.* Charming, sad story about the Clearances.

Dorothy, Dunnet, *King Hereafter.*

Gibbon, Lewis Grassic, *A Scots Quair.*

Gray, Alasdair, *Lanark.*

Howarth, David, *Shetland Bus.*

Mackay, Colin, *The Song of the Forest.* A beautiful piece of contemporary writing, giving a picture of life in the Dark Ages. *The Sound of the Sea* is equally well written.

Mackenzie, Compton, *Whisky Galore*, and any of his other novels.

Profumo, David, *Sea Music.*

Scott, Walter: his vast output includes: *Waverley*, his first novel, about Jacobites; *Redgauntlet*, about how Prince Charlie returned to Scotland to try his luck once more; *Fair Maid of Perth*, set in Perth at the end of the 14th century; *Old Mortality*, about Covenanters; and *Rob Roy.*

Stevenson, Robert Louis, *Kidnapped*; and *Catriona* (based on the story of the Appin murder).

Thomas Ellis, Alice, *The Inn at the Edge of the World.*

Poetry

(ed) **Barke, James**, *Poems and Songs of Robert Burns.* With introduction by the author.

Maclean, Sorley, *From Wood to Ridge.* A collection of his haunting poems, in Gaelic and English.

MacDiarmid, Hugh: any of his works.

McCaig, Norman, *Anthology of Poetry.*

McGonagall, William, *Poetic Gems Selected From the Works of William McGonagall, Poet and Tragedian.* Scotland's worst poet—and compulsive reading.

Light Relief

Hedderwick, Mairi, *An Eye on the Hebrides.* An Illustrated Journey.

HRH The Prince of Wales, *The Old Man of Lochnagar.*

Stuart, Jamie, *A Glasgow Bible.* Essential reading for anyone familiar with Glaswegian.

For Children

Hedderwick, Mairi: all the *Katie Morag* books.

Main page references are in **bold**. Page references to maps are in *italics*.

Aberfeldy 62–3
  Black Watch Monument 62
  Castle Menzies 63
  Glengoulandie Deer Park 62–3
Aberfoyle 75
  Scottish Wool Centre 75
accommodation *see* where to stay
Achanlochy 205
Acharacle 122
Achavanich Standing Stone Circle 197
Achiltibuie 153–4
Achnacarry Castle 131
Adam, John 88, 89, 169
Adam, William 63, 88, 89
Aiden 96
Aigas 175
Ailsa Craig 218
air travel 4, 5–6
Alexander I 52
Alexander II 27, 93, 136
Alexander III 27, 212
Altnaharra 207
An Cala Garden 95
Anne, Princess Royal 57
Aonach Mhor 108
Appin 104
Appin Murder **111–12**
Applecross 146
Ardchattan Priory and Gardens 103
Ardelve
Ardentinny 85
Ardkinglass Woodland Garden 88
Ardnadam Heritage Trail 86
Ardnamurchan Peninsula 124
Ardnamurchan Point lighthouse 125
Ardrishaig 98
Ardtornish Castle 125–6
Ardtornish House 125
Arduaine Garden 95
Ardverikie House 132
Ardvreck Castle 155
Argyll's Bowling Green 84
Arisaig 118
Arran **216–19**
  Auchgallon Stone Circle 218
  Brodick 216–17
  Corrie 217–18
  Fallen Rocks 218
  Farm Road Stone Circle 218
  Giant's Graves 219
  Glen Ashdale Falls 218
  Glen Catocol 218
  Glen Iorsa 218
  Glen Sannox 218
  Goat Fell 217
  Isle of Arran Distillery 218
  Isle of Arran Heritage Centre 217
  Kildonan 218
  Kilmory Cairns 218
  King's Caves 218
  Lamlash 219
  Lochranza 218
  Machrie Standing Stones 218
  Pirnmill 218
  Thunderguy 218
  Whiting Bay 218
Arrochar 83
Assynt **154–6**
Auchindrain 90
Auchterarder
Aurora Borealis 2
Aviemore 171
Avoch 180
Ba' Game 300
Badbea 196
Baile an Or 196
Baile Marghair 206
Ballachulish 111
Balliol, John 28
Balloch
Balmoral 56–7
  Crathie Church 57
Balnakeil Craft Village 208
Balquhidder
  Rob Roy's Grave 76
Bankfoot
  Macbeth Experience 58
Barcaldine Castle 103–4
Barra **293–5**
  Castlebay 294
    Kisimul Castle 294
  Dun Bharpa 294
  Heaval 295
  Traigh Mhor 295
Barry, Charles 194
Battle of the Braes 252
Battle of the Clans 49
Battle of the Shirts **132**
battles
  Bannockburn 28
  Carbisdale 155, 187
  Carinish 284–5
  Culloden 32, 166
  Druim na Coup 205
  Flodden Field 29
  Glendaruel 86
  Inverlochy 107–8
  Killiecrankie 67
  Largs 28
  Neville's Cross 28
  Prestonpans 32
  Sheriffmuir 31
  Traigh Gruinart 227
Beaufort Castle 175
Beauly 174–5
  Beauly Priory 174
  Lovat Memorial Garden 175
Beckford, William 217
Bein Eighe National Nature Reserve 147
Ben Arthur 83
Ben Cruachan 91
Ben Hope 207
Ben Lawers 65
Ben Lomond 75–6
Ben Loyal 207
Ben Nevis 108
Ben Venue 75
Ben Vrackie 75
Ben Vraggie 193
Ben Wyvis 178
Benbecula **285–7**
  Balivanich 286
  Borve Castle 286
  Liniclate 286
  Nunton 286
  Rossinish 286
Benderloch 103
Bernera Barracks 135
Berneray 282
  Ruisgarry 282

Index

Bettyhill 205
Birnam
  Beatrix Potter exhibition 58
Black Douglas 92
Black Isle 179–80
Black Isle Wildlife Park/Country Park 180
Black Rock Gorge 184
Black Watch 50, 62
Blackburn, Jemima 122
Blair Castle 68
Blairgowrie 55
Boece, Hector 107
Bonar Bridge 186
Bonawe Iron Furnace 103
Borve Castle 205, 206
Boswell, James **39–41**, 88, 89, 125, 135–6, 138, 140, 162, 233, 236,
  240, 243, 260, 261, 262, 263
Boyle, George Frederick 215
Braemar 55–6
  Braemar Castle 56
  Braemar Royal Highland Gathering 56
  Invercauld Arms 56
Braemore Junction 150
Brahan Seer 43–4, 182, 207
Breadalbane 62, 73
Bressay 315
Bridge of Balgie 65
Bridge of Cally 55
Brig o'Trams 200
Brora 194
Brough of Birsay 303
Brown, John 57
Brown, Lex 123
Bruar Falls 68
Bryce, David 68, 99, 222, 238, 307
Buchan, John 128
Bucholie Castle 201
Burns, Robert 62, 68–9, 83
Burra 316
bus and coach travel 5, 7
Bute **220–3**
  Ascog Hall Fernery and Garden 222
  Kames Castle 222
  Mount Stuart 221–2
  Rothesay 220–1
    Bute Museum 220
    Rothesay Castle 221
    St Mary's Chapel 221
    Winter Garden 220
  St Blane's Chapel 222
Byron, Lord 130
Cairngorm 171
Cairnwell 55
Caithness *see* Sutherland and Caithness
Caledonian Canal 107, 163
Callander 73–4
Cameron, Donald ('the Gentle Locheil') 131
Cameron-Head, Francis 122
Campbell, Colin, of Glenure ('the Red Fox') 111
Campbell, Marion 99
Campbell, Mary Maxwell 117
Campbell, Robert, of Glenlyon 113
Campbeltown 100
Canmore, Malcolm 27, 56, 100, 185
Canna **247–8**
canoeing 14
Cape Wrath 209
car travel 5, 7
Carbisdale Castle 187
Carnegie, Andrew 192
Carrbridge 171
Carrick Castle 84
Castle of Mey 203
Castle Stalker 104
Castle Sween 97
Castle Tioram 123, 132
Castle Varrich 206
Cawdor
  Cawdor Castle 169
Céilidh **36**
Channonry Ness 180
Cherry Island 138
Chioccetti, Domenico 305–6
chronology **330–1**
Clan Cameron Museum 131
Clan Gunn Museum/Heritage Centre 197
Clan Macrae 136
Clanranald, Allan Mor 123
clans
  families **321–8**
  tartans **36**
Clansman Centre 138
Clava Cairns 168
Clearances *see* Highland Clearances
climate **10**
climbing 14–16
Clo Mor Cliffs 209
Clootie Wells 44, 147, 180
Cobb, John 141
Coldbackie Bay 206
Colintraive 86
Coll **243–4**
  Arinagour 243
  Breachacha Castle 243
  Totronald 243
Colonsay and Oronsay **230–2**
  Colonsay House 232
  Dun Domhnuill 231
  Kiloran Bay 231
  Oronsay Cross 231
  Oronsay Priory 231
Commando Memorial 130
Comrie 72
  Auchingarrich Wildlife Centre 72
  Drummond Trout Farm & Fishery 72
  Earthquake House 72
Connel Bridge 103
Contin 177
Cook, Captain 303
Cope, General 131–2
Corrieshalloch Gorge 150
Corrieyarich Pass 131, 132
Corrimony Cairn 176
Corryvreckan Whirlpool 230
Cove 148
Cowal Peninsula 84–5
Crarae Garden 90–1
Crianlarich 77
Crieff 70
  Crieff Visitor Centre 70
  Glenturret Distillery 70
  Knock of Crieff 70
Crinan 97
Crinan Canal 97
crofting **37**, 212, 214
  see also Napier Commission
Croick Church 186
Cromarty 181–3
  Cromarty Courthouse 181
  Hugh Miller's Cottage 181–2
Crosskirk 205
Cruachan Power Station 91
Culloden 32, 166
Cumberland, William Augustus, Duke of ('the Butcher Cumberland') 138, 166, 168
Cunninghame Graham, Robert 76
curling 16
Dalwhinnie Moor 69
Darling, Sir Frank Fraser 154
Darwin, Charles 131
Davaar Island 100
David I 27, 50, 190
David II 28

Devil's Cauldron 72
devolution 33–4
Dingwall 183–4
  Town House 183
distilleries
  Ardbeg 225, 226
  Blair Athol 60
  Bowmore 225, 227
  Edradour 60
  Isle of Arran 218
  Glenmorangie 186
  Glenturret 70
  Lagavulin 225, 226
  Laphroaig 225, 226
  Talisker 261
diving 16
Donizetti, Gaetano 50
Donn, Rob 205, 208
Dornie
Dornoch **190, 192**
  Dornoch Cathedral 190, 192
Douglas, Catherine 49
Douglas, Ellen 74
Dounreay Nuclear Power Station 205
Drongs 318
Drummond Castle Gardens 71
Drumnadrochit 141
Dubh Artach lighthouse 230
Dun Dornadilla 207
Dun Telve 136
Dun Troddan 136
Dunadd Fort 95–6
Dunbeath **197**
  Dunbeath Castle 197
Dunblane
Duncan I 27
Duncansby Head 201–2
Dundee, John Graham of Claverhouse ('the Bonnie Dundee') 67, 68
Dunkeld **59**
  Dunkeld Cathedral 59
  Hermitage (Ossian's Hall) 59
  Little Houses 59
  Loch of the Lowes 59
  Wildlife Centre 59
Dunnet Head 203
Dunoon **85–7**
  Dunoon Castle 85–6
Dunrobin Castle 194
Dunstaffnage Castle 103
Durness 208
Durness Old Church 208
Eas-Coul-Aulin 156
Easter Ross **183**
Eday 308
Edward I 28, 193
Edward III 50, 68
Egilsay 308
  St Magnus Cenotaph and Church 308
Eigg **246–7**
  Sgurr of Eigg 246
Eilean-an-Tighe 283
Eilean Ban 144
Eilean Donan Castle 136
Elizabeth, Queen, the Queen Mother 203
Elizabeth II, Queen 85, 280
Ellice, Edward 134
Elliot, James and Archibald 63
Embo 192–3
Erbusaig
Eriskay **292–3**
  Haun 293
Erracht 131
Erraid 236
Eskadale 175
Fair Isle 320
Fairy Flag 260
Falls of Glomach 136
Falls of Measach 150
Falls of Shin 187
families *see* clans and families
Farquharson, John, of Inverey ('the Black Colonel') 56
Fearn 185
Fergusson, J.D. 50, 52
ferry travel 6
Fetlar 318
Finlarig Castle 65
fishing 17–19
Fiunary 125
Flannan Islands lighthouse 276
Flow Country 190
Fontane, Theodor 69
food and drink **10–12**
  eating out 11
  national dishes 10–11
  whisky 12
Forbes, Duncan 168
Fort Augustus **137–9**
Fort George 169–70
Fort William **106–8, 110**
  Caledonian Canal 107
  Inverlochy Castle 107, 128
  West Highland Museum 106–7
Fortingall 64
Fortrose 180
Foula 319
Fowler, Sir John 150
Freswick 201
Furnace 90
Fyrish Monument 184
Gaelic language **37–8**, 214
Gairloch 148
  Gairloch Heritage Museum 148
Gigha **223–5**
  Achamore Creamery 224
  Achamore Gardens 224
  Ardminish 224
  Kilchattan 224
Gilchrist 177
Girnigoe Castle 200
Glassburn 176
Glen Beag 136
Glen Lyon Church 64
Glen Nevis 108
Glen Roy 131
Glenaladale 118
Glencoe
  Glencoe Folk Museum 114
Glencoe Massacre 31, **113–14**
Glendale Martyrs 252–3
Glenelg
Glenfinnan 32, 117
  Prince's Monument 116
Glenmorangie Distillery 186
Glenmoriston 140
Glenshee 55
glossary **332–4**
golf 19
Golspie 193
Gometra 235
Gow, John 303
Gow, Neil 59
Gowrie Conspiracy 49–50
Graham, James Gillespie 63, 131, 217, 254
Great Bernera 276
Great Cumbrae **215**
  Millport 215
    Cathedral of the Isles 215
Great Glen **128**
Grey Cairns of Camster 198
Gruinard 149
Gruinard Bay 149
Gunn, Neil 195, 197
Haakon, King 224, 253, 302
Hamilton, Patrick 185
Handa Island 156

Harald Tower 204
Harris 270, **277–81**
Amhuinnsuidhe Castle 279
Bunavoneadar 279
Hushinish 279
Leverburgh 280
Loch Leossaidh 279
Luskintyre Beach 280
Plocrapool 279
Rodel 280
St Clement's Church 279–80
Tarbert 278
tweed 272, 279
Helmsdale **194–5**
Timespan Heritage Centre 195
Highbridge 130
Highland Clearances 32–3, **38**, 175, 186, 193, 205, 283, 287
Highland Line 1, 52, 72, 216, 220
Highland Mystery World 111
Highlanders Regimental Museum 170
Hill o'Many Stanes 198
Historic Scotland **13**
hitch-hiking 6
Hobbs, Joseph William 128
Hogg, James 77
Holy Island 219
Holy Loch 85
Hopkins, Gerard Manley 76
Horlick, Colonel Sir James 224
House of Bruar 69
Hoy 306–7
Betty Corrigall's Grave 306
Dwarfie Stane 306
Hoy *cont'd*
Melsetter House 307
Old Man of Hoy 306
Rackwick 306
St John's Head 306
Hutcheson, David 94
Hutton, Charles 61
Hydroponicum 154
Inch Cailleach 83
Inch Kenneth 236
Inchbuie 65
Inchmahome Priory 76
Inchnadamph 154, 155
Inner Hebrides *213*, **223–45**
Innerpeffray Library 70–1
Innerwick 64, 65
Inverailort Castle 122
Inveraray **88–90**
Inveraray Castle 89
Inveraray Jail 89
Inverarnan Drovers' Inn 82
Inverewe Gardens 148–9
Inverfarigaig 140
Invergarry 134
Invergarry Castle 133–4
Invergordon 185
Invernaver National Nature Reserve 206
Inverness **160–5**, *161*
area around **166–88**, *167*
Caledonian Canal 163
Cameron Barracks 163
Castle Garrison 163
Eden Court 163
Inverness Museum 163
Ness Islands 163
St Andrew's Cathedral 163
Inverpolly National Nature Reserve 154
Iolaire, wreck of 273
Iona **238–41**
Cathedral 240
Dun I 241
St Oran's Chapel 241
Irvine, Robert 154
Irving, Washington 307
Islands of the Clyde *213*, **215–23**
Islay **225–9**
American Monument 227
Beinn Bheigeir 226
Bowmore 227
Claggain Bay 226
Dunyvaig Castle 226
Ellister 227
Kildalton Crosses 226
Loch Finlaggan 227
Loch Gruinart 227
Machrie 227
Museum of Islay Life 227
Oa Peninsula 226–7
Port Askaig 228
Port Charlotte 227
Port Ellen 226
Rhinns of Islay 227
Jacobite Rising of '45 **116**
Jacobite Steam Railway 116
James I 28, 49
James II 29
James III 29, 298
James IV 29, 71, 104, 124, 186
James V 29, 74, 101, 256, 260
James VI/I 30, 49, 52, 71, 258, 270
James VII/II 31
John o'Groats 201
John of Moidart 132
Johnson, Dr Samuel 1, **39–41**, 82, 84, 88, 89, 125, 135–6, 138, 140, 162, 233, 235, 236, 240, 243, 258, 260, 261, 262
Jura **229–30**
Corryvreckan Whirlpool 230
Craighouse 230
Jura House Gardens 230
Paps of Jura 229
Kames 86
Keil 101
Keiss Castle 201
Kenmore 63
Crannog 64
Taymouth Castle 63
Kerrara Island 93–4
Dunollie Castle 94
Ganavan Sands 94
Kerrysdale 147
Kilberry 99
Kilchoan 125
Kilchurn Castle 91
Killiecrankie, Pass of 67
Killin 65–6
Breadalbane Folklore Centre 65–6
Moirlanich Longhouse 66
Killing Times 67
Kilmartin 95
Kilmorack 175
Kilmory Knap Chapel 98
Kilravock Castle 168
Kingshouse Inn 114
Kingussie **171–4**
Highland Folk Museum 172
Ruthven Barracks 172
Kinloch Rannoch
Rannoch Smokery 61
Kinlochbervie 156–7
Kinlochleven 110
Kinlochmoidart 122
Kintyre **99–102**
Knapdale **97**
Knockfarrel 178
Knox, John 30, 49, 50, 52
Knoydart 120–1
Kyle of Lochalsh **144**
Kyles of Bute 220
Kylesku 155
Lady's Rock 102, 237
Laggan 132
Lairg 187

Lamb Holm 305–6
Burray Fossil Centre 306
Italian Chapel 305–6
Latheron 197
Lauder, Harry 61
Lazaretto Point 86
Ledmore 154
Leiper, William 122
Lennox Castle 83
Leslie, David 101
Leslie, Lionel 238
Lethaby, W.R. 307
Leverhulme, Lord 271, 278, 280
Lewis **270–7**
Ardroil 276
Arnish Moor 273
Arnol 274
Back 274
Black House Museum 274
Bosta Beach 276
Bragar 274
Butt of Lewis 274
Callanish Standing Stones 275
Carloway 275
Carloway Broch 275
Dalbeg 275
Dalmore 275
Europie 274
Garynahine 276
L for Leather 275
Lewis Chessmen 276
Ness 274
North Tolsta 274
Point 274
Shawbost Folk Museum 275
Shawbost Norse Mill and Kiln 275
St Columba's Church 274
St Moluag's Chapel 274
Steinacleit 274
Stornoway 272–3
An Lanntair Art Gallery 273
Lewis Loom Centre 273
Lews Castle 273
Western Isles Museum 273
Thrushel Stone 274
Uig 276
Linn of Dee 56
Lismore Island 102–3
Loch Ailort 122
Loch Awe 91
Loch Dochart 77
Loch Earn 72
Loch Eriboll 207
Loch Etive 103
Loch Ewe 148
Loch Fyne 84–5, **88**
Loch Hope 207
Loch Hourn 135
Loch Katrine 75
Loch Linnhe 107, 110
Loch Lomond **80, 82–3**
Loch Maree 147
Loch nan Uamh 118
Loch Ness 139–40
Loch Ness Monster **139–40**, 141
Loch of the Lowes 59
Loch Ossian 115
Loch Sunart **124–6**
Loch Tay 65
Loch Torridon 146–7
Loch Tummel Forest Centre 61
Lochaber **128**
Lochaline 125
Lochawe 91
Lochearnhead 72
Lochgilphead **98**
Lochinver 154–5
Lochnagar 56
Lordship of the Isles 212, 225, 227–8
Lorimer, Hew 288
Lorimer, Sir Robert 194, 238
Lovat, Simon Fraser, Lord ('the Old Fox of the '45') 119, 174
Lowlanders defeated at Highbridge **130**
Luss 82
Lybster 197
Lyth Arts Centre 201
Macalpine, Kenneth 27, 103
Macbeth 27, 58, 160
MacCulloch, John 236, 256
MacDiarmid, Hugh 246, 298
Macdonald, Alasdair 133
Macdonald, Flora 32, 103, 257, 258, 259
Macdonald, General Sir Hector 183–4
Macdonald, Hugh 258
Macdonald, Margaret 178
Macdonell, Ian Lom 133
MacGregor, James Mor 117
MacGregor, Rob Roy 76–7
Machrihanish 100
MacIan, Alisdair 31, 113, 114
Mackenzie, Compton 291, 295
MacKenzie, Osgood 149
Mackenzie, Roderick 140
Mackinnon, Archibald 100
MacLean, Sir Fitzroy 237
MacLean, Sorley 250, 256, 262
Macleod, George 125, 240
MacMillan's Cross 98
MacNeils 294
MacPherson, Hugh 246
Macpherson, James 74, 203
MacPherson, John 295
Mainland Orkney **300–5**
Bay of Skaill 305
Click Mill 305
Corrigall Farm Museum 305
Gurness 305
Kirkwall 300, 302
Bishop's Palace 302
Earl's Palace 302
Mercat Cross 302
Orkney Library 302
Orkney Museum 302
St Magnus Cathedral 300, 302
Wireless Museum 302
Longaglebe Geo 304
Maes Howe 304
Ring of Brodgar 304
Sandgeo 304
Skaill House 305
Skara Brae 305
Skipi Geo 304
Stones of Stenness 304
Stromness 302–3
Pier Arts Centre 303
Stromness Natural History Museum 303
Mainland Shetland **314–18**
Brae 318
Clickhimin Broch 315
Dore Helm 318
Eshaness 318
Firth 318
Jarlshof 317
Lerwick 314–15
Bod of Gremista Museum 315
Fort Charlotte 315
Shetland Museum 315
Town Hall 315
Up Helly Aa Exhibition 315
Lunna 317
Mavis Grind 318
Old Scatness Broch 315
Quendale Watermill 315, 317
Ronas Hill 318
Sandness 317
Scalloway 316

Mainland Shetland *cont'd*
Shetland Croft Museum 317
Sullom Voe Oil Terminal 318
Sumburgh 317
Sumburgh Head 317
Tangwick Haa Museum 315
Tingwall 316
Toft 318
Malcolm II 27
Malcolm IV 27
Mallaig 120
Mam Ratagan 135
maps **13**
Margaret, Princess ('the Maid of Norway') 193, 306
Martin, Martin 225, 227, 229, 232, 247, 272, 295, 296
Maruma 247
Mary, Queen of Scots 29–30, 68, 76, 162, 168, 219
Mary Ann's Cottage 203
Maxton, James 33
Maxwell, Gavin 120, 136, 144, 255, 289
McSporran, Seumas 224
Melvich
Menzies, Sir Robert 63
midges 10, 147, 246
Miller, Hugh 181–2, 246
Mingary Castle 124
Mingulay 295
Mitford, Unity 236
Moidart 121
monarchs **329**
Moniack Mhor 175
Monk, General 106, 133, 162
Montrose, James Graham, Marquis of 107–8, 155, 187
Morar 119
Morris, Roger 88, 89
Morrison, Dr Thomas 177
Morvern 125
Mousa Island 316
Mousa Broch 316
Moy 171
Muck **248**
Muir of Ord 177
Mull **232–8**
Ardmeanach Peninsula 236
Aros Castle 238
Ben More 232, 235–6
Bunessan 236
Burgh 236
Calgary Bay 234
Carsaig 237
Duart Castle 237
Eas Forss 235
Grass Point 238
MacCulloch's Tree 236
MacKinnon's Cave 236
Mull *cont'd*
Mull Little Theatre 234
Mull Museum 234
Old Byre Heritage Centre 234
Pennyghael 237
Ross of Mull 236
Salen 238
Tobermory 233–4
Torosay Castle 238
Uisken 236
Mull of Kintyre 101
Munlochy Bay 180
Munro, General Sir Hector 184
Munros 14–15
Murray, Sir Andrew 180
Murray, Lord George 53, 68, 172
Mylne, Robert 88, 89
Nairn **170**
Napier Commission **41–2**
National Trust for Scotland **13**
Newtonmore 172
Waltzing Waters 172
North and South Sutors 182
North Ballachulish 110–11
North Kessock 182
North Rona 209
North Ronaldsay 308, 310
North Uist
Aird an Runair 284
Balranald 284
Barpa Langass 284
Ben Langass 284
Blashaval 283
Carinish 284
Clettraval 284
Dun-an-Sticir 283
Feith-na-Fala 285
Hosta 284
Lochmaddy 283
Newton Ferry 283
Pobull Fhinn 284
Scolpaig Tower 284
Sollas 283
Teampull-na-Trionaid 284
Unival 284
Noss 315
Noss Head 200
Oban **92–4**
McCaig's Tower 93
St Columba's Cathedral 93
Ord of Caithness 196
Orkney **299–310**, *301*
Ornsay 253
Oronsay *see* Colonsay and Oronsay
Orosay 291
Orwell, George 230
Ossian's Stone 71–2
Otter Ferry 86
packing **13**
Papa Stour 317
Papa Westray 308, 310
Parallel Roads 131
parliament 33–4
Pass of Brander 92
Pass of Killiecrankie 67
Paterson, John 63
peat 37
Pentland Firth 201, 299
Perth **48–54**, *51*
Art Gallery and Museum 50
Balhousie Castle 50
Branklyn Gardens 52
Bridgend 52
Caithness Glass Factory 52
Elcho Castle 53
Fair Maid's House 50
Fairways Heavy Horse Centre 52
Fergusson Gallery 50, 52
Huntingtower Castle 52
Kinnoull Hill 52
Lower City Mills 52
Perth Hunt Racecourse 52
Perth Mart and Agricultural Centre 53
Regimental Museum 50
Round House 52
Scone Palace 52
St John's Kirk 50
Perthshire *46–7*, **48–78**
piping **42**, 261
Pitlochry **60**
Blair Athol Distillery 60
Edradour Distillery 60
Hydroelectric Dam and Fish Ladder 60
Pladda Island lighthouse 218
Plockton 146
Pontius Pilate 64
Poolewe 148
Port Appin 104
Portavadie 86
Portmahomack 185
Potter, Beatrix 58

public holidays **14**
Queen Elizabeth Forest Park Visitor Centre 75
Queen's View 61
Raasay **262–3**
Castle Brochel 263
Raasay House 262
Raasay Outdoor Centre 263
Rangag Broch 197
Rannoch Moor 115
Rannoch Smokery 61
Rea, Fredrick 291
Redcastle 182
religious differences **42–3**
Rennie, Sir John 97
Rest and be Thankful 84
Rhiconich 156
Rob Roy *see* MacGregor, Rob Roy
Robert I (the Bruce) 28, 77, 101, 103, 218
Robert II 28, 215
Robert III 28, 215
Rogie Falls 178
Rosemarkie 180
Groam House Museum 180–1
Roshven House 122
Ross, Alexander 163
Ross, George 181
Rossdhu House 82
Rough Bounds **116**
Rousay 307, 310
Midhowe 307
Taversoe Tuick 307
Trumland House 307
Roybridge
Rum **245–6**
Kinloch Castle 246, 248
Sabhal Mor Ostaig 214, 254
Saddell Abbey and Castle 101
sailing 19–20
Sand 149
Sanda Island 101
Sandaig 136
Sanday (Canna) 247
Sanday (Orkney) 308, 310
Sandwood Bay 157, 209
Scalpay 278
Scapa Flow 303
Scarp 279
Scathac the Wise 254
Schellenberg, Keith 247
Schiehallion 61
Scott, Sir Walter 73, 74, 75, 207, 247, 255, 260, 306, 317
Scourie **156–7**
Scrabster 204–5
Seaforth Highlanders 183
seers **43–4**
Seil Island 95
Seven Men of Glenmoriston 140
Seven Men of Moidart 118, 122
Shandwick 185
Shapinsay 307, 310
Balfour Castle 307
Burroughston 307
Shetland **311–20**, *313*
Shiant Islands 278
Shiel Bridge (Loch Duich) 135
Shiel Bridge (Moidart) 123
shinty 20
Shinwell, Emmanuel 33
shooting 20
shopping **14**
Sinclair, Sir John, of Ulbster 203
Sinclair Castle 200
Skelbo Castle 193
skiing 20–1
Skinnor, William 169
Skipness Point 101
Skye **249–66**, *251*
Aird of Sleat 254
Annait 259
Armadale Castle 254
Armadale Pier 254
Aros Experience 257
Blaven 255
Braes 252, 256
bridge 144, 250
Broadford 254
Castle Camus 254
Castle Maol 253
Clan Donald Centre 254
Colbost 261
Cuillins 255–6
Dun Beag 261
Dunsgaith Castle 254
Duntulm Castle 258
Dunvegan Castle 260
Durinish Peninsula 261
Elgol 254
Floddigarry 257
Isleornsay 253
Kilmuir 258
Kilt Rock 257
Knock Bay 254
Kyleakin 253
Loch Coruisk 254–5
Loch Mealt 257
Loch Snizort Beag 259
Luib 255
MacCrimmon Piping Heritage Centre 261
Macleod's Tables 260
Monkstadt House 259
Old Man of Storr 257
Ord 254
Portree 252, 256–7
Quiraing 257
Skeabost 259
Skye Heritage Centre 257
Skye Museum of Island Life 258
Skye Serpentarium 254
Sleat Peninsula 253–5
Staffin 257
Storr Lochs 257
Talisker 261
Trotternish 257–9
Trumpan 259
Uig Bay 259
Waternish 259–60
Sma' Glen 71–2
Small Isles **245–8**
Smith, John 98
Smoo Cave 207
Soay 255
'the Sobieski Stuarts' 175–6
Soldier's Leap 67
sorcerers **44**, 190
South Ronaldsay 306, 310
St Margaret's Hope 306
Tomb of the Eagles 306
South Uist **287–92**
Askernish 290
Beinn Mhor 289
Bornish 289
Caisteal Bheagram 288
Daliburgh 290
Flora Macdonald's Birthplace 290
Garrynamonie 291
Hecla 289
Howmore 288
Kildonan Museum 289
Loch Bee 288
Loch Carnon 288
Loch Druidibeg National Nature Reserve 288
Loch Eynort 289
Loch Skipport 288
Lochboisdale 290
Ludag 291
Nicolson's Leap 289
Ormiclate Castle 289

South Uist *cont'd*
Our Lady of the Isles 288
Rubha Ardvule 289
South Lochboisdale 290
Usinish lighthouse 289
Spanish Armada 320
Spean Bridge
special-interest holidays 8
specialist tour operators 8
Speyside Way 16
sports and activities **14–21**
St Adamnan 64, 122, 139, 160, 239
St Barr 294
St Bean 176
St Ciaran 124
St Columba 26–7, 59, 96, 123, 124, 139, 160, 172, 176, 230, **239**
St Columba's Cave 98–9
St Cummein 137
St Duthus 179, 185
St Fillan 65, 77
St Fillans 72
St Finnan 117
St Kilda **295–6**
Hirta 296
St Maelrubha 146, 147
St Magnus 300, 303
St Margaret 176
St Molaise 219
St Moluag 102, 263
St Mungo 59
St Ninian 26, 197, 239
St Ninian's Isle 316–17
St Oran 230, 253
Stac Pollaidh 154
Stack Islands 293
Staffa
Fingal's Cave 234–5
stalking 20
Stevenson, R. L. 111, 199, 236
Stewart, Alexander ('the Wolf of Badenoch') 59
Stewart, Earl Patrick 302, 304, 316
Stewart, James, of Acharn 111–12
Stone of Destiny **34**, 96, 103
Strath Affric 176
Strath Cannich 176
Strath Farrar 175
Strath Glass 175
Strathardle 55
Strathnaver Museum 205
Strathpeffer 177–8
Eagle Stone 178
Water Sampling Pavilion 178
Strathy Point 205
Strontian 124
Struy 175
Stuart, Charles Edward ('the Young Pretender') **32**, 68, 117, 118, 122, 131, 134, 140, 166, 168, 171, 172, 206, 252, 257, 258, 259, 262, 271, 273, 278, 286, 289, 293
Stuart, James Edward ('the Old Pretender') 31, 32
Suilven 155
Summer Isles 154
superstition **44**
surfing 21
Sutherland, Scott 130
Swanson, John 246
Tain **185–6**
St Duthus Collegiate Church 186
Tain Peninsula 184–5
Taransay 280
Tarbat Ness 185
Tarbert 100
Tarbet (Argyll) 83
Tarbet (Highland) 156
tartans **36**
Taymouth Castle 63–4
Taynuilt 103
Telford, Thomas 59, 95, 97, 107, 152, 163, 199
Thomas the Rhymer 43
Thomson, James 199
Thurso **203–4**
Harald Tower 204
St Peter's Church 204
Thurso Castle 204
Tighnabruaich 86
Tiree **244–5**
Ben Hynish 244
Dun Mor Broch 244
Gott Bay 244
Hynish 244
Scarnish 244
Skerryvore Museum 244
Wave Classic 244
Tobar nan Ceann 133
Tomatin 171
Tomnahurich 163
Tongue 206
House of Tongue 206
topics **36–45**
tour operators, specialist 8
tourist offices **22**
Toward Castle 86
tracing your ancestors **22–3**
train travel 5, 6–7
Treshnish Isles 234
Lunga 235
Tronda 316
Trossachs **74**
Tyndrum 78
Ullapool **152–3**
Ullapool Museum & Visitor Centre 152
Ulva 235
Unst 318
Haroldswick 318
Muckle Flugga lighthouse 318
Urquhart, Sir Thomas 181
Urquhart Castle 141
Vallay 283–4
Vatersay 294
Victoria, Queen 55, **56–7**, 60, 64, 67, 68, 82, 84, 90, 97, 114, 117,
132, 147, 183, 194, **234–5**
Wade, General 1, 62, 130, 138, 172
walking 14–16
Wee Frees 148, 272
Wemyss, John, Earl of 53
West Highland Way 77, 106
Devil's Staircase 114
Westray 308, 310
Noltland Castle 308
Whaligoe 198
Whalsay 318–19
Benie Hoose 319
Standing Stones 319
where to stay **23–4**
see also under individual places
whisky 12
Whisky Galore 291
White Corries Ski Centre 114
Whiten Head 207
Wiay 286
Wick **199–201**
Caithness Glass Factory 200
Heritage Museum 200
Oldwick Castle 200
Pulteneytown 199
wildlife **39**
William I (the Lion) 27, 49, 182
Wolsey Lodges 24
Wordsworth, William 67, 72, 74, 76, 84
Wyre 307
Cubbie Roo's Castle 307
Yell 318
Younger Botanic Garden 85
youth hostels 24
Zucher, Gerhardt 279